Modern
Social
Science

Modern
Social
Science

ROBERT BIERSTEDT
Department of Sociology and Anthropology
New York University

EUGENE J. MEEHAN
Department of Political Science
Rutgers University

PAUL A. SAMUELSON
Department of Economics and Social Science
Massachusetts Institute of Technology

McGraw-Hill Book Company
New York
San Francisco
Toronto
London

Modern Social Science

Library of Congress Catalog Card Number: 63-21776

05242

3456789 UL 9876

This book is set in Caledonia, a type face designed for linotype by the American graphic designer W. A. Dwiggins. The boldface headings are Trade Gothic and the chapter titles are Caslon italic.

Preface

This text is intended for use in a two-semester or three-quarter course in general social science. Though it is not, in the strict sense of the term, an "integrated" text, the three disciplines represented (sociology, political science, economics) are bound together by various common threads. Each discipline, of course, is concerned with human behavior, though each surveys social behavior from its own particular viewpoint. More important is the general method of approaching the subject matter embodied in the parts of the text: each part is concerned with the exploration in depth of the fundamentals, with the development of a basic framework that can be used for further study in the field. This we feel is the most valuable service that a textbook can perform.

Responsibility for the various parts of the text is almost self-evident but deserves to be spelled out to avoid any possibility of confusion. Part 1 (Chapters 1 to 5) and Chapter 18 were condensed from Robert Bierstedt's *The Social Order*, 2d edition; Part 2 (Chapters 6 to 10) and Chapter 19 were prepared by E. Meehan especially for use in this text; Part 3 (Chapters 11 to 17) and Chapter 20 were condensed from Paul A. Samuelson's *Economics: An Introductory Analysis*, 5th edition. Responsibility for selecting and condensing the material in sociology and economics lies solely with Meehan, though both Bierstedt and Samuelson shared in the process and gave their approval to the completed work.

A great many persons, too many to enumerate, offered advice, suggestions, and editorial assistance during the preparation of the text. We would like particularly to acknowledge the work of Felicity Skidmore and Michael Taussig in the preparation of the economics section, and of Robert Getz in the preparation of Chapter 19 of the political science material.

To those publishers who granted permission to make use of excerpts from their publications we also extend our thanks, and suitable acknowledgments will be found in the body of the text.

R.B.

E.J.M.

P.A.S.

Contents

Preface

Part 4   Contemporary Problems: Social, Political, Economic

Introduction

Man dominates the earth on which he lives, bending all other living things to his wishes. This much is simple fact. Though other animals are stronger, faster, more agile, hardier, and longer-lived, none seems likely to dethrone man from his position of supremacy. To what does man owe his superiority? Clearly, and above all, to his intelligence. Man is born with an enormous intellectual potential—a capacity to learn and adapt. No creature living on earth can match him in this respect. Even the most assiduous of thinkers uses only a fraction of his total capacity, and the human brain represents an untapped resource of incredible dimensions. Man's intelligence makes possible the subtle and complex forms of communication and thought that he has developed, and it supplies the ideas and concepts that inform his communications with meaning. Intelligence marks the boundary between the hive of bees, driven by inexorable instinct, and the human social group, which is almost infinitely plastic and flexible. Men are intelligent creatures, living in close relations with others, able to communicate with them, and able to form their own principles in these interactions. This is the foundation from which all social science springs.

Man and society. If man is an intelligent animal, so also is he a social animal, and it is hard to say which is the more significant of these two facts— if they can be separated. In order to live, and in order to be a man, man must live in the company of others of his kind. This is the second of our prime landmarks. Man's need for society is fundamental. From that need spring the kinds of activities that the social sciences investigate. Because man must live with other men, he must adapt his behavior to them, whether he is seeking his livelihood or merely amusing himself; life without regard for others would soon become impossible. In association with others, man finds the protection, sustenance, companionship, and satisfaction which he must have; he also generates a need for rules of behavior to guide and control these relations and to keep them within manageable bounds.

Broadly construed, the social sciences are concerned with the social life of man. Human society has no peer as an object of study, for it offers a richness, a diversity, and an intrinsic interest that no other subject matter can match. This has long been recognized, of course, and some of the earliest of all human writings are directed to the relationships that arise between men and between societies. They are thus treatises in the social sciences, however much they may differ in approach or language from the social sciences of the present day.

Modern social science is relatively new. In the present century the systematic study of the various aspects of human society which began in the nineteenth century has expanded greatly; vast piles of information have been accumulated in each of the major divisions of social science. As a consequence of this accelerated activity, the subject matter of social science has been divided and then divided again, forming new, more specialized subdisciplines. Much remains to be done, and it seems unlikely that the topic can be exhausted. Social life among men, unlike the behavior of bees, is "open-ended" in that it is not fixed once and for all by the limits of instinct. New forms and relationships are always possible. Men devise new social structures, new goals, and new means of attaining them just as they produce new instruments and new tools. Thus the study of human society seems likely to hold its interest for man far into the future, and perhaps indefinitely.

The social sciences. The text that follows offers the student a general introduction to three of the major subdivisions in social science: sociology, political science, and economics. Although there is very much more to social science than these three subjects, and although the subjects themselves depend in some measure on information derived from other disciplines, they are the hard core of most social science curricula. In the text, each subject is treated as a whole, ignoring the more specialized subdivisions which have appeared, each requiring further intensive study for mastery. The point is that human society is such an enormously complex subject that no single volume and no single discipline can do justice to its intricacies. The material in the text provides a foundation on which further study can be based—a systematic conception of society and its operation on which further understanding of particular aspects of social life can be grounded.

In these days of specialization, swift communication, and rapid social change, the importance of a firm grasp of the basic principles of social relations hardly needs additional emphasis. Men fear what they do not understand, or what they misunderstand, and there is complexity enough without adding to the burden by failing to grasp essentials. To be able to understand the particular within the broad framework of the general, to appreciate the social context as well as the individual context, to be able to evaluate what happens to us as individuals in terms of broad principles of social action— these are important goals in any educational process. The basic purpose of the text is to provide a framework that makes this sort of comprehension possible.

Two aspects of the subject matter of the text bear mentioning, since they condition the attitude we take toward our studies. In the first place, the three disciplines considered in the text are overlapping and interrelated in many broad areas. The sociologist is concerned with all human societies, wherever they occur and whatever purpose or function they serve. His task is to examine, classify, compare, and, if possible, explain how and why society functions and why one mode of operation is used and not another. The political scientist is concerned with a more restricted phase of social life— the function of government, a phenomenon which is peculiarly difficult to define but everywhere recognizable. The economist too deals with one limited phase of social action—man's use of time, energy, and resources to provide the goods and services he needs and wants. Sociology is thus more general than political science or economics; the latter are more specialized and detailed. In the text, we move from the broad and general outlook of the sociologist to the specific interests of the political scientist and the economist, and the student should note carefully the types of questions considered at each level of generalization and the kinds of answers that each discipline proposes. The answers are, of course, different, for the disciplines survey society from different points of view. But that does not mean that one or another is prior, that it is more desirable to learn one than the other. Each discipline sets its own goals and seeks to explain its own phenomena, and the success of the effort must always be judged in terms of these objectives, not according to some other standard.

A second related point bears on the tendency to specialization that has developed recently in modern academic work as well as in modern business. Until some two hundred years ago, all three of our disciplines were comprised in the mother science—philosophy. Sociology appeared as an independent field of study in the nineteenth century; political science and economics were linked together as the study of "political economy" until the present century. Yet in a relatively brief period of time, specialization has overtaken all three fields. Specialization is very fruitful, but it has its dangers. For one thing, increased specialization tends to increase interdependence; as economists or political scientists specialize, they in fact become more dependent upon others for information excluded from the narrow confines of their specialty. In the social sciences, there are many points of view which may be considered legitimate points of specialization, and no single viewpoint can claim priority over all others. Information of importance to our understanding of social behavior can be found in many different fields—psychology, geography, biology, or even astronomy. Thus the reconciliation of the trend toward specialization and the need for social scientists to be aware of the contributions being made in other fields poses a genuine dilemma for the modern scholar. We cannot solve it here, of course, but an awareness of the problem on the student's part will mitigate some of the more serious dangers inherent in the current trend toward more and more specialization.

The text. This textbook is intended as an introduction to three of the major disciplines in the social sciences—sociology, political science, and economics. Like any book, it had to be written, and in the writing some subjects were selected for detailed treatment and others were omitted. On what basis was the material selected? What function is expected of the text? These questions are significant for both student and teacher, for every book is designed to serve some purpose, and knowledge of that purpose is essential if the book is to do its work properly.

Let us begin with the general question, "What function does an introductory textbook serve?" An academic discipline can be defined as a particular body of subject matter which is studied systematically by a group of scholars. Their aim is to accumulate information about some particular group of phenomena, to analyze and explain these phenomena as fully as possible. The results of their scholarship—the data, theories, and hypotheses developed by the discipline—are usually put into writing where they can be read and criticized by others interested in the same subject matter. In this way, academic investigation moves on continuously, and the findings of one generation are passed along to the next for further study and criticism. The basic aim of an introductory text is to supply the student with the tools and information needed to understand and appreciate scholarly activity in a given field of study.

The problem is somewhat complicated, however, by the fact that introductory texts must serve two distinct types of students. First of all, there are those who plan to continue their studies in a particular discipline. Obviously, they must have the tools and data needed to comprehend more advanced work in the subject matter. A second group of students who do not plan to become specialists in the subject, still have a real need to understand the subject matter of the discipline. The needs of these two types of students are somewhat different, but both can be served by a well-designed text.

To take an illustration, an introductory course in economics must obviously provide the student with the tools and equipment needed for further study. What is involved in this task? Clearly, the subject matter must be defined precisely. The student needs to learn the technical terminology used in the discipline and the basic techniques used by economists to attack their subject matter. The fundamental conceptions used in economic analysis must also be taught (the laws, theories, etc., that are used to explain economic behavior), and the student should learn to use them properly. Basically, the student should learn the questions asked by those who study the subject, the means used to find answers to these questions, and the kinds of answers that have been proposed. From this beginning, he can continue into more detailed and precise work in specialized areas of the discipline.

The student who does not intend to become an economist also has a vital interest in the work of economists, and he and the future economist are both concerned with the same basic questions. All of us, in our everyday lives, must concern ourselves with economic subject matter—indeed with all social science subject matter. Without some knowledge of what economists, sociologists, political scientists, psychologists, etc., have been able to learn about their respective subjects, we cannot hope to deal with our own social affairs in an adequate manner. The introductory course in social science, then, has the obligation to inform the student of these matters so that he can think clearly about them as they impinge on his own social behavior. In most if not all cases, this involves learning precisely the same types of information and skills that are imparted to the prospective specialist in the discipline. It is a profound error to believe that one way of thinking about economic or political matters is appropriate for the economist or political scientist and another for the nonspecialist. They may differ in the degree of sophistication they impart to their work, in the complexity of the concepts they employ, and so on, but the framework which is valid and useful for the specialist is also the best framework available for the general reader.

Our next question is, "Where can this information be found and how is it best imparted?" Fortunately, this is not a very serious problem, and there is no need for an author to sit down and work out anew all of the basic definitions, skills, techniques, conceptions, etc., to be taught in each of the social sciences. That has already been done, or is in the process of being done, in every academic discipline. There are standard introductory texts in all of the social sciences, each containing the information and skills needed to understand current work in the discipline. The content of these texts is not set for all time, of course, for as new information appears or new approaches to the subject matter prove fruitful, they are speedily introduced into the texts and used in the training of incoming students. Hence at any given time, the texts that are most widely used and approved by professional scholars in a field will tend to provide the student with the kind of foundation that is needed to study the subject matter, based on current trends and movements within the discipline.

Where an introductory course is limited to a single subject and offered for a full year, such texts provide the best available foundation on which to begin our studies. However, it is not always feasible to devote a full year to the study of each of the social sciences, and some of the subjects are often combined in a single course that is shorter and more intensive than the full-year course. The texts designed for the year course are not entirely suitable for a combined course. They are often large and expensive, and they probe more deeply into the subject matter and techniques of study than the student can be expected to go in a shorter time period.

The obvious solution to this dilemma is to condense and combine standard texts of high quality, producing a text which is shorter in length, more selective, less detailed, but covering a wider range of subject matter. That is what has been done in the text you are now reading. Perhaps the finest introductory text in economics now available (Paul A. Samuelson, *Economics: An Introductory Analysis*) has been combined with one of the best standard introductions to sociology (Robert Bierstedt, *The Social Order*) and with an introduction to political science, specially written to parallel the approach to the subject matter taken in these two volumes, to form a single introduction which spans the three major disciplines in the social sciences. The goal was a text which is readable, soundly conceived, and widely endorsed by specialists in the various fields. The completed condensation was exposed to professional criticism in each of the three areas prior to publication to ensure that the goal had been achieved.

The student who uses the text is therefore assured that the material is up to date, that the approach to the subject matter is well conceived and widely accepted in each of the specialized areas. The condensations are not as full and detailed as the originals, and students planning to specialize in one of these subjects should seek a fuller treatment of the material. But the basic questions asked in each of the disciplines, the ways of handling various kinds of information, the fundamental conceptions used to investigate particular social phenomena, and the major problems facing specialists in the field at the present time have been presented as fully as space permits. The result, we believe, is a text that can be used with profit by everyone.

PART 1

The
Social
Order

Although he may be approaching the subject for the first time, the reader of this book already knows something about sociology. He has been a member of society since birth, and he has had continuous personal experience with social relationships. He knows in addition that he has inherited a long tradition of Western civilization and that many of his ideas and customs had their origin in prior societies. Finally, he knows that in some respects he is like all other people, in certain respects like some other people, and in some ways unique— like no one except himself. All this is sociological knowledge. His participation in social relationships, his sharing of a social heritage, and his awareness of likenesses and differences between people all give him some insight into the subject that now engages his attention. But they do not make him a sociologist. He may not yet know, in fact, what sociology is, and so we begin our discussion with this first basic question.

The story of sociology. Sociology has a long past but only a short history. Since the dawn of civilization society has been a subject for speculation and inquiry, along with the other phenomena that have agitated the restless and inquisitive mind of man. There is warrant indeed for saying that *The Republic* of Plato is the first great sociological treatise in the Western tradition, and the *Analects* of Confucius its counterpart in the East. But it is only within the last hundred years that the study of society has become an identifiable academic discipline.

Various strains and tendencies, some intellectual and some ethical, combined to form the science of sociology. Two factors of major importance were, on the one hand, an interest in social welfare and social reform, and on the other, an interest in the philosophy of history. How they together produced something called sociology is a fascinating story, but one that cannot be told in an introductory text. It will suffice for the student to know that these separate and indeed somewhat disparate strains did enter into the formation of the new science. In the United States, particularly, in contrast to the European countries, sociology has been associated with an effort to improve the social conditions of mankind; it appears as an active agent in eradicating the problems of crime, delinquency, prostitution, unemployment, poverty, conflict, and war. That this identification, which is widely accepted by the general public, is not currently correct, or is correct in only a very special and partial sense, will become clear as we proceed.

In the nineteenth century, a French philosopher named Auguste Comte worked out, in a series of books, a general approach to the study of society. He believed that the sciences followed one another in a definite and logical order, that human inquiry went through certain historical stages, arriving finally at the last or scientific stage. He thought that it was time for all inquiries into social problems and social phenomena to enter this scientific stage, so he recommended that the study of society become the "science of society."

The name that Comte gave to his new science was "sociology," and this was, from a number of points of view, an unfortunate choice. "Sociology" is composed of two words: *socius,* meaning "companion" or "associate"; and *logos,* meaning "word." Thus the term formed from the two parts means talking about society, as geology (*geos,* earth) means talking about the earth. Unfortunately, however, *socius* is a Latin word, and *logos* comes from the Greek, and the name of our science is thus an "illegitimate" offspring of two languages. John Stuart Mill, a nineteenth-century English philosopher, proposed the word "ethology" for the new science, and though this term had the merit of being all Greek, it never appealed to other writers. When, in the latter half of the century, Herbert Spencer developed his systematic study of society and frankly adopted the term "sociology" in the title of his work, this became the permanent name of the new science, and sociology, especially with Spencer's own contributions, was well launched on its career.

Sociology developed rapidly in the twentieth century, notably in France, Germany, and the United States, though it advanced in somewhat different directions in the three countries. In spite of the fact that both Mill and Spencer were Englishmen, the development of sociology, for some reason, has been nowhere nearly so rapid or extensive in England as in other countries. In the United States, Yale, Columbia, and Chicago Universities, closely followed by the universities in the Midwest, were in the vanguard of a vigorous sociological movement, and sociology is today firmly established in the American university system. All major American universities offer instruction in the subject and all but one have independent departments of sociology. Most colleges also include sociology in their departmental organizations and curricula.

When we recall that none of this American development significantly antedates the twentieth century, that Harvard, the oldest of our universities, had no department of sociology until 1930, and that Princeton still has no independent department, we can appreciate how new the science of sociology is. It is not yet in all respects a mature science, and the student will therefore find in it more divergent points of view and perhaps less system than in such older sciences as physics, astronomy, and biology.

The nature of sociology. If we look at sociology now from the point of view of its internal logical characteristics, we shall find some clues that help to locate the subject for us and indicate what kind of science it is. We already know that sociology is a social and not a natural science. This, however, is a distinction in content and not in method. It serves to distinguish those sciences which deal with the physical universe from those which deal with the social universe—it distinguishes sociology from astronomy, physics, chemistry, and so on.

In the second place, sociology is a *categorical,* not a *normative,* discipline; that is, it confines itself to statements about what is, and not what should be or ought to be. As a science, sociology is necessarily silent about questions of value; it cannot decide the directions in which society ought to go and it makes no recommendations on matters of social policy. That is not to say that sociological knowledge is useless for purposes of social and political judgment, but only that sociology cannot itself deal with problems of good and evil, right and wrong, better or worse, or any others that concern human values. Sociology can and does, in a categorical fashion, state that at a certain time and in a certain place, a particular group of people adhered to certain values; but it cannot, in normative fashion, decide whether these people ought to have held these values in preference to others. There is no sociological warrant, nor indeed any other kind of scientific warrant, for preference in values. It is this canon that distinguishes sociology, as a science, from social and political philosophy and from ethics and religion.

Closely related to the above point is a third canon, and one that is sometimes difficult for the student to grasp. Sociology is a pure science, not an applied science. The immediate goal of sociology is the acquisition of knowledge about human society, not the utilization of that knowledge. Sociologists do not determine questions of public policy, do not tell legislators what laws should be passed or repealed, and do not dispense relief to the ill, the lame, or the poverty-stricken. Sociology, as a pure science, is engaged in the acquisition of knowledge that will be useful to all sorts of persons, but sociologists do not themselves—except, of course, in their capacity as citizens—apply the knowledge that it is their duty and profession to acquire. Sociology thus stands in the same relation to administration or legislation as physics does to engineering, or biology to plant and animal husbandry. Sociology is clearly and definitely concerned with acquiring the knowledge of society that can be used to solve some of the world's problems, but it is not itself an applied science. These comments mean neither that sociological knowledge is useless nor that it is impractical. They mean only that there is a division of labor involved and that the persons who acquire sociological knowledge are not always those who can use it best, and that those who use it are not usually those who have the time, the energy, and the training to acquire it.

A fourth characteristic of sociology is that it is a relatively abstract science and not a concrete one. This does not mean that it is unnecessarily complicated or unduly difficult. It means merely that sociology is not interested in the concrete manifestations of human events but rather in the form they take and the patterns they assume. Thus sociology is not concerned with particular wars or revolutions, but with war and revolution in general as social phenomena, as repeatable and recurrent processes in history, as types of social conflict. Similarly, sociology is not interested in particular associations or societies or particular groups of people; it is concerned with the fact that all people, no matter how diverse their origins and no matter how disparate their beliefs and attitudes and ways of doing things, have nevertheless formed themselves into human societies that exhibit, in all places, the same general structural characteristics. It is in this simple sense that sociology is an abstract and not a concrete science.

A fifth characteristic of sociology is that it is a generalizing and not a particularizing or individualizing science. It seeks general laws or principles about human interaction and association, about the nature, form, content, and structure of human groups and societies, and not, as in the case of history, complete and comprehensive descriptions of particular societies or particular events. It is not interested in the discrete historical fact that Italy under

Mussolini once made war on the Ethiopians, but in the sociological principle that external aggression is one way to intensify the internal solidarity of a group, a principle of which the Ethiopian conquest is only one of many thousands of examples.

A sixth characteristic of sociology is that it is both a rational and an empirical science. Since this is a methodological issue, we shall ignore it here and consider it in the next section, which is devoted to the method of sociology.

Finally, a seventh characteristic of sociology is that it is a general and not a special social science. Although this distinction has been a matter of some controversy among sociologists themselves, it seems fairly clear that social relationships and social interactions between people occur in all the affairs of human life, whether these affairs are primarily economic or political or religious or recreational or legal or intellectual, and there is no separate category of the social apart from all of these others. In other words, sociology studies those phenomena that are common to all human interaction. In all human intercourse, there are social factors, and it is on this level that sociology operates. Note that we do not say that sociology is *the* basic social science—that is too large a claim—nor that it is *the* general social science, but only that it is *a* general rather than a special social science and is interested in social factors in any social context, political, religious, or any other. The focus of sociology may be a special one, as is the focus of every other science, but its area of inquiry is general.

We may now, for quick reference, arrange these categories or canons in a series of opposing pairs and italicize those logical characteristics that pertain to sociology:

Social	Natural
Categorical	Normative
Pure	Applied
Abstract	Concrete
Generalizing	Particularizing
Rational	*Empirical*
General	Special

Sociology is thus a social, a categorical, a pure, an abstract, a generalizing, both a rational and an empirical, and a general science.

The method of sociology. Scientific investigation is characterized by a number of qualities, including objectivity, relativism, ethical neutrality, parsimony, and skepticism. In addition, there is in any science a willingness to bow to the facts, to expose one's conclusions to all of the force of contrary and even hostile criticism, and a resolution that enables one to work arduously over long periods of time with no apparent results. These attributes are found in all inquiry that merits the name of science, no matter what the subject matter under investigation.

Is sociology a science? Are the social sciences, and sociology in particular, sciences? Clearly, this depends on what we mean by a "science." Although the term is widely used, it is not really easy to define, particularly as the level of sophistication of the definition is raised. Science cannot be defined by its objects—a scientist is not someone who studies particular things—nor can it be defined by its techniques—a microscope can be used most "unscientifically." Perhaps the best general definition of a science comes from Professor Ernest Nagel, "The distinctive aim of the scientific enterprise is to provide systematic and responsibly supported explanations." The physical scientists have a great advantage here, for they are more or less agreed on what constitutes a "responsibly supported explanation," while the social scientists are not. The question, "Why does a balloon filled with helium rise into the atmosphere?" can be answered to the satisfaction of every scientist. The question, "Why do men behave in this particular way?" is much more difficult to answer satisfactorily. Can we give a "scientific" answer to such questions? Perhaps not, but we can, as social scientists, make use of the method by which the physical scientist approaches his subject matter; we can be objective, relativistic, ethically neutral, skeptical, and very careful to avoid some of the common fallacies in human thought. These aspects of scientific work commend themselves to the social scientist, and it is generally agreed that the social sciences would benefit enormously by adopting them.

Objectivity. To be objective is to eliminate from one's conclusions the influence of such factors as race, color, creed, occupation, nationality, moral preferences, or political predispositions. Objective inquiry is independent of the subjective desires of the investigator and his personal preferences. In the social sciences, objectivity is essential but difficult to achieve. The student is always a part of the system he studies, and the terms in which his findings are reported are open to the influence of his predispositions in a way the student may not even realize. We are, as human beings, peculiarly liable to certain kinds of errors in observing and reporting, errors summarized more than three centuries ago by the English philosopher, Francis Bacon (1561–1626), into four categories which he called the "Idols of the Tribe," the "Idols of the Cave," the "Idols of the Market Place," and the "Idols of the Theater." The terms may sound quaint, but the classification is excellent and still worth our attention.

    1. The Idols of the Tribe are the errors we commit because we belong to a particular species. It is normal for human beings to believe what they

wish to believe and disbelieve what displeases them, and as members of the species we all commit this error. It is, for example, always easier to find material that proves our argument than to find data that disprove it.

2. The Idols of the Cave are the mistakes we make because we are *particular kinds* of human beings—Americans, Russians, liberals, conservatives, Easterners, Westerners, etc. We all live in a kind of cave, and when we peer outside at the world, we tend to see only what our experience inside the cave has taught us to see, and to judge it accordingly. Our social experience, in other words, has an obvious influence on our social, political, and economic beliefs and judgments that we must learn to avoid.

3. The Idols of the Market Place are perhaps the most troublesome of all human errors, for they arise out of our choice of words and our need to use words to communicate. Words are like women—seductive, inconsistent, unpredictable, frequently faithless, and full of hidden meaning. Without them we cannot think at all; with them, we often think inaccurately or imprecisely. Scientists have become so acutely conscious of the ambiguity of words that they use mathematics and carefully defined symbols to eliminate the use of ordinary words whenever possible.

4. The Idols of the Theater are the "received opinions" we inherit with our culture. We all tend to assume that old ideas, or widely accepted ideas, are correct, that "Fifty million Frenchmen can't be wrong." The scientist questions all beliefs, old or young, and truth is not a matter of majority opinion. In fact, "universally accepted" premises are perhaps the most dangerous and misleading elements in social thought.

It need hardly be said that the student of sociology, or any other subject, must learn (and it takes conscious effort) to avoid the errors spelled out in Bacon's "Idols."

Relativism. The search for "truth" is an essential feature of any academic discipline, but the sociologist who seeks to be "scientific" in his work will never be tempted to spell truth with a capital "T." He works in the understanding that today's facts may be questioned or disproved tomorrow. Nothing is sacred; there are no privileged propositions, no absolute truths. Anyone may question anything and seek to disprove it. This attitude of mind is absolutely essential to scientific activity in the social sciences as in physical science.

Ethical neutrality. Characteristically, the physical scientist deals with facts and with theories that explain the facts; such propositions have no moral significance. They indicate no approval, no disapproval; they neither enjoin nor enforce. Thus the scientist, qua scientist, does not take sides in issues that involve ethics or values; such questions are left to the moral philosopher. Logically, the "scientific" social scientist ought to accept the same position, but there is some dispute within the social sciences about this point. Some feel that moral argument is an essential part of any social science; others believe that "scientific" social science is a more limited enterprise which cannot seek to answer every question that may arise. The student must work out his own position for himself.

Skepticism. Skepticism, carried to extremes for its own sake, leads to absurdity. But a willingness, or even an eagerness, to question before accepting, however strong the authority, is the mark of a well-trained mind. The good student must be convinced; he must assure himself that the evidence justifies the proposition he is asked to accept. This is an important feature of any field of study, for it leads to the correction of errors and mistakes. Critical and skeptical inquiry is in fact the heart of any academic endeavor.

Fact and theory. If we measure the distance between two lines, the figure we obtain from our measurement is an *empirical fact;* it has been observed by standardized techniques. If we produce a formula into which all of the empirical facts related to some particular phenomenon can be fitted, we obtain a theory, or a law. The law of gravity, for example, is a general mathematical formula into which all of the particular empirical facts about the relationship between two bodies, their "mutual attraction," can be fitted. It is called a "law" because a very large number of facts are "explained" by the formula, and none of the facts that science has produced contradict it. This is a very useful property, the ability to explain particular facts, and theories or laws play an important part in any scientific explanation.

The point to note here is that neither facts nor theories are worth very much alone. We can collect mountains of facts but cannot use them until they have been fitted together or brought under some general rule or theory. Facts without theories have no meaning. On the other hand, theories which are not based on facts are also meaningless; facts are needed to verify or disprove theories. The ability of a theory to relate facts gives it value in explanation. The sociologist must concern himself with both fact and theory, obviously. True, one student may spend a lifetime gathering facts, and another may spend his lifetime attempting to formulate general theories. Neither has the "right" approach to the subject, taken alone. Both kinds of activity are essential.

Words. Words, as Bacon noted, are deceptive. In academic work, words are often given technical meanings to eliminate some of these problems. That is, most academic disciplines have a specialized vocabulary which the student must learn to use precisely.

Unfortunately, the words that are widely used in social science are not always defined in this precise way. Freedom, democracy, socialism, and many other such terms are highly ambiguous as used in everyday speech, and their use in academic work is also imprecise. Thus sociologists use "culture" to mean something quite different from taste or refinement, and economists define "perfect competition" in a very special sense. The beginning student may not find this difficult, but anyone who reads extensively in the social sciences will find "word problems," special meanings attached to everyday terms that must be mastered.

Empiricism and rationalism. We have asserted that sociology is both a rational and an empirical science. The empiricist collects facts; the rationalist seeks to order and arrange them. The two must work together to produce fruitful explanations, for if the empiricist works alone, he acquires masses of facts without order, and if the rationalist works alone, he has nothing to discuss.

In that part of philosophy known as "epistemology," or theory of knowledge, these two doctrines are radically opposed. Most Western philosophers have been either empiricists or rationalists, and not both. Yet in science, both doctrines are combined and made to work together, and science cannot dispense with either of them. A theory unsubstantiated by hard facts is nothing more than opinion; facts by themselves, isolated and discrete, are meaningless and useless and even trivial. One may paraphrase the great German philosopher, Emmanuel Kant, and say that theories without facts are empty and facts without theories are blind.

All modern sciences in practice make use of both empirical and rational resources, and sociology is no exception. It happens that American sociology has remained rather close to empiricism as compared with German sociology, for example, which tends toward a wider use of rationalism. It also happens that over periods of time, sociology, like other disciplines, shifts its emphasis in one direction or the other. The empirical bent of American sociology has produced an enormous compilation of facts, so many facts indeed as sometimes to be embarrassing. One of the major needs of sociology in the near future is some means to transform these facts into orderly and systematic theories. And that is why we say, without by any means solving all of the problems involved, that sociology is both a rational and an empirical science.

The second methodological issue concerns the use of language. In most subjects, and particularly the physical sciences, the student begins to acquire a new and technical vocabulary almost immediately after beginning his study. In sociology, the situation is somewhat different—or at least it appears to the introductory student to be different. After two or three weeks of study he will have acquired few if any new words, for he already knows terms like "society," "culture," "role," "association," and so on. It is very important, therefore, for the student to realize that although the words look and sound the same as ordinary language terms, the sociologist in fact gives them a very precise meaning which may be quite different from ordinary discourse. For the sociologist too has a technical vocabulary. The words he uses are taken from ordinary English, but he gives them a special technical meaning, and the words do not necessarily mean what the student has been accustomed to think they mean.

It must be admitted that the technical vocabulary of sociology is not so firmly established as the technical vocabularies of some of the older sciences. Sociologists do not always use the same words in exactly the same way. This presents no problems for the introductory student, but it is possible that some of the words used in the following chapters will not be used in precisely the same sense in other sociology books, and there is nothing to be gained by concealing the problem. Where differences in usage may lead to confusion, we shall inform the student of other usages. Where such usages are only of incidental interest, or where a knowledge of them might confuse or impede the inquiry, we shall simply ignore them. In any event, we shall conform to the terminological practices of the majority of contemporary American sociologists.

A definition of sociology. We have not yet offered, in a single sentence or proposition, a statement that defines sociology. Some writers prefer to omit such a definition altogether on the ground that definitions are difficult to construct and easy to misunderstand. One might contend, with some cogency, that this entire introduction is an extended definition of sociology. The student may nevertheless find a short, summary statement useful. We shall therefore adopt as our own a definition contributed by P. A. Sorokin in his advanced systematic text. "Sociology," says Professor Sorokin, "is a generalizing science of sociocultural phenomena viewed in their generic forms, types, and manifold interconnections."[1]

The uses of sociology. We have asserted that sociology is concerned primarily with the acquisition of knowledge, not its utilization, that sociology as such is a pure and not an applied science. Does this imply that sociology is altogether devoid of utility? Of course not. However "pure" a science it may be, sociology has intellectual consequences for anyone who studies it.

In the first place, sociology is a liberating discipline. It releases the student from the provincialisms of color and class, region and religion. It encourages him to consider society as a natural phenomenon, as natural as any other phenomenon in the universe. It helps him to take an objective view

[1] P. A. Sorokin, *Society, Culture, and Personality,* Harper & Brothers, New York, 1948, p. 7.

of his own society, to learn that it is one among many, to see the manner in which his own groups interact and combine with others to form the great society in which he lives, to understand that the social forces that built the civilization of ancient Egypt and those that built the civilization of contemporary America are, in essential characteristics, the same. Sociology thus gives a perspective to history and an insight into the life of man on earth. Man, as Aristotle noted long ago, is a social animal. Everything he is or does or thinks is related in some fashion to the fact that he lives with other people and is never, except under unusual conditions and then only for a short time, alone.

In the second place, sociology can help the student to recognize and to appreciate the social factors in the environment that surrounds him—his relations with his fellows, the life of the community in which he lives, and the nature of the greater community and the larger society in which he finds himself at this particular juncture of historical circumstances. Society, after all, is no local phenomenon. It is universal and as permanent as the life of man.

For the student who decides to specialize in sociology, the more practical, as distinguished from the intellectual, consequences of this program of study are readily apparent. Sociology is a profession in which technical competence brings its own rewards. Sociologists, especially those trained in research procedures, are in increasing demand in business, government, industry, city planning, race relations, social work supervision, administration, and many other areas of community life. A few years ago all a sociologist could do with his sociology was to teach it. Although teaching, especially in colleges and universities, will always draw sociologists, sociology has now become "practical" enough to be practiced outside academic halls. Careers apart from teaching are now possible in sociology, and expertly trained people are needed to work in many of its sectors and subdivisions. The various levels of applied sociology, in short, are coming more and more into prominence on local, state, national, and international levels. Sociology has come of age.

The ultimate goals of sociology. Enough has now been said about the nature of our subject to provide a rough indication of the immediate goals and purposes of sociology. It is the immediate goal of sociology to acquire knowledge about society; it is the immediate purpose of sociological reasoning and research to describe in detail the structure of society, to exhibit the eternal recurrences and regularities in society, and to analyze the social components in all human activity.

Like all other sciences, however, sociology must go beyond descriptions, exhibitions, and analyses. It has a more remote and ultimate purpose. It seeks also the causes of things. The final questions to which sociology addresses itself are those that have to do with the nature of human experience on this

earth and the succession of societies over the long centuries of human existence. The rise of man and the succession of his civilizations—is this a process
that has rhyme and reason in it, or is it merely a cosmic accident in which
no order and regularity can be discerned? "The glory that was Greece and
the grandeur that was Rome"—are these purely chance phenomena, forever
insusceptible to logical and causal explanation? What are the factors responsible for the disintegration of one social structure, such as that of the medieval
world, and the coming into being of another? Do human societies, like the
individuals they comprise, grow old after a while, and weary, and finally
disappear from the face of the earth? Is there an ebb and flow in the affairs
of men, a systole and diastole of human history? These too are problems of
sociology. No one can answer such questions today, and men who speculate
about them are called philosophers of history. But someday, if the science of
sociology, through its intimate analyses of the dynamics of society, can achieve
some understanding of problems of this order and contribute to their resolution, it will fulfill its initial promise and its ultimate destiny.

CHAPTER 1

Natural Conditions of Human Society

Before we enter into our study of human societies themselves, it is desirable to consider certain nonsocial or natural conditions—geographic, biological, and demographic—that make societies possible and that have something to do with the similarities and differences to be discerned in them. Thus geographic factors may locate human societies and condition their mode of operation very extensively; the biological factor sets limits to social possibilities and helps to determine the form and structure of society; and the demographic factor tells us much about the characteristics of society as they already exist by revealing the statistical aspects of human populations. Natural influences of this kind are themselves shaped and molded by social and cultural factors, for the latter can alter the face of the earth and affect the structure and function of the human body. Massive influences of this sort can seldom be generalized in a simple fashion.

THE GEOGRAPHIC FACTOR

The nature of the earth as a planet has much to do with the societies that appear upon its surface, and no serious attempt to understand society can be successful without an examination of this influence. The importance of geography in human life seems self-evident, but men have differed in their opinions on the matter, some arguing that geography explains human life, others that geography explains nothing. Here we shall take the view that if the geographic factor is seldom decisive, it is seldom negligible either and is therefore a necessary consideration in any study of society.

DEFINITION. As Pitirim A. Sorokin has defined them, geographic factors include:

. . . all cosmic conditions and phenomena which exist independent of man's activity, which are not created by man, and which change and vary through their own spontaneity, independent of man's existence and activity. In other words, if we take the total environment of a man or that of a social group, and subtract from it all environmental agencies directly or indirectly created or changed through man's existence and activity, we will have left approximately what is known as geographical environment.[1]

To list these factors individually would be an impossible task, for we would have to include the sphericity of the earth, its position, movement, composition, atmosphere, and rotation, the winds that play upon its surface, its animals and plants, and so on through an endless list. But some factors are functions of other factors, and we may classify geographic influences into four main groups: (1) the sphericity of the earth, (2) the distribution of land and water masses, (3) climate, and (4) natural resources. We shall examine the manner in which each of these major factors exerts an influence upon society.

First of all, however, it is appropriate to admit a proposition that is not susceptible to denial or contradiction: A proper conjunction of cosmic conditions is necessary for the existence of life upon this planet. An examination of the conditions necessary for life is a problem for biology, not for sociology. Even where there is life there may be no human life and consequently no human societies. There are no societies on the tops of the highest mountains and none in the centers of the seas. The size of the earth itself and the number of acres of arable land set limits to the number of people who dwell upon it. We may therefore draw a preliminary conclusion that will help us to assay the role of the geographic factors in general. Geographic factors are limiting factors; they set limits to the variation of social phenomena; they determine the boundaries within which social events occur. In this sense at

[1] Pitirim A. Sorokin, *Contemporary Sociological Theories*, Harper & Brothers, New York, 1928, pp. 101 and 102.

is a necessary but not a sufficient condition for the production of naval power.

It would, of course, be erroneous to assume that geographic factors, particularly those which have to do with the relative arrangements of land patterns and water patterns on the surface of the earth, are sociologically negligible. Maritime peoples do tend to develop maritime occupations, and prairie people do cultivate the soil and become farmers. The commerce of the world tends to follow the arteries cut by geology because these are the geographic paths of least resistance. Mountains and rivers and lakes have been barriers to travel and trade and settlement. But man has learned to conquer them all. He now digs holes through the mountains to make a turnpike, and climbs over broad rivers on roadways of steel and concrete. Political boundaries commonly follow natural boundaries, but frequently they do not. Cities grow where natural conditions are favorable. Thus the City of New York enjoys one of the finest natural harbors in the world and owes much of its preeminence in international trade and commerce to the geographic advantage, but in colonial times New York was inferior as a port to both Boston and Philadelphia. If it later surpassed these cities, its growth was due in part to another geographic factor, the vast and rich hinterland now connected to the city by railroads. The harbor, river, and hinterland have existed for centuries, for geographic conditions are constants or nearly so. It is the social and cultural factors that vary. And the most elementary logic teaches us that it is impossible to explain a variable by a constant.

With respect to the influence of scenery upon the human temperament, there are as many theories as there are varieties of scenery. The mountaineer, says Ellsworth Huntington, is resentful and quarrelsome, and much bolder than the plainsman. He envies the wealthier denizens of the lowlands and often tries to steal a share of their possessions. And it is true that such raids by mountaineers occur often at harvest time in Persia and Afghanistan. In addition, feuds are more common in the mountains than in the lowlands, and they may continue for many generations. The tendency to steal and maraud Huntington attributes to the poor quality of mountain soil, for this forces the mountaineer into poverty and desperation. The tendency to feud and quarrel arises out of the natural isolation of mountain life and the lack of access to justice. "Such things would not happen if the isolation of the mountains had not forced people to look out for their own rights."[3]

The mistake here is to regard isolation as a geographic rather than a social conception. The reader can easily see that one can be as effectively isolated from human companionship in the middle of a heavily populated city as in the trackless wastes of the wilderness or on the rim of a high mountain. Geographic conditions may make social interaction difficult, but they

[3] Ellsworth Huntington, *Principles of Human Geography*, 5th ed., John Wiley & Sons, Inc., New York, 1940, pp. 223–224.

cannot prevent it completely or the species would fail; they may facilitate social interaction, but they cannot assure it. Physical distance is one thing and social distance another, and much more research is needed before theories like these can be admitted to the science of sociology. Important as the arrangement of land and water masses may be, its influence is negative and not positive. It may determine what can be and what cannot be in society, but not what actually is. And so we find increasing support for an imminent conclusion that geography governs the possible, not the actual.

Climate. Of all the geographic factors we have mentioned, climate is possibly the most important, and we shall therefore discuss the ways in which it exerts its influence on society and human activities. Again, we find that Ellsworth Huntington has emphasized more than any other writer the influence of climate upon civilization. He introduces figures to show that physical strength, mental activity, and health are correlated with variations in temperature and humidity. From his studies of productivity of workers in New England textile factories and of the daily mathematics grades of West Point cadets, Huntington notes that there is an optimum temperature for mental work and another optimum for physical work. The optimum figure itself fails, however, when the climate is monotonous, for changes of temperature, provided they are not too great, are more stimulating than uniformity, and a fall in temperature, in some climates, is more stimulating than a rise.[4]

One could continue with many more examples. Crime, suicide, morbidity, and mortality rates are all affected by climatic factors. There is no reason to suppose that other human phenomena are not similarly affected. Anyone who has tried to do his daily work in the middle of an enervating heat wave knows for himself that such factors are important. It is easy to be lazy when the temperature is abnormally high, and society itself supports our indolence. During the heat waves that frequently assail much of the United States in the summer, automobile workers in the factories of Detroit and clerical workers in the offices of Manhattan are excused from their labors and permitted to go home and rest.

Despite the acknowledged influence of climate on behavior, we must conclude that even in this respect climate is of relatively minor importance when compared with all of the social factors that influence the activity of men. Regional variations in climate are large in the United States. But the societies and civilizations in the various states are in all essentials the same. The same subjects are taught in the schools and the same general occupations

[4] Ellsworth Huntington, *Civilization and Climate*, Yale University Press, New Haven, Conn., 1915, especially pp. 79 and 119. Various factors, such as football games, holidays, etc., had to be eliminated from the results before the correlations of achievement and climate held good.

are pursued by the people. The main streets of the small towns and cities of Nevada and North Dakota are virtually indistinguishable from those of Arkansas or Minnesota. Where there are differences they are attributable, for the most part, to other than climatic factors.

Ellsworth Huntington has drawn maps showing that regions of the earth which have an equable and temperate, but variable, climate are also distinguished by a high productivity in the arts that we ordinarily associate with civilization. But even he has conceded that great nations have appeared in widely diverse climates and that areas with very similar climates (like Illinois and Southern Mongolia) differ enormously in civilization. The fact that we find the same kinds of societies in widely different climates, and different kinds of societies in the same climate, encourages us to conclude that if climate is one of the natural conditions that make human societies possible, it does not determine in any inevitable manner the infinite details of those societies.

Natural resources. Natural resources like uranium ore are not, of course, evenly distributed over the face of the earth; some nations have more of them than others and some have none at all. And it is perfectly obvious that the nations which are rich in uranium deposits may be more powerful in a political and military sense than those which have none and that this natural factor has much to do with diplomacy and international relations. We have to say, therefore, that natural resources have a great deal to do with the wealth and comparative position of nations. And even further, natural resources have something to do with the general state and condition of society. It is difficult to imagine contemporary civilization existing without iron or coal or oil. In order to make something, one must have the ingredients; the old recipe for rabbit stew begins, quite properly, "First, catch your rabbit. . . ."

It must be apparent, however, that it is not the presence of natural resources in the crust of the earth that is important but the use that is made of them. Without use, resources are quite devoid of sociological significance. The precious metals and common ores were part of the earth long before the Industrial Revolution, but they had little influence on early human society. The largest supply of uranium in the world is useless to a society that lacks the technological skills needed to use it. Again, the natural condition acts as a limit—uranium cannot be mined where it does not exist—but not as a creative factor.

We cannot conclude without mentioning the greatest of all natural resources—the resources of the soil itself. Most of our food comes from the soil, directly or indirectly, and without a proper combination of rain, sun, and soil, the earth would not yield sustenance for man. The land is one ultimate source of all wealth, and the difference between rich land and poor land has much to do with the prosperity and power of nations. But if exhausted soil supports no societies, neither does virgin soil that is not tilled. No matter how productive the land may be, it is the use that men make of land that gives it its significance for sociology. The natural resources of the earth, including its soil, are susceptible to both use and misuse by men. By themselves, the natural resources set limits to the societies men may construct and the activities in which they may indulge. But they do not in themselves determine the kinds of societies, nor the kinds of activities, that these shall be. Geography supplies the natural conditions for the answers to some of our sociological problems, but it cannot supply the sufficient conditions that wholly satisfactory answers require.

Geographic factors and civilization. The role of geographic factors in the origin, development, and disintegration of the great civilizations has fascinated sophisticated minds from ancient time to the present. Why is it that some societies rise to the level that we should be inclined to call "civilized"— a word that in its etymological and nonevaluative sense means simply "urban-ized"—whereas other societies remain in a state of primitivism and contribute nothing to literature and science and philosophy? We may argue that success in war is an essential feature of all such dominant civilizations, and no one can read the chronicles of war and fail to attribute some importance to the geographic factor. Can it be that differences in literature, religion, law, art, or philosophy can also be attributed to the influence or operation of geographic factors?

The geographer can here make a case that, on the surface at least, possesses a high order of plausibility. We may speculate, for example, that where geographic conditions are too favorable the people have no incentive to invent the arts and instruments of civilization, using some of the South Sea islands as illustrations of the point. There may be such a thing as an environment that is too propitious, one that in its very luxuriance fails to stir the natives into the restless striving that results in the development of a civilization. It is sometimes said, in jest, of course, but perhaps with some measure of truth, that the British Empire was developed by Britons striving to escape from the horrors of the English climate. Where geographic condi-tions are too unfavorable, they may require the expenditure of too much human energy simply to survive, as in the case of the frozen lands of the Eskimo; here, too, no high level of civilization can be expected to develop. This theory appears a plausible one, certainly, and it has been elevated into a philosophy of history by the speculative sociologist, Arnold J. Toynbee.

Toynbee believes that civilized societies arise as a "response" to certain "challenges," among which the environment is initially most important. Thus Toynbee declares that each of six early civilizations—Egyptian, Sumerian, Chinese, Mayan, Andean, and Minoan—arose in response to an environmental challenge, the desiccation of the soil, jungle and swamp, flood and extremes of temperature, overabundance of tropical forest, a grudging earth, or a hostile sea. These examples illustrate "the truth that, in the genesis of civilizations, the interplay between challenges and responses is the factor which counts above all others."[5] Toynbee, no extremist, notes that in the genesis of other civilizations social rather than geographic factors presented the principal challenges to man, and that in the incidence of some civilizations no direct physical challenge is present or apparent, and that even where physical challenges are present, they may have been accompanied by human challenges now concealed forever in the unknown recesses of history. But he leaves the impression that "ease is inimical to civilization," that the adversities of the unfavorable environment are an historical advantage, and that only men who must master these adversities to survive can create a civilized society. Of course, such adversities may be too harsh to overcome, as in the frozen north; hence the challenge must be reasonable, and within human capacity, to produce optimum results.

The colonization of the North American continent provides Professor Toynbee with a typical illustration. The "winning of the West" was accomplished by Yankees who had already conquered the stern coasts and stony soils of New England and not by the inhabitants of Virginia or the Carolinas. Toynbee deduces from this that the Mason and Dixon line constitutes a southern limit to the area in which man is challenged sufficiently to respond and produce civilization. Below that line, the challenge is not adequate. He also discovers a northern limit, a point beyond which the challenge is too great, and this limit he places in New England. He acknowledges the contribution made to American civilization by Massachusetts as beyond compare, then goes on to say that:

Maine, on the other hand, although actually a part of Massachusetts, until her establishment as a separate state in 1820, has always been unimportant, and survives today as a kind of museum piece—a relic of seventeenth-century New England inhabited by woodsmen and watermen and hunters. These children of a hard country now eke out their scanty livelihood by serving as "guides" for pleasure-seekers who come from the North American cities to spend their holidays in this Arcadian state, just because Maine is still what she was when many of these cities had not yet begun to arise out of the wilderness. Maine today is at once one of the longest-settled regions of the American Union and one of the least urbanized and sophisticated.[6]

Environmental factors, which reach an optimum in Massachusetts, thus reach the point of diminishing returns in Maine. The environment grows pro-

[5] Arnold J. Toynbee, *A Study of History,* abridged by D. C. Somerville, Oxford University Press, Fair Lawn, N. J., 1946, pp. 68–79.
[6] *Ibid.,* p. 147.

gressively more hostile as we move north until in Labrador we find conditions so severe that civilization cannot survive.

The down-Easterners and the Dixielanders who read this book can doubtless supply their own answers to this theory without any assistance from the author. If Toynbee is saying that the geographic factor sets limits to the kinds of human societies that can appear upon this earth, we have already agreed to this earlier in the chapter. If he is implying, however, that a civilization is an inevitable function of an optimum conjunction of geographic circumstances and challenges, his conclusions are running ahead of the supporting data. A thoughtful student may be inclined to wonder why, if the severe climate of New England stimulated the colonists to build a great civilization, it did not similarly stimulate the indigenous North American Indians who inhabited the region long before the Pilgrims arrived in 1620. Toynbee's reply to this criticism would be that the "prodigality of nature" disposes of more challenge than men can take up; hence it was in this case simply wasted. But the biological analogy is somewhat less than satisfactory.

Similar theories have been constructed on different bases to account for the disintegration as well as the construction of civilizations. Huntington, for example, believed that the decline and fall of the Roman Empire could be explained by climatic changes, particularly the decline of rainfall. He obtained his correlation by using the growth patterns of Sequoia trees in California, the only living things old enough to record changes in the days of the Empire. To sociologists, the theory seems more like astrology than geography. Another general theory is based on the observation that the capital city of each successive civilization has been located north of its predecessor. This is attributed to a gradual increase in the temperature of the earth, and the theory is used to explain the emergence of Russia as a great power. Again, this is highly conjectural, and there are not enough data to support the conclusions.

Social and geographic factors. We may conclude by emphasizing the fact that geographic influence is not a one-sided affair. Throughout the course of his existence, man has steadily and systematically altered the face of nature. Geographic factors of many kinds exert an influence on human society but human society in turn influences these same geographic factors. Climate conditions culture and culture also conditions climate. Thus man cannot initially control the chemistry of the soil or the configuration of the land or the duration of the seasons. To all these and many more geographic factors he must adjust and in some measure adapt his life. But he changes these factors as he adjusts to them. He cultivates the soil and thereby changes its composition. He can quite literally move mountains. If he cannot determine the climate, he can at least build shelter from the elements and condition the air that surrounds him, warming or cooling it to suit his needs and his fancy. He can reclaim a desert for agriculture, or even take land from the sea. The mark of man is upon the earth in all but the most inaccessible regions, and modern man can inhabit lands in which primitive man could not survive.

The process of civilization may be looked upon as a constant accumulation of instruments that insulate men and their societies from the forces of nature. The geographic factors exert their most direct and immediate effect upon the most primitive societies. As men develop a culture, from the time they begin using the skins of animals to cover their nakedness to the stage when they install air conditioning to cool their apartments in summer, they exert an ever greater control over nature. The dangers that beset man in the twentieth century are seldom, and then only in small part, attributable to the inclemency of the elements. A heavy snow may disrupt a great city for a few days, but a strike of transportation workers can have the same effect. A hurricane may level a small city, but so can a squadron of bombers. The dangers that man must face today are largely attributable to the inclemency of man himself. Few readers of this book have ever been seriously threatened by wild animals; all live under the shadow of a radioactive cloud.

What we are trying to say here is that if societies are never wholly independent of the operation of geographic factors, neither are these factors immune to social and cultural influences. Nature is vast and man is puny, but this, of all comparisons, is the least significant. Every item of culture that man devises or invents is a new sentence in his declaration of independence from nature, and although it can never be complete, it is incommensurably greater than that enjoyed by any other animal. It enables him to assert his own dominion over the earth that sustains him and gives him life.

THE BIOLOGICAL FACTOR

A noted American anthropologist is reputed to have remarked that "your carcass is the clue to your character." An equally noted American psychologist steadily maintained, in flat contradiction, that the human child is infinitely plastic and that from any infant he could produce on demand a doctor, lawyer, merchant, or chief—given of course, the proper environment and training. Here, clearly defined, is an argument between an anthropologist and a psychologist about the role to be assigned to biological factors in the development of adult men and women. The importance of biological factors is seldom denied, but it has always been a problem to estimate their influence in the never-quite-finished product that is a human being.

Sociology is not concerned with individuals as such, either with their behavior or their character or their personality. Concerns like these belong to the psychologist and social psychologist. But sociologists do need to inquire into the biological attributes of social processes, to seek the biological foundations of social phenomena, and to discover if possible the biological ingredients in human and historical events. We have already learned that human societies are what they are, to some extent at least, because of the operation and influence of geographic factors over which men have little or no control. Are they also what they are because of a comparable operation and influence of biological factors? Again, we shall anticipate our conclusions by suggesting that the biological, like the geographic, factors are a limiting and not a determining influence, that they are a necessary but not a sufficient explanation of human society and its operation.

By biological factors we mean those having to do in general with the genetic constitution of the human organism. They concern the things we have and do because we are members of a particular species, because we share the planet with other species, and because we live in a somewhat delicate ecological balance with these others. Like the geographic factors, biological elements are relatively autonomous, relatively independent of our wishes and desires. Man is a species of animal life, a species somewhat presumptuously called "sapiens," and the nature of this "wise" species has something to do with the societies that men construct. A race of morons could not possibly produce a society in which the science of mathematics would become an admired achievement—although it must immediately be said that a most gifted people might also fail to produce such a science in the absence of factors of a different kind.

To be more specific, some of the questions we wish to explore concern the respects in which societies do or do not resemble a biological organism; the role of race and racial differences in society; the biological basis of race; race mixture; the relationships between brain and intelligence, anatomy and character. In short, we seek to discover the role that biological factors play in the social life of man. In the present state of our knowledge, the conclusions will lack precision, nor can we expect a comprehensive answer. But if our discussion is neither precise nor comprehensive, we want it at least to be suggestive, to indicate the importance to society of the fact that its members also belong to a biological species.

Organisms and organismic analogies. The view that society itself is an organism, conforming to the laws that govern other organisms, will doubtless seem curious to the contemporary student. This idea, however, can be found throughout Western history, and it received a special impetus in 1859, with the publication of Charles Darwin's *Origin of Species*. For a considerable period thereafter, organic analogies were popular in sociology, and the early sociological vocabulary was filled with such terms as "organism," "heredity," "instincts," and "struggle for existence." The notion that occupies us here is not that society is *like* an organism, but that society actually *is* an organism. This conception was particularly important in the latter part of the nineteenth century and in the early part of the twentieth.

In the works of some writers of this persuasion, we find assertions that society has the same characteristics as a biological organism, including multiplication, growth, differentiation, illness, death, regeneration, integration of parts, cohesion, purposivity, spirituality, structural perfectibility, and energy transformation. We find the view that the cell is the basic unit, the tissue is a complex of cells, the organ a complex of tissues, and so on until society becomes the highest form of organism, organism being defined as "a united mass of living substance which is capable of preserving itself under certain exterior conditions." We find too the view that social phenomena, such as armies, police, roofs, etc., are "protective social tissue," corresponding to the epidermal tissue of animals. We find the belief that society, like any other organism, has organs to serve it and that the state is masculine and the church feminine. And we find the conclusion that "since society is composed of living creatures, it can be but a living creature."

It was ridiculously easy for the writers of this school to discover social counterparts for the nervous system, the respiratory system, etc. In the works of the great Herbert Spencer himself, we find a chapter entitled "A Society Is an Organism," with such additional chapters as "The Sustaining System," "The Distributing System," and "The Regulating System." It was Spencer who attempted to transform a biological theory—the theory of evolution—into a theory of society. The Darwinian conceptions of evolution, natural selection, and the survival of the fittest came in this period to be applied not only to societies, as in Spencer's works, but also to art, literature, music, philosophy, and almost every other achievement of the mind of man. "Evolution," in fact, became the key word in all intellectual inquiry, and Darwin and Spencer were the key names of an era in the history of thought, particularly in the social thought of the United States.

No one today considers society a biological organism or derives any but a momentary profit from so regarding it. Biological *analogies,* on the other hand, will doubtless persist; for it is often convenient to say that in certain respects society or some part of it is like an organism or some part of it, that some social processes *resemble* some biological or physiological processes, and that some social functions can be compared to or are analogous to some organic functions. Thus, for example, it does no harm to refer to the communications system in the United States as the nerve network of American society. It does no harm, that is, if we always realize that such a comparison is merely an analogy, a manner of speaking, a literary device with no intrinsic significance. In particular, the temptation to refer to the rise and fall of nations and of empires in terms of the life cycle of organisms will probably never be ~~wholly resisted by philosophers of history. But the reader of these theories,~~ like the sophisticated student of sociology, will recognize that he is dealing with analogies, not identities, and that where similarities of this sort arise they are superficial and external. However well they may serve to illustrate, they can seldom explain.

Race. So much has been written about racial differences, and so much suffered because of them, that one begins a discussion of the subject with trepidation. In the histories of all societies some of the darkest chapters tell of torture and terror inflicted because some people who lived in them, or in other societies, were recognizably different. And some of the fiercest pride has been taken in characteristics, genetic in origin, with which people themselves have had nothing to do, which are not human achievements but only biological accidents. All peoples in fact have dreamed of a racial "purity" when there is no such purity anywhere in the world, except possibly in the most primitive and isolated of societies. It has taken us thousands of years to learn that there is only one species of mankind on earth and that we all belong to it.

The notion that "blood will tell" is both old and erroneous. One finds it in ancient religious writing, in classical literature and philosophy, in the sacred books of the East, and indeed in the expressions of all peoples. It is a belief retained by many people today, even in our own "enlightened" country and century, and particularly by those who for one reason or another have been denied the benefits of education. It is not necessary to trace the history of an idea so persistent. Suffice it to say that this belief was given perhaps its clearest intellectual expression in the nineteenth century in the writings of Count Arthur de Gobineau and Houston Stewart Chamberlain. The work of these two men in particular, one a Frenchman and the other an Englishman, found its way into the Nazi political philosophy and gave to Adolf Hitler the catastrophic delusion that an "Aryan" was somehow superior to a Jew. In his *Essai sur l'inégalité des races*, de Gobineau stated his final conclusions as follows:

Passing from one induction to another, I was gradually penetrated by the conviction that the racial question overshadows all other problems in history, that it holds the key to them all, and that the inequality of the races from whose fusion a people is formed is enough to explain the whole course of its destiny.

and further:

I convinced myself at last that everything great, noble, and fruitful in the works of man on this earth, in science, art, and civilization, derives from a single starting point; it belongs to one family alone, the different branches of which have reigned in all the civilized countries of the universe.[7]

Similar reasoning led de Gobineau to conclude that races are in fact unequal, that some are superior and others inferior. The first carry the torch of civilization; the second are condemned to helplessness and historylessness. The latter are unfortunately in the majority, yet they have produced nothing of cultural significance in thousands of years.

By superior race, of course, de Gobineau meant the so-called "Nordic," "Aryan," or "white." This, in the age of the gods, was the one absolutely pure race, but the infusion of foreign blood has constantly contaminated it, and it has suffered degeneration. Although "the white race originally possessed the monopoly of beauty, intelligence, and strength, by its union with other varieties hybrids were created, which were beautiful without strength, strong without intelligence, or, if intelligent, either weak or ugly." Race mixture was thus anathema to de Gobineau, and he felt great apprehension about the mixture that had already occurred and the possibility that men would end up all alike, like a herd of sheep.

Chamberlain was an English aristocrat who admired the German heroic composer, Richard Wagner, and married his daughter. His writings followed the pattern laid down by de Gobineau, with less pretense at scientific exactitude. Chamberlain was particularly influential in promulgating the myth that the German people had a special mission on earth, a mission touched by divinity, which gave them both a right and a duty to subjugate other peoples.

De Gobineau and Chamberlain are representatives of a point of view that has an ancient and dishonorable history. The notion that civilization is in any way synonymous with blood, or a function of biology, is one for which there is no evidence. When one considers the number of people who have devoted their lives to seeking such evidence, one must be impressed by the fact that they have consistently been unsuccessful, that none of the evidence they have produced has remained immune to refutation or failed to collapse under the most elementary scientific criticism. There is not the slightest reason to suppose that racial factors have anything to do with the rise or fall of nations or that, in the absence of other differences, there will be a substantial difference in the societies created by the different racial groupings of mankind.

The biological basis of race. We have just denied that race produces significant differences in human capabilities; we do not deny that racial differences do exist, that the members of the human race can be classified into

[7] Quoted in Frank H. Hankins, *The Racial Basis of Civilization*, Alfred A. Knopf, Inc., New York, 1926, pp. 34–36.

subgroups in terms of known and sometimes visible physical differences. Many sociologists, appalled by the political uses to which racial differences have been put, have denied, perhaps in an excess of idealism, that races exist or that discernible differences have a biological base. They have been tempted to tell us that the notion of race is a myth or a superstition. The error may be on the side of the angels, but it is an error nevertheless. Race may be a dangerous concept, but it is hardly mythical. How do we know this? Experiments have shown that there is a definite correlation between racial classification and the ability to taste such substances as phenylthiocarbamide (PTC for short), and the ability to do so is inherited. Similar correlations obtain in the incidence of certain blood types among the races, or the presence or absence of the Rhesus factor (Rh factor) in the blood. But we do not make a classification of people on this basis, for we find that there is no relationship between the three, and people who are similar in blood type may be quite different in skin pigmentation or tasting ability. To select any one factor as *the* basic classification standard would be a purely arbitrary choice; we could give no reason for making the selection.

Probably the most common "classification" of races is based on color of skin, or pigmentation, yet skin color is perhaps the poorest basis on which to argue racial superiority. One might argue that those whose blood had a different Rhesus factor than our own were inferior or harmful to the race, just as those with different blood types are "incompatible" so far as transfusions are concerned. No such argument can be constructed on grounds of pigmentation. True, it is sometimes argued that the "white" race has evolved further than the Negro race, that the Negro is closer to the primates than the white man. Yet whites usually have thinner lips, straighter hair, and much more body hair than Negroes; in these characteristics, then, whites are clearly more similar to the order of primates than are Negroes. This conclusion is seldom drawn, of course. Arguments which asserted a differential in intelligence between the white and Negro races were for a time based upon intelligence tests administered to inductees in World War I, for the white soldiers made higher scores than Negro soldiers. Yet further investigation showed that Northern Negroes made higher scores on the average than did southern rural whites, and the factor of education and opportunity clearly overwhelmed the racial factor, and one more bit of "evidence" for racial superiority went into the discard.

Mankind—one species. Red squirrels and gray squirrels in the forests of this country do not interbreed with each other. They constitute two different species in the same biological genus. Since there is no interchange of genes between them, they are said to be in a situation of reproductive isolation. Various factors can cause reproductive isolation. Copulation may be impossible because the genital organs do not fit (mechanical isolation). The breeding seasons may not coincide. And even if copulation does occur, there may be no effective interchange or conjunction of genes. First, the sperm may not fertilize the ovum. Again, the resulting hybrid may not live, or it may be sterile if it does live (the mule, for example). Although reproductive isolation is common in the animal world, it is unknown to mankind. Every kind of normal man on earth can mate fruitfully with every kind of normal woman, producing offspring who are viable, and who, at sexual maturity, will have a similar facility. Various peoples are geographically isolated from others, and this separation, over long periods of time, has resulted in the differences we can today observe between South African Bushmen, let us say, and Polar Eskimos, between American Indians and the Arabs of North Africa. Such differences come about through natural selection and through the perpetuation of certain mutations that appear to be favorable, or at least not unfavorable, in certain geographic regions. But there is not, and so far as we know has never been, reproductive isolation among humankind. The organs fit, and sex knows no season. In other words, all men now on earth belong to one and the same species.

The races of mankind are thus seen to be subspecies rather than species, the reasons being the absence of reproductive isolation and the small degree of genetic differentiation. As Paul A. Moody concludes: "Modern races are descendants of ancient races, but probably no one modern race is the descendant of any one ancient race alone. Our inability to draw any clear-cut lines between races gives added confidence that such is the case. The genes have been continually 'reshuffled' as time, in geologic copiousness, has gone by."[8]

What are the subspecies of the human race? Most authorities now classify them into four groups that exhibit geographic and minor genetic differences: Mongolians, Caucasians, Negroes, and Australoids. They were never "pure" races, and in any event their differences are probably doomed to ultimate extinction. The world has become so small that race intermixture is increasing rather than decreasing, and even pockets of relative geographic isolation are disappearing.

So far as race is concerned, the current inhabitants of the United States of America, including presumably all of the readers of this book, are the most thoroughly jumbled of all peoples. Unless they are direct descendants of American Indians, their ancestors came in recent times from every continent. Most came from Europe, where ancestry is also mixed. The Irish, for example, are a mixture of Picts, Scandinavians, Asturians, Spaniards, Celts, Campignians, Angles, Normans, and Norsemen. The origins of most other national

[8] Paul Amos Moody, *Introduction to Evolution,* Harper & Brothers, New York, 1953, p. 234.

groups are similarly diverse. The end products in present-day America are thus mixtures of mixtures, though they may now claim the same nationality. But there is no American race, a point that is perhaps easier to see than the assertion that there is no German race, though both are fictions.

It would be pleasant if we could conclude our discussion of race with these biological observations. Unfortunately, as a distinguished sociologist, W. I. Thomas, once said, "If people define situations as real they are real in their consequences." If people believe that one race is superior to another, their belief has consequences, and the consequences are social rather than biological. The *fact* that there are biological differences between the races of mankind has nothing to do with the societies these races construct. The *belief* that the differences are important can have a great deal to do with the character of their societies.

Brain and intelligence. One biological factor would seem to have a great deal to do with human actions and would normally elicit the sociologist's attention. We refer to brain size, or cranial capacity, for there are significant differences in the relative capacity of man and other creatures. But the construction of indices which can reveal significant information about brain capacity is most difficult. If weight alone is the standard, then whales and elephants have an advantage over men. If we reckon the ratio between brain weight and body weight, the results seem closer to everyday experience. Yet even here there are quirks, for the ratio in birds is 1 to 35, and in newborn infants, 1 to 6, while in adult man it is 1 to 50. The brains of adult males are significantly larger than the brains of adult females, but female brains are somewhat larger in proportion to total body weight. Brain size seems, in short, to have little direct relationship to intelligence. Further, there has apparently been little change in the size of the human brain in the last 200,000 years. On the other hand, people in various parts of the world are growing taller, on the average; American college students of the present generation are both heavier and taller than their parents, and today's coeds have bigger feet than yesterday's. All of this has very little to do with the type of society we are producing.

Physical type and social career. If neither race nor brain size has anything directly to do with social phenomena—that is, if these biological factors do not produce social results directly—can we find any other physical characteristics that do? We have to concede, of course, that a certain collocation of biological factors is required for the appearance of a particular social effect. It is unlikely that a tone-deaf person will ever become a virtuoso on the violin. There is no certainty, on the other hand, that talent will express itself in the absence of social opportunities to do so. And it is clear that persons with absolute pitch do not automatically become violinists, any more than persons with large muscles automatically become shot-putters. Again, it seems that biological factors supply the necessary but not the sufficient conditions for the appearance of particular social phenomena.

The quest for biological correlates of social phenomena has never ceased. Psychologists, for example, are always interested in possible relationships between physical types and temperament. The practice is very old: remember Shakespeare's Caesar and his suspicion of the "lean and hungry" look of Cassius, for "such men are dangerous." Efforts to supply a link between physical characteristics and personality still appear. Ernst Kretschmer divided men into three physical types, which he called "asthenic" (lean), "pyknic" (fat), and "athletic" (athletic!), plus a "dysplastic" classification for those who did not fit the others. These "types" were supposedly associated with personality differences. The more recent theories of W. H. Sheldon had a rather extensive contemporary vogue. Sheldon wished to "somatotype" the universe, that is, to classify all people into three bodily types which he claimed were related to three temperamental types and to three psychiatric types. It is unnecessary to discuss this new variety of an ancient doctrine, for "characterology" lies, if anywhere, in the province of the psychologist. The sociologist, however, does want to know whether certain bodily or physical characteristics are correlated with social phenomena. Is there any situation in which it can be asserted that a particular biological factor *A* causes a particular social phenomenon *B*? Let us consider the question with respect to the social phenomenon of crime.

Anatomy and crime. The first serious social scientist to maintain that criminal behavior has an organic origin was the Italian scholar Secare Lombroso. According to him, criminals can be identified by certain physical traits or stigmata, including a slanting forehead; prognathism, or jutting jaw; heavy eyebrows; and either excessive hairiness or no hair at all. This theory, though it was found to be erroneous, proved to have important consequences in the stimulation it gave to studies in criminal anthropology. Every so often someone resurrects the theory and strives to find another organic basis for criminal behavior. In our own generation the most important theory of this kind has been propounded by the late Earnest A. Hooton, for many years a professor of physical anthropology at Harvard University.

Hooton and his associates devoted twelve years to a painstaking study of the bodily characteristics of criminals in an effort to find anatomical differences between them and noncriminals. They measured a criminal population of 13,873 male convicts in ten different states and a control, or noncriminal, group of 3,203. In these studies, such indices as chest breadth, head circumference, upper face height, nose height, and ear length, among many others,

were carefully recorded. At the end of their labors the investigators concluded with enthusiasm that criminals, in comparison with noncriminals, were
deficient in all these indices. They went further and attempted to discover
correlations between different racial types and kinds of crime, concluding,
for example, that Mediterranean types are high in crimes of violence, such as
murder or rape, and low in forgery, whereas Nordic types are high in the
commission of fraud but low in crimes of violence.

It need hardly be said that if such efforts as these could succeed they
would indeed indicate the importance of biological factors in the incidence
of criminal behavior. Unfortunately, none of these attempts has managed to
resist rebuttal. The notion that criminals are somehow biologically or organ-
ically inferior and that this inferiority is the cause of their criminal behavior
rests upon the shakiest of empirical and rational foundations. Using precisely
the same reasoning as Hooton follows, one could contend that males, since
they commit ten times as many crimes as females, and since they are biologically different from females, ought systematically to be weeded out of the
population.[9]

In other words, the association between delinquent or criminal behavior
and bodily type, in spite of the best efforts of serious scholars and scientists,
has at the moment to be awarded the Scottish verdict of "not proven." We
do not yet know whether there is a relationship between these two variables,
or if there is, whether it is merely coincidental or genuinely causal. There
may be a tendency for people with certain bodily malformations to become
freaks, so to speak, in circus sideshows and in carnivals, and here the linkage
is a reasonable one, but a similar relationship does not, so far as we now
know, exist between "organic inferiority" and criminal conduct. Indeed, the
critics of Hooton have exposed the circularity of the reasoning he uses to
deduce this relationship. He infers the "organic inferiority" from the criminal
conduct and then posits the former as the cause of the latter.

Animals, insects, and microbes. This is not, unfortunately, the place
to do it, but a fascinating tale can be spun about the influence of animals and
insects and microbes upon human beings and their societies. The planet, after
all, does not belong solely to us, the species that studies it and writes about it.
It belongs also to herrings and hyenas, lice and lions, cows and corn borers.
We are only one species among many and we exist in a kind of delicate
ecological balance with the others. We prey on some of them and they, of
course, return the compliment. Nature exhibits an endless cycle of eating and
being eaten, and from this process our own kind is not exempt. As a great
bacteriologist has somewhat unpleasantly put it:

[9] This facetious suggestion is made by the late criminologist, Edwin H. Sutherland, in a
devastating review of Hooton's book, *The American Criminal.* See the *Journal of Criminal
Law and Criminology,* vol. 19, pp. 911–914, March–April, 1939.

There is probably as little conscious cruelty in the lion that devours a missionary as there is in the kindhearted old gentleman who dines upon a chicken pie, or in the staphylococcus that is raising a boil on the old gentleman's neck. Broadly speaking, the lion is parasitic on the missionary, as the old gentleman is on the chicken pie, and the staphylococcus on the old gentleman.[10]

The point is that there is a balance between the human, the animal, and the insect kingdoms, and any alteration in one will in some way affect the other.

Does it follow that insects, animals, and other life forms on earth have an influence on human society? Dr. Hans Zinsser's choice of book title, *Rats, Lice and History*, clearly indicates his belief that they have a great deal to do with history and accordingly with society. Certainly the story of human epidemics, from the earliest times to the present, would shed some light upon human events not obtainable from another point of view. A study of the bubonic plague alone, the Black Death that ravaged Europe toward the end of the fourteenth century and killed, according to some estimates, as many as twenty million Europeans, would suggest that bacteriological phenomena may not be ignored as an influence in society.

Similarly, the distribution of various species of animals and fish can exert an influence in society, particularly upon the occupations of men and the economies of nations. Richard Lewinsohn offers an example in the fish trade of the late Middle Ages, which was operated on an international basis by the Hanseatic League, an organization of North European cities. The main catch was herring, which the League supplied to Europe. Lewinsohn maintains that the rise of Amsterdam was made possible by the herring industry, and goes on to say:

Meanwhile the Hanseatic League had been enjoying a virtual monopoly in the Black Sea. In about 1500, however, the herring stayed away, disappeared completely. To this day, no one knows whether it was marine currents, the depredations of larger fish, or a plague that brought about this catastrophe. In any event it was a terrible blow to the Hanse. Many historians believe that this biological event, rather than later political conflicts, started the downfall of that great commercial organization.[11]

Only historians who have given detailed and diligent study to this period of history can decide the question, of course, and they exhibit no unanimity. Nevertheless, the possibility that herring had something to do with one of the earliest and most successful efforts at international economic cooperation, and its subsequent decline, is not altogether to be discounted.

[10] Hans Zinsser, *Rats, Lice and History*, Little, Brown and Company, Boston, 1935, p. 8.

[11] Richard Lewinsohn, *Animals, Men and Myths*, Harper & Brothers, New York, 1954, p. 140.

DEMOGRAPHY

We turn now to a third approach to the study of human society, the science of demography, which concerns itself with statistical study of the human population. Since the statistics demographers produce relate to ourselves, they are among the most interesting in the world. The very first demographic question, one supposes, concerns the size of the population. How many people live on the earth today? How many were there one hundred years ago? How many will there be in ten years? A hundred years? Questions like these, though prominent, are still rather primitive so far as demography is concerned. The size of the population may be much less important than its location, its rate of growth, the causes of change in growth rate, the distribution of population, and similar questions. If we know that almost half the world's population lives on 5 per cent of the land area, and 57 per cent of the land area contains less than 5 per cent of the population, we are able to deduce some rather significant conclusions from our knowledge.

The subject of demography is not, however, without its hazards, both political and intellectual. One would think that the study of population could be more objective than almost any other. People, after all, can be counted; births and deaths can be recorded; other characteristics of the population taken as a quantity can be measured with great accuracy. Yet this is not really the case, for the findings bend this way and that, depending upon the demographers' optimism, religious views, nationality, and general intellectual attitude.

Development of demography. Demography, like sociology, is fairly new as a systematic and scientific study, but very old as a general body of questions to which men have sought answers. Ancient writers often considered the ideal relationship between the size of population and land area, between population density and efficiency, and similar questions. They pondered population growth, and population failure, and the various devices that might be used to limit them. The total size of the population much concerned early Greek writers, and Plato went so far as to specify the exact number of citizens in his state (5,040), choosing the number because its mathematical properties appealed to his own love for arithmetic and because the number was adequate for defense and maintenance of community expenses. His pupil Aristotle investigated many of the same questions, particularly the overall size of the community and the means of controlling increase, including rewards for marriage, rebuke for those who fail to marry, and migration of excess populations to form new colonies (a common Greek practice).

Not until the seventeenth century do we find the beginnings of analytic rather than merely descriptive demography. The mercantilists were interested in the population problem because of its effect on national strength, and advocated, among other things, a continual growth of the population. Already we find budding demographers investigating regularities in population statistics and learning that the death rate is higher in urban than in rural areas, that male births exceed female births, and that the death rate is higher for the young and the old than for those in between. All of these principles appear in the works of John Graunt (1620–1674), and a German, Johann Peter Sussmilch (1707–1767), wrote a comprehensive work in which he related variations in mortality rates with variations in age, sex, residence, and so forth, estimated the population of the earth of his day, and offered a hypothesis on future population growth. It is worth mentioning that Benjamin Franklin also wrote a book on demography in which he suggested that overcrowding, which interferes with acquiring the means of subsistence, is the only real limit on population growth.

Thomas Malthus. In 1798, an English clergyman named Thomas Malthus published one of the most influential and important books in the entire history of sociology. Men like Charles Darwin, David Ricardo, and many others have tilled the field that Malthus first cleared and found something there of use to them. Malthus's book, entitled *An Essay on the Principle of Population as It Affects the Future Improvement of Society, with Remarks on the Speculations of Mr. Godwin, M. Condorcet, and Other Writers,* has become a landmark in demography. Malthus was concerned with the doctrine of human progress he found in the writings of Condorcet and Godwin, and hence with the notion of human perfectibility, of an end to inequalities and animosities among men. These men were optimists and Malthus thought their enthusiasm misplaced.

Briefly, Malthus believed that the heart of poverty and misery was revealed only through the study of population as a whole, not through an investigation of the qualities of individual men. If the population was allowed to increase without any restraint, it would double every twenty-five years, and hence increase in a geometric ratio according to the series 1, 2, 4, 8, 16, 32, etc. The food supply, on the other hand, could not possibly increase more rapidly than an arithmetic ratio, e.g., 1, 2, 3, 4, 5, 6, 7, 8, 9, etc. From this, Malthus concluded that "in two centuries the population would be to the means of subsistence as 256 to 9; in three centuries as 4,096 to 13, and in two thousand years, the difference would be incalculable." Something would have to give.

It was the formula and not the fact that gave the theory its impact. Others before Malthus had noticed the relationship between the productive powers of the earth and the reproductive capacity of man. The mathematical ratio, however, seemed more exact and compelling than any verbal argument could possibly be. What Malthus did was call attention to the relative properties of arithmetical and geometric series, which differ in an awesome manner.

Of course, population does not increase unchecked, as Malthus himself realized full well. There were positive checks, which might affect any species and shorten the natural life span—such checks as epidemics, diseases, wars, famines, and climatic exposure. And there were preventative checks, which men themselves employ, either deliberately or accidentally, to reduce population growth, including celibacy, late marriage, sexual continence, or "moral restraint" as Malthus called it, though he pointed out that it "does not at present prevail much among the male parts of society." Since Malthus thought the need for sexual gratification second only to the need for food, the outlook for the future did not appear to him to be very bright.

Although things have not worked out quite in accordance with Malthus's formula, and neither the food supply nor the population has followed the predicted pattern, his work remains fundamental in importance. He could not anticipate the peculiar situations that at times have prevailed in the United States, for example, where the food supply (or rather, the capacity to produce food) has grown much more rapidly than the population. But Malthus did realize, and this is the vital point, that there is a limiting relationship between population and food supply, and his dramatic essay captured the attention of those interested in social science. With his essay, we enter on a new era in writings on population. In fact, much of modern demography may be phrased as a conflict between Malthusians and anti-Malthusians, and the conflict has not yet been settled. Karl Marx tended to accept Malthus's argument, but contended that it was true only of capitalistic societies. In this context, the policy of the Chinese Communists in recent years is interesting, for they at first attemped to stimulate population growth, and then, more recently, have returned to birth control and attempts to limit the rate of growth of the population. Perhaps the Chinese Marx is turning to Malthusianism?

The census. A census, or head count, of the population began as an instrument of Roman taxation, and was very unpopular for that reason. Early efforts to count the population were usually limited to certain categories of people, and since the information had military significance, the results are not known to us in most cases. In general, estimates of population in early history are only estimates, however ingenious they may be. Attempts to produce an accurate head count began in the United States, Canada, and Sweden about the middle of the eighteenth century; no one is certain which country first made the attempt. By the end of the nineteenth century, the practice of taking a census was common in most of Europe. By 1930, it had been extended to cover some two-thirds of the world's population. In 1960, the United Nations was able to report population statistics for over one hundred countries and territories. How accurate these figures may be, say, in

China or India, is another matter, but the presumption is that they are now reasonably accurate in most cases.

World population. We hear a great deal these days about population "explosions," and if we consider the growth of world population from the inception of man to the present, or even for the past hundred thousand years, then it may truly be said that an explosion has occurred in modern times. For thousands and thousands of years, the population was sparse and thinly spread in small settlements of a few dozen persons. The rate of increase for each generation was also small—almost insignificant. If we take 600,000 B.C. as a reasonable starting point, we discover that from that time to the present some 77 billion people have enjoyed a sojourn here. Only about 12 billion of these people lived before 6000 B.C., so 99 per cent of the time span produced only 6 per cent of the population. In the remaining 1 per cent of the time, 94 per cent of the total population of mankind was produced. More impressive is the fact that about 4 per cent of all the people who have ever lived on the earth are alive today.

By early modern times, the world's population had risen to some 500–550 million persons, but the growth trend was neither large nor continuous nor uniform. The general pattern of development from the Middle Ages to roughly the seventeenth century may be summarized in three groups: (1) In China, India, Mesopotamia, the Near East, and Egypt we find wide fluctuations, a relatively small net increase and in some cases a decrease in population. (2) In Greece, Spain, and the Danube region, there are similar but less violent fluctuations, with a trend toward population increase. (3) A pronounced increase occurs in Central and Eastern Europe. A small overall increase is generally assumed after the seventeenth century, but no one knows the rate or how it compares with earlier population trends. The data given for the period are usually "educated guesses" rather than settled facts. However, the experts tend to agree with a reasonable margin as we can see from the following chart.

POPULATION OF THE WORLD, 1650–1900

Date	Willcox	Carr-Saunders
1650	470,000,000	545,000,000
1750	694,000,000	728,000,000
1800	919,000,000	906,000,000
1850	1,091,000,000	1,171,000,000
1900	1,571,000,000	1,608,000,000

SOURCE: W. F. Willcox, *Studies in American Demography*, Ithaca, 1940, and A. M. Carr-Saunders, *World Population, Past Growth and Present Trends*, Oxford, 1936. Both sets of figures are taken from *The Determinants and Consequences of Population Trends* (Population Studies, no. 17), United Nations, New York, 1953.

The difference here is not very large and we can therefore accept either set, or a compromise figure between them, with a good bit of confidence.

When we come to the most recent period of history, the population figures tell a startling story.

POPULATION OF THE WORLD, 1920–1960

1920	1,834,000,000
1930	2,008,000,000
1940	2,216,000,000
1950	2,406,000,000
1960	2,901,834,000

The rate of growth *by decades* is becoming incredibly large, for population grew as much from 1950 to 1960 as in the whole century and one-half from 1650 to 1800. If we produce a graphic representation of population growth in the past 100,000 years, we obtain a picture which shows all too clearly the present population trend. The change is dramatic, and has many implications.

The crowd. As in Malthus's time, we are assailed on all sides by the great debate over population. Are there too many people in the world? Should human productivity be restrained? Does the concept of overpopulation make sense? What occurs if the death rate is lowered and the birth rate remains unaffected? Will the problem disappear with the coming of the Marxist state? Obviously these are questions that cannot be given a clear and definitive answer.

However, let us examine the situation in the worst possible light, as the neo-Malthusians see it. The figures have already been given in outline; the question is, what shall we make of them? From the origins of man until 1830, the population of the earth did not exceed 1 billion persons. One hundred years later the population had doubled. And how long will it take to reach 3 billion? Only thirty-one additional years. At the present rate of increase, a fourth billion will be added in another fifteen years, and ten years more will add a fifth. By the end of the present century, the world's population will rise to some 6 billion if allowed to proceed unchecked.

The impact is not uniform from one country to another, of course, but consider some miscellaneous items relating to population in various areas. India is adding 8 million people to its total every year; China adds 1 million each month, or 12 million per year. The population of Mexico will double in the next twenty years. Every year in the sixties, the earth acquires another 46 million people—enough to populate modern France. Yet two-thirds of the people in the world go to bed hungry each night, and every morning about 150,000 more infants are clamoring for food.

If statistics are more understandable, or more palatable, in smaller doses, consider that some 6,000 babies are now born every hour—which means 100 each minute, day or night. And each day, the number increases, and the rate of increase is alarming, for we are truly beginning to learn something of Malthus's geometric increase ratio. There are more people on earth than ever before, and the rate at which the number is increasing is alarming. The earth is becoming a thickly populated planet.

The United States. The population of one particular country has no more intrinsic interest for sociology than the population of any other, though population problems will tend to be solved at the national level so long as the present political organization of the world is retained. Sociology is concerned with phenomena or processes that appear everywhere, and this relatively abstract view distinguishes it from history or ethnography. Nevertheless, the population trends discernible in the United States are a useful illustration of the problem at hand, and since data are readily available, we will make use of the illustration. This is also a useful remedy for anthropocentrism, since Americans are easily persuaded that the difficult problems of mankind always happen elsewhere and that our own country is relatively immune from social processes that affect less-developed or less well endowed nations. It is true, of course, that we are favored in many respects, but it is not true that our natural advantages enable us to escape the problems that beset all other societies.

Let us begin with the facts. On November 30, 1961, the population of the United States reached 185 million persons, a figure far greater than the estimates made by demographers prior to World War II. The increase from 1960 to 1961 was 3 million, a figure larger than the total population of any American city except New York and Chicago. At this rate, we shall produce enough people every 2½ years to populate another New York City. The population of the entire country is expected to reach 196 million by 1965, and 214 million by 1970. A child born in 1957 who lives a normal life span can expect to see the population soar to 400 million.

Two points command our attention here. First, only three countries in the world have a larger total population—China (583 million), India (384 million) and the Soviet Union (215 million). The United States is the fourth most populous country in the world today. If we examine population density, the ranking changes somewhat. India goes to the top of the list with 317.2 persons per square mile; China is next with 172.7, the United States third with 50.5, and the Soviet Union fourth with 24.1. The United States is thus twice as "crowded" as the U.S.S.R. It is interesting to note that more than half of the world's population lives in one or another of these four countries.

A second point is that in our growth from roughly 4 million people in 1790 to 63 million in 1890, the figures duplicate with curious precision the geometric increase that Malthus predicted for all populations everywhere in the absence of positive or preventative checks. In this century, the population of the United States did double every twenty-five years, and the curve of population growth coincides almost exactly with the Malthusian projection. From 1890 to the present, our rate of increase has declined, partly because immigration virtually stopped, and partly because the birthrate declined.

In any event, the most palpable of present facts about the population of the United States is that it is increasing at a rate that some people, not all of whom are looking for a place to park, regard as something more than comfortable. With immigration relatively static and with no important emigration, the changes that occur are attributable to a continued increase in the birth rate and a continued decrease in the death rate. The rise of the birth rate after World War II is puzzling, for it means that younger Americans are producing larger families than their parents. In 1950, for each 1,000 women of childbearing age, 154 children were born; in 1960, this number increased to 180 children. The decline in death rate can be explained, for the most part, but it is very difficult to say with certainty why people have more children. For our purposes, it is clear that the population problem is not limited to underdeveloped nations of Asia and Latin America. It is also an American problem.

What of the future? We can approach the future of populations by two different routes. We can make population *projections*, using only statistical materials; or we can make *forecasts*, introducing nonstatistical variables and estimating their influence. Forecasts, of course, are far more hazardous than projections. It is impossible to predict with certainty the influence of depressions, wars, or even social changes such as the removal of a religious taboo on contraceptives. It is not always possible to distinguish between projections and forecasts, and in what follows we shall move beyond both to what is sheer speculation, for we want to consider some of the things that can happen, that are not beyond the realm of possibility, as the future unfolds.

The first possibility is that there is an automatic check built into the reproduction process, some natural means of preserving the ecological balance between the species and its food supply, something that is wholly natural and does not require the intervention of human plan or design. Reproduction rates may be a function of population density, for example; they may decline when the density becomes too great, and thus ensure the continuation of the species yet protect against excesses.

It must be said at once that such theories enjoy little evidence in their support. Such data as we have come chiefly from the lower animals, and even in this area, they have not been accepted unanimously. Some naturalists assert that glandular secretions in the lower animals alter with population changes, thus increasing or decreasing factors like susceptibility to disease, resistance to infection, fertility, or milk production. This phenomenon has been observed among some of the animals, and not among others. Yet it is certain that some animals maintain an ecological balance. A four-year study of woodchucks in Pennsylvania, for example, shows that the population tends to stabilize at one woodchuck per acre approximately, and this balance is quickly restored when the total population is altered, or even reduced by half. This too is believed to be the outcome of hormone change.

Whether such phenomena, if true of the lower animals, also apply to men, we cannot know. We merely want to suggest the possibility that an increase in population density may be detrimental to population increases, and thus operate as an automatic check. But as opponents of such theories point out, those parts of the world with high birth rates are also most densely populated. There are too many other factors at work for any simple theory to operate, however attractive it may be.

The second possibility is that present trends may be reversed. The history of population growth shows many regressions, surges, and retreats of population in the past. Long-range predictions are therefore quite risky, and the demographers may be wrong again—and they may not. If a reversal of trend is to occur, it seems likely that national policy will in some way be involved in the change, though it is also possible that people themselves, if sufficiently concerned, may reverse the trend without direction. Parents who are desperately short of food do not, given a choice, usually produce a large family which increases the problem. Similarly, when it is difficult to support a family, men marry later in life, thus reducing the potential size of the family.

Finally, there is a paradoxical kind of solution to the population problem —war. Unfortunately, it is so effective that it may also finish off the whole of mankind. But nuclear warfare is quite capable of taking care of excess populations, either by direct destruction or by sterilization or the production of lethal mutants. Whether the solution is more terrible than the problem must be left to the individual moral judgment of those concerned with the question.

Summary

In this chapter, we have indicated a number of ways in which geographic, biological, and demographic factors influence human societies; we have also stressed the extent to which this influence is sharply limited by the nature of those societies and by the social and cultural factors which are the products of human ingenuity. What these social and cultural factors are we shall explain in detail as we proceed, for they constitute the central theses of sociology. But we have now finished one of our preliminary tasks, an exhibition of the relationship between the earth and the societies it supports.

The principal geographic factors affecting human society arise out of the sphericity of the earth and its movement in orbit, the distribution of land and water masses on earth, climate, and natural resources. Each of them is important, and none may be ignored, for together they make possible the existence of society. But none of them singly, nor all of them taken together, can explain the infinite variations in human societies. The geographic influence, then, is limiting but not determining. Geographic factors are necessary but not sufficient to explain human social organizations. To ignore them is to commit a serious sociological error. But to give them more significance than they warrant in each particular situation is to commit an error equally serious. As human societies grow in complexity and as culture accumulates, geographic factors decrease steadily in sociological significance. Geography, in short, governs the possible, not the actual.

Biological factors also have a role to play in human society, for society is what it is, to some extent at least, because the human organism is as it is. No thoroughgoing sociology can neglect certain basic biological facts, like bisexual reproduction, or deny their influence in society. But society is not itself an organism, and the organic analogy is both false and misleading.

We have also examined some of the ingenious and even desperate attempts to associate civilization with one color of skin rather than with another. Such efforts, like organic analogies, are devoid of scientific significance or cogency. That there are small biological differences between various groupings of mankind cannot be denied, but it is impossible to maintain for long that these differences have anything to do with the differences in their societies. Nor can we find a close correlation between physical type and social phenomena, such as crime, in spite of astonishingly diligent and even brilliant attempts to discover them. Even increases and decreases in population, though they depend upon biological activity, are not autonomous biological factors; they are susceptible to the reciprocal influence of human device and design.

Finally, we have had a brief look at population trends, at the science known as demography, tracing its growth from the work of Thomas Malthus and his observation that population and food supply grow at different rates. The trends in population growth current everywhere in the world, not excluding the United States, are a matter of interest and significance to every educated man. Difficult though it may be to assess their significance, the facts are becoming more and more available, and they all indicate a steady surge in population, particularly in recent decades. Here, doubtless, is another problem that will occupy the attention of sociologists, economists, and political scientists in the future.

Review questions

1. Outline briefly and accurately the doctrines or theories associated with each of the following persons. Give the approximate date of their writings, and know the criticisms that have been made of their theories.

    a. Arthur de Gobineau
    b. Houston Stewart Chamberlain
    c. Ernst Kretschmer
    d. W. H. Sheldon
    e. Hans Zinsser
    f. Earnest A. Hooton
    g. Arnold J. Toynbee
    h. Thomas Malthus
    i. Ellsworth Huntington

2. Give an adequate justification for the view that single-factor theories are unlikely to be adequate to explain society.

3. Give some examples of the manner in which geographic factors affect society and are overcome by society, using the United States as a model. Try to take examples from various aspects of social life (economic, political, etc.) rather than from one single area.

4. Differentiate between the view that society *is* an organism and the view that society is *like* an organism, explaining the uses and dangers of each view.

5. List the major known differences among the races and discuss briefly the significance of each of them for modern society.

6. Differentiate between a population forecast and a population projection and explain the uses of each.

7. List the major questions that can be answered by population statistics and comment on their significance for the sociologist.

8. Discuss the significance of Malthus's doctrine for present-day American society, indicating factors which might increase or lessen its validity.

For further study

1. What would be the effect of a scientific discovery that clearly established the superiority of one of the races?

2. Prepare a comparative demographic study of the United States and the Soviet Union, including information about population density, rate of increase of population, urbanization, relation of total population

to various other social and economic factors, etc. Attempt to draw meaningful conclusions from the information you have compiled.

3. In the long run, will an idea that is false lose its significance? Why?

4. Does an increase in technological skill decrease the influence of geographic factors on society? Can you cite evidence for either side of the question?

CHAPTER 2

Basic
Aspects of
Human Society

We are now ready to turn directly to the central themes of sociology and to treat in detail the factor of *culture*, the factor which above all others exerts a positive and determining influence in society. Culture is one of the most important concepts in contemporary social science: it appears in psychology, social psychology, economics, political science, and many related studies. We are concerned first with its meaning, with the qualities that make up a culture, and then with its content, with the beliefs, capacities, artifacts, etc., that society actually produces.

THE MEANING OF CULTURE

An American high school student learns that the square of the hypotenuse of a right-angled triangle is equal to the sum of the squares of the other two sides. He also learns that bodies attract each other with a force that is directly proportional to their mass and inversely proportional to the square of the distance between them. He does not, usually, learn how to catch a seal or sew a parka hood or make a kayak. An Eskimo child will not learn the things in the first group, but will usually know how to perform the operations necessary in the second. How are we to explain these differences? It is fairly obvious that no examination of climate or topography or any geographic factor can provide a satisfactory explanation. For if it is true that seals do not grow everywhere, nevertheless, mathematics can be taught anywhere; yet it is not. Nor can we find an answer by examining the human brain or the living organism that we call man. We must seek our explanation in another factor, the factor of culture.

Nearly everyone makes use of the term "culture" in everyday speech, as we commonly differentiate between a "cultured" and an "uncultured" person. In this sense, the term has something to do with personal refinement, and possession of culture implies the knowledge needed to conduct oneself properly in all of the social situations to which he is likely to be exposed and in which he participates. It means, as Matthew Arnold once said, a knowledge of the best that has been thought and said in the world, an ability to see life steadily and to see it whole. It is not easy to say precisely what culture is in this sense, for common usage has produced overtones which are not easily differentiated. But in any event, this is not the sense in which the word culture is used in sociology.

A DEFINITION. In the interests of simplicity, we shall provide an initial definition of the meaning of culture, but the definition will be expanded as we move along and the implications and qualifications which must attach to the definition are made clear. We shall say initially: *Culture is the complex whole that consists of everything we think and do as members of society.* This is only a point of departure, not a final definition.

Some synonyms for culture.

We can clarify the nature of the phenomenon that sociologists call culture by considering some of the terms that are used as synonyms for culture, as expressions that give exactness to its meanings.

Learned behavior. The first of these is the phrase "learned ways of behavior." When it is identified in this way, culture is not behavior as such but the "channels" in which human behavior proceeds. Unlearned behavior like the eye-blinking reflex or the knee-jerk reflex are purely physiological and therefore not cultural. Shaking hands and shaving, on the other hand, are learned and are therefore part of culture. The emphasis upon learning is important. Man is poorly supplied with instincts, compared with the other members of the animal kingdom. Unlike the bees and birds, he must learn most of his behavior patterns. There is no instinct or biological endowment that teaches man to tie a shoelace, boil a potato, or fry an egg; such things must be learned, and learned from other men. A bird, supplied with materials, will build the right nest at the right time even if no other bird is present to emulate. This simply is not true of man; in the human being, all but the most simple of reflexes, such as the sucking reflex which is present at birth, must be learned. Whether or not we learn particular behavior patterns, if we are normal individuals, depends not upon genetic constitution but upon our being members of a society in which the behavior occurs. We learn to sew and read and build kayaks because we are born in a society in which sewing, reading, and kayak building take place.

Culture, in other words, is transmitted by learning, not through the chromosomes and the genes. And learning requires social interaction. We can illustrate this fact easily by noting that individuals who are deprived of society, of the companionship of other people, do not acquire a culture. A case of this kind has been observed and described by Kingsley Davis; it involved Anna, an illegitimate child found in the attic of a Pennsylvania farmhouse. The child had been given no attention, no training of any sort, no exercise, and just enough food to keep her alive. When discovered, she could not walk or talk or even sit upright, and she was believed to be both deaf and blind. As Professor Davis commented, her condition showed "how little her purely biological resources, when acting alone, could contribute to making her a complete person." By the time Anna died, at the age of ten, she had learned how to follow directions, play with beads, identify colors, build with blocks, keep her clothing clean, wash her hands, and brush her teeth. Thus, although she never "caught up" with others of her age group, she did make notable progress in spite of her overwhelming and ultimately fatal handicap.[1]

This case and others like it indicate that no one can acquire culture without associating with human beings and that once culture is acquired it can gradually be lost through deprivation of the association. Extraordinary as it may seem, human beings need other human beings in order to become human and remain human. We are not born human but become so by acquiring the culture of our society. The man without a culture, in this sociological sense, is a feral man, a "wild" man, more like an animal than a human being. The human child, whom someone has wittily and sensibly defined as an alimentary canal with a lot of noise at one end and utter irresponsibility at the other, must literally be "domesticated," and the process of domestication is the process of acquiring culture.

The social heritage. A second synonym for culture is "the social heritage." If culture must be learned, even where learning is unconscious imitation, so

[1] Kingsley Davis, *Human Society*, The Macmillan Company, New York, 1949, pp. 204–205.

also it has to be taught, even if the teaching is unconscious instruction. If a generation fails, for one reason or another, to transmit a part of its culture to the succeeding generation, that aspect of culture will simply disappear and may have to be reinvented or rediscovered at a later period. Thus there are various things that people living in an earlier age knew how to do that people living centuries after them can no longer do. No one today, for example, knows the secret of Egyptian embalming. And no one today knows the formula for making the stained glass used in medieval cathedrals. Contemporary technicians know how to stain glass, but some part of the formula has been lost through a failure of transmission. Though we have learned to do many things that were quite unknown to our predecessors, we have forgotten some things that were commonplace to them.

Culture may, in these terms, be conceived as a kind of stream flowing through the centuries from one generation to another. When we think of it this way, it becomes synonymous with the "social heritage" of man, and some sociologists use this term rather than the term culture. Each generation contributes something to the stream, and in each generation something is left behind, some "sediment" drops to the bottom and is lost to society. For the most part what is lost is no longer required; it disappears because it has become obsolete. But in some cases, it may be possible to lose a social heritage of real value through neglect or failure to realize the importance of particular parts of culture. Our museums are full of relics of all kinds from earlier civilizations, just as our books are full of earlier ideas, many of which have disappeared from current use.

Although metaphors are dangerous, especially when taken too literally, we may say that the social heritage, or culture, is the memory of the human race. Few of us today, perhaps, would have the wit to invent a wheel or the genius to devise an alphabet if the concepts themselves were missing. Fortunately, we do not have to do these things, for all of them were part of our culture when we were born. It is instructive to think about what society would be like without this accumulation of culture, what our lives would be without it. Human beings as we know them would not in fact exist; man would simply be another species of animal. It is culture, par excellence, that distinguishes us from other animals, and if animals of some species, such as the anthropoid apes, have the ability to learn, the fact that they have no language prevents them from transmitting what they learn to the next generation. Language is, of course, the most important of all vehicles for transmitting culture, and without language, culture cannot accumulate.

To digress a moment, we ought to point out that culture in the sociological sense is something that is shared, and not something that one person alone can possess. An isolated inventor may produce a gadget that does all sorts of wonderful and useful things, but if no one but himself ever uses it, it does not become part of culture. Similarly, if new ideas never find public expression and if new ways of doing things are not adopted by other people, they may as well never be conceived or devised. For culture is shared. It is something adopted, used, practiced, believed, or possessed by more than one person. It depends upon group life for its existence.

Man—like all of his cousins in the animal world—must ultimately adjust to his physical environment; he can develop and vary only within limits set by that environment. Unlike the other animals, man does not adjust to the physical environment directly, for culture always intervenes and in most cases aids the process of adjustment. Just as our houses shelter us from the storm, so culture insulates us from natural dangers and helps us to survive. And few of us indeed could survive without culture, though early man must have been able to do so. For us, nature does not exist "in the raw," and we do not need to respond to it alone. We have the aid of our social heritage. A modern civilized man going naked into the wilderness, without knife or ax or match, might possibly survive and might even thrive. But if he were also without a single scrap of knowledge, his survival would be problematic. And the knowledge that would make survival possible would have its source in his culture. Thus Robinson Crusoe took his culture with him when he landed on his ocean isle, and he did not have to "start from scratch." Nature, however, sometimes reminds us that culture alone is not enough for survival when it hurls winds, cold, water, or shock at us; but without culture, survival would be difficult even in the best of weather or with a minimum of natural hazards.

The superorganic. A third synonym that is sometimes used for culture is the "superorganic," so called because of its independence from organic and inorganic factors. This implies that there are three orders of phenomena—organic, inorganic, and superorganic. The first of these is investigated by the biological sciences, the second by the physical sciences, and the third by the social sciences and humanities. The term "superorganic" was introduced into the literature by Herbert Spencer, and it is unfortunate, in a sense, for it implies that somehow culture is "superior" to nature, or that what is cultural is not natural. The modern city is, of course, just as natural as the anthill, and the implication here is clearly false. Yet the term "superorganic" is useful if it implies that a phenomenon which has one appearance from the physical or biological point of view may look quite different when approached through culture. A piece of cloth may be used as a headdress in one society, a diaper in another, and a flag in a third. A tree means one thing to the botanist, another to the gardener who tends it, and still another to the motorist who collides with it or the farmer who picks its fruit. The same physical objects and physical characteristics, in other words, may constitute a variety of quite different cultural objects and cultural characteristics. On the other hand, the same cultural meaning may be objectified in a variety of physical objects, as the flag has significance whether printed on paper, hung from a pole, or stamped in metal.

The same considerations apply to the relationship between organic facts and their cultural significance. How men are garbed—whether as priests, soldiers, miners, prisoners, professional baseball players—has a great deal to do with how they are viewed by society. But so far as biological type is concerned, an admiral may be quite indistinguishable from a bishop or a swindler. Thus the adage that clothes make the man is full of sociological meaning.

The word "superorganic," therefore—if we refrain from attaching metaphysical connotations to it—fixes our attention upon the social meaning of physical objects and physiological acts and emphasizes the fact that this social meaning may be relatively independent of physical and biological properties and characteristics.

Other synonyms for culture. Finally, we may note that various simpler and less precise terms are sometimes used as substitutes for the term culture. Sometimes, for example, culture is taken to mean simply a "way of life" of a people or a "design for living." This concept of culture is particularly useful in distinguishing one society or group from another. For the reference here is not to culture in general but to particular cultures. Thus the "culture" of the Mexicans is different from that of the French and the culture of the contemporary Soviet student is different from that of the American reading this book. There is an American way of life that is important to Americans; it is our design for living. Similarly, other peoples have their own way of life which is important to them and which they cherish.

"Way of life" is superficially a simple term, but the conception is really quite complex when it is carefully examined. For culture in this sense is capable of almost infinite variety within the limits set by biology and geography, and cultures as they appear on earth need not coincide with political boundaries or with historical eras and epochs. But it is permissible to speak of the American way of life as American culture and the Japanese way of life as Japanese culture and so on. All peoples have their design for living, and this, in a very general sense, is what we can also mean by their culture.

The importance of culture. It is almost impossible to exaggerate the importance of culture in human life. Neither a single individual, nor a particular social group, nor an entire society can be understood without reference to culture. It is culture that distinguishes individual from individual, group from group, and society from society. It is culture that distinguishes us as a species from the other animals. It is culture that makes us human. What each individual contributes to culture is small indeed; what he takes from it is beyond all possibility of measurement.

In some respects we are like all other people, in some respects like some other people, and in certain respects like no one except ourselves. The first of these comparisons is the proper concern of biology and physiology, and the last of individual psychology. Sociology is especially interested in the second, in the respects to which we are both like and unlike other persons, and this is, obviously, related to our culture.

It may seem obvious that seeing is a purely physiological act and that what we see depends upon what is in front of us when we open our eyes. Actually, what we see depends upon our culture, for strange as it may seem, we must learn to see, and what we learn to see depends to a large degree upon the society in which we mature. A blind man who suddenly recovers his sight will not be able to distinguish between a cube and a pyramid by sight, though he can make these distinctions readily by touch. He must learn to interpret what he sees. Indeed, the spectacles that some of us wear to correct our vision actually "correct" the world that presents itself to our eyes. And spectacles, of course, are a cultural item unknown to some societies.

Even more dramatic, perhaps, is the fact that people all over the world see different things in the same object, such as the moon. Americans see a man in the moon, and sometimes another man looking over the first man's shoulder. The natives of Samoa see in the moon a woman who is weaving the stuff that clouds are made of. Native American Indians of the North West see such things as a duck, an eagle with outstretched wings, and a horned toad. To the Indians of the East the moon contains a little gray rabbit with long ears and outstretched paws. And loveliest of all, perhaps, Irish legend tells us that the young girl who drinks white wine and rosewater and then looks at the moon through a silken handkerchief will see there the face of her future bridegroom.[2]

If what we see depends upon our culture, so also, and much more obviously, does what we wear, and indeed whether we wear anything at all. Variations in costume are immense and can almost always be used to distinguish societies from one another as well as to distinguish different groups and strata within the same society. Similarly, culture decides what sort of structures men build for shelter and what food they will eat. The French consider water fit only for washing, and regard milk drinking by adults with horror. Some people live mainly on fish, others on meat, others on cereals. Obviously, these distinctions are cultural, not natural or biological. Biology may demand that we have food, but it cannot tell us that a lizard is a delicacy while cattle are sacred and should not be eaten. Geography may limit the materials available for building houses and other buildings, but it does not tell us whether we should build large apartment buildings or small houses or skyscrapers.

[2] The author is indebted for these facts to Mary Gene Evans, "What's in a Moon?" *The New York Times Magazine,* Oct. 12, 1947, p. 34.

One might be tempted to think that shedding tears, like other expressions of emotion, is a physiological process to be accounted for in terms of the functioning of the tear glands when excited by the appropriate stimulus. There is no evidence to show that glands are constructed differently or function differently in different societies, though there are minor variations attributable to age and sex. But a physiological examination of the glands and their nervous connections, no matter how minute, will not explain why they operate on certain occasions in some societies and not on similar occasions in other societies.

American men do not, as a rule, shed tears in public except on the occasion of bereavement, or possibly at the loss of an important football game. Weakness in this respect is culturally tabooed, and boys in our society are taught as early as possible to restrain their tears in circumstances of sorrow or anger or pain. American men, however, are permitted grimaces, if not tears, in certain situations, say, in the dentist's chair. In certain American Indian tribes, on the other hand, the young braves were subjected to an ecstasy of torture, and they passed the test only when they endured it without a flicker of facial expression. It cannot be maintained that there are constitutional differences in the ability of men of different societies to withstand pain. The answer again is cultural. When we reflect that the adult American male is permitted to laugh in public but not to cry, that the adult Iroquois male is permitted to do neither, and that the adult Italian male is permitted to do both, we can easily see that other than physiological factors are at work.

It is often maintained that for physiological reasons, some peoples are more aggressive and warlike than others, yet here too we find that it is culture that matters and not physiology. The contemporary American student may think it quite "natural" to read these lines from left to right and is likely to imagine that any other way of reading would be wrong. He has forgotten, of course, that he was once taught to read in this direction, and that he did not do so automatically or naturally. A little reflection will convince him that the explanation is cultural, for the Hebrew and Persian read from right to left, and the Chinese from top to bottom beginning at the right, and these directions seem equally natural to them.

If what we do is so greatly conditioned by our culture—eating, drinking, building, laughing, reading and writing, and all of the other activities in which we indulge—so also is what we think. Once again we have a subject on which many books could be written, and have been written. Of the many illustrations of the point, then, we must confine ourselves to only a few.

As a first consideration, what we think about may already be determined in large part by the particular language which is so essential a component of our culture. We cannot think at all without words, and words are bits of culture. It may be that an entire attitude toward the universe—what the Germans call a *Weltanschauung,* or world view—is already contained in the language that we learn because we are born in a particular society at a particular period of history. How, for example, could we ponder such philosophical problems as quantity, quality, relation, substance, and causality if these words did not belong to our language and if the ideas corresponding to them did not belong to our culture? How a language itself gets to be what it is and to contain the words that it does is again a function of culture. The Eskimos, for example, have many words for "snow," whereas we have only one in English, and we qualify it by using adjectives. For the Eskimo, drifting snow, falling snow, light snow, heavy snow, wet snow, and melting snow all have different names. Similarly, the Arabs have different names for kneeling camels, standing camels, old camels, young camels, and pregnant camels, whereas we use adjectives rather than nouns to announce such differences.

All societies seem to have ideas that are peculiar to their culture and that cannot be precisely translated into the language of another society. For this reason translations from one language into another are at best difficult. One has to sacrifice either the flavor of the original or its meaning. Further, the same word may have two quite different meanings in two different languages. As a famous French translator has said, "Les traductions sont comme les femmes. Quand elles sont belles, elles ne sont pas fidèles; et quand elles sont fidèles, elles ne sont pas belles." (Translations are like women. When they are beautiful they are not faithful and when they are faithful they are not beautiful.) An obviously culture-centered epigram. And some words cannot be translated at all into another language, except by circumlocution, because there is no word in the second language that corresponds to them. The German word *Weltanschauung,* for example, cannot be rendered exactly into English and is usually translated literally as "world view," though it implies in addition an entire philosophy of life. The French word *rapport* likewise cannot be translated into English and we make use of it in the French. The Greek *polis,* which is usually translated as "city-state," is still another example of a word that is perhaps best retained in the original because of what is lost in translation. Nor is American easily translatable into other languages, and a sports headline—"Cubs Cool Bums"—would baffle a European who spoke excellent English. Further, the famous headline—"Stix Nix Hix Pix"—in *Variety Magazine,* which circulates mainly through the entertainment world, is probably unclear even to most Americans, for it means, roughly, that motion pictures of rural life do not sell well in rural areas.

If what we think and what we say are functions of our culture, so also is what we learn. We can obviously learn only what our culture can teach, and in a complex society, only a small part of the total in any case. The Eskimo adolescent learns how to conceal a bent sliver of bone in frozen meat as a means of catching a polar bear. The American boy learns natural history and political history, algebra and geometry, roller skating and bicycle riding, perhaps how to play baseball, and generally, how to drive an automobile. Whether we learn or how much we learn is, of course, a function of intelligence. But what we learn is a function of culture. Not everybody in our society can become a famous mathematician or musician, despite the fact that mathematics and music are a part of our culture. A certain amount of native talent is required for accomplishment in these fields. On the other hand, no one can learn mathematics or music if the subject is not part of the culture, and we have no way of knowing how many unsung geniuses exist or have existed in other parts of the world whose native talents in music, mathematics, or other fields could find no expression because such achievements were not part of their culture. Nothing that we know about intelligence permits the conclusion that an Eskimo cannot, in another cultural setting, learn the elements of calculus as well as an American college student. The differences here are cultural and not biological.

Not only our knowledge and our education but also our goals and our aspirations are set for us by the culture of our society. What we are and what we want to become can therefore be understood only with reference to culture. No Zuñi Indian wants to be a successful bond salesman, no Eskimo wants to win the Nobel prize for literature, no Andaman Islander wants to run the four-minute mile, at least not as such, though he may at times be interested in generating maximum velocity for escape purposes. Similarly, no American wants to become a witch doctor. Occupational choice is restricted by the number of statuses from which the choice may be made. In a complex society, there is a wide range of statuses available, but among nonliterate peoples, there may be only a few statuses and the choice must be made from among them. Literate peoples have the great advantage of numerous cultural alternatives. But in all cases, goals and aspiration must be defined by the possibilities which the culture offers. We could illustrate the point by further examples, but this would soon become tedious. We have said enough, surely, to satisfy the most skeptical student that culture is the key concept in all attempts to explain and understand the social life of man.

Culture and biology. If we look at the world's societies from past to present, from primitive to civilized, and from East to West, we shall be impressed with the almost illimitable variations that they display. They are all made up of human beings who live in groups with one another, but their ways of doing things, their patterns of living—their cultures, in short—exhibit thousands of differences in detail and in design. As biological specimens, all people are pretty much alike. They all have two eyes, two ears, four limbs, a nose, and a mouth; further anatomical observation discloses only the most superficial and indeed inconsequential differences. It is in the realm of culture, not biology, that the differences become significant and consequential. There are therefore certain relationships between culture and the organism that we now wish to examine.

Sometimes cultural and biological factors operate in harmony; sometimes they work against each other. It is obvious that the imperious needs of the body may force us to violate the standards of our culture and to commit antisocial acts. A man who is starving is not one who is overly impressed with the sanctity of property under existing law or with the theoretical benefits of the economic system in which he functions. A society under siege, where physical mobility is limited, or in the crisis of famine, does not exhibit the same cultural patterns as a "normal" society, nor does it even follow its own normal pattern. Further, when the individual is under great stress, or physically impaired or damaged, he too will not respond in his usual manner. These are obvious facts which require no elaboration.

What may not be so obvious is the influence that cultural factors exert upon biological factors, even altering their fundamental character. A striking and terrifying illustration of the point is the effect of man-made radiation upon animal reproduction, including human reproduction. Cultural influences may even determine what is biologically "normal," as in the case of epilepsy, which may confer special privileges upon the afflicted in some societies. Those afflicted with paranoia (delusions of persecution) may also be considered normal in some societies and at certain times. Problems of this sort have an intrinsic fascination, but their study is a task for the anthropologist and social psychologist and we cannot pursue it further here.

It is important for us to recognize, however, that cultural patterns may have deleterious effects upon the physiology and anatomy of the human organism and that practices which culture approves or even requires may be biologically harmful. Thus stretching and piercing the lips, filing the teeth, inducing obesity, and various other devices for torturing the flesh in the name of adornment are all culturally approved. Initiation rites into particular societies, even in so-called civilized societies, and perhaps even upon the campuses where this book is read, may involve mutilation of the flesh by flogging, forced ingestion of strange foods and drugs, or body-racking ordeals of hunger and thirst. People have starved in the midst of plenty because the food available to them was for one reason or another culturally tabooed. Diet is a cultural and not a psychological phenomenon.

The effects of cultural activities on the anatomy need not be disastrous to be recognized. The blacksmith possesses, on poetic authority, a mighty arm; the marks of the professional pugilist are widely recognized; athletes suffer from enlarged hearts as a general rule, and baseball pitchers suffer a number of ailments not regularly encountered in the general population, including bursitis, calcium deposits on the tendons, unusual fractures, and a severe pain known inelegantly as "pitcher's elbow." College professors as a class almost universally develop impairment of vision, and spectacles are practically a badge of the profession. All of these cases and many more illustrate how occupations may alter and even damage the physical apparatus with which we are endowed at birth.

Cultural influence may also produce its deleterious effects more insidiously. For example, the high incidence of ulcers in our society, occurring more often in males than females, is most cogently explained by reference to the competitiveness of contemporary culture. It has been remarked that for women, competition ceases at the altar, while for men, it begins at that point. Of greater interest, perhaps, is the harm that American women do to their bodies in order to conform to cultural standards of feminine beauty. Diets are a direct interference by cultural factors in physiological functioning. High, spiked heels are plainly inimical to healthy feet and directly affect the anatomy of the arch, yet no coed would dream of wearing loafers to the junior prom on these grounds. Nor are men totally immune from the influence of fashion, for no more idiotic apparatus can be conceived of than a tight collar and necktie, binding the crucial blood transmission centers of the neck; yet no male student would present himself to an employment manager of a corporation without both, though the interview is more than likely to raise blood pressure and activate the sweat glands. The frequent use of perspiration repressants, eye makeup, girdles and corsets, restrictive brassieres, and so forth, doubtless has an influence on the physiological apparatus.

It is very interesting, for the male student at least, to note that the standards of feminine beauty are cultural standards and not physical standards. They are susceptible to incredible variations from one society to another and, in the course of time, within the same society. Certain African tribes value most highly the fattest of their females, and obesity is sought after by all young girls. When they reach marriage age, they are taken to encampments where they are stuffed with rich and heavy food, rubbed with butter, and in other ways urged to acquire excess poundage. If the young lady gains so much weight that she can hardly walk, the regimen is a whopping success and she has no trouble finding suitors when she returns to the tribe. But it is not necessary to go to Africa for illustrations. In our own American society in as short a time as twenty-five years, the standards of feminine beauty have changed incredibly. The sex is the same, but the appearance it presents is quite different. In the twenties, the ideal was a hipless, boyish figure with lines approaching the vertical; more recently, the idealized figure seems neither hipless nor boyish. Doubtless the subject requires a more exhaustive analysis than the author can manage here, but any alert male whose senses and intellect are not totally benumbed by the demands of the studious life can easily acquire the needed data and complete the details for himself.

In other words, the human body is itself no mere physiological organism but a mixture of biological and cultural influences, each intermingling with and affecting the other. The human body has a different meaning for different people in different times and places. The diseases that afflict the body, the demands that are made upon it, and all the trials and tribulations that it encounters can be understood only when culture is added to physiology. The body may be either a noble and splendid temple of physical beauty, as in the Greek ideal, or a somewhat bothersome shell for an immortal soul, as in early Christian thought, or a combination of both; but what it is will be determined by culture alone. The human body may be a physiological fact, but it is a cultural value.

Cultural diffusion. We have remarked that differences in culture distinguish one society from another. We shall later have occasion to emphasize these differences as a means of distinguishing one group from another within the same society. But culture does not come in sealed containers; rather it is carried in a sieve. So long as people move restlessly over the face of the earth, they scatter bits of culture from one place to another. Travelers and traders, soldiers and settlers, missionaries and migrant workers—and many more—have been instrumental in the process known as *cultural diffusion*, the spreading of culture into areas in which it is not indigenous. By means of this process, culture comes to be widely distributed, and what is invented or discovered by one society is spread to other societies at various spots on the globe. Modern techniques of communication and transportation have facilitated the process to such an extent that some things can now be found in nearly every society except the most isolated and primitive of tribal systems. Thus the African explorer finds a tribe of isolated natives never before seen by white man, and one is sitting upon a Standard Oil can. The author of this section of the book, traveling some years ago in central Czechoslovakia, found few villages in that region without Ford tractors, Singer sewing machines, and Eastman Kodak cameras. As is well known, Coca-Cola can now be purchased in almost every part of the world, much to the dismay of the French. Swiss watches, French wines, English tweeds, German machinery, Spanish sherry, and many other cultural items can now be found in most parts of the United States.

Cultural diffusion does not include material objects alone; ideas are spread just as widely as things. The Christian religion, for example, has spread from its place of origin in the eastern Mediterranean to almost every part of the globe. Scientific knowledge, in the absence of political restrictions, moves easily and rapidly from one society to another. So do ideas about fashions, automobile design, and politics. Astronomical data have been exchanged between scientists whose countries were at war at the time; important books are usually translated into many different languages. Every ship, book, airplane, and person who travels from one place to another is an agent of cultural diffusion, either in material objects or in ideas and customs. The important lesson for us is that none of the complex societies found on earth today created more than a few of the cultural elements found in it; all have borrowed from other societies. Indeed, Ralph Linton has estimated that in no case does the number of indigenous or native elements exceed 10 per cent of the total culture.

THE CONTENT OF CULTURE

Thus far in this chapter, we have emphasized the fact that people in different societies all over the world have different cultures. They think different thoughts, do different things, and use different implements and utensils. For this reason their lives run different courses and the cycles of day and year and season wear different aspects. The natives of Polynesia and the citizens of Paris accumulate different kinds of knowledge and cultivate different arts. The Eskimo and the Ethiopian nourish themselves on different foodstuffs and indulge in different ceremonies. The Spartan and the Spaniard worship different deities, find their enjoyment in different pursuits, and relax and play in different ways. Men of different cultures, and women too, lead different lives, entertain different ideas, have different values, and seek different goals. Neither physiology nor geography can explain these differences or even approximate them. They are the effects of differences in culture and nothing else.

Culture is a complex and comprehensive phenomenon, as we have tried to suggest briefly above. In order to use the concept as a tool for sociological analysis, we must do more than define it and insist that it is important; we must also break it down and consider its various components. We continue, therefore, to inquire into the structure of culture and its content.

One of the principal goals of sociology is to discover the sources of the fundamental order that society exhibits, the order that makes it possible for human beings to interact with one another and to live together in the same house, the same town, the same country, and the same world. The key to the riddle is culture. For it is apparent that there are certain cultural similarities that underlie all of the cultural diversities and disparities throughout the world as it now is and as it has been throughout the course of history. People may worship different gods in different ways, but all people have a religion. People may pursue different occupations, yet the task of earning a living is ubiquitous. The vocal cords may vibrate in different rhythms, but all men speak a language. Ideas about the universe and its contents may differ, but all men have some answer to the question of why there is human life and what is its destiny. The rituals and ceremonies of mankind are so diverse they defy exhaustive description, yet every society and group has its rituals and ceremonies. The material culture of society may be quite simple by American standards, or very rich and abundant, but all societies have a material culture. We have chosen in the previous material on culture to emphasize differences and discrepancies; we now want to demonstrate that culture everywhere can be broken down into the same categories, that everywhere it has the same component parts.

Many sociologists have classified the content of culture into two large components: material culture and nonmaterial culture. One sociologist, William Ogburn, has used this distinction as the basis for an impressive theory of cultural change, which we shall discuss later. The concept of material culture is clear enough; but the concept of nonmaterial culture is not quite so clear except in the sense that it is a residual category, including everything that is not material. However, "everything that is not material" may include items of different kinds, and this residual definition tends to obscure significant distinctions which need to be made. We shall therefore adopt a threefold classification of the content of culture. Our classification stems directly from the definition of culture as a complex whole that consists of everything we think and do and have as members of society. Thinking and doing and having are three of the most fundamental categories in the grammar of any language. They give us the three components of culture—*ideas, norms,* and *things.* Things make up the material component of culture. Ideas and norms are both nonmaterial, but we distinguish them because they perform different functions in society and operate in different ways. We thus have the three major categories or headings under which we can later locate the detailed items that make up this comprehensive phenomenon. The basic table which we shall build looks like this:

CULTURE

Ideas (Thinking)	*Norms (Doing)*	*Materiel (Things)*

As we move through our discussion of the three categories, we shall attempt to complete the chart or table.

Ideas. If it is impossible, as we shall see, to count the material possessions of a given society, it is inconceivable that anyone could take an inventory of their ideas. No questionnaire, no matter how extensive, could disclose them all. Many of them may be subliminal, in the sense that the people themselves are only dimly aware of them or not aware of them at all. In literate societies ideas are recorded and written down and stored in books and libraries, and ideas therefore make up the literature of the society in the broadest possible sense of the term. In nonliterate societies they constitute the lore and the legends of the tribe. The sociologist is not interested in the truth or falsity of the notions that prevail and help to determine the unique character of the lives that people live in these societies. It matters not whether these ideas are compounded into myths or into scientific truths about the universe, although we shall later make a distinction between ideas, on the one hand, and ideologies, on the other. Men and societies are sustained by false notions and true notions alike, and what may seem true in one society may seem false in another, and the other way around.

The Greeks believed in many gods, gods of both sexes, who loved and disported themselves like human beings as they lived on Mount Olympus. The Pilgrims who settled the first English colony in Massachusetts believed in one god, a male deity, who frowned upon pleasurable pursuits and who particularly did not like to see his people wasting their time and their substance. The Eskimos believe in several gods, but the most important one is a beautiful female deity named Sedna who lives with her father at the bottom of the sea and who, when she is pleased with her people, sees to it that they get enough to eat. The Russians, officially at least, believe in no god. All of these notions are but variants in the religious ideas to be found in human society. The minor variations on the same theme are infinite.

We find a similarly vast and heterogeneous collection of political ideas. Some peoples believe that their chiefs or kings are divinely ordained to rule over them and to lead them to power and glory. Others believe that the strongest should rule, or the wealthiest, the wiliest, or the most excellent and most wise. Still others believe that government should represent the wishes of the majority of the population of the society. Finally, some adhere to the hereditary principle and attach the right to rule to a particular family.

The people of some societies have ideas that are totally lacking in others. Some people do not, for example, know that there is any connection between sexual intercourse and the birth of a child, and some believe that repeated intercourse is needed to make the child grow in the womb. Some others believe that the birth of twins is a certain sign of adultery on the part of the mother. It is impossible to imagine, let alone record, the ideas that have appeared since the beginning of human history. But it is easy to see that each society has its own collection and that the ideas of one society differentiate it from all others. What people think is a vital component of their culture and helps make that culture unique. Whether or not it is the most important component is a matter that we shall return to later.

We have already remarked that some of the ideas entertained by the members of a society are true and others are false, and some, of course, may lie beyond our capacity to prove or disprove. Sociologically speaking, it is important to realize that both kinds of ideas, the false as well as the true, influence human conduct and illuminate the contours of society so long as they are believed and acted upon. Thus the false notion that twins are evidence of adultery may lead to punishment for the mother. The notion that the world is coming to an end at a specified date periodically induces the members of certain religious sects to sell all their possessions and climb to the top of the highest hill to prepare for their transfer to another, better, world. The false notion entertained by many Americans that the Negro is somehow inferior to the white man results in patterns of prejudice and segregation. All ideas which are acted upon are important, whether or not they are intrinsically true or false.

We may generalize the point and say that there are three classes of ideas: those which are false, those which are true, and those whose truth or falsity has not been determined. All three exert an effect when they are entertained and acted upon. From another point of view we may classify ideas into such categories as scientific propositions, legends, myths, superstitions, proverbs, and aphorisms. The number of scientific ideas is unfortunately but necessarily always less than the total number of ideas in the culture. When no scientific explanation is available to satisfy the human desire for knowledge, other explanations are constructed. More important, perhaps, is the fact that some of our ideas include judgments which cannot, in the nature of things, be scientific propositions.

At this point, we have begun to complete our table of culture, and we find the following additions:

CULTURE

Ideas	Norms	Materiel
Scientific truths		
Religious beliefs		
Myths		
Legends		
Literature		
Superstition		
Aphorisms		
Proverbs		
Folklore		

Norms. The concept of norms, one of the most significant in contemporary sociology, serves as a label for the second major component of culture. When we use this concept we refer to ways of doing and not to ways of thinking. Most of the things we do as members of society, and most of the things we refrain from doing, are cultural in character. When we talk about what people do in society, we are interested, as sociologists, not in their behavior as such but in the type of behavior that is considered socially acceptable or unacceptable.

Behavior may be mere impulse or response; conduct, on the other hand, implies the presence of norms. Our conduct conforms to certain standards, standards which are considered appropriate in the society in which we live. These standards and rules and expectations are what we call norms and there are several kinds of norms. Norms are the "grooves" or "channels" through which conduct normally runs in society. Without norms social life would be impossible and there could be no order in society. Without norms we should never know whether to shake hands with a new acquaintance, rub noses with him, ignore him, or knock him down. Society is a kind of order that is made possible by the presence of norms; they are the essence of social organization.

Imagine for a moment that eighteen men are attempting to play baseball, yet each man carries his own rule book and each of the rule books is different. Thus the first batter hits the ball on the fly to the second baseman, whips out his rule book, and announces that under *his* rules, he is entitled to two bases. The second batter knocks the ball over the right-field fence, and the pitcher then shows him a rule book in which it is clearly stated that he is out. And so it goes, for there are eighteen interpretations of each possible action taken by the players. In effect, they are attempting to play without rules, for eighteen sets of rules are worse than no rules at all, since in the latter case it is obvious that rules will have to be agreed upon before the game can proceed. It is perfectly apparent to everyone that baseball, or any other organized game, would be impossible without rules. An attempt to play under such circumstances could only lead to confusion, pandemonium, or chaos. Baseball has rules; therefore it has norms. For rules and norms are the same thing.

What may not be apparent is that what happens in the stands is also subject to rules; both spectators and players must have norms. The spectator pays a stipulated price for the right to enter the stadium through certain gates and perhaps occupy specified seats. Usually, women precede men through the gates, and men, not women, purchase the tickets needed for entry. Tickets are sold by ticket sellers, and not by policemen or peanut vendors. Some people, not necessarily the strongest or even the richest, occupy the box seats, while others, not necessarily the weakest, occupy the less-desirable bleachers. The hawkers who sell peanuts, popcorn, candy, and liquid refreshments will accept particular kinds of material objects in return for their wares, and not others. The spectators do not attempt to clamber into the dugout, nor do they try to take a turn at bat, except occasionally, and on such occasions, the police intervene with much promptitude. Spectators are, however, permitted to offer advice to anyone on the field, and this they do with enthusiasm and such vocal power as they command. Baseball watching is an organized activity, and like every other organized activity, it has its own norms or rules, though they are less clear than the rules that govern the behavior of the players.

And so with all the situations in society. Society is not a game, but the operation of society requires rules. Not all of the rules of society are enforced by umpires or other officials; some are enforced by those subject to the rules, as we shall see. Further, there are various kinds of rules and many of them operate somewhat differently from the rules of baseball. But everywhere and in all societies rules are found, and these rules make up social norms; they are ways of behaving that cover almost all situations that we confront in our lives. There are norms that determine our communications with others, whether by letter or telephone or conversation. There are others that govern the way in which we take books from the library, set a table, buy groceries, park a car, eat a meal, and so on through the myriad of social activities that are so much a part of our daily lives. We grow so accustomed to these norms that we are likely to forget that they exist or that other peoples may accomplish the same social interactions by an entirely different set of rules.

It is apparent that the norms of one society are different from the norms of another. When we greet a person in our society we are likely to shake hands and not rub noses. American males do not kiss each other when they meet—the notion is abhorrent to us—but the French or Italian or Greek peoples may do so upon some occasions. It is quite acceptable to cheer loudly or rudely at a baseball or football game, but not at a county cricket match or at a "test match" in England. It is rude to walk ahead of a female companion in some societies and quite acceptable or necessary in others. Even the rules of grammar are norms, and it is not good English to carelessly split infinitives, and prepositions are poor words to end sentences with.

There is a serious question in regard to norms that we shall have to consider later, i.e., whether there are universal or absolute norms that are binding upon all men at all times. Here we want only to emphasize that norms, like the other major factors in social life, tend to vary from one society to another and from one time to another even within the same society. We need only pause to consider the norms relating to the behavior of the female sex over the past fifty years to see how much they can vary. Norms are of central concern to sociology because they regularize human conduct and contribute order and stability to human societies. A norm, in brief, is a standardized mode of procedure, a way of doing something that is acceptable within society. It thus corresponds to the second of the verbs in our definition of culture.

Materiel. We have now discussed ways of thinking and ways of doing and are ready to introduce the third major component of culture—what we *have* as members of society, the things that make up our material culture. We shall call this category *materiel*. Materiel is the most tangible and the most obvious and most easily understood of all the components of culture. This category includes all of the material items that the members of society have and use. It would be an impossible task to list all of the material in even a very small and simple society, and utterly so in the large and complex social structures to which we are accustomed. No one could possibly, even with every conceivable item of equipment, take a complete inventory of all the material things to be found in the culture of the United States in the twentieth century. Neither the Sears and Roebuck catalog by itself nor all the catalogs together would begin to exhaust the list of material possessions of the American people—the things they have and use. It would be hard enough to make such a list for a single household, for materiel has a way of accumulating, and each generation in a complex society has more than its predecessor, just as our present generation possesses aircraft, automobiles, television sets, etc., which were unknown a century ago.

When an archaeologist digs up an ancient city or village it is only the remnants of material culture that he finds. The norms of the people who once lived there have disappeared together with their ideas and beliefs. But these norms and ideas can, to some extent at least, be inferred from the material remains, and this enables the archaeologist to reconstruct the life of the society. This indicates the close connection of ideas and norms and material things.

Quantitatively speaking, some societies have a much richer collection of materiel than do others. We may be inclined to call the former more "advanced" and the latter more "primitive." But such judgment should not imply that one society is therefore superior to another. Gadgets and "gimmicks" do not necessarily contribute to happiness, prosperity, or well-being, though they may facilitate the performance of certain tasks. For one thing, the tasks may not be worth doing. But if we cannot evaluate societies fairly in terms of material culture alone, we can compare and differentiate them on this basis. For each society has its own collection of material culture traits, and this collection, in spite of the effect of cultural diffusion, helps to differentiate it from all the rest. We do not find spark plugs in Bali, a monastery in Iceland, a swimming pool among the Eskimo, or an igloo in the Congo.

Some sociologists do not like to include materiel under the concept of culture on the ground that culture consists only of ideas, or that it has a meaning only after it has been "internalized," so to speak, and becomes a customary part of the conduct of the members of a society. We ourselves, in discussing the superorganic as a synonym for culture, pointed out that the same material objects may have quite different meanings for members of different societies. Beads may be a medium of exchange or an ornament, depending upon the society in which we are living. But it is necessary to point out that the material culture of a society precedes the birth of a given individual in that society, and material culture is one of the factors to which he must adjust his life. Our own children learn to skate, to ride wagons and tricycles, and later to drive automobiles because these items are part of our material culture; in other cultures, the learning pattern may be quite different, and hence the effect on the individual will change. Our lives are influenced in many ways by material culture, by the size and shape of our houses and their rooms, by the arrangement of buildings, highways, knives and spoons, by our school facilities, and so on. Materiel is inexorable in its own way, and in some senses at least it is more rigid and unyielding than ideas or norms. The question of "internalizing" this culture is in many cases academic because there is no real alternative.

Our table of culture, as constructed up to this point, now looks like this:

CULTURE

Ideas	Norms	Materiel
Scientific truths		Machines
Religious beliefs		Tools
Myths		Utensils
Legends		Buildings
Literature		Roads, bridges
Superstitions		Artifacts
Aphorisms		Clothing, furniture
Proverbs		Vehicles
Folklore		Foodstuffs, medicines

Ideologies. We have now discussed, in a preliminary fashion, the three major components of culture—ideas, norms, and materiel. Some kinds of culture may not fit clearly into only one of these compartments, but may belong rather to two or even three of them. A work of art, for example, may partake of the nature of all three. Thus it has the materiel component, the pigment and canvas, the idea that informs it, and the aesthetic norms to which it conforms. We also find phenomena that relate two of the components of culture and in a sense stand between them. One of the most important is the combination of ideas and norms that we call an "ideology," which appears in our table as follows:

CULTURE

Ideas	Norms	Materiel
Ideology		

When we are presented with an idea, we are likely to ask whether it is true or false, and we have already had occasion to observe that true and false ideas alike exert an influence in our societies. When we are presented with a norm, a way of doing things, on the other hand, we are likely to inquire whether it is "right" or "wrong," "good" or "bad," "efficient" or "inefficient." In some cases we raise questions about ideas too. We want to know not only whether certain ideas are true or false but also whether they are good or bad, and frequently this second question is more important than the first. Ideas that are evaluated in this way are what we should call "ideologies," though some writers prefer to call them "values." More precisely, an ideology is an idea supported by a norm. We are encouraged to believe it, not because it is true, but because such belief is regarded as right and proper in our society. Let us examine this a little more closely.

Some of our ideas, particularly those we should include in the category of scientific knowledge, are morally neutral. Thus the Pythagorean theorem is true in terms of the axioms and postulates of Euclid. We do not ask whether it is a "good" theorem in addition; the question is in fact meaningless. No one, except perhaps our geometry teacher, exerts any pressure upon us to believe it, nor do we gain moral stature when we declare that it is true. The situation is the same with respect to the ideas contained in the whole of mathematics, the various science texts, almanacs, telephone directories, catalogs, statistical tabulations, and historical records. These ideas may be true or false, but not good or bad, proper or improper; they are not ideologies, and we gain no moral approbation by accepting or rejecting them.

There are other ideas, however, that we are expected to believe, not because they are demonstrably true—indeed the truth of the proposition contained in the idea may be impossible to determine—but because they are considered right or good or proper in our society. These are the ideologies, the ideas that we have a social obligation to believe, the ideas that we are required to believe if we wish to remain in good standing in our social groups. All societies exert pressure upon their members to adhere to some beliefs and reject others. Propositions asserting, for example, that there is only one God, that the human soul is immortal, that monogamy is the preferable form of marriage, that atheism is wrong, that premarital sex experience is immoral, that anarchists are dangerous, that free enterprise is good, that infant industries ought to be protected by tariffs, and that Communists are wicked—all these, and hundreds more, are ideologies. Those who share the contemporary culture of the United States are expected and indeed required to hold these beliefs, and the man who publicly challenges any one of them will be given short shrift by most of his associates and by the members of his larger social circle. An almost sacred quality adheres to these ideologies, and any deviation in principle is regarded as "un-American."

The Declaration of Independence, known to every American and celebrated on the Fourth of July, states as a self-evident truth that all men are created equal. This proposition is an ideology, not a scientific truth. Indeed, we know on scientific grounds that it is false. Men are not equal. Some are tall, some short, some fat, some thin, some are black and some white, some are rich and others poor, some are stupid and some intelligent, and so on through a catalog of individual differences. But such considerations are obviously irrelevant to the proposition. The proposition means that all men are equal in the sight of God and should be equal in the sight of their government. In this sense the proposition is ideological rather than scientific, and one expresses his "Americanism" by supporting the ideology; belief is a patriotic obligation. We are proud to acknowledge the proposition and we regard the Declaration that contains it as one of the ringing documents of human history.

It is apparent that all societies, even the most primitive, have ideologies and that these ideologies are an intimate and important part of their culture. Each society regards its central ideologies as sacred and tolerates no skepticism with respect to them. Indeed, it is a significant sociological fact that the pressure to believe them is frequently stronger than the pressure to conform to the norms of conduct to which they are related. Thus, in our society, it is easier to commit adultery than it is to advocate adultery. Bertrand Russell, the British philosopher, once recommended that the taboo on adultery be reconsidered, and though he himself did not commit adultery, he was denied a position instructing in mathematical logic at the City College of New York because of the protests aroused by the appointment.

In all religions, similarly, sinners may sometimes be saved, but unbelievers never. The sinner may live a life spotted with infamy, but appropriate penance may absolve him from its consequences. The heretic, on the other hand, may lead a pure and virtuous life, perhaps almost saintly in character, but his conduct will not necessarily save him from damnation. Thus it is pardonable here to violate the norms only if one accepts the ideology. It is unpardonable, however, to reject the ideology no matter how closely one conforms to the norms. Skepticism, in short, is more serious than "sin." This sociological fact, evident in every time and society, is a paradox. We mention it because it indicates the very great importance of ideologies in the social life of man.

Technologies. Between norms and materials we find another set of phenomena, which we shall label *technologies,* although they are sometimes labeled technical norms or merely techniques. Thus it is not enough to have the material, to own the tool, to possess the utensil. One must also, in the convenient American phrase, have the "know-how." It is considered inappropriate, and indeed it is usually inefficient, to use a chisel as a screwdriver, or a screwdriver as a chisel. To do so violates a technical norm. We are therefore admonished to use the right tool for each job. Technologies, like other aspects of culture, differ from one society to the next, and societies may be compared meaningfully with reference to the level of technological achievement. We shall deal with this question in more detail toward the end of the text.

Subsidiary culture concepts. We may also encounter, in the field of sociology, various subsidiary conceptions that have to do with culture. When sociologists discuss a very small bit of culture, for example, they generally speak of a *culture trait* or *culture item*. A group of culture items, arranged and organized, is called a *culture complex*. Combinations of culture complexes become *culture patterns* and *culture configurations*. Thus a spark plug is a culture item, and an automobile engine is a culture complex, and automobiles and gasoline form a part of the culture pattern that we call the "machine age" or "mechanically minded society." These are shorthand terms, used to attain speed and accuracy in sociological writing, and the student ought to be familiar with the concepts they involve.

OTHER ASPECTS OF CULTURE

We shall now examine some of the remaining cultural conceptions that sociologists employ, illustrating them briefly.

Acculturation. The process of acquiring the culture of a different society is called *acculturation*. When in Rome, we must do what the Romans do, acquire Roman culture. If acquired patterns last and become part of our regular behavior (an accent, eating habits, etc.), we have become acculturated. The American student in England who learns to like tea in the afternoon is becoming acculturated, and he brings some of his acquired culture back to his native land when he returns.

Acculturation occurs on a large scale when one society is invaded and conquered by another. The conquerors attempt to impose their way of life upon the conquered; the conquerors also adopt some of the practices of the conquered. The process is inevitable when peoples meet on a large scale. Societies jealous of their own culture try to prevent acculturation by forbidding "fraternization" or by erecting obstacles to social intercourse, but such attempts are rarely successful and never completely accomplish their goals. Sometimes, of course, the traits of one culture do not harmonize well with those of another, and transmission is resisted. Thus the American Indians eagerly adopted firearms and "firewater" but were reluctant to embrace the colonist's religion or attitude toward work.

The process of acculturation is not always a smooth and easy one, and some peoples are acculturated more readily than others; yet it never fails to happen when people of one culture have social relations for any extended period of time with people of another culture. The Englishman may continue to dress for dinner even in the steaming jungles of Malaya, but he is not wholly exempt from Malayan customs. Usually, we acquire the culture of our own society through education. We acquire the culture of other countries through contact, through travel and residence abroad, through books and writings, the theater, and all the various means of social communication.

Cultural lag. The sociologist uses the term *cultural lag* to refer to a situation in which one phase of culture lags behind another and causes imbalance and disharmony in the society. Traffic congestion, for example, results from a cultural lag between the accumulation of material culture and societal adjustment to it, when highway construction and urban traffic engineering simply have not kept pace with the increase in automobiles. In other cases, the speed limit may be adjusted to the automobiles of twenty years ago, or courtship patterns may suit the "sitting-room" sofa but may not the sports car. Bathing suits became briefer, usually, more rapidly than the law could keep up, or down, with them. The law is generally a laggard, not always keeping up with social requirements. Advances in communication, as in television, for example, may far outstrip our ability to use them properly. A device or invention may appear centuries before it is actually used by society. New words enter the dictionary only after they have come into widespread use. Endless illustrations of cultural lag may be found in every society, and we shall return to the question again.

Cultural survival. Sometimes culture traits, items, or complexes survive in a society long after their original function has disappeared and sometimes after the initial reason for their establishment has been forgotten. The sleeves of men's jackets still have three or four buttons at or near the cuff, but these buttons serve no function whatever except, possibly, decoration. Military drill, once important as a means of moving soldiers from one place to another quickly and for bringing maximum firepower to bear on a given target, is merely a cultural survival in the age of rockets and jets and atomic weapons. It may still have a function in inculcating discipline and in making habitual and unthinking obedience to orders a part of the normal equipment of the soldier, but this was not its original purpose. Our readers will doubtless be able to supply many more examples of cultural survival from their own knowledge and experience. Which parts of university life, for example, may be classed as cultural survivals?

Culture conflict. The term *culture conflict* is an ellipsis; that is, it is people who are in conflict not cultures. Their contention, however, usually or often has a cultural base, and it is commonly referred to as a cultural conflict. Religious wars, which have filled so many sorry pages in the history of Western nations, are good examples of culture conflict. In the Hindu culture, the cow is a sacred animal, but not in the Moslem culture. In India, where

Moslem and Hindu live side by side, this one subject produces perennial conflict. Similarly, where Protestant and Catholic live side by side, as in the United States, their differences on censorship, contraception, and education are fruitful sources of conflict. Numerous other examples will suggest themselves readily.

Ideal culture and real culture. The *ideal* culture is the culture that the members of a society think they have; the *real* culture is the culture they actually have. In all societies there is a discrepancy between the two. If an American citizen were asked to tell a visitor from a foreign land something about how Americans think and live, his description would probably be somewhat less than realistic. He might say, for example, that the United States is a democracy, that all men are created equal, and that all have the same legal rights and social privileges. He might neglect to mention, however, that some Americans, whose skin color happens to have a darker hue, do not enjoy these rights and privileges equally with other citizens. He might say that Americans believe in and practice monogamy, but the divorce and remarriage rate might lead the visitor to suspect that Americans actually practice something that could better be described as serial polygamy.

The distinction between ideal and real culture is expressed by some anthropologists in terms of *overt culture* and *covert culture*, or *explicit culture* and *implicit culture*. Indeed, these latter terms may be preferable since the former are laden with philosophic connotations that are quite irrelevant to the question at issue. The terminology, in other words, is not currently settled or consistent, but there is no difficulty about the distinction that is meant. The student of sociology is primarily concerned with differences between the real and the ideal, the overt and covert, whatever the label used to identify them.

Cultural relativity. We often have a situation in which the norms of one society contradict the norms of another. The Eskimo may lend his wife to another as a gesture of genuine hospitality; in our society, this constitutes the sin of adultery. What is right in one society is wrong in another and vice versa. As we look at societies throughout the world and throughout the course of history, we find many examples of this conflict. It is difficult, if not quite impossible, to find any absolute standard to which all societies adhere. Standards are always relative to the culture in which they appear. This is the principle of *cultural relativity*. In its simplest terms it means that actions that are moral in some societies are immoral in others, that propositions which one society considers true are considered false in another, and that conduct which is approved and even required in some is disapproved or forbidden in others. This principle, which anthropological investigation of nonliterate societies all over the world has helped to support, has been known to social thinkers since the earliest times and was given a complete and lucid expression by Boethius (ca. 475–525) in *The Consolation of Philosophy,* when he said: "The customs and laws of diverse nations do so much differ the one from the other, that the same thing which some commend as laudable, others condemn as deserving punishment."[3]

The principle of cultural relativity raises questions that cannot be answered in an introductory text. One is the question of universal norms. Are there any actions that are commended alike in all societies or condemned alike in all? In short, are there any absolute norms? The evidence is inconclusive, and there is no complete agreement on the subject. One might assume that premeditated murder is forbidden by the norms of all societies and of all human groups. But the norm does not, in so-called civilized societies, apply to the soldiers of a country with which one's own country is at war. Indeed, the soldier who kills the largest number of the enemy is decorated for valor. In many primitive societies, the norm does not apply to the stranger, and wanderers risk their lives entering the outskirts of tribal villages not their own. If the murder of strangers and enemies is permitted under specified circumstances, one might assume that the premeditated murder of a friend is not, that such an action is always prohibited. But here again there are exceptions. Some societies support the killing of a friend under certain conditions— for example, if the "friend" is found *in flagrante delicto* with one's wife. And whether or not wives are to be considered "friends," they too may be justifiably done away with in some societies for actions that may or may not be considered offenses in other societies. Even in a civilized society with a long tradition of law, it is difficult to get a jury to convict a man who murders the seducer of his wife. Thus, there is no universal taboo against homicide, and circumstances that proscribe it in certain societies may prescribe it in others.

Perhaps the closest we can come to a universal taboo is the taboo against incest, that is, against sexual relations between close blood relations—brother and sister, mother and son, or father and daughter. And yet, incest is known to occur in all societies, not excluding our own. The reasons for this taboo, so nearly universal, have fascinated psychologist and anthropologist alike, but no thoroughly satisfactory explanation has been discovered. Furthermore, the taboo is "officially" relaxed in certain cases. Brother and sister marriages have been required in the ancient Egyptian royal house and the ancient Hawaiian royal house in order to preserve the purity of the royal blood line.

One might speculate that cruelty to young children would be another universal taboo. But infanticide, especially female infanticide, is practiced in a number of nonliterate societies. In most literate Western societies, children were forced to work long hours in factories under incredible conditions during the early stages of the Industrial Revolution and for some time afterward. The taboo is far from complete.

In other words, it is not only difficult but, in the present state of our

[3] *De Consolatione Philosophiae,* Loeb Classical Library, vol. II, p. 215.

knowledge, apparently impossible to find a single universal taboo—the prohibition of a single act in all circumstances at all times in all societies. As far as our knowedge goes, the norms are always relative to a particular culture and a particular set of circumstances. They are never absolute.

It is important in this connection to distinguish between a cultural absolute and a cultural universal. It is conceivable that some norms could become universal without at the same time becoming absolute; that is, it could happen that at some time in the future all peoples in every society in the world would adopt the same general type of clothing that is now worn by Western European and American peoples. We should not infer that because, in this hypothetical instance, a practice had become universal it had also become absolute, that there would then be only one right kind of clothing to wear. On the other hand, the ethical philosopher might say that there are indeed absolute values or norms even though they are not universal, that underlying all the diversities to be found in the range of culture there is an abstract principle of right and wrong, of good and evil. The religious philosopher would certainly say so. But here at least this important question must remain open, for the problem belongs properly to ethics and not to sociology.

Ethnocentrism. The concept known as *ethnocentrism* is a corollary of the principle of cultural relativity. It means the ethnic-centered tendency to evaluate other cultures in terms of our own. It means that the ways of thinking and ways of doing that we observe in other societies are measured and judged in terms of the ideas and norms prevailing in the society with which we are most familiar. Thus the Eskimo practice of placing aged parents on the ice to die seems abhorrent to us, and we would place it in the category of homicide, or more precisely, geronticide. From the Eskimo point of view, however, the man or woman who becomes too old to keep up with the tribe, to travel the vast distances that must be covered in the course of a year in search for enough food to keep alive, jeopardizes the continued existence of the community; and the existence of the community is considered more important than the survival of the individual.

On the other hand, certain practices of ours, such as catching a seal and using only the oil, discarding the rest, seem to the Eskimo to be wasteful to the point of immorality. Likewise, the Eskimo can understand how one man may kill another in anger, but he is totally unable to comprehend the phenomenon of organized war, and when informed that white men indulge in this practice, he is somewhat incredulous and tends to regard it as ridiculous. Poor benighted Eskimo!

There is one possible solution to the dilemma which ethnocentrism poses. We might judge societies, if we are inclined to judge them at all, in terms of the degree to which they conform to their own norms rather than the degree to which they conform to ours. We could evaluate them according to the relation between their real culture, on the one hand, and their ideal culture, on the other. By this test, of course, we might find our own society "inferior" to many others, and especially to those societies that we usually call primitive. On the other hand, the notion that we ought to practice what we preach may be an ideology taken from our own culture and one that is quite irrelevant to others.

In other words, the ethnocentric predicament in sociology is as hard to avoid or resolve as the egocentric predicament in philosophy. In any case, it is a problem for advanced sociological theory and especially for the sociology of knowledge. Introductory students are advised merely to guard against the tendency to judge other cultures in terms of our own and to assume that some exotic custom is unseemly or immoral in another society simply because those objectives are applied to it in our society.

Temporocentrism. The temporal equivalent of ethnocentrism is called *temporocentrism;* it has been defined as "the unexamined and largely unconscious acceptance of one's own century, one's own lifetime, as the center of sociological significance, as the focus to which all other periods of historical time are related, and as the criterion by which they are judged."[4] All of us are inclined to believe, or rather to assume without question, that the present is more important than the past and that the whole of historical time is significant only for what it means to us. We thus tend to judge earlier societies in terms of criteria that are relevant to our own rather than to their age and to weigh their virtues and defects in terms of standards drawn from our contemporary era.

This temporocentric tendency induces us to place what must, in the long course of history, seem to be an exaggerated emphasis upon our own era. We assume, for example, that the crisis of our age is somehow more "critical" than the crises of other ages. We are afflicted with a sense of urgency, a feeling that our tasks, our problems, need to be undertaken before it is too late. The stark warning, "It is later than you think," seems to be directed to our own age rather than to previous or subsequent periods. We believe that what we do here and now will have an overwhelming impact on future centuries. This belief could conceivably be warranted, but on the other hand, we may later be viewed as only a minor ripple in the stream of history. Finally, we are continually impressed with the fact that we live in an "age of transition"; so might Adam have remarked to Eve on the occasion of their departure from Eden.

Temporocentrism, in short, results from a lack of historical perspective.

[4] Robert Bierstedt, "The Limitations of Anthropological Methods in Sociology," *American Journal of Sociology,* vol. 54, no. 1, pp. 27–28, July, 1948.

It afflicts in large measure the untutored man who has had no opportunity to study history. But it also afflicts the social scientist who out of concern for the present seems to lose all respect for history. Much of contemporary sociological research in the United States is concentrated on the "specious present" to the neglect of an extended temporal orientation. This tendency can even be detected in some anthropological literature. Sociology needs the deepening sense of time that only the study of history can supply. Travel is generally conceded to be broadening. But it is not often noticed that we can travel in time as well as in space and that such travel is relatively inexpensive. We may spend the day with Socrates in ancient Athens or Shakespeare in Elizabethan England for a trifling cost. He who knows no other society, to paraphrase Goethe, who made the same remark about languages, knows nothing of his own. Only by avoiding the perils of both ethnocentrism and temporocentrism can we hope to escape from our own time-bound, space-limited, and culture-constructed experience and begin to appreciate the nature of human society, and through them, the nature of man.

Summary

We began this chapter with an attempt to explain the meaning of "culture," one of the basic analytical tools of sociology. It refers, in its technical use, to the entire complex of human thought and action within the framework of society. It includes all of the ways of living and doing and thinking that have been passed down from previous generations and are accepted as part of society. It is culture, above all things, that distinguishes man from the other animals, and the human child from the feral child. Culture makes man human.

Various synonyms for culture have been employed in the study of society, particularly (1) learned behavior, (2) the social heritage, (3) the superorganic, and (4) design for living. Each of these expressions emphasize a different aspect of a complex phenomenon, focusing our attention on different characteristics of the same basic concept. Culture plays a role in human life that cannot be overemphasized. Excepting isolated societies, much of culture derives from other societies, through cultural diffusion.

It is useful to conceive of culture in terms of three large compartments—ideals, norms, and materiel—and two combinations of compartments—ideologies and technologies. Such divisions allow us to treat the wealth of available facts more systematically. Further, we can examine specific aspects of culture—traits, items, complexes, patterns, and configurations—and arrive at still greater precision of definition. We also find it useful to introduce such phenomena as acculturation, cultural lag, cultural survival, culture conflict, and ideal and real culture, which indicate observable regularities in human society. Finally, we make use of such principles as cultural relativity, ethnocentrism, and temporocentrism to indicate certain "bundles" of cultural characteristics.

All of these topics deserve a more extended treatment than is possible in an introductory text. They embrace, in fact, a large part of the literature of anthropology and sociology. We have said enough, however, to give the reader some appreciation of the meaning and content of culture.

Review questions

1. What are some of the synonyms that are used for the term "culture"? Give illustrations of each synonym from your own experience.

2. Define each of the following terms and give suitable examples from your own experience:

    a. cultural transmission
    b. cultural diffusion
    c. ideology
    d. technology
    e. culture trait
    f. culture complex
    g. culture pattern
    h. cultural lag
    i. acculturation
    j. cultural relativity

3. Differentiate between the following pairs of concepts, giving examples for each member of the pair:

    a. ideal culture and real culture
    b. norms and laws
    c. ethnocentrism and temporocentrism
    d. folkways and norms

4. What are the three major components of culture?

5. What are some of the more important social elements that aid in the transmission of culture?

6. List some of the techniques by which culture is diffused.

7. In what way can culture influence biological inheritance? Is the converse also true?

8. What is the relationship between ideologies and norms?

For further study

1. Prepare a brief paper dealing with the different manner in which different societies deal with the same social process, e.g., marriage or division of work, and discuss possible reasons for these differences.

2. If Robinson Crusoe were born alone on a desert island, and managed to survive, would he acquire culture?

3. When Friday appeared on Crusoe's island, did he bring culture with him? Did he acquire culture from Crusoe? Did Crusoe acquire culture from Friday?

4. Is the relative lack of instinctive behavior patterns in man an asset or a liability? Under what conditions would it be one or the other? What are some of its social consequences—for the family, for example?

5. Would it be possible to speak of an "animal culture"?

6. Can you think of any types of human behavior that are relatively unaffected by culture?

CHAPTER *3*

The
Acquisition
of Culture

We have emphasized the importance of culture in everything we think and do and have, and indeed we used these verbs in the derivation of our definition of culture. We now want to take a slightly different view of the matter. We want to look at the individual and see how he acquires the culture to which he is exposed, to learn if possible the mechanisms that operate in this process in all societies, and to watch the development of personality in the interaction of the person and his culture. We want to look, in short, at what has come to be called the "socialization process," the process by which original nature is transformed into human nature, the process in terms of which every human individual becomes an acceptable member of his society. In exploring this subject we shall have occasion to deal with the nature of the interaction between self and society, with the self as subject and as object, with the old question of heredity and environment, with the agencies of socialization, with personality itself, and with the self as an actor and role player in the drama that all of us are destined to endure and enjoy.

THE ENCOUNTER: SELF AND SOCIETY

Strictly speaking, the initial encounter is not between self and society, because at the first stage, as we shall see, the self does not yet exist. Here, however, we want to suggest that the infant at birth, the organism that is to become human in its exposure to culture, is not simply a lump of material that receives impressions and is shaped, like clay on a potter's wheel, by external influences and instruments. The organism is not wholly passive, wholly inert, wholly malleable, and no one who has ever seen an infant in action would believe it to be so. There is response, of course, but there is impulse too. The organism not only responds to the stimulus but also seeks it out. The baby roots around for the nipple to which it will then respond by sucking movements of the lips—movements indeed that precede the discovery. We are not saying that the stimulus is altogether absent, but only that it may be internal—like, for example, the peristalsis of the walls of the stomach, which stimulates the search for food—and not a part of the culture as such. The organism is an engine, in short, with its own motive forces, and this in effect, as Aristotle noted long ago, is what distinguishes an animate from an inanimate object; this is what it means to be alive. The organism not only receives the culture; it also, so to speak, goes to meet it.

The nature and number of these motive forces have puzzled philosophers for centuries and they are still largely unresolved problems in psychology and social psychology. In the early years of the present century an instinct theory prevailed. The first two books published in the field of social psychology, one by the sociologist E. A. Ross and the other by the psychologist William McDougall—both in the year 1908—subscribed to this theory and indeed gave it great impetus in the social and psychological sciences. The existence of instincts somewhere in the organism made the explanation of human behavior an exceedingly simple process. Why do men and women mate? Because of the sexual instinct. Why do they have children? Because of the philoprogenitive instinct. Why do they live in groups? Because they have a gregarious instinct. Why do they earn money? Because they have an acquisitive instinct. And why do they save it? Because they have a hoarding instinct.

All this was very simple and very easy—until someone, notably the sociologist L. L. Bernard, noticed that it was too simple and too easy. For it became clear after a while, as the number of instincts multiplied, that the instinct theory could explain everything and therefore could explain nothing. For, as we shall have occasion to remark again in this book, a theory that explains too much is as useless as one that explains too little. The questions and answers above seem reasonable enough. But similar answers to additional questions begin to sound a little strained. Why do people play games? Because they have a competitive instinct. Why do they play baseball? Because they have a baseball-playing instinct? And why do they study sociology? Because they have a sociology-studying instinct.

It became obvious, in short, that the instinct theory was rather like a large warehouse in which every conceivable kind of instinct was stored. Whenever it became necessary to explain any snippet of behavior one had only to enter the warehouse and find the appropriate instinct—and thus one had the explanation. The number of different kinds of behavior was almost limitless, but then so was the number of instincts in the warehouse. It became fairly obvious in fact that until and unless one found a physiological correlate or a biological base the instinct was nothing but an artifact—a label as it were—that might serve as a descriptive tag but was wholly devoid of explanatory power.

One solution to this problem, when the instinct theory was discarded, was to find instead a small number of "prepotent reflexes," "unlearned drives," or more currently, "wants." A contemporary textbook in social psychology, for example, lists in its treatment of motivation an affiliation want, an acquisitive want, a prestige want, a power want, an altruistic want, and a curiosity want.[1] Once again, however, whether we use reflexes, drives, or wants—or interests, propensities, or urges—we have merely a series of synonyms for instincts. What we have thrown out of the front door reappears at the back in a different dress, and the problem remains unsolved.

Whatever the answer to the difficult problem of motivation may be, the organism clearly has motions of its own and meets its environment in various ways. It also has various unlearned reflexes—the Babinski, the knee jerk, and the blinking reflex—which serve as indicators of physiological normality but are not important for our present purposes. We have said before in this book that, compared with other animals and insects, the human infant is poorly supplied with instincts, but there are things nevertheless that it does not have to learn, such as anger at constraint, fear of falling, the need to eat, and later on, the urge to sexual expression. The life of man in society is thus a confrontation of organism and culture, each of which contributes something to the behavior that results. The point is that man encounters his culture and in a sense has a tussle with it. He does not merely receive it.

Heredity and environment. If organism and culture each contributes something to the human being the individual will become, then we would

[1] Like all such lists, this one has its problems. No one wants curiosity, for example, as one wants prestige. Curiosity is simply a synonym for wanting to know. If there is any want involved it is a wanting to know, or, in the authors' jargon, a knowledge want. Incidentally, the philosopher James K. Feibleman has long maintained that the desire or drive to know must be ranked with such other basic drives as hunger and sex. How else can we explain the ubiquity of curiosity, the eagerness to learn a secret or listen to gossip, the desire to be what David Riesman has called an "inside-dopester," to be "in the know"?

seem to have the problem of heredity and environment, or heredity versus environment, to be perhaps a bit more accurate. Today, however, one must almost apologize for using so ancient an expression. For the controversies that raged forty and fifty years ago over which of the two was more important have long since ceased. The battlefield is quiet now, the war forgotten. Without the organism, the culture would be only an archaeological relic, as dead as the ruins of Pompeii or the lost city of Petra, half as old as time. Without the culture, on the other hand, the organism would remain an organism, a feral, not a human, being. Both are obviously necessary to create a human person with the attributes and faculties, the conduct and characteristics, we associate with our species.

The question did arise, in a less-sophisticated era of the social sciences, as to which of these two distinguishable things, heredity and environment, is more important, which makes the major and which the minor contribution. The question, in these terms, is unfortunately phrased. It is like asking about a breakfast of ham and eggs, which contributes the most, the ham or the eggs.

There are more serious difficulties. One cannot be sure, when the problem is sufficiently refined, that the two things, organism and environment, are in truth as distinguishable as they may superficially seem to be. An American writer of a generation or more ago, A. F. Bentley, a gentleman farmer who distinguished himself in three fields (political science, social psychology, and philosophy), once published a paper with the facetious title, "The Human Skin: Philosophy's Last Line of Defense," in which his question, like ours today, is far from facetious. At what point does a custom that is cultural, and therefore external to the organism, become a habit that is physiological, and therefore internal to it? Where now is the dividing line, the point of transition? When does the custom of brushing our teeth or of using a knife and fork become a habit and therefore a "natural" activity of the organism? When does the pleasant custom of smoking become a habit that is hard to break, and when does the sad practice of drug taking become an incurable addiction?

And when, seen from the other side, does what is internal to the organism become an item of culture? At what point do the orator's words or the singer's notes cease to belong to orator and singer, as it were, and become objective phenomena in an external world? When do the words that flow from the tip of a writer's pencil onto a piece of paper cease to be a part of him and become instead a part of a larger universe so external that others can read them and then internalize them again? Where is the dividing line between words that begin as ideas and end as ink? We have here, one would suppose, another riddle. It is a riddle we do not propose to solve, but merely to state in order to indicate that things are not so simple as they seem and that what is clearly distinguishable when seen from one point of view may be blurred and confused when seen from another.

The sociologist Sorokin has suggested one of the best analogies perhaps of the relationship between the individual and culture, or the individual's heredity and the culture's environment. It is something like the relationship between the phonograph and the record. What the phonograph will play depends upon the record that is placed upon its turntable. It is the record that determines whether the music will be popular or classical and whether the language that issues from it will be Italian or French—and so on through all the varieties of records. But how well the music will be played, the quality of the tone, depends upon the phonograph. The same record will sound quite different when played upon a phonograph that is a child's inexpensive and squeaky toy and upon one that is a massive and costly instrument designed for high-fidelity reproduction. And so also for individuals. Whether they speak French or Italian, salute this flag or that, worship one god or many, depends, as we have seen, upon their culture. But the quality of their performance, its timbre and tonality, so to speak, depends upon their hereditary talents and capabilities. Some will be better at music or atomic physics or pole vaulting or ice skating than others, but they can be neither good nor bad at them in societies where these activities are not pursued.

We need not argue, therefore, about which is more important, heredity or environment, because both are important in ways that defy a quantitative comparison. As we have indicated before, a Mongolian idiot has no chance of becoming a mathematician, but neither has the most gifted individual in a society in which there is no mathematical science. The biologist will continue to study the mechanisms of heredity—whether in Indian corn, fruit flies, race-horses, or human beings—and will particularly try to find connections between genes and certain attributes, chromosomes and certain characteristics. But there is no longer any quarrel between biologist and social psychologist about which is more important, heredity or environment.

THE SELF AS SUBJECT

Everyone who is alive, in any society, has a consciousness of self. The self is what he means, in the English language, for example, by the word "I" when he is not thinking of himself. The stipulation of not thinking is important because as soon as he thinks of himself, or of his use of the "I" or even of "I" in quotation marks, the self becomes object rather than subject and the essence of the "I" disappears. The nature of the self, as seen by the self, subjectively and from the inside, is one of the great mysteries to which neither science nor philosophy has anything but partial and inadequate answers. As soon as we say "the nature of the self," as in the preceding sentence, we have already made an object of it, and the self as subject has vanished into a limbo where there is no language and where words are redundant. The self as subject is a self that transcends the possibility of explanation. It is as difficult to identify this self as it is to find it and to give it a location.

Let us consider the problem of location for a moment—and let the author who I am talk to the reader who you are in the first person. Let us ignore the usual formality, in short, in order to get closer, if we can, to the self as subject. Of all of the pronouns it is the "I" that is most baffling and complex. I know perfectly well what you are—for one thing I can see you and listen to you talk (I can imagine you reading this book)—and I know what he is and she is and they are (we both do) for similar reasons. I even know what we are because "we" surely means the two of us or the three of us or all of us, as distinguished from the rest, the others, the ones that the "we" excludes. But what am I? When I say that I do not know what I am, I do not even know whether there are three different "I's" in that expression, two different "I's," or only one. One reason for my difficulty is that any effort to think about it—i.e., my "I"—already turns it into an "it," an object, and that is precisely what, at the moment, I do not want my "I" to be.

But let us proceed to the problem of location. If I do not know what I am, can I not at least say where I am? This too is difficult. I think that I am somewhere behind my eyes—at least I have the impression that I look through them when I see—but now that I have put the words down on paper the notion seems a bit ridiculous. I know the eyes are mine (the left one, for example, has been nearsighted for years), but now I am confused again about what the "mine" might refer to. Modern surgical techniques could transfer them to someone else. But nothing could transfer the "I" that now owns them to someone else, and if it could be done the "I" would probably no longer be me but rather someone else.

I am surely dependent upon my body because I did not exist before my body did, and it is a genuine (and religious) question whether I shall continue to exist when my body dies. And so, you see, I have something to do with my body. But if I look for me somewhere inside this body there is no particular place that I can find myself. In fact, this whole body is mine to do with what I want. I can feed it, fill it and empty it as the Greek philosopher got tired of doing, lay it down for a nap (in which case I disappear for a while), run it up or down the stairs, take it swimming, or make it—one hand of it that is—move a pencil across a sheet of paper. All of these things *I* can do to *it* and therefore I cannot be identical with it but rather something else. I am never far away from my body, it is true, except perhaps in revery, and what I should do without it I really do not know. I have the impression that it is always somewhere around, where I am, and I should no doubt be quite uncomfortable without it. But that seems only fair, for sometimes it is quite uncomfortable with me, as when I give it too much to eat or drink or make it work too long without rest.

My body has changed a great deal since I—or it—was born, but I think somehow that in spite of these changes I am still the same I, not a different one, and that I shall continue to be the same I until I die. But what accounts for this sameness, this continuing identity through all these changes—graying hair, for example, and increasing weight—I really do not know. This problem is the problem of identity, with which the philosophers often struggle. In the eighteenth century three "coffeehouse intellectuals," Pope, Arbuthnot, and Gay, wanting to make fun of the philosophers, wrote anonymously a book called *The Memoirs of Martinus Scriblerus*. In this book they told the tale of a sock. This sock, after it is worn a while, gets a hole in it. You darn the hole, wear it a while, and then it gets another hole. You darn this hole and wear it some more and soon there is another hole. And so on. There will come a time, after continuous darning, when not a single one of the original threads remain. The question of Martinus Scriblerus then becomes—Is it the same sock?

This question, of course, can be asked about me and my body. I do not exist without my body and yet every single cell of my body reproduces itself, it is estimated, every seven years. This means that no part of my body seven years ago is part of my body today, and I am puzzled therefore about what has happened to me in the meantime. Am I the same I or a different one?

I think it is time to stop this speculation about me. You have the problem, too, or at least I think you have. Who are you anyway? I don't mean what is your name, what is your street address, what is the color of your hair, or whether you are tall or short or fat or thin. I mean who are you? Do you also have an I that baffles you when you try to explain your being to your self? Have you ever been tempted to think that you might have had another body than the one you have, say a body of a different color or a different age? Isn't it curious, when you stop to think about it, that you are you today and that there has never been another you in any period of history? How strange that you should be you, and I I, and that there is no confusion of identities between us. Suppose the arrangements of life and consciousness and existence were such that when we became dissatisfied with our body we could thrust ourselves into another and then continue both to be ourselves and to have ourselves permanently, through all of future time? Would we then be able to know more about this ineffable self that refers to itself as I?

Lawrence Durrell, in the first of the novels in his Alexandria quartet, has one of his characters—Pursewarden, a writer—ask still another question about the self. He wonders whether it is continuous or whether it exists only in successive moments of self-consciousness. But this is only an echo of David Hume, the Scottish Skeptic, who long before said that when he sought this mysterious thing he never found a self as such but only a succession of sensations.

Observations like these, tantalizing as they may be, have of course no end to them. All of them are speculative, some seem surrealistic, and others may come close to nonsense. What I am from my point of view and what you are from yours are questions not open to inquiry. The subjective self is mine, or yours, and that is all we can say. As soon as we start to talk about it, it turns into an objective self and it has then disappeared as subject. It becomes the object of our concern, as it does in the section that follows.[2]

THE SELF AS OBJECT

We now leave the subjective self to the solipsists and turn to the only self that can be an object of inquiry—the objective self. Where does this self arise? Are we born with it or is it something we have to learn to recognize and to know? Is it something the individual brings with him as he confronts society or is it something that he receives from society as a gift in the confrontation. How, as the English philosopher W. J. H. Sprott engagingly puts it, do little Shirley and little Raymond begin to absorb their culture? How, more importantly for present purposes, do they acquire their Shirley-hood and Raymond-hood?[3] This at least is a question to which social psychology and sociology have some answers.

One of the earliest of sustained attacks on this problem was made by Charles Horton Cooley, a sociologist who dedicated his entire career to the advancement of two primary propositions—one, that the mind is social, and two, that society is mental. The second of these propositions is quite out of fashion and no one subscribes to it in Cooley's terms; but the first is of over-riding importance and has won the general assent of all of his successors, even when they have demurred on its details. A characteristic passage appears at the very beginning of his book, *Social Organization,* where he insists that "self and society are twin-born, we know one as immediately as we know the other, and the notion of a separate and independent ego is an illusion."[4] Indeed, Cooley objects to the famous formulation of Descartes—*Cogito ergo sum* (I think; therefore, I am)—on two grounds. Before mentioning them let us examine the cartesian situation.

René Descartes (1596–1650), the inventor of analytical geometry and

---

[2] One may wonder in addition whether the difference between the subject and the object is a fact in the universe, hard and obdurate, or whether it is something that occurs only because of the exigencies of language. Is it only the nature of language and not the nature of the universe that requires us to differentiate between subject and object? Is this because the sentences we speak have subjects and predicates? Or do our sentences have subjects and predicates as an accurate reflection of the nature of the universe—a universe that actually contains subjects and objects? These questions belong to the philosophy of language and to the sociology of knowledge, but they can occur, of course, to any thoughtful mind.

[3] W. J. H. Sprott, *Social Psychology,* Methuen & Co., Ltd., London, 1956, p. 126.

[4] Charles Horton Cooley, *Social Organization,* The Free Press of Glencoe, New York, 1956, p. 5. The book was originally published in 1909.

the founder of modern philosophy, was also a gentleman soldier of some repute. In the year 1619, while on his way to join the army of the Emperor Maximilian, then in winter quarters, he found himself in a little village near Ulm, in a sheltered hut with its comfortable fire. He fell to musing about the potentialities of human reason and indeed began to wonder if he could prove his own existence by reason alone, without recourse to observation and experience. He began by trying to doubt the existence of everything in order to discover what, if anything, would remain when the doubting had been pushed to its ultimate limit and had exhausted all of its possibilities. He doubted first the existence of the external world. This could be an illusion for it seems to be dependent upon sensations that could be erroneous or misleading. The water that is warm to cold feet, for example, is cold to warm hands, as Plato had noticed long before. Next Descartes doubted the existence of God, a doubt that was similarly fortified by philosophical precedent. Finally, he doubted that he himself existed, and this too he convinced himself that he was able to do. There was one thing, however, that he could not doubt, and that was that he was doubting. To doubt is to think; to think is to be; therefore—triumphantly—I am. *Je pense, donc je suis* (I think; therefore, I am).

One of the flaws in this argument is in the restoration of the "I." The end product of the doubting was only doubting and it was a dubious leap from an unspoken premise that permitted Descartes to assume that doubting required a doubter and that it was he (whose existence he had doubted) who was doing the doubting. How did he know, moreover, having doubted everything else, that a predicate or a participle required a subject and that that subject was himself? Once the first step was taken, however, Descartes found it comparatively easy to restore the other things that he had doubted— God, by an argument reminiscent of St. Anselm in the eleventh century, and the external world as a corollary of the existence of God. As the American philosopher Morris Raphael Cohen once pointed out, no one who uses the method of cartesian doubt is ever satisfied until he has recovered everything he has doubted.

Whatever the logical flaws in this procedure, Cooley objected to it: "In the first place it seems to imply that 'I'-consciousness is a part of all consciousness, when, in fact, it belongs only to a rather advanced stage of development. In the second it is one-sided, or 'individualistic' in asserting the personal or 'I' aspect to the exclusion of the social or 'we' aspect, which is equally original with it."[5] In Cooley's view self-consciousness can arise only in society, and indeed is inseparable from social consciousness. Self-consciousness does not in fact appear in children until they are about two years of age and then only in conjunction with the consciousness of others as well. The self, in short, is social.

[5] *Ibid.*, p. 6.

In the earlier of Cooley's two major works, *Human Nature and the Social Order* (1902), he contributed a number of useful and indeed striking insights, together with his famous "looking-glass" conception of the self. The first of the insights that attract our attention is that "I" is, after all, a word, that a word is a part of a language, and a language is a social product.[6] Without society there would be no communication, without communication no language, and without language no "I." "To think of it as apart from society is a palpable absurdity."[7] A second insight, less relevant to his central thesis but interesting nevertheless, is Cooley's observation that we sometimes transfer the "I" to an inanimate object with which we are closely associated and which is ours. Examples would be a golf ball or an automobile, as in "I am in the rough to the left of the green" and "I am in Parking Area C." The first of these examples is Cooley's and he quotes with approval the somewhat similar observations made by William James in his *Principles of Psychology* (1890): "A man's self is the sum total of all he can call his, not only his body and his psychic powers, but his clothes, and his house, his wife and children, his ancestors and friends, his reputation and works, his lands and horses and yacht and bank-account. All these things give him the same emotions."[8]

More important, however, is the looking-glass conception mentioned above. The way we imagine ourselves to appear to another person is an essential element in our conception of ourselves. Thus, I am not what I think I am and I am not what you think I am. I am what I think you think I am. The proof of this view seemed clear to Cooley from the consideration that "we are ashamed to seem evasive in the presence of a straightforward man, cowardly in the presence of a brave one, gross in the presence of a refined one, and so on."[9] That we exhibit a different self in different social groups is fairly clear and it is only a small step therefore to the inference that we *are* a different self in different groups; to the additional inference that we depend upon the presence of others for our conception of our selves; and to the conclusion again, now strengthened by this additional evidence, that the self is social and that self-consciousness would not exist in the absence of society. These, at least, are Cooley's important contributions to the problem.

The role of others in self-perception was the fruitful starting point for the theory of the self propounded by George Herbert Mead (1863–1931), the philosopher and psychologist who taught and wrote for many years at the University of Chicago. Mead agreed wholeheartedly with Cooley that it is absurd to look at the self or the mind from the viewpoint of an individual organism. Although the self may have its focus in the organism, it is without

---

[6] *Human Nature and the Social Order,* The Free Press of Glencoe, New York, 1956, p. 180.

[7] *Ibid.,* p. 181.

[8] *Ibid.,* note to p. 170.

[9] *Ibid.,* p. 184.

question a social product and a social phenomenon.[10] What are the specific mechanisms, then, in terms of which this social self comes into consciousness? One suggestion comes from the realization that almost all behavior is behavior in interaction with others and therefore involves adjustments and adaptations to them. This is the way it is when dogs are fighting, cats are playing, and people are conversing. Everything that one of the participants does is a response to what the other one does, for this is the nature of interaction. So far we have consciousness by each of the other, but not necessarily as yet any self-consciousness. The more we interact with others, however—and interaction increases in the process of living itself—the more we learn to anticipate the responses of others and to learn, for example, the future significance of present gestures. We watch for signs of pleasure or displeasure in the other person and learn to interpret them correctly. These signs ordinarily take the form of gestures and facial expressions, and after a while these gestures and expressions indicate to us what we are expected to do in a given situation.

In this way, in reverse so to speak, our own gestures become meaningful to us. That is, we learn the meaning of our own gestures through the responses to them ourselves, implicitly, as the other does explicitly. The gesture, in short, evokes in ourselves the response we intend to elicit from the other—we take the attitude of the other. Thus we are always replying to ourselves, silently, when we are talking to others. This tendency is apparent in teaching, for example. We have to restrain ourselves from blurting out the answers to the questions we have asked of those we are trying to teach. One result of this process, in the course of our normal interactions, is that we begin to carry on an internal conversation, a conversation with ourselves, not in the manner of the village idiot, who talks aloud to himself and answers questions no one has asked him, but rather as one who is responsive in anticipation to one's own words and gestures. It is in this process, according to Mead, that we find the genesis of the self and the origin of self-consciousness. For, as Sprott remarks in discussing this point, unless we make the very large assumption of a primal selfhood, it is difficult to see how a self-consciousness could otherwise arise except in the process that presents ourselves to ourselves as something somehow different from others.[11]

The next step is to notice that, although we take the attitude of the other in order to discover the self, the others with whom we interact are different others and we respond to them differently. We take the attitudes of a number of others, just as we engage in a number of different interactions. We do not, however, become a different self with respect to each different other—although we do, of course, respond to different persons differently—

[10] George Herbert Mead, *Mind, Self, and Society*. The University of Chicago Press, Chicago, 1934, p. 133.
[11] W. J. H. Sprott, *op. cit.*, p. 129.

and Mead now has the difficult problem, therefore, of explaining the continuity of the self—its consistency, so to speak—throughout these changing interactions with different others. He solves the problem with the quite original suggestion that we consolidate all of these different others into a "generalized other" and this generalized other in turn is identical with the social group or the community to which we belong. The responses that finally result in selfhood are not the discontinuous responses to different others but rather the continuous responses we make to a generalized other. The situation is exactly like that found in every one of us when we say, or more likely think, "What will people think if I do this or that?" The "people" in this expression is not any particular person but rather a generalized person, a generalized other, that is coextensive with the community of our associates. In this way the social explanation of the self is complete.

There is at least one other notion in Mead that merits a moment of attention and reflection, and that is his distinction between the "I" and the "me." The "I" is what we have called above the subjective self, and the "me" is the objective self. The "I" is both subjective and spontaneous, the "me" results from a recognition of the self as the bundle of attitudes and responses that is derived from the generalized other. The "I" initiates action, but it becomes, in cognition and memory, the "me." We do not, as we have seen in our earlier discussion, ever know the "I," because as soon as we know it—i.e., cognize it or recognize it—it has already become an object, and thus the "me." It is the "I" that is unique; the "me" is the product of the generalized other. The "I" is spontaneous, therefore, and the "me" conventional. The "me" cooperates with the community, so to speak, because the community is its source and origin as the generalized other.

The separation of the self into an "I" and a "me" can serve as a transition to the Freudian view of the matter, to which we now briefly turn. If Mead used these two components, Freud used three—the id, the ego, and the super-ego or, as they appeared in the original German, the *Es,* the *Ich,* and the *Über-Ich.*[12] The id represents our appetites, those inborn drives that prompt us to act. It seeks pleasure and avoids pain—and gives added resonance to the famous sentence of Jeremy Bentham (1748–1832) that "Nature has placed mankind under the governance of two sovereign masters, Pain and Pleasure." The id furnishes the impulse, the impulse to do what we want because it is what we want to do, without regard to friends or society, conscience or morality.

---

[12] Philip Rieff suggests that the Latin words, now used invariably in English discussion, as contrasted with Spanish and French, for example, have contributed to the complexities of the Freudian "rhetoric" and obscure what a simple pronoun usage would otherwise make clear. See his study *Freud: The Mind of the Moralist,* Anchor Books, Doubleday & Company, Inc., Garden City, N. Y., 1961, note to p. 64.

We are not, however, permitted to do what we want. We are not allowed to steal the steak in our neighbor's freezer, to initiate conversation with the prettiest of passing females, or to hit the person who infuriates us with his willful stupidity. We are required to adjust our desires to the reality of a world in which they may not be fulfilled. It is the second mechanism of the mind, the ego, that helps us to do this. It mediates, so to speak, between the impulses of the id and the moral exigencies of the world in which we live. It is the ego that weighs the claims of the id against the demands of society, making now some space for impulse and then some reins for restraint, and thus contributing to the long-term adjustment of the individual. The ego is thus the manager of the self.

The moral restraint that society imposes also has its agent in the self—and this is the superego. The superego tells us what is right and what is wrong; it is the "Sunday school" of the mind, the conscience of the individual. It tells us what we ought and—more frequently perhaps—ought not to do. It imposes upon us the moral imperatives of society. It prohibits the freedom of impulse. The id and the superego then stand in opposition, the one to the other. If all of our impulses cannot be gratified, however, neither can they all be restrained without serious harm to the individual. It is the task of the ego then to serve as the umpire in this contest.

The contest, incidentally, is an internal one and is not identical with the process, to be described in the following chapter of this book, in which the sanctions applied by our companions induce us to conform to the norms. This, on the contrary, is the self in conflict with itself, as Philip Rieff so clearly expresses it:

No small part of Freud's impact upon the contemporary moral imagination derives from his idea of the self in conflict. He conceives of the self not as an abstract entity, uniting experience and cognition, but as the subject of a struggle between two objective forces—unregenerate instincts and overbearing culture. Between these two forces there may be compromise but no resolution. Since the individual can neither extirpate his instincts nor wholly reject the demands of society, his character expresses the way in which he organizes and appeases the conflict between the two.[13]

The id meets the superego head on as it were. They are always on a collision course. It is in this contrary juxtaposition that the awareness of self arises and it is this conflict that gives us our conception of self. It is in the repression of impulse that we become conscious of the fact that there is something else in the universe than our selves, and it is this consciousness that gives us also the sense of self.

There are thus certain similarities in the theories of Cooley, Mead, and

[13] Philip Rieff, op. cit., p. 29.

Freud. All three, however different their intellectual orientations, arrive at a theory of the self that requires society. For none of the three is self-consciousness possible without the presence and, in one case, the repressions of society. Thus in three writers we have a view of the self that is explicitly sociological. The individual has a self only because he first acquires a society.

It may be that the reader of this book will be reluctant to accept any such sociological theory of the self. The trouble is that the demonstrable facts we have on this subject are insufficient to support a general theory and the theories therefore still have in them some flavor of speculation. It may be that in spite of Cooley, Mead, and Freud, there is a primal self-consciousness after all, a subjective self that has an initial and permanent independence of all external influences whether these latter originate in the inhibitions of a society or in the obduracies of the physical universe. We have no disposition to argue the case, either here or elsewhere, because, as Nietzsche said, "One's own self is well hidden from one's own self." However this may be, we should doubtless all agree that, whether or not we have a primal self-consciousness, we need a language to make it articulate—even to make ourselves aware that we have it—and language is both a product and a vehicle of culture. We cannot know the meaning of "I" and "me" and "mine" until there are such words in the language as "I" and "me" and "mine," and we learn these meanings only in intercourse and association with our fellows—with you and yours, and them and theirs. The subjective self, the elusive self, may not require any cultural assistance for its existence, but the objective self cannot dispense with such assistance. To this extent at least the self is social.

PERSONALITY AND CULTURE

On the first page of this book we made the now rather common observation that in certain respects we are like all other people, in certain other respects like some other people, and in still others like no one except ourselves. We have said that the second of these propositions is particularly appropriate to sociology, and we shall see later that people do fall into similar groupings, depending upon their possession of common characteristics. A logical inference from this proposition would be that all those who are exposed to the same culture are alike and it would be difficult to explain therefore how each human personality could be unique. The truth is that not everyone is exposed to exactly the same culture, not even those who are children in the same family. We need therefore to explore this complicated situation in a little more detail in order to see how culture is related to personality.

Let us notice first of all that culture is not a monolithic entity, a hardened mold into which each individual is poured at birth, a cookie cutter designed to produce innumerable individuals all exhibiting exactly the same traits and attributes. Culture is not a uniform pattern that impresses itself alike upon all who are exposed to it, nor is it a uniform that all must wear. Consider, for example, the regional differences in culture that occur within a single society. There is a difference between a Middlewesterner and an Easterner in the United States, a Highlander and a Lowlander in Scotland, a Prussian and a Bavarian in Germany, a Venetian and a Sicilian in Italy, and so on, in addition to such other differences—in size or place or religion—that they might exhibit. There are different traditions born of different regions, and these tend to create different personalities and a different temperament. The Middlewesterner is opener, friendlier, breezier, as it were, the Easterner more reserved, and some would say, more dignified in his contacts, especially initial ones, with other people. These differences are fairly obvious and there is no need to expatiate upon them except to say that any culture that is shared by a large number of people reasonably distributed in space is a mosaic of subcultures—subcultures created by region and religion, class and occupation, education and political belief. Not all of the children in the same society confront the same culture because of the many subcultures that every complex society contains.

In the second place, the culture may present alternative lines of action that are equally acceptable and yet one of them may affect the personality in one way and the second in another. In our own culture, for example, babies may be breast-fed or bottle-fed, and both procedures are in conformity with the norms. There are those who would contend that breast feeding is preferable to bottle feeding on the ground that the greater intimacy with the mother contributes to a greater emotional security. Whether or not this is true, few would doubt that there could be a differential effect upon personality. Similarly, infant feeding may be periodic or permissive, on either a definite or a "demand" schedule, and again both alternatives are permitted by the culture and may exert slightly different influences upon the personality. The point is that there are cultural alternatives as well as cultural specifications and not all cultural patterns are cultural imperatives.

Newly arrived members of a society do not confront the same culture for still another reason. Culture does not transmit itself. It is transmitted only by individuals and these individuals have absorbed different bits and pieces of the culture to which they in their turn were initially exposed. No two sets of parents, even of the same race, religion, and region, will transmit to their offspring the same cultural items and traits. One of the problems of marital adjustment in fact stems from the circumstance that the two individuals involved, even when they have the same ethnic antecedents, the same religion, the same social-class background, and a comparable education, will bring to each other different cultural emphases and will conform to slightly different norms. One of the couple will squeeze the tube of toothpaste from the bottom (as it should be squeezed!) and the other at the top. And after the adjustment is made—a continuous process—and the children come, the culture that one pair of parents transmits will be different in perceivable particulars from the culture that is being transmitted to the new generation next door in the same housing development. Each family, in a sense, has its own subculture.

If the cultures exhibit these slight discrepancies, so also does the social situation in which the infant finds himself and which also has an effect upon the development of personality. The social group that the only child belongs to in his family is clearly not the same social group in which two children are members—or three or five or eight. A child that has brothers only is in a different social and cultural situation from one that has only sisters, and his own sex is an additional variable in the situation. Birth order is still another factor that can affect the personality, and it is obvious again that first and last children have both advantages and disadvantages that do not accrue to the middle children. Closely related to this last is another variable, the age of the parents, and once more it is easy to see that a child of young parents has a better chance to learn to water-ski, for example, than the child of older parents. Even with roughly the same culture, in short, the social situation in a single family is different for each of its younger members, and consequently the personalities that develop will be different too.

Variety is endless in human life, and various also are the influences to which the developing personality is exposed. Several other factors that encourage idiosyncrasy require a remark or two. We have not yet said that if the culture is not uniform, neither is it static. In the complex societies that we know best, culture is changing all the time and, so far as we can determine, without fixed points for comparison, at a rapid rate as well. Even if the ages of parents could be held constant, children born into the same family a decade apart would encounter a different culture and in some respects a dramatically different one. Culture is a dynamic, changing thing; it presents with every passing period new facets and a "new frontier."

We have to notice too that the original material that comes to the culture to be shaped and formed and conditioned and directed is also highly variable. No two biological organisms, no two newborn babies, are exactly alike in every talent and attribute and trait—although identical twins come close to being an exception. There are biological differences, too, genetic and hereditary, that make every human infant different from every other and able, in consequence, to respond in different ways to the same or similar cultural stimuli. We should not overstress the biological basis of personality, but we must not understress it either. As we have said before, to the developed personality that is an adult human being both heredity and environment have their share to contribute.

The culture itself can place a greater emphasis upon individuality than upon conformity. As we have said, a culture can offer alternatives as well as specifications, and its norms, as we shall see, are areas of permissiveness as well as guides for conduct. Initiative, inventiveness, originality, adaptability to new situations can all be values that are ranked high in a particular culture, just as their contraries can be ranked high in others. Wherever we find an emphasis upon individuality we have a cultural factor operating to diminish what would otherwise be cultural uniformity.

We have offered a number of reasons why culture does not sculpture personalities into a common mold: (1) cultures themselves lack uniformity in their spatial distribution; (2) cultures are transmitted atomistically as it were by persons who possess different collections of their items and traits; (3) the social situations in which personalities are acquired produce additional cultural varieties; (4) cultures may change rapidly even in brief periods of time; (5) the organic constitution accounts for its share of variation; and (6) the culture may encourage individuality and even, in some respects, idiosyncrasy. For all of these reasons there may appear in a given culture a wide range of variation in personality type, and indeed this tends to be the case.

There are those who maintain nevertheless that the relationship between culture and personality is quite close and that culture encourages the development of certain types of personality and discourages certain others. They argue that cultures are congenial to the development of certain kinds of personalities because of the ideas and ideologies they contain. In some the virtues of humility, modesty, and withdrawal, for example, may win rewards in personal esteem, and in others the contrary traits of boastfulness, self-acclaim, and aggressiveness may win esteem. Some may stress order and efficiency and neatness, whereas in others these attributes receive only a secondary emphasis if indeed they are considered important at all. Still others may give a high priority to ambition, material success, and "getting ahead." Different goals, aspirations, hopes, and fears may all receive a different stress; in this way a particular culture may encourage the development of a particular kind of personality. Those who support this view offer as evidence the case of our own culture, where there is a sharp differentiation of sex roles and where boys, therefore, are taught to be masculine—that is, to develop those personality traits associated with "maleness"—and girls are taught to be feminine. That these differences are culturally determined, however, is a theory that we treat with some skepticism in another chapter of the book.

Other evidence comes from studies of cultures quite different from our own and appears in the literature of anthropology. The most famous of these studies perhaps are Ruth Benedict's *Patterns of Culture* and Margaret Mead's *Sex and Temperament in Three Primitive Societies*, both of which were published in 1935. In these books we are told that the Zuñi Indians are calm, the Kwakiutl competitive, the Dobuans suspicious, the Arapesh amiable, the

Mundugumor treacherous—and these differences in temperament are attributed to the culture. Similarly, writers like Abram Kardiner and Ralph Linton have utilized the concept of a "basic personality structure" that is supposedly congenial with the total range of institutions to be found in a given culture.[14]

The cogency of these claims for the cultural determination of personality would seem to depend very largely upon one's definition of personality. Writers in this field have different conceptions of it, and among the various definitions we find such expressions as "an integration of habit systems," "a totality of physiological and psychological reaction systems," "a cultural mold," "the events whose locus defines the individual in relation to surrounding individuals," "the individual's social stimulus value," "a structural whole, definable in terms of its own distinctive structural attributes," "a structural organism-environment field," "a primordial stuff," "a pattern of accidentally imposed conditionings," "an achieved inner structure," and "the dynamic organization of those psychophysical systems that determine the individual's unique adjustment to his environment." These expressions are partly paraphrases and partly quotations culled from a variety of places, including the writings of G. W. Allport, Edward Sapir, Harold D. Lasswell, Mark A. May, and Gardner Murphy. Some of them, as can be seen, stress the organic and some the environmental, some the individual and some the social, some the personal and some the cultural—and indeed these adjectives may be regarded in this context as three sets of synonyms.

Now it is fairly clear that if we define personality as "a cultural mold," then we can easily accept the view that personality is determined by culture. It is true by definition. If, on the other hand, we regard personality as some kind of "primordial stuff," then we must reject this view. It is false by definition. Our own conclusion would go to neither of these extremes. We would tend to subscribe to an intermediate position and say that neither psychology, with its emphasis upon individual differences, nor sociology, with its emphasis upon cultural similarities, can by itself give an adequate account of personality. It would seem to be a superior strategy to regard personality as a biosocial phenomenon, the study of which belongs properly to a social psychology or—what is the same thing, though a more awkward expression—a psychological sociology.

We should like, however, to stress two facts about the confrontation of the individual and his culture: (1) that it is a two-way process, not like the pouring of an infinitely plastic substance into an unyielding container, and (2) that the process is a continuous one, not something that begins in infancy and ends at adulthood. One might say with respect to the first of these

[14] See Abram Kardiner et al., *The Psychological Frontiers of Society,* Columbia University Press, New York, 1945; and Ralph Linton, *The Cultural Background of Personality,* Appleton-Century-Crofts, Inc., New York, 1945.

observations that the word "process" is too mild, that actually there is a struggle going on that frequently results, for the individual, in frustration and anxiety. "One lives," as Ernest van den Haag has poetically expressed it, "in the tension between society and solitude,"[15] and this is the tension too that gives pertinence to the Freudian theory of the self. Sometimes the cultural impress does not "take," sometimes it stimulates the individual to "counter-attack," sometimes even when cultural patterns are apparently accepted, tensions may flare up later and result either in personality disorders or in an effort to change the offending part of the culture.

Furthermore, individuals react in different ways to these cultural pressures and impressions. As Gardner Murphy suggests, "One child is easily molded with regard to food but fights constantly against socialization of his aggressive impulses; the reverse may be true of another child."[16] Complete uniformity and a total absence of innovation would be the stagnant result of a process in which every individual bore the unchanging imprint of a monolithic culture. It is easy, in short, to exaggerate the effect of culture upon personality—an exaggeration that was fashionable in the culture and personality theories of a few years ago. Personality is not a passive creation of culture—as the differing temperaments of siblings should have shown us. On the other hand, one cannot wholly ignore the influence of culture either. However useful the concept of "basic personality structure" may be, there is a difference between the typical Englishman, the typical German, the typical Turk, and the typical Brazilian. The trouble is that so few of these Englishmen, Germans, Turks, and Brazilians are typical.

The agents of socialization. Personalities do not come ready-made. The process that transforms the primitive organism—the puking, mewling, bawling, caterwauling infant—into a reasonably respectable human being is a long process and one that is apt to be arduous for all concerned. As sociologists we are inclined to see the culture on the one side and the individual on the other and wonder what effect each has upon the other. To look at the problem in this way, however, is in part erroneous and in part artificial, because on the one side—the individual—we have a concrete entity, and on the other—the culture—we have an abstraction. How an entity interacts with an abstraction is not a meaningful question. We can give it meaning, however, by eradicating the abstraction as it were and by emphasizing something we have previously recognized, namely, that culture is always transmitted by people in interaction. It is transmitted through the communication they have with one another, and communication thus comes to be the essence of the

[15] In Ralph Ross and Ernest van den Haag, *The Fabric of Society*, Harcourt, Brace & World, Inc., New York, 1957, p. 73.

[16] Gardner Murphy, *Personality*, Harper & Brothers, New York, 1947, p. 905.

process of culture transmission. It is the basic—though not the only—instrument of socialization.[17] And a versatile instrument it is, too, since it operates between those who do not know one another as well as between those who do. Let us consider this instrument in a little more detail so that we may disclose the specific kinds of communication through which the child acquires his culture.

It must be fairly apparent that the process of culture transmission begins for every one of us in the family, and that the parental—and especially the maternal—influence upon the infant is the most important of all. Given the basic abilities that are genetically present and transmitted through the germ plasm, this most intimate of all human relationships, that between mother and child, must be accorded the largest significance in the socialization process and in the shaping of these abilities and capacities in ways that the culture helps to determine. The father, of course, is important too, but his role is defined somewhat differently in different cultures, and in some, as will be seen in a later chapter on the family, the father is less important than the mother's brother. Nevertheless, it is the father in most societies who transmits to his sons the knowledge and the skill in particular activities that males in these societies are expected to acquire. In any event, these are the communications—with mother and father—through which the child receives an introduction to his culture, an introduction which, in advanced societies, is somewhat prolonged in time. He receives additional communications from his older siblings, who have gone through the same process—with certain differences due to birth order, as we have already recognized, and to the number and sex of the siblings.

The role of siblings in the socialization process leads us by an easy transition to the role of peer groups. Peer groups, as the word implies, means those groups made up of the contemporaries of the child, his associates in school and in Sunday school, in the playground and in the street. He learns from these children, as indeed they learn from him, facts and facets of the culture that they have previously learned, at different times, from their parents. The members of peer groups have other sources of information about the culture—their peers in still other peer groups—and thus the acquisition of culture goes on, with much of the socialization process a function of precisely these kinds of groups.

As time goes on, of course, the peer group surpasses the parental and family group in importance, and by the time children are in high school, in our culture, they have begun openly and candidly to reject parental influence in favor of the obvious superiority of the information and guidance they receive from their contemporaries. This seems to be an inevitable occurrence

[17] There are other mechanisms, too, for example, imitation, which was treated so brilliantly by the French sociologist Gabriel Tarde (1843–1904).

in rapidly changing societies—it might be called the displacement of the parents by the peers—and no one doubts that it occurs in ours. The teen ages are the ages par excellence of parent-child misunderstanding. Mark Twain gave his own inimitable recognition of this fact when he said, "When I was sixteen my old man was so stupid I could hardly stand to have him around; but when I got to be twenty-one I was surprised to see how much he had learned in the meantime."

Certainly it is true that the peer culture takes precedence over the parental culture in the adolescent years, and the advice of one's contemporaries, whether overtly or covertly communicated, sets the standard in almost every aspect of conduct. We should not assume, therefore, that the socialization process is completed by the time the teen ages are reached. On the contrary, this is the time when the pressures for conformity are perhaps at their height, when deviance in the ordinary affairs of life is punished most severely by one's associates, when conformity is required with a daily and almost hourly insistence. The American high school might be described, in fact, as a "hotbed of conformity." No one who suffers it is competent to write about it, and those who write about it can no longer remember it with precision.

Parents and peers, however, are not the only agencies of the socialization process; there are teachers, too, and thus the school comes to play an important role. It is hardly necessary to discuss that role, so obvious is it in every society that has an institution of education. In the school the culture is formally transmitted and acquired; the lore and the learning, the science and the art, of one generation is passed on to the next. Not only the formal knowledge of the culture is transmitted there, but most of its premises as well—its ethical sentiments, its political attitudes, its customs and taboos. The children in the earlier school may uncritically absorb the culture to which their teachers give expression; they may in the high school respond with increasing skepticism. But wherever they are, and at whatever age, the communications they receive from their teachers help to socialize them and to make them finally mature members of their societies.

There is another source of socialization, one that appears only in literate societies, and that is the printed word. The civilization that most of us share is constructed of words. Words rush at us in torrent and cascade; they leap into our vision, as in billboard and newspaper, magazine and textbook, and assault our ears, as in radio and television. "The media of mass communication," as our commentators, sociological and otherwise, like to call them, importune us with their messages, and these messages too contain in capsule form the premises of our culture, its attitudes and ideologies. The words are always written, and the people who write them—authors and editors and advertisers—join the teachers, the peers, and the parents in the socialization process. In individual cases, of course, some of these influences are more important than others, and in any case there are inconsistencies and even contradictions among them. The responses can also differ. Some of us respect tradition; others fear the opinions of their peers; and still others prefer to listen to the "thousand tongues of conscience." In the words of David Riesman, persons in the first group are tradition-directed, those in the second other-directed, and those in the third inner-directed. In Riesman's theory these three groups have different orders of preponderance under different historical conditions, but all three modes of socialization result in conformity of a kind and all three thus contribute to the transmission of a culture by some and its acquisition by others.[18]

Summary

In this chapter we have tried to take the mystery out of the process by which culture is transmitted from one generation to another in human societies. Here we turned to the individual and suggested that what is culture transmission from the point of view of the society as a whole is socialization from the point of view of the individual. We have endeavored to show how association with others is the underlying mechanism by which culture is acquired.

It is necessary to recognize, however, that culture is not a simple, monolithic entity that is transmitted en masse and all of a piece to every new human individual who is exposed to it. Culture is a complex and variable thing—flexible, loose, not always integrated, sometimes rigid, sometimes permissive, sometimes inconsistent in its parts, and in truth amorphous. Socialization, in short, involves a partial, not a total, culture, because human beings are involved and human beings have their whims, their idiosyncrasies, and their infinite variety.

The socialization process raises a number of issues and problems. The organism that confronts society and that is receptive to its culture is not, after all, an inert and passive organism. It goes to meet the culture. The forces that motivate it have never been altogether clear, either in physiological or sociological terms, and the problem of motivation, therefore, remains unsolved. We can, however, indicate some of the difficulties associated with it and describe what happened with respect to one of these theories, the instinct theory that enjoyed so long a reign in the history of psychology.

[18] For Riesman's theory see his famous book *The Lonely Crowd*, Yale University Press, New Haven, Conn., 1950. Also, abridged, in Anchor Books, Doubleday & Company, Inc., Garden City, N. Y., 1953. The book was written in collaboration with Nathan Glazer and Reuel Denney.

Although we have previously considered the biological factor in society we thought it appropriate to look once again at the ancient issue of heredity and environment, primarily because it occupied so much of the time and attention of social scientists and psychologists in the earlier decades of the century. A number of problems remain, of course, but they no longer engage the passions of partisans who would claim that heredity is more important than environment, or the other way around. In the socialization process we may say that the attributes of the organism are necessary conditions and the culture a sufficient condition to explain the personality that develops.

The chapter also dealt with the problem of self—both the subjective self and the objective self. The first is a matter of almost pure speculation, and it abounds in paradoxes; the second, the objective self, is rather more amenable to investigation. We explored the theories developed by Charles Horton Cooley, George Herbert Mead, and Sigmund Freud, and found in all three the belief that the self is social, that it requires society for its full explanation, and that our consciousness of it—our self-consciousness—arises in our interaction with others.

The view, fairly popular in recent decades, that culture is the determinant of personality, though it is plausible on the surface, presents nevertheless many difficulties. These difficulties seriously affect the concept of a basic personality structure, especially when we consider the variations in both the cultural and the social situations that face the individual in his developmental career. A culture would have to be much less variable than it is, and social situations would have to be much more constant, in order to construct this basic structure. Some attributes of personality are indeed traceable to culture. National and religious differences, to mention only two, encourage the development of different personality traits. But again, individual differences and variations in social situations make it difficult if not impossible for consistent personality types to emerge—to say nothing of different initial constitutions. The story of personality is one of the most complex of all the problems belonging to social psychology. We do our sociology no service when we make personality entirely a function of culture. Personality in truth is a biosocial phenomenon and one that can be understood neither by psychology nor by sociology in independence of the other.

We concluded, briefly, with an emphasis upon four of the most important of the agents of socialization—parents, peers, teachers, and the mass media—suggesting how each contributes its share to the never-ending process that begins with the human infant, only barely qualified for admission to the human race, and ends with his acceptance as a member of society. In between the initial material and the end result there is the socialization process, the process by which all of us acquire the culture that we shall, in turn, transmit to the next generation as it arrives upon our scene with its own pressing need to be socialized.

Review questions

1. Discuss the theories of self-knowledge or motivation associated with the writings of each of the following persons. (Include the approximate date at which each was writing.)

   a. E. A. Ross
   b. William McDougall
   c. René Descartes
   d. George Herbert Mead
   e. Sigmund Freud

2. What is meant by the "instinct theory" of motivation, and what are the grounds on which it can be criticized?
3. Why is it particularly difficult to distinguish the effects of heredity from the effects of environment?
4. What part do others play in our conception of ourselves?
5. Why is the distinction between the self as subject and the self as object important?
6. If culture is all-important in human life, why do people develop individual differences within the same general cultural environment?
7. What are the prime agencies for the socialization of man? Which elements of culture does each transfer to the developing person?
8. In what sense can books be considered a means of cultural diffusion as well as socialization?
9. Why does a theory that explains everything explain nothing?

For further study

1. Sketch the major differences in socialization that one might expect in the development of an "only child" and a child with brothers and sisters. Which do you feel has the greatest advantage? Why?
2. Give reasons why the discussion of the relative significance of nature and nurture (heredity and environment) in the formation of personality is pointless.
3. Discuss the likelihood that the personality traits developed in the young child cannot be changed when the person grows older. What arguments can be used on each side?
4. Could the role of the family in socialization be carried out easily by another agency—say, a governmental kindergarten for all children?
5. Discuss the possible differences between a rural upbringing and an urban upbringing and their effect on personality.

CHAPTER *4*

Social

Organization

In this chapter, we approach the vital center of sociology. When we turn from culture to social organization, however, it is important to realize that we are not changing the subject but changing our perspective. Social organization is as much a part of culture as art, science, philosophy, or kitchenware. Social organization begins with the *norms;* they contribute order and stability to society; hence we will begin our discussion of social organization with them. But norms alone are not enough, for norms are not "free-floating"; they are attached to something, and that something we call *status.* The network formed by norms and statuses makes up a large part of the structure of social organization. We then turn to the general types of social structure, beginning with *groups* which are formed out of combinations of norms and statuses, and continuing with the *associations* and *institutions* to which groups give rise. The chapter as a whole should provide the reader with a firm sense of social structure and a knowledge of the factors that contribute order and stability to human society wherever it appears.

NORMS

Social relations are almost miraculously orderly and stable; that is a social fact. How does it happen that social relations among people of all kinds and varieties, all ages and both sexes, run along as smoothly as they do? The answer is supplied by the norms that prevail in every society and that constitute an important component of its culture. To this point, we have left the column labeled "Norms" in our cultural table vacant; we can now begin a more detailed discussion of norms that will supply the material that is missing.

The nature of a norm. We introduced the concept of norms by making reference to a baseball game in which it was obvious that play could not proceed until the rules of the game had been established. These rules constitute the norms of the game and we might say that they constitute the structure of every game, including game watching. The norms of baseball are enforced by umpires on the field and special policemen in the grandstand, but, as we shall see, police action is not the only way of encouraging conformity to norms. What is true of baseball is generally true of all societies. Whatever order and regularity they exhibit is attributable to the presence of norms that are binding upon the members of society. A norm, then, is a rule or a standard that governs our conduct in social situations. It is a societal expectation, a standard which we are expected to respect whether we actually do so or not. It is a cultural specification that guides our conduct in society, a way of doing things set for us by society. It is also, as we shall see, the essential instrument of social control.

A norm is not a statistical average. It is not a mean, a median, or a mode. It does not refer to average behavior in a number of persons, but to expected behavior, the behavior that is considered appropriate for everyone. One norm of our society, for example, is to say "Please" when requesting a favor and "Thank you" when a favor is received, but no statistical count of the frequency of occurrence of these polite expressions is available, nor would such a count be relevant. The norm is the standard procedure whether or not it is observed by particular persons on particular occasions.

Norms and the individual. We are frequently admonished by our elders and our teachers to think about what we are doing. The late philosopher Alfred North Whitehead once remarked that this advice is nonsense if it is meant to apply to the ordinary affairs of life. As a matter of fact, he continued, the more things we can do *without* thinking the better off we are. If we had to reflect and deliberate about what we are going to do when we enter a store, ticket line, or classroom or when we meet a teacher or cashier, we should be able to accomplish only a very little each day. The principal function of the norms is thus to reduce the necessity of innumerable individual decisions; without norms the burden of decision would be intolerable. Further, if there were no social norms, social relations would be haphazard and chaotic and perhaps even dangerous. Normlessness, or anomy, would be quite intolerable, for this is anarchy, the absence of society, and men could not long endure under such conditions. That is why the norms conduce to stability; they in fact produce order, and make society a reality.

Varieties of norms. There are many different kinds of norms, and we can begin to complete our cultural table by listing the various phenomena that belong to this column.

CULTURE

Ideas	Norms	Materiel
	Laws	
	Statutes	
	Rules	
	Regulations	
	Customs	
	Folkways	
	Mores	
	Taboos	
	Fashion	
	Rites	
	Rituals	
	Ceremonies	
	Conventions	
	Etiquette	

The listing is obviously unsatisfactory as a systematic approach because some of the words are nearly synonymous and there is a great deal of overlapping. Unfortunately, there is no standard classification of the norms and each sociologist makes use of a somewhat different list. We can avoid verbal quibbles and semantic complications, however, if we merely say that all norms may be subsumed under three major concepts—*folkways, mores,* and *laws*—and we shall examine each of them in turn.

Before we do this, we want to make two preliminary observations. The first is that the norms are both prescriptive and proscriptive; that is, the norms both prescribe and require certain actions and proscribe or prohibit others. We are required to wear clothing (prescribed) and forbidden to go naked through the streets (proscribed). Very often, prescriptions and proscriptions are paired; we are required to do something and forbidden not to do it, or forbidden to commit an act and required to omit it. Proscriptive norms, when they are not legal prohibitions, are known familiarly as taboos.

The second point is that some of the norms pervade an entire society while others prevail only in certain groups. We shall call the former *communal* norms and the latter *associational* norms. The custom of shaking hands upon meeting a new acquaintance is a communal norm, for it appears throughout our society. The special handshake employed in some fraternities, on the other hand, is an associational norm limited to the members of the fraternity. The classification of norms into associational and communal norms cuts across the classification of prescriptive and proscriptive norms, obviously, and the distinction between the two needs to be borne in mind as we proceed.

Folkways. The term "folkways" was introduced into sociology by the late William Graham Sumner of Yale, one of the earliest of American sociologists, in a famous book by that name. Literally, the word means the ways of the folk, the ways people have devised for satisfying their needs, for interacting with one another, and for conducting their lives. Each society has a different set of folkways, just as each has different ideas and material things—thus each has its own culture. The more familiar word for the practices of the folk is "customs" and we shall use the two terms, folkways and customs, as synonyms.

Folkways, in short, are norms to which we conform because it is customary to do so in our society. Conformity to folkways is not required by law nor is it enforced by any special agency of society. No law requires us to wear shoes, to eat breakfast in the morning, to sign our letters, to drink water from a glass and coffee from a cup, or—if we are male—to retrieve the handkerchief that a young woman adroitly drops before us. And yet we do all these things, and thousands more like them, without thinking. It is a matter of custom, a matter of usage, to which we are trained from childhood. These are our folkways. People who live elsewhere in the world may do none of these things, in which case, their folkways are different.

There can be no comprehensive list of folkways, obviously. They are far too numerous. We can, however, note that folkways are a universal characteristic of human societies and that society cannot and does not exist without them. They are a basic part of every social structure, and they perform the function of any social norm: they produce order and stability in human relations.

Mores. The mores differ from the folkways in the same sense that moral conduct differs from merely customary conduct. Our society requires us to conform to the mores, though there is no special agency to enforce conformity. The word *mores* is the Latin word for customs, but we use it as synonymous with morals; it is in fact the Latin source of the word "morals." This word too comes to us from William G. Sumner, for he said that the mores are those practices which are believed to conduce to societal welfare, whereas folkways do not have the connotation of welfare. It is hard to see, for example, how the custom of tipping conduces to societal welfare, though it is part of the folkways. The situation in respect to sexual behavior is quite different, for deviations in this sphere are regarded as threats to the family and consequently to society. The man who supports both a wife and a mistress in our society, though not necessarily in others, is regarded as immoral. It would be a mistake, however, albeit a common one, to limit morals to the sexual sphere. The cadet who violates the honor code at the United States Military Academy by cheating on an examination is also regarded as immoral by his associates. The man or woman who pushes to the head of the line and buys a ticket out of turn is similarly violating one of the mores. The author who uses the expressions of other writers in his work without giving due credit to them also violates the mores, as does the person who is cruel to children or animals. One may recognize a legal right, moreover, and still regard the action as immoral; the classic illustration is the villain of the "Gay Nineties" who foreclosed the mortgage on the old homestead, laughing to himself as he did so—perhaps the addition of laughter made the scene immoral to its audience.

Laws. The norms that we call "laws" are perhaps the most familiar of all. Nevertheless, not all societies have laws, though all have folkways and mores. Laws appear only in societies which have a political organization, a government. They are expressly enacted by legislatures or decreed as acts of legitimate authority by political officials, and some societies are too small to maintain this apparatus. Laws are always written down and recorded in some fashion; hence they cannot possibly appear in nonliterate societies. This conception of law is not always accepted, though we use it here because of its precision. Some writers expand the meaning of law to cover all of the customs whose observance is somehow required and enforced by recognized authority, in nonliterate as well as literate societies, and in this sense there can be a primitive law. In sociology, however, it seems desirable to limit the meaning of law to formally enacted and recorded norms, particularly because it then becomes possible to maintain the important distinction between laws, on the one hand, and folkways and mores, on the other. Folkways are *crescive*—they just grow; laws are enacted. The common expression "the unwritten law" actually refers to the mores and not to the laws. Further, laws are enforced directly by the state acting formally, and not by social opinion acting informally as is the case with mores.

Sanctions. Sanctions support the norms. They are the punishments applied to those who do not conform and the rewards given to those who do. Negatively, they may be anything from a raised eyebrow to the electric chair; positively, anything from a smile to an honorary degree. The negative sanction for violating one of the folkways is to be considered odd or queer or boorish;

the negative sanction for violating one of the mores is to be considered immoral. There are more or less subtle ways in which social disapproval may be exhibited. One of the less subtle is ridicule, a powerful social sanction because no one likes to be considered ridiculous by those whose opinions he values. We conform to both folkways and mores because we dislike being different, because we do not like disapproval from our friends, because, in fact, we need their approval in order to be able to live with ourselves.

To be told that something or other "just isn't done" is in most cases a more powerful sanction than any official penalty could be. Similarly, when we do as others do we are rewarded with approval, and approval is therefore a positive sanction that encourages us to conform. The ultimate negative sanction for both mores and folkways is ostracism, a studied refusal to communicate with the violator, the banishment of the offender from the groups to which he wants to belong. No one likes to be exiled from groups that he considers his own, from his circle of intimates and friends, and ostracism is therefore one of the cruelest punishments known to man.

The negative sanctions applied to violators of the laws are usually clearly stated in the laws themselves. They include fines, imprisonment, deportation, and for some offenses, the loss of life. Although the sanctions may differ in degree and sometimes in character for the different norms, they all tend to separate the errant individual from his group and to cast upon him the spell of loneliness. Citizens who conform—and most of us do—are usually unaware of the strength of the pressures that operate to induce this conformity. Only when one is himself the victim of ostracism is it possible fully to appreciate the seriousness of this sanction. The records of history provide countless examples of individuals who were exiled from their groups for not conforming to ideologies that the groups held sacred. One of the great philosophers of modern times, Baruch de Espinoza, or Benedict Spinoza as we have come to know him, refused to conform to the religious ideology into which he was born, and was in consequence excommunicated with much solemnity and bitter curses and imprecations. All members of the faith were forbidden to speak, communicate, live, or eat with him or to serve him or approach within a given distance of him henceforth. This is typical of the dire consequences of ignoring or flaunting the basic ideology of society.

Associational norms. The state, which embraces and supports the legal norms or laws, is only one of the associations of society. All organized groups have their own rules and regulations, their formal statutes that set out the obligations and responsibilities of the members to one another and to the association itself. These norms we call *associational norms*. They pertain, of course, only to the members of the association. Frequently, they are more stringent and more comprehensive in their regulation of behavior than are the laws of the state. Thus a monk in his monastery, the member of an Olympic swimming team, and the teacher in her public school—each enjoys more privileges, perhaps, but also suffers more restrictions than do those who are merely citizens. Each association imposes its own set of norms upon the persons who belong to it, and these are our associational norms. Some are more rigid than those made by the state, and some may even conflict with the laws of the state.

The sanction for violating associational norms is quite clear—dismissal from the association and withdrawal of rights and privileges of membership. The physician who violates the associational norms of the American Medical Association may be expelled in accordance with carefully specified regulations—a very powerful sanction.

The principal difference between laws, which are the norms of the state, and the norms of other associations, is that the former apply to everyone in the country, including noncitizens, whereas the latter apply only to members of the association. One assumes the obligation to conform to the latter by formally joining the association, and a formal agreement to obey the rules and regulations of the association is usually a condition of membership in the association. One can withdraw from a voluntary association and cease to be bound by its rules, but political laws are omnipresent, and if we leave one state and move to another, we simply come under a new set of laws. There is also a difference in the kinds of sanctions applied by the state and those applied by other associations, for the state may not expel its members, nowadays at least, and the state is the only association which may legitimately apply the death penalty to those who violate its laws, or use force to assure compliance with them.

Relationships between the norms. There are some exceedingly interesting relationships between folkways, mores, and laws. First, each of these norms is supported by slightly different sanctions, but we should not assume that the mores are necessarily more powerful than the folkways, or that laws are necessarily more coercive than mores. The negative sanctions of mores and folkways may in some cases be much more severe than the sanctions used to support laws. Further, even where the penalty established by law is severe, the severity does not ensure greater conformity. And it need hardly be said that a small fine may be much less severe than ridicule.

Although we may violate certain laws without fear of punishment, for there are many laws which are redundant or hardly enforced, we usually think twice before violating the folkways and mores, for sanctions are swiftly applied in such cases, and they have the support of the community. None of the readers of this book would come to class in a bathing suit or appear at a dance in dirty sport clothes, yet no law forbids such practices. In other words, laws are not necessarily more effective instruments of social control than are the folkways and mores. In certain instances, such as taxation, they are more effective, but in many others they are not.

Societies so primitive that they lack government obviously have no laws in the sense in which we have defined them. But all societies have folkways and mores, for no society could exist without them. The laws that appear in complex societies are in some respects a crystallization of the mores of society. They support the mores, or certain of them, with an added sanction—the state and its police power. The mores thus gain formal recognition in the laws. But the mores precede the laws, and may change while the law remains in force. Cultural lag between law and mores is quite common. Sometimes, of course, laws are enacted before their provisions have the support of the community, and in these cases, it is difficult if not impossible to enforce them. The laws of India, for example, wiped out the caste system legally, but have not yet eradicated its consequences; laws dealing with integration are encountering the same difficulty in the United States. The folkways, in contrast, are considered more changeable than the laws and mores. Folkways associated with fad and fashion may change from year to year or even more often. Most folkways, moreover, are not formally recognized by the laws and hence are not subject to this additional stabilizing influence.

The existence of cultural lag between law and mores often produces a conflict between the two. Obsolete laws illustrate the point well. Sometimes the conflict assumes a dramatic significance; sometimes it is merely funny. The city attorney of Wilmington, Delaware, once decided to enforce the "blue laws" then current which forbade work of any character on Sunday. The result was pandemonium, for newspapers, milk, bus lines, drugstores, etc., were all affected, and the life of the city was threatened with complete stoppage. The lesson was obvious and quickly learned.

Oddly enough, when there is a conflict between laws and mores, it is the laws which must give way. The historical evidence in support of this proposition is overwhelming, and it was noted as long ago as Roman times by the historian Tacitus in a famous question—*Quid leges sine moribus?* (What are laws without mores?). We cannot infer from the principle, however, that laws are not necessary, as is sometimes done on the grounds that when laws are not supported by mores they cannot be enforced, and when the mores are adequate, there is no need for laws. The law may not be needed in very small communities where everyone knows everyone else, but in large societies they are absolutely essential, for social relations are a function of status rather than personality, and there is much overlapping of social groups which must be regulated and controlled.

In our own society, for example, there are some who would not join the Army and others who would not pay taxes if these practices were not required by law. As members of a complex society, we recognize the need for such actions and the mores support the laws requiring them. But the mores cannot by themselves ensure conformity, because their sanctions cannot operate effectively in such situations. Some persons may fear the consequences of membership in the Army more than they fear moral disapprobation incurred in the attempt to evade this responsibility. If one were subject to no legal penalty for nonpayment of taxes, he could violate the mores in this respect with impunity. His associates would not discover his offense and could not therefore express disapproval. Some offenses can be secret, and thus evade the publicity that brings moral pressure to bear in support of the mores.

Furthermore, a complex society is composed of many social groups each with different mores and different folkways; complex societies are not homogeneous. When the norms of these diverse groups conflict, as often happens, some more pervasive authority representing the entire society is needed to adjudicate between them, and this is the prime function of the laws.

However, it is true that when the mores are inadequate, the laws are useless. When the mores of the majority are strongly opposed to the laws, the laws cannot be enforced. The history of prohibition legislation in this country is a perennial example of this fact. There appear to be certain areas of life that are immune to legislation and that the laws cannot successfully invade. Control in these areas is reserved to the mores and folkways. Where the mores do not support the laws, no political authority on earth, including that represented by all the resources of the totalitarian state, can for an indefinite period enforce them. The achievement of law may be the apex of civilization, but sociology teaches us still to remember, with Dr. Johnson:

> How small of all that human hearts endure,
> That part which laws or kings can cause or cure!

Why we conform to the norms. We have seen that society, as represented by our associates, exerts a tremendous pressure upon us to conform to the norms and that in some cases (laws) these pressures are institutionalized and applied by special agencies. It is easy to see that we do not enjoy the disapproval and displeasure of our fellows, that we can hardly sustain the pain of ostracism from our own groups, and that we thoroughly dislike the loss of mobility occasioned by imprisonment. It is easy to see in addition that we do enjoy the approval and approbation of our fellows. But the hope of reward and the fear of punishment are not the only reasons we conform to the norms of our society. There are other bases for conformity which we need to explore. In particular, we need to examine (1) indoctrination, (2) habituation, (3) utility, (4) and group identification as forces which enforce conformity to the mores of society.

We are indoctrinated, taught to conform to the norms, from our earliest childhood. Like other aspects of our culture, norms await us when we arrive on the human scene, and we accept them as we accept the ideas and material of our culture, without thought or reflection. The "socialization" of the child, in effect, is the process of learning the norms of his own society. After a while, these norms seem to him the right and proper way of doing things, and sometimes, indeed, the *only* way. Often, therefore, we conform to the norms because we know no alternatives, for the same reason, for example, that we use English and not Hindustani. This is the process of indoctrination, a process that is constant and continuous from the beginning of our lives.

We also become habituated to our norms. Learning to use a knife and fork "properly" (as defined by our society, for others may do this differently) is difficult, but once learned it is not really easy to use a knife and fork "incorrectly." Repetition has thus produced a habit, and the folkway becomes rooted, in a sense, in the organism. When one is habituated to a practice, he observes it automatically, without effort or reflection. From this time on, it is more difficult to violate the habit than to conform, and if the habit embodies a folkway, the folkway is also strengthened.

In some cases, we appreciate the utility of norms, and obey them for that reason. As reflective individuals we can see the use of the norms—we recognize that an orderly line or queue is a superior social device to a disorderly rush in which the weak may be trampled. We may even recognize the efficacy of norms when we do not conform to them; that is, we may on occasion "run a stop sign" when we are in a hurry and so invite the possibility of an accident, but we do not therefore advocate the abolition of stop signs.

Conformity is also a means of group identification. We may conform to the norms of our own social groups rather than to those of groups to which we do not belong, not because we regard our own as superior, or even because we are indoctrinated or habituated to them, but because in conforming to them we express our identification with these groups. Our folkways may not always be rational—the Eskimo shoe, for example, is superior to our own on rational evaluation, for it produces fewer fallen arches—but we conform to them because they are our own, because they identify us with our own society and our own social groups.

Bohemians and Babbitts. It must be apparent that there are varying degrees of conformity to the norms of societies and groups. Some people conform closely to them; others not so closely. Thus we have "conformists" and "nonconformists" in all societies. There are "deviates" even in primitive groups where the norms, and indeed the total culture, have a universal application throughout the community. We may refer to those who are relatively nonconformist as Bohemians, and call those at the opposite end of the scale, who are relatively conformist, Babbitts. The word "Babbitt" comes from the famous novel of that name by Sinclair Lewis. The principal character in the novel is George F. Babbitt, a "realtor" in the fictional city of Zenith, Ohio. Babbitt may grumble and even try to rebel against the folkways but in the end he always conforms. The process by which his groups bring him back into line is brilliantly portrayed by the novelist, and sociologists owe Sinclair Lewis a large debt for this service.

Anyone who deviates too much, of course, challenges the order of his society and will suffer the sanctions that we have already discussed. But it should also be observed that we do not ordinarily approve of people in our society who are "sticklers" for the rules, who seem to consider the norms absolute standards to be observed no matter what the situation or what extenuating circumstances it may contain. In other words, those who conform too closely to the *ideal* culture, as opposed to the *real* culture, may also be subject to ridicule. Caspar Milquetoast, the creation of the late H. T. Webster, is the caricature of such a conformist.

In the ideal culture and in the ideal society, everyone conforms to the norms to the same degree. In the real culture, there are many degrees of conformity. These two kinds of culture produce two sets of norms, one on the ideal pattern, which everyone professes, and another in the real pattern, to which people in fact conform. The norms do not, then, bear equally upon all the members of a society. There would be no variety in a society in which all were Babbitts; there would be no order in one in which all were Bohemians. In practice, even the Bohemians conform to the norms of their own Bohemian groups, though the norms themselves may differ from the surrounding community's norms.

Differential norms in a multigroup society. One does not conform to all of the norms in a complex society but only to the norms of his own group. This introduces a complicating factor into any treatment of norms. For each society is made up of many diverse groups with different and even contradictory norms. Thus a member of the Catholic Church may not eat meat on Friday without violating a norm (for him); this norm has no effect upon the Friday menus of most Protestants. To conform to a norm set by his fraternity, the college student may have to violate a norm set by his family group. To conform to a religious norm, a man may have to violate the law.

The diversity of norms belonging to different social groups sharply sets off a complex society from a primitive society. Primitive societies in general do not have more than one set of religious beliefs and practices; they do not have several political parties or political points of view clamoring for recognition; their members conform or do not conform, as the case may be, to a single code of morality; they lack a series of diverse standards for judging the artistic achievements of their members; and so on throughout the list of norms. They thus present a more or less unified picture to the observer, and their culture exhibits a high degree of integration. Although individuals may deviate, as they do in all societies, their deviation is from a single set of norms.

The situation is quite different in complex societies. Such societies, including our own, comprise an almost infinite variety of different groups, all of which, as we have seen, have different norms to which they are expected to conform. What is deviance in one group may in fact be conformity in another. A Babbitt may rebel against the norms without becoming a Bohemian. And the man who rebels against *all* norms is not usually a Bohemian but a hermit who separates himself completely from society. A complex society, then, can never exhibit the degree of cultural integration that is characteristic of primitive societies. Our differential norms and ideologies give us a many-faceted culture, and, we might say, provide more room for individual idiosyncrasies.

Societies with many different sets of norms create special problems for the individuals who live in them. The same person may belong to different groups and be expected to conform to different norms. When the norms conflict or contradict one another, the individual is forced to make a choice between them, a problem that seldom arises in primitive society. What does the pacifist do, for example, when he is ordered to report for induction into the Armed Forces? Conformity to one norm is tantamount to violation of another. In a rapidly changing society such as our own, the norms of succeeding generations often conflict, creating stresses on the individuals in both generations. Some sociologists believe that such conflict situations are largely responsible for the high incidence of mental disease in our society. It is not that there are too many norms to which the individual must conform, but too many contradictory norms. Business, religion, family, state, politics—each may produce norms which are conflicting. Individuals are thereby presented with problems that would not occur in simpler social structures, and they accordingly spend much of their lives attempting to adjust to these conflicts.

A third consequence of the multiplicity and variety of norms in a complex society is that they introduce a barrier into social intercourse which may be difficult to scale. The language barrier is the most common example of such barriers, and there are many others. Differences in norms are barriers to understanding, and they may be sources of irritation and conflict.

Miscellaneous norms. Although folkways, mores, and laws are the principal kinds of norms that we find in society, there are others to which we now devote a brief discussion. Among them are fashion, rite, ceremony, ritual, and etiquette. All of them might be included in the folkways, but for the most part they are the ways of selected groups within the society, not of an entire folk. They nevertheless function as folkways for limited groups and are supported by similar sanctions.

People prefer to be like their associates and friends; they also like to be different. They conform to norms because in doing so they identify themselves with their groups; they also want to express their individuality. Fashion is a device beautifully suited to reconcile these opposing tendencies, the desire to conform and the desire to be different. Fashion can be defined as a permitted range of variations around a norm. It operates in many spheres, but is most familiar in women's dress. The requirements of fashion are very general indeed, and many variations are possible within the basic pattern. These variations—style, color, design, etc.—permit the expression of individuality. The norm is thus not a thin line but an area of permissiveness. If one dresses too radically or too conservatively, the group sanction of disapproval comes into play, but within the area defined by the norm, variations are both possible and desirable. Fashion is thus a device that enables us to be both like and unlike other people, to conform to norms and at the same time express our individuality, to be different without breaching the customs of our contemporaries.

The vagaries of fashion in dress constitute much too large a subject for us to pursue in detail. But it would be an error to limit fashion to matters of dress. Fashion extends its sway over many areas of conduct and belief, from amusements to foods, and from books to diseases. There are fashions in art, literature, science, and religion, and even psychology and the other learned professions. Certain subjects of inquiry, certain modes of interpretation and analysis, certain kinds of problems attract attention for a while and come into style only to recede in favor of something else. When changes are relatively rapid or superficial or trivial, they are called fads rather than fashions. In any case, fads and fashions alike are constant phenomena of social life; people follow them and conform to their requirements; hence they operate effectively as norms.

Rites, rituals, and ceremonies lend dignity and a kind of special significance to various events of social life. By investing particular events with extra importance, they help to sustain the orderly processes of society and to break the tedium of monotony. They mark some occasions with solemnity and introduce gaiety into others. Above all, they serve to identify the individual with his groups, his community, and his nation, thus supporting and intensifying his social loyalties.

The function of ceremony is quite clear. We tend to ceremonialize the exploits of our fellows, along with the major crises or transitions of life. Births and deaths and marriages are accompanied by some ceremony in all societies. The ceremony gives public recognition to the event. It may mark the transition from one state to another, living to dead, or childhood to adulthood, in which case it is called a *rite de passage* or rite of passage.

Different societies ceremonialize different events, of course. The return of a channel swimmer would, in some societies, be considered unworthy of recognition; Americans have been known to ceremonialize such a "return" with showers of ticker tape, presentation of keys to the city, and a public welcome by a prominent official. In some societies, a girl's first menstruation is made the occasion of a joyous ceremony; in others, such as our own, puberty is awarded no celebration, and all public mention of menstruation is tabooed, prohibited by the mores.

Ceremony actually plays an important part in the life of society and the individuals in it. It regularizes and standardizes situations and offers an appropriate guide for action. Ceremonies often cloak genuine sentiment and allow for its expression, as in funerals or formal weddings. Such norms solve the problems encountered in crisis and relieve us of an otherwise intolerable burden of decision.

Rites and rituals serve similar purposes; rite and ceremony are often used as synonyms. Sometimes, however, the term "rite" conveys a sense of secrecy, of practices secured from prying eyes. Initiation ceremonies in fraternal associations or lodges are usually referred to as rites. Rites are not, in this sense, open to the whole community, but are hidden from public view and reserved for members of particular groups. Ritual too is a kind of ceremony, but this word carries the additional connotation of repetition; ritual is a ceremony that is periodically and regularly performed, like the observation of "holy days" or holidays. Various groups, churches or business clubs, have their rituals, like the Catholic Mass or the weekly meeting of the Rotary Club. Ritual introduces temporal regularity into many of the events of our social life. Hence it induces a sense of group identification and group loyalty.

Etiquette shares with ritual the property of precision. It is a code of precise procedures that govern the social interaction of people. Like other norms, it contains the notion of propriety; it is "proper" to give or send a gift to those whose weekend hospitality one has enjoyed or to wear formal attire on certain occasions, and so on. Sociologically speaking, etiquette is a system of norms which has three primary purposes: first, it prescribes standard procedures to be followed on specific occasions; second, it is symbolic of social distinctions that some members of society may wish to preserve, as Robert MacIver has pointed out; third, it maintains social distance where intimacy and familiarity are not desired. Etiquette serves as a standard means of discouraging intimacy of social relations and as a formal structure for promoting and regularizing them.

STATUSES

The order and regularity of social interaction are attributable to the existence of norms which guide and canalize the relations people have with one another. It is the norms that give predictability to those relations, form them into patterns, and thus give structure to society. We now wish to discuss another phenomenon, intimately related to the norms, that also accounts for much of the order that we see in society. That is the phenomenon of status. For the norms, as we said, do not "float free" in society; they are "fastened down" by being attached to statuses. Society, then, is a network of statuses, and status is the key to our understanding of the activities of groups and associations. The concept of status is one of the more powerful analytical tools at the disposal of the sociologist.

The importance of status. A status is simply a position in society or in a group. Every society and group has many such positions, and every individual occupies many statuses in different groups and associations. A significantly large number of the social interactions between people in a complex society such as ours are status interactions, and not personal interactions, and this gives status its great importance in the study of sociology. For example, it is likely that the new student at a university knows none of the administrative or academic staff. Nevertheless, even without such personal knowledge, he manages to register for his courses, rent a room, pay his fees, purchase his athletic book, and begin to attend classes with instructors whom he has never seen before. Registration alone, with its attendant red tape, is a miracle of social organization. Hundreds or even thousands of freshmen interact with dozens of university officials, and none of them knows more than a few of the others personally. In this situation, not even the names of the individuals concerned have any initial importance; the operation is conducted solely in terms of statuses and the norms attached to them. These norms and statuses make it possible for the student to know what to do and how to behave with persons whom he has never seen and does not know at all personally. For norms are attached to statuses, and not to individuals, as are the rights, duties, privileges, obligations, and prerogatives which determine human behavior in social interaction.

We want to exaggerate this point a little for purposes of emphasis. Our friends the psychologists like to think of social relations in terms of the character and temperament of individuals, their likes and dislikes, laying stress upon their personalities. This is both appropriate and necessary in so far as primary-group relations are involved, that is, when people interact with members of their intimate and friendship groups and evaluate one another intrinsically and personally. In secondary-group relations, however, which are so numerous in complex societies, the situation is different. Here the relations are determined by the statuses of the individuals involved, by the fact that one person is a dean and the other a freshman, not by personal characteristics. Statuses of this sort have nothing directly to do with the character and temperament of the individuals themselves but are components of the social structure.

The point is that those of us who do not live in small hamlets where everyone is personally acquainted must every day interact with dozens of people whom we do not know, and such relations must be conducted in an orderly manner. We may ride on a bus or subway knowing nothing of the personality, domestic situation, or marital preferences of the guard or driver. The subway motorman we seldom see. We buy cigarettes and newspapers from total strangers. And at work we may deal with many other strangers. All of this is possible only because of what we have deliberately called the "miracle" of social organization. It is possible because people occupy statuses, and the statuses define the terms on which relationships can proceed in the absence of personal acquaintance. All of this is really very simple and very obvious, but like many simple and obvious things, it usually escapes our attention.

When we meet a new person the determination of status is usually the first order of business, whether we realize it or not. The sex status of the individual is apparent and the age status equally so, but such questions as "Where are you from?" and "What do you do?" are designed to uncover status (regional and occupational); only after such information is elicited does one know what norms to apply as conversation continues. Furthermore, if we are single males of a certain age and the new acquaintance is a female of a certain age, we may be most interested to see whether the young lady is wearing a particular type of ring on the third finger of her left hand. Other conditions being favorable, the presence or absence of a symbol of marital status will determine whether or not we ask her for a date. Her status and ours, quite literally, determine the direction of the future relationship.

Status and role. Status is a position afforded by group affiliation, group membership, or group organization. It is in the structure of the group or of the society before a given person comes along to occupy it. Thus the Presidency is a status determined by the political structure of the United States, and a "leader" can be a status in an informal boy's group. Each status is occupied by a person. The person, however, does things as occupant of the status. We say that he plays a *role*, and it is obvious that the role played will depend upon the individual occupying the status. Thus the role is the dynamic or behavioral aspect of status. A role is the manner in which an individual fulfills the obligations of status and enjoys its privileges.

Let us take the American Presidency as an illustration. There are many different norms attached to this status, and they define the duties, rights, privileges, etc., attached to the status. They are always attached to the status and not to the individual occupying the status. Nevertheless, different persons who occupy the status may play quite a different role while so doing. The roles played by Herbert Hoover and by Franklin D. Roosevelt were quite different from the role played by Harry Truman. The status remains roughly the same, but there are great variations in the role. One individual may choose to emphasize one group of rights and privileges while another places his emphasis differently. One may conceive the obligations of the status differently from the other. All of this adds up to significant differences in the role played by different occupants of the same status.

We may pause for a moment to point out that the different interests of sociology and social psychology appear clearly in the distinction between role and status. Status is a sociological concept; role is a concept in social psychology. Individual idiosyncrasies in personality and ability and behavior account for the fact that different individuals play different roles in the same status. Both role and status are dynamic and constantly changing. The role obviously changes with each new incumbent in a status. The status changes as new norms are attached to it. Vigorous role playing may expand the functions of a status, and sometimes these functions change because of exigencies in the system of which the status is a part. Both status and role are dynamic elements in the life of society. But the former is cultural and the latter behavioral.

It is possible, of course, to have a status without a role, for any unfilled position in an association fits the requirements. Is it also possible to have a role without a status? Yes. Many women, for example, play the role of nurse when a member of the family is ill. Nurse is a status in a hospital, but in the home it may be simply a role. To state the point formally, we may say that a status is an *institutionalized* role, a role that has become regularized, standardized, and formalized in the society at large. Historically speaking, the role always comes first, but at any given moment in a complex society a status precedes the incumbency of a given individual. Thus if status and role are correlative and closely related phenomena, it is possible to have one without the other. The structure of society, however, is composed of statuses and not roles. It is statuses, together with norms, that produce the formal, stable structure of society.

Ascribed and achieved statuses. When status derives from membership in an involuntary group, such as an age group or sex group, we call it an *ascribed* status. The individual does nothing in particular to acquire the status. When status is derived from voluntary groups, then it is *achieved*. The individual has acquired status through some effort on his own part, be it feeble or considerable. Thus the status of President of the United States is an achieved status, as are marital status and educational status. National and regional and sex statuses, on the other hand, are ascribed, for the individual can do nothing to gain them or indeed to repulse them.

Statuses may change, of course, Thus membership in a religious association may be ascribed originally, then altered to an achieved status later. Class status is likewise ascribed at birth, and a different class status may be achieved later in life.

Statuses that are achieved in some societies may be ascribed in others. In medieval society, for example, religious status, class status, and usually occupational status were ascribed. They could not be achieved, nor could the original ascription be changed. In a totalitarian society political status may be ascribed, and it may be difficult or dangerous to attempt to achieve political status. In societies with rigid class structures and little social mobility, class status is ascribed and cannot be changed. In a caste society such as India, caste status was also a function of kinship status and remained a permanent ascription. In highly fluid societies, on the other hand, where the class structure is relatively open and where social mobility is possible, class status may be achieved. In other words, societies differ in the proportions of ascribed and achieved status that their structures contain. We are inclined to say that one mark of a free society, in the political sense, is the large number of achieved statuses that its organization makes possible. In a free society the number of voluntary associations, and consequently of achieved statuses, is at a maximum.

The individual and his statuses. It is apparent that each individual in a complex society occupies many different statuses during the course of a single day and an extremely large number of different statuses during the course of his life. Male, foreigner, student, motorist, pedestrian, patient, customer, athlete, clerk, barber—all these and many more are common statuses in most of our lives. This diversity is one of the distinguishing marks of life in a complex society. The smaller and simpler the society, the fewer the statuses that an individual can have.

The individual does not, as a rule, create the statuses he occupies; they are already part of the structure of society. The student who sees and understands this point has grasped a basic and genuine sociological insight, for this phenomenon helps give society its stability. One may, of course, beat new paths and branch out in new directions, playing roles not played before, and after winning social acceptance for them, creating new statuses. But for the most part, the individual finds the statuses that he may occupy already established in the society in which he is born.

Some statuses are more important than others in deciding the individual's position in society, and each society has its own criteria of importance. For this reason, the sociologist E. T. Hiller has introduced the conception of "key status." This is the status that assumes greater importance than, or takes precedence over, all others. In our American society, the key status tends to be occupational; that is, what usually interests us most about Mr. Smith is, what is his occupation? The answer to this question will not only tell us his occupational status but give a clue to several other statuses, for example, his social status and class status. Thus we can say that in our society it is the individual's occupational status that occupies a key position. In other societies kinship status, religious status, or even political status may be more important and thus become the key status. In primitive societies, sex, age, and kinship are usually dominant statuses. In India, caste status was once of primary importance. In contemporary Russia, political status is all-important. In ancient China, that academician's delight, the intellectual status of man took precedence, and it was the wise and the learned who received the veneration of their fellowmen.

Some status relations. Many of the statuses in society are linked in a somewhat constant relationship with others. For example, we have parent-child, doctor-patient, lawyer-client, husband-wife, coach-player, foreman-worker, and thousands of other relationships that are tied together in this way. This illustrates the extent to which our relations with other people in a complex society are status relations rather than personal relations, although they may, of course, be both. The norms attached to status pairs of this sort may be quite specific and different from other statuses in society. There is, for example, a powerful taboo on nudity in our culture. This taboo does not, however, apply to some of the status relationships which have appeared in society. A doctor, in other words, can, *in that status,* ask a young woman to remove her clothing while she occupies the status of patient. In the status relations of husband and wife, artist and model, the taboo is similarly absent. To inquire in another direction, we all realize that the norms applied to the relationship between penitent and priest, patient and psychiatrist, and lawyer and client have been recognized in the law to be of a different order from personal relations, and information passing between the two statuses is privileged and cannot be disclosed. None of these special norms has anything to do with the personal traits or character of the persons involved. They are sociological phenomena, arising out of status relationships that have been formalized.

Status conflicts and reversals. What occurs when an individual occupies two statuses whose norms are contradictory, when conforming to the norms attached to one status violates the norms of the other? This is a familiar problem in complex associations. The Quaker who receives an induction notice from his draft board is faced with a conflict between the norms attached to his status as citizen and the norms attached to his religious status. Here, the law provides an alternative solution, but the individual is not always so fortunate. A California high school teacher was once dismissed for criticizing the members of the school board. The grounds for dismissal were that no teacher has the right to indulge in such criticism. The teacher was also a citizen, and citizens do have this right. But this argument did not save the teacher her job. The privilege attached to one status is not necessarily attached to other statuses held by the same individual, and may, as in this case, be denied to him in the latter position. Thus a member of the British Cabinet cannot, in that status, criticize the policies of the government openly, though he is free to do so as a citizen and as an ordinary member of the House of Commons. By tradition, he must first resign his Cabinet post and then he may criticize as much as he likes.

The point of the illustration is that different norms are attached to different statuses, and an action permitted in one may be prohibited in another. The same action may be obligatory in one status and proscribed as a crime in another. No one but a medical doctor, for example, may administer a drug to a patient, and he may legally be charged with negligence if he fails to administer it under the appropriate circumstances.

Sometimes we find interesting reversals in status privileges and obligations. The President of the United States is at the very top of an organizational hierarchy. Nevertheless, he takes orders from the officers of the Secret Service who are legally charged with guarding the security of his person. An admiral may likewise take orders from a junior officer in his status as patient to the junior officer's physician status. Authority is thus determined entirely by status and the relation between statuses, and the same persons may find their relationship reverses when they occupy different statuses.

Obviously, we grow accustomed to the norms of our dominant status, and it is often difficult to adjust to the norms of a new status. Confusion is the normal effect of status transitions, and the period of adjustment may be quite long. The young man who is accustomed to civilian status may find it difficult to conform to the norms of the Armed Forces; conversely, once indoctrinated to military status, he may find it difficult to return to civilian life. Some persons in fact never manage to make a complete adjustment to what is in effect a new society and a new culture.

Symbols of status. Some statuses, especially those of age and sex or skin color, are highly "visible." But others do not depend upon biological distinctions and are not easily recognized. Nationality, for example, can sometimes but not always be established by dress and language or accent. Regional status may be identifiable by idiom. A title on an office door or below the signature in a letter serves as a specific symbol of both status and rank, and the status of wife is symbolized in our society by the wedding ring and in other societies by distinguishing costume, headdress or other ornament. Occupational statuses especially are frequently symbolized by various kinds of costume. These vary all the way from a complete uniform to a distinctive kind of cap or hat and on to a badge of one sort or another pinned to the lapel. Policemen, priests, soldiers, and nurses, for example, may easily be distinguished by their dress, when they are garbed for their occupation, of course. Briefcases are status symbols for attorneys, professors, and diplomats. Rank within an occupation, moreover, may also be designated by differences in dress. The classic illustration is the distinctions in dress made between ranks in the military services.

Where no distinctive uniform or other kind of dress or ornamentation indicates occupational status, other signs may appear. Frequently these signs of status are special kinds of material culture traits. The male secretary of a corporation executive may be indistinguishable in dress from his "boss," but his desk will be smaller and its appointments less luxurious. He may or may not have a private office, but if he does it will be smaller, perhaps much smaller, than that which the corporation executive occupies. In any case, a stranger walking into any business office seldom has any uncertainty about the positions that the various employees occupy in the hierarchy. In general all these status symbols are perfectly clear in our complex society and confusions arising from misinterpretation are relatively rare, and usually slightly humorous when they occur. Hollywood has done its best by the mistaken status with pictures involving rich sons and poor but honest working girls who labor under the misapprehension that the rich son too is poor and honest.

Status succession. Statuses, as we have seen, are highly differentiated in complex societies. They also tend to be arranged in such a manner that individuals occupy them in regular sequence. One is a freshman before he is a sophomore, an undergraduate before he is a graduate student. Military ranks and faculty ranks present the same order of succession and it is rare indeed that an individual passes from his initial rank to the highest rank without occupying, in turn, all of the intervening ranks. Exceptions do, however, occur. In business organizations too there are regular progressions, though the situation is more fluid than in the military services.

The fact that statuses are not only differentiated, or set off from one another, but stratified, or arranged in various ranks in a "stepladder" pattern which is known to everyone, is most important. It has even been suggested that so far as the individual is concerned the total course of life represents a certain regular progression in statuses. At birth, one acquires certain ascribed statuses. From childhood to late middle age, there is a steady accumulation of statuses, a rise in the number of statuses achieved. Old age represents a period of relinquishment of statuses. One does not, of course, relinquish ascribed statuses, but achieved statuses tend to diminish in later years. Many statuses become "inactive" and others are surrendered altogether. The corporation president retires and is given the somewhat honorary and less functional status of chairman of the board. The professor retires and is given, with or without ceremony, the title of professor emeritus.

In one sense a new status of this sort is still achieved, but it is largely honorific and inactive. It may be an important achieved status, but the role accompanying it has a diminished significance. Obviously this means that the period of status relinquishment is a period of severe adjustments for the individual. It is a problem that in our own society is increasing in importance because of the changing age composition of the population. The time that the individual must retire, however, is determined by cultural as well as biological factors. A professional baseball player relinquishes his key status in his thirties at the latest; a university professor in his late sixties. A professional philosopher may be young and promising at the biological age of forty-five or even more.

Private and public statuses. Although we may occupy a number of statuses simultaneously and continuously, we play roles in them only intermittently. The meter reader, for example, is a meter reader only when he is reading meters, when he is on the job. Before duty and afterward and on the weekends and holidays, he does not play the role attached to that status. This is true with respect to many of the occupational statuses in society. They are significant only when we are playing the accompanying roles. These are what have been called by the sociologist Max Weber *associational statuses;* that is, they have relevance only within an association or organized group.

Certain other statuses, on the contrary, carry over into the community and have relevance to both associational and extra-associational situations even when we are not playing the roles demanded by them. Thus the priest is always a priest in all his social relations, and not only when he is celebrating the Mass or hearing confession. We will call these latter *public statuses* in contrast to the former, which are *private statuses*. Public status, in other words, carries over into the community and operates even when the individual is outside the association. Society thus has both private and public statuses, associational and communal statuses. A further distinction is useful. A bank official's status is banker so far as the public is concerned; within the bank he may be the chief cashier. Thus both a public and a private status attaches to the same individual, depending on the point of view from which we describe his status.

Multiple statuses in a single group. The members of a single small group in society may represent a large number of statuses, and the relations between these members may be conducted sometimes in terms of some of these statuses and sometimes in terms of others. In the relation between a group of workers and their foremen, for example, the statuses involved include sex status, religious, recreational, occupational, nationality, residential, marital, union membership, and so on through an endless list. Obviously, much time would be needed to discuss adequately the status relationships involved in the life of a very small group.

If multiple statuses appear in a single group, it is also true that many people in different groups have similar and even identical statuses. Every criminal trial in a court of law, for example, exhibits the same formal pattern. The personnel in two trials may be quite different—but the statuses are usually the same—judge, jurors, attorneys, bailiffs, defendant, witnesses, newspapermen, spectators, prosecutor. Without identifying any of these individuals, without naming them, knowing only their status, we immediately know a great deal about what they will do, how they will interact with one another, what kinds of authority will be exercised, and even where they will sit in the courtroom.

Social situations, in other words, are structured, and the structure can be reproduced in terms of statuses and norms. When we know the statuses involved, and the norms that are attached to these statuses, we know the general procedure that will obtain in the situation. We do not need to know the personalities of the individuals involved, nor do they need to know one another, and the latter point is most important. If a trial occurs in a large city, the people in the courtroom may never have seen one another before, and when the trial is completed, they may go their separate ways and not see one another again. This is another of the "miracles" of social organization, brought about or made possible by the fact that society is a network of statuses.

Status relations and personal relations. If we were to maintain that social relations between people proceed *only* in terms of statuses, we should be guilty of gross exaggeration, not to say a clear contradiction of fact. Norms and statuses make it possible for people who do not know one another personally to interact efficiently, and this makes complex society possible. But in other cases people do get to know one another. They evaluate one another, to use E. T. Hiller's terms, both "intrinsically" or "personally" and "extrinsically" or "categorically." People do occupy statuses, but they also play roles in these statuses, and some play the role in one manner and some in another. People respond emotionally and temperamentally to other people and not only formally and officially. People grow fond of some people and grow hostile or remain indifferent to others. Social relations have a psychological character as well as a sociological character; they occur in terms of social structure and in terms of the structure of personality.

Parent-child relations, for example, are not only status relations, but relations involving total personalities. Parents have obligations and responsibilities toward their children, and in turn enjoy certain privileges of authority over their immature decisions and pride in their growth and development. They also normally love their children. The relationship is full of complex emotional commitments on both sides. In this situation, the purely status character of the relationship recedes into the background, even though it is never wholly without significance and even though it is ultimately defined in the law. In such relationships character and temperament and personality take precedence over status.

We also need to indicate that what are initially status relations may in time come to be personal relations. Initial interactions between customers and clerks, for example, are status relations, independent of the personal characteristics of the individuals involved. But customers often come to know personally the clerks with whom they have frequent transactions. Clerks and customers begin, after a while, to evaluate one another both intrinsically and categorically. Customers have favorite clerks and clerks have favorite customers. This sort of thing happens in many social relationships. Certain bus drivers are more cheerful than others and we are glad to ride with them. Teachers have favorite students, not necessarily the most brilliant, and students have favorite teachers, not necessarily the most brilliant. But we should not overemphasize the relationship. The status relationship remains important in such situations, for the butcher does not lower his prices for his favorite customer; that remains governed by the seller-buyer status relationship.

Further, personal factors are not completely absent from even the most rigid and highly organized associations. In all such groups, an informal organization arises to take its place beside the formal structure, and the relation between these two social arrangements is beginning to engage the systematic attention of sociologists. The analysis of status that we have just completed will serve as a foundation for our own subsequent treatment of this complex and fascinating subject.

GROUPS

Sociologists have not yet achieved a satisfactory classification of social groups. The task is difficult. The student can appreciate one of the difficulties by pausing to reflect upon the enormous number of groups that a complex society contains. Indeed, there are probably more groups in any sizable society than there are individuals in the society. Obviously, this will depend upon the manner in which we define a group. If we say that all those born at 5 A.M. on a Tuesday, for example, constitute a social group, then the number of groups is infinite, since there are an infinite number of moments which can be used to define a separate group. If we say that any collection of people on any street in any city or village in the world constitutes a group, then once again the number is infinite. We may argue that this kind of definition is nonsense because some groups are significant and others are not, but we are then faced with the complicated problem of differentiating between significant and not significant. Clearly there are issues of great complexity here, and it is our responsibility to attempt to resolve them. In this section of the chapter, then, we confront the problem of groups and their classification.

"No man is an island." No man normally lives alone. With the exception of hermits, shepherds, lighthouse keepers, prisoners in solitary confinement, and possibly a few others, no human being lives alone for any extended period of time. So necessary in fact is association with our fellow human beings that survival is problematic without it, for personality deterioration accompanies its absence and total ostracism is probably the worst punishment man is called upon to endure.

The large majority of us consequently live in groups—all kinds of groups. Inevitably, most of us are, or have been, members of a family. We have friends, or at least acquaintances. We live in a certain place, and accordingly our street, our neighborhood, our city, our state, and our country represent kinds of groups. We are male or female, old or young, and so we belong to at least two groups based on biological characteristics. All those who profess the same religion, salute the same flag, have the same ethnic origin, are in the same income tax bracket, "root" for the Dodgers, subscribe to the same newspaper, and so on are in some sense members of a group.

The problem of classifying all of these groups, actual and potential, real and imaginary, is difficult. It would serve no good purpose to pursue it in all of its intricate detail in an introductory text. All sociologists, at one time or another, are concerned with the problem and many of them have made impressive attempts to solve it. We shall not even recommend that the beginning student familiarize himself with the more prominent of these attempts, for such a task is more appropriate to a senior course or graduate seminar. We shall instead offer a classification of our own with the hope that it will be of some preliminary use and serve the purposes of this first course.

A classification of groups. We are members of some groups through the circumstance of statistical arrangement. We are members of other groups because we are conscious of having something in common, some shared attribute or characteristic, with other people. We are members of still other groups because we enter into social relationships with other people. And, finally, we are members of groups because we join them and have our names inscribed on the membership rolls. These observations provide the foundations on which we can distinguish four different kinds of groups: (1) the statistical, (2) the societal, (3) the social, and (4) the associational. These may not be the best possible names or labels for the different kinds of groups, but they are descriptive and useful. Let us examine them in order and explain them in some detail. Note particularly that they arrange themselves on a kind of logical continuum depending upon the presence of certain important sociological properties: (1) consciousness of kind, (2) social interaction, and (3) social organization—properties that result in groups that have fundamentally distinct characteristics.

1. *Statistical groups* are not formed by the members themselves; they are the work of sociologists and statisticians. The members of such groups are not usually conscious of belonging to them, and indeed "belonging" is too strong a word, for membership in such groups carries with it neither obligations nor privileges. Thus there is no consciousness of kind, no social interaction among the members of the groups, and no social organization. We can chart the statistical group, then, as follows:

GROUPS

Type	Consciousness of kind	Social interaction	Social organization
A. Statistical	No	No	No

Some sociologists do not include statistical groups in their classification on the very reasonable ground that since there is no social interaction there are no social relations and social relations are the specific business of the sociologist. It is perfectly true that one can construct a large number of statistical groups that have no sociological significance whatever. All of the people born on Tuesday and all those who have seen the Mississippi River are two statistical groups which are absurd and without meaning. Nevertheless, many purely statistical groups have more than a mere statistical significance and much to do with the entire character of society.

Thus it may be very important to know how many persons in society fall into the statistical group that we call illiterate members of the population. Statistical groups composed of particular ages are also significant, for a society with a large part of the population in the age group over fifty would be quite different from a society with only a small part of the population in that group. The number of persons afflicted by particular diseases influences the allocation of funds for research, though having the disease does not conduce to social relations. One should not demean the importance of statistical groups of this kind. Many such groups, especially when they are majorities of the total population, have much to do with the total character of society. They constitute a demographic rather than a social arrangement, in strict terms, but they cannot be ignored in any thoroughgoing sociological inquiry.

2. We apologize for the awkward sound of *societal groups,* but they differ from statistical groups in one important sense—consciousness of kind, a term introduced by Franklin Henry Giddings to explain a phenomenon that every observer of society has noted, i.e., that we always find people in association with one another. The fact is that people do recognize that there are others like themselves, and they want to associate with them, as a new child on the block seeks playmates and perhaps for the same reasons, though this we do not know. Whatever the cause, people do live together and are aware of each other. Consciousness of kind is a strong stimulus to social relations. We tend to move into groups which share a common trait with ourselves. Consciousness of difference, on the other hand, will have a quite different influence on social intercourse as we shall see later.

Societal groups, then, are composed of people who have a consciousness of kind, who are aware of the similarity or identity of the traits or characteristics that they all possess. There is usually some external and visible sign of similarity which can be recognized, such as age, sex, language, accent, style of clothing, response to particular symbols, etc. This does not imply that women associate only with women and plumbers with plumbers, but consciousness of such similarities is a powerful stimulus to social relations and to the formation of organized groups.

When we add the societal group to our table, then, it appears now as follows:

GROUPS

Type	Consciousness of kind	Social interaction	Social organization
A. Statistical	No	No	No
B. Societal	Yes	No	No

3. In the term "social group," we use "social" in its narrowest sense to imply social contact and communication, social interaction, and social intercourse. Once again the label is somewhat awkward but there seems no better one at hand, and the concept itself is reasonably clear. In any event, social groups are those in which people actually associate with one another and have social relations with one another; hence our table now looks thus:

GROUPS

Type	Consciousness of kind	Social interaction	Social organization
A. Statistical	No	No	No
B. Societal	Yes	No	No
C. Social	Yes	Yes	No

Social groups can be of many kinds—friendship, classroom groups, crowds, audiences, congregations, play groups, neighborhood groups, and many others. In these groups there is not only a consciousness of kind or of some like interest but also social interaction, which may be polite conversation or mutual awareness or a very close and intimate relation. We are not merely members of social groups—"membership" is in any case too formal an expression. These are groups in which we live, composed of people whom, for the most part, we know personally and either like or dislike. In other words, the social group is more than mere consciousness of kind; we have here a genuine social relation and social interaction.

4. The associational group differs from the others in that it is organized while they are not. Associational groups are far and away the most important kind of group in modern complex societies.

GROUPS

Type	Consciousness of kind	Social interaction	Social organization
A. Statistical	No	No	No
B. Societal	Yes	No	No
C. Social	Yes	Yes	No
D. Associational	Yes	Yes	Yes

The associational group possesses a formal organization or structure. We all belong to many such groups—college, YMCA, Red Cross, Army, fraternity, city, church. Indeed, every formally organized group to which we belong falls into this category. Associations are groups of people who are joined together to pursue certain interests, and the interest may be anything under the sun from mining metal to undermining an empire. They may even be formed for the purpose of ensuring privacy or discouraging intimate social relations.

To indicate how these groups can grow out of one another, let us consider an example. Redheaded people do not ordinarily associate with one another simply because they are redheaded. All people who have red hair, nevertheless, do constitute a statistical group, and it is important for clothing manufacturers, dress designers, hairdressers, and various others to know roughly how many people there are in the group. The group is statistical at this stage, and its sociological influence is negligible.

Suppose, however, that the government, through some capricious legislation, should impose a tax upon redheaded persons. They would then become a societal group, a group rather conscious of their kind, for they would be united both in the possession of red hair and in their opposition to the tax. They would begin to greet each other as fellow sufferers, always a point of mutual interest sure to generate conversation. Soon, they would become social groups in our special sense of the term; they would have social relations with one another. If they would then take the final step and organize and establish a Redheaded League à la Sherlock Holmes to resist the legislation and further their own interest, the cycle would be complete and a new association would take its place among many others, some even more farfetched.

To return to the question of group classification, it is not always easy for the sociologist to decide what a group is and how the term should be used. If social interaction is to be the criterion or if some measure of mutual awareness is required, as some have maintained, then important phenomena are omitted from our study. A rather different kind of problem arises out of the nature of groups themselves. It is often difficult to draw the line between groups with precision, even though the definitions are agreed; the social fact being described may change. Subway passengers in New York, for example, are notoriously indifferent to one another. But only a slight stimulation is needed to transform the societal group in the subway car into a social group. The writer was in a fairly crowded car one evening when a very young, very tipsy Scandinavian sailor happened to stroll in from the adjoining car. He began to sing aloud in his native tongue, a gay, pleasant song, and the passengers, roused from their reveries and their newspapers, responded warmly to his effort and began to exchange smiles with one another. With unexpected and unusual solicitude for subway passengers, several of the men in the car asked the sailor where he wanted to go and made sure that he did not ride past his destination. After he left, the remaining passengers, augmented now by others who were strangers to the episode, returned to their reveries and their newspapers. The spell was broken. But for a few transitory moments, a societal group had become a social group, and a dull ride was made more pleasant for the change.

The form and content of groups. Keeping in mind the basic classification of statistical, societal, social, and associational groups, we shall now alter our viewpoint and consider the distinction between the sociological *form* of a group, on the one hand, and the sociological *content* of the group, on the other. It should be apparent that form and content are distinct characteristics. We can ask whether a group is large or small; that is a purely formal question. Or we can ask what the purpose, function, or principal activity of the group is, and this is a substantive question, the reply to which is a matter of sociological content. By using these two basic distinctions, we can approach the subject of groups in a way that enables us to enumerate their more important properties.

Let us consider sociological content first. This is the characteristic that the layman would ordinarily employ if he attempted to classify groups. He would want to know whether a given group was a basketball team, a labor union, a charitable organization; he would want, in brief, to know the purpose of the group. This is, of course, sound procedure, and many sociologists maintain that the function or purpose of a group is its most significant characteristic, the feature which best distinguishes it from other groups. Certainly this property of a group cannot be ignored, but we also need to recognize that function or purpose, important though it undoubtedly is, is only one property of groups, and this does not and cannot exhaust the possibilities of sociological analysis. Groups also have formal properties, and only with the aid of these formal properties can we grasp the fundamentals of group theory in modern sociology. The formal properties themselves are usually divisible into two categories, which we shall discuss in turn. We are particularly interested in the distinction between primary and secondary groups, in-groups and out-groups, majority and minority groups, and similar classifications.

Primary groups. The concept of *primary group* was introduced into sociology by Charles Horton Cooley, who identified it as the intimate, personal, "face-to-face" group in which we find our companions, comrades, family, and daily associates. These are the people with whom we enjoy the more intimate kinds of social relations, not those whom we know merely by acquaintance or reputation, but those with whom we have a close and constant relationship. The concept is discussed very clearly by Robert M. MacIver and Charles H. Page:

> The simplest, the first, the most universal of all forms of association is that in which a small number of persons meet "face to face" for companionship, mutual aid, the discussion of some question that concerns them all, or the discovery and execution of some common policy. The face-to-face group is the nucleus of all organization, and, as we shall see, is found in some form within the complex systems —it is the unit cell of the social structure. The primary group, in the form of the family, initiates us into the secrets of society. It is the group through which, as playmates and comrades, we first give creative expression to our social impulses. It is the breeding ground of our mores, the nurse of our loyalties. It is the first and generally remains the chief focus of our social satisfactions.[1]

The expression "face-to-face" should be interpreted with a modicum of caution. It is possible to have face-to-face relations with people who are not members of our primary groups, and conversely, we may not have face-to-face relations with those who are members of our primary groups. Bank tellers and barbers, for example, are not necessarily members of our primary groups, though we see them face to face; on the other hand, all of us correspond with close friends whom we have not seen for years, as we grow older at least. The primary-group designation indicates a degree of intimacy, or social distance, rather than a physical relationship. In short, the primary group is a personal one, the secondary group an impersonal one; we have

[1] Robert M. MacIver and Charles H. Page, *Society: An Introductory Analysis*, Holt, Rinehart and Winston, Inc., New York, 1949, pp. 218–219.

personal relations with members of the first and status relations with members of the second.

We may observe that primary groups are not constant in their composition throughout the lifetime of the individual. The intimate relations we have as children with our brothers and sisters, for example, may not continue through the years of maturity. Distance and dissimilar interests may finally create barriers to social intercourse, especially in a society in which kinship relations receive little emphasis. Friends of a decade ago may have followed a course of life quite different from ours and greet us now, if at all, with a yearly Christmas card. The membership of our primary groups thus changes constantly. But wherever we are, at whatever age, we are members of some primary group—unless we have become hermits or solitary wanderers on the face of the earth.

The primary group is always a small group. It may take several columns of *Who's Who* to list all the organized secondary groups of an unusually prominent person, but the untraveled man or woman who dwells in some remote hamlet may have as large a primary group as the President of the United States. Indeed, because the prestige so formally attached to the latter position constitutes a barrier to intimacy, a President may be the loneliest man in the world. The primary group is made of intimate, informal relations, and this does not depend upon prestige and status.

We are constrained to suggest, finally, that the growth of secondary relations in complex societies neither diminishes the need for the primary group nor reduces its membership. No matter how large the groups of which we are members, no matter how rigidly organized they may happen to be, we shall always come to know some of the members more personally than others. Some will become friends. Some, in short, will become members of our primary group. The need for intimacy and for primary-group response is a constant. It is here that we find the sense of "belonging," and it is here that we are evaluated for what we are and not merely for what we can do.

Abrupt changes in the primary group, which occur when we leave home to attend college or take a job, may produce a severe reaction in the individual. What is commonly known as "homesickness," an almost universal reaction to changed surroundings, is really nostalgia for a primary group from which our ties have suddenly been severed. It is this factor that makes adjustment to a new situation difficult, whether a new job, a new school, a new regiment in the Army, or a new neighborhood in the city. Those with strong primary-group ties are better fortified against the outside world, and psychologists have found that soldiers in this category resist battle strain or domestic infidelity more easily. And it has been shown again and again, first by the great French sociologist Emile Durkheim, that the incidence of suicide is highest in those whose primary-group ties are weakest.

The primary group, then, has all sorts of consequences for our social life. It is always, in terms of our classification, a social group and not a societal or associational group. It molds our opinions, guides our affection, and subtly influences our actions in many ways. Its importance can hardly be exaggerated, for this is the group in which we live. Secondary groups, by contrast, are a residual category that has no significance in and of itself. Because a large part of our social relationships in a complex society takes place within the framework which secondary groups provide—status relationships—they play a large part in our lives, but the part is always impersonal and not primary.

In-groups and out-groups. A second subclassification of groups which interests us here is the *in-group* and the *out-group*. Basically, the in-group includes all of the persons we mean when we use the term "we"; an out-group those who are designated by "they." The groups may be quite small or very large, depending upon the context and our intentions. When we say "we" this may include only the members of our immediate family, or it may mean everyone in the United States, and even everyone in the "free world." In-groups and out-groups are not actual groups except in the sense that a person may create them for himself by his use of the pronouns "we" and "they." This simple distinction, however, has considerable sociological significance, for it enables us to construct two basic principles of social relations which we shall now proceed to examine.

1. The first of these principles is that members of the in-group tend to stereotype those who are in the out-group. They tend to evaluate personally those in the in-group and evaluate categorically those who are not. We react to members of the in-group as individuals, and to those in the out-group as members of a class or category. We tend to notice the similarities among the members of the out-group and the differences between those in the in-group. To Americans of occidental origin, all Chinese look alike and are quite indistinguishable from one another. The converse is true from the Chinese viewpoint. Similarly, we accept ethnic and nationalistic stereotypes about the out-groups, such as the propositions that the English have no sense of humor, that all Frenchmen drink wine, and that all Germans are fond of sauerkraut. The propositions are false, but the stereotypes are widely accepted.

Unfavorable generalizations and stereotypes are not limited to persons of other nationalities. In this country whites often accept unflattering stereotypes of Negroes and vice versa. It is only recently that Hollywood has become aware of the injustice involved in casting Negro actors and actresses in these stereotyped roles. Many whites, too many certainly, continue to think of the Negro male in terms of the Stepin Fetchit type—shiftless, lazy, untrustworthy —and the Negro female in terms of the Hattie McDaniel type—the big-bosomed, cheerful Aunt Jemima who appears on the pancake packages. One could as easily cast the stereotype in the mold constructed by Ralph Bunche, one of the most brilliant of our diplomats, or Lena Horne, one of the most beautiful and talented of living women, but always the least respectable traits found in the out-group are included in the stereotype—never the most flattering.

Perhaps the prime reason why in-groups produce stereotypes of out-groups is the social distance between the two groups, for this encourages the categorization and discourages individual differentiation. That is, both the sociologically naïve and the sociologically sophisticated tend to react to members of our in-groups as individuals and to those in the out-groups as members of a class, and to do so thoughtlessly and without premeditation. Knowledge of the principle involved helps make us conscious of the practice, and thus may reduce its unfortunate effects and eliminate some of the barriers to easy intercourse among all peoples.

2. The second principle that follows from the in-group–out-group distinction is that any threat, imaginary or real, from an out-group tends to intensify the cohesion and solidarity of the in-group. This principle can be illustrated at all levels and in groups of any size. In the normal family, for example, brothers and sisters quarrel among themselves freely, but a slighting remark from someone outside the family immediately binds the family together to repel the intruder. Similarly, it is seldom wise to interfere in a quarrel between husband and wife, for both may turn on the peacemaker and remind him that this is a private fight. Again, we find that the members of a given military unit may gripe to their heart's content about the personnel, policies, and equipment of their unit, but woe to the representative of another unit who dares to impugn either the personnel, policies, or equipment of the in-group. The illustrations that can be drawn at the international level are obvious.

Dictators have proved most adept at utilizing the principle, and many a tottering regime has been saved by the pretense that the state is menaced from without and a potential victim of aggression. Mussolini condemned the dastardly Ethiopians for menacing the power and glory of the Italian empire, and Hitler made use of the Jews as an out-group. And in current Soviet jargon, the "theory of capitalistic encirclement" represents a formalization of the in-group–out-group distinction.

The out-group need not always be hostile. The presence of even a friendly representative of an out-group will exert a positive influence on the solidarity and cohesion of the in-group. The presence of a foreigner will emphasize the consciousness of kind and stimulate social intercourse among nationals. Or to take a slightly different facet of the same effect, a slight acquaintance can ripen into friendship when two persons meet in a strange country many miles from home. The essence of this in-group–out-group relation has been captured magnificently, and in glowing prose, by H. G. Wells's description of a botanist:

[The botanist] has a strong feeling for systematic botanists as against plant physiologists, whom he regards as lewd and evil scoundrels in this relation; but he has a strong feeling for all botanists and indeed all biologists, as against physicists, and those who profess the exact sciences, all of whom he regards as dull, mechanical, ugly-minded scoundrels in this relation; but he has a strong feeling for all who profess what he calls Science, as against psychologists, sociologists, philosophers, and literary men, whom he regards as evil, foolish, immoral scoundrels in this relation; but he has a strong feeling for all educated men as against the working man, whom he regards as a cheating, lying, loafing, drunken, thievish, dirty scoundrel in this relation; but so soon as the working man is comprehended together with these others, as *Englishmen,* he holds them superior to all sorts of Europeans, whom he regards. . . .[2]

Group size. We may also make a useful sociological distinction between *large* groups and *small* groups, for the size of the group will affect its internal characteristics. Further, the growth of a group can produce social phenomena of a recognizable sort, as can a reduction in size. For some purposes, small groups are obviously more effective than large, and for others the reverse is true. Yet there may be an optimum size which is neither large nor small, depending upon the purpose. Fifty students and ten professors would hardly produce a university, yet when universities grow too large they lose some of the virtues of the small college, though they may acquire new ones to replace them; that is, better library facilities, a strengthened faculty, more equipment, etc., may replace the virtues of informal, close, and frequent contact between instructor and student.

Some of the effects of the size of a group may be mentioned here briefly. For one thing, as the size of a group increases, so also does the division of labor. In small groups, all of the members may perform the same functions and indulge in the same activities. In large groups, this becomes impossible, and functions are differentiated and activities specialized. The teacher in a small school may teach several subjects, for example, whereas the teacher in a large high school may be limited to teaching one portion of one subject (modern history, for example).

A second consequence of increasing the size of associational groups is that their structure becomes more rigid. More organization is needed, additional norms are produced, and the total effect is an increase in what we generalize as "red tape." Small groups may perform informally, but in large groups, successful operation demands that a minimum performance be obtained with certainty from each member of the organization; hence the formal

[2] H. G. Wells, *A Modern Utopia,* Chapman & Hall, Ltd., London, 1905, p. 322.

rules of the association must specify precisely what each status in the organization must produce.

Finally, it follows as corollary to these two principles that social relations in large groups are more formal and less personal than they are in small groups. An increase in size brings with it an increase in the number of secondary or status relationships but no increase in the number of primary relationships. Indeed, the latter may actually decrease. Thus there are more secondary relationships on a battleship than on a destroyer, and in a large city than in a small village, as, of course, we might expect.

Related to the gross factor of size, but not identical with it, is the characteristic that determines whether the group is a *majority* or a *minority*. Neither a majority nor a minority is an absolute and the terms are always relative, for a majority may be very small (two of three friends) and a minority very large (the Negro population in America). Even in the same group, the meaning of terms may be different, for a majority of a group of 100 may be as few as 51 or as many as 99; hence the distinction tells us nothing of absolute size.

The property of being a majority or a minority has important consequences in social life and particularly in political matters. Ethnic-group tension or conflict, for example, is least when the majority group is very large and greatest when the difference between majority and minority is slight. The political consequences of majorities and minorities have long been recognized, but the sociological implications of this condition have not yet received sufficient study.[3]

The duration of a group, its span of existence, is also a major property of the group. Some groups have only a brief and momentary existence; others last for centuries. Some, like the crowd that gathers at the scene of an accident, vanish after a brief period; others, like the class of '28 at "dear old Siwash" last as long as their members live; still other groups have an existence independent of the lives of particular individuals for they have a flow of people in and out of membership, as do universities or national states. Finally, some groups live to be very old, like the Parliament of Iceland and the Church of Rome.

Some groups are voluntary—we join them of our own free will; others make us members willy-nilly, without choice. Our age, sex, ethnic, and national groups are involuntary groups, as are all groups based upon biological properties; our occupational groups, recreational and educational groups, indeed all interest groups, are voluntary. In some societies, of course, the listing would be quite different.

Groups may also be defined as open or closed, depending upon the ease

[3] For a more extensive discussion of this subject, see Robert Bierstedt, "The Sociology of Majorities," *American Sociological Review*, vol. 13, pp. 700–710, December, 1948.

with which they are joined. Almost anyone of voting age, for example, can easily become a member of a political party, and any one can contribute to the Community Chest. Families, on the other hand, are closed biologically and legally. The professions, trades, and skilled occupations are relatively closed. The Princeton Club of New York is closed to all except Princeton graduates. When the qualifications for membership are only biological, we are inclined to say that the group is open; when additional qualifications are introduced, the group becomes, to that extent, closed. In politics, this is an extremely important point, as we shall see in Chapter 7.

Groups may be distinguished into those which select their members from a single social or economic class and those whose members come from all social strata. The sociologist terms the former "horizontal groups" and the latter "vertical groups." Religious associations are usually vertical groups; country clubs tend to be horizontal groups, particularly those which are very expensive. In politics, the distinction is extremely important in relation to class rule as we shall see below.

Another simple distinction among groups is their degree of independence. Some groups, like banks, private colleges, etc., are independent; many others, like branch offices of corporations or state colleges, are dependent upon a larger organization or group. The distinction is useful because the behavior of the two groups is not quite the same; the dependent group is not really a free agent, since it must operate within bounds created by another group.

We may also distinguish between those groups in which the members are bound together by a single tie and those in which more than one tie is shared. P. A. Sorokin has described these as "unibonded" and "multibonded" groups, respectively. National groups are unibonded, for example, while kinship groups are multibonded. Sorokin thought the distinction might be used to produce a kind of "chemistry of groups" in which units were defined and used to build more complex multibonded structures, indicating tendencies to attract or repel one another depending upon the character of the unit.

Finally, we must distinguish between organized and unorganized groups and the distinction here is really important. Statistical, societal, and social groups just exist—they happen to be. The associational group, however, comes into existence through a formally articulated process that we call "organization." Without defining the term strictly at this juncture, we can point out that organization is the factor in society which permits those without personal acquaintance to carry on complex relationships with one another. It creates social authority; it determines who shall command and who shall obey; it is the factor that confers permanence on some groups. The organization factor, in brief, makes possible the very existence of large, complex, technological societies to which we all belong. Organization demands our detailed and analytic attention, and it is to this subject that we now turn.

ASSOCIATIONS AND INSTITUTIONS

Since sociologists make use of the term "organization" very often indeed, especially when they seek to explain the structure of society, they call the groups that are organized "associations" rather than organizations. An association, as we have said earlier, is simply an organized group. We have now to explain precisely what organization means and how a university (which is organized) differs from an ethnic group (which is not). Before launching into a definition of organization, we need to consider briefly two preliminary points.

First of all, we ought to note the function that organization plays in our lives, for we literally cannot do without it. We could neither think nor understand nor communicate without organization, for speech is organized sound, and writing is organized markings, and thought is the organization of basic concepts into unified wholes (ideally, at least). Organization transforms noise into music, and musicians into an orchestra; it makes teams of individual players, a national state out of a collection of people, a machine out of raw parts.

Secondly, there are degrees of organization; there are not just two distinct opposites, organization and unorganization. Instead, these are extreme limits on a continuum with wholly unorganized groups at one end and highly organized associations at the other. Groups may be ranged at any point between the two extremes, and the point on the continuum which they occupy is extremely significant, particularly, perhaps, in politics. Highly organized groups are almost totally independent of their personnel; they can survive a complete turnover without expiring. As organization diminishes, the group becomes increasingly dependent upon its personnel, and very tenuously organized groups may collapse on the departure of a single key person from the ranks. We may state this as a general principle—the dependence of the group upon particular personnel varies inversely with the degree of organization of the group. We shall have occasion to refer to this principle again and again as we proceed.

The criteria of organization. We distinguish an organized group from an unorganized group by the presence of certain specific factors in the former and not the latter. These factors are as follows: (1) a specific function or purpose, (2) associational norms, (3) associational statuses, (4) authority, (5) tests of membership, (6) property, (7) a name or other identifying symbols. We shall examine each of these factors in turn.

1. Every association is formed for the pursuit of a particular interest or activity. There are almost no limits on what the activity may be, and a group interested in keeping bees may be just as well organized as a political association. Further, associations need not be limited to a single interest or func-

tion. They often embrace a number of different or related functions, and in rare cases all of these functions are major. More commonly, there is a principal function and certain auxiliary or subordinate activities. The principal function of a church, for example, is religious instruction and worship, but it may also be involved in ethical, recreational, educational, social, or even political activity. The functions of the association have the property that they cannot be pursued by the individual alone. In other words, interests of this kind are possible only because people can and do act in concert with their fellows. Hence such interests have their origin in society and are pursued only in society. Here we see the basic reason why associations arise. They make possible what is not possible for the individual otherwise.

2. Every association also has its own norms. Certain types of conduct are appropriate for each association, whether it is a church, a university, a factory, a government bureau, or a military unit. The procedures or norms that are established by each association distinguish it from the others, and also distinguish it from the more or less amorphous community in which it appears. Of course, the members of an association, say, a factory or an office, also follow communal norms which are not specific to the association; hence not all norms observed inside an association are association norms. But certain modes of conduct and certain procedures will be found only within the association, and they constitute the associational norms.

3. If associations have their own norms, obviously they must have their own statuses to which the norms are attached. These statuses are, like the norms, unique to the association. A right fielder is found only in the association we call a baseball team; this is not a communal status. This special group of statuses constitutes the organization of the association and determines the social relations which members of the association have with one another. This indicates one of the important phenomena of associations, the division of labor, and it explains in large measure the difference between organized and unorganized groups. In a sense, organization is synonymous with division of labor, and associations relate their statuses in a manner which reveals and orders that division. We cannot, for example, have a baseball team consisting only of pitchers or outfielders. The organized action that we call baseball is only possible because there is a division of labor, recognized and solidified in the organization of statuses within the association. Division of labor and specialization of function characterize modern associations. Even football teams have specialists in kicking, passing, pass catching, blocking, running, and so on. Specialization is even more clearly apparent in modern medicine. One may regret that the personal touch of the old family physician is disappearing in the new clinical conditions arising out of specialization, but no one can deny that specialization contributes to the greater expertness of medical care.

4. Although we usually relate the concept of authority to the phenomenon of government, authority actually appears in every association, and not only in those whose function is government. In one sense, every association has its own government; there is a political quality to all associations. For organization creates authority. It gives to certain members of the association the authority to call meetings, increase salaries, employ workers, change pitchers, schedule examinations, or give out grades. Such authority does not exist in an unorganized group. Authority, in other words, implies the ability to produce certain kinds of behavior in others, and to have the others recognize the right to determine this behavior. This is the essence of organization.

Authority is always attached to status, never to the individual; further, the exercise of authority is a function of the norms that attach themselves to statuses. An individual exercises the authority of a status only so long as he occupies that status; when his term expires, the President of the United States ceases to occupy that office and becomes once again a private citizen without political authority, at least in the formal sense. Since authority is attached to status, it clearly has no relationship with personal superiority. It is superiority of status, or hierarchical position in an organization, that confers authority, and this may not be related to personal abilities or talents. Authority, then, is quite different from personal leadership. Leadership has its center in the personality traits of the individual; authority derives from status and is a sociological not a personal phenomenon. Leaders do not always occupy the statuses which would give them authority commensurate with their capacity to lead, and this can, of course, create serious problems within an association.

In summary, authority is an inseparable component of organization, attached to statuses which are in all cases stratified in some way. The stratification or ranking of statuses produces a differential in authority between levels which is purely organizational and not based upon the personal capacities of those playing the different roles in the organization. Further, the statuses which exercise maximum authority are always few in number, while those which have little or no authority are many. Thus the structure of organized societies is always pyramidal; there are a few statuses at the top and many at the bottom. A little thought will show us that it is utterly impossible for organization to be conducted in any other manner.

5. All associations require certain qualifications, however minimal, for membership, even those associations which are involuntary. To become a citizen of a state is usually simple for those whose parents are already citizens, but may be quite difficult for others. To join the military services in wartime may be very easy, for when associational needs are urgent, minimum signs of life may be adequate qualifications. The condition of membership, the minimum to which every person joining the association must agree, is to respect the exercise of authority within the association, to agree to abide by the rules

of the group. This raises some puzzling questions for involuntary associations such as the state, which we shall deal with in due course.

6. Most associations, particularly those operating in complex societies, have property of their own. Dues collected from the members belong to the association, not to the treasurer, and such sums are expended on behalf of the organization by those authorized to do so. For practical purposes, an association becomes a separate "person," a collective entity, and so long as we realize that it is not really a person which is completely separate from its members this can do no harm. It is most important to note that ownership of property, and even the exercise of authority, is always carried on in the name of the association as an entity.

7. Related to this is the fact that every association has a name, or some other identifying symbols. It may be the United States of America, or Local No. 22 of the Beanhoers Union, or the United States Steel Corporation, but some means of identification of the group is essential. It serves a most useful function. For the symbol makes it possible to discuss the actions of a large group of persons, *when they are acting in their capacity as members of an association,* in a simple manner. It is much easier to say the "X Club built a tennis court" than to say the "John Doe, Richard Roe (and so on through the whole list of members of the association), acting in their capacity as members of the X Club, performed Y function." In addition to the name, there may be symbols, slogans, mottoes, crests, seals, flags, and other devices that serve to identify the association and its members and distinguish them from others (in-group–out-group differentiation).

Formal and informal organization. We have already mentioned that a status relation, like the relation between butcher and customer, can change into a personal relation given time and frequent contact. This phenomenon appears in every association, for the relations between the members, which may begin as status relationships, may also be transformed into personal relations. There thus arises, in every association, an informal organization which parallels, and may even supersede, the formal structure. This distinction between formal and informal organization is extremely important. The former involves status relations, and is easily investigated; the latter is a mixture of status and personal relations and may be of bewildering complexity, particularly in an old association.

Let us discuss this distinction in the language of sociological analysis. The formal organization of an association consists of the formally recognized and established statuses of the members in accordance with the rank of the offices and other positions they occupy, together with the rules and regulations that set out the obligations, duties, privileges, and responsibilities of these positions. The statuses of nonofficeholding members, their duties and privileges, are of course part of the formal organization, for they are recognized as a condition of membership. Social relations between the members are conducted formally in terms of these statuses, in conformity with explicit norms, and in impersonal or "extrinsic" and "categoric" evaluations of persons. Statuses in formal organizations have differential prestige independent of the persons who occupy them.

Since this independence is difficult, if not impossible, to maintain in the dynamics of associational life, an informal organization arises to exist alongside the formal. The informal organization consists of roles rather than statuses, of the patterns of dominance and submission, affection, hostility, or indifference that form among the members in accordance with their intrinsic or personal evaluations of one another. These role patterns may or may not coincide with or conform to the status hierarchy of the formal organization. In the informal organization social relations occur on the basis of the esteem that the members have for one another as persons. Formal relations proceed on the basis of prestige attached to statuses; informal organization proceeds on the basis of esteem attached to the person.

In some associations, the formal and informal organizations may be very closely related; in such cases, statuses that carry the highest prestige are occupied by persons who carry the highest esteem of the membership. On the other hand, there may be a wide discrepancy between formal and informal organization. The occupant of a prestige status may therefore lack esteem and become a figurehead if he possesses the formal authority but lacks the informal influence sustained by esteem. It is apparent that any organization functions best when the informal organization supports the formal organization, and if the two are antagonistic, the continued existence of the association is endangered.

We can see this more clearly, perhaps, if we list the attributes of formal and informal organization side by side:

Formal Organization	*Informal Organization*
Associational norms	Communal norms
Statuses	Roles
Prestige	Esteem
Authority	Leadership
Superordination	Dominance
Subordination	Submission
Extrinsic evaluation	Intrinsic evaluation
Status relations	Personal relations
Positions	Personalities

Clearly the principal attributes of the formal organization are essentially sociological in character; those which appertain to the informal organization are personal and temperamental, and appertain more to social psychology than to sociology.

The importance of this distinction frequently escapes the attention of those who are interested in the problems of motivation. The nature of formal organization has a great deal to do with matters ordinarily consigned to psychology. For example, victory in the World Series goes to the team that wins four of seven games. Since the financial returns to the players are great, players would be motivated to stretch the series to the last game, even unconsciously, to increase their return from the series. But the norms of the World Series prevent this possibility, for the players are paid for the first four games only; thus it is to their advantage to finish the series as rapidly as possible. If more than four games are needed, the players are literally playing for nothing at a time when, having worked all season, they are anxious to get away. Here the norms clearly influence motivation.

We can now make two general observations about the relationships between formal and informal organization. The first of these is that the best conceivable formal organization will not suffice to make a successful association unless it receives support in the informal organization; that is, the most orderly and efficient structure does not automatically produce a successful associational administration if the members have no good will toward one another, if there are personal hostilities, if, in short, the members do not like one another and cannot "get along." The exercise of authority in such situations brings nothing but resentment, and resentment makes the orderly operation of the organization difficult if not impossible. In the extreme case, authority itself disappears and nothing remains but force.

The second observation concerns the reverse situation, for the best good will in the world is insufficient for the successful pursuit of associational goals if the formal structure is deficient. For this reason formal defects in organization, such as divided responsibility at the top or overlapping authority, or responsibility without concurrent authority, should be avoided at all costs.

Institutions. An association, as we have said, is any organized group, whether large or small. Because it is organized it has structure and continuity. It has, in addition an identity and a name. An institution, on the other hand, is not a group or an association; it is *an organized way of doing something.* An institution is a formal, recognized, stabilized way of pursuing some social activity. As R. M. MacIver has defined the term, an *institution* is an established form or condition of procedure characteristic of group activity. Succinctly, then, an institution is an organized procedure, while an association is an organized group. An institution is also a norm, but it differs from other norms in a way we shall come to presently.

Human beings perform thousands of actions during their lives, and some are institutionalized while others are not. To take baseball as an example, sandlot games played ad hoc are quite different from a World Series; the former is not institutionalized, and the latter is. A similar distinction obtains between the things one is taught while a member of an informal group and what one is taught in the classroom by a professional teacher; in the latter, education or teaching has been institutionalized. An institution is a definite, formal, and regular way of doing something, an established procedure. Different societies, of course, institutionalize different activities. In very simple societies, institutions are relatively undifferentiated, and priest, medicine man, and political leader may be indistinguishable. As societies grow, differentiation occurs, and with it a growth of institutions.

Unlike folkways and mores, institutions depend upon specific associations to sustain them. Wherever we find an institution, there also will we find an association, or many of them, whose function it is to pursue the institutionalized activity. We can perhaps see this somewhat more clearly by studying the following list, in which associations and their related institutions are contrasted:

Associations	*Institutions*
A corporation	Business
An army	War
A college	Education
A church	Religion
A newspaper	Journalism
A family	The family
A government	Government

One may obviously join or belong to any of the associations listed in the left-hand column; one may not, however, join the institutions listed at the right, for there is nothing to join.

As an illustration, let us reiterate that *a government* is an association, whereas *government* is an institution. The Government of the United States is a very highly organized group composed of elected and appointed officials and other persons. Governments have members, persons who make political decisions, enact and enforce laws, etc. Government, the institution, is a regular and recognized way of making political decisions, enacting laws, and maintaining order in society. All complex societies, at least, have an institution of government, and a corresponding association, a government, that supports the institution and carries on the institutionalized activity.

In concluding this discussion of associations and institutions, we should like to make one final observation: that several associations may serve the same institution and that a single association may have a number of institutionalized activities. The contemporary American university, for example, is primarily dedicated to the institution of education. But it also has something to do with the institution of intercollegiate athletics, and it is often involved with the institution of business and the institution of government. A large university, in other words, represents many more institutions than education. We have here, in the growth of institutional functions served by a single association, an important sociological phenomenon in complex society. As an association grows in size it tends to increase its institutional activities, and the number of institutions represented by a single association is usually a direct function of its size. This is a most useful sociological principle.

Summary

The norms, the patterns of expectation or rule governing our social conduct, are a central concern of sociology. They give structure and stability to society and without them social interaction would be dangerous, difficult, and chaotic. Some norms are proscriptive, others prescriptive; some are communal while others are associational. In general, norms can be divided into folkways, mores, and laws.

The norms are supported by sanctions which may be positive (rewards) or negative (punishments). The laws too are ultimately enforced by the folkways and mores. People conform to the norms for various reasons, principally indoctrination, habituation, utility, and group identification. Of course, there are varying degrees of conformity—Bohemians and Babbitts exist in every society. Extreme conformity can be subject to disapproval just as extreme nonconformity is disapproved, and most of us function somewhere between these extremes.

Because different societies have different norms, and large societies contain many groups with varied norms, conflicts can arise both within and between societies.

The norms do not "float free" in society; they are attached to status, and the total meaning of most social situations depends upon the statuses involved. Every complex society exhibits thousands of different statuses, and they can, taken together, explain the nature of social organization and social relations. Status enables us to interact in an orderly and harmonious way with countless individuals whom we do not know personally.

The distinction between status and role is needed to explain behavior, for status is a structural concept while role is behavioral. Although status and role usually appear together, they can appear separately. People occupy statuses; they play roles. The norms, however, are attached to statuses and not to roles.

Statuses may be either ascribed or achieved. In a complex society, each individual occupies many statuses, some ascribed and some achieved. Usually there is a key status, which can vary from one society to the next; in our society, this is usually occupational status. Some statuses are paired, and the norms attached to such pairs may be quite different from the norms attached to individual statuses, as is the case in a doctor-patient relationship. On the other hand, an individual may simultaneously occupy two statuses which are incompatible, and the conflict arising out of this condition introduces some vexing problems into the life of man in complex society.

Some statuses are biologically "visible," like sex and age; others are not and are often demonstrated by symbols, such as badges or costumes. Statuses are in any event usually stratified and differentiated, forming regular patterns. There are status progressions and successions, periods of status accumulation and relinquishment that mark the lives of men living in society.

The next step in the construction of a regular pattern of social organization is the examination of human groups, for no man lives alone for his entire life. There are, in fact, probably more groups than individuals in a large, complex society. Classification of such groups is difficult, but we can distinguish between (1) statistical, (2) societal, (3) social, and (4) association groups. The distinction depends upon three factors: (1) consciousness of kind, (2) social interaction, and (3) social organization. All modern societies contain these four kinds of groups.

The content of a group, in the sociological sense, is its function or purpose; the form depends on the sociological properties of the group. These properties can be treated in pairs as follows: (1) primary or secondary groups, (2) in-groups or out-groups, (3) large groups or small groups, (4) majority groups or minority groups, (5) long-lived or short-lived groups, (6) voluntary or involuntary groups, (7) open or closed groups, (8) horizontal or vertical groups, (9) independent or dependent groups, (10) unibonded or multibonded groups, and (11) organized and unorganized groups.

Without organization, most complex forms of social activity would be utterly impossible. An organized group can be distinguished from an unorganized group by seven characteristics: (1) a specific function or purpose, (2) associational norms, (3) associational statuses, (4) authority, (5) property, (6) tests of membership, and (7) a name and other identifying symbols. Organization may be either formal or informal, and both are usually present. In formal organizations, members evaluate one another extrinsically and categorically in terms of authority attached to their statuses; in an informal organization, the evaluation is intrinsic and personal, in terms of affection, hostility, or indifference. The operation of any association is thus a subtle combination of informal and formal organization.

Institutions are organized ways of doing things, modes or procedures. People may belong to associations; they cannot belong to institutions, though certain associations may be closely related to particular institutions. Associations have a locus while institutions do not. The structure of an association represents an institutionalized mode of social interaction. Many activities are not institutionalized, others may be institutionalized in part, one institution may be represented by many associations, and a single association may represent many institutions. Associations and institutions are thus closely related but nevertheless distinct phenomena.

Review questions

1. Identify and give examples of each of the following concepts:

a. norms   *g.* fashion
b. statuses   *h.* rite
c. folkways   *i.* ritual
d. mores   *j.* ceremony
e. laws   *k.* etiquette
f. sanctions

2. Differentiate between each of the following pairs of concepts, giving suitable examples:

a. mores and laws
b. communal norms and associational norms
c. prescriptive norms and proscriptive norms
d. Bohemians and Babbitts
e. status and role
f. achieved status and ascribed status
g. public status and private status
h. statistical groups, social groups, societal groups, associational groups.
i. primary group and secondary group
j. associations and institutions
k. formal organization and informal organization

3. What are some of the more common reasons why people conform to social norms?
4. What is meant by the concept of dominant status? What is your own dominant status? Are there any symbols associated with this status?
5. List six groups to which you presently belong and establish your status in each group.

6. What are the criteria that distinguish the organized group from all others?

7. What are the principles that distinguish the behavior of in-groups?

8. Discuss the transition from status relationships to personal relationships, using an illustration from your personal experience.

9. Why are laws needed when we know that all societies have mores and folkways?

10. In what sense are status and role independent of each other?

11. What is the effect of size on the behavior of the group?

12. What are the social consequences of a conflict between the informal and formal organization of a group?

For further study

1. Try to prepare a sociological analysis of your college or university, considered as a community. List the major groups involved in the community, the important statuses in these groups, the principal mores and folkways of the society, etc. Try to associate these structures and rules with the particular purposes for which they were intended.

2. Select one smaller group on your campus for intensive analysis, following the same general pattern.

CHAPTER 5

Social Differentiation

Society is not composed of an amorphous mass of individuals, "windowless monads" in a sea of faces. Nor is society a single entity, a monolith rigidly molded and solidly integrated. It is made up, rather, of knots and nodes, of changing clusters, of *groups* of people in ever-fluctuating relationships with other people, some of whom are like and others unlike themselves. It is with reference to this diversity within society that we use the phrase "social differentiation." Our next task, then, is to consider some of the more important differentiations in society, the distinctions between men and women, between city and country, between color and creed, and between associations and institutions, which mark the reality of social structure and process. We shall see that out of the juxtaposition of different groups we obtain a "profile" of society, a glimpse of the pattern that emerges out of a shifting background of social interaction.

WOMEN AND MEN

We have two sexes. Not one, not three, but two only. This is one of the brute facts of the universe and of society. The biological differentiation between the sexes produces what is also one of the most important of all social differentiations, the distinction between men and women. In no society do the same norms apply with equal force to these two groups. In no society do they indulge in identical activities, share identical aspirations, or pursue identical goals in identical ways. One could argue with only a slight exaggeration that these two cultures are quite different. More precisely one might say that every society has three distinct cultures, one male, one female, and one shared by the two sexes. In any event, the biological fact of sexual differentiation has manifold social consequences which we shall attempt to explore.

The dominant sex. Certain movements of thought in the twentieth century, including feminism and behaviorism, have tended to underemphasize differences in sex and to attribute them in any event to the influence of cultural, rather than biological, factors. It has been contended, for example, that the dominance of the male is by no means a universal characteristic of human societies, that where it exists it is culturally induced, and that it is never based upon a biological advantage. It is argued that male dominance is in some societies replaced by female dominance, that the women initiate sexual behavior, are the aggressors in courtship, and make the marital decisions. Finally, it has been maintained that differences in the size, shape, and strength of men and women are determined solely by cultural conditioning and "will disappear slowly but surely when equality of rights is established."[1]

The well-known anthropologist Margaret Mead has adopted at least part of this theory of the relation between men and women. In her studies in the South Seas, she discovered within a single 100-mile area three tribes which seem to her to illustrate the thesis that patterns of sexual behavior are not fixed in the physiological properties of the organism but are resultants of cultural factors.[2] To writers of this school or this point of view, it is culture and not biology that ultimately explains the distinctive thoughts and actions, the disparate passions and possessions, of men and women. The notion of an infinitely plastic human nature is thus extended even to similarities and differences between the sexes.

[1] Mathilde Vaerting and Mathias Vaerting, *The Dominant Sex,* George Allen & Unwin, Ltd., London, 1923, p. 115. Quoted in Amram Scheinfeld, *Women and Men,* Harcourt, Brace, & World, Inc., New York, 1944, p. 7.

[2] "Preface," *Sex and Temperament in Three Primitive Societies,* Mentor Books, New American Library of World Literature, Inc., New York, 1950. Published originally by William Morrow and Company, Inc., New York, 1935. See also Margaret Mead, *Male and Female,* William Morrow and Company, Inc., New York, 1949.

Other evidence casts considerable doubt on the cogency of this conclusion. Perhaps the social sciences themselves, with their emphasis upon the importance of culture, have exaggerated the manner in which sexual differences in society are matters of social achievement rather than biological determination. In previous chapters we have ourselves emphasized the importance of the cultural factor, in most cases at least, as against the biological factor. Nevertheless, we need to explore the possibility that biological factors may have more to do with the norms and statuses that pertain to sex than many writers have hitherto been willing to acknowledge. In other words, sexual differentiation in society may be more of a biological phenomenon and less cultural than has recently been supposed.

Our sex, after all, is perhaps the most important thing about us. In most situations, our conduct is bent one way or another, depending upon the sex of those with whom we are in contact. How much of this difference is biological; how much is due to culture? Mr. Amram Scheinfeld confesses that when he began to work on his book, *Women and Men,* he was completely dedicated to the cultural point of view. The evidence, however, conflicted with accepted explanations, and the book, to his surprise, produced questions which could not be answered by an appeal to cultural explanations. Some of the facts that proved so puzzling are summarized below.

The weaker sex. Maturation is of course a biological as well as a cultural process; in fact, maturation can be conceived as a combination of two processes, more or less coordinated with one another. It is an ineluctable fact that the process proceeds at a different pace in the male and the female. The evidence is inconclusive, but it seems likely that the gestation period for male babies averages five to nine days longer than for female babies. At birth, the girls are better developed than the boys. Their bones are stronger, their reflexes better coordinated, their skulls in better shape, for the soft spot, the fontanel, closes more rapidly in girls. Bones and muscles generally develop more rapidly in girls. Finally, wrist movement, finger movement, and manual dexterity are decidedly superior in the young female.

The difference in rate of growth continues through childhood, and a discrepancy of some two years appears by maturation time. Puberty occurs in girls at an average age of twelve, in boys at an average age of fourteen. Girls are usually physically mature at about the age of eighteen, two or three years ahead of their male contemporaries. The same disparity appears when we consider intellectual and emotional maturity. We may have here a clue to the cultural fact that men tend to marry women younger than themselves. For our purposes, it is clear that if maturity is a cultural definition it is also clearly a biological process, and the latter is much less variable than the former. Think of the significance of these data for our educational system, particularly for the principle of coeducation, which presumes that chronological age and intellectual maturity go hand in hand for both sexes.

If doubt remains that men are the weaker sex, let us attend to the statistics of disease and health. It is a fact, however explained, that at every age of life more males than females contract diseases and die. This is a difference between the sexes that appears before birth and continues to advanced ages. Death, though it is no respecter of persons, is clearly a respecter of sexes, and the female is definitely favored at every age of life, except of course, the very latest when, because women too are mortal, the differential disappears.

The sex ratio at birth is 105.5 males to 100 females; at the end of the first year of life it has dropped to 104–105 to 100. Consider what this means. It means that a great many more male than female babies die and that the first year of life is especially hazardous for the male. At puberty, males enjoy only a 2 per cent advantage over females, in contrast to the 5½ per cent advantage at birth, and at maturity the ratio is about equal. At later ages females make rapid proportionate gains and pull ahead of the males in absolute numbers. By the early seventies, females outnumber males by 6 per cent, after seventy-five by 18 per cent, and after ninety by 50 per cent. The disparity of numbers in the older groups must be attributed to both biological and cultural causes, of course, for it can be argued, as an example, that the pressures of competitive society bear more heavily upon men than women and take a correspondingly higher toll.

It appears, then, that some basic biological inequity exists between the sexes and that no matter what the cultural arrangements may be, males are more susceptible to disease and early death than females. If there is a lesson here, it is that women should take good care of the men in their lives, wait on them, serve them diligently, and never let them exert themselves, nursing them carefully at the slightest sign of indisposition.

A curious phenomenon which Mr. Scheinfeld calls the "mysterious mortality seesaw" also appears in the statistics. When the death rate for infants is very high, about as many male as female babies succumb. The differential is slight. When the infant mortality rate is low, however, the percentage of deaths among male babies is greater than among female babies. Apparently, as standards of sanitation, hygiene, etc., improve, both sexes gain, but the females gain disproportionately, and in that sense, the males lose. Here too is more evidence that the male is the weaker of the two sexes.

What now is the situation concerning life expectancy for the two sexes? Again we find a startling fact. Consider the following figures:[3]

[3] These figures are rounded off and apply only to whites.

Year	Males	Females	Difference
1900	48	51	3
1952	66	72	6

SOURCE: *Statistical Bulletin of the Metropolitan Life Insurance Company*, vol. 36, no. 2, p. 6, February, 1955.

As these statistics dramatically indicate, life expectancy has increased proportionately more for the female, though both have gained. Again, it is impossible to account for the disparity by cultural factors, without placing a great strain on the imagination, yet biological differences account for it quite easily.

The stronger sex. In one sphere, the superiority of the male is not in serious question—muscular strength. The male is physically stronger than the female; only he can perpetrate rape, or open the lid of the pickle jar. The disparity is not only obvious, it is nearly universal in the animal kingdom. In athletics, for example, women simply do not excel men, whatever the sport. This is also true when skill takes precedence over strength, as in tennis or golf. The national woman champion may well beat most men, but she is no match at all for the national male champion. Whereas some women may be better than the majority of men in a given sport, they are never as good as the best men. To this observation there appears to be no exception. Men are clearly stronger, more agile, better coordinated.

Sex and intelligence. Here we tread dangerous terrain, for intelligence testers have exhibited a curious but understandable reticence in the area. All the tests are inconclusive. One reason for this, perhaps, is that they have been constructed to meet a bisexual need. It appears, however, that in some respects boys are superior to girls (mathematics and mechanical reasoning, for example) and in others girls are superior to boys (manual dexterity, for example). It is really impossible, in any case, to devise a culture-free intelligence test, and we cannot discover from the tests we do have whether girls or boys are superior in intelligence. In other words, we can arrive at no valid general conclusion.

Achievement and genius. Genius, as measured by actual achievement, is a rare thing in history. It seems impossible to doubt that it is even more rare among females than among males. Men of genuine distinction appear in positive profusion in comparison with women of the same talent. Where, for example, do we find women equal or even comparable to men in statesmanship and war? The reply will be that women have not been permitted to function in these areas, but it is only superficially cogent. Why, in that case, have not women contributed where they may, for surely some fields are congenial to women. But where in the arts do we find a female Bach or Brahms or Beethoven? Where is the woman philosopher of first rank? The woman who can rank with Rembrandt? Leonardo? David? We do not really expect women to build bridges, but why not write symphonies, compose music, perform music, produce philosophy?

Let us look for a brief moment at literature. Some outstanding things indeed have been accomplished by women in poetry, the novel, the drama. But no woman has the rank of the Greek dramatists, or Dante, or Milton, or Shakespeare, or Montaigne. At no time has literary activity seriously violated the norms for women, yet the difference in results obtained from the two sexes is so great that it is almost impolite to mention it.

We conclude this sad recital with the observation that men have excelled even in those activities which we ordinarily associate with women. The great chefs, the leading hairdressers and designers of clothes have been—men.

The facts are not here in question; what is the explanation? One, somewhat psychoanalytic in character, attributes the superior creative achievement of the male to a kind of compensation, or overcompensation, for his inability to create human life as woman does. Both Dr. Karen Horney, the neo-Freudian psychologist, and Ashley Montagu, make use of this "explanation." The reply is simply that men too contribute to the process of biological creation and that their contribution is not altogether negligible, if somewhat different. Such explanations are in any case too fanciful in the present state of our knowledge.

A more reasonable explanation comes from Mirra Komarovsky, a woman and a sociologist. She concedes the situation described above and goes on to suggest a factor possibly associated with it:

Where are the women geniuses? When it comes to truly great cultural innovations, the record of women is unimpressive. While for some this slender yield constitutes prima facie evidence of women's limited capacity for creative achievement, the inference is by no means conclusive. We are reminded that many male geniuses were not deterred by poverty, discouragement, and even persecution and that, consequently, women who had it in them would also have surmounted environmental handicaps. But the environment that counts is not merely the external one of favorable laws and opportunities. It is the inner environment, the self-image and the level of aspirations, which is at the root of motivation. This self-image, subtly molded by society, has been and still is, inimical to the full development of whatever creativity women may possess.[4]

Miss Komarovsky argues furthur that the fierce concentration essential to creativity cannot thrive on "self-doubt" and that internal skepticism suffices

[4] Mirra Komarovsky, *Women in the Modern World,* Little, Brown and Company, Boston, 1953, pp. 29–30. Reproduced with permission of the publisher.

to explain why women have not attained the highest circles of accomplishment.

Clearly, this is a cultural answer to the question, for self-doubt can only have its source in society. She would presumably agree, therefore, with an explanation utilizing our own concepts, to the effect that society ascribes to women statuses to which contradictory norms are attached and that the resulting conflict precludes the kind of creativity that men, who experience no such conflict, are able to exhibit. There is a certain cogency to this point of view. It is difficult to accomplish what society does not encourage. Whatever else may be said, no woman has yet even approximately achieved the stature of the great men of the past and present. In the empyrean regions of state-craft, art, literature, science, and philosophy, it is the male who reigns supreme. We may have here the intrusion of brute biological fact; we may be dealing with an upper and sex-limited segment of the normal probability curve; we may have to conclude that for this phenomenon, the phenomenon of genius, the cultural explanation does not suffice.

The woman problem. We are left, then, with the woman problem. This in itself is a curious expression, for we never speak similarly of a man prob-lem. Books are written about women and their special problems, but no one writes books about men. If there is a woman problem, and the intensity of the denials merely confirms the facts, it exists because biology places certain limits upon woman's cultural aspirations. To reconcile two careers, one based upon physiological fulfillment and the other upon cultural creativity—that is the "woman" problem to which our society has so far found no satisfactory solution. Women and men alike occupy many different statuses, but for women the norms attached to these statuses pull them more frequently in two different directions and leave them caught in conflict, caught between contra-dictory demands. A woman can never forget her sex. A sequence of momentous physical changes punctuates the life of woman—menarche, the end of vir-ginity, pregnancy, birth, and menopause—each reminding her that she is female and interfering with her attempts to be anything else. While there is an opening here for exaggeration, of the kind sometimes made by feminists, there can be no doubt that basic biology and physiology tend to set limits for the female which the male need not observe. How extensive the implications of this fact may be we simply cannot tell at the moment.

The sexual division of labor. It is highly improbable that the sexual division of labor was ever determined in a deliberate way. But the division exists in all societies, and it is fairly uniform from one society to another. The notion that sex roles, especially vocational ones, are reversed in some societies is entertained by only a minority of anthropologists. Because of the ineluctable fact that it is the woman who must bear and nurse the babies, the sexual division of labor has a firm biological base. Cultural differences in sex statuses can vary only within limits of physiological capacities, and among these the most important are the reproductive function of the female and the physical strength of the male. Culture may determine the interest which the father takes in the children; it cannot change the basic biological status.

Nor is the sexual division of labor limited to complex societies. George Peter Murdock once studied 224 nonliterate societies in an effort to discover regularities in the sexual division of labor.[5] In these societies, warfare, metal-working, hunting, fishing, trapping, and trade were all predominantly male activities. Cooking, the manufacture and repair of clothing, pottery making, and fire making were predominantly female activities. Agriculture was shared almost equally by the two sexes. In civilized society we find a similar division. Few women work on railroads, none sits on the Supreme Court, few are house painters, plumbers, electricians, carpenters, masons, meter readers, bus drivers, jazz musicians, engineers, or professors. Few men, on the other hand, teach elementary or nursery school, relatively few become ballet dancers, and none is a recognized ecdysiast (stripteaser). Discrimination against women for professional and vocational preferment is steadily decreasing in many societies. We would like to suggest, however, that a sexual division of labor is likely to remain one of the constants of human society.

Voluntary associations. In view of the growing equality between the sexes in our own society is it not surprising to note the large number of voluntary associations which limit membership to one sex or the other? We have "Cubs" and "Brownies," Boy Scouts and Girl Scouts, YMCA and YWCA, men's and women's colleges, and so on through many of the groups in which men and women do approximately the same things in separate associations. In other words, in spite of decreasing emphasis upon sexual criteria in many of the occupational statuses of our society, single-sex groups persist. Even in those informal groupings of people that spring up now and again in society there is a tendency for the sexes to segregate themselves. A group initially mixed will, after a time, tend to produce a bipolar condition, with the men at one end of the room and the women at the other.

Sexual differences stand immutable, unchangeable, immovable. They are a kind of differentiation that is destined to last so long as human societies, and human beings, endure. Few would not have it that way. Someone in the French Parliament, hearing a debate in which the speaker complained that women should not be enfranchised because of the differences between women and men, sang out in a loud, clear voice, "Vivent les différences!" Long live the differences—whatever problems they may produce. There may be anger

[5] George P. Murdock, "Comparative Data on Division of Labor by Sex," *Social Forces,* vol. 15, May, 1937.

and hostility between the sexes, but there is also love and affection; there is seldom indifference. Let Aristophanes tell us that we can live neither without women—nor with them. Let our own James Thurber write episodes in the perennial war of the sexes. The sociologist is content to suggest that at least we have here one of the most important of all social differentiations, one that will warrant discussion until the reader of this book has long since joined his ancestors, together with the author.

THE FAMILY

Of all the groups that affect the lives of individuals in society none touches them so intimately or so continuously as does the family. The family is the first social group that we encounter in our inchoate existence, and it is the group with which, in one form or another, we shall have the most enduring relationship. Every one of us, with statistically small exceptions, grows up in a family, and every one of us, too, with perhaps a few more exceptions, will be a member of a family for the larger part of his life. The family gives us our principal identity and even our very name, which is the label of this identity, in the larger society of which we are a part.

The family, curiously enough, is not an easy subject to study. In spite of our personal experience with the family, or perhaps because of it, most of us are ill equipped to view this group as a social phenomenon. It is too close to us, our contact with it is too intimate, to permit us to view it with objectivity. Anything a sociologist has to say about the family, therefore, is inevitably tempered by his own experience. Within these limits, our discussion will be confined to the family as a social phenomenon and will move along on a sociological level. We are interested in the family both as an association and as an institution, but we offer no counsel on how to be happy though married.

The universality of the family. The family is the most permanent and the most pervasive of all social institutions. There is no human society in which some form of the family does not appear, nor, so far as we know, has there ever been such a society. It is idle to inquire into origins, for no one knows, or can know, when or how the family began, if indeed the question has any real meaning. Furthermore, it is safe to surmise that the family will remain with us in the future as a central and nuclear component of society. Some speculative writers have constructed societies in which the family as we know it does not exist, as does Aldous Huxley in *Brave New World*. Perhaps it would be possible to live in this environment, but it is still unlikely that the family will be abandoned as an institution; it offers too much to man himself to be cast aside lightly.

The biological basis of the family. A superficial observer might believe that the family is to be explained in terms of biological factors—the existence of two sexes and the sexual character of reproduction in the human species. The family seems a "natural" outcome of the human sex drive, a phenomenon solidly based on the human organism. But a little reflection suggests that biological factors in fact do not explain the family. The sexual need can, after all, be satisfied outside the marital relationship, and often is so satisfied in many societies, including our own. It is also possible to beget and rear children outside of a marital and family relationship, though it is remarkably inconvenient to do so. Even if biology could explain marriage and the family, it could hardly explain the variation in these institutions as they appear in different societies. Sex, as someone has observed, can explain mating but cannot explain marriage. Even the relatively long period of pregnancy and subsequent lactation, which renders the human female unfit in a biological world in which the fit survive, is not an adequate explanation, though it is said that this forces the male to feed and protect the mate and her offspring.

These arguments have a degree of plausibility and would seem on the surface to answer the question from the point of view of the female. Unfortunately, however, no one has yet been able to find in the male any biological need or physiological propensity to perform these services. The females of other species suffer the same disabilities without similar results appearing. If the human male accepts these responsibilities, as he does in all societies (with important exceptions, of course), the reason must be that he is induced to do so by sanctions of one kind or another and these sanctions have their source in society and not in biology. The biological explanation is insufficient, however presented. Indeed, biology gives a curious kind of support to the facetious comment that all women should marry, and no men.

We omit various other arguments which emphasize the biological explanation of the family. Clearly no full explanation is possible without reference to society and culture. If there were such a phenomenon in the human species as bisexual reproduction, it is doubtful that the family would ever have come into existence; this much we can concede to biology. But this is a necessary and not a sufficient condition, for bisexual reproduction is possible without the family. The sufficient conditions lie in society itself. As we shall see, the family performs a number of functions that no other group can perform so well.

A NOTE ON NOMENCLATURE. Before proceeding further, it seems desirable to clarify the words we use in talking about the family. We must be clear about the distinction between the family as an institution (standardized procedure) and the family as an association (organized group). *The* family is an institution; *a* family, an association. We can all belong to *a* family; we cannot belong to *the* family as an institution. We must also introduce a second distinction between the family in which we are a child and the family in which we are a parent. The first of these is called the *family of orientation,* the second the *family of procreation.* Virtually everyone belongs to a family of orientation, and most of us will someday belong to a family of procreation. The first of these, we should note, is a social group; the second an organized group or association. Further, the family of orientation is an involuntary group, while the family of procreation is in our society a voluntary association; we have no choice about joining the first, but we enter the second of our own free will, at least in our society, and this practice is spreading in other parts of the world. Still, there are places where marriages are arranged by the family, and even in the United States this probably occurs in fact if not in law.

Variations in family forms. The bewildering variety of family forms observed in human society now and in the past is a cultural phenomenon of considerable interest. Some societies follow *matrilocal* marriage customs, while others are *patrilocal.* (*Mater* and *pater* are of course the Latin words for mother and father.) In a matrilocal society, the young married couple takes up residence in the home, tribe, or village of the bride's parents; in the patrilocal society, in the bridegroom's home. Our own culture is patrilocal in that it gives the husband and not the wife the right to choose the place of residence after marriage. If she refuses to accompany him to his choice of location, assuming that he wants her to go along, then she, not he, is ordinarily guilty of desertion.

Similarly, where descent is traced through the female line it is called *matrilineal;* where it is through the male line, *patrilineal.* If the mother's name is taken, *matronymic;* if the father's name, *patronymic.* Our own society traces descent through both lines, and is patronymic, but neither practice is universal. In government, *matriarchy* refers to government by women, and *patriarchy* to government by men, generally with the connotation that the women or men are aged.

Matriarchy is sometimes used to refer to a society in which the maternal line is emphasized and the mother, or her brother, exercises authority over the household. Here the distinction between the *conjugal family* (parents and children) and the *consanguine family* (either parent and her or his blood relatives) becomes important. Matriarchal societies sometimes stress consanguine family more than conjugal, resulting in a sharp separation of biological and social fatherhood. A man in this system owes his primary obligations not to his own children but to his sister's children; his biological children, on the other hand, are the responsibility of his wife's brother. This may seem odd, or even reprehensible. But it has advantages. Biological parentage, which is hard to prove, loses its significance and all children have status through their mother. Divorce or separation cannot interfere with the care of the children, for this is guaranteed by the mother's brother and her consanguine family. Finally, quarrels and confusion about property inheritance are much more easily avoided, as you can see merely by sketching the relationship in diagram form.

Turning to the variations in family form once again, we find that the number of spouses that the individual may have at one time is also subject to societal variation. The two major forms, among a limited number of mathematical possibilities, are monogamy and polygamy. Monogamy, which now prevails in most of the world, means singular marriage, one man and one woman. Polygamy means plural marriage, and takes several forms. *Polygyny* (one man, two or more wives) and *polyandry* (one woman, two or more husbands) are most common. In another form, several men, usually brothers, marry several women, usually sisters, but this is relatively rare. Finally, there is the form typified by Hollywood practice, in which several men marry several women, but one at a time; the form, being still nameless, is hereby christened "serial polygamy."

Societies also vary greatly in their prescriptions and proscriptions with respect to marital selection. Some societies require marriage *within* prescribed limits (endogamy) while others require marriage *outside* prescribed limits (exogamy). All societies, with rare and minor exceptions, require marriage outside the immediate family, but incest is not always defined in the same way. Some societies permit the marriage of first cousins, for example, while others prohibit this marriage. Hamlet bitterly accused his mother of incest because she married his uncle, but in some societies a man is required to marry his deceased brother's wife (the *levirate*). The *sororate* is another custom which requires a woman to marry her deceased sister's husband.

With the exception of the incest taboo, endogamous rules are more common than exogamous ones. In all societies people are required, at the very least encouraged, to marry within certain groups, and these endogamous norms define the difference between an "acceptable" and an "unacceptable" marriage. One may be expected to marry within his own tribe, village, nationality, religion, ethnic group, or social class. In fact, most religions attempt to enforce strict endogamy. In our own society, marriage of people of widely different ages, though entirely legal, tends to excite endogamous disapproval.

We cannot hope to exhaust the full range of cultural variations in marital and family arrangements in a short discussion. There are further differences in the manner in which marriage is contracted, the method of betrothal (abduction, purchase, parental agreement, partnership agreement, etc.), courtship practices, duration of courtship, wedding ceremony, ease of divorce, remarriage rules, relations with family, brother-sister relations, and so on.

The functions of the family. The family owes its existence as a social institution to a number of functions that it performs both for society and for the individual. There is no standard list of these functions, and from one point of view they are all interdependent and an arbitrary list may do violence to the actual situation. However, some family functions are sufficiently independent to be specified clearly enough, and these we can enumerate.

First, of course, the family provides for replacement of the species, and the survival of mankind depends upon efficient performance of the function. There is no logical reason why this process cannot be left to haphazard biological impulse, but this would certainly lead to confusion. For the sake of order, if for no other reason, the process of reproduction is institutionalized in the family, where it assumes a regularity and stability that all societies recognize as desirable. Doubtless this accounts for the fact that promiscuous parenthood is everywhere deplored and the family actually introduces the element of legitimacy into reproduction. Freedom of sex expression may be permitted, but freedom of conception falls under an almost universal prohibition. Society surrounds the reproductive process with stringent norms and supports them with powerful sanctions.

From the point of view of the individual, the family of orientation satisfies a correlative if unconscious need. The family gives him life and a chance to survive. Children conceived outside marriage often perish through abortion or infanticide, even in the most civilized of societies. It is the family, in these terms, to which we owe our lives.

A second major function of the family is to control the sexual impulse and regulate its operation. Although sex alone cannot explain the family, we have here nevertheless the most intimate association between biological reality and social design. There is no possibility that any male who is physiologically mature can get along without some kind of regular sexual release until such time as age reduces his responsiveness. When we ponder this almost irresistible force, we begin to wonder, not why there are deviations from sexual codes, but how there could ever be any conformity. Somehow, society must cope with this powerful force; it must construct a code of conduct in sexual affairs and control and regulate sexual activity by commandment and taboo so that it is not destructive. Fortunately for social stability, the task was accomplished. The achievement is more than a sociological phenomenon—in a sense it is a sociological miracle. And there can be no doubt that the institution that played a central role in the process was the family. Marriage is society's way of regularizing the sexual relationship. The family obviates the chaos that would otherwise be the inevitable accompaniment of an urge so ineluctable, a drive so demanding. A family, initiated in the established manner by marriage, thus serves as a sanctioned locus for the satisfaction of the sexual impulse and reduces the disorder that would otherwise prevail.

If the family serves as a means of sexual control, it serves the individual also as a locus of sexual opportunity. Men and women need stability in their sexual relationships, and they gain it in marriage. As Bernard Shaw once remarked, marriage combines a maximum of temptation with a maximum of opportunity, and if the first part of the statement is open to question, on the ground that familiarity breeds contempt, the second cannot be questioned. Yet marriage offers much more than satisfaction of the sexual desires of the moment. It offers a satisfaction that can endure for many years and become what the distinguished sociologist, Florian Znaniecki, has called a lifelong erotic relationship. The significance of this service can be grasped most readily by considering how precarious the sexual situation would be for the individual if there were no such institution as marriage. It is thus in the family that appropriate recognition is given to the importance of the sexual aspect of human life.

In a more speculative vein, we may ask whether the family may not serve to sanction the claims of women that they would be unable to assert for themselves in a purely biological world. We do not mean to imply that women are devoid of sexual weapons, but only that sex is a right that they could not demand if there were no institution of marriage. Marriage recognizes the reciprocal obligations of both sexes, confers a legitimacy of expression on the part of the male, and sanctions a claim to expression on the part of the female. The institution of marriage, in short, gives social recognition to the sexual needs of the female.

The third function of the family serves both society and the individual in essentially the same way. We may summarize it in a single word—maintenance. The family maintains the child for the society into which he is born. Maintenance could, of course, be institutionalized in quite different ways. Children could be maintained, for example, by the state or the church, by hospitals or asylums, or even by the army. It is doubtful, however, that any of these alternatives would work so well as the family. Although the state, say, might in many instances be better able than the family to provide for the material needs of children, the family combines an intimate, personal response with social care, and this is a combination that no other institution can successfully challenge. From birth to maturity, the individual requires, and the family provides, the physical maintenance and economic support that no other institution of society can so efficiently offer, and as society becomes more complex, the period of dependency is prolonged. The subsistence obligation, furthermore, is never really removed from the family. As someone has facetiously remarked, home is a place where, if you go there, they have to take you in. It would be difficult in any event, seriously or facetiously, to overestimate the significance of this maintenance obligation.

The family also serves as an instrument for the transmission of culture from one generation to the next. A very considerable part of culture, even in a society whose members are mostly literate, is of a nonliterate or nonliterary variety, and this part of culture must be transmitted in some manner to the next generation. Clearly, the family is marvelously well suited to perform the task, and is indeed the only agency engaged in the task during the early years of life. The family thus guarantees cultural continuity of the society. The mores and ideologies and ideas of society are particularly well suited for this type of cultural transmission. The family teaches the child what is right and what is wrong, what is good and bad; it helps the child to choose goals and the appropriate means to attain them. It teaches the child how and what to win or lose, what to desire, when to stand firm, what to learn and what to ignore, and so on through the entire catalog of attitudes and ideas we must have for social existence. Each family, in short, transmits the mores and folkways of society to its children.

The family also has its own private folkways, and these are intimate and dear to its members. It has its own possessions, its house and furniture, its ornaments and heirlooms, its prizes and trophies, and these too are passed from generation to generation. All these things and many more contribute solidarity and cohesion to the family group and give meaning for its members that cannot be duplicated by any other association in society.

If the family serves as an instrument for culture transmission, it also serves the individual as an instrument of socialization. A family prepares the child for participation in a larger world and acquaints him with a larger culture. With a curious and almost unique mixture of love and authority it introduces the child to an equality of rights and an inequality of privileges—a situation which, paradoxically, is characteristic of all societies. The family is society in miniature, in some respects, and familiarity with its paths and customs initiates the child into the labyrinth of social relations that are needed for social life in complex modern society. Perhaps more important still, the family introduces the child to the ideas of love and authority, generosity, sharing, and property; it transforms the infant barbarian into the civilized adult.

Finally, the family performs two other functions which we must note—status ascription for society and societal identification for the individual. Most of the ascribed statuses that we acquire, excepting sex and age which are biological, come to us from the family. Our ethnic status, nationality status, religious status, residential status, class status, and sometimes political status and educational status are all conferred by the family, and though most may be changed later, it is in terms of these ascribed statuses that we first gain social recognition. As simple and as obvious as this function may be, it nevertheless requires specific acknowledgment. Status ascription and societal identification (for we take our names from the family) are two facets of what is in effect the same process seen from two different points of view, and the importance of the family in this respect is paramount.

Family, church, and state. It is apparent that the family as an institution is related in a number of intimate and interesting ways to other institutions in society. Among these other institutions we may note particularly education, business, religion, and government, the last two of which merit some attention here. The family is in no sense an independent institution. Our own Western history has exhibited a constant competition between church and state for control of the family, and the struggle has by no means reached a conclusion as we approach the twenty-first century. In countries where there is an established church, as in Spain and Israel, the state itself enforces religious norms, among which endogamous rules are perhaps most important. In countries where church and state have separated, some modus vivendi must operate which gives superiority to one or the other (in our case, to the state).

It is sometimes difficult to grasp the extent to which the state controls the family. Consider the following remarks by MacIver and Page on the subject:

> One peculiarity of the marriage partnership is that the state exercises over it a more stringent control than it generally exercises over any other partnership or association. It does not leave the form of the contract to the will of the members. They cannot prescribe for themselves its conditions or its duration. It fixes a minimum age for marriage. It determines degrees of relationships within which people must not marry. It treats certain violations of the contract (bigamy, for example) as criminal offenses. It defines the economic and other responsibilities of the husband toward his wife and of the parents toward the children. It treats the property of the partners as, in some degree, not individual but family possessions, limiting in the name of the family the freedom of bequest. These regulations vary considerably in different states of this country, but everywhere the state is an important determinant of the form and character of the family.[6]

Whether or not the state should exercise this much detailed control over marriage and the family is a matter for moral, political, and social debate. Some argue that protection of the children of marriage is the only substantial ground on which the state may claim authority to regulate these matters, but such arguments are normative in intent and conclusion and perhaps belong more properly to the sphere of social philosophy.

CITY AND COUNTRY

This is the paradox of the city. It has everything that is tawdry and everything that is sublime. It holds both hope and despair. It encompasses millions of people yet it can be the loneliest place on earth. Its noise is some-

[6] Robert M. MacIver and Charles H. Page, *Society: An Introductory Analysis,* Holt, Rinehart and Winston, Inc., New York, 1949.

times deafening, but it produces the ideas that change the world. It is the vital center of every civilized society, and it is so lacking in essential resources that it can subsist only with the continuous support of its countryside. It is the magnet that draws the ambitious from thousands of miles away and the goad that drives them back again to the peace and quiet of the country. The banker lives here, and also the beggar, the diplomat and the derelict, the actor and the accountant, the censor and the clown, the Philistine and the philosopher. Its structure contains every status, and its groups every norm. It is both a place and a state of mind.

The history of every civilization is the history, not of its countryside, but of its cities and towns. Civilization means the city, and the city means civilization. Man originally built the city, and the city in turn civilized him. He became a citizen when he became a member of a city-state.

City and country, the town and the land, the capital and the province; this is one of the basic kinds of social differentiation. The city man and the countryman do indeed adhere to two different views of the world, have different rounds of activity, sustain in different ways the progression of the seasons, indulge in different kinds of work and play, and spend their lives in different surroundings, looking upon different horizons and seeing different things there.

The growth of cities. Most of the world has been rural most of the time; until quite recently the percentage of the world's population that lived in cities was small indeed. Before 1800, moreover, the cities themselves were small. Those who live in New York City can now greet, with satisfaction or annoyance, the news that one out of ten Americans lives within commuting distance of Broadway and 42nd Street. For that matter, New York and London together now contain 1 per cent of the entire population of the world, while they occupy 1/20,000 of the earth's habitable land. Statements like these can be made for the first time in history in our own twentieth century. The metropolitan community, in short, is a new experience in human living arrangements and one to which we have not altogether learned to adjust.

The city is culture par excellence; it is the epitome of culture. It is mankind's greatest work of art—and of artifice—because it contains all others. In the city, unlike the country, both the tools and the objects to which they are applied are almost invariably cultural. A natural environment surrounds the countryman and governs his life; a manufactured environment surrounds the city man. In the city everything is culture—even the parks, which are planned and tended by a department of government. Nature frequently intervenes, of course, with rain and snow and flood, heat and cold, but for the most part man adapts himself to conditions of his own creating. The city is his own product and his own achievement.

The earliest cities were small, and the trends that brought them into being did not accelerate very much in ancient times. For technological reasons (the low productivity of agriculture and slow transport and communication systems), augmented by political and social reasons (danger of revolt in large cities, traditional ties with the land, absence of sanitation facilities in cities, etc.), urbanization proceeded slowly. Few ancient cities numbered their inhabitants in the hundred thousands, and the population of Rome, the largest city in ancient times, was certainly below the million mark, and perhaps reached only half that size. With the collapse of Rome, cities declined, not to revive until the Middle Ages began to wane. Not until the Industrial Revolution did cities of any size or consequence arise, and the cities we know today are in truth a new phenomenon in history.

A NOTE ON DEFINITION. "Urbanization" and "urbanism" sometimes cause confusion. We shall here follow Bergel, who refers to urbanization as a process and urbanism as a condition; that is, urbanization is the process by which rural areas are transformed into urban areas; urbanism is the condition that results from urbanization. The distinction has the merit of grammatical correctness and logical clarity.

Urbanism is more than a simple statistical concept, and it cannot be correlated simply with the percentage of people in a given state who live in cities. Thus the percentage of population living in cities is greater in Chile than in Canada, but every other index of urbanism would suggest that the former is less urban in total characteristics than the latter. Nor is the size of the principal city a reliable index; Ireland, for example, would ordinarily be regarded as a more urban nation than Mexico, though Mexico City is six times as large as Dublin. Considerations like these suggest that purely statistical comparisons, useful as they are, have certain limits in articulating the nature of a sociological phenomenon.

A second point is that "rural" and "urban" represent two gradations on a linear scale, and the gradations between them cannot be set with precision. We are dealing with a gradient rather than a set of separate categories. Villages shade imperceptibly into towns, towns into cities, and cities into metropolitan regions. Furthermore, it is impossible to rely upon the census for differentiations. A city of more than 150,000 population, like Des Moines, Iowa, is more "rural" in many respects than a suburb like Rye, New York, with a population of only 10,000. The more than 370,000 people who read *The New York Times* each day, wherever they may live, are at least as urban in their tastes and customs as the 420,000 people who live in Indianapolis, Indiana.

Homogeneity and heterogeneity. The countryside presents a sameness to those who dwell on the land. The city alters its attractions with every passing block. Soil and cement are two different environments, and of the two cement has more shapes. The countryman's corner of the earth imposes upon him a more homogeneous round of activity than his cousin in the city pursues. He responds more directly to the hours of daylight and the hours of night, follows more closely the progression of the seasons. The earth gives him a dominant mode of occupation and determines his time of work and time of sleep. The countryman pursues his lifespan in intimate relationship with the physical forces that make the day and the year, the weather and the wind. In contrast, the city man pursues his work independent of the vicissitudes of the wind and the alterations of the season. Nature affects them differently.

The land offers only one, or only a few, vocations. The city, in contrast, offers an almost limitless range of ways to earn a living. Indeed, it is impossible to describe the diversity and heterogeneity of occupational life in the large city. Here is found every trade known to man, every skill and talent, every opportunity. Trade, commerce, finance and industry, and research thrive in the city as they cannot in the country, and the city consequently is the locus of occupational variety.

Yet there is a paradox here, for the farmer living in the country where a single mode of occupation is dominant cannot be a specialist. He must cultivate different crops, of course, but he must also build, repair, breed, mend, dig, fix, haul, and do all of the thousand jobs that must be performed on farmland. In the city, on the other hand, each man is a specialist, performing essentially the same job day after day. Occupational heterogeneity, then, stimulates specialization, while occupational homogeneity fosters eclecticism in skills.

It must be recognized, of course, that some of the sharp contrasts between city and country are now softening, at least in complex societies, and that twentieth-century developments in agricultural technology, in transportation and communication, are diminishing the differences between the two, making the city more homogeneous with respect to certain kinds of conformity and the country more heterogeneous with respect to certain kinds of stimulation. The American farmer was always a pioneer and not a peasant, and therefore more closely tied to the political and social life of society. Finally, mass production and specialization are now coming to agriculture as well as to the city. We now have enterprises with vast acreages and fantastic machinery for preparing and seeding the soil, harvesting and processing the crops. The consequences of these changes are unpredictable in detail, but it seems almost certain that the density of rural population will diminish still further in the future, and cities will receive an additional growth stimulus.

Primary and secondary groups. Even under the best of circumstances there are only a relatively few persons with whom a given individual in society has intimate and personal relations—that is, primary relationships. No man, however gifted or prominent, has more than a few dozen others whom he admits to his primary social circle. In this respect the countryman and city man are as one.

The difference between the two social conditions appears in a striking fashion, however, in their secondary relationships. The relationship between the urban dweller and others is very largely a status relationship and not personal; the countryman tends to deal with most of the people he knows on the personal level. The city man may go from one end of the region to another and know no one whom he meets en route. He interacts with them according to the norms attached to their statuses. This predominance of secondary relations, status relations, over primary and personal relations, is one of the significant characteristics of city life.

It is not only the relationships themselves but the groups of which we are members that exhibit this contrast. Group life in the country tends to display few of the organizational rigidities that characterize group life in the city. For the farmer, organized and unorganized groups are generally the same; he knows the members of the former as well as he knows the members of the latter. They are the same people, his neighbors and friends, whether he meets them in the fields, at church, at the grange hall, at a community festival, or in politics. The city man, a broker, for example, may interact with his customers all day, and know them only by name. Similar observations can be made about the clerk at his counter, the policeman at the intersection, and the doctor in his ward. All of these activities, well structured as they must be, involve hundreds of highly organized associations, and secondary rather than primary contacts, status rather than personal relationships. And the associations that contain these statuses are the locus of the city man's life, the place where he earns his living, and the nodal points in the web of his society.

We should not conclude this section with the implication that there are no primary groups in the city apart from families and circles of friends. If a man lives in the same neighborhood for any length of time, he will come to know his newsdealer, the salesman at the cigar store, the pharmacist, the grocer, the butcher, the bartender at his favorite tavern, elevator operators, and many others. These will be segmental relationships, it is true, relationships initiated through status rather than through personality, but these too may ripen after a while and take on a genuine warmth even in the absence of intimacy. The city seems unfriendly only to the visitor, the tourist, the stranger, the people who seek its superficial pleasures and never learn the folkways of those who call the city home and spend their lives in quiet neighborhoods, far from the milling crowd.

A final distinction between city and country is the amazing number of voluntary associations that city life appears to breed. This characteristic is a corollary of the predominance of status relations and the sheer number of people congregated at one place. No matter what a man's interest may be, no matter how trivial or esoteric or profound, he is almost certain to find others in the city who share it and who, in all probability, have formed an association to pursue it. In a small town, only one or two persons will have an enthusiasm for, say, stamp collecting. In New York City, 50,000 people will pay admission to an exhibition of stamps on a single day. Whether the interest is stamps, foreign automobiles, tropical fish, chess, poetry, space travel, or match folders, there will be an association in the city to aid in its pursuit, and if there is no association, an enthusiast can usually find others who are interested and initiate one. No one can speak confidently about the durability of such associations, but there is no doubt of their profusion.

Formal and informal social control. Social control in the city presents a striking contrast to its counterpart in the country. In the former, it tends to be formal and secondary; in the latter, informal and primary. The gossip that keeps the individual member of the small community "in line" and that operates as a potent sanction inducing conformity to the norms has little relevance in the city. Social pressures of this kind work steadily and inexorably in primary groups. Ostracism is much more serious when there is no alternative group to which the individual may turn. We need not elaborate on the function of gossip as a means of social control. It is the instrument which permits the prompt application of sanctions to those who fail to conform to the norms of the small community.

It is apparent that gossip can have no such function in the metropolis. The primary groupings in which it operates so effectively in the village have no definite locus in the city; they exist, but not at a given place. An individual may withdraw from them easily, or otherwise avoid them. If the city provides privacy, it also furnishes anonymity to those who desire it. One may escape the primary social controls altogether at the price of dispensing with group affiliations, both formal and informal. On the other hand, the formal social controls in the city—the law and the police—are very much more in evidence. No one is immune from the parking regulations, none from the traffic ticket. The sanctions of the law press equally upon all who are tempted to stray from its requirements and they are applied, if not with complete impartiality, at least with impersonality.

At the same time, it is apparent that the city exhibits more tolerance for certain kinds of conduct and for individual idiosyncrasies than does the small community. The reason is simple. The city is a place of contrasts; its very heterogeneity suggests that there will be many different sets of norms, that the citizens will be exposed to variegated cultures and diverse ways of working and worshiping. The countryman, on the other hand, is likely to greet the unfamiliar with suspicion and even with hostility. It poses a threat to his way of life and may call into question traditions and beliefs to which he has always been deeply if unconsciously committed. Exposure to social differentiation itself induces tolerance of diversity and sometimes even understanding, and it is in the city that differentiation reaches its extremes.

Social mobility. The society of the city, in contrast to that of the country, is a fluid one. Its social strata may be more apparent, the lines more clearly drawn, but the individual can move up, and down, more freely. Kingsley Davis's comments on this phenomenon are very much to the point:

> Just as the city requires and promotes great geographical mobility (of persons, goods, and ideas), so it requires and promotes great social mobility as well. Its elaborate division of labor, its competitiveness, its impersonality—tend to emphasize the achievement rather than the ascription of status. Recruiting a heterogeneous population whose origins are obscure and rewarding them on the basis of uniqueness, eccentricity, novelty, efficiency, and inventiveness, it necessarily judges status according to what the individual does and how he looks rather than to whom he was born. The urban person can therefore raise or lower his status to a remarkable degree during his lifetime, and the competition for status (and with it the insecurity of status) becomes a perpetual preoccupation.[7]

Cities differ, of course, in this characteristic, depending upon the rigidity of the class structure of the larger society of which they are a part. But where there is any mobility at all it is certain to be accelerated in the city.

Davis's statement has a particular application to American cities. The penniless immigrant who becomes a millionaire, the impoverished graduate student who later achieves the presidency of a college or university, the clerk in the corporation who later becomes chairman of the board—these and many similar instances are phenomena of the city. There are more "escalators" there, and more people riding them. The division of labor and the differential evaluation of occupational endeavor, which give rise to the social class in the first place, paradoxically make possible a greater individual mobility than a less highly differentiated situation can offer. This is doubtless one of the reasons why the American city in particular attracts the able and the ambitious from great distances in the hinterlands.

Specialization and localization. In the country almost all activities are subsidiary to one dominant concern—agriculture. One may roam far and wide over the land, with its sprinkling of villages and towns, and see everywhere, despite regional variations in crops, essentially the same modes of work. In the city, this sameness disappears, and we meet again the endless diversity to which we have repeatedly referred. Diversity makes for specialization, and the specialization we now want to mention is of two kinds.

[7] Kingsley Davis, *Human Society,* The Macmillan Company, New York, 1949, p. 318.

First, cities themselves tend to be specialized, so that different cities emphasize different functions and activities. In our own country, for example, we associate Detroit with automobiles, Hollywood with motion pictures, Hartford with insurance, Norfolk with the Navy, Pittsburgh with steel, Scranton with mining, and Chicago with meat-packing. Each city except the very largest tends to have its own special reason for being and comes to be associated with its own dominant activity.

In the second place, certain areas within the city also become specialized, and as a result certain groups and certain activities are localized there. In New York City, for example, the financial district is at the southern tip of Manhattan Island. Wall Street, a short, narrow canyon with a graveyard at one end and a river at the other, symbolizes finance for the entire country. The fashionable shopping district is on upper Fifth Avenue. Surrounding Carnegie Hall, on 57th Street, are the studios and the music shops. The garment workers ply their trade in the few congested blocks between 34th and 42nd Streets on Seventh Avenue. The theater district, of course, is Broadway, although most of the theaters are actually located just off this famous thoroughfare. And Madison Avenue is the street of the "hucksters" or advertisers, as nearly everyone in the world now knows.

Residential localization is also characteristic of the city, and it may proceed in terms of different variables, especially the ethnic group, nationality, and social class. Taking the first two together, every city of any size has its districts in which people of Negro, German, Spanish, Italian, Irish, Polish, Greek, Chinese, or Russian ancestry congregate and live. Similarly there are neighborhoods of the wealthy and neighborhoods of the poor, often in close proximity geographically. These divisions change character, and what is at one time an area of costly residences may ultimately give way to slums, rooming houses, or new developments. Concurrently, new "desirable" locations within the city are developed. These differentiations and transitions provide the sociologist, the city planner, and the urban architect with a fruitful source of data and an endless series of special problems.

Still another change which occurs in the larger cities may be called the depletion of the middle class. New York City, for example, and especially Manhattan Island, is a place in which the extremes of income are represented in greater numbers than the normal probability curve would indicate. It is a matter of serious concern that only the rich and the poor continue to inhabit the city; those of the middle class tend to escape to the suburbs where they try to recapture the values of small-town living and spend their free time painting and repairing their houses and fighting a losing battle against the crabgrass in their yards.

We have now sketched some of the principal sociological differences between the rural and urban ways of life. Although no sharp line can be drawn between them, particularly in our own country, they have traditionally represented two different cultures, each with its own ideas and norms and materiel. Vast changes in technology since the Industrial Revolution began have reduced the disparities between them, and it may be that as urbanization continues, the differences will continue to diminish in significance. But some differences, we may be sure, will remain, giving one cast to the country and another to the city. In this respect, we have to think of country and city, not in the geographical sense as two different places, but in the sociological sense as two different kinds of groupings and two different modes of life. In any event, the stereotypes of "rube" and "city slicker" are no longer valid, and such stereotypes now belong in the attic with the children's old comic books.

The suburb. Urbanization has brought with it a new phenomenon—the suburb and the process of suburbanization. Actually, it is not so new as people in general and sociologists in particular sometimes suppose. It is attributable to a cultural lag in political organization, and from one point of view it is not a new phenomenon at all.

Every city has grown by increasing its area, along with its population, and many localities that are now urban were once suburban. Thus what is now 14th Street in New York City was once a region of isolated farms for the early Dutch settlers. As the city grew, each area in turn went through a comparable transformation. The suburbs at any given time are merely the less densely populated areas at the edge of the city. If there were no political boundaries, and therefore separate municipal governments, suburbs as such would not exist. Again, our concept is neither geographical nor political but sociological. The suburb, in short, is simply another residential district in the city whose separate existence is attributable only to a lag in political arrangements.

State boundaries are greater barriers to the integrated political organization of a city than are county lines within the state. Some of the problems that arise when a city lies in one state and its suburbs fall in another can be solved by the creation of interstate governmental agencies, such as the New York Port Authority, which builds and operates bridges, tunnels, airfields, grain, truck, and bus terminals, and other facilities serving New York and New Jersey. But larger problems are likely to appear in the future, in fact, within a generation or two, as a new phenomenon appears—the consolidated or continental city. Population on the Eastern seaboard of the United States is now virtually continuous from Bridgeport, Connecticut, to Washington, D.C., and a few years should expand this "built-up" area from Boston to Norfolk. The city of the future may well include this whole complex, nine states and the District of Columbia.

Though the suburb can be considered simply another part of the city, it does have its own distinctive social characteristics. In the first place, it contains more than its proportionate share of families and less than its share of single adults. The suburb is the home of parents—particularly young parents—and their children—particularly young children. The reason for this is patent. In the second place, suburban families belong largely to the middle and upper middle classes. The poor cannot afford the luxury of trees, and the rich can enjoy them in a second home in the country. Hence the middle-income groups largely populate the suburbs. A third characteristic, which is corollary to the first two, is the predominance of the single-family dwelling, of houses, in suburbia, in contrast to the apartments and tenements of the city. Finally, the fact that adult males who live in the suburbs usually work in the city and therefore commute in the morning and evening has its own interesting ramifications. The suburb during the day is a "city of women" and we may remark, half-facetiously, that it thus may come close to being the only genuine matriarchy in the history of human society.

The suburb obviously deserves more attention than we can manage in a brief preliminary survey. As a subject of inquiry, it will doubtless attract more sustained sociological investigation as time goes by. Meanwhile, we may conclude this brief section with a note on a new phenomenon, the "exurb" discovered by a popular writer. It lies beyond the suburbs, and attracts a higher income group thán does the suburb. Further, it has its own, different, culture. Its inhabitants—writers, artists, publishers, advertising executives—do not ordinarily have to commute to the city each day, they enjoy more independence and suffer more competition in their jobs, and they spend even more time keeping up with one another than the ordinary citizen spends keeping up with the Joneses.

CLASS AND CASTE

Society is composed not only of different groups but also of different strata, an observation that means some groups are evaluated "higher" or "lower" than others. Our knowledge of the structure of any society will have to include some understanding of this stratified arrangement, for stratification produces our classes and our castes. We will here confine ourselves mainly to American society, hence chiefly to class and not to caste, but the phenomena are themselves universal.

The universality of class. Class is almost, but not quite, a universal phenomenon in human society. It is absent only in the smallest, simplest, and most primitive of societies. All societies of any size, including the U.S.S.R.

and the United States, have a class structure. Although the origin of class structures is obscure, we are relatively safe if we assume that social stratification has something to do with two factors—the size of the society and the division of labor within society. Since the division of labor, in terms other than age or sex, itself is a function of size, it seems probable that this is the real clue to stratification. As society grows larger, groups form within the larger structure, producing different statuses as labor is divided, and leading to a differential in the prestige attached to different statuses, and this could account for the development of social classes. The evaluation of status, it is suggested, stems from the different contributions which the various occupations make to the total society. Some statuses, in other words, are important to the community and perhaps hard to fill. The healing arts, for example, have been so closely linked with survival that their functional importance is great in all societies, and accordingly the status of medicine man carries high prestige in both primitive and modern societies.

It is not necessary that these evaluations be "rational" in any sense of the word. Some societies have evaluated accomplishments very highly that we would regard with indifference and even distaste. On the other hand, some members of our own society place a great value on activities that would hardly excite the approval or even the interest of the more "primitive." Nevertheless, certain statuses or clusters of statuses come to be evaluated positively in all societies, among them the status of chief, medicine man, priest, and sage or professor. These clusters begin to form a foundation for the class structure of society and to constitute its strata.

But stratification of statuses alone does not produce a class structure. Class is a group phenomenon and depends upon the juxtaposition of groups in some order or rank. We need another condition of class before we can assign sufficient reason to this phenomenon, and that is the extension of the prestige of the status to the family of the person occupying it. That is, the prestige attached to status must be enjoyed not only by the occupant but also by his family and descendants. Here the family unit has played a vital role. The occupational prestige accorded to the status of an adult male in a patriarchal society comes to be accorded also to his wife and to all their children. In this way, the stratification of statuses comes to be a family or group phenomenon. Later on, the status ascribed to the family becomes hereditary, and ultimately it exceeds occupational status in importance. What is first a function of occupational status thus tends to become an hereditary function of family membership. At a given time in the life of a society, therefore, family status based upon ancient occupational prerogatives and prestige may take precedence over present occupational status in determining an individual's position in the class structure.

Obviously, we cannot outline a complete theory of social class and marshal the evidence to support it in a brief introduction. The preceding observations on class should therefore be construed as suggestions which may shed some light on the process of class formation.

Open and closed class systems. The distinction between class and caste, or between "open" and "closed" class systems, is a matter of rigidity. A class structure may be barely perceptible in a small community in which all or most social relations are primary. In all complex societies it appears much more strongly. Descriptively, we can discern two major forms of class system, differing from one another in degree. In an open class system vertical social mobility is possible. This means that there are no restrictions, or only very mild restrictions, on movement up and down by individuals. A closed class system, on the other hand, is one in which vertical mobility is severely restricted or even prohibited entirely. Obviously, the family will play a crucial part in both, but in the closed system it is much more important than the personality of the individual, while in an open system, the significance of the individual is greater. A society with a closed class system is likely to emphasize the family more than an open system (which will emphasize individual achievement).

Class in American communities. When we look at so territorially vast a society as our own, a society composed of so many heterogeneous groupings of people, the problem of illuminating its class structure—if indeed it has only one class structure—takes on considerable complexity. Before discussing the possibility of a general class structure, let us first take a look at some particular class structures discoverable in different American communities.

1. Middletown can be found in the state of Indiana. As the name implies, it is an average, middle-class, middle-sized American city, with a population of around 30,000. It was studied, first in 1925 and then again in 1935, by two sociologists, Robert S. Lynd and Helen Merrell Lynd, and the two books they published about it, *Middletown* and *Middletown in Transition*, are among the most famous community studies in sociology.[8]

We have suggested that no examination of any community of significant size can fail to disclose social classes. People in Middletown simply do not associate on equal terms with one another. They have different incomes, they work and play and eat and drink with different people, they follow different occupational pursuits, and they have different styles of living. The Lynds found it convenient to divide the people into two major classes, the business class and the working class. The working class earns a living by working with

[8] Both published by Harcourt, Brace & World, Inc., New York, the first in 1929, and the second in 1937.

things, the business class by working with *people*. Although this division has the advantage of simplicity, it blurs the position of many people, as the Lynds well knew.

Ten years later, the Lynds altered their simple two-class scheme somewhat, though they continued to emphasize the "long arm of the job." Some major changes had occurred in Middletown, not least of which was the impact of the Depression. Further, they attached rather more importance in the second volume to the position of the X family, whose power and influence were characterized by one of the "lesser citizens" as follows:

> If I'm out of work, I go to the X plant; if I need money I go to the X bank, and if they don't like me I don't get it; my children go to the X college; when I get sick I go to the X hospital; I buy a building lot or house in an X subdivision; my wife goes downtown to buy clothes at the X department store; if my dog stays away he is put in the X pound; I buy X milk; I drink X beer, vote for X political parties, and get help from X charities; my boy goes to the X Y.M.C.A. and my girl to their Y.W.C.A.; I listen to the Word of God in X-subsidized churches; if I'm a Mason I go to the X Masonic Temple; I read the news from the X morning newspaper; and, if I am rich enough, I travel via the X airport.[9]

Here we have a class phenomenon of a different order, a family that belongs neither to the working class nor to the business class but one that exerts its influence over both of them. This influence extends into every sphere of the city's life—business, education, medical care, philanthropy, housing, real estate, leisure, journalism, and religion. First-generation wealth, as the Lynds suggest, becomes second-generation power, and this has far-reaching effects on the stratification of the city.

2. Let us now move to a small village somewhere in the Middle West, called simply Plainville. It was studied by James West prior to World War II.[10] The population in 1939 was 275, and one reason for the study was the assumption that it would be devoid of class stratification. Indeed, the inhabitants themselves thought they were "one plain old class of common working people." Nevertheless, West soon learned that he would have to deal with a "discrimination system of enormous complexity."

> Friends began to warn and instruct me about whom I should or should not visit and be seen with, if I wanted to gain correct information and maintain the respect of the "worthwhile" people. Judgments of neighbor on neighbor, and all evaluations of individuals, appeared to be repeating patterns of great uniformity, despite the wariness with which they were phrased.[11]

[9] *Middletown in Transition*, p. 74.
[10] James West, *Plainville, U.S.A.*, Columbia University Press, New York, 1945.
[11] *Ibid.*, p. xii.

Without following the detail of the study, it will suffice to say that West found a clearly articulated social class structure in his small community.

[This structure] provides for every person living there a master pattern for arranging according to relative rank every other individual, and every family, clique, lodge, club, church, and other organization or association in Plainville society. . . . It provides also a set of patterns for expected behavior according to class, and a way of judging all norms and deviations from these norms in individual behavior.[12]

Plainville, then, exhibits two distinct social classes, with minor gradations on each side of the dividing line. Each class contains roughly half the population. The upper class is made up of "good, honest, self-respecting, average, everyday, working people," and when this entire expression is used, there is no doubt where the people belong. The members of the lower class are not described in the same way. The top third of this class is "respectable" and "decent," but poor; the middle third is no longer "respectable," and the third level is comprised of "people who live like animals."

By what criteria were the classes of Plainville distinguished? West discovered that there were six: place of residence (prairie people versus hill people), technology (modern methods of agriculture versus "patch farming," hunting, fishing, trapping, and wood chopping), lineage, wealth, "morals," and "manners." The last two of these seem most important and it is interesting to note that "manners" also includes knowledge. Religion and membership in certain voluntary associations, such as the Masons, also serve as class distinctions.

Three of West's observations invite special attention because of the insight they afford into the nature of class structure in general. First, there is a great disparity between the ideal culture and the real culture, so far as class is concerned. In the ideal culture, there is no such thing as a class structure; in the real culture, there is a distinct and influential class system. The second point is that it is possible for a class structure to evolve in a very small community where everyone knows everyone else personally; hence, class may be based on personal relations or can be found with social relations based on personality. Finally, the line between the two classes is almost impossible to cross. West found only three illustrations of vertical mobility, two upward, and one downward.

3. The city of Newburyport, Massachusetts, has been the subject of a novel by John P. Marquand (*Point of No Return*) and a sociological study by W. Lloyd Warner and Paul S. Lunt.[13] Both make clear the extent to which

---

[12] *Ibid.*, p. 115.

[13] *Point of No Return* was published in 1949 by Little, Brown and Company, Boston. "Yankee City" is the "short" title of a four-volume work by Warner and others, of which the first volume, *The Social Life of a Modern Community*, was published in 1941 by the Yale University Press, New Haven, Conn.

the city is stratified. Warner and Lunt propose six separate and distinct classes in the city, and though this has been criticized as perhaps unrealistic and overprecise, the content of the classes is still interesting. The upper-upper class is comprised of the "old families" whose ancestors arrived prior to the Revolutionary War and acquired wealth in shipping and whaling. They live in the "Hill" section and are known as "Hill Streeters," though not all of them live on the street in question. The lower-upper class is made of later arrivals who would qualify as upper-upper except for this fact. They may have larger incomes, automobiles, and houses than the upper-uppers.

The upper-middle class comprises merchants and professional men and their families, some well-to-do, who do not qualify for the upper classes by virtue of the location of their residence, their associations, and their general activities. The lower-middle and upper-lower classes are hard to distinguish, for they live together in a section of town apart from the higher classes, and many of these, oddly enough, can trace their families back to the halcyon days of whales and sailing ships. At the very bottom of the pile are the River-brookers, who live where the river runs into the sea, and whose "morals" are not what they should be.

Marquand's novel deals with the closed structure of the upper-upper class in the city, a point made by the sociological investigation as well. It revolves around a New York banker, born in the city, who falls in love with a member of this exalted group. Her family had been shipowners; his, ship captains. Marquand recounts in detail a futile attempt to break down the barriers of the traditional class system, and the manner in which the tradition is enforced.

Sociologists and novelists have studied and written about many other communities. Some have had more classes, some fewer; the criteria of class have differed, and the rigidity of the structure has varied. But in all cases, a class structure appears. In no society anywhere in the world do people associate with one another on strictly even terms. There is always deference and sometimes obedience, on the one hand, and condescension and sometimes command, on the other. The society that makes possible the multifarious relationships which people have with one another always provides a means of limiting these relations and confining them within certain stratified patterns.

The criteria of class. Among the various criteria of class that have appeared in our own society, the following merit brief discussion: (1) wealth, property, and income, (2) family or kinship, (3) location of residence, (4) duration of residence, (5) occupation, (6) education, and (7) religion. They are, of course, interrelated.

1. If we were forced to choose a single criterion for the class structure of *our own* society, financial resources would probably be the successful candidate. Few will doubt the importance of wealth, not only in itself but for

what it enables the owner to do. Wealth multiplies living choices and life opportunities, and provides a wider range of possibilities in many aspects of living. It serves as a symbol of success, a means of stabilizing family influence, and a prestige symbol in the community. But wealth alone does not always suffice, even in our own monetary-minded society. For one thing, income must actually affect the style of living of the owner, and wealthy but obscure individuals who make no use of their wealth during their lifetime may acquire no social prestige by virtue of their acquisitions. Further, inherited wealth may be evaluated more highly than earned income, and earned income itself may be divided into more or less desirable brackets. This brings us to the occupational factor, which is another matter.

2. The evaluation of status made by society is often applied to the family as well as to the individual holding the status. Class status is generally a family phenomenon, as we have seen. It also tends to be hereditary. This makes kinship or family an important criterion of class position. Even in a society in which social mobility is present, initial status is ascribed and tends to be retained. When class endogamy—marriage within one's class—is encouraged and practiced customarily, class status can be perpetuated over long periods of time. Some societies symbolize the position by titles of rank or nobility.

3. We have suggested that there is always an ecological corollary of class status, a "hill" and a "prairie," a Beacon Street and a South Boston. It is not purely geographic, but location of residence, in the absence of other criteria, can be an index to class position. People strive to move into the sections of town that are considered desirable from this point of view. Again, these locations may change from one era to another, and other considerations may override location as a determining factor in class status.

4. The acquisition of substantial property or wealth does not automatically produce an accepted class status, even when it is accompanied by residence in the "best" section of town. There is also the matter of duration of residence, for most societies make a distinction between the "old" families and those who are more recently arrived. Sometimes it takes half a lifetime to be accepted into the upper stratum of a community, and it is sometimes necessary to have been born there, or to be able to claim several generations of residents in the family tree. The stranger is always classless, and remains so for varying periods of time. It is not easy to say why this should matter, except that newcomers are usually expected to "prove" themselves, to demonstrate their capacities and give others the opportunity to judge their performance against prevailing standards, whether in the game of baseball or in an established community.

5. It is clear that what people do for a living has a great deal to do with their class position, excepting, perhaps, the very top classes of society. Those with high occupational rank will usually have social status that is appropriate. High political and diplomatic officials, professional men in education, law,

medicine, etc., are usually accorded a high social position independent of their actual income or wealth. Evaluations differ from one society to another, of course. Generals and admirals are accorded higher status in Germany than in the United States, for example, while the status of university professors has never been evaluated so highly in the United States as in Europe.

6. The attitude that applies to the status of university professors can be applied to education in general, or to the possession of knowledge. In all societies, learning, whether sacred or secular, is a distinguishing mark. For one thing, its acquisition requires effort, and for another, its possession permits the performance of tasks that are otherwise impossible. The evaluation made of these conditions is variable. In Old China, education bestowed a level of prestige obtainable in no other way; in modern times it is less significant, usually, than other factors.

7. Finally, though we should not wish to overemphasize the importance of religion as a criterion of class, candid investigation of the subject discloses that it may not be altogether ignored. In our own society, for example, the Unitarian and Episcopalian churches carry more prestige than does the Church of God or the Holy Rollers. It is possible that in the United States as a whole, Congregationalists and Presbyterians rank a little higher than Methodists, who in turn rank a little higher than Baptists. It is doubtful that an Irish Catholic could ever become a "proper Bostonian" even if he were a millionaire many times over and his family had lived in Boston for many decades. Evaluations of religious status change from community to community, certainly, but there is little question that we have here a factor not wholly unrelated to class.

Commensalism as a symptom of class. Throughout this discussion, we have emphasized that in no society can any single factor be used as a sole criterion of class status. Nor can we say that in general in human societies some criteria are more important than others. Some combination is always involved, and the combination exhibits subtle differences from society to society. It is obvious that the criteria are related to one another and that people who rank high in several tend, more frequently than not, to rank high also in others, though here the criterion of kinship seems an exception. When we take them all into consideration we can usually make an accurate guess about a person's social class.

All of these various criteria, taken together, make up what sociologists have called a life style or manner of living. And there is one almost infallible symptom of a shared life style that enables persons otherwise unknown to one another to recognize that they belong essentially to the same class. This symptom has to do with the culture of eating and might be called, somewhat jocosely, the "alimentary index." We shall call it *commensalism*, that is, the sharing of a common table. For few human activities show class distinctions so readily as the culture of the table. It is a common but nevertheless curious observation that persons will have sexual intercourse with, and permit their children to be suckled by, people with whom they would in no circumstances share a common table. The question of who eats with whom, therefore, will almost invariably disclose the strata of society.

A critique of class analysis. We need to examine briefly, before we leave the subject of social classes, one criticism that has been made of community studies of class. It is argued that if we are interested in the class structure of an entire society we may be misled if we look for it on the local community level. Such studies as we have cited here, then, are not the proper locus for inferences regarding the class structure of American society in general. Indeed, the question whether or not there is a generalized class structure in the United States, or whether there are class structures of particular American communities, is often raised. Since they are two separate questions, however, we might answer the first question in the negative and the second in the affirmative, and there is good reason to believe that this is the proper reply.

Inferences from the class structure of particular locations to the class structure of whole societies are based on two assumptions, both questionable: first, that the class structure in one community is comparable or even coincidental with the class structure of another; second, that a particular community is society in microcosm, that it represents society at large. But it is clear that there may not be any "carryover" from one community to the next; the structures we have been discussing are not only local phenomena, but they are in a sense limited to the local community. We cannot, for example, infer that in every American society there are two classes, hill people and prairie people, simply because that phenomenon appears in particular areas. If every American lived his whole life in the community in which he was born, the inference might be warranted. But the extreme geographic mobility of the American people, to say nothing of the influence of our mass-communication system, prevents the formation of a rigid class structure and contributes to the fluidity of society.

Further, the assumption that the local community is the entire society in microcosm is even more questionable. Many Americans who are highly mobile, for occupational or other reasons, may not identify themselves with the local community at all. The local community may also be devoid of many occupational statuses. Hence the local community picture is almost invariably incomplete.

Finally, we must point out that class is not merely a social phenomenon, but a *power* phenomenon as well. As such, it has consequences which community studies cannot disclose. There is an overlap, of course, between class as prestige and class as power, but they are two different things.

COLOR AND CREED

The complex societies of the modern world contain many different kinds of people, and that, of course, is what makes them complex. Throughout the text, we have emphasized the fact that society comprises differences of all sorts, and this creates a situation which has both virtues and vices. Imagine, for example, the monotony of living in a society in which all of the people were alike. It is ridiculous, of course, to suppose that they could all be alike in age and sex. But could we have a society made up entirely of Chinese farmers, or Catholic physicians, Irish policemen, or Swiss watchmakers? The notion is equally fanciful, but for sociological rather than biological reasons. Even if it were possible, such a society would seem to most of us deplorable. One of our oldest sayings is that variety is the spice of life, and it is also the spice of society.

There are those, however, who prefer their fare less highly seasoned than some others, and some would prefer less differentiation in society than others. Some who would concede the biological necessity for differences in age and sex might still prefer that all of us were of one color, one creed, one complexion, or one belief, one race or one religion. In smaller and simpler societies, such conditions often obtain, but uniformity of this kind is almost impossible in so-called civilized societies, such as our own. Differentiation is one of the prices we must pay for civilization; it is one of the costs of complexity. We are of different colors, and we hold different creeds, and the consequences of these differences we want now to explore.

Consciousness of kind and consciousness of difference. We have already encountered the conception of "consciousness of kind" as an explanation of group membership and social interaction. It is the similarities that people recognize in one another that induce them to seek one another out and form groups, either consciously for the purpose of social action or unconsciously because others, who are different, consider them alike and react to them as belonging together. It is not too much to say that we have social groups in the first place because certain people are similar, because they have physical traits or common interests, and because they are conscious of what they share. But if we are like some persons, we are also unlike others, and consciousness of our differences from others also has social consequences.

If consciousness of kind encourages a man to greet his neighbor, consciousness of difference cautions against the stranger; it inhibits social intercourse. The first quality invites, the second condemns; the first leads to unity, the second to disunity. When we recognize that some people are different from us we are ordinarily less ready to admit them into the small circle of our intimates and ascribe to them the virtues that distinguish "people like us"; we are in fact more likely to assign the sins of society to "people like them." Once more, in other words, we have the tale of the "we's" and the "they's," the in-group and the out-group. And unfortunately, we more often deal with this situation in terms of stereotypes than in terms of personalities or real knowledge. We may not even have met members of the groups from whom we feel consciously different. Lack of personal knowledge does not diminish the passion of "we"-"they" conflicts. Rather it makes them possible, for personal experience would often eliminate suspicion and hostility, given time.

As we become members of some groups, so do we, in the same process, exclude ourselves from others. As certain statuses are ascribed to us, so also are certain others denied. And so we arrive at a society made up of different groups, in always-changing juxtaposition with one another, their members moving in and out of them, qualifying themselves for some and at the same time disqualifying themselves for others. As soon as we join with some people we separate ourselves from others. We are always conscious of our kind, and conscious too of those who are not our kind. And furthermore, it is always *they* who are different—*we* are ourselves always. Since no group is an island, societal groups inevitably come in contact with one another; the setting for conflict is prepared. We thus live in a world in which intergroup tensions are built into the system, to rise and subside again and again. It is a world of Catholics and Protestants, Jews and Gentiles, Hindus and Moslems, Frenchmen and Germans, Negroes and whites, playwrights and critics, authors and publishers, "natives" and outlanders. Different traits and different ideas and purposes create different groups, and the fact of such differentiation can be neither deplored nor denied. Differentiation need not mean conflict, and it does not of itself produce prejudice. At what point then do conflict and prejudice arise? That is one of the most vexing of all sociological problems.

"Pride and Prejudice." Let us concede at the outset that any preference is a kind of prejudice. If preferences are normal and desirable, so are prejudices. It is unreasonable to ask us to take pride in our own groups and their accomplishments and at the same time to refrain from considering them superior. It is the superiority in which we take pride. And if our groups are superior they must be superior to something that is inferior, or language has no meaning. What is a virtue in one sense becomes in reverse a vice, and the attitude that is commended in one situation is condemned in another and for precisely the same reason. Pride means prejudice and it is impossible to have one without the other. The rain that saves the farmer's crops is also the rain that ruins the picnic. It is not possible for us to praise our own country or take comfort in our own religion without being thankful that we have this country and this religion and not some other. If patriotism is a virtue, can prejudice be a vice?

Prejudice in favor of one's own group would seem to be a normal phenomenon in the human species. Prejudice then can mean merely preference or preferment, and need not be anti-anything. To be prejudiced may mean only that we favor our own groups, our own associates and companions. One way, then, to eradicate prejudice is to eliminate such virtues as group loyalty, group pride, and patriotism, for whatever is responsible for one is also responsible for the other. Another way to achieve the same end would be to eradicate or abolish all groups in which a consciousness of difference is exhibited and abolish them so completely that no one will ever be able to identify a given individual as a member of this group instead of that or that group instead of this. The price for this solution might be more than we wish to pay. If there were no Catholics, Protestants, and Jews, there would be no prejudice among them, and to the degree that we insist upon retaining them as separate entities, that is the degree to which we will attract the prejudices of others.

There is little chance, however, that societal groups will disappear. They represent the differences between men, and the differences between men are legion. Men will disagree upon the slightest provocation, and groups have the faculty of emphasizing their differences. It is something of a paradox, however, that when groups are very different, no tension arises between them. The St. Louis Cardinals do not compete with the University of Pennsylvania, nor do chess clubs compete with libraries. As groups become more alike, so do they become aware of their differences. The more aware of their differences they become, the more zealous their adherence to their own creed. Further, when there are no large differences, small ones are magnified; thus the more similar groups become, the more they attempt to magnify the differences that do exist. This may explain why civil strife is often the bloodiest of all, and why enmity between brothers is sometimes so intense. Finally, there is often more bitterness between two factions of the same political or religious sect than between the sect and other sects, provided, of course, that common enemies do not threaten the existence of the whole and thus contribute to its cohesion.

If differences in color and creed seem more serious than those between physicists and literary critics, it is largely because the former represent affiliations from which it is difficult or impossible to resign. Involuntary group memberships and the ascribed statuses that accompany them in a given society are relatively fixed. They can sometimes be changed, through subterfuge or certain other means, but it is difficult to withdraw from some statuses and certain groups. It is difficult to stop being a Negro and start being white, or to reverse the status in the other direction. It is difficult for the same reason to stop being a Jew, even though one embraces another religion, and difficult to become a Jew even though one joins the faith.

Similar observations apply to the fact of national origin. It is possible for a native of Poland to become an American. But he does not wholly cease to be a Pole so long as he retains something of the Polish language and literature, custom, or tradition. And how can he leave these behind him? Assimilation is never complete; it usually requires at least two generations. National origin, as ascribed status, thus separates group from group even when they live together in the same society.

Another type of problem might be called the native-stranger question, or "who got there first?" Wherever they meet, the native and the stranger regard each other with suspicion and distrust. They do not know each other's norms, and each distrusts the other's way of doing things: each thinks the other's customs queer and possibly absurd or "wrong." The native may suspect that the stranger has designs on his territory and will one day displace him. Even when the stranger is welcomed, acceptance takes longer, and the visitor is usually better received than the permanent settler. Those who come first not infrequently attempt to exclude latecomers, even though they are not themselves native to the territory.

We have been saying, then, that prejudice is a normal phenomenon, and in one sense it is little more than a preference. It is doubtful that such a thing as an unprejudiced man can exist. Even those who take pride in being unprejudiced are prejudiced against the prejudiced. Sociologists, for example, are as a rule both personally and professionally as unprejudiced a group as one can find, yet they are prejudiced against the keepers of concentration camps, masters of slaves, oppressors of the poor, religious fanatics, totalitarians, tyrants, racists, chauvinists, and other similar types. And they are prejudiced against them as types, not as individuals. It appears then that we are approaching the conclusion that some prejudices are better than others; unfortunately, those prejudiced in the opposite direction can reach the same conclusion.

Discrimination. Prejudice is one thing. Discrimination is something else. Prejudice is a matter of belief; discrimination is a mode of behavior. Prejudice can be "for" as well as "against"; discrimination is always "against." To discriminate means simply to deny to an individual or a group a privilege or opportunity or pleasure that is thereupon reserved for one's own group. The denial, moreover, is made on irrelevant grounds, for reasons that have nothing to do with the merits of the person in question. Thus a man who possesses all of the qualifications for admission to medical school is denied admission because he is a Jew—that is discrimination. A man with all of the qualifications needed for employment is refused employment because he is a Negro—that too is discrimination. In neither case is there any reasonable relationship between the privilege denied and the grounds on which denial is effected. This is not merely exclusion, in the sense that Democrats may not vote in the Republican primary election or in the sense that infidels are excluded from the Catholic Church. When the tests applied have no conceivable relationship to the purposes or interests for which the group exists, denial of access to membership amounts to discrimination.

Discriminatory practices range from the ludicrous to almost inhuman cruelty. Consider the following sad catalog of cases chosen pretty much at random from our own social experience:

ITEM: In the state of Mississippi a bill was once introduced in the legislature requiring that the textbooks used in Negro schools be stored in separate warehouses from those used in white schools.

ITEM: There is a soft-drink vending machine in use in this country with separate coin slots marked "white" and "colored."

ITEM: "In . . . 1947 Fletcher Melvin, a twenty-four year old orderly at Provident Hospital in Baltimore, was asleep when the train conductor ordered all colored passengers at Enfield, North Carolina, to move to the segregated coach. On being awakened, Melvin refused to move and was shot and killed instantly by the Atlantic Coast Line Railroad conductor. The conductor claimed self-defense and was freed."[14]

ITEM: At a Northern university a cross is burned in front of the student-union building to remind Negroes to "keep their place."

ITEM: A Jewish family arrives at a resort hotel. They have reserved accommodations in advance and their reservations have been confirmed. The desk clerk informs them, with apologies, that there has been some mistake. The space is not now available. A short time later the accommodations are given to a non-Jewish family without a reservation.

ITEM: A country club at which no Jews play golf. No sign is needed.

ITEM: A house on fraternity row in an American college town. A chapter is threatened with the loss of its national charter because the members wanted to pledge a Jewish friend.

ITEM: In 1955 Dr. Sammy Lee, for thirteen years a medical officer in the United States Army, the world's greatest diver and winner of the Sullivan Award for sportsmanship, attends a luncheon in the White House as a guest of the President. During his stay in Washington his wife is informed by a real estate agent in California that he cannot purchase the house he wants because of his Korean ancestry.

ITEM: Thousands of American citizens, accused of no crime, are rounded up and placed in concentration camps in various locations in the western United States. The citizens' only crime was to have Japanese ancestors. The date was 1942.

This is discrimination. Many books have been dedicated to an effort to explain it and many theories have been offered. None is wholly satisfactory.

[14] From Walter White, *How Far the Promised Land,* The Viking Press, Inc., New York, 1955, pp. 166 and 167.

But before we look at the more promising of these attempts, let us first consider some suggestions that seem unsound or useless both as causes and as cures.

Misleading trails. In the ensuing discussion, we shall put prejudice and discrimination together again and view the latter as the overt expression of the former.

1. The first misleading trail is the denial that race exists. Many writers use this solution, and if there is no such thing as race, it is obvious that prejudice cannot exist either. Those who appear prejudiced, then, are merely indulging in superstition or delusion. However admirable the sentiment may be, the datum is false. The trouble with this strategy is that everyone knows that races do exist, and denying it does no one a service. The strategy does harm instead of good, for it increases the suspicion of the unlearned for the learned, brings scientific inquiry into disrepute, and still fails to solve the problem. It neither suggests a cause nor supplies a cure for either prejudice or discrimination.

2. A related error is the denial, not that races exist, but that their differences are important. It is quite valid of course to deny that the discernible differences between the races are relevant to certain characteristics. There is no evidence, for example, that skin color is in any way related to cultural accomplishment, nor is there any known connection between stature and intelligence. But we refer here to the attempt to convince those who think that racial differences are important that such differences are not important. If some people *think* they are important, they *are* important, no matter what other people say. No amount of emphasis upon the insignificance or irrelevance of racial characteristics will convince the Governor of Georgia that he ought to invite the president of Atlanta University (a Negro university) to dine in the executive mansion. The strategy can succeed only with those who are accustomed to accepting scientific evidence. Scientific evidence showing that segregation does harm to both races is either rejected or denounced as irrelevant by those who wish to preserve the patterns of the past, the norms they have been taught to respect, the conduct they believe is proper. Their answer can always be that, although race differences may not be important to *you,* they are important to *me,* and I'll thank you therefore not to interfere.

3. A third misleading trail arises out of an erroneous assumption rather than a mistaken strategy. Prejudices and their problems have of late been identified with and labeled as minority-group problems. The relationship of minorities and majorities is indeed irrelevant to prejudice, but it is incorrect to conclude that the victims of prejudice are always members of a minority group. Many minority groups are not discriminated against at all, and some majority groups have attracted vicious persecution. Millionaires are a minority

group, but hardly subjected to much discrimination; nor are doctors or residents of St. Louis, Missouri. And if it is easier for the camel to pass through the eye of the needle than for a rich man to enter the gates of heaven, and this is a form of discrimination, it is one that seems not to operate on earth. The problem of prejudice and discrimination simply cannot be reduced to a majority-group–minority-group question.

4. A fourth trail that leads to a dead end involves a logical fallacy that is not so clear in sociology, that is, the belief that to understand prejudice, we must study those against whom prejudice is leveled. To grasp anti-Semitism, we must expend millions on the study of Jews. This is saying that if Group A is prejudiced against Group B, then something must be wrong with Group B. But surely it is more likely that the cause of the difficulty is Group A, and it is here that our studies ought to center. As Gunnar Myrdal concluded in his study of racial discrimination in the United States, the Negro problem is really a white problem. But no one has yet offered a study of the Southern white in whom prejudice against Negroes is so vocal and direct. What makes this man so vehement, so dogmatic, so passionate in his prejudice? That is the question that wants answering.

5. Corollary to this is the observation that groups that are discriminated against are not always free of the faults of the group doing the discriminating. Group B, which is discriminated against by Group A, may in turn use discrimination against Group C, and so on through a complete "pecking order." Recognition that the same group may be both subject and object of discrimination can give us some insight into the problem. And it may produce difficulties of a practical nature.

Once more, the laws and the mores. Our sixth and final misconception requires a section of its own. This is the view, widely accepted, that in order to solve the problems of discrimination it is necessary to "pass a law." The hope that legislation or a judicial decision can solve this social problem, or any social problem, is one of the more prevalent delusions of the human mind. We have already exposed the fallacy of the belief in our discussion of the relation between mores and laws. Laws are impotent when the mores do not support them; "passing a law" may even have a contrary effect of stiffening the mores, and at the same time appeasing the conscience of the community.

This does not mean that the resources of the state ought not to be employed to enforce the peace between different groups or to abolish discriminatory practices when possible. In some respects and in some situations, a law can be both useful and influential. A law, in a sense, serves notice that *this* is the will of the community. In situations where the mores lack definition, the law can introduce a note of clarity and indicate precisely what is proper conduct. Where the community is divided, as on the segregation issue in the

United States, the law can hasten a process—not without some intensified opposition—that is in any event inevitable. Even more important, the law can operate as an instrument of education, lending dignity and rectitude to a course of conduct that might not otherwise be openly approved or candidly pursued.

The relation of law and mores can be approached from another direction—by emphasizing once again the distinction between prejudice and discrimination. Prejudice is an attitude of mind and as such is quite beyond the reach of the law, the policeman's club, the robed decision. No force on earth can induce a courageous man to change his mind on what is to him a matter of principle. The Supreme Court of the United States can help to end segregation, but no decision of that court, however unanimous, can force the Governor of Mississippi, for example, to like integration. It would be folly to pass a law forbidding anyone to dislike Jews or Protestants, Catholics or Negroes, just as it would be silly to require them by law to prefer football to baseball. But it is neither folly nor foolishness to enlist the sanction of the law and the sovereignty of the state to assure that all children, whatever their color, enjoy the same privileges in school and the same rights in society. Acts, in short, are susceptible to legal treatment; attitudes are not. Discrimination can be abolished by law, and by legally sanctioned force if necessary, but neither law nor force can sweeten hospitality or encourage kindness.

Indoctrination. Having warned against several misleading trails, we now want to take a positive approach and indicate some of the more likely sources of prejudice. One of these sources is indoctrination, the process by which an individual absorbs the culture that surrounds him. When prejudice is part of the folkways, the individual will take it in and make it a part of him in precisely the same manner in which he makes all of the other components of culture a part of him. If a white child grows up in a group in which anti-Negro sentiments are steadily expressed and anti-Negro discrimination steadily practiced, it is much too much to expect of him that he will easily rid himself of his feelings. One might as well expect an orthodox Jew to take gustatory pleasure in a pork roast or an orthodox Catholic to dine willingly on meat on Friday.

It should not be necessary to explain, in discussing this point, that prejudice is not innate. One is not born with a dislike or distrust of another group of persons, nor with the urge to discriminate. Babies are wholly free of prejudice, as they are free of every other idea, good or bad, that they will acquire later simply as a matter of belonging to a certain social group. Prejudice is learned, just as culture in general is learned. Indoctrination and habituation, responsible as they are for inducing conformity to the norms are thus responsible also for inculcating patterns of prejudice and discrimination, when they too are part of the culture.

To remove this kind of prejudice it is quite useless to attack the individual. It is necessary instead to change the norms that guide the discriminatory practice. It is in this respect that legislation and judicial decision can be especially effective. They can indicate that in the larger society the norm no longer possesses the appropriate sanction and that the majesty and dignity of the law, in fact, are on the other side. By slow degrees, the norm can thus be changed.

Frustration. Prejudice is not always a matter of conformity alone. Sometimes it is the outcome of personal frustration as well. One's own failure in the face of another's success is a common and one might say a normal cause of frustration; and frustration frequently expresses itself in aggression. It is not too difficult to understand how, in a period of economic crisis or severe depression, a father desperately seeking work in order to support his family would look with disfavor upon Negroes or Jews who managed to hold on to their jobs after he had been dismissed. Similarly, one who loses an honor of some kind, a promotion, an increase in salary, a job, or a business deal to a competitor who can be identified with some other ethnic or religious group against which there is already some prejudice or discrimination in society, is more than ready to ease his frustration by accusing the winner of trickery, dishonesty, deceit, and mendacity. He goes further. He then attaches these unpleasant characteristics to the entire group to which the latter belongs. The successful man, the confident man, the serene man, on the other hand, does not need to discriminate.

It is, briefly, always easy to blame others for the faults we perceive in ourselves, and what could be more convenient than to blame those who already occupy a privileged position. This is especially useful when we have no means of retaliation at our disposal. There is no malady of society, whether it be poverty, war, depression, "radicalism," corruption in government, crop failure, or international tension, that has not been blamed on some ill-fated ethnic group or religious group. A scapegoat is needed, someone to blame, someone on whom to project one's own responsibility and guilt. Aggression follows frustration as blame follows failure. When this happens to groups it begins to explain some of the tension, the unpleasantness and hostility, that exists between them. In this way did the medieval Christian blame the Jews for everything from the plague to the poisoned well, and in this way too did the Nazi blame them for every catastrophe in German history. In this way indeed a similar plight can befall any group in society.

The vicious circle. Sensitive students of prejudice have noticed an interesting phenomenon in connection with its causation. They discovered that prejudice itself is one of the causes of prejudice. Ordinarily an assertion of this kind means nothing and serves only to illustrate the fallacy of circular reasoning. We know that naming something is not equivalent to explaining it, that a cause cannot be included in the definition of the effect, and that a phenomenon cannot be explained by itself. Nevertheless, it makes sociological sense to say that prejudice is one of the causes of prejudice. We can appeal to Robert M. MacIver for an explanation of the principle and for an illustration of it:

> We can now turn to the patterns of causation in which a series of conditions or forces sustain, confirm, and generate one another. Each of the forces so interacts with the other conditions as to promote and perpetuate them and thus the whole system they together constitute. These patterns exhibit something more than the interdependence of factors that obtains in every established system. To take the simplest possible case, if you begin with condition *a* it sets in motion condition *b,* and *b* in turn keeps *a* going. The system, in other words, embodies the principle of circularity.

And the illustration:

> A rumor spreads through a community that a particular bank is insolvent. There is a run on the bank. Since no bank can immediately liquidate its resources—apart from outside help—so as to honor all claims upon it, the bank closes down. The rumor is self-confirming.[15]

This is precisely the manner in which the view that Negroes are inferior contributes to their inferiority, and the assertion is a factor that helps produce its own confirmation.

Northerners are often informed that they "do not really know" the Negro. Actually, we are sometimes told by Southern apologists, the Negro clearly belongs to the station to which he is consigned. He is an inferior, dirty, shiftless, stupid, uneducated, and immoral creature. He is fit only for the menial tasks of society and then under close supervision only. But those who argue so fail to realize the extent to which this is true because they believe it to be true. Why is the Negro inferior? Because he is ignorant. Why, then, don't you educate him? Because he is inferior. And so the vicious circle turns. Discrimination means unequal treatment, which results in poverty, which means poor education, which means inferiority, which breeds discrimination. The circle may be large or small; the effect is the same.

What can we learn from the principle of the vicious circle? Professor MacIver's conclusions again are so eloquent that we shall quote them more extensively:

> Besides the more special inference that we have already drawn there are

---

[15] Robert M. MacIver, *The More Perfect Union,* The Macmillan Company, New York, 1948, pp. 61–62.

certain broad lessons we can derive or reinforce from a study of the causal chain called the "vicious circle." In the first place such study should broaden and correct ideas about the nature of prejudice. Prejudice is not a simple thing. It is not a mere expression of human blindness and bias. Prejudice, so to speak, is not altogether prejudice. It has a rational element combined with an irrational one. The irrational element is often sustained by a response to observed behavior that might be accounted fair and proper if the observation were not so selective or if the observed behavior were the whole evidence. The proportion of the two ingredients, the rational and the irrational, will vary according to the kind and degree of prejudice.

It is true—let us say it "without prejudice"—that some Negroes are dirty and careless and immoral and lazy. It is true that some Eastern Europeans who have migrated to these shores are rude, uncultivated, venal, with narrow interests. It is true that some Jews are vulgar, ostentatious, ready to advance themselves by illicit or underhanded methods; and some Jewish groups are clannish and socially inbred. Nor is it an effective answer to charge that the members of the dominant groups display equally undesirable or unpleasant attributes. No headway can be made by that kind of "you're no better."

When, however, we have admitted these things—though avoiding the gross exaggerations, generalizations, and distortions of them that are the concomitants of prejudice—we have not weakened but rather have strengthened the case against discrimination. This is the lesson of the "vicious circle." We should not discriminate against Negroes because some of them are shiftless or irresponsible. Nor against Bohemians or Italians because some of them are uncouth and their votes can be cheaply bought. Nor against Jews because some of them are prominent in the black markets, and so forth. Instead, we should seek to comprehend that our very discrimination disposes them to these ways, and that *the more severe the discrimination the more evidence it will provide to justify its own perpetuation.* In other words, if we dislike the traits that we condemn we should know that the best contribution we can make toward their removal is to cease our discriminating. Whereas if we continue to discriminate we are doing all in our power to fasten them on the groups in question and on our own community.[16]

But if the circle can turn in one direction it can also, happily, turn in the other. If discrimination is one of the causes of discrimination, so also can tolerance serve as a cause of tolerance, and fair play breed fair play. If one of the variables in the circle is altered in a favorable way, others too will change, and ultimately favorable consequences will follow. A higher income for the Negro, for example, will mean a higher standard of living, which in turn will mean a better education, which will make a still higher income possible, with prejudice decreasing all along the line. If segregation increases prejudice, so also does desegregation decrease it. As discrimination in general disappears, so also will prejudice subside. The circle can be "beneficent" as well as "vicious."

[16] *Ibid.,* pp. 77–78.

The true believer. So far, our discussion of discrimination and prejudice has dealt principally with color rather than creed, but before we conclude the discussion we should like to give brief attention to the significance of belief and the manner in which differences in ideological commitment separate man from man and group from group. We have already seen that ideologies operate as norms, giving guidance to conduct and moral sanction to belief. Among these ideologies, political and religious convictions tend to be especially intense, and perhaps the latter are the most pervasive and most intimately personal of all.

Adherence to religious beliefs has an emotional tone, and the tone causes trouble and dissension between groups and encourages their members to entertain a mutual prejudice. In a society in which only one religion flourished, religion would hardly be a source of suspicion. In a society where many religions exist side by side, each claiming to represent the truth, conflict is almost inevitable. Indeed, it has been remarked about our own society, for example, that it is never so segregated as it is at eleven o'clock on Sunday morning, when people are in church.

Religion is not always a barrier to social interaction, certainly, and in an ideal society it would never be such. But we do not live in an ideal society, and our society has no ideal inhabitants. We are asked to believe that there is only one true faith—our own. If this is indeed the case, then those who differ from us must be wrong. Since they have precisely the same opinion of us, a conflict situation exists. Each group views the other with apprehension and insists upon the truth of its own beliefs. Creeds are precious things, but only ours is believable; yours is simply the measure of your stupidity.

Such is the strength of creeds, such the devotion that ideas can arouse, and such the passions that flow from them. Men are exiled for their ideas more readily than for their deeds. The man who is wrong about an ideology is both wrong and dangerous, as Stalin so often said. He is a threat to the existence of the group. He must therefore be exterminated, or at the very least brought to his senses, e.g., persecuted until he recants his heresies. What a sad chapter in human history has been written by those who hold this attitude, and it is nearly universal. The true believer is the fanatic; his contrary is not the false believer, but the skeptic. As a matter of fact the intensity of a belief often creates more havoc than the content of the belief, and few creeds are held more strongly than those that appertain to religion. No religion, if we except Confucianism, which is not, strictly speaking, a religion, has ever been able to tolerate an adverse idea. As George Santayana has defined him, the true believer is the man who "redoubles his efforts after he has forgotten his aim."

Fanaticism is of course destructive to intergroup harmony. Strong attachments, however admirable they appear to the in-group, attract the hostility of the out-group, and appear to the neutral observer as unfortunate, for they lead to intolerance. This is the reason for the tension we find between religions. What is sacred to one is profane to another, what is clean for one unclean for another, proper for one, improper for the other, and true for one, false for the other. And so we have the great insoluble, the great surd that prevents a rational solution to the social equation. The man of unswerving principle wins the plaudits of the crowd; the fanatic attracts its jeers. Yet they are often the same man.

Summary

Various foundations are used for social differentiation. One of the most important is differences in sex. In no society do males and females do the same things, occupy the same statuses, conform to the same norms, etc. Some writers claim this is a consequence of cultural influences, others have asserted the importance of biological distinctions. The available evidence seems to support the latter position, though cultural factors assist the differentiation or channel its direction in some measure.

Another basic factor in human association is the institution of the family, which is pervasive and universal. Is this a biological phenomenon? The answer seems to be negative, for the family, though rooted in the sexual characteristics of the species is nevertheless a social and cultural phenomenon. There are two kinds of families—the family of orientation and the family of procreation—and many kinds of organization. That is, families may be matrilocal, patrilocal, matrilineal, patrilineal, matronymic or patronymic, depending on the extent to which emphasis is placed on the consanguine or the conjugal family. Again, families may stress endogamous or exogamous norms, becoming monogamous, polygamous, polyandrous, or polygynous.

The functions of the family are so important and so numerous that they defy summarization. No other institution can perform these functions so well, which leads us to suppose that the family as an institution is quite likely to remain with us in the indefinite future.

A common form of social differentiation can be made between the countryman and the city man; it exists in all except the most primitive of societies, and it symbolizes two different ways of life, or even two different cultures. Here we have touched only on some of the major and perhaps obvious facets of this fascinating and complex subject.

Differentiation based on caste and class are also commonplace in human society. Two authentic examples of caste in contemporary American society are the line between Negroes and whites and the one between officers and enlisted men in the Armed Forces. How rigid are class and caste lines? This is a difficult point, with arguments on both sides and no satisfactory answer. Some of the famous studies that have been made have produced criteria used for class differentiations, among them: (1) money, wealth, income, (2) kinship, (3) occupation, (4) location of residence, (5) duration of residence, (6), education, and (7) religion. Obviously, they work in combination and not singly.

There are several serious limitations on our study of social classes in America: (1) the strata of one community do not necessarily coincide with the strata of another, (2) mobile members of the population may lack community attachments yet occupy highly evaluated statuses in society at large, and (3) in the larger society, class is not only a prestige phenomenon but also a power phenomenon, and these conditions, though related, are not the same.

Two further criteria for social differentiation are color and creed, which are also elements in class distinctions. We have traced the etiology of prejudice to consciousness of kind and consciousness of difference, and to pride in group membership. Since pride is a form of prejudice, it is inherent in the very structure of social life. Discrimination, which expresses prejudice in conduct, is more than a mere preference. It implies action, ranging from discourtesy to outright cruelty. If prejudice is inherent in society, the same is not true of discrimination, and we have suggested some of the means by which it may gradually be eliminated.

At this point, we end our general discussion of the basic characteristics of human society, returning to the sociologist's point of view in Chapter 18 when we consider the problem of social change. The discussion is of course incomplete. No single text, and no series of texts, can do full justice to the awful complexities of human society. But what has been done may serve the student as a framework or set of guideposts for the more detailed discussion of the two major types of social activity —the political and the economic—that follow.

Review questions

1. Differentiate between the following pairs of conceptions:

   a. family of orientation and family of procreation
   b. conjugal family and consanguine family
   c. polygyny and polyandry
   d. endogamy and exogamy
   e. levirate and sororate

f. prejudice and discrimination

g. class and caste

h. matrilineal and patrilineal

2. List as many of the significant differences between men and women as you can and try to enumerate their social consequences.

3. In what ways does the political association now intervene in the affairs of the family here in the United States?

4. Illustrate the meaning of the concepts of consciousness of kind and consciousness of difference and show how they affect human behavior.

5. Distinguish between the primary group and the secondary group. Compare their relative significance and function in the country and in the city.

6. Contrast the city and the country as regards the following:

a. means of social control

b. degree of specialization

c. size of primary and secondary groups

7. What is meant by commensalism? How can the conception be used?

8. List the more common errors made by those who discuss race and its consequences.

9. List the more common bases on which class distinctions rest.

For further study

1. What role does kinship play in social differentiation?

2. How would a society in which social differentiation was extensive and sharply defined differ from a society in which differentiation was comparatively slight?

3. Does it seem possible that consciousness of kind could extend to the whole of humanity under any circumstances short of an invasion by creatures from some other planet? Explain.

4. What is the effect of a gradual breakdown of the differential between city and country on the whole society?

5. Is it conceivable that class distinctions can be totally eradicated from society? By what means?

6. What role does education play in social differentiation?

SELECTED READINGS

Chapter 1: Natural Conditions of Human Society

Calder, Ritchie: *The Inheritors: The Story of Man and the World He Made,* William Heinemann, Ltd., London, 1961.

Clark, George L.: *Elements of Ecology,* John Wiley & Sons, Inc., New York, 1954.

Cook, Robert C.: *Human Fertility: The Modern Dilemma,* William Sloane Associates, New York, 1951.

Eversley, D.: *Social Theories of Fertility and the Malthusian Debate,* Oxford University Press, Fair Lawn, N.J., 1959.

Firey, Walter: *Man, Mind and Land,* The Free Press of Glencoe, New York, 1960.

Halbwachs, Maurice: *Population and Society: Introduction to Social Morphology,* Otis Dudley Duncan and Harold W. Pfautz (trans.), The Free Press of Glencoe, New York, 1960.

Hauser, Philip M., and Otis Dudley Duncan (eds.): *The Study of Population: An Inventory and Appraisal,* The University of Chicago Press, Chicago, 1959.

Hofstadter, Richard: *Social Darwinism in American Thought,* University of Pennsylvania Press, Philadelphia, 1945.

Huntington, Ellsworth: *Principles of Human Geography,* 5th ed., John Wiley & Sons, Inc., New York, 1940.

Lewinsohn, Richard: *Animals, Men and Myths,* Harper & Row, Publishers, Incorporated, New York, 1954.

Markham, S. F.: *Climate and the Energy of Nations,* Oxford University Press, Fair Lawn, N.J., 1947.

Osborn, Frederick: *This Crowded World,* Public Affairs Committee, Inc., New York, 1960.

Scheinfeld, Amram: *The New You and Heredity,* J. B. Lippincott Company, Philadelphia, 1950.

Vogt, William: *People: Challenge to Survival,* William Sloane Associates, New York, 1960.

Wagner, Philip: *The Human Use of the Earth,* The Free Press of Glencoe, New York, 1960.

Zinsser, Hans: *Rats, Lice and History,* Little, Brown and Company, Boston, 1935.

Znaniecki, Florian: *Cultural Sciences: Their Origin and Development,* The University of Illinois Press, Urbana, Ill., 1952.

Chapter 2: Basic Aspects of Human Society

Benedict, Ruth: *Patterns of Culture,* Houghton Mifflin Company, Boston, 1934.

Edel, Abraham: *Ethical Judgment: The Use of Science in Ethics,* The Free Press of Glencoe, New York, 1955.

Faris, Ellsworth: *The Nature of Human Nature,* McGraw-Hill Book Company, Inc., New York, 1937.

Feibleman, James K.: *The Theory of Human Culture,* Duell, Sloan & Pearce, Inc., New York, 1946.

Herskovits, Melville J.: *Man and His Works,* Alfred A. Knopf, Inc., New York, 1948.

Hobhouse, L. T., G. C. Wheeler, and M. Ginsberg: *The Material Culture and Social Institutions of the Simpler Peoples,* Chapman & Hall, Ltd., London, 1950.

Huizinga, J.: *Homo Ludens,* Roy Publishers, New York, 1950.

Kluckhohn, Clyde: *Mirror for Man,* McGraw-Hill Book Company, Inc., New York, 1949.

Kroeber, A. L.: *The Nature of Culture,* The University of Chicago Press, Chicago, 1952.

Linton, Ralph: *The Study of Man,* Appleton-Century-Crofts, Inc., New York, 1936.

————: *The Tree of Culture,* Alfred A. Knopf, Inc., New York, 1955.

Malinowski, B.: *A Scientific Theory of Culture,* The University of North Carolina Press, Chapel Hill, N.C., 1944.

Murdock, George Peter: *Social Structure,* The Macmillan Company, New York, 1949.

Pieper, Josef: *Leisure: The Basis of Culture,* Pantheon Books, a Division of Random House, Inc., New York, 1952.

White, Leslie A.: *The Science of Culture,* Farrar, Straus & Cudahy, Inc., New York, 1949.

Chapter 3: The Acquisition of Culture

Brim, Orville G., Jr., David C. Glass, David E. Lavin, and Norman Goodman: *Personality and Decision Processes: Studies in the Social Psychology of Thinking,* Stanford University Press, Stanford, Calif., 1962.

Cooley, Charles Horton: *Human Nature and the Social Order,* The Free Press of Glencoe, New York, 1956.

Erikson, Erik H.: *Childhood and Society,* W. W. Norton & Company, Inc., New York, 1950.

Faris, Ellsworth: *The Nature of Human Nature,* McGraw-Hill Book Company, Inc., New York, 1937.

Faris, Robert E. L.: "Reflections on the Ability Dimension in Human Society," *American Sociological Review*, vol. 26, pp. 835–843, December, 1961.

Freud, Sigmund: *The Basic Writings of Sigmund Freud*, with an introduction by A. A. Brill (trans. and ed.), Vintage Books, Random House, Inc., New York, 1938.

Goffman, Erving: *The Presentation of Self in Everyday Life*, Social Sciences Research Center, University of Edinburgh, Edinburgh, 1956. (Available also in Anchor Books, Doubleday & Company, Inc., Garden City, N.Y., 1959.)

Hall, Calvin, and Gardner Lindzey: *Theories of Personality*, John Wiley & Sons, Inc., New York, 1957.

Inkeles, Alex: "Personality and Social Structure," in Robert K. Merton, Leonard Broom, and Leonard S. Cottrell, Jr. (eds.), *Sociology Today*, Basic Books, Inc., Publishers, New York, 1959, pp. 249–275.

Kardiner, Abram, et al.: *The Psychological Frontiers of Society*, Columbia University Press, New York, 1945.

Klapper, Joseph T.: *The Effects of Mass Communication*, The Free Press of Glencoe, New York, 1960.

Kluckhohn, Clyde, H. A. Murray, and D. M. Schneider (eds.): *Personality in Nature, Society and Culture*, Alfred A. Knopf, Inc., New York, 1954.

Linton, Ralph: *The Cultural Background of Personality*, Appleton-Century-Crofts, Inc., New York, 1945.

Mead, George Herbert: *Mind, Self, and Society*, The University of Chicago Press, Chicago, 1934.

Mead, Margaret: *Sex and Temperament in Three Primitive Societies*, William Morrow and Company, Inc., New York, 1935.

Rieff, Philip: *Freud: The Mind of the Moralist*, Anchor Books, Doubleday & Company, Inc., Garden City, N.Y., 1961.

Rose, Arnold M. (ed.): *Human Behavior and Social Processes*, Houghton Mifflin Company, Boston, 1962.

Shibutani, Tamotsu: *Society and Personality: An Interactionist Approach to Social Psychology*, Prentice-Hall, Inc., Englewood Cliffs, N.J., 1961.

Sprott, W. J. H.: *Social Psychology*, Methuen & Co., Ltd., London, 1956.

Strauss, Anselm (ed.): *The Social Psychology of George Herbert Mead*, Phoenix Books, The University of Chicago Press, Chicago, 1962.

Turner, Ralph H.: "The Problem of Social Dimensions in Personality," *Pacific Sociological Review*, vol. 4, pp. 57–62, Fall, 1961.

Chapter 4: Social Organization

Albig, William: *Modern Public Opinion*, McGraw-Hill Book Company, Inc., New York, 1956.

Aristotle, *Politics*.

Berger, Morroe, Theodore Abel, and Charles H. Page (eds.): *Freedom and Control in Modern Society,* D. Van Nostrand Company, Inc., Princeton, N.J., 1954.

Blau, Peter M.: *Bureaucracy in Modern Society,* Random House, Inc., New York, 1956.

Cartwright, Dorwin, and Alvin F. Zander (eds.): *Group Dynamics: Research and Theory,* Harper & Row, Publishers, Incorporated, New York, 1953.

Etzioni, Amitai (ed.): *Complex Organizations: A Sociological Reader,* Holt, Rinehart and Winston, Inc., New York, 1961.

Feibleman, James K.: *The Institutions of Society,* George Allen & Unwin, Ltd., London, 1956.

Gouldner, Alvin W.: *Patterns of Industrial Bureaucracy,* The Free Press of Glencoe, New York, 1954.

Gross, Neal, Ward S. Mason, and Alexander W. McEachern: *Explorations in Role Analysis,* John Wiley & Sons, Inc., New York, 1958.

Haire, Mason (ed.): *Modern Organization Theory,* John Wiley & Sons, Inc., New York, 1959.

Hart, H. L. A.: *The Concept of Law,* Oxford University Press, Fair Lawn, N.J., 1961.

Homans, George C.: *The Human Group,* Harcourt, Brace & World, Inc., New York, 1950.

————: *Social Behavior: Its Elementary Forms,* Harcourt, Brace & World, Inc., New York, 1961.

Key, V. O., Jr.: *Politics, Parties, and Pressure Groups,* 3d ed., Thomas Y. Crowell Company, New York, 1952.

LaPiere, Richard T.: *A Theory of Social Control,* McGraw-Hill Book Company, Inc., New York, 1954.

Lerner, Daniel, and Harold D. Lasswell (eds.): *The Policy Sciences,* Stanford University Press, Stanford, Calif., 1951.

Linton, Ralph: *The Study of Man,* Appleton-Century-Crofts, Inc., New York, 1936.

MacIver, Robert M.: *The Web of Government,* The Macmillan Company, New York, 1947.

———— and Charles H. Page: *Society: An Introductory Analysis,* Holt, Rinehart and Winston, Inc., New York, 1949.

Merton, Robert K.: *Social Theory and Social Structure,* The Free Press of Glencoe, New York, 1949.

Parsons, Talcott: *The Social System,* The Free Press of Glencoe, New York, 1951.

Petrazycki, Leon: *Law and Morality,* Hugh W. Babb (trans.), Harvard University Press, Cambridge, Mass., 1955.

Presthus, Robert: *The Organizational Society,* Alfred A. Knopf, Inc., New York, 1962.

Riesman, David: *Individualism Reconsidered,* The Free Press of Glencoe, New York, 1954.

———— with Nathan Glazer and Reuel Denney: *The Lonely Crowd,* Yale University Press, New Haven, Conn., 1950.

Rose, Arnold M. (ed.): *Human Behavior and Social Processes,* Houghton Mifflin Company, Boston, 1962.

Russell, Bertrand: *Authority and the Individual,* Simon and Schuster, Inc., New York, 1949.

Simon, Herbert A.: *Administrative Behavior,* 2d ed., The Macmillan Company, New York, 1957.

Truman, David B.: *The Governmental Process,* Alfred A. Knopf, Inc., New York, 1951.

Weber, Max: *The Theory of Social and Economic Organization,* A. M. Henderson and Talcott Parsons (trans.), Oxford University Press, Fair Lawn, N.J., 1947.

Whyte, William F.: *Street Corner Society,* The University of Chicago Press, Chicago, 1943.

Whyte, William H., Jr.: *The Organization Man,* Simon and Schuster, Inc., New York, 1956.

Williams, Robin M., Jr.: *American Society: A Sociological Interpretation,* Alfred A. Knopf, Inc., New York, 1951.

Znaniecki, Florian: *Cultural Sciences: Their Origin and Development,* The University of Illinois Press, Urbana, Ill., 1952.

————: *The Social Role of the Man of Knowledge,* Columbia University Press, New York, 1940.

Chapter 5: Social Differentiation

Allport, Gordon W.: *The Nature of Prejudice,* Beacon Press, Boston, 1954.

Amory, Cleveland: *The Proper Bostonians,* E. P. Dutton & Co., Inc., New York, 1947.

Anshen, Ruth Nanda (ed.): *The Family: Its Function and Destiny,* Harper & Row, Publishers, Incorporated, New York, 1949.

Baber, Ray E.: *Marriage and the Family,* 2d ed., McGraw-Hill Book Company, Inc., New York, 1953.

Barber, Bernard: *Social Stratification,* Harcourt, Brace & World, Inc., New York, 1957.

de Beauvoir, Simone: *The Second Sex,* H. M. Parshley (trans.), Alfred A. Knopf, Inc., New York, 1953.

Bergel, Egon Ernest: *Social Stratification,* McGraw-Hill Book Company, Inc., New York, 1962.

Bernard, Jessie: *American Community Behavior,* The Dryden Press, Inc., New York, 1949.

Ditzion, Sidney: *Marriage, Morals, and Sex in America,* Bookman Associates, New York, 1953.

Dobriner, William M. (ed.): *The Suburban Community*, G. P. Putnam's Sons, New York, 1958.

Dollard, John: *Caste and Class in a Southern Town*, 2d ed., Harper & Row, Publishers, Incorporated, New York, 1949.

Elliott, Mabel A., and Francis E. Merrill: *Social Disorganization*, 4th ed., Harper & Row, Publishers, Incorporated, New York, 1961.

Gottmann, Jean: *Megalopolis: The Urbanized Northeastern Seaboard of the United States*, The Twentieth Century Fund, New York, 1961.

Greer, Scott: *The Emerging City: Myth and Reality*, The Free Press of Glencoe, New York, 1962.

Hoffer, Eric: *The True Believer*, Harper & Row, Publishers, Incorporated, New York, 1951.

Hoyt, Homer: *World Urbanization: Expanding Population in a Shrinking World*, Urban Land Institute, Washington, D.C., 1962.

Kahl, Joseph A.: *The American Class Structure*, Holt, Rinehart and Winston, Inc., New York, 1957.

Kenkel, William F.: *The Family in Perspective: A Fourfold Analysis*, Appleton-Century-Crofts, Inc., New York, 1960.

Kirkpatrick, Clifford: *The Family as Process and Institution*, The Ronald Press Company, New York, 1955.

Komarovsky, Mirra: *Women in the Modern World*, Little, Brown and Company, Boston, 1953.

Lipset, Seymour M., and Reinhard Bendix: *Social Mobility in Industrial Society*, University of California Press, Berkeley, Calif., 1959.

Lynd, Robert S., and Helen M. Lynd: *Middletown*, Harcourt, Brace & World, Inc., New York, 1929.

———— and ————: *Middletown in Transition*, Harcourt, Brace & World, Inc., New York, 1937.

Mead, Margaret, *Male and Female*, William Morrow and Company, Inc., New York, 1949.

Mills, C. Wright: *The Power Elite*, Oxford University Press, Fair Lawn, N.J., 1956.

————: *White Collar: The American Middle Classes*, Oxford University Press, Fair Lawn, N.J., 1951.

Mosca, Gaetano: *The Ruling Class*, Arthur Livingston (ed.), McGraw-Hill Book Company, Inc., New York, 1939.

Mumford, Lewis: *The City in History: Its Origins, Its Transformations, and Its Prospects*, Harcourt, Brace & World, Inc., New York, 1961.

Myrdal, Gunnar: *An American Dilemma*, rev. ed., Harper & Row, Publishers, Incorporated, New York, 1962.

Nimkoff, Meyer F.: *Marriage and the Family*, Houghton Mifflin Company, Boston, 1947.

Park, Robert E., Ernest W. Burgess, and R. D. McKenzie: *The City*, The University of Chicago Press, Chicago, 1956.

Parsons, Talcott: *Essays in Sociological Theory*, rev. ed., The Free Press of Glencoe, New York, 1954.

Pirenne, Henri: *Medieval Cities*, Frank D. Halsey (trans.), Princeton University Press, Princeton, N.J., 1946.

Reissman, Leonard: *Class in American Society*, Routledge & Kegan Paul, Ltd., London, 1959.

Scheinfeld, Amram: *Women and Men*, Harcourt, Brace & World, Inc., New York, 1943.

UNESCO: *Race and Science: The Race Question in Modern Science*, Columbia University Press, New York, 1961.

Weber, Max: *The City*, Don Martindale and Gertrud Neuwirth (trans. and eds.), Collier Books, a division of Crowell-Collier Publishing Co., New York, 1962.

Winch, Robert F.: *The Modern Family*, Holt, Rinehart and Winston, Inc., New York, 1952.

Wood, Robert C., with Vladimir V. Almendinger: *1400 Governments: The Political Economy of the New York Metropolitan Region*, Harvard University Press, Cambridge, Mass., 1961.

Young, Kimball: *Isn't One Wife Enough?* Holt, Rinehart and Winston, Inc., New York, 1954.

Zimmerman, Carle C.: *Family and Civilization*, Harper & Brothers, New York, 1947.

Znaniecki, Florian: *Modern Nationalities*, The University of Illinois Press, Urbana, Ill., 1952.

PART 2

The
Political
Order

The study of political affairs is one of the oldest of all academic disciplines, though modern political science is a child of the twentieth century. Both Plato and Aristotle, for example, produced systematic treatises on politics more than two thousand years ago, and they apparently taught the subject in their respective schools in Athens. Nearly every generation has added something to our store of political writings, yet the subject remains fresh and significant—the basic questions have not been answered for all time. Perhaps this is the major reason why politics retains its interest; it is obviously important, yet the problems it poses cannot be solved once and for all. Each new generation is entitled to look upon politics as a new problem, a new game which offers opportunities to try new players, new strategies, and new techniques. So long as men continue to live in society, the need for political institutions will remain, and with it the perennial need to ponder and discuss political affairs.

In this section of the text, we attempt to identify the basic problems in politics and indicate the factors that must be considered when man seeks to solve them. We can also see how men have solved their political difficulties in the past and perhaps suggest some of the consequences of the many different approaches to politics that have appeared in our history. The aim, in brief, is to lay a foundation for more detailed study. We cannot, of course, produce anything like a final solution in politics.

Approaches to politics. Political science, which is the discipline concerned with political associations and institutions and practices, has grown very rapidly in the past half century, particularly in the United States. For the student, this rapid expansion has some important consequences. In the first place, growth has led to specialization and concentration and to an enormous increase in the amount of specialized information available in the many academic publications. A modest university department of political science may offer as many as two or three dozen separate courses in politics, ranging from political parties and local government to international organization or political philosophy. The subject matter has been divided and then divided again as specialization increased until it is now almost a hopeless task to attempt to summarize all of the work being done, even in the major branches of the discipline.

A second problem arises out of the proliferation of "approaches" to the study of political affairs in the past two decades. Before World War II, political scientists were usually oriented to the study of political institutions and their operation, and most political science materials were grounded in political history. More recently, dissatisfaction with institutional studies and concern for methodological problems have led to the development of various alternative approaches to the subject. The result has been a certain amount of confusion and the development of "schools" of political science, each taking a rather different approach to the subject matter. Again, the consequences are too complex to attempt to deal with them comprehensively in an introductory text of this sort.

Though an exhaustive treatment of the different approaches to political science cannot be made here, the student ought to be aware of certain basic methodological problems arising in political science and the manner in which they are being attacked, for they will probably appear in any further reading that may be assigned. The point at issue here is really fairly simple, though the solution may be complex. Every academic discipline must deal with two fundamental problems: it must collect information or data and it must organize or structure its data to provide explanations that are meaningful. Each of these tasks poses some serious obstacles for the student, particularly in a new discipline where the most suitable approach to the subject matter has not yet been decided.

With regard to the data collected, there are two possible areas of disagreement: first, the *type* of data to be collected; and second, the *quality* of the data that ought to be demanded. That is, political scientists may look for information through historical studies, they may examine institutional arrangements in various political associations, they may seek an explanation of the manner by which society makes its political decisions, or they may concern themselves with the psychological, cultural, and other factors that bear on the political process, among others, and each kind of emphasis will lead to a slightly different kind of information. Since the discipline is still new, there is no real agreement on the type of information that ought to be considered, and some political scientists stress one type of investigation while others seek information by different channels. This need cause no serious difficulty so long as we realize that no single group has a monopoly on political study, that no particular approach to politics is exclusive and final. But it does make it difficult to produce a standard approach to politics which can be used to introduce the student to the subject.

At another level of investigation, the political scientist must decide whether or not he will limit himself to empirical evidence, which the physical sciences, for example, would accept, or whether the study of human society demands a different qualitative standard of evidence. Some political scientists argue that the study of politics should be limited strictly to empirical evidence; others believe that this is too constricting and that subjective evidence must be accepted. Again, this is not easily decided, and there are eminent authorities on both sides of the question.

An even more serious difficulty arises when political scientists attempt to organize their information into meaningful patterns. At one extreme, some scholars argue that it is not really possible to produce structured explanations of politics because such patterns presume that there is some absolute political pattern, like the pattern of planetary movements, which is to be discovered, whereas no such model exists in human society. But others believe that meaningful intellectual structures are possible and have attempted to produce them. One such approach suggests that politics is best considered as a "game" between competing players pursuing goals which are antithetical within a given framework of rules. Another seeks to structure political information into "systems of action" which take into consideration the various influences at work in the political sphere. A third concerns itself with the process by which political decisions are made, and attempts to formulate its data so as to arrive at a better understanding of decision making. Others, more traditional perhaps, are concerned with power relationships within society, or with the manner in which political associations define and protect their vital interests. All of these approaches to politics provide insights into the political process that may be useful, and so long as no single approach is maintained dogmatically, the practice of attacking political problems by diverse methods is probably salutary, but it does add to the problems of the textbook writer.

Finally, there is considerable disagreement within the discipline over the use that should be made of value judgments, or normative arguments, in political science. Some "scientific" scholars aver that political scientists ought to follow the physical sciences and make no effort to provide normative criticism of political institutions and practices. Others believe that politics is essentially a process for making value judgments and that political science has some obligation to exercise its critical faculty in this area too. The difficulty lies in the fact that value judgments cannot be derived logically from factual data, but must be justified by some other means; they are not either true or false in the empirically verifiable sense. Again, there is no way in which the discussion can be settled; each student must choose for himself that approach to the problem which satisfies his conception of the proper role of political science in modern society.[1]

Under these conditions, it seems unlikely that an agreed approach to political science will appear for some years. It is hardly surprising, then, that introductory texts in political science vary greatly in form, in content, in emphasis, and in the kind of analysis of political affairs that they use. The approach taken in this textbook is somewhat traditional in that it seeks to avoid a commitment to any one particular approach to political study, and, at the same time, seeks to provide the student with an understanding and appreciation of the kinds of problems that politics involves and the manner in which their solution may be attempted.

The aim of the text. In a preliminary text, we cannot hope to produce a complete summary of the vast area encompassed by modern political science or even to indicate the results that have been obtained by the use of different techniques of political analysis. Nor can we undertake a detailed examination of our own political system; that is best left to a course in American government. But political life, in every society and in every age, is characterized by the search for a solution to certain broad general problems, and their importance is no less great in our own time than in previous eras. A clear understanding of the manner by which man has arrived at his present stage of political development, of the key issues which have had to be resolved in the historical development of present institutions, seems a necessary prerequisite to any detailed analysis of present-day political affairs. Furthermore, if we can

[1] For further consideration of the kind of problem raised here, see, for example, Roland Young (ed.), *Approaches to the Study of Politics*, Northwestern University Press, Evanston, Ill., 1958; Charles S. Hyneman, *The Study of Politics: The Present State of American Political Science*, The University of Illinois Press, Urbana, Ill., 1959; S. Sidney Ulmer (ed.), *Introductory Readings in Political Behavior*, Rand McNally & Company, Chicago, 1961; David Easton, *The Political System*, Alfred A. Knopf, Inc., New York, 1959.

grasp the fundamental value structure implicit in different kinds of political arrangements, past or present, it becomes much easier to keep the basic issues of political life in their proper perspective. It is the aim of this text to provide this fundamental substructure, to produce a foundation on which further knowledge and appreciation of political affairs can be built.

In the present state of political science, an eclectic approach of this kind seems unavoidable. Detailed concern with the problems of methodology and technique, or with the operation of particular political associations, is more appropriate to a text devoted entirely to the study of politics. Here, we need to examine political science as one of the special branches of social science, a discipline which deals with a particular kind of social organization, with a particular type of social problem. The discipline lies somewhere between the study of economics and the study of music or philosophy. Political science is much less precise than economics but more exact than the humanities. It most closely resembles sociology, and might really be considered a special branch of that discipline. Politics, in other words, lies suspended somewhere between the arts and the sciences, sharing a little of each. Some political scientists prefer to emphasize the scientific aspects of their discipline, emulating the sciences; others are more conscious of the less precisely definable aspects of politics, tending to regard the discipline as more of an art than a science.

A preview. We are concerned here with politics as a whole, with the entire complex of associations and institutions and practices which are involved in political action, and not with politics in one particular society or of one particular type. Viewed broadly in this way, man's political life is as rich and varied as his physical environment. Political associations may be large or small, rich or poor, liberal or authoritarian, democratic or dictatorial, peaceful or violent. Virtually all men live in the form of political association that we call the modern state, yet some men live as free citizens, relatively unhindered by the activities of the state, while others are subject to state control and direction in almost every phase of their existence. We must, it seems, seek a framework which will permit us to make meaningful comparisons of political associations—basic questions which will underline and emphasize the fundamental distinctions among the various political associations.

The first set of problems arises out of the very existence of the modern national state, for it is a relatively recent phenomenon, and it differs greatly from the kind of political organization previously found in Western civilization. How did the modern state develop? How does it differ from its predecessors? What are its more important characteristics? These problems occupy our attention in Chapter 6, where we attempt to trace the development of the state system and outline the major features of the state in our own day.

The second set of questions that must be considered is related to the fact that political organization creates political authority, and the manner in which authority is allocated and employed is of great moment for those who live in society. How much authority does the state claim over its citizens, for example? All states claim to be sovereign in their own territory, but all states do not actually exercise sovereign authority over every phase of social life. How much sovereign authority is left to the individual? This is one of our best indications of the extent to which human freedom is meaningful in particular political associations. How is authority justified? How is it allocated among the various statuses in society? Is it concentrated in a few hands or dispersed among many? Are there many levels of government, each with meaningful authority, or only a single all-powerful central authority? How is authority limited? Is it divided among different political offices, one serving to check the other? Is there a constitution, a fundamental document which prescribes the limits on political authority and its use? Such questions have immediate, personal significance for those who must live subject to political authority, and the manner in which they are answered will greatly affect our evaluation of the political association being studied. They form the central topic of Chapter 7.

A third major problem that arises in every political association has to do with the political process, with the manner by which political authority is transferred or used and the role of the population in the process. Is the franchise meaningful? How widely is it dispersed? Do political parties operate as instruments of the state or as free organizations which the citizenry may use to seek political power? Is violence a commonplace in the political process, or is it eschewed as a means of acquiring power? If the system makes use of elected representatives, are they bound by the wishes of their constituency, or are they free to make their own best judgments? Broadly, we are asking whether the political process is "open" to the citizens, or whether it is in some manner "closed" or limited to particular groups or individuals. This congeries of problems is considered in Chapter 8.

The fourth major problem area in modern politics is concerned with the relationship between political authority and the economic system which the society employs. What role does the state play in economic affairs? Is it limited to defining the rules by which economic activity is conducted, or does it interfere in economic affairs to redress injustices that may arise out of the operation of the economic system? Is political government responsible for maintaining the economic system and preventing stagnation and widespread misery? We find that there are four major approaches to the problems of political-economic relations in modern times: one is typified by the United States, which combines an open political system with a modest regulatory function over economic matters; a second, exemplified by British democratic socialism, suggests a combination of political democracy with some measure of government ownership of industry and a substantial welfare program; a third solution, identified with the writings of Karl Marx, combines a fully controlled economy with a closed political system in which the population has little or no voice; and finally, the fascist solution attempts to combine a militant political dictatorship with a private capitalist economic system, controlled by the government through giant corporations. These political-economic problems are considered in Chapter 9.

A fifth basic group of political problems, which has increased greatly in significance in modern times, arises out of the relations among national states, out of international affairs. Here, we need to ask about the basic characteristics of the state system as it has developed in modern times. What institutions do governments use in their relations with one another and how well do they function? What, for example, is the function and purpose of international organizations, of diplomacy, of war? Such questions are concerned with the total system: They give us a bird's-eye view of the operation of the system of states in which we live. We can also look at international affairs from the standpoint of the single state—at foreign policy. We need to ask how foreign relations are managed; where authority is vested for making foreign policy and how it is exercised; what role the general population plays in foreign relations, even in an open society; and what part military necessity may have in the behavior of particular states. Here we can use our own country as an illustration, examining some of the major problems that have arisen in recent decades. Discussion of these matters is reserved for Chapter 10.

These five problem areas could, of course, be greatly augmented. But they are sufficient for a basic analysis of political affairs and the problems arising out of them, and they set the stage for a discussion of contemporary political problems in Chapter 19.

CHAPTER 6

The Changing Pattern of Politics

Long before men began to write history, or even to produce the artifacts of archaeological study, political institutions were playing a vital role in the life of man. There is no need to ponder the origins of the political association, for it arises "naturally" out of the needs of social life. Where men live together in groups, the actions of one man necessarily impinge upon the actions of another, and some social instrument is needed to regulate and control common affairs. Of course, this "political" regulation can be performed by associations that we would not today consider political, and this was doubtless the case in the past. The family, for example, was responsible for detecting and punishing crime in many societies until quite recently, whereas today we assume that this function is proper to a political association. Virtually every human group on earth has produced some form of political association and formalized its functions and authority, though these associations differ enormously in detail. In this chapter, we are concerned with the salient characteristics of modern political associations and with the major phases in their development, particularly in Western Europe.

GENERAL CONSIDERATIONS

In the political history of man, it is the "glamorous" events like war and revolution that capture our attention; they are the landmarks by which we chart a course through the maze of history. Yet we must not lose sight of the fact that these great explosions are usually the culmination of a sequence of less notable events. As an illustration, it would be foolish, for example, to assert that World War I began *because of* the assassination of the Austrian Archduke, for that was only one trifling incident in a very complex historical sequence. Political change proceeds slowly and steadily, though the pace may quicken from time to time, and it is very difficult to determine the trend of politics in the age in which one lives. If we are aware of the dynamic nature of politics, however, we may look for signs of change in our own time, not in terms of great outbursts, but in that gradual alteration of political structure and process that is so persistent a factor in every political system.

The modern state, for example, appeared on the scene only a few hundred years ago, and already it has gone through a number of phases of development, each different from its predecessors. Furthermore it seems likely that the national state, as presently constituted, is unlikely to fill man's needs in the indefinite future, for there are already signs of weakness in the structure. Very often, contemporary criticism of the state system has been coupled with naïve and unrealistic demands for an immediate "world government" of some sort, and this has tended to reduce its effectiveness by making "crackpots" of the critics. Yet the national states themselves have admitted the inadequacy of the state system to the extent that they have produced international organizations of various sorts to cope with problems that the state cannot manage alone. Furthermore, many such organizations are concerned with very fundamental matters, such as national security and national health, which are considered the prime responsibility of the political association. In other words, there seems already to be a genuine need for political associations—perhaps of a type quite different from the modern state—which can perform functions beyond the state's competence. Whether this need will force a change in the state system we cannot say with certainty, but the future of the national state is today much less secure than it appeared perhaps a century ago.

Political institutions tend to develop according to the way they are used, according to the demands that are made upon them. When the existing political structure cannot perform the tasks which society demands, it will almost certainly change. An obvious example is the extent to which political systems alter during periods of crisis such as wars or natural disasters. Such changes may occur in either the formal or the informal political structure, but they are more likely to appear in the latter. The formal position of the British Crown, for example, has altered little in centuries, but in practice the king today "reigns but does not rule." The informal political system severely limits the authority of the monarch. Similarly, the formal political system in the United States has remained fairly constant since the Constitution was adopted, but the informal political system has altered greatly.

Political institutions are also strongly influenced by the physical and social environments in which they develop. The influence of geographic factors, such as climate, resources, and topography, is fairly obvious. The Soviet Union is a very large state, but it has a serious agricultural problem because, lying in roughly the same latitude as Canada, much of its land is too cold, too dry, too mountainous, etc., to be used for food production. British political development has been influenced in various ways by the fact that Britain is an island, separated from the European mainland by the English Channel. The history of the United States would be quite different if we were located nearer to Europe, or to Asia, or if our resources were different. Modern technology can, of course, compensate for some physical handicaps, but even technology is helpless if the basic resources needed for technological advance are not present.

The physical environment is an important influence molding the pattern of political activity of man, but the social environment cannot be left out of our calculations. It is often said that the American "way of life" cannot be exported, particularly to the newly emerging nations in Africa and Asia, because the physical conditions in these countries cannot support it. This is certainly true, but we must bear in mind the fact that social traditions may also inhibit the transfer of political structures from one nation to another. We can see this easily if we reverse the process. The political institutions of Saudi Arabia could hardly be transferred to the United States, not because the physical resources needed to support it are lacking, but because it would be incompatible with our social and political traditions.

The point is that political institutions are deeply embedded in the total structure of human society, in the social, economic, military, religious, and other practices of human groups. Identical political machinery may function quite differently in two different environments: both the United States and the Soviet Union, for example, are formally federal systems, yet the resemblance is only superficial and not meaningful. As political scientists, we must attempt to isolate the political, leaving other aspects of society to the sociologist, the economist, the anthropologist, and other social scientists. The separation is always artificial, and it generates inaccuracies and incompleteness. As an academic device, it is useful and even necessary, but we must remember that it is only a device, and not a reflection of some "true" condition of society.

The diversity of political systems. The diversity of political institutions, the variety of political associations, is one of the more striking features of modern politics. This makes the task of the political scientist more difficult, for he must be reasonably systematic if he is to be meaningful, yet his approach to political questions must be broad enough to encompass the significant variations in structure and process that appear in the various political societies. The political scientist faces a world filled with "beasts" of various descriptions, and unlike the zoologist, he has not yet managed to produce a definitive system for classifying them. In zoology, animals are classified together on the basis of similarities and differences in form, structure, and function, and grouped into a regular pyramid in which every animal has its place. Thus far, no one has produced a similar taxonomy for political associations, nor can we develop one here.

However, it is possible to introduce some measure of order and arrangement into political study, so long as we realize that our classification is incomplete and that other approaches to the problem may also be quite useful. Karl Marx, for example, decided that the economic structure of society, the ownership of the means of production, was *the* key to political institutions, and he built his system on that basis. As *one* approach to politics, Marx's scheme is both interesting and useful, for it underlines the importance of economics in political development; as the *only* approach to politics it is faulty and misleading, for there is more to politics than economic relations.

Of the many attempts that have been made to classify political associations, we will mention only one more very early and very famous example. The Greek philosopher Aristotle, in a book entitled *Politics,* divided all governments into three basic types: (1) rule by one person, (2) rule by a few persons, and (3) rule by many persons. Each type had two alternate forms, one "good" and one "perverted." Thus the good form of rule by one man he termed kingship; the perverted form he called tyranny. Rule by the few could be aristocratic (good) or oligarchical (bad). Rule by the many could be a democracy (bad) or a polity (good). Aristotle's low opinion of democracy is largely due to his definition of the term, for democracy meant, to him, rule by the poor in their own favor. His "polity" is somewhat closer to the modern democratic ideal, though they are not identical. Using this classification system, Aristotle produced a detailed and often acute analysis of the changes that occurred in the political societies of his day, and many of his comments are still useful and penetrating.

In this text, we will concentrate upon the modern state as a basic political structure and attempt to deal systematically with the major political systems that have developed within the broad framework which the state provides. Thus the present chapter attempts a brief summary of the development of the modern state as a whole, indicating the major stages of its history, and some of the principal features of each stage. In the chapters that follow, the modern state is examined in greater detail, stressing the fundamental differences that have appeared within the state system and some of their consequences. This will not, of course, produce a zoologist's classification of political systems, but it can provide the broad framework which is needed for understanding the political process of our own time.

CITY-STATES

Western man has had a fascinating political history, and it has been paralleled in many respects by the political history of non-Western nations, such as China. Some knowledge of the major features of that history can help us to appreciate the complexities of our own age; history illuminates the present, whether or not it is a guide to the future. Very broadly, we can identify three major stages in the political development of the West, each marked by characteristic structures, processes, and values. The first stage is marked by the appearance of the *city-state,* which emerges in Greece some seven hundred years before the birth of Christ, and lasts, in modified form, until the collapse of the Roman Empire in the fifth century. The second stage, which we refer to as the *feudal system,* appears in Western Europe after the collapse of the Roman Empire and remains the dominant structure for several centuries. The third stage, the *modern state* system, appears in Europe around the beginning of the fifteenth century, and remains, in modified form, the dominant political institution of the present age.

This historical division must be used with care. Many of the political systems which preceded the Greek city-states in time shared various characteristics of the later form of political association, and there were great differences among the city-states themselves. Feudalism too is a loose and awkward term, for it differed from country to country and from one time to another; it was not a single, clearly defined structure. And the differences among modern states will already be known to the reader, though perhaps not systematically. In other words, each of these divisions is a broad range or spectrum, and particular associations may fall anywhere on the range. Our task, then, is to define first the general characteristics of each stage of development, and then indicate some of the major variations that appeared within this framework.

The role of the city. Before proceeding to a detailed discussion of the city-state, we ought to give some attention to the role of the city in the political life of man. Politics, after all, has been and continues to be centered in the city, whether we discuss ancient Greece or modern America. The development of cities has paralleled the growth of civilization and the diversification of culture, and political institutions have their roots firmly embedded in the needs of city life.

Until modern times, the city served man as a natural center for his economic, social, political, and military activity. The city was a defense center, the goal of attacking armies, and the focus of economic activities, such as trade and commerce, banking, and manufacturing. It is no accident that most ancient cities lay along the great trade routes; access to transportation is still an important factor in city development. Cities were a natural center for government, for cities require governing. The intensification of social relations in cities, magnified by the effect of close economic and social relationships, unquestionably demands more social regulation than rural regions require. The laws of large nations are directed mainly toward the kind of activity that we associate primarily with urban life, and not toward the social relations that characterize the rural area. The city is now and seems likely to remain the center of political life.

The city-state. The city-state was a social arrangement which combined the population of a central city with the residents of the surrounding countryside into a single coherent social unit. It originated in Greece, perhaps because the mountainous terrain generated natural divisions which encouraged the formation of small-scale associations. Originally, the city was probably a fortress, just as many American cities originated as a stockade constructed by the early settlers for protection against attack. Doubtless the city also served as a center for religious observance, and in time as a political, economic, and cultural center. But the Greek cities were not the first cities, and we need to ask why the Greek city-state is entitled to be considered a new political form.

There is no simple answer to this question. Doubtless, the accomplishments of the Greeks in philosophy and learning have much to do with the respect they are accorded in Western civilization. But it is also true that the city-state system gradually replaced the earlier tribal systems of government as the fundamental political unit in the Western world, bringing with it a new concept of political association. It is one thing for an emperor to rule a vast territory, collecting taxes and tribute from subjects. It is another matter for a group of men to consider themselves *members* of a political society, to believe that their personal fortunes are inextricably bound to the rise or fall of a particular association. The Greeks, in a word, brought us the concepts of citizenship and of politics—our very word for politics comes from the Greek language.

In the early stages of the development of the city-state, the line between tribal association, religious association, and political association is hard to draw—they were intermingled. Gradually they were merged in the wider context of a political association which was all-encompassing; the term citizen came to denote a religious, a tribal, and a political relationship of and by itself. At the zenith of the city-state era, the individual Greek thought of himself as a citizen of a particular city, and this settled his tribal status and his religion, for religion was a function of the city. The city thus became the focus of human life, for the citizens at least, as we can see in the famous Funeral Oration of Pericles. Not until modern times was a similar phenomenon to appear once again in political society.

The city-state, then, produced the same sense of pride in membership, the same in-group feeling, that the modern national state produces in its citizens. The ancient Greeks were "nationalistic" in relation to their cities in a way that medieval man never was, which may explain why it is easy to understand Greek political argument and so very difficult to grasp the point of medieval scholasticism. The Athenian took the same sort of vicarious pride in the beauty and accomplishments of his city that the present-day citizen of the United States takes in the performance of his country; indeed, the Greek was willing to make considerable personal sacrifice in his city's interests. The principal difference between the city-state and the modern state is the size and technology of the society; modern nationalism was an impossibility until some means of standardizing education, information, and social values could be produced and applied to a very large territory. Even the Romans, with their immense empire, were unable to consolidate their holdings into a tight political unit, though the size of the in-group was maximized by judicious granting of citizenship. England, for example, was never an integral part of the Roman Empire in the same sense that Texas has become a part of the United States. The various parts of the Empire remained conquered territories, controlled by an imperial administration and Roman troops. In most essentials, Rome remained a city-state until its demise.

The solidarity of the early Greek city-states doubtless originated in a shared religion. In an interesting if somewhat dated book, Fustel de Coulanges has described the basic significance of religion in the early cities, and his conclusions are still largely acceptable.[1] The rulers of the early cities were a combination of priest, king, and warrior, and the Roman Emperor remained *pontifex maximus,* or chief priest, even at the peak of his political power.

---

[1] Fustel de Coulanges, *The Ancient City,* Doubleday & Company, Inc., Garden City, N. Y., 1956. This is a reprint of the 1873 edition.

Unlike some oriental rulers, the Greek kings seldom regarded themselves as gods personified, but the religious function of the king remained primary for many centuries. In time, as Gilbert Murray points out, the real religion of the Greeks became devotion to the city, and the power of this binding force can be felt in the works that Greek writers, poets, and playwrights, as well as politicians, left behind.[2] The military, political, and religious functions of the king became separated, the former passing to the aristocracy, while the latter remained with the king. The religious ceremonies themselves were formalized, losing their original connections with harvests, fertility, and other natural phenomena. They were attached now to the city-state itself, or to persons associated with its growth, and religion tended to become a ritual by which the citizen expressed his respect for society and its institutions, quite different in conception, of course, from the mystic and personal experience that Christianity today accepts as normal.

The Athenian experience. A brief sketch of the development of Athens, though not representative of all of the Greek cities, for they were highly diversified, will illustrate the general pattern of city-state growth. In the dim recesses of history, the Athenians had a king, who was religious leader, military commander, and political ruler. His military function was taken away and placed in the hands of a polemarch well before the seventh century B.C., and in time the royal house itself was overthrown and an archon or regent assumed power. By the seventh century B.C., the Athenians were ruled by an aristocracy, and the religious, military, and political functions had been separated. The political function seems to have been mainly judicial, and the archon was supreme judge in all civil suits. An aristocratic council, the Areopagus, was the deliberative center for the society.

Economic distress, arising out of changed economic circumstances and a drastic separation of wealthy and poor, led to growing unrest toward the end of the seventh century B.C. The Greeks then resorted to an extraordinary legislator to revise their social structure, first in the code of Dracon (ca. 621) and then in the legislation of Solon (ca. 594–593). Solon in particular made some drastic changes in the system, annulling all debts, freeing the slaves, limiting land ownership, and opening membership in the assembly to the lower classes. The power of the Areopagus continued, however, and Athens remained far from the democracy she was to become later.

Following a period of tyranny (rule by a single person), Athens undertook another set of reforms, beginning with the work of Cleisthenes, who reorganized the subordinate associations of the city in such manner as to

---

[2] Gilbert Murray, *Five States of Greek Religion,* Doubleday & Company, Inc., Garden City, N. Y., 1955. A reprint of the 1951 edition.

break the power of the older tribes. He also instituted the use of the lot for election to the various councils and the use of ostracism as a weapon against citizens seeking personal power at the expense of the community. In the fifth century B.C., under the leadership of Pericles, Athens reached its peak as a democracy. The Council of Areopagus was stripped of all except its ceremonial powers, the archons became paid officials of the state, and all citizens were made eligible for the office. All offices were filled by lot from amongst all of the eligible citizens, and payments were made for services, permitting the poorer citizens to serve. The Athenian democracy became one of the crown jewels in the Western political tradition, an ideal that excited the admiration of men for centuries thereafter. Unfortunately, it was not to endure, partly because of the incessant warfare that raged through Greece and partly because the city-state as an institution could not withstand the imperial armies of Alexander of Macedon, and later of the Romans.

It is interesting to note that the economic division between rich and poor (and the social conflict it created) was a commonplace in the ancient world and a problem that was never satisfactorily solved. The Greek city-states, and Rome as well, suffered from this disease. Some cities like Sparta attempted to eliminate the division into rich and poor by sumptuary laws and by forbidding the use of money or the alienation of land, but to no avail. Land reform was carried out to relieve the tension when it bordered on revolution, both in Rome and Greece, but the effect seemed never to last very long.

It must also be said that the development of a democratic system in Athens was exceptional and not the rule. Not all of the city-states moved toward political democracy, and democracy often degenerated into mob rule, followed by tyranny. It was democratic Athens, after all, that put Socrates to death for leading the young astray with his pernicious doctrines. Internal unrest, or the fear of danger from without, frequently led to the concentration of power in the hands of a single ruler, producing what the Greeks termed a tyranny, and if some tyrannies were benevolent, others were harsh and despotic. In other cases, the weight and power of numbers and the threat of revolution generated a new political force—periods of democratic rule in which the voice of the mass of citizens was dominant. Not many of the Greek political structures would qualify as democracies in the modern sense of the term, of course, but in a few, such as the Athens of Pericles, there appeared a political ideal which still fires the imagination. Here we find the view that government is responsible to the governed, that authority derives from the body of citizens, that law and not the vagaries of individual caprice ought to govern human affairs, the belief that each citizen can and should have an opportunity and an obligation to take part in civic affairs, and that government ought to be conducted in the interests of the entire community. It is an ideal that has done much to shape the direction of modern Western civilization.

The city-state and the citizen. For the Western reader, the relation between the city-state and its citizens, even in an enlightened democracy such as Athens, appears relatively totalitarian. The life of the citizen, his goals, his pleasures, his success, his social activities—all were identified with the life of the city. The Greek citizen acquired his position by birth, and with his citizenship he acquired a religion, economic and social status, and his *raison d'être*. His personal life was subordinated to community life to a degree that would now appear excessive and strange. Each city had its own gods, its own ceremonies, its own rites; each citizen had a part to play in them. Citizenship implied a merger of family, religion, economics, and politics in a single monistic relationship; the life of the citizen was political life. Service to the state was mandatory, extensive, and often expensive. Each citizen shared the burden of maintaining the city, though not always equally; the state could and did demand the citizen's property, his children, and indeed his life or talent or time, to meet its needs. The citizen could be forced to serve in the military establishment, to adorn the city, to provide a trireme for warfare, or to serve in some political capacity when chosen by lot. The Greeks thought this perfectly natural and considered any other political structure primitive and uncivilized.

Today, this type of social arrangement would be deemed collectivism, and in the United States, with its formidable individualistic tradition, the term is used to criticize. But so long as the city proved able to satisfy the social and private needs of man, the Greek was quite content with it. How much he was able to accomplish within that framework we need hardly review here. But the expansion of Macedonia put an end to the independent Greek city-state, and the Roman Empire doomed all city-states save one to impotence. Then we find the Greeks turning to another source for their inspiration and ideals.

The Hellenistic era. The period between the collapse of the Greek system and the growth of the Roman Empire is known loosely as the Hellenistic age. It produced a concept of the aim of human life which was divorced, for the first time, from the particularism of the city-state. Glorification of the city was rather futile in view of its obvious lack of significance in an age of great empires. The ideal of service to the city declined, and belief in political activity as the highest form of human endeavor was abandoned. They were replaced by a philosophy of *individualism*, an emphasis upon personal rather than communal goals, upon individual self-satisfaction as an end for human life. There was, in effect, a revolution in Greek thought which had the effect of transferring the emphasis in human values from society to the isolated man. The new attitude originates with the school of philosophers known as the Cynics, who denied the primary importance of the tie between the individual and society and asserted instead that man was bound equally to every member of the human race but was responsible primarily to himself. The Stoic philosophers, who followed the Cynics in time, expanded this conception and passed it along to the Romans. They taught extreme individualism and an utter disregard for social affairs, urging instead a concept of universal citizenship and the brotherhood of man. This is a philosophy for the defeated and frustrated, and not for the strong and the victorious, of course, but it has found a firm place in the Western tradition, remaining influential down to the present age.

The Hellenistic era also marked the origin of the doctrine of *natural law,* i.e., the belief that there are "laws" of nature which govern the social behavior of man in the same way that physical laws govern the behavior of inanimate objects. Such laws are to be learned by the exercise of human reason or through divine revelation. In time, the law of nature became roughly equivalent to the "Law of God" and it maintained this quality until the revival of faith in reason that marked the Enlightenment of the eighteenth century.

The influence of Christianity strengthened the notion of natural law and the movement toward individualism, for Christ had preached the value of the individual in the eyes of the Creator, and the notion of divine law is inherent in all Christian doctrine. To be sure, Christianity stressed the religious and spiritual aspects of individualism rather than its material aspects, and it could tolerate slavery, as an example, because it believed that the soul remained free whatever the condition of the body. Early Christianity was weak and lacked the power to assert and enforce a view of the material life of man that would parallel its conception of his spiritual individuality. Later, when the church obtained the power to enforce its views, its position was somewhat compromised by its own material needs. In general, nevertheless, the Christian influence tended strongly to support individualism, rather than collectivism, and natural law as a final, divinely inspired corrective on the laws and actions of men.

The city-state legacy. It is always difficult to assess the importance of an historical tradition. The influence of Greece and Rome was undoubtedly slight during the period from the fifth through the eleventh centuries, and even today it is questionable that political practice in the West is very heavily indebted to the experience of the ancient city-states. It is easy to take a romantic attitude toward Periclean Athens and proclaim it as the fountainhead of modern liberal and democratic theory. Yet to do so is to ignore the inheritance of the Middle Ages and the many other factors that contributed to the development of modern politics. The classic Greek ideal of a free, informed citizenry, participating actively in political discussion and decision making, ruled for the benefit of all, with due respect for law, freedom of discussion, and freedom of thought, is attractive. But there are concepts embedded in modern liberal-democratic thought which are quite foreign to Greek practice, e.g., respect for the person, belief in the basic equality of mankind, belief in the worth of the individual as an individual. Such notions would be quite out of place in classic Greece.

The Roman contribution, if we except the field of law, was slight. The revival of Roman law was certainly influential on the European continent where most legal systems are codified on the Roman pattern. Roman political practice was soon lost. The Roman belief that the Emperor was *legibus solutus,* the sole source of law and above the law, was revived in the later Middle Ages and survived through the age of absolutism, though it has now been abandoned. The great ideal of natural justice embodied in the Roman Law, the concept of a law of nature apprehended by reason and applied impartially, remains today mirrored in the belief that governments of laws, not men, are most just. We may also note the concept of a world empire, which remained as a model of the universal state, kept alive by the unwieldy structure of the Holy Roman Empire (revived in 800 A.D. with the crowning of Charles the Great) and inspiring medieval writers like Dante, or, in our own time, political leaders like Mussolini.

It is also true that the social and political questions to which the Greeks and Romans devoted their time are still part of our political heritage, for they are timeless questions, and to some extent the Greeks in particular set the frame of reference in which they are discussed even today. The Greek solution to these social problems, arising as it did out of the city-state system, has only a limited applicability in the modern world, but this need not diminish our respect and admiration for the speculative genius that first proposed to answer universal political questions in a reasoned manner. The Greeks failed to see the limits of their own system; perhaps we too are guilty of the same short-sightedness. But what they did see, they saw with almost startling clarity and objectivity, and the concept of intellectual activity which they left behind has remained an inspiration and model for the Western world.

FEUDALISM

There are many parallels between the modern state and the Greek city-state, so long as reasonable care is exercised in making comparisons. But when the modern state is compared with the political structure that appeared in Europe in the Middle Ages—to feudalism—we find that the latter exhibits few of the characteristics that are today associated with the activity of the state. Indeed it can be said with much truth that the state simply did not exist in the Middle Ages, though this does not imply the absence of politics in the period. Curiously enough, modern political conceptions, such as representation, belief in limited government, the rule of law, and the doctrine that government rests on the consent of the governed, are apparently derived from medieval politics, for they do not appear in the classic age, yet they are firmly rooted in normal medieval practice.

Feudalism, as we shall use the term here, was a politico-economic system that appeared in Western Europe between the tenth and fifteenth centuries. The political structure of the early Middle Ages, from the fifth to the tenth centuries, is too little known for extensive generalization. In fact, it was known to history as the "Dark Ages" for many years until historians became overly sensitive to the term and abandoned it. In any case, we are here concerned with feudalism at the peak of its development, and not with its origins, which are very obscure. The principal drawback to a brief discussion of feudalism is the need to oversimplify rather drastically. We must deal with feudalism as a whole, whereas, in fact, French, English, and German feudalism differed considerably. The distinctions are here ignored, but the student is warned that medieval politics was quite as complex and variegated as classic or modern political activity and no brief summary can hope to convey the flexibility and character of the system accurately and satisfactorily.

The system. The key to understanding the feudal system is to grasp the connection between economic authority—the right to possession and use of land, mainly—and political authority. Of course, social status and blood lines were also significant in medieval politics, but it was the landholding system that set the basic pattern for the exercise of political authority. After all, the two great problems in the lives of most people are the need to be safe and to be able to earn a living. Feudalism solved these problems reasonably well.

The economic foundation of feudalism was the transfer of the right to possess and use property in return for service, which might be military or economic or personal. Thus the king granted land to the great lords in return for their aid and support; the lords in turn granted rights of use to lesser lords and exacted aid and support in return. We can picture a great pyramid of socioeconomic relations in which there were obligations running from the top to the bottom—obligations to protect the rights that had been granted or had come into being through usage—and other obligations—obedience and service—running from the bottom to the top. The system operated on a very primitive economic base, for money was seldom used, trade was much constricted, and there was little manufacturing. It was bound together by oaths and pledges between successive levels of landholders, those above promising to protect and maintain, those below agreeing to support and obey. It contained, therefore, an implicit contractual relationship with obligations on both sides. Political activity was carried on within this broad framework, very often by violent means.

Citizenship. The concept of citizenship that we found in Greece and Rome, the attachment to the abstraction of the city, disappeared in the Middle Ages. It was replaced by a "personal" relationship, by loyalty to one's overlord, and in an ultimate sense to one's king. Further, the identification of political, religious, and economic society with the state disappeared, and religious obligations were separated from politics—"Render unto Caesar that which is Caesar's." Political authority and political obligations came to rest on a contractual relationship between individuals, or individuals occupying particular statuses, in which one side promised obedience in return for protection and economic support. A failure on the part of one side to carry out its obligations was a breach of contract, and medieval practice provided a remedy of sorts. It was on these grounds, for example, that the English barons forced King John to sign the first version of Magna Charta in 1215, reaffirming their traditional rights and his traditional obligations. The change from social to individual political loyalty—the decline of a sense of "belonging" to society, along with the departure from a monistic and unified social structure which encompassed the whole of human life—is perhaps the most basic change in the transition from classic to medieval politics.

Church and state. Much has been written about the relationship between the church and the state in medieval society, largely because the conflict between the Papacy and the Holy Roman Empire tends to focus attention on this aspect of medieval life. Yet in normal medieval thought and practice, the church and the state were separate institutions, though related. Traditional Christian doctrine argued that Christ had been both chief priest and king, that he had held in his hands the "two swords," one secular and the other religious. When Christ left the earth, one sword fell to the church, the other to the political ruler. They must cooperate, of course, and it might be necessary, as St. Augustine argued, for the state to support true religion, but the structure was not unified. Religious belief and political loyalty were two entirely different matters.

At various times in history, the secular rulers attempted to dominate the activities of the church, and at times they succeeded; at other periods, the church sought deliberately to expand its control over secular government, and succeeded at least partly. That was the essence of the conflict between the medieval church and the Holy Roman Emperor. But the normal view was that the church concerned itself with matters of the spirit, with affairs that were "higher" than politics, and that it was improper for the state to interfere in these matters, just as it was improper for the church to engage too extensively in mundane political affairs. A few writers in the later Middle Ages argued that the church ought to be subordinate to the state, and Henry VIII created a national church in England which was his own creature, but the general rule in the Middle Ages was a clear separation of the two.

Law. We have said that in the Middle Ages the conception of a limited political authority was widely and commonly held. The basic instrument used to maintain those limits was law or custom. The Romans had held that the ruler possessed absolute political authority, which he derived from the people of Rome but which the people could not retract. Nothing could be further from medieval practice. The law, in the Middle Ages, was not produced by an act of legislation. It was largely customary law, taken as the expression of the will of the community, and in some sense the will of God; it was a manifestation of the "right" order of things. The law, or custom, was binding upon king and commoner alike, and a ruler who violated the laws and traditions of society was a tyrant, and in some cases could be deposed.

Consent. In a society where changes occur slowly, the law is seldom capricious; where law derives basically from custom, change is slower still. The medieval kings could on occasion enact special legislation, but even here the right of the king to produce law was limited, particularly in German practice; he could do so only with the advice and consent of his subjects or the principal men of the realm. Thus consent and, later, representation were firmly embedded in normal medieval politics.

Most students are familiar with the operation of the king's councils, for remains of these bodies survive today as representative institutions like the British Parliament. But we are likely to overlook the extent to which representative assemblies appeared in the Middle Ages, with full power to listen and agree to the king's proposals. The Cortes in Spain, the States General in France, and the English Parliament, to mention only three of the more famous of these bodies, had a long and significant history in the political process developed in their respective territories. In many cases, of course, the representatives were expected to listen and then agree automatically, but even the right to listen implied the right to refuse, as many a royal master found to his sorrow. During the age of absolutism, in the seventeenth and eighteenth centuries, representative institutions lost much of their power and prestige, yet they retained sufficient respect in tradition and custom to serve as a focal point for the challenge to absolute kingly authority, and they were the prime instruments used to bring about the end of absolutism in Western Europe.

Divine right. Royal absolutism, the belief that kings ruled by "divine right," was unknown, in theory at least, in the Middle Ages. The "divine right" theory asserts that the ruler is the representative of God on earth, divinely appointed to rule over his kingdom, and hence that any resistance or argument is a violation of the heavenly mandate and sinful. The origins of this curious doctrine are rather obscure. Gregory the Great had asserted something very like this view in his eulogies of the Roman emperors, but the notion seems then to have disappeared until the sixteenth century. Christianity taught that all authority *originates* with God, and this was commonly accepted in the Middle Ages, but the two concepts are not identical. The normal Christian position comes from St. Paul's Letter to the Romans, where he said, "Let every person be subject to the governing authorities. For there is no authority except from God, and those that exist have been instituted by God. Therefore he who resists the authorities resists what God has appointed, and those who resist will incur judgment." Taken literally, as sometimes happened, this could be made into the divine right theory, but that was not the normal medieval interpretation. Instead, the concept followed in the Middle Ages was that enunciated by St. Augustine, who had said that political rule was a divine remedy for human sinfulness. This implied, of course, that the people should not protest against unjust rule, for tyranny was doubtless punishment for great wickedness, and tyrannicide was sinful. But Augustine also taught that there was a vast gulf between the spiritual and the temporal worlds, and the notion that the king was a vicar of God, as was later claimed by extreme supporters of divine right, would have been quite repugnant to him.

The political process. The governmental process we find in the Middle Ages has little resemblance to modern government; in fact, it was more like estate management or property administration than what we call government today. The medieval kingdom was really the property of the king, in the modern sense of the word property. He acquired it by conquest or inheritance, and dispensed it as we dispense property at the present time. The king's rights were limited, of course, by the rights of others, based on tradition and custom, and these rights were not easily violated. But within the general framework of property rights, the king could rule his kingdom as he managed his personal estates. Not until early modern times did the kingdom become a formal association, separated from the personal domain of the king.

All too briefly, then, the normal medieval political structure was a kingdom, acquired through hereditary bequest or by conquest, in which the ruler was clearly limited by sovereign law derived by reason from the principles of God and nature, and expressed in the customs and traditions of the community. The relationship between ruler and ruled was a mixture of the economic and the political founded upon reciprocal obligations resembling our modern contractual relationship. Law was held in great esteem, and custom could not be violated with impunity. The modern concept of law as legislation was seldom observed, and when the king did legislate, it was with the advice of his councils. Ultimately the law expressed the will of the community in some sense of the term.

The political relationship was individualistic and personal; there was no conception of nationality, no loyalty to an abstraction, such as the state; loyalty was to the person or office. Church and state, though interdependent and complementary were separate in function, the former being "higher," since it was concerned with matters of the spirit and not with mundane temporal affairs. Government was financed and directed by the king and was, in effect, a form of household management, with no sharp distinction between affairs of state and the private affairs of the king, whether related to internal or external matters. Wars were personal, and often dynastic, and they left the bulk of the population unaffected and uninterested. Armies were made up of those owing service to the king or the king's lords. Thus the king was the key figure in an intricate network of personal, economic, political, and family relationships, each with its own sets of rights and privileges and its own obligations.

THE MODERN STATE

The transition from medieval feudalism to the modern state system did not occur overnight. In fact, it is very difficult to mark either the beginning or the end of the transition period. People did not awaken early one morning and shout, "Huzzah, the Middle Ages are ended!" Yet the transition was marked by a major social, political, and economic upheaval—perhaps the greatest in the history of mankind. It proceeded slowly, but it ran deep. Very often the people were hardly aware of changes taking place around them; when they were aware, they often decried or lamented the changes. The pace varied from one society to the next, and the final result—the modern state—was seldom the same in detail, though the rough outlines of the state appeared everywhere in due course. Each region remained to some extent unique, and these distinctions are with us still in most of Europe. Thus northern Italy was "modern" as early as the fourteenth century; Russia remained medieval until the nineteenth century; England and France effected their transition in the fifteenth and sixteenth centuries. By the age of the Tudor kings, England was a modern state, as was France. We shall deal mainly with these two countries in our discussion of the change from medieval to modern life, for they set the pattern for those who came later, and their experience is a significant part of our own social heritage.

The scope of the upheaval. Few periods in human history can match the impact of the transition from medieval to modern times. The changing pattern of politics was only a small part of a total social upheaval and the political structure engendered by the change was much affected by developments occurring in nonpolitical aspects of social and economic life. The whole foundation of Western society was overturned in a few short centuries, and a way of life that stretched back to the classic age disappeared. We may almost say that man has yet to completely adjust to the new conditions—social, economic, and political—that appeared in the early modern era. The economic basis of human life was overturned, and this undermined the political structure that had taken shape on the basis of the older economic system. The family, education, religious institutions, and the vocations and avocations of men—all shared in the general reshaping of human culture, generating a new system of human values and a new attitude of mind. An intellectual revolution of the first order accompanied, and perhaps led at times, the social transition, and this in turn had repercussions in every other phase of human life. The soaring architecture of medieval Gothic gave way to a new mode of artistic expression; painting found new life in the use of perspective, which freed the painter from the conventional symbolism of medieval art. The medieval allegories of Dante were replaced by the stark realism of Machiavelli and the lusty naturalism of Boccaccio and Cellini. Medieval Latin was replaced by national languages, and a vernacular literature appeared which appealed to more than the tiny fraction of the population competent in the classic tongues. The printing press made possible a wider public than ever before. Modern science, with its new conception of man and the universe made its first hesitant appearance, then speedily found its own special niche in Western society. The pessimism and morbidity of the Middle Ages gave way to optimism, humanism, and curiosity about the world in which man lived and about man himself. Fearful concern about the life hereafter was replaced by a sunnier attitude, by more concern with the nature of life on earth. The stylized and formal routines of the medieval court were superseded by a more individualistic, a more capricious and personal set of human relations. The catalog of fundamental changes could be extended almost indefinitely.

An age in which the foundations of an old social order are being laid to rest and a new set of primary beliefs are being established is at once a stimulating and a challenging period in which to live. It forces some men to retreat to the shelter and safety of past tradition; others it stimulates to new creativity, idiosyncrasy, and experimentation. Some men refuse to question anything in the existing order; others question everything. The fifteenth and sixteenth centuries are for the most part alive and teeming with activity— economic, political, intellectual, and religious. Europeans shook free the medieval shackles and began casting about for new worlds to conquer, new walls to storm. The men and women of the Middle Ages scarcely come alive, perhaps because we lack information about them and their lives; they are preperspective drawings on the fabric of history and they lack flesh. The men and women who lived through the age of transition are creatures of flesh and blood; they live, they sparkle, whether as rogues or saints. We can understand them, appreciate their problems, and if occasionally we see flashes of an age which is strange and incomprehensible, they are for the most part people like ourselves—they are modern.

Economic revolution. To attribute the change from medieval to modern life to economic causes alone would be to say too much, but there is no doubt that the drastic alteration of the economic structure in Europe, which began as early as the eleventh or twelfth century, was a very influential factor in the transformation. The medieval landholding system, based upon a contractual relation involving rights and obligations for both parties, was the rock on which medieval politics and economics were built. Between 1300 and 1500, this landholding system was transformed into a capitalistic system which differed fundamentally from the old order.

Although the cause of the economic revolution cannot be ascribed with any degree of certainty, its consequences are fairly clear. The older system of payments in kind or in service was replaced by a money system and by rents. There was a vast expansion of trade inside Europe and with overseas territories. Manufacturing flourished, and the power of the medieval guilds, which had controlled and restricted production, pricing, and worker entry into industry, was gradually broken. The invention of the joint stock company, which resembles the modern corporation, made possible the accumulation of large stocks of venture capital for further enterprise. The slow-moving agrarian economic system of the Middle Ages gave way to a capitalistic system, which was still far removed from modern industrialization, but a great advance over the past. A further technological revolution, particularly in power production and in machinery, was needed before modern industrialization could begin, but the direction was set for the future. A new economic class appeared, comprising the merchant and the trader, which acquired economic power quickly and began pressing for political rights and for an end to the restrictions on enterprise lingering from the feudal period. The rise to power of the new entrepreneur class helped pave the way for the emergence of the modern state.

Historically, the modern national state was a product of the joint efforts of the merchant classes and the king. In the Middle Ages, the king had usually been *primus inter pares*—first among equals; in a relatively short time he became absolute—first with no equals. The opposition of the nobility and the great landowning classes was overcome with the aid of the new middle class, the product of the new economic system. The merchant and trading classes supported the royal house against the nobility; in return, the feudal privileges of the nobility, particularly those which restricted economic activity, were limited. In the process, loose feudal confederations were united into a single political unit ruled by the king.

Social change too followed on the economic revolution, for interdependence grew as trade revived and it became more economical to depend on others for some goods while specializing in the production of others for money payment. The attitude of the general population toward materialism and luxury changed, and the ascetism of the Middle Ages was replaced by an almost inordinate fondness for finery and personal adornment. Economic affairs occupied an increasing part of the attention of the political rulers as well, and royal influence in economic matters soon filled the gap left by the displaced nobility. *Mercantilism,* the belief that economic activity ought to be conducted in such manner that it would add to the glory and greatness of the state, was a natural outcome of these changed circumstances. In time, mercantilism too became a restriction on private economic activity, and the efforts then made by the merchants to shake off mercantilist influence played an important part in the diminution of royal power, particularly in France.

Intellectual change. Behind the economic and political superstructure which emerged during the transition to modern politics lay a new mental outlook whose importance can hardly be exaggerated. Man's knowledge of the universe expanded enormously and rapidly as men took to scientific activity with real enthusiasm. Modern science was born early in the sixteenth century with the work of Copernicus in astronomy; it matured quickly, reaching a pinnacle with the publication of Sir Isaac Newton's findings in astronomy and physics. There was a general revival of learning, an upsurge of university life in which the leavening influence of humanism began to loosen the ties of medieval scholasticism and to interest man once again in human problems. Man became more adventuresome, intellectually as well as physically, more speculative in thought as in action. There was a decline of superstition, the irrational fear of the unknown and inexplicable, and a concurrent rise in man's faith in his own ability to explain. There was a change in general outlook, a new attitude toward the problems of living and the purposes that life could achieve, and it affected man's political outlook as well as his social and cultural and religious behavior.

In the sixteenth century, the intellectual revolution struck the religious life of Western man, producing a challenge to the Catholic Church and its claim to speak for the whole of Christianity. The Reformation dissolved the medieval ideal of a universal church, and the relation of church and state was redefined once again in the period that followed. An attempt to institute state control over religion failed, particularly in France and Britain, and the outcome was a slow movement toward religious toleration as the only position compatible with political stability and peace. The new Protestant groups tended to ally themselves with the national rulers, particularly in Central Europe, and thus add their support to the development of the modern national state. They also fitted nicely into the newly developing capitalistic spirit, as R. H. Tawney and Max Weber have demonstrated.[3]

Political transition. The appearance of the modern, unified, national state as a coherent social entity is without question the most significant consequence of the demise of medieval feudalism. In the process of transition, the scattered personal loyalties of the feudal system were replaced by a single loyalty to a centralized political system, personified by the king. Personal loyalty to the feudal lord was replaced by loyalty to the king, and then by loyalty to the state. National sentiment and national pride and arrogance developed rapidly. The modern parallel can be found in the changing pattern of loyalty in the American Colonies following the Revolution; loyalty to the nation as a whole eventually overshadowed allegiance to the individual state—the Virginian became an American, and the psychology of the change is quite complex. In Europe, a similar process, working perhaps more slowly, made Frenchmen of the men of Burgundy and Touraine and Picardy, and made Englishmen of Yorkshiremen, Londoners, and Lancastershiremen. The consolidation was nearly completed in England by the time of the first Tudor King, in France by the age of Louis XI, and in Spain by the early sixteenth century, when the marriage of Ferdinand and Isabella (1469) united the two largest political units in that country. National sentiment was carefully nurtured by the royal houses of Europe, and we may judge the success of the effort by the virulent nationalism that appears in Elizabethan drama. A new political institution, the national state, came into being; it also brought a new type of ruler, the absolute monarch, ruling, in some cases, by "divine right."

The character of the political system. Let us look more closely at the political changes that occurred as Europe passed from medieval to modern times. We find that they affected every facet of politics, from the theoretical

[3] R. H. Tawney, *Religion and the Rise of Capitalism,* Harcourt, Brace & World, Inc., New York, 1926; Max Weber, *The Protestant Ethic and the Spirit of Capitalism,* Charles Scribner's Sons, New York, 1958.

to the practical, from the mundane to the fundamental and basic. Europeans produced a new justification of political authority, a new concept of law, a new political process, a new locus of political power, and so on through a long list of fundamentals.

Political authority. The usual medieval conception of political authority was drastically modified in the transition to modern society; indeed, it is hard to see how the modern state could emerge on any other basis. Medieval writers accepted government as a divine remedy for sin, took for granted the kingly form of government, and severely inhibited the right of the population to protest against misrule. Most people believed that a political society was impossible outside the true religion and that one of the prime functions of the state was the protection and expansion of the church. The authority of the ruler was limited by law and custom, and by the natural or divine law, as well as by incipient representative institutions. Legislation, as a deliberate exercise of authority, was rare, and national political institutions were almost nonexistent.

Modernization altered the entire pattern of thinking about political authority, extending its scope enormously, reintroducing the concept of legislation as a deliberate act of will, and amending the fundamental justification of political authority. The influence of Greek political writings, particularly the *Politics* of Aristotle, helped turn men to the belief that society was a natural form of human association and not a divinely inspired creation. This created a serious theoretical problem, for if political associations were natural, how was the authority to rule others to be justified? The question puzzled political theorists in the early modern period no end. One school of thought, bent on supporting the absolute authority of the king, turned to a religious foundation for political authority, arguing that the king was divinely appointed to rule. One ardent royalist, Sir Robert Filmer, even managed to trace the authority of the King of England to the parental authority of Adam over his children, and John Locke devoted the whole of his first *Essay on Government* to the demolition of this vapid proposal.

In the long run, the view that political associations were natural won out, though not before a fairly extensive period in which the divine right of kings was widely accepted. In consequence, some very complex, and unnecessary, explanations of the foundations of political authority appeared in the seventeenth and eighteenth centuries. Some held that government was needed to restrain the inherently evil impulses in men. Others held that men were good and political institutions made them evil; hence government was the devil's work. In time, most Western political thinkers came to agree that the best possible source of political authority, and perhaps the only legitimate source, was the consent of those over whom authority was exercised—that just government must rest on the consent of the governed. There remained the question how consent was to be given, and how often it was needed, but that can be left to the following chapter.

The concept of law, and law making or legislation, also underwent a substantial revision during the transition period. In the medieval view, law was the custom of the community, augmented and justified by the will of God as expressed by reason and embodied in the law of nature. Customary law had been adequate in a static society where fundamental institutions changed but little over the centuries. In a period of social upheaval, customary law proved a serious handicap to society, and the older practice of direct positive legislation was revived. Again, this produced difficult theoretical problems. Who had the right to make law? Under what conditions? What laws might be made? Must the law be obeyed at all times? What if law and custom were in conflict? Was the king bound by the law? Could the king be deposed if he made harsh laws? Could he be put to death? Such questions were of great moment in the early stages of modern history, however academic they may now appear.

They were answered in various ways. The supporters of loyal absolutism argued simply that the king was *legibus solutus*, as the Roman Emperor had been; hence he was the sole source of law. Others held that legislation was only valid if it reflected the will of the community; hence the consent of the community, through representatives, was required. Some believed the king bound by all laws, and others felt that he was bound only to the law of God. Some felt that natural law could be enforced only by God himself; others were willing to hasten judgment and make applications of natural law by a trial of peers.

Natural law in fact proved to be an immensely powerful weapon against the absolutist kings. The Middle Ages had regarded natural law as synonymous with the law of God and used it mainly to support customary practices; it was essentially a conservative force in society. But the concept of natural law also held a latent capacity to work in a more radical manner, and from the early eighteenth century onward it became a weapon of radicalism in the attack upon royal prerogative. The concept was reshaped into a demand for the right to select the rulers of society, for the right to certain basic personal freedoms and rights, for limits on the power and authority of government, and for the right to participate fully and meaningfully in the political process. The medieval use of natural law to preserve existing rights was transmuted into a demand for the creation of new rights. Natural law had been an instrument used to protect the many against their masters; it now became a device which the new propertied classes could use to justify their demand for freedom of enterprise and a partnership in the political system. Most Americans are familiar with a number of illustrations of the modern conception of natural law, for the Declaration of Independence is almost a classic statement of the eighteenth-century tradition. A still more radical concept of natural law appeared in France, asserting the brotherhood of men and their natural equality, as in the French Declaration of the Rights of Man (1791).

The changing political process. In virtually every case, the termination of feudalism marked the beginning of a period of royal absolutism, the accumulation of political authority in the hands of the king. The political process under the absolutists was little more than a continuation of the medieval practice of household rule over a personal domain. The key to political authority, in such conditions, was family connections, together with access to the king's person. The peculiarities of the system are well illustrated by Shakespeare's treatment of Falstaff, who expected great things when his princely drinking companion mounted the throne, though in this case Henry V failed to live up to expectations. This is still fundamentally a medieval conception of political action. From that point, the political systems of Western Europe tended to develop in one of two directions: first, toward democratic or open societies in which the population participated actively and meaningfully in the political process; second, toward totalitarian or closed political organizations in which the general population was excluded from political activity as far as possible. We may take Britain as a prime example of the first of these trends and the Soviet Union as an exemplar of the second. In general, British political institutions evolved slowly and gradually without excessive turmoil, perhaps because the fundamental revolution came early in British history. The transition in Russia and in France came differently and much later, bringing violence, bloodshed, and a massive disruption of society. These distinctions have left their mark on the present political structure in these countries, as we shall see in a moment.

The first step in the transition to a modern political system in Britain was the depersonalization and institutionalization of government. The bureaus and agencies of government, though still responsible to the king, became *national* institutions; they were removed from the king's personal household. The transition has been well documented by British historians. In the reign of Henry VIII, while Thomas Cromwell was in control of the political administration (between 1530 and 1542), the machinery of government was thoroughly overhauled. Cromwell produced a well-defined bureaucracy, still responsible to the king, of course, but of a different character than before. Offices that had been part of the king's personal retinue for centuries were transformed into national institutions, leaving Britain with a government, and not only a king.[4] The king remained absolute, but in another century, most

[4] See G. R. Elton, *The Tudor Revolution in Government*, Cambridge University Press, London, 1953.

of the political authority of the ruler was transferred to the two houses of Parliament.

The second step in the process of creating modern politics was the overthrow of the absolute monarchy. Here England took the lead, for the Revolution of 1640 virtually ended absolutism in England, and the Glorious Revolution of 1688, in which William and Mary were brought to the throne by Parliament, clearly inaugurated a limited constitutional government. In other parts of Europe, the process was slower. The French royal house remained absolute until the Revolution of 1789. World War I terminated absolutism in some countries, such as Russia; World War II brought it to an end in still others. In a few, it remains active today. Of course, many of the countries were liberated from one form of absolutism only to be imprisoned in another; we cannot assume that the overthrow of absolutism automatically leads to the development of an open, democratic society. Even today many of the so-called underdeveloped areas of the world are learning the bitter lesson that one absolutism can lead to another as overthrown colonial regimes are replaced by domestic tyrannies.

Once political authority in Britain was centered in Parliament, that body became the locus of political struggle. In the seventeenth century, both the House of Lords and the House of Commons were controlled by a combination of church leaders, landed aristocrats, and wealthy merchants. The landed gentry, were, in effect, substituted for the absolute monarchy, though the latter still retained some measure of political power.

The new economic class thrown up by the Industrial Revolution in the late eighteenth century was much strengthened by the economic impact of the Napoleonic wars, and a struggle for political power began early in the nineteenth century between the landed aristocracy and this new economic group. Faced with the possibility of revolution, the aristocracy capitulated, in stages, beginning with the Reform Bill of 1832. This opened the House of Commons to the new economic leaders, though it did nothing to enfranchise the masses, and the House of Lords remained a bastion of the landed groups until 1911.

The final stage in the evolution of British democracy came in the twentieth century. Between 1850 and 1920, a new force—the mass organization—appeared on the economic scene. Trade unions were formed early in the nineteenth century and expanded rapidly after 1880 into large mass unions. By 1914, organized labor was a powerful economic force and a political force of some consequence. As new legislation opened the franchise to all persons, a combination of political and trade union leaders, acting through the newly formed Labor party, managed to organize and direct the voting power of the masses into a coherent political force. In 1924, Labor was strong enough to form a minority government with Liberal support, and in 1929 it made the same attempt, only to founder disastrously under the impact of the Great

Depression. Not until 1945 did Labor win a decisive victory at the polls and produce a majority government. In a sense, the general election of 1945 marked the coming of age of mass politics in Britain. The system is open, in the sense that there are no restrictions on political action which differentiate the population on a class or economic basis.

The French experience was quite different. When the Bourbons were overthrown late in the eighteenth century, France did not follow Britain into moderate and gradual channels. Violence and extremism flourished to the general disrepute of the entire structure. It is difficult now to recapture the turbulence, the violent and passionate hatred, and the vengeful spirit of the revolution, yet no adequate conception of the political problems of modern France is possible that does not probe the currents of this tumultuous age. The demise of moderation, the terrors of Jacobin rule, the monstrous bloodletting under Robespierre, the impotence of the Directorate, and the final *coup d'état* by Napoleon led to an expansive, dictatorial, nationalistic, and even chauvinistic tradition that is quite at odds with the British temper. Since Napoleon's downfall, France has literally been torn by irreconcilable forces, often equally potent, and where factions have not been strong enough to rule, they have managed to prevent others from ruling. The precarious balance of forces has not always been maintained, as the brief regime of Napoleon III demonstrates. The spirit of the "man on the white horse," the great leader who can once again carry France to the heights of glory and eminence sits above French politics almost like a vengeful spirit. Democracy lives a precarious existence in such surroundings, as France has turned now in one direction and now in another seeking a solution to her political difficulties.

By comparison, the direction of politics in Russia or China has been simple, clear, and decisive. When the despotic Russian Tsar was overthrown in 1917, a period of absolutism extending deep into Russian history was brought to an end. The moderate Kerensky regime was speedily undermined by a determined and ruthless faction led by Lenin and Trotsky. Whatever the theoretical ambitions of the group that seized power in the October Revolution, the political system they established has been closed and dictatorial from its very inception. Only a small part of the population has any political significance, and the real locus of power has remained the tiny oligarchy that controls the party mechanism. No one may aspire to rule in the U.S.S.R. with impunity; political activity is expressly forbidden and the machinery which makes popular government possible simply does not exist. This is a closed system par excellence. The procedures by which political authority is acquired and exercised in Russia and China are even today relatively obscure in detail, though the broad outlines of the system are known, for the process is cloaked with secrecy, and the information needed to understand the operation of the system is not allowed to circulate.

The modern state, then, has developed along two quite different lines.

On the one hand, there has been a movement toward mass political systems in which political rights are widely dispersed, and individual freedom is maximized; on the other hand, many modern states have moved in the direction of authoritarian and dictatorial rule, severely limiting participation in politics. The conflict between these two concepts of political activity is one of the dominant themes in contemporary politics, and the issue is as yet far from resolved. What is involved is two different sets of political values, justified by two quite different explanations of the role of politics in the life of man. The issue cannot always be set forth in black and white terms, but the overall relationship is clear. We return to this question in Chapter 8, where we examine the rationale used by supporters of each of these conceptions, and perhaps suggest a basis on which the two systems can be compared meaningfully.

The state and the individual. When we turn our attention to the relations between the individual and the state we find a third major area in which there have been drastic changes in the transition from medieval to modern politics. Medieval man had virtually no political rights, and his personal rights were in many cases severely limited. Yet the nature of the feudal system offered some guarantee of a man's customary and traditional privileges, and if his freedom to change his position was limited, he did retain a definite status in society and that status was in some respects protected and guaranteed. This social protection was gradually stripped away, leaving man to shift for himself in a competitive social and economic system. But if man is to be responsible for his own welfare yet does not have the power and authority to provide for that welfare, he is left in the most frustrating of social conditions. What is to be done in this case? The modern state has produced two basic solutions to the problem. In closed societies, the state has deprived man of responsibility and vested it in the community, producing a situation which is very much like medieval life. In open societies, responsibility remains with the individual, but the society has attempted to create a set of conditions which make the self-realization of man possible. By treating all men as equals, particularly in the vital areas of political rights, freedom of association, and freedom of personal choice, and by accepting the desires of men as a limit on the activities of collective society, open societies have moved in the direction of a social system which makes it possible for man truly to be master of his own destiny. The ideal has not yet been achieved in practice, of course, but some states have gone far toward creating a society in which men are accepted as equals—in politics, in economics, and in all other areas of human life; others have simply accepted human inequality and institutionalized it.

In most cases, the key to differentiating between open and closed societies is the extent of the political rights granted to the citizenry. Where political rights are equal and meaningful, where the activity of the state is subject to the direction and control of its citizens, the basic instrument needed to create an open society is available. For it is society—the state—which controls the conditions of human life within its borders. If the activity of the state is to be carried on by a select group in utter disregard of the wishes or desires of the body of citizens, then man can hardly be held responsible for his own condition, and the basic premise of medieval life has been re-created. Political rights, in other words, offer man a means of rationalizing his own freedom and responsibility, a means of creating the conditions in which the satisfactory life may be pursued. Meaningful political rights, vigorously exercised, can create the conditions under which the social, economic, and individual life of man can move in the direction which man himself desires. The one major difficulty here, which we shall examine later, is the possibility that the intent and purpose of some other society may render it impossible for open societies to maintain internal conditions as they might wish. The maximization of political rights may be incompatible with the maintenance of the security of the society. This is a problem which every open society in modern times must face.

The open society, then, is predicated upon equality of members and maximization of the political rights of members; the closed society presumes inequality and a severe reduction of the political rights of members. There is a further distinction to be made. The open society begins with a conception of society that is individualistic, that sees society as a collection of individual parts. While the society may have interests which conflict with the interests of the individual member, it is assumed by those who accept this conception of society that the function of the state is to promote the best interests of the individuals who form the state. On the other hand, it is possible to view the state as an organic entity, to make an analogy between the state and the living organism, and to postulate for the state a life, a will, and a set of goals which may be quite indifferent to the desires and interests of the individual members of the association. Thus Jean Jacques Rousseau, an eighteenth-century French philosopher, argued in *The Social Contract* that there was a "general will," which desired the "true" best interests of the whole society, and that society ought to be directed by this general will, even though it might differ from the particular wills of the members of society. The organic view of society, and any social theory that exalts the interests of the collective above individual interests, requires the subordination of individual desires to the interests of the whole. That the organic analogy is false we need hardly repeat. But a very large part of the world's population today accepts the view that certain collective interests are desirable enough to sacrifice the welfare and even the life of particular individuals, and the degree to which this view is compatible with a belief in sovereign, responsible individuals needs careful examination.

Living in a society in which freedom of association is more or less taken for granted, we are apt to overlook its immense importance to man. In a world that is large and complex, the voice of the individual is likely to be very small and perhaps overlooked. If the individual is to be heard, he must have the right to associate with others of like mind, to create an association which will further his interests. It is not surprising that closed societies tend invariably to restrict free association and deliberately eliminate competing organizations, while open societies have recognized, though imperfectly, that competing organizations are a necessary feature of large complex modern societies. A recent text in political science begins with a chapter dealing with "The Alleged Mischiefs of Faction," in which a strong argument in favor of faction and group interests is presented.[5] The extent to which freedom of association is present in society is a vital matter, and to ask whether the state controls economic, recreational, religious, social, and political associations is to ask a crucial question.

Finally, we need to be aware of the great importance of individual freedom of choice in personal affairs when we examine the structure of society. The difference between open and closed society, between a free society and a totalitarian society, appears most clearly in the delineation of areas where free choice by the individual is permitted. No state can allow absolute freedom of choice, of course, and remain viable; no state can eliminate all freedom of choice, for if nothing else remains, the individual may choose between life and death. But the spectrum between these extremes is quite clearly marked. In one case, the state determines the choice of occupation, residence, living standard, clothing, amusements, and even basic thinking (by controlling education, economics, information, and social organization). Such a society is rightly called totalitarian, for it seeks "total" control over individual thought and action. At the other extreme is the social life envisioned by the anarchist, in which no individual is coerced into any activity to which he does not agree willingly. A careful examination of those areas in which the will of the individual is sovereign and final can provide us with an extremely useful index to the character of a political system and a practical guide to the manner of life which that society encourages.

Government and economics. The relationship we find between government and economics is a part of the overall relationship between the state and the individual, but it is so important in human life that it deserves separate treatment. Economic activity affects the life of man in a direct and immediate fashion, and the relationship between economics and politics is almost organic. One need not be a Marxist to realize that regulation and control of economic affairs is one of the most important functions of political government. In

[5] David B. Truman, *The Governmental Process*, Alfred A. Knopf, Inc., New York, 1951.

Chapter 9, the relationship is examined in detail, for the distribution of economic power in society may have important political repercussions, while the use of political power may have a substantial influence on the operation of the economic system. Here we are concerned only to trace briefly the development of political-economic relations in the period following the demise of feudalism.

We have already noted that the transition to modern times involved an economic revolution of massive proportions. The economy of Western Europe was converted to capitalism: the means of production became privately owned and economic activity came to be based upon the pursuit of profit. The distinction here lies with the private profit factor, for the state may own an enterprise which shows a handsome profit, and other enterprises, such as cooperatives, may be owned privately and yet not operated on a profit-seeking basis. In many parts of the world, both private and public profit-seeking enterprises appear, as in the United States, where state-owned liquor stores operate at a profit alongside private business in other fields. In the early modern period, the king, who was usually the wealthiest person in the kingdom, often became an entrepreneur in both his private and public capacity. Louis XIV of France, for example, owned nearly one hundred different manufacturing establishments in the early part of the eighteenth century, and other royal rulers were involved in economic matters on an equally large scale. At the beginning of the modern period, then, the economic policies of the political ruler played a vital part in the development of the economic system.

Mercantilism, which we have already mentioned, aimed at the development of national power and economic self-sufficiency through control of imports and exports and manipulation of commercial relations. Thus some domestic industries were repressed, while others were fostered by state subsidies and protective tariffs or by state purchases. Jean Baptiste Colbert, finance minister for Louis XIV of France, was one of the most famous advocates of mercantilist theory, and we can see the effects of mercantilism very clearly in his policies. Roads and transport were improved at state expense, certain types of goods needed internally could not be exported, certain classes of skilled workers were not allowed to emigrate to other countries, high tariffs were deliberately imposed to exclude foreign goods from French markets, and many industries were heavily subsidized. Overseas colonies also had a part to play in the economic process both as planned sources of supply and as means of achieving a favorable balance of trade—an excess of exports over imports which would cause gold to flow into the country. And all of this activity forced the French to maintain a large navy at considerable expense to protect overseas trading interests. This is almost a classic illustration of mercantilism in action.

Obviously, mercantilism could produce some galling and obnoxious restrictions on private economic activity. When mercantilist policies were combined with the remnants of feudal rights and privileges, the result could be highly complex and confusing. In France, an elaborate system of internal tariffs made domestic commerce a tiresome and expensive matter. And for the Colonies, as Americans know only too well, mercantilism placed an aggravating body of restrictions on free economic activity, many of which seem to defy common sense—for example, the requirement that goods intended for the West Indies be first shipped to London and then reshipped to the nearby islands.

Early in the eighteenth century, the precepts of mercantilism were challenged by a group of French economists who became known as the *physiocrats*. The group, which included Jacques Turgot, the finance minister to Louis XV, and François Quesnay, denied that the wealth of a nation depended on trade and an influx of gold bullion into the country. Wealth, they asserted, came from the land, from farming and agriculture. The best way to increase national wealth was to eliminate all restrictions on trade and commerce, particularly within the national borders, and permit the individual free access to markets and goods. One of the physiocrats, Jean Claude Gournay, coined the phrase, *Laissez faire, laissez passer* (in effect, "let us alone"), which became a slogan for the physiocratic movement. They believed that economic activity was subject to natural laws which government ought not to alter; that government was best when it governed least. The physiocrats were very influential, particularly in the eighteenth and nineteenth centuries, for they were the progenitors of Jeffersonian democracy and of the classical school of economists in Britain.

The physiocrats' demand for *laissez faire* was taken up by a Scottish professor, Adam Smith, in a very famous book entitled *The Wealth of Nations*. Smith argued that economic activity was regulated by an "invisible hand" which guided and directed affairs so long as free competition existed. Each man, by pursuing his own good, was thus led to further the common good of all. Although Smith placed some limits on laissez-faire theory, his followers tended to disregard them and Smith's book became a bible for those who advocated a "hands-off" policy in economic matters. Free trade, free competition, and the inviolability of private property became the guiding principles of the new school of economic thought—what is usually called "economic liberalism."

Economic liberalism was peculiarly well suited to the economic needs of Western Europe and the United States in the early nineteenth century. It emphasized the importance of individual competition, freedom to exploit natural resources, freedom of contract, free trade, and a free market; thus it fitted the individualistic temper of the age. These ideals were seldom if ever achieved in practice, but as theoretical goals they proved satisfactory for an era in which rapid industrialization was the general rule. However, the application of laissez-faire policies in America and Europe produced social abuses that aroused a storm of protest from humanitarian elements in society and led to a wide variety of reform activity, ranging from political control of economic actions sufficient to prevent gross abuse through complete state ownership of the means of production. We treat the proposals for reform in another chapter; hence we can leave the development of economic-political relations at this point and turn to the problems arising out of interstate relations.

Relations among states. Few aspects of contemporary political life command so much attention as international affairs, and rightly so, for the future of man may well hinge upon his ability to control the exercise of state power in its relations with other states. Interstate relations have a history as long as the history of states, of course, and the "normal" condition in this area was for many centuries a state of war. Thus the attempt to limit and channel international conflict has been a crucial part of interstate relations since the beginning of written history. Some thirteen hundred years before the birth of Christ, we find the king of the Hittites and the king of Egypt agreeing in a formal treaty to a state of perpetual peace between them, renouncing war as an instrument of policy, and organizing a mutual defense system. The terms have a modern ring, and the problems they were meant to solve are as yet unsettled. We do not imply that international relations deal with nothing but war and conflict, but that war and conflict have been the central issues of international relations for so long as we have a record.

Modern international relations began with the revival of the city-state in northern Italy in the thirteenth century. In time, a very elaborate and formal diplomatic system developed in that region, with permanent ambassadors, treaty systems, complex alliances, international organizations, intrigues, and the inevitable wars. Here *Realpolitik*, the amoral pursuit of national self-interest, reached its peak, as we can see from Machiavelli's *The Prince*, which is literally a handbook for international behavior. It was in this period that the laws of Venice forbade the ambassador to take his wife on a diplomatic mission, lest she divulge his secrets, and commanded him to take along his cook, lest he be poisoned. The injunction was symptomatic of the age. Though there have been states which departed from the Machiavellian principle in international politics, it seems that there has always been some state at hand to uphold the tradition and, usually, to force the others (in the last analysis) into armed conflict.

The central concept that shaped the structure of international relations in modern times has been sovereignty—the belief that each state is answerable to no other in its conduct of foreign and domestic affairs. This notion of sovereignty, which first appears in the writings of the sixteenth-century Frenchman, Jean Bodin, became the rock on which the behavior of states was justified. Of course, there were others who refused to accept the notion of unfettered individual sovereignty for each state. Hugo de Groot, for example, argued in his great book, *De Jure Belli ac Pacis* (Concerning the Law of War and Peace), that states were limited by natural law and a law of nations which could be derived from existing practices in diplomacy and from the rule of reason. De Groot's work earned him the title "father of international law" but few followers in the state system. All too often, the rules of reason and the "laws" of international behavior have been ignored when they came in conflict with self-delineated conceptions of national interest.

How important conflict and war have been is perhaps most clearly demonstrated by the history of the seventeenth and eighteenth centuries. An absolute holocaust swept Europe at the beginning of the seventeenth century in form of the Thirty Years War (1618–1648), which culminated in the Peace of Westphalia. The war involved nearly every country in Europe, and left a trail of blood and wreckage across the continent that took years to repair. Yet virtually nothing was accomplished, for France emerged as the dominant power on the continent and spent the remainder of the century, and most of the next, trying to extend its hegemony across Europe. Britain emerged as the leader of the opposition, seeking to counter each move made by the French by alliances or economic pressures, and resorting to arms when the exigencies of the moment demanded it. Religious toleration, which was accepted in principle by the nations at Westphalia, was perhaps the only valid accomplishment of the peace settlement.

Out of the seventeenth century came the concept of *balance of power,* which meant simply that any time one nation attempted to obtain sole control of the European continent, the others banded together to prevent it. The basic principle has endured to the present. The eighteenth century became almost a personal duel between France and Britain, the former seeking to gain a preponderance of power, the latter attempting to prevent it from doing so. The War of the Spanish Succession (1701–1713) rocked both Europe and the American Colonies and succeeded in preventing the union of France and Spain. Other wars were to follow.

Meanwhile, the character of the system was changing. By the end of the eighteenth century, or before, Spain was reduced to the rank of a second-rate power. In Central Europe, the power and authority of Prussia increased steadily, though Germany remained a mass of petty principalities. In the East, the Russian bear was beginning to stretch its muscles and take an interest in West European affairs. England, France, Russia, Prussia, and Austria remained in a precarious balance, the dominant powers in Europe and in the world. In the nineteenth century, the last and perhaps the most formidable attempt at French supremacy was made under the direction of the redoubtable Napoleon.

When he failed at Moscow and capitulated finally at Waterloo, a stage of European international history was past. Europe settled down to a century of peace, for there were no major wars in the years from 1815 to 1914. Europe occupied itself with the "Eastern question" (Russo-Turkish affairs); Italy achieved unity as a nation in 1861; Germany was unified under Bismarck a few years later. There was sharp competition in empire building as the European nations rushed to obtain concessions, protectorates, spheres of interest, and colonies in Africa and the Far East. Finally, the balance-of-power structure was crystallized, and a very elaborate set of alliances was produced toward the end of the nineteenth century which partially determined the alignment of powers in the first of the great world wars of the twentieth century. Here we may leave the dismal history of international affairs for the moment, returning to it once more in Chapter 10.

Summary

In this chapter, we have taken a long and somewhat complex journey, tracing the development of the modern state system from early Greek city-states through feudalism and down to the modern national state. We have summarized briefly the outstanding characteristics of the city-state and of feudalism, and indicated the areas in which the modern state differed from its predecessors. Further, we have generalized the development of the modern state into two broad channels, the one leading to an open political society, in which the citizens are actively concerned with the political process, the other a closed society in which political participation is extremely limited. Probing further, we found that open societies differ from closed societies in the political rights they grant to their members, in the extent to which they accept the principle of human equality, in their willingness to accept freedom of association, and in their attitude toward political-economic relations. To these particulars we shall return in the chapters that follow as we begin a detailed examination of the fundamental characteristics of the modern state.

Review questions

1. Outline the major similarities and differences of city-state, medieval, and modern politics.

2. In what sense is the modern state inadequate as a political instrument?

3. List some of the major factors that condition the organization and functioning of political associations.

4. Give Aristotle's definition of the various forms of political association and one modern example of each type.

5. Write a brief essay on the role of the city in politics.

6. Compare the role of the city in the life of the Greek citizen with the role of the United States in the lives of its citizens. How are the roles similar, and in what ways do they differ?

7. What was the principal difference between Greek political conceptions in the Age of Pericles and in the Hellenistic era?

8. What does *legibus solutus* mean?

9. What are some typical examples of representation in medieval times?

10. Contrast the medieval concept of law and the modern concept of law.

11. List the major areas in which the modern state differs from medieval feudalism.

12. Identify and contrast mercantilism, capitalism, and the doctrines of the physiocrats.

13. Explain how natural law can be conceived as either a conservative or a radical doctrine.

14. What is meant by *laissez faire?*

For further study

1. "Economics is what politics is all about." Comment on this assertion.

2. What difference does a gradual versus a radical social transition have on subsequent political behavior?

3. Does the history of international relations give us any room for optimism about the future?

4. What do you think are the primary individual freedoms, those which are essential above all others? Give reasons for your answer.

5. Is it possible to conceive of a return to a system of the past, such as medieval feudalism? Why?

6. Why did some political societies develop in the direction of an open political process while others turned toward closed political systems?

7. Do you feel that "what people think" has an important effect on their actual social behavior? Discuss.

8. Do you believe that the separation of church and state in modern times has given rise to political instability? Why?

CHAPTER 7

Political Authority in the Modern State

We begin our discussion of the character of the modern state with an inquiry into the nature, scope, justification, organization, and control of political authority. The topic may seem forbidding at first glance, but the concepts involved are actually quite simple and are familiar to everyone who has taken part in organized social action. Consider the problems facing a student's club. Should the club be informal, or should it have a formal, written fundamental document? Should it have the authority to collect dues? Expel members? Punish infractions of the rules by other means? What rules should be made for club members? What officers are needed and how much authority should each of them have? What means should be used to legislate for the club? Why is it necessary to have authority to punish members? What purposes should the club serve? These are all "political" questions, and they arise in every social organization. Each of them has to do with the scope, justification, organization, and control of authority within the club. They are basic social questions, and until they have been answered it is not really possible to form an organized society. The state is an organized society, and in every state these questions have already been answered, though the answers may be quite different from one society to the next. Our purpose in this chapter is to identify the basic questions that society must ask and to indicate the manner in which the modern state has answered them, together with some of the relationships and consequences that flow from these answers.

THE NATURE OF AUTHORITY

Defined as simply as possible, authority is the capacity to create and enforce rights and obligations which are accepted as legitimate and binding by those who are subject to the authority. Authority is different from power in that the former implies acceptance by those to whom it is applied, whereas power means simply the capacity to enforce a particular form of behavior upon others, whether they accept it or not. Authority carries a connotation of legitimacy, even when it is associated with power or force.

Rights and obligations. To create a right is to grant freedom to act without hindrance within the scope of the right. To create an obligation is to require some person or group of persons to permit the free exercise of certain rights, even where they are affected by the process. Thus rights and obligations are reciprocals; every right that is created creates an obligation to respect the right. Let us take an illustration. If I agree to lend one of my books to a student, I create for the student the right to make use of the book, and I create for myself the obligation to permit the student to exercise that right. If the student and I lived alone on a desert island, that would be the end of the matter. But since we live in society, we must inquire further, for it remains to be seen why I have the "right" to create the right to make use of the book. The answer is that our society has granted me this right with reference to my own property, suitably defined by law; hence I have a right, within the limits of the law, to create further rights contingent upon my own. Should a third party interfere in the process and attempt to prevent the student's exercise of the right which I granted, I would attempt to remedy the situation, and failing that, I would call upon society to protect and enforce the right which it granted me over the book. Similarly, if anyone attempts to make use of the book without first acquiring the right to do so from me, I may call upon the state to prevent that use and return the book to my possession. Society, by granting me rights of possession and use, has agreed to protect those rights and has done so by placing an obligation to respect them on all other persons subject to its authority.

Obviously, this conception of "rights" has nothing to do with "natural rights." It implies that all rights are fundamentally social rights or, to state the point differently, that the term "rights" can be used meaningfully only to designate those freedoms of action which society, directly or indirectly, is willing to guarantee. It follows that what society can grant, society can take away or limit, unless there is some fundamental limit on the authority of the society—a constitutional principle, for example. Society may grant me freedom of speech and create an obligation on everyone to respect my exercise of that freedom. But the courts, which are instruments of society, may abridge or limit that right by requiring me to exercise my freedom of speech in a responsible manner, within the limits, say, of the laws of libel. Society is also peculiar in that it can create rights for itself by creating obligations for all those subject to its authority. Thus the state commonly takes for itself the right to control the behavior of some of its citizens for specified periods of time by creating the obligation of military service for all those who fall into the class defined for this purpose. Society, then, is the fountainhead from which all rights and obligations flow, for even when the individual creates rights against himself for others, he must do so within the framework that society lays down. I cannot, for example, grant another person the right to end my life, at least not within the present legal framework, for the state will punish him if he acts upon the right I have "created."

Legitimacy. We have said that authority is accepted as legitimate by those who are subject to it. Let us now examine this aspect of authority more closely. Clearly rights and obligations cannot be created which go beyond the scope of authority. I cannot grant the right to make use of books that are not my property, for society will not recognize my authority to do so—it would not be legitimate. Authority always has limits which may be either practical or theoretical, and a precise definition of the limits of authority is of the utmost importance in politics. In British law, for example, an administrative official who exceeds the authority granted to him by Parliament is said to be acting *ultra vires;* hence his actions are illegal, and he may even be liable to prosecution. But this does not help to define the authority of Parliament, and that is the really crucial question. Is Parliament omnipotent? Theoretically, this would appear to be so. Yet in practice there are very definite limits that Parliament may not exceed, and these limits can be defined, though not precisely. Further, the government of the United States—and the government of the U.S.S.R.—are also limited in their authority, for there are things which their respective people would not accept as "legitimate" exercise of authority—though there are great differences between the two limits.

This is not meant to imply that a failure on the part of society to create certain types of rights or obligations means that authority to take such action is absent. The fact that the American government does not create certain rights does not mean that it does not have the authority to do so if it chooses. Nor does the fact that rights are created but not used or respected mean that the authority which created them is faulty. A student, having paid the appropriate fees, may have the right to make use of the library and attend lectures at a university, and the fact that he chooses to do neither does not bring the authority of the university into question. In politics, there are similar situations. We are obliged, in our society, to come to a full stop when driving an automobile through an appropriately marked intersection. This obligation is frequently violated, but the offender does not deny the validity of the obligation or question the authority of those who placed the sign at the intersection requiring him to halt. He is much more likely to plead, if that is the right word, that he failed to see the marker, thus implicitly accepting the authority on which his detention is predicated.

It is true that some men have disputed the authority of society to make rules which they personally found obnoxious. The nineteenth-century American man of letters, Henry Thoreau, produced such an argument in his paper *On Civil Disobedience*, where he stated the view that men should be able to renounce society, together with its rights and obligations, whenever they desired. The anarchist likewise believes that social rules ought not to be enforced by coercion, and he asks that we depend upon education and good will and voluntary cooperation to accomplish social objectives. Whether or not such attitudes are viable in a complex society is a question best left to the reader, though it may be worth pointing out that only a tiny minority of the population can entertain them at a given time without dissolving the society.

Coercion, force, and consent. Authority always implies the capacity to coerce, even though the "punishment" involved may be trivial. It would be pointless to create "rights" and "obligations" which could not be enforced or guaranteed. In fact, this is impossible by definition, for authority carries the implication that the rights it creates are in some manner guaranteed; otherwise the term is without meaning. Authority carries with it the power to apply sanctions or punishment, and to have the punishment too accepted as legitimate. The driver who passes the stop sign without stopping pays his fine in the belief that the authority which made the act improper has the capacity to punish in an appropriate manner. The term "appropriate" is necessary here, for a $10,000 fine imposed for passing a stop sign would certainly be contested, and, under the terms of the United States Constitution, voided.

If authority depends ultimately upon the capacity to apply sanctions, is the supreme authority in society that which possesses the strongest sanctions?

John Locke argued in his *Second Treatise on Government* that the mark of a political association was its ability to apply the death penalty to citizens, implying that this is the case. But there are problems involved in this point of view, as we learned in our discussion of sociology, particularly when the laws and the mores clash. In practice, authority that is wisely employed does not attempt to enforce what cannot be enforced. The limit is not the same for all societies, and rules that may be perfectly acceptable in one society may be politically impossible in another. The attempt made by the United States government to prohibit the sale and consumption of alcoholic beverages is a good example of this type of limit. No one disputed the authority of the government, for the Eighteenth Amendment was definitive. Yet large numbers of persons disobeyed the law, enforcement was impossible, and the attempt at regulation proved a failure.

The lesson implied in the illustration is clear. Social authority exists where it can be enforced, and authority can be enforced only when it is accepted, or at least not actively resisted. When those subject to political authority refuse to accept its laws, coercion is impossible unless the group that resists is small enough to be coerced easily; government cannot coerce the entire population. Political authority, then, is defined in scope by the outcome of a kind of tug of war between government and population, the former attempting to extend its authority over particular matters, and the latter either accepting or resisting the attempt.

This relationship is particularly important when government seeks to expand the scope of its authority. The response it elicits from the population will depend upon the past traditions of society and its present circumstances. A people conditioned to authoritarian rule may accept without question an exercise of authority that would lead to rebellion in a free society. And even in a democracy, an economic or military crisis may lead to an expansion of political authority which would be impossible in normal circumstances. This is a serious problem in modern times, for crises have become more frequent, and with them have come demands for more authority; the end of a crisis does not always lead to a diminution of that authority and a return to the *status quo*. There has been, therefore, an absolute increase in the authority of government in the past half century, and some writers believe that this has endangered the future of democratic society by accumulating excessive amounts of authority in the hands of political rulers.

Authority and revolution. It is an easy matter to overestimate the role of coercion and force in the control of society, and the man in the street is quite likely to take it for granted that totalitarian and authoritarian systems of government wield power solely because they control the *force majeure* in society. Granted that force is needed to maintain order and that the threat of force is implied in all political action, it seems obvious that very large parts of the population cannot be coerced if they act in concert. The attempt at coercion would in fact create conditions which we would recognize as revolution—a violent struggle for control of the political association.

The mass of the population of a society need not give active support to the government, but it must at least remain neutral and not be actively hostile to political authority. In fact, politics could be defined as the efforts of an active minority to attain authority over an inactive mass of people. And a closer examination of the political process may lead us to doubt that force is useful even against determined minorities, however small they may be. In a democracy, majority disapproval is a far better instrument of social control than the imposition of rules by physical coercion. And the experience of invading armies leads us to believe that massive physical force is of little use against an active, hostile, and ruthless minority. The German armies that overran the Soviet Union in 1941 commanded all of the physical force needed to coerce any part of the population, yet in those areas where guerrilla warfare was widespread they found it almost impossible to maintain control over the occupied region. Physical force simply will not work against skillful and active minorities who refuse to come to a trial of strength. The Chinese Communists made use of this basic principle for many years in their struggle for control of China, and the same tactics have been used in both Greece and Asia to harass legal governments. If experience is a guide, it seems that such small groups can virtually nullify the authority of government in particular areas, forcing the government to expend its strength in futile attempts to eliminate the guerrilla groups.

The power to dissolve. We can generalize what has been said into a very useful principle—the membership of any society has the inherent and unalienable *power* to dissolve that society by refusing obedience to the constituted authority of society. An organized society is a group of people who are subject to the rules produced by specified authority. When the membership refuses to accept a particular rule, the rule is not enforceable, however much force may be applied. When the members of a society refuse all obedience to authority, the society is for practical purposes dissolved. If all of the members of a club refuse to recognize the existence of the club, then the club is dissolved, and the same point can be made with reference to political associations. Perhaps the extreme case will make the position clear. Imagine a society in which all of the members are subject to the will of a single individual, and give the ruler the power to put to death any or all of his subjects at will without assistance from anyone. The fact remains that if the members of society choose to disobey the ruler, the society will still dissolve. True, the ruler may put to death all of the members of society, but beyond this he cannot go. And if all of the members of society are dead, then society is dissolved, for the ruler has no subjects. Of course, in practice it is one thing for society to refuse to obey a particular rule, and another thing to deny the authority of the state in the face of certain death, but the possibility is inherent in the nature of society. The power to dissolve is seldom used, for it is a drastic remedy, and very difficult to arrange. We need only try to imagine how hard it would be to arrange for every person in the United States or in the Soviet Union to refuse obedience to the state at one time to appreciate the difficulties. Such action would require a social organization perhaps larger than the government itself.

In practice, revolution is not so complex as this. An effective revolution can often be carried out by a small part of the population, though much depends upon the structure of government and the traditions of the society. Further, the threat of revolution, real or imagined, is in itself a powerful social force which may act to limit governmental action without bloodshed or violence. But this is a relative matter. In a society such as China or Russia, where authoritarian rule is customary, measures which would cause a revolt in Western Europe pass with scarcely a ripple on the surface of society. In such associations, coercion can be exercised on a much broader scale than liberal society will tolerate. A Stalin or a Mao Tse-tung may coerce or even kill millions of persons while collectivizing agriculture, uprooting homes and families and disrupting traditional relationships without causing mass disaffection. Such political behavior would be quite impossible in Britain or the United States. Each society has its own unique characteristics, and they determine the extent to which coercion and force may be used by those who rule without causing a social upheaval. But in all cases, the members of society retain the theoretical power to dissolve the structure.

Authority and opinion. What we are saying here is that public opinion, however tenuous it may be, is nevertheless a factor of considerable significance in every political association, whether it is ruled democratically or in an authoritarian manner. When the government of a state attempts to create rights and obligations which conflict with fundamental and cherished beliefs it comes face to face with a social force that is extremely powerful and only partly amenable to coercion. Just which beliefs will arouse antagonism will depend upon the society and its past traditions. In Britain, the government is unable to obtain regulations which permit mass fingerprinting of the population, even though fingerprinting might be very advantageous; in the United States, fingerprinting is done casually and with little opposition. Some people are violently opposed to inoculations; some have religious beliefs which they will not see violated. The basic ideology of society is a tricky thing to define, but every society has some prized beliefs which it will not see impugned.

THE SCOPE OF POLITICAL AUTHORITY

We have seen that social authority is always subject to some ultimate limits, that no government may act so that the whole population refuses obedience, or even so that a major part of the population rises in revolt. But this is hardly useful in practical terms, for it is at best only a protection against extreme tyranny, and when a population is inured to harsh government it may fail to protest even against gross maltreatment. Though some countries have an educated public and a system of government amenable to public pressure, much remains to be done before public opinion can be considered an effective weapon against misgovernment everywhere in the world. Perhaps the first task is to arrive at a clear definition of the kinds of laws that government ought not to be permitted to promulgate or, seen from another vantage point, at a definition of the rights of citizens which government ought not to infringe.

Authority and purpose. Usually, though not always, the need for authority is judged by the purposes which authority serves. A college professor may schedule examinations when he chooses, but he does not ordinarily control the diet of the students, and the reason why he does not is fairly clear—control over student diet simply is not essential to the professorial function. The authority attached to a status, in other words, is usually defined in terms of the function of that status in the society. When the function is clearly defined, there is usually no difficulty in deciding on the scope of the appropriate authority. But when the function is not clearly defined, or when different conceptions of function are held by different members of the society, then the task of fixing the scope of authority may be almost impossible.

The principal difficulty encountered in defining the scope of political authority arises out of our fundamental inability to state precisely the purpose of political government. People differ in their views of the function of government; hence they differ, and very strongly, about the amount of authority which government ought to possess. When one man argues that government ought not to engage in business while another argues that the government ought to have the authority to engage in business, the argument between them cannot be settled until we know what each person believes to be the proper role of government in the social life of man. If one argues that it is the purpose of government to maintain full employment at all costs, then the argument in favor of government-owned business may be valid; if the opponent argues that it is not the purpose of government to guarantee full employment, then government ownership of business may be quite improper.

But, you may ask, *does* government have the responsibility for maintaining full employment? There is no definitive answer to this question; that is, whatever answer we give, it is neither true nor false. It is a normative assertion, a statement of values. Government is not some absolute concept which has ends of its own; government is an instrument and it can be used for many purposes, some of which may be contradictory, just as a surgeon's scalpel can be used to heal or to kill. The only answer we can give to questions of this order is that if the people of a society believe that government ought to maintain full employment, then it is certainly possible to use government for that purpose. In this case, the authority needed to accomplish the desired goal would have to be granted.

Why do people believe that government ought to be used for some purposes and not for others? Why do the people of Britain, for example, believe that the government ought to provide medical care for everyone in the country while many Americans do not accept this as a legitimate function of government? Why do some persons believe that the Federal government ought to provide assistance in education while others argue fiercely that this would be dangerous and improper? In many, and perhaps most cases, there are no adequate reasons for such opinions; they are learned in the family or taken from the press or from one's social group. "Reasons" which are convincing for some people are unconvincing for others.

The dilemma arises because the argument is normative, or concerned with values; it appears in every form of social dispute. When two physicists argue about natural phenomena, the argument can either be settled by determining the facts, or clarified sufficiently for both sides to agree on the nature of the problem. Physicists have standards by which to judge facts, and they have techniques that can be used to prove or disprove theories. In no case are they concerned with values. But the social scientist has no standards for settling arguments about social values except his own judgment and feelings. He can insist that we argue about social goals without personal animosity, and he can provide evidence which may be useful to both sides. But there is no guarantee that agreement will be reached, even when the facts are clear. This is probably the most serious problem in the study of politics at the present time—the fact that men are unable to agree on social values even when the facts are not in dispute.

Sovereignty. How much authority does a political society need? What limits should be set on that authority? In modern times, every major political association—each national state—claims to be sovereign, to be able to order and arrange its internal affairs without interference from another state, and to be the supreme authority over all affairs within its borders. For the most part, that claim is recognized, and it provides a useful beginning for generalizations about the scope of political authority.

The need for sovereignty. Political associations do not exist alone. They are part of a complex and variegated system of social relations which is growing increasingly interrelated as modern technology provides new means for integrating our lives. Each person lives at the center of a web of social relations, subject to the authority of a variety of social organizations. A man may belong to a family, and have a family of his own. He may belong to various economic associations, cultural and recreational associations, and he is usually subject to the authority of one or more political associations. Each of these organizations, however informal it may be, exercises some authority over its members. Some associations claim the right to limit the behavior of their members very substantially; others have only a very limited claim to make. In addition, man also claims some measure of authority over his own person, some right to determine matters according to his own wishes.

Since all of these claims to authority—political, economic, cultural, family, personal—are focused upon the same individual, it would be a miracle if some conflict did not arise among them. What is to be done when the wishes of the individual conflict with the demands of the state? What happens when the claims of the church conflict with the claims of the state? Should the individual reserve certain minimum rights over his own behavior to his own control? And most important of all, who is to resolve these conflicts? The individual? The church? The state? These are not abstract questions, for they arise every day, and history is full of major conflicts between political, religious, and family institutions, to say nothing of conflicts that arise when economic matters are brought into the discussion.

Clearly the answer to this predicament is some authority within the social framework that can override all others, some "supreme court" which can render a final decision or act as a court of final appeal in all cases of controversy. In modern times, the state claims this right when it insists that it is sovereign. To be sovereign is to be able to give a final decision, *if one chooses to do so.* The proviso is important, for few political societies attempt to control all aspects of human life, though some make rather stronger or wider claims than others. But for each bit of inhabited territory there is usually one political association which insists that it is the final arbiter of internal disputes. This does not mean that political society is absolute, though that is the meaning which Jean Bodin gave the term "sovereignty." The United States government is sovereign in relation to all other states, hence it is the sovereign authority within the United States, but it does not, either in theory or in practice, wield absolute power.

Sovereign authority in the United States. The various facets of sovereignty can be illustrated from current American practice, and at the same time we can demonstrate the immense significance of the distinction between the *claim* to sovereign authority and the *exercise* of sovereign authority. It is one thing to say that a final answer to social questions must be possible in society; it is another matter to insist that the state has the last word. Because the United States is sovereign externally, it can solve its internal problems without reference to any other state. That is the case with any member of the family of nations. But within our society, the final word may come from various sources, and not from the government alone. In some cases, of course, final answers are given by the Federal government, but in others the final word may come from a subordinate association such as the church, the family, or the individual himself. The question who answers what type of question with finality is extremely important when we begin discussing individual freedom and its relation to politics.

In the United States, a man may, with some rare exceptions, choose his own mate, his friends, his church, his place of employment, his place of residence, and so on, without any interference from the government. The government simply does not rule on these matters; they are left to the individual. Hence we can say that in these matters, and many others, the individual is sovereign, in the sense that he can, if he likes, give final answers to such questions. In theory, a sovereign state could, if it chose, make decisions in these areas. But in fact the rules of society leave these decisions to the individual over a very wide range of personal matters, and this is extremely important. In matters relating to religion, to take another case, the state is theoretically sovereign, yet our government is constitutionally bound to allow the churches to exercise sovereign authority in religious matters. Similarly, the businessman is sovereign in some but not all of the aspects of his business life. In the political field, the Federal government is sovereign in some areas, the state governments in others, and local governments in their own more limited province. In other words, when the society is internationally sovereign in relation to all other societies, it may give sovereign answers to social questions in its own way, and the manner in which the exercise of sovereign authority is delegated is a matter of first importance in politics. Even in political matters, there is no single final authority which is in all cases supreme.

This approach to sovereignty has the effect of identifying the sovereign differently for each particular question, and this often puzzles the European student of American government. In Britain, for example, Parliament is the single supreme authority in all matters, though Parliament does, of course, allow the individual a considerable area of sovereign authority. There is no parallel to this element of government in the American system, and British students are fond of playing a little game called, "Let's find the sovereign," and then announcing that there is no sovereign in the United States. That is simply a misconception, for the American system can and does supply sovereign answers to social questions just as the British system does, but the source of the final solution will depend upon the particular question at hand. Perhaps the closest thing to a single absolute sovereign in the history of man was the medieval religious order, for in some cases its authority extended even to matters of thought. In modern times, there is no parallel to this kind of sovereign authority and it would be a waste of time to look for it.

Individual sovereignty and personal freedom. One of the most basic questions that can be asked about any political association is the extent to which meaningful questions are left for sovereign decision by the individual citizen—or the extent to which the state claims the right to sovereign control over individual behavior. Here is a very useful means of comparing the degree of freedom for the individual in two different societies. All political associations fall somewhere on the scale between absolute individual sovereignty and absolute social control of human thought and action. Neither extreme is possible; they are approached as asymptotes or limits. As political associations move toward complete control over their members, they become authoritarian; as they move in the opposite direction, maximizing the sovereignty of the individual, they tend toward free or liberal societies. This is not the same as the tendency for all political decisions to be centralized in a single body, as in Britain, or decentralized among many bodies, as in the United States. We may designate these two tendencies as collectivism (tendency for decisions to be made by society collectively) and individualism (tendency for decisions to be left to the individual), if we bear in mind that the terms are not limited to economic thinking. Collectivism, in this sense, tends toward authoritarianism; individualism tends toward liberalism in the broad sense of the term.

Comparing political systems. It is useful to illustrate this distinction by the political practices of two different states, such as the Soviet Union and the United States. In the United States there are large numbers of nonpolitical associations of all sorts, unrelated to the state and vested with sovereign control over particular kinds of activity; in the Soviet Union there are very few associations which are not either directly connected with the state or indirectly instruments of the state power. Thus the United States is clearly *pluralistic*, while the Soviet Union is *monistic;* we can use these terms as a shorthand system to save time, so long as their meaning is perfectly clear. Further, there is a tendency for all social activities in the U.S.S.R. to be controlled by a single central political agency, while in the United States there are various levels of government, each exercising real authority. We say, in political shorthand, that the Soviet system is *centralized* or *concentrated* while the American system is *decentralized* or *dispersed*. Finally, the Soviet Union tends to make its decisions as a group, not only in economics but in social and cultural matters as well, whereas the United States attempts to maximize the role of the individual in economic, social, and political matters. Thus the Soviet system is *collectivist* while the American system is *individualistic*. Each of these generalizations provides us with some meaningful information about the nature of the two systems.

When we discuss centralization, unification, or collectivization of authority in society we are in fact discussing the manner in which sovereign authority is exercised. To the degree that a social system is unified, centralized, and collectivized, sovereignty is exercised by a smaller group on behalf of the whole society, or to look at the same point another way, the sovereign authority of the individual is minimized. Where the system is characteristically dispersed, decentralized, and individualistic, the authority of the individual is maximized. There is, briefly, more freedom of choice for the individual, whether in economic, social, or political matters. Obviously there is more personal freedom in societies where sovereign authority is delegated to the individual in as many areas as possible.

The distribution of sovereign authority in society can also be used as a framework for studying the development of a particular society over a period of time. To use the United States as an example, a comparison of the allocation of sovereign authority in 1800 with the allocation prevailing at the mid-twentieth century indicates that a remarkable transformation has taken place and tells us something of its nature. Clearly, society has moved in the direction of monism and centralization and collectivism during the past 150 years. The Federal government has gained in authority at the expense of state and local government. The family has lost authority over some of its activities to the state. The influence of the state over economic and social affairs has increased immeasurably. And the sovereign authority of the individual has declined very substantially. The facts are clear enough. But does this mean that the trend is dangerous or harmful? Political science cannot answer the question meaningfully. Perhaps the most useful thing that can be done is to determine the extent to which such trends are necessary, or whether they can be reversed. If the trend toward centralized, monistic, collectivist society is a necessary consequence of social and economic change and growing complexity in social relations, then it seems probable that man must learn to live in a new and different framework, and perhaps to pursue different values within that framework, seeking his satisfactions within the realm of the possible, and if he can, avoiding irreversible decisions that may have catastrophic results in the future. Political science, in other words, may point out the trend, but it has not the knowledge to decide on the ethical worth of the alternatives.

In general, the American tradition is hostile to monism, to centralization, and to collectivism, whether in economics or in social affairs. The principal source of this bias against central authority is fear of the misuse of power, coupled with a belief that possession of great power invariably leads to misuse.

The attitude was fundamental with the founding fathers and it is still a significant element in American thought. The problem has been aggravated by modern technology, which places immense power in the hands of those who control its products, and at the same time makes it difficult for the population to control those who exercise political power. Much of democracy proceeds on faith, and faith is always open to abuse. The difficulty is that the consequences of abuse are now potentially greater, even if we leave aside the destructive potential of atomic weapons. The possibility of thought control, genetic control, psychological and pharmaceutical tampering with human thought, educational conditioning, etc., is real and frightening. The possibility of a society in which there would be no need to inhibit free criticism, in which no one would criticize since the very foundations of criticism had been destroyed, is real, and, for anyone who values the human being individually, horrible. The American tradition has been oriented to the individual, and human freedom has meant, above all else, freedom for the individual—free access to information, free discussion, free association, and so forth. It has been an article of faith in Western civilization that man, given access to ideas and freedom to discuss them, will seek a liberal solution to his social problems. It is in this context that the demand for maximization of individual sovereignty, and the fear of a further reduction in the sovereign authority of the individual, becomes meaningful.

JUSTIFICATION OF POLITICAL AUTHORITY

If we are asked, "Why do we have political authority?" the question sounds foolish and simple, for the obvious answer is that political associations are necessary. But if the question is pressed, we arrive at a question we have met before, "Why are political associations needed?" This, as we have seen, is a very difficult question to answer. It does not mean that political associations ought to be dissolved until men can discover why they exist and what their purpose may be, for that would misrepresent the problem. Society is necessary, in some form or another, but social organization is a man-created tool which can be used for many purposes, and man does have the problem of selecting those purposes. Society can be justified by various arguments, and if the point sounds academic, it is nevertheless very important to note that the argument by which society is justified makes a great deal of difference to those who live under its authority.

Let us see why that is so. The Greek city-state, the polis, was held to be a natural arrangement like the family, and indeed, Aristotle thought it was an extension of the family. In the Middle Ages, political writers usually thought of society as a divinely appointed remedy for sin. In modern times, man has returned to the view that society is natural and necessary. The difference between the two points of view is very broad, but its implications are practical and immediate. For if government is a divine remedy for sin, what is to be said by the governed if the ruler is arbitrary, harsh, or cruel? Unless we are willing to assume that an infallible deity has erred, the oppressed must take it for granted that the punishment is deserved, that they are peculiarly sinful and merit the treatment meted out. But if society is natural, a harsh ruler is an unnatural ruler, using the analogy with the family, and protest is in order. The relation between government and governed, the concept of legitimacy in political affairs, is substantially different as seen from these two points of view.

Basically, every justification of society begins with a conception of the nature of man and his relation to society. If man is naturally good we obtain one justification of social systems; if men are evil, the arrangement will be different. It is like the difference between a maximum-security prison and a detention home meant for rehabilitation. Beginning with a conception of man, political theorists proceed to the goals of society, to the social values that society ought to seek. These too will vary widely according to the concept of man from which the theory begins. Obviously, it would be impossible to summarize all of the justifications of political authority that have appeared in Western civilization, but a brief outline of some of the major theories and their consequences will indicate the importance of the question.

Thomas Hobbes. The seventeenth-century English philosopher, Thomas Hobbes, argued that man in a state of nature, without government, would be forced to fight for his very life against all other men. There could be no peace, no security, no time to enjoy one's possessions and family. To escape from this hellish existence, men were forced to join together and make a social contract, giving over their authority to a government. Men, in other words, are evil and selfish, and without social authority they are little better than jungle animals. The social contract that Hobbes visualized took a peculiar form, for every man was party to it, but the government created by the contract was not included in the bargain. Men agreed to obey government, but government, or the sovereign, did not agree to anything. The task of the sovereign was to eliminate the chaos of the natural order. In effect, Hobbes produces an absolute ruler, limited only by the ultimate power of the people to rebel. The system will produce order and stability, and since Hobbes wrote during a period of English history when the social order was being racked by civil war, this was doubtless one of his primary goals. Hobbes, then, postulates order and stability as the fundamental goal of social organization, and he is willing to pay the price of absolutism to obtain it. In fact, he sees no alternative, given the nature of man.

John Locke. Another seventeenth-century Englishman, John Locke, who wrote somewhat later than Hobbes, denied Hobbes's contention that men are naturally warlike, aggressive, and selfish. He held that all men were bound by the laws of nature, whether or not they lived in society; hence the war of all against all that we find in Hobbes was not necessary. Why, then, were political associations formed? Locke argued that natural law did not contain any provision for dealing with property; hence in a state of nature man could not enjoy the fruits of his labor in peace. He therefore joined together in a social contract with other men in order to stabilize the use and possession of property.

Now, if the goal of society is to protect the property rights of individuals, it is clear that society may not be ruled by an absolute sovereign, as Hobbes believed necessary, for a ruler of this sort could then do as he pleased with individual property rights. Locke, in other words, must postulate a limited sovereign ruler in order to maintain his fundamental premise about property rights. He does this by assuming that there were two contracts: in the first, men joined together to form a society; in the second, they contracted with the ruler, consenting to be ruled in return for guaranteed rights in property. Locke's views, which were very influential in America, thus include three main points: first, all government is limited; second, all government rests on the consent of the governed; third, the principal purpose of government is to protect property. The social order is here used to provide conditions that the individual cannot guarantee alone, but it does so within a framework that is provided by the needs of the individual.

Jean Jacques Rousseau. A third point of view which has had great influence in the modern world comes from the writings of the eighteenth-century French, or Swiss, philosopher, Jean Jacques Rousseau, particularly the work titled *The Social Contract*. Rousseau accepts Locke's view that man in a state of nature was bound by natural laws and enjoyed his natural freedom. But man reached a point where the natural condition could not be maintained, and he was forced to join society. By doing so, man placed himself under the control of the *general will* of society, trading his natural freedom for social freedom. This "general will" is a peculiar concept which is basic to Rousseau's theory. It is not the same as the will of each and every member of society. It is the will of the *people when they were willing their own collective good,* and Rousseau believed that it was infallible (by definition) and sovereign. If the individual willed contrary to the general will, he was willing wrongly and society could force him to accede to the general will, and by so doing society made him free. Freedom, in other words, means agreeing with the general will of society.

Rousseau is a highly controversial figure in political thought, some writers holding that he is a source of modern democratic thought, others that he is the precursor of totalitarianism. We are here concerned only with his justification of society and its consequences, and we cannot enter into this broader question. The point that is significant for our purposes is that the general will is essentially a mystique, and Rousseau provided no means by which the general will might be known. That is, Rousseau claimed that there is a "correct" course of action for every society, known to the general will or expressed as the general will, and that society must follow it, just as Plato argued in the *Republic* that the philosopher-king would know what was good for society and act accordingly. Unfortunately, the common citizen has no way of knowing whether one claim to speak the general will is better than another, for he has no standard by which to judge—his individual will is insufficient.

Georg Wilhelm Friedrich Hegel. Finally, we should mention the very influential justification of political authority that appears in the writings of the early nineteenth-century German philosopher Hegel and his most famous disciple, Karl Marx. Hegel argued that the modern state was the end result of an immutable historical process which he called the dialectic. That is, from the beginning of human history, every idea (*thesis*) generated its own opposite (*antithesis*), and the interaction between thesis and antithesis produced a new and different conception, which he called a *synthesis*. The synthesis then became a new thesis and the dialectic was repeated once again. The driving force behind this historical process is a mystical entity that Hegel calls "spirit"—a concept that closely resembles the Christian deity. Particular nations at given times in history become the vehicle which "spirit" uses to attain its ends, and under its direction, they move the dialectical process forward. The state is therefore a necessary and immutable consequence of an inexorable historical process moving toward a final and perfect end. Hegel thought that in his own day the world spirit resided in the German people, and this led him to a glorification of the Prusssian state which sounds suspiciously like the mutterings of Adolf Hitler. However, Hegel also thought that the United States was next in line for the honor, and some nineteenth-century American literature makes it appear that some Americans at least agreed with him, though that is beside the point.

Marx retained the general outlines of the Hegelian dialectic, but changed the foundation. For one thing, he substituted material things for Hegel's ideas, and altered the driving force of the system from a mystical spirit to a materialist economics—the dynamics of production. In his philosophic foundations, Marx ends by denying the state, because it was an instrument of class oppression, and substituting for it an economic order. Nevertheless, Marx too believed that the unfolding of the dialectic process was moving man toward an ultimate order of some sort, an order in which the state would "wither away" and only the economic system would remain.

Individualism and collectivism. In all theories justifying political authority, two basic approaches can be discerned: one group of thinkers, typified by John Locke, begins with the individual member of society and accepts as a first principle that the basic goal of society is the satisfaction of individual needs; the other group, of which Rousseau is typical, begins with society as an organism or organic entity, and considers the effect of social policy upon the collective. We can refer to these two points of view as *individualist* and *collectivist,* respectively, so long as we bear in mind the fact that no individualist can ignore social needs completely, and no collectivist can be totally unaware of the individual. The difference between them is a matter of emphasis, though it is no less important on that account.

The individualist view of society is fundamentally atomistic—it sees society as a collection of parts or units, and the parts become more important than the whole because the whole can have no other reason for existing than to serve the parts. Individualists tend to evaluate the use of political authority according to the way in which it affects the life of the individual, beginning, usually, with the ideal of an individual who is completely free, and granting authority to the collective grudgingly and sparingly. In general, individualists are suspicious of social authority, considering it a necessary evil; it should be kept to a minimum, for each accretion of social power means a corresponding loss of individual freedom. The role of society is therefore conceived largely in negative terms. Lord Acton's famous dictum, "All power tends to corrupt; absolute power tends to corrupt absolutely" is a good illustration of the individualist attitude.

The collectivist begins with the whole, with a society that is somehow more than the sum of its own parts and not merely different from them. In the collectivist view, society has its own goals and its own rationale, and hence its own values. The individual is judged according to the contribution which he makes to the operation of the whole structure, and the good of the whole is taken as the goal of social activity. There is no fear of collective authority; a collective has nothing to fear from itself. The decline in individual freedom that is characteristic of collectivism is sustained by the argument that real freedom can be found only inside society, that the isolated individual cannot be considered free except in a trivial sense. This attitude was common in the Greek city-state, and it has begun to appear with increasing frequency in modern times.

Earlier in the chapter, we found it useful to discuss the scope of political authority in terms of the amount of sovereign control vested in the individual and in society respectively. The same framework has now been used to discuss the justification of political authority. In each case, emphasis on the importance of the individual leads to a social structure, a set of social values, that is quite different from that found where emphasis is on the importance of society as a whole. Without attempting to judge between them, for the moment at least, let us now go on to examine the manner in which political authority is organized and allocated within the social structure, for here too we can see the influence of this fundamental dichotomy between the individualist and the collectivist outlook.

ORGANIZATION AND ALLOCATION OF AUTHORITY

A great deal can be learned about the operation of a political society by examining the organization and allocation of power and authority within the system. There are various points to look for, various questions to ask about the structure. Is authority concentrated in a single central agency or is it dispersed among a number of autonomous or semiautonomous bodies? Within a given agency, is authority vested in a single status, a few statuses, or many statuses? How far is the system dependent upon the talent or wisdom of a single person? What is the relation between the formal and informal organization? We can ask, in other words, whether political authority is concentrated or dispersed, centralized or decentralized, formalized or informal, personal or institutional. There are many examples to choose from. In France, the political process is highly centralized, and local administration is tightly controlled by the national government. In the United States, political authority is widely dispersed among state and local governments, each in some degree autonomous and independent. In Stalinist Russia, political authority was concentrated in the hands of a single individual to such an extent that no major decision could be made without the personal approval of the ruler. This was true also in Nazi Germany. In Japan, before World War II, real political authority was almost completely divorced from the formal political system. Each of these conditions has its own political consequences, and each in turn derives, to some extent, from either a collectivist or an individualist base.

Leadership: personal political authority. Sociology tells us that authority is attached to status and that the individual who occupies the status plays a role which is appropriate to the status though different from the role that another person might play in the same position. In these terms, the extent to which the personality of the incumbent influences the authority and behavior of the American President is a commonplace, and every status is subject to some measure of personal influence of this sort. But there are exceptional cases in which authority seems to attach to the person, to an outstanding leader, for example, not because of his status but because of his personality. Max Weber gave the name "charismatic" to those leaders who are believed to possess a mystic insight into the aims and problems of political society and who are supported by the population for that reason. Both Hitler and Mussolini, for example, were charismatic leaders, "divinely inspired," in the eyes of their followers, and each acquired enormous authority as a person. Though the authority was formalized in the office of *Führer* or *Duce,* it was not really transferable. Many other similar cases appear in Western political history, from Oliver Cromwell to Napoleon, or to the attempt to foster the "cult of Stalin" in Russia, dramatizing the personal element in Stalin's leadership rather than his institutional position.

Charismatic leadership is a particular form of collectivism, for it involves the making of decisions for the whole by a single person. It is essentially mystical, for it depends upon the belief that the person designated is truly able to perceive destiny in a way that the ordinary man cannot fathom; hence the only suitable role for the latter is blind and unquestioning obedience. Further, it is extremely difficult to curb once under way, for if the first message from beyond is accepted, how can another be denied, or if superiority is granted in one case, how can it be questioned in the second? Nor is it possible to limit the authority of the charismatic leader in the ordinary manner, for his role is not part of an institutionalized system. For these reasons, among others, personalized authority has been extremely hazardous in the past, and the society which has come under the personal rule of a charismatic leader has more often than not come to grief. In fact, the list of political leaders who fit this category reads like a rogues' gallery of the recent political past— Hitler, Mussolini, Perón of Argentina, Napoleon, Stalin, and so on.

The power behind the throne. A second type of political situation which is fraught with danger for society involves a sharp separation of formal political authority and real political authority. The study of informal political structures is perhaps the most difficult part of comparative political study since it is virtually impossible for the uninitiated to comprehend the informal system; the influence of the formal structure may be greatly overrated in consequence. Some type of formal system always exists, of course, whenever men form organized societies. But when real authority passes into the informal political structure, responsible government becomes impossible.

Let us look at a few examples. In Japan, the Emperor has been the formal head of the Japanese government for centuries; in theory he is inviolable, sacred, and vested with unrestricted authority. Yet the Emperor has in fact seldom if ever ruled Japan. Real authority has rested in the hands of small groups of leaders who possessed no formal status whatever. Political power belonged to military leaders, elder statesmen, powerful family dynasties, and even to a fanatical group of junior military officers, at one time or another. A similar condition is found in the Soviet Union, where the distinction between formal and real authority is based on the close association of state government and political party. Status in the Communist party, not in the formal political structure, is the key to power in the U.S.S.R. Even the United States has not been immune to the problem, for the political "boss" was in effect an informal locus of real political authority. In all these cases, responsibility for political decisions is difficult or impossible to fix. Before we can have a government that is responsible in any meaningful sense, it must be possible to collate authority and responsibility, and this requires a reasonably close relationship between the structure of authority in both the formal and the informal social organizations.

A related problem, which is growing in importance in this century, arises out of the need for those who hold authority to seek advice, and to accept it, on matters for which they are responsible. In some special cases, as in England, for example, there is no particular problem involved. The Crown never acts without advice, and is not responsible for its political actions; the minister who advises the Crown, usually the prime minister, has both the authority to act for the Crown and the responsibility for the action, which seems a reasonable solution to the problem.

But the political official seeking expert advice is faced with a rather difficult situation. The responsibility he retains, but it is not certain that he has as much discretion about accepting advice as we might like to think. The American President, for example, must accept advice in the field of foreign relations, though responsibility is his alone. This is only one of many burdensome tasks that go with the presidential office, and the complexities of the subject make it unlikely if not impossible that the President can remain fully informed on all aspects of American policy abroad. His chief assistants are, for the most part, personal appointments for whose work he is also responsible. When the President must act, and he has been advised to act in a particular manner by his informed subordinates, is he in fact free to act without reference to such advice? Formally, of course, the answer is affirmative. But surely only a foolhardy President would ignore advice without excellent reasons, and he is unlikely to have excellent reasons in more than a few areas where he believes himself to be personally competent. This poses a difficulty for those seeking responsible government, for it may not be enough to allocate responsibility and authority together if it is in fact impossible for the individual who has authority and responsibility to exercise them in a meaningful fashion.

Centralized and decentralized authority. As the loose, highly dispersed structure of feudal authority was modernized, it was also centralized, more power passing into the hands of the king at the expense of the decentralized nobility. With a few exceptions, the trend has been toward maintaining or even increasing centralization in political associations. In some few cases, as in the United States, a group of separate independent states have merged to form a single political association, and the component parts have attempted to maintain their political integrity and retain a decentralized system. They too, however, have been caught in the swelling tide of centralization in recent years.

Efficiency. The principal advantages of centralized political authority, or, of course, disadvantages of decentralized authority, can be stated in terms of efficiency. A single central government can eliminate duplication of effort, overlapping jurisdictions, and internal confusion and conflict. There need be only one court system, one body of legal principles; taxes can be identical for all citizens in the same classification; and the whole system can operate more equitably and efficiently than a complex structure with many conflicting jurisdictions. In the United States, to take an example, each state makes its own laws regulating divorce, incorporation, roads, schools, and even voting, subject to certain broad principles laid down by the Constitution or the Federal government. The result is chaotic, conflicting, and in a sense unfair, for it means different standards of behavior for citizens of the different states, variations in the quality of education, and other inequities. Further, a centralized system is in a sense easier to control, for it is much easier to keep track of political affairs when they are all conducted in a single forum, such as the British Parliament, than to stay abreast of political policies when they are carried on meaningfully at a half-dozen different levels. Centralization, then tends to be more efficient, simpler, easier to follow, and perhaps more equitable.

Against these advantages we must weigh at least three major disadvantages of centralization: first, the increased danger of misuse of power; second, the possibility that local idiosyncrasies will be ignored; third, the probability of producing a large bureaucracy.

Dictatorship is quite impossible in a decentralized political system. Here, in a nutshell, is a very important political principle. In a highly centralized structure, seizure of power by a military *coup d'état,* or the exercise of dictatorial power, is comparatively simple; in a decentralized system, it is by definition impossible. Totalitarianism must first centralize, then exercise power. In the United States, for example, there can be no palace revolution, for there is no palace. Seizing control of the national capital is only one part, and a small part, of gaining control of the total political apparatus of the country. Of course, there are many other factors in society which predispose the population to accept or reject totalitarian government, but a decentralized system contains a built-in safety factor which cannot be overlooked.

The second difficulty with centralized governments is more easily seen in very large territories, such as the United States or Russia. The question is whether a single government can deal adequately with an area that includes such gross variations in economic and social life. The United States contains regional groups as different as the people of Norway and Spain; can they be reconciled in a single administrative structure? And if the central government attempts to meet this problem by decentralization and regional groupings, what has been gained through centralization?

Finally, centralization usually means the accumulation of a large administrative organization, even after the duplication of decentralized structures has been eliminated. This too may make the process of government more unwieldy—ignoring expense—and the multiplication of administrative levels between the political policy makers and the population increases the possibility of error and the amount of time needed to implement political decisions. Again, this can act to reduce the efficiency of the total structure.

Unification of political authority. A related but not identical question has to do with the desirability of concentrating or unifying political authority, whether or not it is centralized. Thus the American Federal government is divided into three main branches, according to the so-called separation of powers theory, each branch holding some political authority autonomously. A structure of this sort clearly disperses authority, even within a centralized system. France has a highly centralized system, but authority at the center is divided between the President and the Parliament in some degree. Britain has both a centralized and a unified system, for the central government at London is supreme in all matters, and the authority of the central government is in fact exercised largely by the Cabinet.

What is to be said for these two conditions? Again, we may note that totalitarianism is by definition impossible outside of the unified system, but a centralized or unified system is not necessarily a dictatorship, for Britain is both, yet remains one of the most democratic nations on earth. The authors of the American Constitution quite deliberately introduced dispersion of authority within the central government as a means of resisting tyranny and excessive concentration of authority, yet Britain has accomplished the same purpose without resorting to a dispersion of authority.

In terms of efficiency alone, a unified government is doubtless superior to a dispersed system—the more highly unified the better, for a single dictator can make decisions very rapidly indeed while a large committee usually cannot. Doubtless it is this factor which causes countries with highly dispersed systems to reorganize their affairs during periods of emergency so as to produce a more concentrated structure. The Romans often appointed a dictator to deal with extraordinary problems, and the emergency powers of the American President allow him to override, almost literally, the other two branches of government. But against this must be balanced the possibility of overhasty decisions and a resulting tendency toward instability. Furthermore, it is possible to overstate the gain in relative efficiency, for dispersed governments can act very rapidly when the need is urgent, just as a large committee can decide quickly in an emergency. The principal difference in the two approaches to allocating authority probably lies in the amount of risk involved in each. Unification introduces more risk of excessive concentration of power but tends to produce more efficiency; dispersion may reduce efficiency but it also reduces the risk element.

Obviously, the amount of risk involved in any political system cannot be measured by the degree of unification alone. It is one thing to give supreme power into the hands of a megalomaniac, such as Hitler, and another matter to expand the powers of an elected President, such as Roosevelt, who is bound to seek reelection within a stated time interval. Furthermore, concentration of authority can lead to greater responsibility on the part of the rulers, since it becomes possible to fix responsibility with greater precision than can be achieved in a dispersed system. Thus the framers of the Constitution separated the executive from the legislature, thereby reducing the authority of each, and the risk of tyranny, but a price was paid for this safety factor in the form of decreased responsibility. Would it have been better to make the President responsible to Congress, as was suggested at the Constitutional Convention? Would it be better to have the President's cabinet made up of members of Congress, responsible to Congress? Such questions need to be pondered closely before a final judgment is made on the comparative advantages of unification and dispersal of political authority.

Some special problems. The complexity of modern society has produced a tendency in contemporary government to create special agencies to deal with particular social questions, and this type of allocation of authority creates some unique problems for the student and for society. In the United States, for example, there is now a vast network of special agencies—the Federal Communications Commission, the Atomic Energy Commission, the Tennessee Valley Authority, and so on. Each agency has very considerable authority in its own area of competence, and none is directly responsible to the general public. Some of these special bodies are responsible to the executive branch of government, though most are responsible to Congress. Most of them deal with highly technical problems, which makes political control especially difficult, and there is often little effective supervision of their operations. Obviously, such agencies are a valuable adjunct of government, for they are flexible, can be used for a wide range of purposes, and are capable of focusing expert knowledge on areas where it is needed. But the difficulty of allocating responsibility concurrent to and commensurate with the authority that is vested in such agencies is a serious problem in government and one that deserves careful attention.

Delegated legislation. A very similar problem arises out of what is called *delegated legislation,* which means that the legislative body has granted to the executive the authority to carry out a particular program without specifying the manner in which the job will be done. These legislative "blank checks" are common in modern times, for legislatures cannot possibly anticipate all of the details that will arise in the administration of a complex social program; hence they deliberately phrase legislation in broad terms, leaving particular points to the discretion of the administrator. It is easy to criticize this practice on the ground that it places authority in the hands of persons who are completely without responsibility to the general public. Yet it is equally impractical to insist that legislatures should spell out each bit of legislation in great detail, for that too would produce a rigid and unworkable system, if indeed it produced anything at all.

Bureaucracy. In a more general sense, a modern government, with its gigantic bureaucracies, creates enormous difficulties in controlling the allocation and use of political authority. The special case of foreign relations has already been mentioned; it can be multiplied many times over. Accusations against the bureaucracies have appeared in every country in Western Europe in recent years, alleging that they have tended to control political policy as well as administration. Doubtless, there is some truth to such allegations, for policy making and administration are not easily separated, and the complexity of the political system forces the elected official to rely heavily upon the permanent civil servant, like it or not. Of course, the implication that the civil service is involved in a gigantic conspiracy against the popular will goes too far, so far as actual evidence is concerned, yet there is just enough truth in the point to warrant a great deal more detailed investigation.

Military-Civilian relationships. A very interesting and influential special case of the power of a bureaucracy arises out of the relationship between military leaders and those who exercise political authority. In the United States, there has been a long tradition of political neutrality on the part of military officers and of strict subordination of military to civilian authority, and these principles are generally respected in the formal political system. The President is Commander in Chief of all military forces and the Secretary of Defense is a civilian official responsible to the President. Yet in an age when international problems are couched largely in military terms, the opinions of military leaders must in the nature of things have a substantial influence on political policy, and military needs are given a very high priority on our list of national goals. The task of any military establishment is to advise the head of government on the best means of maintaining the integrity or security of the national state under existing conditions. That such advice is offered seems quite normal and ordinary.

The problem arises out of the peculiar nature of such military estimates. There is some question, for example, whether the term "national security" can be given any explicit meaning and whether the means of achieving this ephemeral goal can be more than vague conjectures. If General A asserts that 500,000 men and 10,000 aircraft are needed for security whereas General B argues that these figures should be doubled, and if Admiral X claims that a substantial part of military spending ought to be directed to augmenting the naval establishment, while General Y makes the same claim for the air force, how is political leadership to choose between them? When military require-ments are phrased in budgetary terms, as indeed they must be, how are civil-ians to offer criticism of the manner in which such monies are spent? Must the political leaders be reduced to asking the chiefs of staff how much money is needed to keep the country safe, then handing it over without question? If not, what terms must be stipulated in the request for funds that will make adequate criticism possible? It is possible, of course, that money estimates are literally meaningless, though it is not necessary that this be the case. The fact is that government must act, and it ought to act on the best available informa-tion. Here too is a problem that requires considerable attention.

LIMITING POLITICAL AUTHORITY

The sorcerer's apprentice took advantage of the sorcerer's absence to make use of the magic broom. Knowing the right words, he started the broom carrying water, but when the task was done, he was unable to halt the process, with disastrous consequences. It is a relatively simple matter to decide how much authority is needed and how it shall be allocated when there is no need to keep within bounds; one simply allocates much more than enough author-ity or even absolute authority and that is the end of the matter. But if absolute government is an unsatisfactory solution to the political society, some means must be devised by which government can be given enough authority to carry out its essential functions, yet controlled and limited sufficiently to prevent the system from degenerating into tyranny and totalitarianism. Government cannot be fettered within bounds that leave it unable to act; that was the prime error of the American Articles of Confederation. Yet the capacity to do good implies the power to do harm, and authority may be used either beneficially or harmfully, depending upon the skill and intent of the user. Government must have authority to perform its necessary function; the use of that authority must be bounded in some way. This is a perennial problem for human society. Let us now look at some of the techniques which men have employed for this purpose.

Custom and tradition. Perhaps the oldest limits on the use of political authority are custom and tradition. In the Middle Ages, and in societies such as traditional China where the pace of social change was slow, respect for custom and tradition could be elevated into a limit on political authority and maintained with moderate success. The difficulty, of course, is that custom and tradition are not always clear about what is and what is not legitimate, particularly when innovations are being introduced and the machinery for enforcing customary rights is flimsy and inadequate against a determined ruler. Finally, as the rate of social change increases, or as new societies are born, custom and tradition fail completely. Relatively young and fluid societies like the United States have little in the way of a tradition that can be upheld. And newly emerging nations may actually turn against tradition because it is associated with periods of foreign domination or colonial rule.

Constitutionalism. In modern times, custom has been replaced by constitutionalism, in most cases by a formal written constitution which states the scope and limits of political authority and the manner in which it is used. Most states now have written constitutions, and those like Britain which do not have a single written document are nevertheless in possession of a strong tradition which serves the same purpose. Constitutions usually include a list of "do's" and "don't's" for government, particularly a list of fundamental rights that cannot be invaded by those who exercise political authority. In addition, they often specify particular arrangements for exercising political authority, which serve as a limit on the unfettered use of power. Some of the more common of these techniques are federalism, separation of powers, and checks and balances. Each has its uses and limits.

Federalism. A federal system of government is comprised of a number of independent political units, which may be called states or provinces or some other term, joined together to form a single political entity. There is a central government for the entire structure, but each subordinate unit also has a government and retains a certain degree of independence. Federal systems usually originate as separate independent states which join together for mutual convenience; only rarely are they created artificially from above. The independent units cede a part of their authority to the central government, keeping the remainder for themselves. The federal government usually has authority to deal with common affairs such as foreign relations, postal systems, roads, military affairs, etc., while the subordinate units may retain control of education, political activity, economic activity, etc. There is no single system of allocating authority that defines a federal system, and a broad range of possibilities can be explored. The agreement which establishes the federal system is usually written, and one of its principal provisions is that which allocates authority to the central government and the subordinate governments, respectively. One essential, however, is that the federal government be unable to coerce the subordinate units in those areas where sovereign authority is reserved to them; this is the basic limiting device on the power of the federal system. No necessary limit on the authority of the subordinate unit is implied.

Can federalism offer the individual citizen real protection against tyranny? Clearly, the answer must be affirmative, though certain additional conditions must also be met. For one thing, federalism prevents an excessive concentration of authority, and as we have already noted, tyranny and decentralization are not companions. The subordinate political units, being smaller than the large system, are at least theoretically more amenable to popular control than the federal structure; hence they can serve as a roadblock against unwanted legislation. Obviously, the smaller units must maintain their integrity if they are to perform this function. The authority of the central government is easily augmented at the expense of the state, and federalism alone is not enough, as the Soviet experience demonstrates. If the subordinate units become mere instruments of the central government, then the value of federalism as a political safeguard is lost. Of course, society must pay a price for this form of insurance, in terms of increased complexity of structure, probably greater expense, some duplication of effort, etc.; but if the system is successful men may feel that it is well worth the cost.

Perhaps the greatest danger to the federal principle comes from its fundamental conflict with efficiency. When a number of subordinate units are involved in a single problem, it is doubtless more efficient to pass control of the problem to a unified central government. When local political units are duplicating work already done by the federal government, there is a strong tendency to eliminate one or the other from the arena in the interest of economy. Similar pressures can arise in every phase of governmental activity. How far should they be resisted? It depends upon the value we place upon federalism as a principle, the price that we are willing to pay to maintain it. In the United States, for example, historical events of the nineteenth century tended to make the citizen regard the Federal government as the friend of the individual while the state government was conceived as an enemy, particularly in rural areas. The Midwestern farmers, for example, finally lost patience with railroad-controlled state legislatures and turned to the Federal government for aid, helping to increase the authority of the latter at the expense of the states. This is but one example of the complexity of the interrelationship of citizen, local government, and federal government, and the type of problem that is met when we attempt to apply and maintain the principle of federalism intact.

The difficulty arises when crisis strikes. In normal conditions, it is a comparatively easy task to maintain a federal system, with all its inefficiencies, but in times of emergency there is a tendency to cede principle in the interest of getting things done. Thus in wartime, and during the Great Depression of the 1930s, the Federal government garnered immense power at the expense of the states. It is not federalism alone that suffers during such periods of crisis, of course; all of the checks and limits on political authority tend to lose their urgency when the entire society is faced with emergency conditions. The executive tends to gain authority at the expense of the legislature, the Federal government at the expense of the states, and the Supreme Court becomes something less than perfect as a protector and defender of the Constitution. Unfortunately, authority granted in time of war is all too seldom rescinded when peace returns, and a prolonged period of national emergency can virtually "normalize" extraordinary political powers. It is very difficult to see how these trends can be avoided, but they do raise a serious question about the efficacy of federalism, or any theory of limited government, in an age where crisis is the rule, national emergency a daily matter, and tension between states overshadows the everyday affairs of men to an unprecedented degree.

Separation of powers. In the United States, the separation of powers is combined with a federal structure, but the two need not be used together; it is possible to have a separation of powers within the framework of a unified political structure. The principle itself is simple: divide authority into two or more parts and insist that the parts concur before the authority is exercised. A common everyday illustration of the principle is having two or more persons sign checks on behalf of a large organization. This spreads authority and guarantees that no single individual or group can wield political authority without consulting others and obtaining their agreement. In the American system, this technique is used at almost every level of government. Authority is divided between the states and the Federal government (the federal principle); the authority of the Federal government is divided into two main parts, and the exercise of authority by one requires the concurrence of the other. Finally, one branch of government, the Supreme Court, is by custom charged with the responsibility for maintaining the integrity of the fundamental Constitution through the process known as *judicial review,* the comparing of acts of government with the principles of the Constitution and refusing to enforce all acts which conflict with the Constitution.

Procedural limits. Various formal devices may be used as a minor check on the use of political authority. For example, political actions may be classified into different categories, and the more important categories may require a more difficult procedure before they can be carried out. Thus a routine measure may pass through a legislature by a simple majority vote, whereas other measures may require an absolute majority, a two-thirds majority, or perhaps a three-fourths majority. A very elaborate system is used to amend the American Constitution, requiring a two-thirds vote in both houses of Congress and ratification by three-fourths of the states. Such complex procedures certainly do inhibit the use of power; witness the relatively few amendments that have been made to the Constitution despite the fairly large number that have been proposed. Procedure prevents hasty and frivolous judgments. But once again we should not underestimate the ability of complex machinery to operate at high speed in times of crisis. Most of the constitutional amendments that have passed, omitting the original Bill of Rights, were sent through the amending process during periods of crisis, and at such times, amendment can be obtained with startling rapidity.

Informal limits. Almost every constitution has built into it a set of formal limits on the exercise of political authority, but the actual effectiveness of such provisions depends on factors outside the formal system. In American history, constitutional limitations have at times been very effective, and at other times almost meaningless. In some South American countries, the formal system is admirable, but it has no significance in practice; the same comment applies to the formal structure in the U.S.S.R. This suggests that formal institutions are less significant than the traditions and practices of society, and the British system, which depends heavily upon informal and conventional practices, would seem to bear out this assumption. In Britain, Parliament is theoretically supreme; there is no separation of powers, no system of checks and balances, no federal structure, no written constitution in the American sense. Yet the government is severely restricted in practice. The limits arise from a long tradition, a politically conscious general public, and an alert and free press. The combination has been formidable, and it has often succeeded in protecting the governed against the misuse of power much more effectively than the more legalistic and formal schemes employed elsewhere.

Responsibility and authority. To approach our problem from a slightly different point of view, it may be said that one principal problem in politics is to organize and allocate political authority in such a way that it is always exercised in a responsible manner. We search for responsible government, and the various techniques we have been discussing are meant to obtain that result. We ought, perhaps, to conclude by stressing a feature of responsible government which is easily overlooked, the role of the general population in any responsible political system.

Someone has said that the price of freedom is eternal vigilance, and there is much truth in this hoary aphorism. A population which guards its rights and privileges actively, with a clear understanding of their meaning and importance, is probably its own best guarantee against the misuse of political authority. Unfortunately, this is true only of those political systems in which individual political rights have already been established and the conditions needed for their operation already obtain. When the existing system is authoritarian, this remedy is not available, and the only means open to the population appears to be the drastic solution of social revolution. This is discouraging, for the history of social revolutions in modern times seems to indicate that the outcome of a revolution is likely to be as authoritarian as the ousted regime or perhaps worse. That was certainly the case in France after 1789, in Russia after 1917, and in China from 1911 to the present; in modern times only the United States has really escaped the authoritarian aftermath to revolution. The point is particularly significant for the newly emerging nations in Africa and Asia, for here we find authoritarian colonial rule refusing to give way except under pressure, and it need hardly surprise us to find that native rule after liberation is not infrequently authoritarian too. India is an example to the contrary, perhaps, but even in India there were periods in the transition from colonialism to independence that were not meritorious.

The same point can be made differently. The best guarantee against tyranny is responsible government; the best guarantee of responsible government is an alert, interested public. Without this solid foundation, all of the apparatus of democratic rule—elections, rotation in office, constitutions, etc.—can do little. The techniques are necessary, of course, for they help bind the elected to the electorate and thus increase the element of responsibility in government. The techniques must be meaningful, and not, as in the U.S.S.R., a sham. Elections that have no meaning are worthless. Within that framework, the political authority of the society can be so organized that its holders are amenable to as much control by the general public as one may wish.

It may be argued, of course, that tyranny is an ill-defined concept and perhaps nothing more than a meaningless phrase. That it is difficult to state clearly the condition inveighed against is doubtless true, but it is equally true that men have condemned the unfettered exercise of political authority, the regulation of political affairs without regard to principle, since the beginning of history. Hatred of tyranny is very old, and the study of the causes of tyranny dates at least to ancient Greece. Yet in every stage of man's history, the tyrant appears, and he is always recognized as such. In every case—Nero, Hitler, Stalin, Mao Tse-tung—they have brought catastrophe and ugliness in their train. Tyrants are difficult to anticipate, but always recognizable when they arrive.

The difficulty lies mainly in our inability to see tyranny developing; political authority contains the seeds of tyrannous rule in its very nature, and hence the possibility is always with us. Congressional committees may investigate the process of government, or the state of society, and produce information which enables us to remedy evils and correct mistakes. Other committees, armed with equal power, may produce terror and persecution without any concurrent benefits. Are there then to be no more committees? The suggestion has been made, but surely this is a coward's approach to the problems posed by political authority; benefits are seldom obtained without risk. Nevertheless, it is not unreasonable to attempt to minimize risk, to ensure against catastrophe, and this requires a nice balance of judgment and an eye for the significant principle. Here the crux of the problem lies. No society can reduce government to a cipher to ensure against tyranny; nothing would be more likely to produce the very condition that society seeks to avoid. But it is not possible either to abandon all principle in the interest of expediency. Somewhere, each society must strike a balance suitable to its own character and temperament and to the conditions of the times. It may be precarious, but it is the best that can be obtained.

Summary

Some of the basic characteristics of the modern state can be demonstrated by examining the nature, scope, justification, organization, and control of political authority. We find that there are two different approaches to political authority, one emphasizing the collective aspects of social affairs, the other stressing the importance of the individual. This emphasis is associated with such factors as the concentration and dispersal of power in society, the amount of sovereign authority left to be exercised by the individual, and the type of justification of political authority that is used. This is particularly significant when we attempt to limit the authority of the state, whether by custom or by constitutional and mechanical means. The problem is to find a means of making government responsible without rendering it impotent.

Review questions

1. Define authority, using the concepts of rights and obligations in your definition. Differentiate authority from power, and sketch the relationship between the two.

2. What is the role of coercion or force in political society? How do they relate to consent?

3. What factors determine the extent to which government may exercise authority in any given society?

4. Differentiate between the *right* of revolution and the *power* to revolt.

5. Why is the scope of political authority particularly difficult to define?

6. What is the role of sovereignty in political society? How does this differ from Jean Bodin's concept of sovereignty?

7. List some of the questions to which the individual American citizen can give sovereign answers. Those answered ultimately by the Federal government.

8. Differentiate between a monistic and a pluralistic political system. A centralized and a decentralized system. A collectivist and an individualistic system. Illustrate each definition.

9. Define the justification of political authority associated with Thomas Hobbes, John Locke, Jean Jacques Rousseau, and Karl Marx.

10. List the fundamental differences between the individualistic and collectivistic approaches to social authority.

11. What is meant by charismatic leadership? Give illustrations.

12. What are the respective advantages and disadvantages of centralized and decentralized political systems?

13. What is delegated legislation and why is it important?

14. What are some of the means that have been used to limit political authority? Criticize each of them for effectiveness.

For further study

1. Is it possible for any government to rule by sheer force? Explain.

2. What constitutes "legitimate" government tends to be defined differently by every society. Is there no single conception that can be applied to *every* society?

3. What view of human nature is implied in anarchist thought? Do you agree with it? Why?

4. How would you define "political"?

5. Is revolution really possible in a modern state such as Russia or the United States? Why?

6. What is the role of education in politics?

7. List the areas of life in which the American citizen is sovereign, make a similar list for a citizen of the U.S.S.R. How do the lists differ?

8. What type of political organization do you prefer to live under? Why?

9. Is efficiency one of the goals of good government? Is it possible that "good" government might conflict fundamentally with efficiency? How can "efficiency" in government be measured?

10. Define what you mean by a responsible government. What conditions have to be met?

CHAPTER *8*

The Political Process

So far as we now know, all men are mortal, not excluding those who wield political authority, and all rulers must eventually be replaced. The transfer of political power from one person to another is a part of the political process which has a fascinating history in the Western world—and in the Orient. In the Middle Ages, for example, a young man of blood might simply gather an army and sally forth in search of a kingdom to conquer, for that was accepted practice then. In other times and places, men have inherited political authority, along with their father's other possessions, or have acquired political authority along with religious status. Some few men have been selected to rule by the members of their society in open balloting. And the skillful application of violence and coercion has produced many a ruler; the death of king or emperor has not infrequently led to prolonged and fearful strife. Even the failure of the ruler to depart this life as speedily as the heir apparent thought suitable has led to various schemes designed to speed the laggard on his way and hasten the political process. The transfer of political authority has been effected on the battlefield, in the anteroom, in daylight and in darkness. The tools of politics have ranged from stealth to seizure, from the poisoned cup to murder and marriage, from execution to election. Many of these quaint political customs survive to the present day.

The making of rules or laws for society, the exercise of political authority, has been carried out in equally varied ways. The command of the ruler, quite unfettered and unlimited, has served men as law, as have custom and tradition and common practice. Societies have at times insisted that one or more representative agencies, or even the whole community, give their assent to laws; in other cases, laws have been made *in camera* and rigidly enforced, though they remained unpublicized and unknown. The procedures employed in lawmaking have ranged from simple enunciation to complex and elaborate rituals involving various agencies of government, each charged with some meaningful and responsible part in the process.

The political process, then, is an intricate affair in most modern societies. It consists, essentially, of the procedures and regulations which govern the transfer of political authority, and those which regulate the use of political authority. Many factors may affect it, directly or indirectly—personal, social, traditional, etc. Obviously it would be impossible to examine the multitude of present-day political systems in detail. Instead, we shall divide modern states into two basic types: one, which we shall designate an "open" society, is characterized by self-government and free participation in the political process by the citizens; the other, which we shall call "closed," restricts or limits the number who may take part in politics on one or another ground. Roughly, the "open" political process occurs in modern liberal democracies such as Britain or the United States; the Soviet Union can serve as our model of a "closed" system.

GENERAL CONSIDERATIONS

The study of politics can be a treacherous and deceiving business, and no aspect of politics is more likely to give rise to confusion than the political process and its related topics. Hence it is desirable to set forth at the outset certain general considerations which can guide our steps and help us to avoid some of the more obvious errors in interpretation.

Anthropocentrism. We are so accustomed to the political practices of our own age and our own society that we are here peculiarly liable to the influence of Bacon's Idols of the Cave. Our own political premises are by no means universally valid, as a little thought will demonstrate. In the United

States, political authority is not inherited or acquired by virtue of religious status, but in other parts of the world these ancient means of acquiring power remain in force. In Tibet, for example, political authority is acquired fundamentally through religious status, and in the Middle East, it is still inherited along with other forms of property. Similarly, we are unlikely to regard violence as a "real" political technique, and we would certainly regard authority acquired through violence as in some way tainted. Yet violence and coercion are commonplace in much of the world, both in the acquisition of political authority and in its exercise; hence their use must be taken into consideration in any general study of political practices. The American political system is atypical; it is not really representative of the kind of government that obtains in much of the world beyond our own continent.

Theory and practice. The difference between theory and practice, between formal and informal practice, seldom appears more clearly than in politics. The United States and the U.S.S.R. are formally constitutional federal systems; the reality, of course, is quite a different matter. Societies claim to share the same ultimate goals, but pursue them by widely divergent means; others share their means, but aim at goals that are scarcely compatible. We must, then, give our attention to both the formal and the informal, the real and the ideal. To concentrate on the formal and ignore the practical is certainly naïve, as everyone knows; but it is equally naïve to ignore the theoretical, the ideals of society, and concentrate on brute facts. For the ideal too tends to mold and condition political practice even where its influence seems slight and intangible.

Influence of social values. We should note particularly that the general value system inculcated into society has a great influence on the political process, even though that influence may be indirect. No political system can endure that does not produce viable results, and to produce viable results means to so govern that the political process and its consequences are acceptable to society. It follows that the influences in society which act to determine what is acceptable and what is not are an important part of the political process. A society that tolerates dishonesty in social or economic affairs, that disdains intellectualism or regards it with suspicion or indifference, can hardly expect to obtain a political process marked by rigid honesty and high idealism or intellectual vigor. Social values seem to follow the operation of a "Gresham's law"; values of a lower quality tend to drive out of the community its higher values. In other words, societies tend to get the kind of political process they deserve—a frightening possibility.

In practical terms, the value structure influences the political process in innumerable ways. It would be foolish to seek political authority by violence in a settled community such as Great Britain where the population simply would not accept the outcome of violence. From another point of view, the general value system of the community will reflect the status and prestige attached to political office and political activity and thereby influence greatly the type of person who engages in politics. In countries where the communal value system prescribes a political career for the well-educated or the wealthy (often the same people), a great deal of talent may be brought into the political arena that would not appear if the mores of society were different. The political process, in short, is affected by a number of factors that are not, strictly speaking, political.

Apathy. As a general rule, political societies suffer from the same lack of interest, or apathy, that afflicts other forms of social organization such as labor unions or educational institutions. In effect, only a very small part of the membership of the society actually takes an active interest in the operation of the society, not only in those associations which restrict participation in the political process, but even in associations which encourage participation very strongly. There is probably no simple explanation of this phenomenon, no one reason why the bulk of the members of most associations take only a nominal interest in associational affairs. But the effects of apathy are quite clear, particularly in the political process. It is a rare society indeed that commands the interest of its members to such a degree that more than half will cast a ballot in an election, let alone seek office. Even American presidential elections, which are the most "glamorous" of our political events, seldom attract as many as two-thirds of the eligible voters, and often bring out less than one-half of the total. Participation in state and local elections during "off years" when there is no presidential race is often very small indeed.

The consequences of apathy in the political society are quite grave, for the extent to which apathy appears casts doubt upon the basic premises on which democratic self-government rests. Are men really capable of self-government when only a small number of them attach sufficient importance to their political rights to exercise them? No conclusion can be drawn, and it has been suggested that this is not really the way to look at the question; but at the very least, apathy seems to imply a serious gap between political ideals and political realities. What is potentially a democracy may in fact operate as an oligarchy, not because the structure is necessarily oligarchical but because apathy makes it so in practice.

Elitism? Political apathy is a social fact. How are we to interpret it? Some modern writers believe that apathy is simply an indication of the necessity of elitism, though they differ to some extent on the conclusions to be drawn from their premise. A famous group of Italian elitists, including the sociologist Vilfredo Pareto and his compatriot Gaetano Mosca (and the sociologist Roberto Michels, who spent most of his life in Italy and Switzerland), produced an explanation of elitism that has been widely read and pondered. Pareto's argument, which is typical of the group, asserts that all societies can be divided into elites and masses and that one of the elites is concerned with governing. The political process, then, is explicable in terms of the activities of the governing elite and the efforts of others to obtain entry into that elite. The members of the elite, on the other hand, seek to maintain themselves in power. Violence is an acceptable means of conducting the political process, for it hastens the departure of decaying elites and makes room for new blood among the rulers.

Now Pareto's thesis certainly sounds like an accurate summary of the political process as it occurs in some societies, but that is not what Pareto had in mind. His point is that there is no way of avoiding elitism, or as Michels stated the position in his famous "iron law of oligarchy," elitism is inherent in the very nature of social organization. This is, of course, a repudiation of the traditional principles of liberal democracy, particularly the notion of equality. Pareto in fact thought that democracy was both impossible and undesirable as a way of governing. More recently, E. E. Schattschneider has argued in a provocative and interesting book that though the political process may, as Pareto argued, be elitist at root, this is no reason to deny the democratic premise; what is needed, he believes, is a redefinition or reevaluation of democracy that will bring it into accord with existing political facts.[1]

The transfer of political authority. The movement on the part of the modern national state toward either the open or the closed political system has been fairly well defined since the beginning of the modern era, and its effects can be seen quite clearly in both the means used to transfer political authority and the use made of political authority once acquired. In Britain, Western Europe, Scandinavia, Australia and New Zealand, the United States, and Canada, to mention the outstanding examples of open society in the contemporary world, the political system has altered gradually to make possible and encourage mass participation in the political process. In most of the rest of the world, politics has made use of processes which are in varying degrees closed. We shall take our illustrations of closed society from the government of the Soviet Union, but the principles are equally applicable in Communist China, in Eastern Europe, and in much of the Middle East and South America.

A perfectly open or perfectly closed society is almost impossible to con-

---

[1] E. E. Schattschneider, *The Semisovereign People,* Holt, Rinehart and Winston, Inc., New York, 1960.

ceive, and certainly no case of either exists in the present day world. It is a matter of degree, though no less significant for that reason. To decide whether a particular society is open or closed we need to ask meaningful questions about the political process in that society and then use our answers to range that society along a scale of possibilities. We shall, in our examples, use extreme cases where distinctions are made fairly easily. But in practice it is sometimes very difficult to make a judgment. Switzerland, for example, does not allow women to vote. Does that imply that Switzerland is a closed society? In one sense, it would be partially closed, in that the franchise is denied to a particular section, and a large one, of the population. Yet in many other respects, Switzerland adheres very closely to the ideal of the open society. We must, in other words, be careful to avoid hasty conclusions based on partial evidence.

The open society. The open society is a political ideal, a goal which men seek through politics, not an accomplished fact. It implies acceptance of a number of basic assumptions about man and his relation to society, and on these assumptions the remainder of the structure can be erected. It implies, first of all, the belief that man is capable of governing himself and that he should govern himself. This is sometimes stated as the principle of *popular sovereignty,* the belief that political authority derives from the consent of those over whom it is exercised and from no other place. The open society further implies the belief that men ought basically to be regarded as equals in the eyes of the law and in the rules of the political system. Equally important, it implies the belief that government ought to be carried on in the best interests of the governed, not in the interests of some particular person or group. The political devices of the open society—political parties, representative institutions, free courts, constitutions, guarantees of personal freedom, etc.—are intended to achieve these political ideals; they are not goals in themselves.

Political decisions, for example, are customarily made by majority rule in open societies, but majoritarianism is avoided by accepting the basic premise that the rights of the minority are not to be infringed by the majority and that minorities are free to seek support for their views and if possible become majorities themselves. There is a further ameliorating principle implied in the belief that no political goal is so certain that it justifies the use of any means at hand to achieve it. Much of the horror of modern politics has been the work of men who were absolutely certain they knew the end of political activity and were willing to countenance almost any measure of tyranny to achieve their goals.

The open society, then, is committed to the principle of free self-government and to maintaining the conditions that make it possible. It follows necessarily that freedom of speech and of publication, freedom of association, and political freedom should be equal and universal in an open society. The right to oppose, to criticize, and to condemn with impunity, are corollary, as are freedom of access to an unbiased education, freedom of information, and the various personal freedoms needed to make the exercise of self-government meaningful. There is also implied some measure of willingness on the part of members of society to make self-government work, a willingness to accept defeat and still retain the system, and a willingness to pay the cost of self-government in the form of time and energy and care. If the loser in every election took to the hills and harassed the government with guerrilla warfare the system would soon lose its vitality and collapse. An open society is possible only when almost everyone accepts its value and seeks to preserve it, even at cost to themselves.

The requirements of this approach to politics affect much of the structure of society. The population must concur in the belief that men are essentially equal in worth and dignity. That is, the open society is fundamentally egalitarian, in social matters at least. The open society is individualistic, and not merely in economic affairs, for it seeks to maximize the benefits to the individual and not the gain of particular elements of society or of society as a whole. Open societies are committed to the "utilitarian" outlook, to use the phrase associated with the school of nineteenth-century English philosophers who followed Jeremy Bentham. In Bentham's terms, the aim of government was the "greatest happiness of the greatest number," and if this maxim has proved difficult to define and apply, there remains a basic commitment to the *individual* happiness which it connotes.

Clearly, the open society which has been described here is no different from the liberal democracies that have developed in Western society, as in Britain or the United States. We favor the use of "open society" as a neutral term that avoids emotive commitments, but liberal democracy can be used as an accurate synonym for the ideal.

The closed society. The closed society proposes quite a different sort of ideal for mankind, and it produces a society that differs fundamentally from the open society—in organization, in process, and in consequences for the individual citizen and perhaps for the entire world. The capacity of man for self-government is repudiated, either explicitly (as in Nazi Germany) or implicitly (as in the Soviet Union). It asserts that men must in fact be led by those who are better, richer, genetically superior, wiser, or better able to see the future. In consequence, representative institutions and their corollary parts of the political process are eliminated from the scene in practice if not in theory. The franchise may be limited severely or rendered meaningless by dissociating it from the actual transfer and use of political authority. The personal freedoms on which the open society thrives are anathema to the closed society and must be restricted or abolished entirely. The value of the individual must be denied, again implicitly if not explicitly, and replaced by the value of the collective or the welfare of future generations. The ideal of peaceful change and respect for order is replaced by hatred and distrust for existing institutions and a willingness to resort to violence to accomplish political ends. Indeed, violence may even be lauded as a "purifying" element in social life and indulged for its own sake. Not infrequently, the closed society takes the path to war in pursuit of its "destiny" or its alleged "right" to rule others.

Briefly, the closed society replaces the liberal ideal of an individualistic, tolerant, self-governing community, with the ideal of a disciplined, obedient population led by an authoritarian government which is in no way responsible to the population for its actions. The dignity of the individual is replaced by the ideal of service to the state; the ideal of self-government gives way to the ideal of obedience. The description here is extreme, perhaps, but it is not inaccurate when applied to Communist China or to the U.S.S.R. Indeed, a substantial part of mankind lives in societies which are much closer to the ideal of closed society than to the liberal democracy to which Americans have grown accustomed.

The distinction between open and closed political societies is more easily seen when we turn to specific details of the political process. Using Britain and the United States as our model of the open society and the U.S.S.R. as the paradigm for closed society, let us examine some of the more specific ways in which they differ. What kind of political environment has society created? What part of the population is enfranchised? Are elections meaningful? Where is authority located and how is it transferred? The answers to these and other similar questions will help to define a set of standards by which political societies can be differentiated, and will provide a useful index of the kind of political life which the citizen leads in each type of society.

THE POLITICAL ENVIRONMENT

Politics does not operate in a vacuum, and the political atmosphere is a significant index to the quality of political society. In particular, open and closed societies differ radically in the extent to which their citizens are allowed freedom to speak and write critically about their government, freedom to associate together for political purposes, and free access to the information needed for meaningful political action.

Freedom of criticism. In an open society, the individual citizen is free to criticize his government and he must have all of the corollary freedoms implied in the right to criticize. In a closed society freedom of criticism is seriously inhibited or eliminated altogether. Few societies are completely open in this sense. In the United States, for example, the law does not permit a citizen to advocate the overthrow of the government by violent means if an overt action is associated with such advocacy. The precise limits of the restriction are not perfectly clear; it was aimed at the American Communist party and presumably was intended as a limit on that group alone. However, it could be applied to other political views, presumably; hence it acts in a restrictive manner on complete freedom of criticism and advocacy. The difficulty with laws such as these, of course, is that when the group advocating the overthrow of the government is large enough to accomplish its goal, it will succeed whether it is permitted or not; if the movement lacks enough support to succeed, then the restriction is not needed. It is therefore hard to see what can be gained through the enactment of such laws. Beyond this rather uncertain point, however, legal restrictions on free criticism in the United States are governed mainly by the laws of libel.

In the closed society, control of both public and private criticism of the government is undertaken on a large scale. This means a large administrative apparatus charged with the task of repressing criticism—a good indication of a closed society. Censorship is common, and surveillance of political views by secret police is widespread. Even the services of children have been used as a means of inhibiting criticism, and denouncing one's parents for political deviation has been elevated into a patriotic duty in some of the more severe dictatorships of this century.

The closed society usually exercises careful control over the educational system, the book publishing industry, and the mass information media, such as radio and television. This does not mean that all nations which control radio and television services are dictatorial; in fact, only the United States, of the major countries of the world, has a privately owned radio and television system. Private ownership of the press, on the other hand, seems an absolute need for open society; no open society has a government-owned press, and all closed societies either own the press outright or control it very carefully. Information and education are equally sensitive areas in politics, and extensive state control over the educational system is usually an indication of a closed society, particularly when the state is heavily involved in the content of the textbooks and the type of information taught in the classroom. Administrative and supply services to education are, of course, another matter.

Freedom of association. In a large-scale political society, social organization is needed before the voice of the individual can be heard; hence the right to associate with others for political purposes is a fundamental necessity in open society. A major distinction between open and closed societies, then, is the degree to which they permit autonomous organizations within the framework of the state. For example, we find that the labor unions, professional associations, and even recreational associations in the Soviet Union are really creatures of the state and not agencies through which the individual citizen can make his voice heard. They are instruments of the state, not instruments of the individuals who belong to them. An even more significant case, of course, is the political party, which is essentially a creature of government in a closed society, and a means of acquiring political authority in an open society. We shall deal with the problem of political parties in more detail below; here it will suffice to say that the right of free association is a common mark of open society and that that right is usually limited in closed society.

Freedom of information. Freedom of information, the right to know what government is doing and why, is also an essential feature of open society, and is obviously unsuited to closed society. But in practice, it is not always easy to measure the degree to which government controls the free flow of information. All governments restrict the free flow of information in some measure, if only for security reasons. Closed societies tend to restrict information in *all* areas of government, whether or not they have military significance, whereas the restrictions imposed by open societies tend to be limited to a few areas which are obviously related to defense. In the U.S.S.R., it is almost impossible to obtain accurate information about living standards, agricultural and industrial production, foreign affairs, government finance, and a wide range of related subjects. In the United States or Britain, information is available in carload lots, except in the two major areas of defense and foreign affairs, and even here the open society habitually publishes far more information than the closed society is willing to concede.

Military and foreign affairs pose a peculiar problem for the liberal democracy. Few persons argue that a government should have *no* military or foreign affairs secrets, but many are concerned with the amount of information actually reserved in these two areas. The difficulty stems from our comparative inability to define vital information with reasonable accuracy. What really is essential to national defense or national security? This is a very difficult question to answer; indeed, we may argue that it has never been satisfactorily answered. We shall deal with the problem at greater length in Chapter 19; here we simply note its existence and the nature of the difficulties it creates.

Secrecy in foreign relations is perhaps less easily justified than secrecy in defense matters, and this aspect of the restriction of free information has been attacked very strongly by liberal writers. In the early part of the century, American opinion was indeed clearly committed to the view that secret diplomacy was in part responsible for the major political problems the world then faced, and the demand for "open covenants, openly arrived at," which President Wilson took to the Versailles Peace Conference was a reflection of prevailing opinion, or was at least widely applauded. This feeling has now died out, for the most part, and it was certainly a naïve attitude for a major world power to adopt. American experience with "summit meetings" and United Nations Security Council meetings has shown all too clearly that the glare of publicity is not really conducive to meaningful negotiation. Open international meetings tend to become sounding boards rather than negotiating sessions. Most experts now agree that secret negotiations are essential for diplomacy, though open societies still maintain that the outcome of negotiations ought to be communicated fully to the public as soon as possible.

In practice, then, open societies maintain only a nominal control over information relating to foreign affairs and defense matters, while closed societies are extremely secretive; the difference is one of degree, but very significant nonetheless. Since all information on these matters must come from governments themselves, it is an area which is peculiarly liable to abuse, for even if invidious intent is lacking, the impulse to paint one's own behavior in the best possible colors while blackening the opponent is hard to resist. Such distortions may annoy the purist, but they deceive only the naïve and those who "believe everything they read in the newspapers." In open societies, to take an example, dozens of interpretations, some favorable and others condemnatory, will appear for each major international incident—the Yalta Conference in 1945 is a good illustration. In a closed society, only one version —the official version—appears, and criticism is severely enjoined. The difference is vital.

The franchise. The franchise is not, perhaps, too useful as an index to the degree to which society is open or closed, for most societies today have extended the franchise to most of the population. The really significant point here is the extent to which the franchise has meaning. That is, if the franchise actually does decide the locus of authority in society, then its extent or qualification becomes politically significant; if elections are merely a fraud, then excessive concern with the extent of the franchise would be misplaced.

In an open society, the franchise is widely extended, or as nearly universal as possible. Each citizen counts for but a single vote, and all votes weigh equally in the outcome. It was this principle, for example, that led the British Labor Government to eliminate plural voting by university graduates and business residents of the city of London after World War II. Of course, it is not possible for everyone in society to vote and each society sets some basic qualifications, but in open societies the rules of eligibility are applied equally, whether they deal with minimum voting age, ability to read or write, or some other requirement. The need for equality is obvious, and it helps explain the amount of concern generated by the civil rights issue in the United States in recent decades.

In closed societies, a number of techniques are used to limit the franchise. Perhaps the most common is to render the electoral system meaningless by transferring and using political authority through some other structure, such as a political party. The U.S.S.R., for example, has an elaborate electoral system, but the real locus of power is in the Communist party, and positions within the party are not subject to election by the mass of the population. Other restrictions may be based on economic status, sex, race, or religious affiliation. Thus many American states once limited the ballot to those with a certain amount of property, and the Southern states have sought to limit the franchise to whites. Religious beliefs have not been an important factor in the American system since the Constitution was adopted, but the early Puritan Colonies, to take one example, limited the franchise to members of the church. In all cases, such limits are an infringement of one basic tenet of open society— the belief in political equality for all persons. Most of the liberal democracies have either eliminated or seek to eliminate the remaining restrictions from their political systems.

Universal suffrage is a basic principle in open societies, but is not sufficient to establish an open society. Its use can be negated in various ways. If no elections were held, to take an absurd case, then the right to vote would have no meaning. We have already mentioned the technique used in the U.S.S.R. to reduce the significance of the vote. Still other means are available. If the voter is given no choice among candidates for a particular office, the usefulness of the vote is substantially reduced. In Poland, for example, or the U.S.S.R., the voter is faced with a single list of candidates, one for each office to be filled, and no alternatives are open. Clearly, the right to vote is not very meaningful in these circumstances. If the voter is coerced or threatened, as happened frequently in Nazi Germany, or if he is paid to vote in a particular manner, then voting loses its meaning so far as liberal democracy is concerned. Finally, we may note that indirect elections, which occur in many political systems, are a means of reducing the significance of the individual vote, though they do not reduce it to complete insignificance. To the degree that these means are employed, the society moves away from the ideal of open society in the direction of a more closed system.

Elections. Since elections perform quite different functions in open and closed society we must limit our discussion of election procedures and practices to electoral systems which are meaningful—those in which a genuine transfer of political authority is effected by the election. Having done so, we find that some quite useful distinctions can be made among the various electoral systems, that they are in varying degrees open and closed.

Secret ballot? Until the latter part of the nineteenth century, the American voter cast his ballot openly. In mid-century and before, he often came to the polls for the day, spending his time drinking and conversing with his neighbors. When his mind was made up, he announced it publicly to the recorder of votes. The system was open to abuse, obviously enough, and the reform movements that appeared in the late nineteenth century urged the adoption of the Australian or secret ballot. This has now become standard practice in the United States and in many other liberal democracies. The secret ballot has not solved all of the problems associated with voting, of course, for abuse of the system is still possible but more difficult. In practice, the open ballot stands largely discredited (though perhaps something can still be said for its use); hence the secret ballot has become one of the standard practices in democratic—and undemocratic—countries.

Frequency of elections. Since elections do allocate political authority, the frequency of elections is one factor making for responsible officeholding in a political system. Thomas Jefferson, for example, believed that frequent elections and rotation of officeholders were highly desirable, and indeed necessary to the democratic process. How often should elections be held? There are arguments on both sides of the question—some preferring frequent elections, others seeking longer intervals between elections.

Election for life would, in effect, deny the right of self-government. But the argument for a fairly long term in office can be made quite strong. Elections are expensive, for one thing, and frequent elections add to the cost of government. Short terms in office may leave the incumbent no time to learn his job properly. It is often argued, for example, that the congressman can hardly learn his way around the Capitol properly in a two-year term. Further, when elections are frequent, the officeholder must spend a great deal of time preparing for them, effectively reducing the time he can allocate to his elective function. The advantages of the short term outweigh some of these disadvantages, certainly, but the balance is not easily discerned. Frequent election seems likely to increase responsibility in some degree, for example, and to reduce the danger of tyranny—a point that concerned Jefferson greatly.

Practice varies greatly in different parts of the world. In the United States, congressmen serve for a two-year period, senators for six years, the President for four years; justices of the Supreme Court, on the other hand, are appointed for life during good behavior. In Britain, general elections must be held at least once every five years, though they may occur more frequently. The terms of few elective offices run for as long as ten years or for as little as one year. The significance of the time factor will depend upon the office, of course.

Election districts. The kind of election districting that is used, and the manner by which election is decided within the district, will often exert a substantial influence on the political process. The range of choice lies between a small single-member district (most British constituencies, for example) or large districts represented by more than one elected member of a representative body. In general, the single-member district is most widely used. The precise location of the districts, their size, etc., can be very important. In the United States, districting in general seems to favor the rural dweller at the expense of the city dweller; it takes fewer rural votes than urban votes to elect a member of the state legislatures, and large cities like New York are often heavily discriminated against in the state political system. Other devices, like gerrymandering (altering voting district boundaries to benefit one or another of the political parties), present similar difficulties for the person concerned with equality of representation.

Basis for election. With a single-member election district, must the successful candidate obtain a majority or a plurality? The plurality tends to make multiparty contests possible; the requirement for a majority vote tends to work best in a two-party system. In some cases, a runoff election is held to produce the necessary majority, entailing a further outlay of time and money. The basis for election also raises the question of forced voting, since the requirement of an absolute majority of eligible voters could be self-defeating if only a minority of those eligible for the ballot chose to come to the polls.

Some of the difficulties can be illustrated by the position of the Liberal party in Great Britain—traditionally a two-party system. The Liberals have managed to roll up a substantial vote in national elections, yet their representation in the House of Commons has been very small in the post-World War II years. They consider themselves much handicapped by the existing electoral system, and have denounced it frequently as unfair and undemocratic. In 1950, to take one example, the Liberal party polled 2,621,548 votes out of a total of 28,772,672, yet they elected only 9 Members of Parliament out of a total exceeding 600. In comparison, the Conservative party polled 12,502,567 votes and elected 298 M.P.s, and the Labor party elected 315 M.P.s with a total of 13,266,592 votes. The Liberal party received about 9.1 per cent of the votes cast in the election, but obtained only 1.5 per cent of the seats in the House of Commons.

Proportional representation. Probably the most frequent suggestion made by political leaders in the same position as the Liberal party leaders in Britain is the adoption of one or another of the systems of *proportional representation* (P.R.). When P.R. is used, strength in the elective body is proportional to total votes obtained in the election rather than to the outcome of voting in each individual voting district. Minor parties, which may lose a number of districts by small margins, like P.R.; major parties in a two-party system dislike it intensely for they stand to lose by it.

The basic question is whether justice demands that representation be proportional to support among the voters, or whether this is subordinate to the need to obtain a clear-cut decision from the electorate. P.R. does tend to "dilute" the composition of elective bodies by introducing representatives of smaller parties; hence it tends toward a plurality of political parties rather than a two-party system. However, its effects may be different, as we can see by considering its influence in an essentially one-party structure, such as the Southern states in the United States. There is nothing sacred about two-party systems, of course, and multiparty systems are common in many open societies, such as France or Belgium. In a two-party system, one party or another will usually acquire a clear majority and the right to govern. Multiparty systems usually breed coalitions; they offer the voter a wider range of choice, of course, and this factor too may be considered important. We shall return to the question when we consider political parties in more detail. Here we need only to note the complexity of the problems involved in making a choice between one system and another.

Voting behavior. In this connection, a number of the recent studies that have been made of the voting behavior of the citizens of open societies, particularly in the United States, are extremely significant. The relationship between voting patterns and religious preferences, racial groupings, socioeconomic status, education, occupation, and many other factors has been examined in some detail by a wide variety of techniques. Other studies have tried to determine the psychological factors at work in voting preferences, in "ticket splitting," and in attitudes toward particular issues. Since most of the major studies relate particularly to the American political scene, we cannot undertake a detailed examination of them here; they belong more properly in an extended study of American government and politics. But the reader is warned against hasty judgment in matters relating to voting until such time as he has made the acquaintance of some of the major contributions to this literature.[2]

REPRESENTATIVE GOVERNMENT

Direct self-government is now physically impossible, except in local matters, and liberal democracy long ago turned to representative institutions as repositories for political authority. Representative systems are meaningful

[2] For example, Paul F. Lazarsfeld, Bernard Berelson, and Hazel Gaudet, *The People's Choice*, 2d ed., Columbia University Press, New York, 1948; Bernard Berelson, Paul F. Lazarsfeld, and William N. McPhee, *Voting*, The University of Chicago Press, Chicago, 1954; Angus Campbell, Gerald Gurin, and Warren E. Miller, *The Voter Decides*, Harper & Row, Publishers, Incorporated, New York, 1954; Angus Campbell, Philip E. Converse, Warren E. Miller, and Donald E. Stokes, *The American Voter*, John Wiley & Sons, Inc., New York, 1960; and a large number of articles in the *American Political Science Review* between 1955 and the present.

only in open societies, though many closed systems also have an elaborate representative mechanism. Here we are concerned primarily with different standards of eligibility for office, techniques for nominating candidates for office, theories of representation, and means of controlling the representative once he is installed in office.

Eligibility for office. Eligibility for office is usually related to, though not necessarily identical with, eligibility for the franchise. Minimum age for voting and for officeholding may be different, and some offices may carry exceptional qualifications in terms of age or training (presidents and judges, for example). Age restrictions, though galling to the young, seem not to be inherently unfair since they affect the population equally. Other limits on the right to hold office are less egalitarian, e.g., the property qualification, one of the older qualifications for office, which is now removed or being removed in most liberal democracies. We must not overlook indirect property qualifications, such as those which arise when the salary for an office is not sufficient to support the incumbent and private means are needed before the office can be accepted.

In practice, most of the serious limitations on eligibility for officeholding are part of the informal political structure. In the U.S.S.R., the formal requirement for officeholding is minimal, but informally every candidate must either be a member of the Communist party (about three-fourths of the candidates are) or be approved or sponsored by the party. Party membership or approval is therefore a *sine qua non* for holding office even though this does not appear in the formal constitutional structure. In the United States, it seems unlikely that an avowed atheist or a Buddhist could gain election to high office, and until the election of John F. Kennedy, it seemed that some offices at least must be filled by white Protestants. These are informal limits of a special sort, of course, but they can operate very effectively.

Nominations. Even where officeholding is formally open to all citizens, the method used to nominate candidates for office may act as a very effective screening device, as we saw with relation to the Soviet Union. It must be said that in most open societies, control over nominations rests with the political parties. In some systems, such as that used in the Weimar Republic in Germany or in the proportional representation system used in France before World War II, the nomination procedure virtually ensured party control over nominees. In the United States, nominations were made by party caucus in the early days of the republic, but this system was speedily superseded by the convention system. At the present time, nominations may be made through party conventions (the national candidates, for example) or through the direct primary election—a preliminary election in which party members vote for the candidate of their choice, the winner being selected to represent the party in the regular election. Nominations may also be made by petition, signed by a stipulated number of voters.

Has the nomination system been successfully "democratized" in open society? The question is almost impossible to answer. The cry of "controlled nominations" is still raised everywhere, and the success of the direct primary, which was intended to eliminate "bossism" in nominations, is hard to evaluate. Perhaps the best thing we can say is that some societies now have machinery that makes nomination possible on a broad basis but that much of the control over the system still rests with the political parties and those who control them.

Representative theory. As we shall see in a moment, any evaluation of the system of nominations, or of the means used to control representatives once in office, depends fundamentally upon our conception of the proper role of the representative, of his relation to his constituents and to the government. Who does the representative represent? And what is meant by representing? These rather innocent-sounding questions produce a serious dilemma for democratic theorists. The basis of representation is the less serious of the two questions, for representatives commonly represent a given geographic location; hence the British M.P. or the American congressman or senator represents a given district or the people in it. But it is possible to argue that representation ought properly to include interest groups, religious associations, ethnic groups, castes, racial groups, and so on.

The basis of representation. Our evaluation of the best basis for representation will obviously depend in large measure upon the social context in which the political system operates. If the national state contains two large ethnic groups, as did Czechoslovakia before World War II, representation that took into account this ethnic division might make for a more workable political system. Federal structures commonly allow representation of the state's point of view in the councils of the federal government. In Britain, the old universities, and the city of London, were for many years entitled to separate representation in the House of Commons, but this was eliminated because it involved plural voting. Where a society has a predominant religious group, as in Israel or Afghanistan, it may be necessary to include representation of the religious interests of society to obtain a workable system. Clearly, we cannot assume that representation based upon numbers alone is always adequate, but once qualitative distinctions are introduced, the question becomes extremely complex. This is perhaps the best argument for a simple numerical basis for representation, but it would be idle to pretend that it solves all of the difficulties involved in the question.

The role of the representative. This brings us to the broader question of defining the relationship between the representative and his constituents. What does it mean to "represent" a group of persons? What obligations does it place on each side of the relationship? An illustration may clarify the question involved here. Imagine a congressman who represents a particular district which is populated mainly by farmers. Suppose that the congressman, through his work in Congress, has come to the conclusion that Federal aid to farmers, however beneficial it may be to his own constituents, is in the long run an unwholesome solution to the farm problem. Suppose further that he has sounded his constituents on the question and found that they disagree completely with him despite his best efforts to convince them to the contrary. Then introduce a bill into Congress to continue Federal aid to farmers. Should the congressman vote for the bill? Should he oppose it? Or should he resign his office? The dilemma is clear. The congressman is of one opinion; his constituents hold another. How should he vote?

There are two solutions to this dilemma, each tenable, but in some degree contradictory. Both cannot be held concurrently. One theory of representation holds that the representative is in effect a "mirror" of the views of his constituents; hence his task is to follow their instructions whenever their views are known. The opposing view holds that the representative is the agent or "broker" for his constituents, empowered by them to act as he thinks best, though in their own best interests and not in his. Here are two quite different conceptions of representative government, each of which has found supporters in the past, though the "broker" view is today most widely held, partly because of the practical problems involved in the "mirror" theory.

The representative as a mirror. Let us examine these two theories more closely. The mirror theory begins with the view that men are capable of self-government and that ideally government ought to be conducted by a meeting of all of the citizens in which a vote of all is taken on each measure. This is impossible; hence representatives are needed. But their task, in this context, is to act as though each of the individual voters were in fact present—they must follow the consensus. This concept has the merit of simplicity and directness. But in practice, it may prove complex and cumbersome. How are the views of the constituents to be made known? What occurs when issues arise suddenly that demand a speedy action by the representative? Clearly, it would be virtually impossible to bind the representative absolutely and in all cases to the will of the constituents, for this might easily render him quite unable to act.

These practical difficulties have led to a corollary conception, known as the "mandate theory," which enlarges the sphere of action somewhat. Under the mandate theory, which is widely accepted in Britain, the political party which is successful at the polls acquires a "mandate to rule" according to the political platform on which the election was fought. In 1911, for example, the Liberal party in Britain deliberately held a general election on the issue of the powers of the House of Lords, and when the election was won, it was accepted as an indication of the desires of the sovereign public and the amendment of the Lords' powers was allowed to pass. This is not quite the same thing as the mirror theory, of course, but it is a close relative, inspired by the same fundamental premise.

The representative as agent or broker. The alternative point of view begins at quite a different set of premises, and we cannot do better than quote the eloquent and elegant statement made by the British statesman Edmund Burke to his own constituents in the city of Bristol when he was declared elected to the House of Commons in 1774:

> Certainly, Gentlemen, it ought to be the happiness and glory of the representative to live in the strictest union, the closest correspondence, and the most unreserved communication with his constituents. Their wishes ought to have great weight with him; their opinions high respect; their business unremitted attention. It is his duty to sacrifice his repose, his pleasure, his satisfactions, to theirs—and above all, ever, and in all cases, to prefer their interest to his own.
>
> But his unbiased opinion, his mature judgment, his enlightened conscience, he ought not to sacrifice to you, to any man, or to any set of men living. These he does not derive from your pleasure—no, nor from the law and the constitution. They are a trust from providence, for the abuse of which he is deeply answerable. Your representative owes you, not his industry only, but his judgment; and he betrays, instead of serving you, if he sacrifices it to your opinion.
>
> Parliament is not a *Congress* of ambassadors from different and hostile interests, which interests each must maintain, as an agent and advocate, against other agents and advocates; but Parliament is a *deliberative* assembly of *one* nation with *one* interest, that of the whole—where not local purposes, not local prejudices, ought to guide, but the general good, resulting from the general reason of the whole. You choose a member; indeed; but when you have chosen him, he is not a member of Bristol, but he is a member of *Parliament*. If the local constituent should have an interest or form an hasty opinion, evidently opposed to the real good of the rest of the community, the member for that place ought to be as far as any other from any endeavor to give it effect.[3]

Clearly Burke does not accept the view that the representative is a mere creature of the electorate; he seeks to justify the position of the independent man of judgment, selected by virtue of his competence and free to exercise,

[3] "Speech to the Electors of Bristol on His Being Declared by the Sheriffs Duly Elected One of the Representatives in Parliament for That City." Edmund Burke, *The Works of the Right Honorable Edmund Burke*, Little, Brown and Company, Boston, 1894, vol. II, p. 95.

indeed bound to exercise, his personal judgment. Why? Essentially, because Burke believed that the purpose of Parliament was to protect and extend the *national* interest as against parochial interests and the possibility of errors in local judgment. But that surely is the point at issue. If men have the right to govern themselves, they must have also the right to err. Here Burke is attacking one of the pillars of liberal democratic theory.

Theory and responsibility. An adequate discussion of the points involved in representative theory would occupy too much space in an introductory text; the student can work out some of the implications for himself. If the electors are to choose a competent and qualified person, what basis are they to judge upon? What role is party to play in the whole process? Burke, after all, lived in an age before the modern political party, and he was thinking in terms of a highly personalized political structure; whether his view is tenable in the modern age is most uncertain. Ought the liberal democracies to examine further the possibility of plebescitary government? Modern technology, after all, holds out the hope of informing and perhaps obtaining a consensus from millions of persons in a relatively short period of time.

From another point of view, if each representative is to speak for his own local interests, what happens to the national interest that so much concerns Burke? Or if we turn to the mandate theory, how can it be reconciled with the party system as it appears in the United States? Try to write down all of the arguments, pro and con, and the unresolved questions that have been raised in the text; it is an excellent exercise in political thinking.

The last major point we wish to raise here is the very significant problem of achieving a responsible system of government, whatever the theory of representation that is adopted. If we believe that a free choice of representatives, subject to reelection, satisfies the requirements of responsible government, then one theory of representation will serve our needs. But if choice alone is not sufficient, if the electorate must also have some measure of control over the elected representative in a responsible political system, then a different atmosphere and new machinery may be needed. In the United States, for example, the machinery of government makes possible a free choice of candidate, but the major means of control provided by the system is the right to withhold reelection, and that is surely no more than a partial check at best, for the only penalty incurred by the representative is loss of office *after* his term expires. What is to keep the representative in line *during* his term of office? On the other hand, it is difficult to conceive of a political system that would ensure continuing control over the representative by the population without producing an unwieldy structure. The recall or impeachment can serve this purpose, but they are at best extraordinary measures which are not easily adapted to frequent use.

It is perhaps for this reason that modern representative theory tends to support the broker or agent theory of representation, to consider the representative an agent with full powers who is accountable for his behavior at the expiration of his term in office. Perhaps it is only fair to allow a representative the opportunity to perform for a given time period before assaying his value; too quick a judgment might fail to take into account the difficulties met by the inexperienced man.

Man or party? The broker theory does not solve all of our problems, of course; we must still decide whether judgment will be passed on the basis of party performance or on the basis of individual performance. Much depends upon the political context, certainly—on the party structure, the rigidity of party discipline, and similar matters. We are asking, really, on what basis a representative ought either to be reelected or defeated after a term in office, and it is not an easy question to answer. If a "better" man appears, surely the better man ought to be installed in office. But what constitutes a "better" man in this sense? On what grounds can we judge that a representative has performed his task well? And how do we define this task? Can we count the number of absences from the legislature? The number of sessions attended or the number of committee meetings attended? The number of speeches made? Do we go by the party record? How is that to be judged? These are very troublesome questions, not least for the representative seeking reelection.

In practice, a variety of criteria are used. In Britain, as compared with the United States, the performance of the political party weighs more heavily than the performance of the individual. This is partly due to the preponderant role of the party in British government, the limited facilities available for the individual M.P. to sponsor legislation, etc. Further, party discipline is much tighter in Britain, and the individual M.P. has much less freedom of action in voting, and even in argument, than does the congressman or senator in the United States. Party allegiance is, of course, very important in American politics as well—perhaps, the most important single factor in the electoral process—but the party plays a less crucial role in the work of the American congressman than in the role of the British M.P. It is easier to move against the tide of party allegiance in the United States. For example, in presidential election years, the winning presidential candidate generally draws a large number of party members into office "on his coattails," particularly when there is a great deal of straight-ticket voting. But in every case, there are individuals from the opposite party who manage to survive. We find that some candidates increase their popularity in an election while other members of the same party do very badly.

The trend, however, is toward a judgment based on party allegiance and party performance, and this may be a necessary effect of mass politics and elections in which very large numbers of officeseekers appear on every ballot. In the circumstances, the voter may have little information about the individual candidate, excepting perhaps the major figures seeking national office or high offices in the state. Where information relating to the personal character of the candidate is lacking, party affiliation seems the only possible basis on which a meaningful choice can be made. At the present time, American practice differs in some measure from European practice, for party differences in Europe are more clearly defined, and the parliamentary system is rather easier to control than a divided and complex structure like the American federal system. But the trend toward attaching increased significance to party program is clearly discernible even in the United States with its loose and poorly disciplined party system, and the consequences of the trend could become very important in the near future.

POLITICAL PARTIES

This brings us to the role of the political parties in the political system, and returns us once again to a consideration of the significant differences between open and closed political societies. Some understanding of the role of political parties in politics is essential to sound judgment in any political system, whether it be open or closed, and a knowledge of the differences in the role of parties in open and closed systems gives us a number of useful clues to the operation of closed societies. In an age such as our own, when large-scale organization is essential to successful social action, it is the organized group and not the individual, usually, that carries weight. Hence parties are the real key to political power in both open systems and closed.

What is a political party? Essentially, an organized group which seeks political power by the means which society provides. However, since the social context differs greatly, it is difficult to produce a simple definition of a political party that will satisfy all situations. In the United States, for example, the Communist party has been outlawed. Some persons have protested against this action on the ground that no political group should be driven underground, whatever its creed; others support the measure on the ground that the Communist party is an organized conspiracy and not a political party at all. We might note that the British Communist party, which shares both goals and methods with the American Communist party, is allowed to operate without hindrance, though doubtless not without surveillance, and it has proved unable to attract any substantial support at the polls; nor has it succeeded in undermining the government. Moving to the U.S.S.R., we find that political parties on the American or British model are not permitted to operate because Soviet theory holds that the Communist party is the "vanguard of the proletariat," in possession of the knowledge needed to advance society toward communism, and hence charged with the responsibility for directing the affairs of the nation during the transition. Clearly the concept of political parties is quite different in the two countries (the United States and Russia). Nevertheless, all political parties do seek to gain control over and use political authority by the means open to them, and with that general definition we must rest content.

The importance of the political atmosphere in determining the organization, operation, and goals of a political party can hardly be overestimated. In a harsh dictatorship, the quest for political power may lead men underground, to plots or to violent revolution, since there is no alternative means of political action available. If political action can take no other form, this concept of party activity would probably be accepted in such a society. But in an open society, where there is general agreement on the basic political structure and the need to maintain an open society, political parties tend to seek the same goals by the same means—they compete at a game in which the rules are more or less agreed. In these circumstances, a party which seeks power by means outside the rules of the game disrupts the system and will usually not be tolerated.

Much depends on the degree to which society looks tolerantly upon political differences. When society is not threatened, and most members of society share the same set of ideals, there is little likelihood of serious dispute over such matters. But when society is sundered by totally different ideals, each with significant backing, as in France and Italy and many of the newly emerging nations, gross differences in parties will appear, and tolerance will lessen. If one or more major factions refuse to play according to the rules and insist on their own prerogatives, all rules tend to vanish and the outcome is left for violence to determine. Where differences are irreconcilable, violence follows almost certainly—it is the announcement of the failure of politics, in a sense, or of the transition from peaceful to violent politics.

The number of parties. The number of political parties varies greatly from country to country, but most political systems can be classified as single-party, two-party, or multiparty systems. In general, one-party systems are associated with authoritarian political rule, though it may be possible to have a one-party system that is not dictatorial. The typical one-party states have been the U.S.S.R., Italy under Mussolini, Hitler Germany, and others having dictatorial governments. However, the Southern states in the United States, and some few other states like Maine, have had what amounts to a one-party system in the past, at least so far as the regular elections are concerned. Defenders of these latter structures point out that within the single party there is often a sharp conflict between factions, and they argue that the system **is**

not monolithic, for the voters make an effective choice within the range offered by the single party. The Soviet one-party system, which we shall use as an extreme example, is more clearly defined, for the Communist party is given constitutional status and no other party is allowed to operate. And, as we shall see, the function of the party is quite different in the U.S.S.R. from what it is in the United States or Western Europe.

Britain and the United States are two-party systems par excellence. In both countries, attempts have been made to form a third party, notably in 1948 in the United States, but with little success. The Liberal party in Great Britain has been in existence since the nineteenth century; it was in fact replaced by the Labor party as the second major party in the period after World War I. Thus it was possible to *substitute* parties in the British system, but the importance of the losing party declined very swiftly. In the United States, the legal framework alone offers a formidable hurdle to potential third parties, for it favors the parties already in existence. The great advantage of the two-party system, of course, is the clear-cut decision it renders at election time. This is particularly noticeable in the British parliamentary system where a government rules on the basis of its ability to obtain a majority vote in the House of Commons. Lacking a majority, a coalition government must be formed, and they are notably unstable.

France is the perfect example of a multiparty system. In that country, parties are highly personalized, ill-disciplined, and very much fragmented. Even the large center parties are riddled by cliques and factions. Under such conditions, coalitions do not survive very long, and France has witnessed a steady procession of coalition governments in the past fifty years, often very short-lived indeed. The profusion of parties offers the voter the opportunity to choose a representative who adheres to his own point of view more closely than is possible in a two-party system, but the price seems invariably to be weak government and relative instability.

In general, then, we can associate a single-party system with a closed society, and a two-party or multiparty system with an open society. Perhaps the crucial difference lies in the concept of opposition or conflict between different points of view. In Britain, the party that loses the election is actually given legal status as an "official" opposition (Her Majesty's Loyal Opposition), and members of the "shadow-cabinet" are paid by the Crown for their special contribution. In the United States, unremitting political warfare between the "ins" and the "outs" is traditional—and valuable. It exposes weaknesses in the government's arguments, suggests changes and alterations in measures which the government proposes, and acts as a sounding board for criticism directed at the activities of the rulers. All of these tasks are essential in a self-governing community. Indeed, political parties perform an invaluable service to liberal democracy—it would be quite impossible without them—and the stereotyped view of parties as small boss-ridden cliques is totally inadequate to convey the real contribution which the political party makes as it goes about its task of organizing support for its candidates and its program.

Types of parties. In a pioneer work, Maurice Duverger produced a complex and interesting classification of the various types of political parties found in the modern world.[4] We cannot here follow Duverger into his detailed analysis or examine some of the many excellent books on political parties that have appeared more recently, but the interested reader will find references to a few of the major works in the field in the bibliographical material. We shall here limit ourselves to an examination of three major types of political parties: (1) the typical American party; (2) the British Labor party, a typical "mass party"; and (3) the Soviet Communist party, which is typical of the "cadre" parties as defined by Duverger. The first two types are found only in open societies; the latter is designed to operate in a closed society. The differences between them are highly instructive.

The American political party. The structure of American political parties has been greatly influenced by the type of political system in which they operate. Because the United States has a federal system of government, and because political parties were developed from below by the amalgamation of smaller units into very loosely joined larger groups, the American party is a unique specimen of its kind. Of the British parties, it most resembles the Conservative party, but even here there are significant differences. Obviously, American parties were designed to operate in open society; hence there has been no need for underground operations or private armies. In most cases, the parties were constructed on the basis of personal loyalty and small-scale local agreements, and the locus of power in the parties has never been transferred to the national level. Party discipline has been slight, particularly at the national level, and the kind of tightly organized, centrally directed group that appeared in European politics has found no place on the American scene.

Perhaps the principal point to grasp about American political parties is that it is the local and state organizations that are important. The national political machinery is loose and ephemeral; it tends to blossom every four years in order to conduct the presidential campaign, then lapse into temporary desuetude once again. At the state and local level, organization is better, though still not comparable to European organization, and discipline is tighter. There are various reasons for this point of emphasis. For one thing, most of the legal regulations on parties are made at the state level. For another, there are many more campaigns to be fought at the state and local

[4] Maurice Duverger, *Political Parties,* Methuen & Co., Ltd., London, 1951.

level; hence the need for organization is greater here. Finally, historical development placed control in the hands of state and local organizations and they have been understandably unwilling to cede their authority to a national organization. The national organization is in effect a very loose confederation of state organizations.

At the national level, there is a national committee for each of the major parties, nominated by the national convention that chooses the presidential candidate. One man and one woman from each state are given a place on the national committee, making a large and somewhat unwieldy body. The committee organizes the presidential campaign, collects funds, and in recent years has maintained a full-time staff for research and publicity purposes. The chairman of the committee is nominated by the presidential candidate chosen by the party, and he is in charge of the candidate's campaign. The national committee plays little part in congressional or local elections.

The parties themselves are strictly instruments for organizing votes at election time. At the local level, the informal party organization—the party machine—may sometimes become involved rather widely in general social affairs, but at the state and national level, particularly the latter, vote getting is the real rationale for the party's existence. Once the election is completed, the party virtually disappears, and as an organization it plays little part in the actual governing process or in the lives of most of its supporters. Apart from the professional politicians, who are relatively numerous, the average voter simply indicates his choice of party at time of registration; he has no formal connection with the party organization as such unless he chooses to become active in election campaigns and assist with the party's routine work. There is no "joining" of parties, and there are no dues—though contributions may be made, and both parties seek means of enticing money from the small contributor. Party discipline is weak, for the national organization has few sanctions that it can apply to its members; in Congress, discipline is slightly better, for various means can be used here to persuade members of the party to follow party policy, but even so, the level of discipline falls far short of European practice.

The British Labor party. We can begin to appreciate the relative simplicity of the American party system when we examine the organization and operation of the British Labor party.[5] The Labor party is essentially a federal structure, but it is rather complex since there are really three focal points of authority within the structure. First, there is a national Labor party organization, which consists of affiliated labor unions and local party units. A second

[5] The best single work on British political parties is R. T. McKenzie, *British Political Parties*, William Heinemann, Ltd., London, 1955.

major power center is the national trade union organization, the Trades Union Congress (T.U.C.), which is a federation of labor unions. Finally, there is the Parliamentary Labor party, consisting of all M.P.s elected on the Labor ticket. Traditionally, the T.U.C. sticks to labor problems, and major figures in the unions hold office in the T.U.C. and not in the Labor party. But the unions are affiliated, in most cases, with the national Labor party, and their large membership gives them a commanding vote at party conferences. The nonunion, political membership of the Labor party often complains bitterly of union domination over party policy, and with some justification.

The individual member of the Labor party may be affiliated through his union or through one of the local constituency parties or both. There is a local party organization in every constituency, and it serves a useful role in collecting funds, in propagandizing, and in selecting candidates—and, of course, in "getting out the vote." Membership is formal, by American standards, for the individual who joins the party must sign a pledge accepting the party's principles, and there are small but regular dues to be paid. The party is organized hierarchically, with a large central organization that is engaged in research, fund raising, and organization. A national newspaper (*The Daily Herald*) is owned and operated under Labor auspices, and a large number of books and pamphlets are printed each year.

The policy-making center of the party is the annual conference, and decisions reached there are binding upon the party for the year. Interim guidance of party affairs is achieved through the national executive committee, elected by the party conference. The large "bloc vote" of the unions obviously counts for a great deal at these annual policy conferences.

In recent years, it has become clear that the real center of power in the Labor party lies in the House of Commons. The Parliamentary Labor party is, under the British constitution, not open to direction by the national party organization, and though it tends to follow the program laid down by the annual party conference, it is coming more and more to lead the party conference in a direction which has been set by parliamentary necessity. The Parliamentary Labor party elects its own officers, and has its own policy meetings; when Labor is in the majority, it forms a government. In the nature of things, those charged with the responsibility for laying down "official" policy, either as a government or in opposition, will have a very broad measure of influence over party decisions. The party conference can hardly refute its own parliamentary group by refusing to endorse their decisions—in major matters at least. The relationship is complex, and we cannot examine the details here, for individual M.P.s are often sponsored by particular unions, or by the national party organization, and the loyalties of the individual M.P.s may be quite diverse and complex.

The Labor party is a mass party, resting on a broad foundation of some six million members, about five million affiliated through the various labor unions. It collects a small fee from each affiliated member, which supplies party funds for propaganda and electioneering. It is firmly committed to the democratic process—to gradualism and parliamentary action rather than revolutionary violence—and is now firmly established as one of the two major parties in the country. Its program is broadly socialistic; it inaugurated a very extensive scheme of welfare and social security in the years immediately following World War II and nationalized several of the basic industries in the country. Since its defeat in 1951, it has been somewhat at a loss for planks in the party platform. It is now much closer to the Conservative party in policy than it was in the 1930s, largely because the latter party has accepted much of the welfare and nationalization program established in the late 1940s.

The party is built from the center, highly organized, and very much centralized. The relationship between the individual member and the party is much closer and more formal than in the United States, though British parties too suffer badly from apathy and lack of member interest, particularly among the trade union members who are affiliated through their unions. There is a large central organization and a well-established policy-making machinery centered on the annual party conference. In practice, the activities of the Parliamentary Labor party have become more significant than the party conference in policy making, but the formal structure remains intact.

Since Labor is already committed to a socialist program, there is one clear difference between its political programs and those which appear in the United States. Labor does not seek to placate every interest group in the country; it assumes the hostility of the wealthier classes and deliberately makes its appeal to the working class and white-collar workers. This acts to present the voter with a reasonably well-defined set of alternatives at the polls and fosters the tendency to vote for the party rather than for the man.

A SUMMATION. These two approaches to party organization in an open society produce quite different conceptions of the political process, even though their function is very similar. Americans are always struck by the centralization and discipline of the Labor party, by the formality of party membership, by the permanent organization, and by the role that the party plays in the life of the active member. Perhaps even more important, the Labor party in the House of Commons has the appearance of a well-drilled instrument for passing legislation. Weekly party meetings are held in the House to discuss policy, and here the individual M.P. is allowed to speak his mind without regard to government policy. But once a decision has been reached, the Labor M.P. may not oppose his own party on the floor of the House, though he may abstain when his conscience is troubled by a particular measure. The M.P. who violates the code governing these matters risks his political future, for election to the House is almost impossible without major party backing.

The mass party, as exemplified by the Labor party in Britain, is a political phenomenon that has not yet appeared in the United States. The American party and the Labor party are the outcome of two quite different approaches to party organization and operation. The American system is informal, organized from below, personalized, and lacking in permanent organization, formal machinery, and sanctions to ensure party discipline. At the national level, particularly, there is little effective organization. The Labor party was deliberately created from the center, and it rests on a firm alliance between the powerful trade union movement and the political branch of the party. The American party is a direct descendant of the eighteenth- and nineteenth-century political organization, when political influence was built on personal following; it is more akin to the world of Jefferson and Hamilton than the age of Roosevelt, Kennedy, or Johnson.

Those who support the Labor party are fond of pointing out that it offers a solution to one of the major political problems facing the large democracies—bringing democracy into the parties themselves. The Labor party is an "open" society, in that party organization and policy making follow the same principles of liberal democracy that direct the operation of the whole political society. It is argued that informal parties like the American Republican and Democratic parties are themselves undemocratic in that they offer no machinery for policy making by the membership, etc. In theory, at least, there is much to be said for this argument. The machinery of the Labor party does make it possible for the individual member to make his voice heard in the same manner that he can be heard in the national political association. When a democratic political system is dominated by oligarchical political parties, some limit is certainly placed on the democracy of the whole.

In practice, the Labor party encounters all of the problems that democratic societies meet on a larger scale. Formally, the system is based on equality of members, free criticism, protection of the rights of minorities, etc., but the party is plagued by the same apathy and lack of interest that haunts the democratic society in other fields. There are often bitter complaints about the influence of the unions, and personality conflicts spawn cliques and antagonism. However, the machinery for party government by the membership exists, just as the machinery for self-government in a democratic society exists in Britain and the United States, and people cannot really be forced to govern themselves.

What of the future? Many observers believe that the mass political party is a sign of the times and a portent for the future, an indicator of the degree to which the twentieth century is an age of organization and formal relationships, and a portent of an age in which population growth and social complexity will lead to formalization and institutionalization of relations previously conducted at the personal level. Mass politics, based on universal suffrage, has acted to move the locus of power in politics more firmly in the direction of the political party rather than the individual, the interest group rather than the person. Politics is now conceived in terms of a struggle between rival associations (in open societies, of course), and not the interplay of small individualized factions, except, perhaps, in France. Further, the mass party seems in part a reflection of the stratification of populations along class lines, as reflected in party choice, particularly in Europe. It seems more than likely that the United States is moving slowly in this direction. The growing importance of party affiliation in voting, the increased significance of the party platform, and the growing interest of organized labor in political action portend major changes in the future. American politics is a very long way from the rigidity and formality of European politics, true, but it has also come a long way from the political system of the nineteenth century. The old-style political leader, whose authority rested on his personal following, is slowly dying out. Younger men seek authority through position in organizations, in politics as in industry or commerce. The very complexity of modern politics presses men in this direction. The open society, in other words, is in the process of becoming the organized society, and what that implies for the political process we are still a very long way from knowing.

Political parties in closed societies. The political party operating in a closed society differs fundamentally from the party operating in an open society; it has a different purpose, it operates on a different level, and its organization reflects these aims and methods. In fact, we are entitled to ask whether such parties are not so different from the political parties we have come to know in Britain and the United States that they ought not to be called political parties at all. They are in opposition as they scramble for political power, but after power is achieved they scarcely resemble Western political parties in the liberal democratic sense of the term.

A political party operating in opposition to the existing regime in a closed society is by definition precluded from seeking power by lawful means; that is the meaning of closed society. Hence such parties must turn to conspiracy and underground activity, and eventually to violent revolution as a means of seizing power. This is also true of political parties operating in open societies which refuse to accept parliamentary limitations on their success, as was the case with Mussolini's Fascists or Hitler's Nazi party. In such circumstances, as Lenin pointed out long ago, the political party must be small, tightly disciplined, and obedient or loyal (for the lives of others depend upon it); the party becomes a paramilitary organization. It is a device for seizing power and nothing more. Here is the basic distinction between Western political parties and the "cadre" parties that appear in or foster authoritarian political systems.

What are we to think of political parties that operate in this manner in open society? Basically, parties that turn to violence and underground activities when they prove unable to achieve power by legitimate means are asserting the absolute correctness of their own position and insisting that their goals are sufficient to justify the departure from the principles of open society. That is, they assert that the voters have made the *wrong* choice and claim the right to put matters straight by seizing power. Hence revolution in open society is essentially an admission of failure, just as the Communist party *coups d'état* in Czechoslovakia and other parts of Eastern Europe after 1945 were admissions of inability to attain power by reasoning or arguing with the electorate.

What seems particularly unfortunate in this position is the history of those political parties which began life as conspiracies and ended in control of a modern state. Invariably, they have installed authoritarian regimes, whether in Russia or Eastern Europe, in China, or more recently in Cuba. Sometimes, as in the case of Hitler and Mussolini, there was no pretense involved, for Hitler stated his aims clearly enough in *Mein Kampf,* and if no one chose to take him seriously, that was only an extreme example of political myopia. Whether or not it is really possible for a political movement operating as a conspiracy to produce a liberal democracy when power is achieved we cannot say, but if history is our guide, then it must certainly be considered unlikely.

Once in power, the political party functioning in closed society becomes simply another instrument of government, and not, as in open society, a means of acquiring power. Generally, all other political parties are suppressed, for a closed system permits no opposition to the government's authority. In these circumstances, the function of the political party changes radically. It is a device by which authority is transferred from the top to the bottom in society, and not a means of gathering together the fragmented political authority of large numbers of individuals, as in open society. The political party becomes a means of controlling the population, a technique for carrying out the intentions of government, and a communications system which may carry information from below but cannot carry authority.

The Soviet Communist party.

We can illustrate the peculiarities attendant on the operation of political parties in closed societies by examining the Communist party in the U.S.S.R., or in any part of Eastern Europe. The special position of the Soviet Communist party is recognized in the Soviet constitution; the party is specifically empowered by that document to lead and govern the society. No other party may function in Russia, for the party already knows what is true in politics, and any opposition would by definition be false and misleading. Further, the machinery of the party is fully meshed with the machinery of government, so that party leaders and political leaders are one and the same; but, and it is an important "but," they occupy their positions by virtue of their status in the party, not in the government. Political authority rests with the party, not with the people or even with the formal government of soviets.

The Communist party in Russia is organized from the top down, creating a giant pyramid, with many layers of party organization between the top and bottom. Authority flows from top to bottom, and not, as in the United States, from bottom to top. The primary unit at the base of the pyramid is the cell, which is quite small and may contain only a half dozen members. There are some 350,000 cells in the country, all strategically located for maximum control. The cells are grouped together into districts, and districts are combined to form regions. The individual republics in the U.S.S.R. each contain a number of regions, and the peak of the pyramid is the All-Union Party Congress. The executive authority of the party is vested in a central executive committee, and though the party congress is theoretically supreme (like the annual party conference of the British Labor party), real power lies with the Central Committee, or more precisely, with the smaller Presidium, which is technically a subcommittee of the Central Committee, but in practice contains the real rulers of Russia. The relationship between the Presidium and the Central Committee is interesting, for Khrushchev, when he was seeking to oust Malenkov in 1957, appealed from the Presidium to the Central Committee (which elects the members of the Presidium) and was upheld at that level, even though he was outvoted in the Presidium. Hence the composition of both bodies is evidently quite important. At the very top level of party organization, party and government merge and mingle; the administration of the party and the administration of the state come under the control of the same people.

The officers of the party are elected at the different levels, but the elections are indirect; each level elects the members of the level above, and in practice, control over these elections rests with those at the top. Hence the system is self-sustaining. Theoretically the party practices "democratic centralism," which means, in Communist jargon, that the officers of the party are elected, hence the system is democratic, but those in lower echelons obey those above them, hence the system is centralized. In practice, the structure appears to depend rather more on centralism than on democracy, at least so far as Western observers are concerned.

The Communist party is definitely not a mass party; membership is strictly limited and no attempt is made to recruit large numbers of members.

There is no need for concern over finances, since money comes from the state. Instead, the party seeks to enroll those who are leaders within their groups, those who can direct the workers and control them, those who show aptitude for party work, and above all, those who appear "reliable." Since party membership is the key to office, to educational opportunities, to special privileges, etc., there is no shortage of candidates for party membership, and the screening process can be very severe and lengthy. Only 4 to 5 per cent of the total population actually belongs to the party; membership was expanded somewhat during World War II, but later reduced once again.

It is almost useless to attempt to compare the Soviet party with American or British parties; their purposes are so different that it would be too much to expect them to be very similar. American parties seek candidates who will appeal to the voters; the Communist party seeks candidates who are politically reliable and acceptable to the government. American parties are based upon the principle of conflict and opposition; they disseminate information which they hope will lead to a change in voting behavior. The Soviet party is an instrument of government, has no opposition, and does not criticize the regime in any way. The whole notion of opposition to the government is alien to Soviet political thought, and with its absence much of the rationale of Western political parties disappears. Even when the parties are performing the same function, like rousing the population to come to the polls, the American party acts in its own interest, while the Soviet party acts in the interest of the state. It is these fundamental differences which lead us to wonder whether it might not be better to consider the Communist party in Russia something quite unlike political parties in the liberal democratic sense of the term. Certainly the use of the same term introduces a great deal of confusion into political discourse.

Violence in open and closed societies. Although violence in politics has a long history, it is the essence of liberal democracy that politics should proceed by peaceful means and that the outcome of the ballot must be accepted. That principle applies both to the right of the majority to rule once elected and the right of the minority to remain active and seek power for itself by lawful means. One of the essential distinctions between open and closed societies is the role that violence plays in the political process in each structure. For once politics degenerates into violence, the political process on which open society is predicated simply disappears; when government uses violence and coercion outside the framework imposed by the rule of law, self-government is an impossibility.

It must be admitted at once that violence is an effective means of settling political questions, though our political tradition tends to deny recourse to violence outside the sphere of international relations. When the political machinery needed to make political decisions simply is not present, then the likelihood of violence is great. Doubtless this accounts for the explosions of violence in many of the newly emerging nations. There simply is no stable alternative to violence, or in the same context, not all of the parties involved in political action are willing to accept the outcome of the system that has been established. Western observers are likely to forget, when they condemn the use of force in these areas, that the Western world has had a long period of time in which to grow accustomed to its political system, and there was a time in our own history when public opinion was quite willing to countenance political conclusions reached by the sword or the army.

Violence may take many different forms and be applied by a variety of techniques. Revolution is only one means of using violence to gain political ends. Thus the Fascist march on Rome in 1922 was not a revolution, or even a *coup d'état*, but an effort to arouse demonstrations which would convince those who controlled the keys to political power that Mussolini alone could maintain stability in the state. Hitler, though he came to power by means which were technically legal, used his private army very skillfully both during and after his rise to power, particularly to suppress opposition. A small group of officers in Japan even used systematic terrorism to prevent the surrender of their own government to the Allies in 1945. A still more subtle form of violence appears in political "purges," such as those conducted in Moscow in 1936 or in Yugoslavia after World War II when Milovan Djilas was sent to prison.

The use made of the police force is another index to the role of violence in political society, particularly in Europe where the police are usually under the centralized control of a single minister. It is significant that the Communist members of the coalition governments installed in Eastern Europe after 1945 all demanded control over the ministry of the interior—the agency that controlled the police—and used the police force very effectively during the period in which Communist domination was enforced and expanded. Violence, in other words, may be naked force or subtle coercion. Often it need only be implied, with suitable demonstrations, as in the gangland "shakedown." Such activities are always an indication of a society in some degree closed, for the use of violence is fundamentally incompatible with the assumptions of the open political system.

The courts. Finally, a word remains to be said about the role of the courts in open and closed societies, for the difference here is also striking. In the United States, we are accustomed to think of the courts as guardians of individual freedom and personal rights, largely because the doctrine of judicial review is interpreted to give the courts the right to maintain the scope of political authority within the bounds laid down by the Constitution. The doctrine known as "constitutionalism," coupled with the notion of judicial review, produces a powerful and flexible instrument for calling legislature and executive to account. In this structure, the font of power is taken to be the people, and law is regarded as fundamentally a statement of the will of the community, made known through properly elected representatives and in conformity to the "higher law" of the Constitution itself. In Britain, the doctrine of judicial review is lacking, and no court may refuse to apply a law which Parliament has enacted in legal form, but the concept of rule of law acts as a check on the unfettered exercise of legislative power, and a long tradition acts to protect the "fundamental rights of Englishmen" from encroachment. In France there is even a special set of courts in which the individual citizen can seek redress against members of the administration for alleged misconduct or violation of rights.

In a closed society, the law serves none of these functions, for it cannot limit the authority of government, and the courts are simply instruments of the state. The legal structure of the U.S.S.R. can serve as an example. In Marx and Engels, the law is denounced as merely the expression of will or domination by the ruling economic class, and the high regard for law that is expressed in the liberal tradition has no place in Soviet theory. Early Marxists commonly assumed that the new Soviet society would have no need for law in the traditional sense, and in the 1930s, Soviet legal experts came very close to abolishing what we know as the legal system. Since that time, Soviet law has moved back toward the Western tradition, probably because the Soviet rulers found that law is essential for any stable society, whether communist or capitalist. Nevertheless, the role of the legal system and the concept of law remain far removed from the structures we are accustomed to in Western society.

Under current Soviet law, the law itself is considered an expression of the best interests of the working class, as defined by those in authority. The courts are creatures of the state—administrative organs rather than tribunals for dispensing "justice." There is no belief in the will of the community expressed as law or in a "higher law" to which man-made law should conform. Partly this stems from the absence of any conception of individual rights and interests to be upheld against the state. The Western tradition considers government essentially an enemy and fears the corrupting influence of power; Soviet society cannot accept any real conflict of interest between the will of the state and the best interests of the individual; hence the whole foundation of Western tradition is lacking. Russia does have a formal constitution, of course, but there is no doctrine of judicial review and no belief in the rule of law. The state is unfettered and absolute.

In Western society, the judge is expected to be impartial, to decide cases on their merits, and to pursue as best he can the somewhat abstract conception that we call justice or equity. In Russia, the judge is not expected to be impartial. Indeed, his task is to exercise his "social conscience" and decide how the behavior of the individual affects the whole society; he does not limit himself to consideration of the "rights" of the individual as such. Even when the interests of society are not involved directly, as in suits between private citizens, the judge is expected to consider the impact of his decision on society first, and to weigh the principles of equity afterward. More recently, Chairman Khrushchev has introduced a special form of tribunal called "comradely courts" or social courts. They have limited powers, but they deal with disputes arising in the neighborhood or at work, and they can also call to account particular persons whose attitude and behavior, though not technically illegal, are considered improper or unsocial. Such "courts" resemble the old-fashioned family confab which met to discuss the course of action to be taken with the family "black sheep"; their impact on the personal life of the individual can be devastating, particularly where there are no procedural safeguards.

The law in a closed society, then, serves quite a different function from the law and courts in open society. It is not a stabilizing force, a source of justice and equity, and a protector of individual liberty as the liberal tradition assumes. Instead, the law finds its sanction in the state alone and serves as an instrument of the state to maintain the interests of the *state*, rather than the individual.

THE USE OF POLITICAL AUTHORITY

When we examine the second part of the political process, the use that is made of political authority, we find a similar divergence between open and closed political associations. There is a basic difference in both the kinds of laws that are made and the manner in which they are formulated. The whole process functions in a different environment. We cannot hope to detail all of the factors that influence the decision-making process in each system, but some of the major differences are clear, and they provide us with a useful index to the degree to which society is open or closed.

The locus of power. The first major distinction in the lawmaking process in open and closed societies is the extent to which power in the latter is located outside the formal political system. Most modern states have enfranchised their citizens, and most states now have representative institutions incorporated into their political structure. Thus the American Congress (together with the Presidency), the British Parliament, the Japanese Diet, and the Supreme Soviet of the U.S.S.R. are each the theoretical focus of political authority in their respective societies. And in the open societies, Britain, for example, the Parliament actually is the power center in the political process. But in closed societies, political authority never resides in representative bodies. There is always a gap between theory and actual practice.

Before 1945, the two-house Diet in Japan was merely an advisory agency; supreme power was theoretically vested in the person of the Emperor. But in practice, the Emperor's authority was exercised by various groups who had no place in the formal political sysem. A group of elder statesmen, known as the Genro, who helped inaugurate the Meiji regime in the nineteenth century, for example, was a powerful force in Japanese decision making until the members of the group died off. And in the 1930s, the military leaders, who had direct access to the throne and a surprising degree of autonomy, often functioned in complete disregard for the formal political system.

In the Soviet Union, the indirectly elected Supreme Soviet is theoretically the prime authority in the political system, but once again we find that the reality is quite different. Behind the formal political system lies the Communist party organization, and this is the real controlling element in the country. The Supreme Soviet, under the guidance of the party, elects two smaller bodies. One, the Presidium, is intended as an interim agency which can act when the Supreme Soviet is not sitting; the other, the Council of Ministers, is made up of the heads of administrative agencies—the old Commissars. Membership in both groups is fully controlled by the party, of course. The Supreme Soviet meets for only a few days each year, and plays almost no part in the legislative process beyond "rubber-stamping" decisions already made in these smaller bodies.

In practice, the prime agency of government is the Council of Ministers, which is authorized to issue decrees that are binding and immediate in effect, though in theory subject to approval by the Supreme Soviet. The Presidium can also issue decrees, and it is theoretically able to nullify decrees emanating from the Council of Ministers, though it has never done so. Again, theory tells us that these decrees are only "interpretations" of statutes already passed by the Supreme Soviet, but in practice the Presidium and Council are judge of their own powers, and no decree has ever been eliminated except at the request of the issuing body. In practice, the constitution itself has been changed by decree—a move that is theoretically impossible. In the years since Stalin died, Western observers assume that the party has come into its own; until his death Stalin ruled personally, with little regard for either the state apparatus or the party machinery. In no case, however, has the formal governmental machinery been the real power center in the society.

Executive government. Closed societies, and dictatorships in general, are usually governed by an executive, rather than a legislature. The role played by Hitler and Mussolini in their respective regimes is too well known to require further comment. But the dictatorial regimes in South America or

Spain or the Middle East, are characterized by the same mode of operation. And the executive is always free from interference, control, or ratification by the legislature. In open societies, certain kinds of executive action are certainly possible and even necessary. The American President can make executive agreements with foreign powers and issue executive orders which are binding within the legal framework that delimits his authority. But such actions are always subject to review and some type of control, directly or indirectly. In the United States, the limits of the Constitution, at the very least, are applicable; in Britain, the administrative or executive agent who exceeds the authority granted by Parliament is *ultra vires,* and the courts will not uphold his actions. Indeed, he may become subject to some rather severe penalties if he acts illegally. In general, the open society is associated with legislative supremacy; the legislature, in the last analysis, defines the authority of the executive. In a closed society, the executive functions without limits, for the legislature has no authority.

In this connection, the role of the British Cabinet in the Parliamentary system may require some explanation, for Americans, accustomed to a clear separation between President and Congress, sometimes assume that the role of the Cabinet in Britain amounts to clear-cut executive government. It is true that legislative pressure and a heavy legislative schedule have seriously reduced the number of opportunities for the private member to introduce legislation of his own. Most bills are proposed by the Cabinet, and government business takes up most of Parliament's time. Further, the bills which the Cabinet proposes almost invariably pass, though they may be modified before approval is given. The reason for this is simple. The Cabinet, or the "Government," always commands a majority in the House of Commons, and strong party discipline ensures that governmental measures can be passed. Indeed, if the Government fails to attain the necessary majority it must resign. However, this does not mean that the Cabinet simply produces legislation without reference to the rest of the party and forces it through the House of Commons. There are various phases in the process at which the individual member can suggest, comment, criticize, or even balk outright, and the Government does not introduce legislation that its own members will not support; that would be suicidal. The Government must retain the confidence of the House, whatever it does, and Governments are defeated, occasionally, when their performance engenders opposition within the ranks. Chamberlain's conduct of World War II is the most recent instance of such action. After the fall of Norway, the Conservative majority in the House dropped by over a hundred votes, and this was construed as a loss of confidence; hence Chamberlain was forced to resign (though he still retained a small majority). The House of Commons is not, like the Supreme Soviet, a rubber stamp. Criticism is real and meaningful, and the phrase "confidence of the House" has acquired fairly precise meaning through long usage.

In general, we can say that legislatures which sit for only a few days each year are probably meaningless so far as the legislative process is concerned. The Supreme Soviet is seldom in session for more than a few days, and its activities are largely ceremonial. Working legislatures sit for weeks and months on end, in plenum session or in committee, for no legislature can arrange the affairs of a nation in a short time. Indeed, Congress is constantly seeking means of expediting the massive pile of work it must accomplish each session as the legislative needs of the country grow.

Unlimited government. In an open society, the decision-making process is, for practical purposes, a search for a compromise, a means of reconciling opposing views and different criticisms. Liberal democracy is subject to criticism, opposition, and restraint from those within the system and from without. These features are lacking in closed societies, which operate essentially without fetters of any sort. Here we find another major difference between open and closed societies as they go about the process of making laws and governing.

In most cases, the decision makers in closed societies cannot be removed by ordinary electoral process. They do not attain their positions by democratic procedures, and removal depends on factors which may have nothing to do with their behavior. Indeed, if society is tightly closed, nothing short of revolution will remove the rulers from their control over political authority. This is in sharp contrast to the position of the lawmaker in open society, for the latter is always removable, either on expiration of term in office or more immediately in case of malfeasance.

Furthermore, closed societies lack those constitutional and legal limitations which commonly restrict legislation in open societies. There may be no constitution, or the constitution may be meaningless, ignored by those who frame the laws. The courts may serve as instruments of authority rather than as restrictions on the use of authority. The needs of the state, rather than the rights of the individual, serve as a guide to the legislator. The ability of the rulers of closed societies to control the flow of information to the public strengthens the tendency, and the absence of any real need to explain or justify policy renders the whole political process peculiarly irresponsible by Western democratic standards.

The role of public opinion. Finally, we may note that in an open society the decision-making process, however complex, is conducted largely if not entirely in the public view, and that public opinion, however ephemeral, plays a decisive part in important decisions. That is, the decision maker, whatever the influences that generate his ultimate decision, always keeps one ear cocked for the *vox populi*. If his actions are not acceptable to the public, he is likely to lose his authority. The basic principles of open society—free access to information, the right to know and criticize freely, and ultimate control over those who exercise authority—tend to force this type of political behavior.

In closed societies, public meetings of governing bodies tend to be "demonstrations" rather than genuine instances of lawmaking, and the actual decision-making process goes on behind closed doors. The general public may be totally uninformed about the intentions or even the actions of government. And public opinion may count for little or nothing in the final decision. Indeed, there is a tendency for closed societies to seek to mold public opinion to fit decisions already made on other grounds to support the policies of the government, rather than the converse. Public opinion may, from time to time, be aroused to support or condemn particular issues, but such action flows *from* decisions already made; it does not generate them.

Summary

In this chapter, we have sought to contrast the two major types of political societies by examining in some detail the manner in which the political process is carried out in each. In general, the contrasts have been overdrawn for the sake of emphasis, and in practice some of the distinctions would have to be conditioned by other considerations, for politics is seldom a matter of pure blacks and whites. Nevertheless, a clear demonstration of the significant differences between open and closed societies and how they operate is a necessary part of the equipment of anyone concerned with understanding modern politics.

In any political study, anthropocentrism must be avoided, and the study must extend beyond the formal to the informal and practical aspects of politics; formal systems are highly deceptive. The general social values of society do much to structure the actual operation of the political system, whether it is open or closed. Further, we must take account of the extent to which apathy is commonplace in human society and consider the degree to which this makes elitism necessary in political affairs.

The open society and the closed society are extremes on the political spectrum; they are ideals, stated explicitly or implicitly. They involve a set of goals and the machinery for achieving the goals, and they induce a political atmosphere which either accepts or rejects the notion of conflict and opposition, freedom of information and criticisms, and their various corollaries (free association and freedom of expression). Some of the more difficult problems in these areas arise in the field of foreign relations and national security.

The points that can be used to prepare a meaningful comparison of two political systems are numerous and diverse. In general, we are concerned with the extent of the franchise, the meaningfulness of elections, frequency of elections, type of election districts, voting procedures, and election procedures. In this regard, recent studies of voting behavior are particularly significant.

Within the realm of meaningful self-government, factors like eligibility for office, techniques used for nominating, and theory of representation are especially important, since they provide the foundation on which the system is judged. Open systems differ greatly in the degree to which their governments are responsible and in their degree of "openness"; these distinctions should not be ignored.

The nature and operation of the party system provide us with a particularly useful index to the type of political structure we are examining. In general, we can distinguish three major types of political parties: the American party, the mass party (British Labor), and the cadre party (Soviet Communist party). Each has its own qualities, but they perform quite different functions by different means. The points to observe are the number of parties, the goals of the parties, and their relation to the government.

Two other major distinctions appear between open and closed societies when we examine (1) the function of law and the operation of the legal system and (2) the role of violence in the political process.

Open and closed societies also differ markedly in the means used to make political decisions. In general, closed societies have real power located outside the formal political system, they are usually marked by executive rather than legislative government, they are not accountable, and they operate secretly, without regard for public opinion.

Review questions

1. Give some illustrations of the manner in which broad social values influence the character of the political system.

2. What is meant by apathy? Does it necessarily lead to elitism? Why?

3. What is popular sovereignty? How does it relate to the distinction between open and closed societies?

4. Make a list of the premises involved in open society and mark those which are antithetical to closed society.

5. What are the basic individual freedoms required by open society? Why is each essential?

6. In what ways can the significance of universal suffrage be limited or avoided?

7. What are the basic aspects of elections that distinguish the open from the closed society?

8. What is proportional representation? What are its advantages and disadvantages?

9. What are the principal mechanisms of a representative system of government? In what ways do representative systems differ?

10. What are the two basic theories of representation and how do they differ in their consequences?

11. Distinguish between three basic types of political parties, and list the characteristics, advantages, and disadvantages of each.

12. Compare the role of the political party in open and closed society.

13. Discuss briefly the role of violence in politics.

14. What are some of the principal differences in the use of political authority in open and closed societies?

15. Prepare a general summary of the characteristics of the political process in open and closed societies.

For further study

1. Can you imagine a one-party political system which could be called an "open" system?

2. How important is the role of the political party in a democratic system? Is democracy possible without parties?

3. Discuss the means that can be used to distinguish between societies which are open.

4. What possible solutions to the problem of responsibility are available in open societies?

5. Should a political candidate be judged by his personal qualities or by his party allegiance?

6. Do you feel that the British or the American party structure is most conducive to responsible government? Why?

7. Is the Soviet Communist party a political party?

8. What changes would be needed to alter the American political system from an open to a closed system? How could you recognize the signs of change?

9. Why are defense problems a special difficulty for open societies?

10. What substantive differences would you expect to find in the kinds of law enacted in open and closed societies?

CHAPTER *9*

Politics

and

Economics

We have now completed our examination of two of the major foci of modern politics: first, the organization, distribution, rationalization, and control of political authority; second, the nature of the political process—the allocation and use of authority. In each area, two distinct political attitudes emerge. Some men begin with the individual citizen and seek in politics a means of maximizing the aims and ambitions of the individual; others begin with society as a whole and look for the collective benefits of particular political policies. The choice between them is a matter of personal values, a question of calculating consequences and choosing among alternatives. But the range of choice can be expressed in terms of the dichotomy between individualism and collectivism, liberalism and authoritarianism, or the distinction between open and closed political associations.

In this chapter, we turn to a third basic theme of politics—the relationship between government and the economic system. No economic system can function in the absence of government and no government can ignore economic questions. The two are inextricably bound. It is one of the prime tasks of government to produce the rules which control and regulate economic affairs, whether the economic system is capitalistic, socialistic, or communist. Again, the dichotomy between individualism and collectivism, between concern for the person and concern for the whole group, appears quite clearly. In the nineteenth century, Western Europe and the United States approached economic matters individualistically, from the point of view that is called "economic liberalism." Toward the end of the nineteenth century, the principles of economic liberalism, or laissez-faire capitalism, were attacked with increasing vigor, and in the twentieth century there has been a steady trend in the direction of collectivism, in economic matters as well as in political affairs. The rise and fall of liberalism in economics, which parallels the rise and fall of political liberalism, is therefore one of the most important social changes of the past century, and it sets the stage for the discussion of contemporary political problems in Chapter 19.

PROPERTY

From the political scientist's point of view, the basic concept in economics is property. Property is a social universal, which appears in all societies at all times, and it is doubtful that organized social life is possible without some property concept. *Property* is that set of rights and obligations relating to the possession and use of economic goods, which are defined and guaranteed by political government. Property, in other words, is a set of rights, which may vary considerably but which flow in all cases from the authority of government. Where there is no government there can be no property, and the definition of property rights, and adjudication of disputes over property rights, is a prime function of government in all societies.

For a lone man on a desert island, ownership and possession would be identical; there would be no other person to dispute his possession or use of the goods. But in a society, possession is not the same as ownership, for the latter implies that society will guarantee possession, and society will do that only if the conditions which society postulates for ownership have been met. One may, for example, obtain possession of goods by theft, but such goods are not "owned," for the government will not usually recognize ownership when possession is obtained by this means. When society's conditions have been met, on the other hand, possession is guaranteed by society, and anyone who seizes goods from their lawful owner will be punished and forced to make restitution.

Limits on property rights. Every society limits property rights in some way; they are never absolute. Usually, the definition of legal property includes limits on (1) the manner in which property is acquired, (2) the types of goods that may be acquired, (3) the use that may be made of goods, and (4) the disposal or transfer of property to other persons. Societies differ greatly in the restrictions they place upon property, of course; some, like the United States, are quite liberal while others like the Soviet Union are very restrictive.

Before the state will recognize the existence of property, certain standards of acquisition must be met. No society, for example, will recognize as property goods acquired by fraud. All societies recognize purchase or barter as valid means of property acquisition. Discovery may or may not create property, depending upon the circumstances. And some societies refuse to recognize the acquisition of goods by inheritance, though most societies accept the practice.

The types of goods that may become property are similarly limited. Few societies today permit one individual to possess another as property, and most societies restrict ownership of dangerous drugs, weapons, or materials such as uranium. In socialist countries, certain kinds of capital goods may not become the property of private individuals; in such cases property rights are vested in the state. The question of state ownership versus private ownership is one of the more significant problems in contemporary government.

In a similar manner, all states limit the use that may be made of goods, though the type of limit varies greatly. No society permits the use of property in such manner as to cause harm to others, though the definition of harm is peculiarly difficult. May a factory owner, for example damage the health of his workers by causing them to work with dangerous materials? Today, the answer in most countries is no, but the practice is not universal unless "damage" is very strictly defined. Perhaps the most important limit on the use of property is the willingness of the state to permit the property owner to use his property to obtain profit. Some societies like the United States permit and even encourage the use of property for profit; others discourage or even strictly forbid the practice. Here is a major question in political-economic relations that requires further discussion.

Finally, societies differ in the rules they make governing the transfer of property. Some, as we have said, do not permit transfer by inheritance. Others refuse permission to transfer certain goods to certain persons—by enjoining the sale of alcohol to minors or refusing to allow giant corporations to merge by transferring property from one to the other, for example. The significance of the limit will depend upon the nature of the restriction and the conditions under which it is applied.

When property is defined in this general way, it is obvious that absolute *laissez faire* is a social impossibility. No society can permit every individual to acquire, use, and dispose of any and all things without restriction. If there were no rules whatever to bind individual action and if government did not intervene to define and protect property rights, and to limit them, there would be no real alternative to force as a means of settling disputes. That is the basic function of the law relating to property—to provide a means for settling disputes about property, for ordering and arranging poperty relations, which the community will accept as just and equitable and which will permit economic relations to continue without violence.

Most property law depends upon the general principle that the right to own property also includes a responsibility for the use of that property. One of the great difficulties in modern times arises from the fact that an increasingly complex society has made it very hard indeed to trace the full consequences of particular uses of property, and thus almost impossible to assign responsibility in a just and equitable manner. If, for example, the United States Steel Corporation is to be responsible for the use it makes of its property, then there must be some way to calculate the consequences of particular corporation policies and assign responsibility accordingly. In practice, of course, this is almost impossible; hence government is often unable to control these matters adequately. The direct and immediate impact of property use—on employees, stockholders, etc.—is reasonably clear; the indirect social consequences of property use are at best vague and poorly defined.

The right to profit. It should be clear by now that the concept of property and the concept of profit are two distinct, if related, conceptions. This is an extremely important point, for there is a strong popular tendency to assume that they are identical and this has introduced a great deal of confusion into the discussion of the economic role of government. Property is a bundle of rights which society has created; the right to seek a profit is only one element of that bundle of rights. And the right to seek a profit is not, either logically or legally, a necessary part of the definition of property. One may own property in a full and meaningful sense without being able to use that property for profit. Thus the man who has a right to possess and use a house, the right to repair or mend the house as he sees fit, the right to transfer the house to others as he desires, can be said to "own" the house, surely, even if he is enjoined by law from selling the house to another person at a profit to himself. Of course, we are dealing only with the logical and legal aspects of the property-profit relationship. One may still believe it to be morally wrong to limit the right to profit, but that is another matter.

The role of profit making in the economic system may vary greatly. In a liberal economic system, as in the United States, profit is considered a social good, and profit making is maximized because it is the foundation of economic activity. In another extreme case, as in the Soviet Union, private property is retained but private profit is minimized, though not, at present, completely eliminated. In between are systems like the British, in which certain sectors of the economy operate on a profit basis while others are operated by the government—railroads, and coal mines, for example.

In theory, it is possible to abolish all profit making from the economy. It is interesting to note, moreover, that it would also be possible to retain a profit-making system while divorcing profit completely from the use of private property. Something of the sort occurs when private citizens are allowed to "profit" from lending savings to the government. But if the government owned all property, it might still arrange a system of leases which would permit the individual to earn a profit from their use. The example is farfetched, of course, but it does point up the extent to which property and profit are separate and distinct entities. Too often, what appears as a defense of private property turns out on closer examination to be a defense of profit making.

The absolute need for property. Although it is possible to eliminate profit from the economic system, it is quite clear that private property cannot be deleted from society without producing utter chaos. Whatever the term that is used to designate the relationship, members of society must have the right to uninterrupted possession and use of certain goods; men have an absolute need for property when they live in society. An illustration may clarify the point. Imagine that all of the property in the City of New York belongs to the government, that no individual in the city owns property of his own. Does this mean that every person in the city has an equal right to every piece of property in the city? That simply is not possible, for it would lead to a breakdown of society. If Jones returns to the apartment in which he has been living to find the Smith family ensconced, and if society will not intervene to guarantee Jones the right to stable possession of the apartment, Jones must either look elsewhere for shelter or literally declare war on Smith. The results of this instance, many times multiplied, can be imagined.

The point is that every individual must have some possessions which are attached to him and to no one else during a given period of time. We may call these things his property, or we may use some other words to describe the relationship; that matters little. What is essential is the relationship between the person and the material items. Man has an absolute need for exclusive rights in certain kinds of goods. The family, whether Russian, American, or Chinese, must have a domicile, clothing, and other personal possessions, and they must be able to count on them for the future; their possession must be stable and predictable. From this point of view, it is idle to speak of abolishing all private property, for the term would then have to be replaced by some other term, and the relationship would remain exactly the same.

Of course, the terms that are actually used to describe economic relationships do matter a great deal, for men respond differently to different words, even if the words refer to precisely the same concept. Those who are accustomed to pay homage to such terms as "private property" will protest loudly against any effort to alter the term, very often failing to realize that the term may be maintained but the bundle of rights which it implies may be altered radically. That is, men often protest more loudly over the shadow of social rights than over their substance, perhaps because they begin with a poorly defined conception of the rights involved. In any academic discipline, we must try to move behind concern for such superficial matters as words and get at the social or economic conceptions involved in them, defining them as clearly as possible. The relationship between property and profit is a very good example of the kind of precise definition that needs to be made when cultural values are involved in the terminology.

GOVERNMENT AND PROPERTY

It is obvious, from what has been said, that the manner in which political government defines property rights will determine the character of the economic system. Here society has a wide range from which to choose. It may seek to maximize the rights that define private property or it may reduce them to a bare minimum. It may include profit making in the compendium of property rights, or it may exclude profit making, partly or completely. It may allow private ownership of every possible kind of good, or it may restrict private property to certain carefully defined categories. It may even eliminate the term "property" and produce a new term to describe the minimum necessary relationship between an individual and the goods he needs for social life. All of these variations are possible, and human society has at various times made use of them.

Property is not, then, an abstract self-defining conception which government merely applies to the conditions it finds. Property is a concept which society defines for itself, seeking, through its definition, to attain certain social ends. That is, any given definition of property will tend to produce particular social conditions, and if society dislikes or admires these conditions it will either retain or alter the definition accordingly. Thus in modern times we find two broad trends in the definition of property rights in Western society. The first, which we can identify as *economic liberalism,* was dominant during most of the eighteenth and nineteenth centuries; the second, which we shall call *collectivism* appeared in the nineteenth century and seriously challenged economic liberalism in the twentieth century.

Economic liberalism. The attitude toward property known as economic liberalism is part of a much wider social conception which is often referred to simply as "liberalism" with a small *l*. It is characteristically individualistic, even extremely so, and it views society as a collection of individuals which exists for the benefit of these individuals. Accepting this basic principle, the economic liberal seeks a definition of property rights that will produce an economic system in which rewards are proportional to individual effort, disregarding, for the most part, the consequences of the system for the whole society. This approach to economic matters is derived from the works of the eighteenth-century physiocrats and from the classical economists, such as Adam Smith and David Ricardo, influenced, of course, by the work of Thomas Malthus. In the nineteenth century, it appears as laissez-faire liberalism, as the attempt to maximize the individual's property rights and minimize the right of society collectively to regulate and control the acquisition and use of property.

Collectivism. The opposite point of view, which we shall refer to broadly as collectivism, begins with society as a unit, frequently as an organic entity, with its own goals and purposes. It is fundamentally egalitarian rather than individualistic, and it argues that the economic system ought to be arranged according to its effect on the whole society and not according to its effect on particular individuals. Basically, it argues that men ought to benefit equally from the productive process without regard to personal status. The collectivist believes that no particular individual can demonstrate a clear right to special privileges from the economic order, to any extra share in production. Generally, the collectivist asserts that present economic differentials are only a consequence of historical accident and that gross social injustice is involved in the maldistribution of economic goods arising out of an individualistic economic system.

The nature of the dispute between economic liberal and collectivist is determined by their basic assumptions. The economic liberal begins with the unfettered individual; the collectivist begins with equal individuals, essentially undifferentiated, who form a society. The liberal seeks an economic system in which the individual may advance his own ends by his own means, reaping his rewards when he is successful and paying the price when he fails. The collectivist argues that the liberal is guilty of the fallacy of composition, in that the results of economic activity may have nothing whatever to do with individual merit or capacity. The liberal argues that a free economic system operating competitively is the best means of ensuring maximum production and quality from industry; the collectivist argues that competition is wasteful and damaging to society and ought to be enjoined. The liberal sees political government as a referee over the economic system, ensuring fair play but allowing the game to reach its own conclusion. The collectivist argues that free competitive economics produces gross injustice which it is the responsibility of society to redress. The liberal believes that each man must assure his own economic security; the collectivist argues that this is impossible, that the society must guarantee to each person a fair and equal share of the good things of life. And so the argument goes on.

Difficult as it may be, we must attempt to evaluate these two approaches to economics as objectively as possible, or at least attempt to set forth the arguments on neutral ground. In particular, we need to avoid reference to ourselves, our aspirations, and the consequences we foresee personally out of particular economic arrangements. An economic structure which might suit the reader perfectly could prove untenable as a social solution to the economic order, and an economic system which might prove beneficial to society could be distasteful or even harmful to particular individuals. The reader may, if he chooses, argue against particular economic measures because they are personally distasteful, but he ought properly to be aware of the assumption on which his argument is based, and to do this it is first necessary to separate the argument from personal entanglement.

Laissez-faire liberalism. Absolute *laissez faire* has never been more than an ideal; it may even be socially impossible. But the application of laissez-faire principles, however partial, in the nineteenth century produced the economic conditions on which contemporary argument about the relative merits of liberalism and collectivism is chiefly based. That is, the contemporary argument between liberalism and collectivism is not phrased in classic laissez-faire–collectivist terms. It deals rather with the question which of these alternatives is the best successor to *laissez faire*. A few economists and social thinkers still defend the principles of nineteenth-century liberal economics, but for the most part Western society is committed to the use of significant amounts of governmental authority in economic affairs. The argument is concerned with the amount of authority that should be exercised and the type of economic structure it ought to produce. The moderate combination of classical economic principles and contemporary social necessity that is most widely held in the United States is well argued in the treatment of the economic order by Professor Samuelson in Part 3 of this text.

Liberalism. Liberalism is a very broad term that is commonly applied to a body of social, economic, and political beliefs that appeared in Western Europe and the United States in early modern times and reached its zenith in the nineteenth century. Liberalism is fundamentally an individualistic doctrine, propagated by the middle classes and the wealthy groups who emerged from the Industrial Revolution. It is optimistic, somewhat mechanistic in its conception of nature, and very much a product of the Enlightenment and of faith in reason and the natural order. It is a doctrine for the successful, for the competitive; it has never been very popular with the poorer parts of the population, which may account for the fact that the demise of classic liberalism coincides roughly with the advent of mass political democracy. Liberalism was at the peak of its influence while political power remained in the hands of the propertied classes. There are substantial differences between British, French, and American liberalism which must be ignored in a brief treatment of the subject, but the reader is warned against overfacile generalization based on the limited evidence produced here.

The liberal ideal is the sovereign individual, man free and unfettered, pursuing his own best interests, as defined by himself, according to means of his own choosing. While the liberal is prepared to recognize the need for society, the recognition is grudging; society is a necessary evil and not a blessing, and one basic assumption in liberal thought is the belief that the authority of government, at all times and in all matters, ought to be limited strictly. The task of government, as the liberal conceives it, is to protect the life and liberty of the citizen from foreign invasion and to protect the property of the individual within the society. Liberals therefore proclaim the merits of constitutional, limited government, of the rule of law; they denounce tyranny and indeed the exercise of authority in any area in which it was not needed. They aim at a maximum of individual freedom in politics, in economics, and in personal affairs. Liberalism is individualistic, pluralistic, optimistic; it tolerates diversity, whether in politics or in religion. As John Stuart Mill asserted, should all the world save one man be of fixed opinion, that lone dissenter ought still to have complete freedom to speak his mind, for society would be the loser if his voice was stilled.

Though liberalism was committed to individualism and to limited government, it was not, in its classic period, egalitarian. Liberals did not, and perhaps do not still, believe in the equality of all men. For one thing, liberals accepted as a matter of course that men of property were entitled to special consideration, for they believed that wealth was a sign of superiority of a natural sort. Most liberals accepted the belief that some men were part of a "natural" aristocracy of talent, and they thought it right and proper that the talented ought to be rewarded for their contribution and given more control over social affairs than other men. Though many liberals were reformers, it was not human misery that inspired their criticisms of existing social conditions, but the absence of logic in the system, the failure of social norms to conform to "reason" or the presence of outmoded or medieval conceptions in the law. They desired modern, enlightened government by the people, but the "people" they had in mind were men like themselves; they were not concerned with leveling reformism of the type that produced socialist thought in the nineteenth century.

The liberalism which we have been describing ought to be commonplace to most American students, since the American social system is founded firmly on a liberal base and retains even today more of liberalism than we can find in any other society on earth. French liberalism was perhaps more radical, following Rousseau rather more than Locke, and concerning itself with the humane and emotional rather more than with the empirical. The French liberals were more concerned with ideals and less with the methodical treatment of brute facts than their British counterparts. They shared many things with British liberals, but emphasized perhaps more the ultimate rationality of the universe, and by inference, the need for rationality in human society. Like the British, they were not proponents of mass democracy in the contemporary sense; in fact, many early French liberals were supporters of enlightened despotism.

Liberal economics. The liberal attitude toward political-economic relations is best summed up in the catch phrase, *laissez faire*—in the belief that government ought not to interfere in the natural order of things. Liberal economic principles originate with the eighteenth-century physiocrats, altered suitably to fit the new environment being produced by the Industrial Revolution. The classic liberal believed that economic affairs were regulated by natural laws of the market place in much the same manner that the movements of the heavenly bodies were governed by the laws of motion. They believed that if a free competitive market could be maintained, in which producers sold their goods at a price determined by market demand, the economic system was then functioning "naturally" and any interference with the system was unwarranted and bound to fail or produce evil consequences. Thus they supported free trade and an end to feudal restrictions on economic activity as well as every other form of government intervention, including subsidies, which would affect the operation of the free market.

Since the free market was "natural," and in a sense inevitable or beyond human control, economic liberals were willing to accept the social consequences of its operation, though they realized that some of these consequences were unfortunate for particular individuals. Labor they conceived as a commodity, to be bought and sold on the market place on a competitive basis. This implied absolute freedom of contract between employer and worker, to ensure the operation of the natural law of supply and demand. On these grounds, liberals were opposed to labor unions and all contracts restraining free competition, whether among employers or among workers. Indeed, liberal governments treated labor unions as conspiracies until well in the nineteenth century (1842 in the United States and much later in Britain). Furthermore, Malthusian theories of population growth, which were accepted by most liberal economists, seemed to indicate that all efforts to alleviate the lot of the worker through private charities or government intervention were in any event bound to fail. An increase in wage rates would simply lead to an increase in population, and the latter would absorb the former and soon reduce the worker to a bare subsistence wage once again. Unemployment, in other words, served as a check on excessive growth of the population.

The classic liberal view of economic activity, then, projected a vision of a "natural" economic order, to be attained by minimizing the influence of government and allowing the laws of economics to operate fully and perfectly. Those with superior audacity, foresight, and enterprise would be well rewarded by the system, and in a sense they were the driving force behind the whole structure. Their rewards were deserved, for success was a demonstration of superiority, and superiority ought naturally to be more amply recompensed than inferiority. Those who lacked talent and were forced to labor suffered, by comparison, but the comparison ought not to be made, for they were "naturally" lacking in the prerequisites which the economic system rewarded. Although reformers might consider the position of labor unfortunate, it would be a profound error to tamper with the system. One might as soon think of altering the movement of the planets in their orbit around the sun. The poor were the victims of inexorable laws which governed the operation of the system, impersonal, just and equitable, and unchangeable.

Liberal economics applied. Although absolute *laissez faire* has never been tried in a real society, the governments of Britain and the United States accepted the basic premises of liberal economics for most of the nineteenth century, and in some respects well into the twentieth century. Social and economic conditions in the nineteenth century are generally accepted as a characteristic illustration of the consequences of applying liberal economic theories to real social situations. In some respects, this generalization may be false. It may be, for example, that the massive expansion of production in the nineteenth century cannot be ascribed to the credit of liberalism in economic matters, as liberal economists often claim; it may also be true that the social conditions produced in the nineteenth century, and commonly ascribed to the influence of liberalism, were not entirely due to the application of liberal economic policies. Nevertheless, the generalization is widely and commonly accepted, and liberal economic theories are credited with rapid industrial growth and with rather horrendous social consequences.

The facts of economic growth in the nineteenth century are not questioned. Whether in the United States or in Europe, industrialization proceeded apace, and production rose with great rapidity, particularly under the impetus of the Napoleonic Wars and the American Civil War. Government kept free of the economic arena, except to provide subsidies and tariffs, or a central banking system which helped to stabilize economic activity. Individual entrepreneurs were free to exploit natural resources, to bargain freely in the open market for goods and for labor. Combinations of firms multiplied without restraint, and governmental monopolies were drastically reduced. Technological change flourished, population grew rapidly, productivity zoomed skyward, and urbanization and industrialization matched stride for stride in the rush through the mid-nineteenth century. Sprawling cities mushroomed outward as centers of trade and marketing and manufacturing and transportation. The number of industries increased, and the size of the firm increased; the small producer, like the independent agrarian of Jefferson's dream, was doomed to extinction in the face of changing economic conditions.

As industrialization boomed, economic liberals rejoiced, for the free market was working, nations were growing wealthy, population was increasing, and national income was expanding at a splendid rate. But there were side effects, at first barely noticed. An increasing share of the population earned its daily wage from industry and fed its wages back into industry as purchases of necessities for living. The day of the mass market, born of specialization of labor and interdependence among an urban population, was at hand. Meanwhile, the corporate device made possible the aggregation of larger units of capital and the growth of still larger firms in which the human equation in economics was increasingly lost in a welter of statistics related to profit and loss and efficiency. The relation between employer and employee was depersonalized at the very moment when the employee became almost totally dependent upon his earning power as a worker.

The social consequences of laissez faire. The list of grievances against the social consequences of laissez-faire economics can, and has, filled substantial volumes. The operation of the free market proved singularly unpredictable and not at all orderly and regular like the movement of planets around the sun. The "Invisible Hand" postulated by Adam Smith seemed at times to falter, and there were large and violent fluctuations in the rate of economic activity—the business cycle. As the fluctuations became more frequent, and larger, serious hardship followed for a population increasingly divorced from the stability of rural life. Waves of prosperity and depression, interspersed with sudden and violent panics brought on by irresponsible speculation, surged through society. The spectre of unemployment and serious hardship haunted the factory hand, and even in prosperous times, his wages were seldom adequate for more than the bare necessities of life.

A further cause for concern was the growing disparity between the wealthy and the unfortunate, for it seemed, for a time, that the rich were indeed growing richer while the poor grew increasingly poor. A small part of the population acquired enormous wealth; the mass of the population eked out a bare and perilous existence. This was perhaps more noticeable in Britain in the early nineteenth century than in the United States, because the land supply in America may have acted as a safety valve for releasing extreme economic pressure on the population. Nevertheless America too had its rich and its poor and the gulf between them seemed to be widening.

The rapid growth of cities created further special problems. Appalling slums, blighted tenement areas, overcrowding, filth, disease, and crime, together with all the concomitants of massed poverty, spread through urban areas like the plague. Cities grew more rapidly than the technology of city life, and educational facilities, recreational facilities, fire protection, police protection, garbage disposal, water supplies, and all the other myriad requirements of city life failed to keep pace with population growth. City government fell prey to unscrupulous political interests, and venality became the order of the day.

More directly related to the laissez-faire system proper was the condition of labor in factories. Working conditions were hazardous and unsanitary. Factories were all too often poorly lighted, badly ventilated firetraps. The hours of work were long, leading to fatigue and a high incidence of accidents. Women and children labored under conditions hardly suited to animal life. Words can hardly describe the appalling conditions that appeared in mines and factories of Britain and the United States in the mid-nineteenth century, though they have been amply documented. The total effect on the worker and his family was devastating.

At yet another level, the effects of *laissez faire* were equally dubious. Uncontrolled entrepreneurs built vast industrial empires, horizontal and vertical combinations tied together with interlocking directorates and holding companies which wielded immense social power. Price fixing, rebates, and other devices were employed to restrict competition and bleed the consumer or squeeze out the smaller competitor. Political bribery and chicanery acted to legalize the exercise of power by the giant corporations. The railroads, for example, manipulated the cost of transportation to the point where it was cheaper, at times, to burn wheat than to move it to market. Nor was the general public immune to the depredations of the "robber barons." Immense quantities of natural resources were detached from the public domain by fraud, bribery, and corruption. Politics became a cockpit in which the economic gamecocks struggled for power and advantage. Corruption in government reached amazing proportions as railroads and steel barons "bought" state legislatures, appointed senators, and arranged for the election of governors.

And for the consumer, the public buyer, the general rule was *caveat emptor*—let the buyer beware. No law controlled the sale of food unfit for consumption, or drugs which endangered the health of the buyer, or stocks not worth the paper on which they were printed. Under the circumstances, jobbery flourished, false advertising was commonplace, and many of the products offered the consumer were literally unfit for consumption. The buyer risked money, health, and even his life, when he went forth to make his purchases. Certainly there were honest men in American business in the nineteenth century, but it is at times difficult to believe that they could survive in the grim and remorseless arena of laissez-faire economics. The description above is predicated mainly on the American experience; it can be matched or even surpassed in the cities and mines and factories of Britain, France, Belgium, or any other country of Western Europe.

The demand for reform. Enough has been said, perhaps, to indicate the nature of the problem as it unfolded in the nineteenth century. As the light of publicity found its way into the dark crevasses of industrial, political, and urban life, a storm of protest rang out across the Western world. Even Victorian England was shocked at the revelations of social reformers inquiring into the abuses of the factory system and the conditions of life in the industrial slums. For a time, liberals were able to maintain their belief that the system was "natural" and ought not to be tampered with. But the volume of evidence increased as social workers went to the mines and factories and slums, parading a regular chamber of horrors before the reading public. Demand for reform swelled rapidly, and it is no accident that a standard history of England in the nineteenth century is titled *The Age of Reform*, nor that a similar text in American history dealing with the years after 1890 has the same title. From every quarter except the business district, there came a demand for regulation and control of abuses in business, in politics, in banking, in the factory, in the stock market, and in government.

The conditions that needed regulation were readily apparent to everyone. How was the remedy to be effected? Various solutions were proposed. One small group of thinkers, not without influence, argued that nothing whatever should be done. A more significant element of the population sought in government action the remedy for abuse, calling upon the government to enter the economic arena in order to remedy abuse, protect the weak and helpless, and limit the strong. A third possibility, which we have called the collectivist solution, argued that the entire social and economic structure needed to be revised in order to remove the basic factors in society which led to these abuses.

The social darwinists. Although many persons came to the defense of *laissez faire*, even when its faults were well known, the group known as the social darwinists were unique in that they were unwilling to accept any fundamental change in the economic system. Following the precepts of the English sociologist, Herbert Spencer, social darwinism combined the evolutionary theories of Charles Darwin with classical economic theory to produce an explanation of the social process that ruled out any interference by government or by private agencies. Spencer did not achieve any real following in Britain, but in the United States his doctrines were taken up by such men as Prof. William Graham Sumner at Yale University and widely expounded in the generation just preceding the turn of the century.

The social darwinist thesis was simple. Spencer taught that society was as much subject to evolutionary development as any plant or animal. In nature, according to Spencer, plants and animals struggle to survive; in society, man must do likewise. Some will rise and swim, others will sink. The "poverty of the incapable," the "starvation of the idle," the shouldering aside of the weak by the strong are the "decrees of a large farseeing benevolence." When the misfortunes of the individual are seen in the framework of the good of all humanity, then it is clear that all is for the best. The "fittest" will survive. And they will deserve to survive. And the poor will not, and that too is for the best. Government has no responsibility toward the poor, nor should government aid the poor. That would be detrimental to the human race. As Sumner was fond of telling his classes at Yale, "Root hog, or die." That is the rule of nature. The unfit should be eliminated. On these grounds Spencer opposed state education, charity, state regulations, tariffs, and even governmental postal systems. Sumner argued that the two prime functions of government were to defend the property of men and the honor of women, and he opposed every proposal for reform legislation that appeared in his time.

The liberal-collectivist alternative. The extreme position taken by the social darwinists was atypical; most people agreed that government would have to use its authority to correct economic abuses. The question was, how ought this to be done. Here we reach the crux of the difference between individualist and collectivist. The individualist argued in favor of retaining the basic capitalist economic system, the profit motive, private ownership of the means of production, and the free market, but using the power of government to limit abuses in the system. The collectivist argued that abuses could not be corrected by this piecemeal approach. What was needed was a basic revision of the economic system, collective ownership of the means of production (nationalization of industry) in some or all parts of the economy, planned production rather than free market operations, and economic equality, embodied particularly in a strong social security or welfare program.

We cannot hope to explore all of the problems raised by the individualist-collectivist controversy in economics in a brief space; hence we must limit the discussion here to a few of the basic principles on which the argument hinges. Nor can we hope to settle the argument. The most that can be expected is a reasonable attitude toward the questions being discussed, a willingness to examine any proposal on its merits, combined with a determination to explore the implications of a given proposal before accepting it. It is foolish to bind society to tradition merely for the sake of tradition, and it is equally foolish to experiment merely for the sake of experimenting. Both extremes must be eschewed if the points at issue are to get the attention they deserve.

Conditioning factors. Before beginning a discussion of the relative merits of individualist and collectivist economic proposals, we should clearly understand certain conditioning factors which govern the operation of any economic system. Two in particular, the physical and resource environment in which the economy operates and the political structure which governs the economic system, are peculiarly important. Experience tells us that both an individualistic and a liberal economy can be made to operate, but it is uncertain that they work equally well in all circumstances. Further, certain kinds of economic arrangements may be incompatible with the political and social conditions which the members of society desire to see maintained. If, for example, a collectivist economy is incompatible with a liberal democratic political system, as is sometimes maintained, then it might be rejected by society even though its economic merits were superior.

Where resources are plentiful and the population is relatively small, maximization of individual economic accomplishment by increasing the reward to the entrepreneur may well be the best means of expanding the wealth of the whole society. In a poverty-stricken region, where one man's gain may quite literally be another man's loss, the balance of gains and losses inherent in unfettered individualism may be quite different. One cannot assume that an economic system which operates satisfactorily in one set of resource conditions will necessarily function as well in another. The selection of the economic structure best suited to a particular society will depend upon such factors as population, resources, technological level, savings, and the goals set for the whole society. An agrarian society may function in an impoverished environment if the members of that society are content with a modest living standard. But if that society decides that it must industrialize as rapidly as possible, it may well have to attack its problems collectively if it hopes to accumulate the needed surplus. A society rich in resources may be able to adopt quite a different solution to the problem of expanding production.

A good practical illustration of this problem and its solution can be found in the history of modern Japan. After the Meiji Restoration of 1868, the Japanese government decided that rapid industrialization was an essential national goal. But the private resources available for capital investment were limited, and the society was predominantly agrarian. Hence the resources of the state were used to inaugurate industrialization and speed its pace. The experiment was highly successful, and Japan industrialized at an amazing rate. Later, industrial concerns which began with government capital were sold to private owners, though in Japan the government retained a substantial measure of control over production. There is little doubt that the Chinese Communists, who also seek rapid large-scale industrialization, have adopted the same tactics. Of course, the Chinese government clearly has no intention of turning its industries over to private owners once they have been established.

Similar problems will doubtless arise in many of the newly emerging nations. Here we may note that the decision to industrialize rapidly is fundamentally a political and not an economic decision. In fact, the severe drain on an agrarian economy that is corollary to a heavy industrialization program probably means a decrease in the living standard for the immediate future. In such areas, unless foreign capital can be obtained to begin industrialization, there seems no reasonable alternative to state-sponsored industrial projects. The domestic capital needed for such projects simply does not exist. This is not unreasonable. The industrialization of Western Europe and the United States was much expedited by governmental policy in the eighteenth and nineteenth centuries, and progress was doubtless much more rapid because of this assistance.

An equally important point to be clarified before a meaningful choice between liberal and collective economic principles can be made is that the political environment in which the system operates may condition our definition of an acceptable economic structure. It is quite useless to compare a private enterprise system operating in a democratic society with a collectivistic economy operating under a totalitarian regime. We are much too likely to assume that the effects of the political dictatorship can be attributed to the economic system, or to attribute the benefits of political democracy to the operation of a free economic system. In practice, the separation of political and economic influences is a very difficult thing. Yet collectivism is too often connected arbitrarily with totalitarianism; this leads to the assumption that one is causally related to the other or that democracy is causally related to a free economic system. Neither association is necessarily valid. Yet there is a relationship here that is important. British socialists, for example, are quite willing to concede immense authority in economic matters to the central government, but few British socialists would be willing to do so if that government were not democratically controlled.

Part of this attitude can be attributed to an historical tradition, for economic liberalism has had a pronounced antistate bias since its inception. The men of the eighteenth and nineteenth centuries took for granted the view that the best government was the weakest compatible with its essential functions. It was not liberalism that taught men to look to the state for protection; that was a function of modern mass democracy. The influence of liberalism worked in the opposite direction.

The transition from one viewpoint to the other, from the notion of government as an enemy to the belief that government was a friend and helper, is an extremely important one, for it tended to mark the transition from classical liberalism to modern mass democracy. In the liberal tradition, it was dangerous to place excessive power in the hands of political government; government ownership and control of industry has often been opposed on these grounds, and the belief is more or less traditional among American and British liberals. It is an odd argument, of course, for it implies a genuine lack of faith in popular government. More important still, if the control and direction of economic affairs carries with it so much power that liberals fear to place that power in the hands of social authority, it is difficult to see how retention of so much power in private hands can be justified.

CONTEMPORARY SOLUTIONS

In the continuum of twentieth-century economic thought, we can identify four major proposals for organizing society, each embodying a different combination of political and economic organization, each seeking a somewhat different set of social values.

(1) One group of nations, exemplified by the United States, has moved steadily toward a mass democracy based upon universal suffrage and a wide measure of personal and political freedom, combining this political system with an economic system based upon private enterprise and profit seeking, controlled by the government to the extent necessary to prevent abuse, and marked by a gradually widening social service program.

(2) A second approach, typified by Great Britain, has a similar political system (parliamentary in form but equally based upon mass participation in the governmental process), but rejects liberal economics in favor of a partially socialized, or nationalized, economy and a very substantial social services program.

(3) A third approach was taken by the fascist nations, such as Italy, Germany, or Japan, prior to World War II. Here the basic capitalist system was retained in economics, though the economy was subjected to fairly strict state control and was combined with a totalitarian and authoritarian political system.

(4) Finally, societies like the U.S.S.R. have rejected both liberalism in

economics and political democracy, combining an extreme form of economic collectivism with a totalitarian political system.

We shall examine some of the salient features of each of these contemporary solutions to economic-political organization.

The American solution. The United States is today one of the very few countries which still retains the basic liberal creed in economics—though there have been substantial departures from laissez-faire liberalism. Oddly enough, the courts have played little part in the modification of the economic system— oddly because the courts are sometimes popularly regarded as bastions of liberty and protectors of the individual. In most cases, political and economic reform have been the outcome of mass protest movements, augmented by the rapid expansion of the suffrage in the nineteenth century.

The transition from the limited popular base of the eighteenth century to the mass political base in the nineteenth century was surprisingly rapid. By the end of Andrew Jackson's terms in office, only women and Negroes remained as substantial population groups without the franchise in most states, and the foundations of free popular sovereignty had been laid. The legal machinery needed to enfranchise the Negro was acquired in the Reconstruction period following the Civil War through the Fourteenth and Fifteenth Amendments, but the amendments have yet to be made completely effective. Women were enfranchised in 1920 by the Twentieth Amendment. Of course, it is one thing to produce universal suffrage legally and another to make it work effectively, but the apparatus for popular government was well established in the nineteenth century.

Control and regulation of business. Economic and social reform began in the 1880s with the agrarian reform movement, and continued with the Progressive movement which lasted through the end of World War I. Led by the Midwestern farmers, a serious attempt was made to institute governmental control over the railroads, and, significantly, when the state governments proved unable to curb railroad abuses, the farmers turned to the national government for redress. The result was the Interstate Commerce Act of 1887, followed by the Elkins Act of 1903 and the Hepburn Act of 1906. A second reform target was the giant industrial combinations—the trusts. Fear of the influence of these behemoths also led to restrictive Federal legislation, beginning with the Sherman Antitrust Act of 1890, followed by the Clayton Act of 1914. Though these actions had only limited success, they did mark a change in public attitude and an important new statement of principle by the government. Finally, there was an attack on the unequal distribution of wealth, beginning with the Sixteenth Amendment in 1913, which made possible a direct and graduated income tax. Again, this marked an important change in social theory, for it allowed government to place the burden of social costs primarily on the shoulders of those who could best afford to bear it.

Political and social reform. Both the agrarian reformers and the Progressives were concerned with political reform and social legislation at the state and national level. Under their influence, a civil service reform act was passed in 1883, reducing the impact of the "spoils system" on the civil service. Some states introduced direct primary elections as a means of wresting control of political nominations from political bosses and party conventions. Other laws sought to control bribery and corruption in government. The Seventeenth Amendment provided for direct election of senators, reducing the influence of business-dominated state legislatures. Other laws, such as the Pure Food and Drug Act of 1906 or the workmen's compensation laws passed by several states around the turn of the century, were aimed at the protection of the general public or the workingman. It is symptomatic of the legal thinking of the time that the Supreme Court voided many of these laws, declaring both old-age pensions and minimum-wage laws unconstitutional.

World War I tended to slow the pace of reform, for it was accompanied by great material prosperity. A few steps had been taken in the direction of controlling the large corporation, political corruption, and the social consequences of urbanization, but a great deal remained untouched. An important change in public attitude had taken place, marking a break with the liberal tradition, but the excitement of the war, coupled with the "return to normalcy" that marked the 1920s, tended to inhibit social reform and social speculation.

The New Deal. Beneath the surface of the prosperous 1920s, the economic structure was in dubious condition, and the collapse of the stock market in 1929 signaled the beginning of a depression which was world-wide and frightening in its implications. The Great Depression, perhaps more than any other single factor in American history, unleashed social criticism in America, making possible a profound readjustment of the role of government in economic affairs. The merits of the "New Deal" have been much debated since the 1930s, for the legislation enacted by the Federal government produced much that was new and extremely difficult to evaluate. Yet it must be said that the New Deal was not really an attack on liberalism in economics or an attempt to replace the private capitalist system by a collectivized economy. The New Deal remained from first to last a reform movement and not a revolutionary movement.

One of the principal effects of the Great Depression was the changed attitude of the individual toward the economic responsibilities of government. Traditionally, economic affairs were the responsibility of the individual; the Depression made it clear that though some individuals might solve their economic problems in times of stress, all of the people could not. Men turned to government for assistance. The change in attitude is vital. Liberalism held that the state was an enemy, to be watched with suspicion and mistrust. The power of government was to be held at a minimum. This conception was discarded in favor of the use of state power to promote the interests of the weak and helpless against the strong. The state became a friend and not an enemy. In particular, the government, with the apparent approval of the electorate, took upon itself the responsibility of protecting the individual against the consequences of severe economic fluctuations or personal misfortunes: first by providing ameliorative legislation such as workman's compensation and social security coverage; second, by accepting responsibility for using monetary and fiscal policy to help temper the vacillations in the economy and maintain a high level of employment.

New Deal legislation falls into a small handful of categories, each defined by the particular economic group which needed government assistance. (1) The farmer was provided with a whole congeries of aids and protections: crop loans and easier credit were provided through government agencies; conservation was encouraged; production was to some extent controlled; prices were maintained. (2) Industrial workers were granted the right to bargain collectively, and an obligation was created for the employers to accept labor union activity; working conditions and safety regulations were controlled; the rights of women and children employed in industry were protected; compensation for injuries received at work and for loss of employment was extended; wages and hours were regulated, etc., all, of course, within the limits of the Federal government's authority. (3) Private persons who were unable to support themselves were provided with relief, old-age pensions were established, assistance for the handicapped was made available, and indirect aid through housing subsidies and other devices was provided for the general population. (4) The general public was also offered some broad measure of protection against unfettered individualism in business and finance. The banking industry was regulated more closely, as was the sale of securities and stocks. Public utilities, transportation companies, and other industries which affected the general welfare of the population were brought under closer government supervision. (5) Nor was the entrepreneur neglected. In fact, business benefited greatly from government activity. There were subsidies for shipping and other forms of transportation, free information from the Departments of Commerce and Agriculture and other governmental agencies, financial aid for the small businessman, and government contracts for a wide variety of items, which proved a boon to business. The Federal government also slackened its prosecution of large combinations; the New Deal was in fact a period of great concentration in industry.

In brief, government intervened on behalf of the farmer, the worker, the general public, and the businessman. It became an active member of the economic community. The desirability of this change was far from agreed, some charging that it would lead to "socialism," vaguely defined, or a totalitarian system. Nevertheless, in the years since the New Deal began, the role of government in economic and social affairs has expanded greatly. The authority acquired during the Second World War has very largely been retained and put to social use. The American government now plays a crucial role in the economic and social life of the nation, as purchaser, as controller and regulator, and as an underwriter.

In the contemporary United States, the direction in which governmental influence has moved society is reasonably clear. What is emerging is a society that is sometimes designated as welfare capitalism, or the welfare state, though the latter term properly belongs to countries such as Britain or Sweden. The rights of property have been limited considerably but the fundamental structure has not been altered, nor has the government turned entrepreneur on any extensive scale. Social security has expanded greatly, though it is still antidiluvian by current European standards and grossly inadequate in an inflationary economy. The lot of the worker has improved immensely, largely through labor union activity, made possible of course by friendly legislation such as the Wagner Act. The farmer's lot has been improved and some of the harshness of farm life removed, partly through governmental action, though there are deep economic problems in this area of production that have not yet been solved, as we shall see in Part 3.

Few persons in the United States now desire to return to laissez-faire conditions, but that does not mean that the argument over both the past and the future has ended. The burning questions of the present are matters of degree, questions about "how far" government intervention in economic affairs ought to go, and which areas of human life it ought to be concerned with. Some press for "more of the same" while others demand retrenchment. There seems to have been no definitive ideological direction, even in the New Deal period; American reform has proceeded pragmatically rather than systematically, dealing with abuses as they came to light and not attempting to establish a "system" which will act as a panacea to social ills. This avoids the danger of authoritarian direction in the name of some abstract and absolute human goal, but it also produces anomalies and contradictions and an irritating lack of principle. It is interesting to compare this approach to reform with the thoroughgoing approach of the European Socialist or Communist, who sets out quite literally to remake society in a new image.

Socialism and its variants. European protests against the social consequences of laissez-faire capitalism took various forms. Some turned to the same
reformist attitude that appeared in the United States. Many put their faith
in the broad conception of social organization and function known as "socialism." Socialism includes various branches—anarchism, communism, syndicalism, guild socialism, democratic socialism—each with its own peculiarities.
Broadly, there were two main lines of development: some Socialists attempted
to combine economic collectivism, total or partial, with political democracy;
others pursued collectivist goals in economics by revolutionary means, seeking
first to destroy the existing political system. Anarchism flourished for a time in
nineteenth-century Europe, but has now declined in importance. Democratic
socialism reached its peak in the years immediately after World War II, and is
still a powerful force in European politics. The principal branch of revolutionary socialism still active in the world is, of course, Marxism. We shall, therefore,
confine our discussion to British democratic socialism and Soviet Marxism, but
the interested reader should also inquire into the precepts of French syndicalism
for this is a significant element in contemporary French politics.

Basic principles of socialism. In an age when the conflict of "isms" has produced
strong international tensions and a great deal of emotional involvement, it is
most important to realize that men do not advocate communism or socialism or
syndicalism simply because they want to install a particular kind of machinery
in society. Socialism cannot be described as a simple mechanical process or
explained by some brief slogan. Socialists advocate a particular combination
of social machinery and social purposes, but the machinery is needed to achieve
the purpose, or so they believe. Most Socialists agree on the basic goals they
seek in society, although they have produced an amazing variety of schemes
intended to achieve them. Communal ownership of property and similar devices
are proposed, not because they are intrinsically good, but because they are
means to desirable social ends.

Thus we find Socialists who wish to retain a democratic political structure,
combining it with public ownership of all or part of the means of production.
Some seek to achieve political power through ordinary parliamentary procedures;
others feel that violent revolution is necessary because the bourgeoisie will not
hand over political authority without a struggle. Most Socialists believe that
the world will eventually accept socialist principles, but some wish to hasten
the process by violence or even terrorism. Some Socialists construct elaborate
utopian systems to illustrate their theories; others, like the anarchist Prince
Kropotkin, refuse to discuss the ultimate nature of society on the ground that
it will develop spontaneously out of the cooperative efforts of men freed from
the bondage of the capitalist system. Some socialist theories like syndicalism are
founded upon the trade union movement; others regard unions as useless or of

limited use. There are, in brief, almost as many systems as there are Socialists, ranging from moderate democratic groups to violent or terroristic revolutionaries.

The core of socialist thought, the point at which Socialists meet and agree, is a set of social values, a body of beliefs about the proper relations between man and man. Socialism is egalitarian, for example, in that it is firmly committed to the belief that men are equal and ought to share equally in the benefits that society produces, and, in most cases, ought to share equally in the control of society. To put the point in more familiar terms, Socialists are strongly opposed to inequalities in wealth, income, educational opportunity, social status, etc. Such inequalities, they believe, are not inherent in man, but are simply consequences of a faulty social structure. The system of private profit and private ownership of capital is chiefly responsible for inequality; hence it ought to be abolished, to be replaced by social or public ownership. Private ownership of capital also produced the bifurcation of society into social classes, one owning the means of production, the other earning a livelihood by the sale of its labor. The interests of these two classes are fundamentally antagonistic so long as the owners of capital are able to profit from the system, since the profit of the owner and the wages of the worker are inversely related—an increase in one automatically implies a decrease in the other. The class struggle is a characteristic of the capitalist system, and eventually the conflict between classes will lead to revolution, though democratic Socialists believe that revolution can be "headed off" by voluntary legislation.

The ideal, then, is social control over the fundamental conditions that make the life of man miserable or enjoyable. It begins with men of equal worth and seeks to offer each man the fullest possible opportunity to develop his innate capacities, unhindered by status differentials imposed by an arbitrary economic structure. Equal educational opportunities, freedom from fear of want, the right and the obligation to work, to contribute to society, adequate provision for health and safety and security in old age—all these matters are a fundamental part of the socialist creed in all countries. National socialist movements differ chiefly on the best means of achieving these goals. Of course, the goals are not the property of Socialists alone; most Americans would agree with many of them. The differences appear when we begin delineating the means of achieving the ends.

Early socialist proposals. A brief summary of the major ideas of some early socialist thinkers will illustrate the complexity of the ideal. In the late eighteenth and early nineteenth centuries, utopia builders like the Frenchman Charles Fourier (1772–1837) and the Englishman Robert Owen (1771–1858) were very influential. Fourier sought to promote the happiness of the individual by developing simple agrarian communities, in which men lived together in small groups in peace and contentment. His ideal was a phalanx, a group of some 1,600 persons living on 5,000 acres of land. Although the phalanxes had various communal features, they were not really communistic societies, for special payments were made to those who labored, those who managed, and those who supplied the capital. Owen's model communities were less committed to the agricultural life, for Owen was himself a successful factory owner and manager, but the general principle was roughly the same—men should live together in small communities, cooperatively and without competition, doing the work they enjoyed.

A rather different viewpoint emerges in the work of Comte de Saint-Simon (1769–1825), who was a civil engineer and approached the problem of social organization from the point of view of the engineer. Saint-Simon believed in collectivized society, carefully planned to operate efficiently and maximize production. The collective community should carry out large social projects such as the building of dams and canals. It followed, he believed, that society should be ruled by the technically competent, and he particularly favored leaders of industry or bankers, for these men know the value of technology. Saint-Simon was relatively unconcerned with personal liberty or democracy; he sought efficiency, material comfort, and prosperity through an efficient and benevolent despotism.

One of the founders of French syndicalist thought, Pierre Joseph Proudhon (1809–1865), who was much maligned by Marx, produced quite a different approach to social organization. Proudhon was born of working-class parents and was inordinately proud of his heritage. He was, to the end of his life, a complete individualist, though his influence on socialist thought was very great. Proudhon hated the state and wanted to abolish it, leaving social organization to voluntary associations. Like the anarchists, he was opposed to all efforts to coerce the individual. He thought that men could be set free if the state were eliminated and a vast credit system was inaugurated which made it possible for any man to obtain capital to develop his ideas. Everyone, he thought, should have equal property rights, and economic activity should be conducted by public utility companies or *syndicats* controlled by the workers. Proudhon is the author of the famous dictum that property is theft, but a literal translation of the phrase is misleading; his real hatred was reserved for inequality of property and the consequent differential in the status of individuals.

At yet another extreme we find the teachings of Louis Auguste Blanqui (1805–1881) who was one of the earliest of the pure, violent revolutionaries. Blanqui's program had the virtue of simplicity. He taught that men should organize and train a small revolutionary elite, and when the time was ripe, strike hard and overthrow the existing political system. What then? Blanqui did not profess to know; he was convinced only that the existing system was evil and unjust and that it ought to be destroyed. People would then produce voluntary associations of some sort to carry out their social activities.

Similar in name, but with a totally different outlook, Louis Blanc (1811–

1882) was one of the founders of democratic socialism. Blanc argued that the workers ought to seek control of the state by democratic means and use the power of the state to benefit the working classes. Blanc, then, sought universal suffrage, free education for all, and opportunity to prepare the workers for their task of ruling. Economic activity would be controlled by the community; the worker would control the community through his political power. On this foundation, British and German democratic socialist theories were later erected.

This is only a small sampling of a very wide range of early socialist opinions and programs. Some of these men had a considerable following; others were only voices in the wilderness who soon died away. Utopian socialism lost its appeal in Europe when the uprisings of 1830 failed, but there were more than enough branches of socialism to replace it. The major trends in nineteenth-century socialist thought included: democratic socialism, particularly in Germany and England; Marxism, which was very strong in Germany and in France; anarchism, which had its greatest influence in Spain and Italy; and syndicalism, which was particularly influential among the French trade unionists.

British democratic socialism. Modern democratic socialism in Britain represents a fusion of intellectual constructions obtained from earlier socialist thinkers with social power produced by the development of a powerful trade union movement and the widening of the franchise. The intellectual fathers of the movement were the Fabian Socialists, who organized their society in the 1880s and produced the very influential *Fabian Essays* in 1889. The guiding spirits of the Fabian Society were Sidney Webb, his wife, Beatrice Webb, George Bernard Shaw, and some other highly influential British intellectuals. The Fabians were gradualists from the outset—they abjured revolution in favor of parliamentary action. In economics, they argued for a planned economy subordinated to a democratic political system. In the early years of the society, nationalization of industry was not greatly emphasized, for the Fabians believed that their objectives could be accomplished by tax policy once the movement gained control of political power.

The Fabians functioned primarily as an information bureau, as a source of information and political doctrine. The first step in the direction of a practical socialist political organization came in 1893 when the Independent Labor party was founded and dedicated to the principle of collective ownership of the means of production, distribution, and exchange (nationalization). A Marxist group, the Social Democratic Federation, was founded in 1881, but never achieved much prominence. The trade unions were not, at this time, committed to socialism; they aimed to use direct industrial action (the general strike) to obtain their objectives in society.

Success in politics had to wait upon the combination of labor union power and political activism, all directed toward the achievement of socialism, and that was not easily accomplished. But in 1902, the British courts made the trade unions financially liable for damage or criminal action caused by members during strikes, seriously handicapping the growth of the unions. The unions promptly turned to political action, assessing their members to raise funds, and working more actively with the Independent Labor party. In 1906, the Labor party was formed as a federation which combined individual trade unions and political groups into a single unit, and it soon had a few representatives in the House of Commons. Not until 1918, however, did the Labor party commit itself firmly to socialism, to achieving the most equitable distribution of the fruits of industry for workers by hand or brain through common ownership of the means of production, particularly the nationalization of land, coal mining, transportation, power production, life insurance, and a number of other basic industries.

The vicissitudes of Labor party history we can ignore; its program of action appeared full-blown when it won a sweeping victory at the polls in 1945 and formed the first majority government in the party's history. Basically, the Labor party's program can be divided into three parts: (1) organizing the machinery needed for national planning; (2) nationalization of the basic industries in one sector of the economy, and obtaining authority to control other privately owned industries; (3) a comprehensive social services program.

The planning machinery was established quickly and set to work on a national inventory and the production of long-range plans for the economy. This is an interesting phase of the Labor party's work, which has not received the attention it deserves. The nationalization program, on the other hand, was widely publicized. A few industries considered basic to the economy were purchased involuntarily from their owners: the Bank of England, the coal mines, gas producers, railroads, and road transportation. A later decision to nationalize the steel industry created bitter opposition, and though the industry was legally nationalized, the process was never completed and steel was denationalized (along with road transportation) when the Conservative party returned to power in 1951. Actually, some of the industries, such as the coal mines and the railroads, were in severe straits and probably welcomed nationalization in fact if not in principle. But the success or failure of nationalization as a policy is difficult to measure. Britain was in a desperate economic position after 1945, and the Labor Government really had little opportunity to experiment with massive investment programs. In any case, Labor leaders were themselves uncertain about nationalization by 1951, though some members of the left wing of the party pressed for further action on purely ideological grounds. Whether Britain will undergo further nationalization of industy if Labor again achieves power remains to be seen.

One major accomplishment of British socialism was its welfare program, which seems now to have been accepted by the British people, and by both political parties, at least in principle. A comprehensive social security program offers full protection to every member of the population against loss of employment, ill health, or incapacity for work. Medical and dental coverage is complete; medicine, teeth, glasses, services of physicians, etc., are provided free, as are hospital care, pre- and postnatal care, funeral expenses, financial aid to parents, etc. An important, though indirect benefit to the population flows from an extensive housing program for low-income groups and a comprehensive program of aid for education. The educational system was revised—mainly through an extensive scholarship program—to ensure that all deserving students would be able to attend college whether or not they could afford the expense. Finally, a deliberate attempt was made to reduce the gap between rich and poor by a heavy and graduated tax structure directed at both personal income and inherited wealth. Though much remains to be done, the limiting factor has been lack of resources and not failure of intent.

Since 1951, British Conservatives have been reconciled to this fundamental change in the social and economic structure, and there is now little likelihood of a major change back to the prewar system. The differences between the two parties have narrowed and both remain committed to mass democracy and a liberal society. Labor has put into effect the basic parts of its program of action and seem not to contemplate any drastic changes in the immediate future. There the matter rests for the present.

Marxism. More than a third of the world's population is today governed by regimes that claim to apply the principles laid down by Karl Marx to the social problems of the times. This alone would make Marxism one of the more significant of living ideologies. Whether the regimes in China and the Soviet Union are really following Marx is in one sense irrelevant, for it proves nothing to assert that they are "not really Marxist." Soviet communism and Chinese communism originate in Marxist writings, and what is important and significant is the direction in which these regimes now move rather than their relationship to the writings of the long-dead prophet.

Since Soviet communism is widely associated in the public mind with both Marxism and totalitarian rule, it is worth pointing out that Marxism arose as part of the social protest movement of the nineteenth century and that Marx denounced the same inequities that aroused the ire of American reformers. His frame of reference was different. Marx seldom looked beyond his own conception of the structure of English society in the mid-nineteenth century and this is a serious shortcoming, for it meant that some of his assumptions about the economic system and its operation were already invalid at the time of his death. It is this factor that led to the development of what is called "revisionism" in the Marxist camp—the effort to bring Marx's assumptions up to date. Marx seeks to remedy the effects of industrialization, he inveighs against the monotony of mass production, the use of women and children as laborers, the dehumanization of the industrial worker, the decline of individual freedom, the ignorance, poverty, and filth common in the industrial slums. In sum, Marx shared with the social reformers of his time the same basic data and much the same moral position, though he insisted that he was not concerned with morality and he despised the term "reformer."

What is truly unique in Marx is the explanation that he offers for existing conditions, and the remedy he proposes. He does not follow the usual reformist pattern and discuss particular remedies for particular evils. Instead he takes as his context the whole of human history and attempts to demonstrate that current social conditions are simply another stage in a *necessary* historical process. Marx begins, in other words, with a philosophy of history. He argues that the key to understanding history is to realize that the economic structure, the relation between those who control the means of production and the rest of society, is the fundamental determinant in social development. Control over the means of production means control of society; the state, in these terms, is simply a tool which the owners of capital use to control society. The foundation of social life is an economic arrangement; all of the other social devices are simply a superstructure erected on this foundation. Religion, for example, the "opiate of the people," is merely a device used by the ruling class, the owners of productive capital, to keep the population in line.

Since the owners of capital will resist all efforts to replace them in control of society, the history of politics is the history of a struggle between those who control power and those whom they exploit. Inevitably, the exploited will win out over the exploiters and rearrange society to their own advantage. This is the famous class struggle and its inevitable outcome. The whole sequence of conflicts is only a part of a larger historical process called the "dialectic," which Marx took from Hegel. But Marx substitutes the interplay of economic forces, or material forces, for Hegel's interplay of ideas; hence the whole concept is described as dialectical materialism, the historical development of society out of the interaction of economic forces.

In the world of his own day, Marx had no difficulty in identifying the dominant class; it was the *bourgeoisie,* the owners of capital. The behavior of the *bourgeoisie* was driving all other economic groups into a single unified lower stratum of society, a single mass, which Marx called the proletariat. The proletariat included the industrial workers, of course, but Marx apparently believed that the professional classes, the small merchants, etc., would eventually be squeezed into the same mold, leaving only two classes, *bourgeoisie* and proletariat, locked in a life and death struggle for power. The struggle would lead to conflict, and the masses would eventually win and thus gain control over the means of production and of society.

Marxism is, then, a theory of historical development, of the driving forces that shape human history. Marx spent a great deal of time searching through history for evidence to "prove" his thesis and show that the dialectic really did explain the development of past societies. However, it is not the theory of history that matters today; it is the practical program that Marx devised and the interpretation of Marx's writings in terms related to contemporary economic and political movements. For Marx held that society must change fundamentally, else by definition the superstructure could not be altered. And he asserted further that the economic foundations *would* change because the capitalist system, useful though it had been, contained inherent contradictions which would cause it to collapse.

Marx took as a basic assumption the belief that all of the value in the goods men produce is due to the labor expended in production—this is the so-called "labor theory of value" which Marx apparently borrowed from the classical economist David Ricardo. It followed that justice demanded that the laboring classes be given the full value of what was produced by human labor. But in the capitalist system, the wages paid the laborer were less than the value of the goods he created; the worker earned his wages, or their equivalent value, during a part of his day's labor. What he produced in the remainder of his working day was taken by the capitalist; the "surplus value," the difference between what the worker produced and what he was actually paid, was the basis of capitalist profits. The capitalist could control and take possession of this surplus value because he had a monopoly over the available jobs; hence the worker could be forced to work for wages that were less than the true value of his labor. This meant that the working class, as a whole, was being exploited by the capitalist class in the sense that surplus value was being taken from the worker and used to maintain the capitalist.

But if history provided an explanation of the problem, it also provided a remedy. The capitalist system, Marx said, could not survive. For if the market and labor force remained constant, the taking of profits introduced an imbalance between the cost of all goods produced and the purchasing power generated by the wages paid to labor. Unless the capitalist could find a place to invest his profits, thus returning them to the community and generating more purchasing power, the system would collapse. Capitalism could only operate in an expanding economic system, like the "chain letters" that were popular in the 1930s. But expanding production would produce a surplus of goods; hence the capitalist must constantly seek new markets for them (which led Lenin to argue that capitalism was inherently imperialist in its final stages). Finally, a limit would be reached and the system would simply collapse in revolution.

The gist of the Marxist argument, then, is that human history unfolds in the form of a struggle between classes, with the dominant class controlling the state power. The worker in a capitalist system is simply a commodity, to be bought at the cheapest price. In time this leads to mass misery, the rich growing richer, the poor growing poorer. Eventually, an explosion will occur, and the class struggle will become a violent revolution. It is obviously useless to engage in parliamentary activity, for the state apparatus is controlled by the *bourgeoisie*, which will not relinquish power willingly. Hence violent revolution is necessary. Marx seemed to believe that the revolution would arise spontaneously, but Lenin (and others) later added that the revolution will be instigated, led, and directed by the vanguard of the proletariat—the Communist party. The revolution in turn will smash the ruling class, leading first to socialism and then to a classless society or communism. The state, which is an instrument of class oppression, will become a useless appendage, like the human appendix, and will gradually wither away.

What is a Communist society like? Marx was not very clear about the matter, but the program outlined in the second part of the *Communist Manifesto* may give us some indication of the lines along which he was thinking (though it is in most respects typical of current socialist propaganda and not really unique). Marx demands the abolition of landed property, a heavy progressive income tax, the nationalization of banks, communications, and transportation, the equal liability of all men to work, the integration of agriculture and industry and abolition of rural-urban differences, and the freedom of publication for all. Of the political structure he says nothing, for a classless society will have no need of it.

Here, much simplified, is the essential Marxist argument. It postulates the need for a new, planned society, based on economic equality, the abolition of class distinctions, and the equalization of social benefits. Ideally, each man will contribute to society as much as he can and take from society as much as he needs; that ideal lies in the future—how far, Marx did not say. The argument is interesting and worth examining, for Marx at least called attention to the immense importance of economics in human life and showed how economic and political authority are related. Unfortunately Marxism does not end with Marx, and Marx himself once declared that he was not a Marxist because of his exasperation with some of his "followers." By emphasizing one aspect of Marx's teaching rather than another, latter-day Marxists have often drastically altered the basic structure.

Soviet Marxism. Marxism, as it has developed in the Soviet Union, is an excellent example of this technique of "interpreting" earlier writers. Lenin, who led one of the Marxist factions prior to 1914, found himself *de facto* ruler of Russia in 1917. The task of reconciling a theory produced mainly in exile and without political responsibility with the needs of a large and backward society proved formidable. Understandably, much of the idealism in Marx was lost. The practical problems arising out of the need to maintain the independence of Russia and the power of the Communist party in Russia overrode theoretical considerations. In any case, Marx had stated his theories largely in terms of a proletariat; in Russia the proletariat was tiny. In the struggle to adapt Marx to the special problems which the Bolsheviks faced in Russia, orthodox Marxist terminology was forced ever deeper into a special context; that is, the name was preserved while the thing designated by the name was changed.

Russia was a poor, largely agrarian society, not a capitalist nation. Could her society move directly to socialism or must she first be made into a capitalist system? Lenin decided, not surprisingly, that the transition was possible. Did the success of the revolution in Russia mean that the world stood on the verge of world revolution? Marx had argued along these lines, and the leaders of Soviet communism waited for the revolution to break out elsewhere; in fact, they sponsored some abortive attempts at revolution in Central Europe. When the world revolution failed to materialize, they decided that world revolution was not really necessary; it was possible, apparently, for socialism to succeed in a single country. Lenin also transformed Marx's conception of spontaneous revolution into a made and directed revolution in which the Communist party took the lead, exercising dictatorial power on behalf of the proletariat during the period of transition to socialism. This was most convenient, and indeed necessary, to maintain party rule.

The point is that it is always possible to generalize theoretical constructions to fit practical situations, and it is probably poor policy to afford such impromptu additions to Marxism the status of "theories." Too many Western writers have accepted Soviet slogans at face value and tried to organize them into a coherent creed. Does the term "Marx-Engels-Lenin-Stalin-Malenkov-Khrushchev line" really have meaning, or has the message been garbled in transmission? To read Marx and believe that one is learning something about current Soviet policy is very possibly a serious mistake; to learn current Soviet policy, it seems better to study the present behavior of the U.S.S.R.

One of the great misfortunes of contemporary politics is the fact that the peoples in the newly emerging nations of Asia and Africa are being exposed to Marxist theory and led to believe that they will be governed by the theory if they accept the leadership of the Soviet Union. This is hardly likely to occur. Marxism may be an attractive doctrine to a poverty-stricken people who have little to lose from revolution; Soviet policy is quite a different matter. If the present Soviet regime is denounced on ideological grounds, that is tantamount to accepting the thesis that Marxism and Soviet policy are one; we can hardly blame the uneducated if they then accept the identification and act upon it.

The Soviet government, as might be expected, has made precisely this sort of rationalization within its own borders—to its own people. Russia is today ruled by a ruthless dictatorial group which brooks no interference from outside its own ranks and is relatively indifferent to the plight of the individual. The regime has been marked by militarism, terrorism, repression, and a depressed standard of living. It has justified itself by appealing to Marx, suitably interpreted. Perhaps the best thing that could happen inside Russia, from the Western point of view, would be for the Soviet people to begin judging their regime by its consequences and not by its theorizing. At times, it appears that something of the sort is taking place, as reflected in demands for more consumer goods and protests against the continual restrictions placed on consumption.

After all, it does not really matter whether or not the society presently operating in Russia does or does not resemble the society that Marx envisaged. What is significant is that the Soviet government is authoritarian, illiberal, militaristic, and dogmatic and that the Soviet population is characterized by sharp status differentiations, low living standards, the absence of personal freedom, and a complete inhibition of political activity.

Fascism. The term fascism is used to designate the political regimes that appeared in Italy, Germany, Japan, Argentina, and Spain in the period between the two world wars. It implies a political dictatorship, based on charismatic leadership and absolute obedience, coercion, repression of all opposition, and a strict subordination of the individual to the state. Fascism greatly resembles the present regime in the Soviet Union, though there are theoretical differences in aim and structure, particularly as regards economics.

A fascist regime is invariably directed by a leader, whether he be called *Führer, Duce,* or what have you. The leader is a superman, divinely guided, infallible, with mystic insight into the future. He is a superior being, to be obeyed without question, for he has a destiny to fulfill. He is the great man, come to save the nation, or more commonly, to lead the nation to its rightful place in history. The leader claims absolute political authority on the basis of his personal superiority and denies all public responsibility for his actions.

The result is a peculiar kind of statism in which leader and state merge and both are exalted together, for the state, like the leader has a manifest destiny, a place in the sun. The state is an organic entity, a mystic union, in which the individual must be totally submerged. His only function is to contribute to the destiny of the state—by obeying the leader. For the men, this generally means military service; for women, bearing strong, healthy children—in quantity. Irrational as this may appear, its very irrationality seems a source of strength, for fascism has successfully proclaimed its mystique and found men willing to accept it on faith. It generated emotional responses, not reasoned convictions, carefully fostered by skillful propaganda and well-staged demonstrations. The psychological foundations of this modern political phenomenon we must leave to the psychiatrist, but the manner in which men can be led to obey en masse is a truly remarkable aspect of human behavior.

Fascism is, of course, elitist, for it denies the equality of all men; the notion that man is capable of self-government is regarded as meaningless drivel. Instead, the fascist chooses to emphasize real or imaginary differences among human beings. Besides the obvious difference between the peerless leader and ordinary mortals, the members of society are led to believe that they too are superior vis-à-vis all other people. They are the superior "Aryans" or the heritors of Roman splendor. Often there is a particular scapegoat, a lower order of being responsible for the ills of society, hence to be eradicated or eliminated, as was the case with Jews in Germany. Fascism, in brief, is committed to racism; and the Nazi myth of Aryan supremacy, which is both cultural and biological nonsense, was widely and successfully cultivated.

Fascism makes a cult of strength. "Might is right," might well be the fascist motto. The supreme virtue in man, in addition to loyalty to the leader, is physical strength. The supreme virtue in society is strength. Even moral strength, "strength through joy" was the Nazi phrase, is desirable as a contribution to the strength of society. The regimentation of young life in Nazi Germany and Italy was a means to physical culture as well an introduction to discipline. Mass gymnastics, after all, are hardly the individualist's conception of the perfect sport.

When a well-organized group of people believes firmly that it has a special mission in life, a unique destiny that must be fulfilled, and combines this belief with an exaltation of force and strength, the consequences are likely to be serious. Fascist states have without exception been military-minded and aggressive; most have been little better than armed camps for a good part of their existence. Peace is viewed with contempt. Superiority confers the right, indeed the obligation, to dominate others—for their own good. The fascist state seeks colonies to "civilize," or "lebensraum," or sources of raw materials. In a sense, fascism is imperialist toward everyone, colony or not, who is weaker than itself.

This combination of influences produces an attitude toward war and conflict that is romantic, and a little horrifying. War is exalted, and conflict is proclaimed the stuff of life. War becomes a purifying experience instead of the brutal, monotonous, degrading behavior pattern which men have found when the glamour is stripped away and the advertising on the recruiting posters forgotten. The sacrifice of life, family, property, and principles consequent on the waging of war becomes an act of religious faith, a mystic ritual in the secular religion of statism. The sovereign individual of the liberal ideal is replaced by a cipher, a statistic, a nameless, faceless, and often arrogant sycophant, and a follower.

In economic matters, fascism is not a collectivist repudiation of capitalism; indeed, the capitalist system is retained, together with the profit motive, though an alliance between political leadership and economic leaders is customary. The industrialist usually benefits from state economic activity, so long as he follows the bidding of the leader. Owners of capital were united together in giant corporations and controlled by the state through these corporations. Labor is similarly unified. No conflict between labor and capital is permitted; the state settles disputes by fiat. There is no class struggle in fascism; all classes are united in the service of the state.

The fascist state is totalitarian, with the usual apparatus of dictatorial control. Political activity is strictly forbidden, since any opposition would, by definition, simply be in error. One political party, that which serves the leader, is permitted, and it becomes an instrument of the state and not a means of seeking political power. Indeed, the efficiency with which the single political party serves the state has led many writers to assert that one-party systems are inherently totalitarian, and that more than one political party is absolutely essential in a democratic system.

The state, of course, reaches deep into society to spread its influence and mold its followers. The young are objects of special attention in every totalitarian system, and special training or indoctrination is duly prescribed. The educational system is likewise fully controlled, texts are carefully edited, and education is directed toward a particular image rather than toward a respect for truth. State control over the organs of opinion, press, radio, and publication is complete. The omnipresent police ensure public conformity. Art and science, literature and poetry, are bent to the needs of the state. And even in Germany, with its prestigious scientific tradition, there was no shortage of fawning hypocrites willing to provide "scientific" justification for such theories as "Aryan" supremacy and Jewish inferiority. Every nation has its own pet beliefs, its own sense of superiority, just as every individual is at times emotionally unstable; in these terms, the fascist state is analogous to the paranoid.

No survey of fascism is complete without mention of the role of force, terror, and brutality in its operation. It may almost be said that fascism is spawned in force, maintained by force, and in most cases, has perished by force. Fascists are contemptuous of parliamentary methods, preferring the private army, the "blackshirts" or "brownshirts," to terrorize opposition and lay the groundwork for the *coup d'état*. The labor camp, the secret police, the concentration camp (corrective institution), the extralegal summons, the forced confession are all part of the sorry saga of human inhumanity that fascism has written into the political history of the twentieth century. Fascism has never achieved authority by popular acclaim or by proposing a particular program. Indeed, fascists have no program. They proclaim instead the greatness of the leader, the needs of the hour, the virtues of obedience, the superiority of action over thought, and the need to kill or be killed, the validity of force as the supreme arbiter in human affairs. It is primitive and uncivilized; it appeals frankly to the baser elements in man. As the war crimes trials showed all too clearly, there are always men to whom such motives appeal. If one attempted to explain to a rational creature from another planet that this farrago of nonsense commanded the loyalty of millions of human beings in the twentieth century, it seems unlikely that the tale would be accepted. Yet the phenomenon has appeared in more than one country, under quite different circumstances, and our efforts to "explain" it have thus far proved inadequate.

Summary

In the relation between government and economics, the property concept is central, though it is separate from the concept of private profit. All societies limit property rights in some manner, depending upon the social values they seek to achieve, but no society may dispense completely with private property. In the eighteenth and nineteenth centuries, the dominant attitude toward political-economic relations was liberalism, or *laissez faire*, which was individualistic. The social consequences of *laissez faire* and the rise of mass democracies have amended economic liberalism substantially. In the United States, individualism in economics remains maximized and is combined with political democracy. In Britain, political democracy is combined with a partially collectivized economy. In the Soviet Union, a collectivized economy is combined with a totalitarian political system. And in the prewar fascist nations, capitalism was combined with a totalitarian political system, though the economy was very strictly controlled.

Review questions

1. Distinguish between property and profit.
2. What are some of the common limits which society imposes on property rights?
3. What is meant by *laissez faire*? Economic liberalism?
4. Can private property be totally eliminated from society? Why?
5. What are the principal differences between the liberal and the collectivist approaches to government-economic relations?
6. What were the major consequences of liberal economics in the nineteenth century? What effects did they produce?

7. What is social darwinism? Why is it important?

8. What is meant by the welfare state?

9. Identify the four major contemporary solutions to political-economic organization and list the principal characteristics of each solution.

10. What were some of the major branches of socialist thought and what principles did they support?

11. Identify each of the following: Robert Owen, Saint-Simon, Proudhon, Blanqui, Louis Blanc, Fabian Society.

12. Distinguish between British democratic socialism and Marxism.

13. What are the principal tenets of the fascist creed?

14. Compare fascism with Marxism as it is practiced in the U.S.S.R. What are the major similarities and differences?

15. What part does force and coercion play in fascism, communism, and democratic socialism?

For further study

1. Do you believe that profit is a good or a bad thing? What reasons can you give for your answer?

2. Prepare an argument in favor of government regulation of the economy. What aspects of the economy would you regulate?

3. What are the arguments in favor of national ownership of industry?

4. In what sense does the New Deal represent a major change in American thought on political-economic relations?

5. Is there any necessary connection between collectivism in economic matters and totalitarianism in politics? Why?

6. If you had to choose between a totalitarian political system with a free economy and a democratic political system with a communist economy, which would you choose? Why?

7. Should men be allowed to inherit property from their ancestors? Is this compatible with equality?

8. Do you believe that the American way of life can be exported to the newly emerging nations in Africa and Asia? What reasons can you give for your answer?

9. If the new nations must choose between economic collectivism and a free market system, what factors must they take into consideration when making their choice?

10. Fascism is usually considered an extreme "right-wing" doctrine and communism is considered a "left-wing" doctrine. Does this suggest that political ideas should be ranged around a circle rather than along a straight line? How would you justify your answer?

CHAPTER *10*

Relations
among
States

The importance of international relations and foreign policies in the life of modern man hardly needs further emphasis here. It is not too much to say that the future of man may very well depend upon his ability to resolve the difficulties that arise in the relations among national states without recourse to violence and war. The subject is much studied, both in the United States and elsewhere, yet it is uncommonly difficult to produce a simple treatment of all of the complex and confusing issues involved in international affairs. All we can hope to do here is sketch the broad outlines of the discipline, leaving the student to pursue the subject further in a more specialized course.

NATURE OF THE DISCIPLINE

Perhaps the best way to demonstrate the problem we face is to compare international relations to a game in which the players are sovereign national states. In the "game" of international relations, there are about a hundred players, each differing from the others in size, equipment, power, and resources; each has its own goals and ideals. Since each player is sovereign, he is free to choose his own goals and his own means of achieving them, and he is bound only by those rules he chooses to accept and only for so long as he desires. Each player can change the rules of the game at any time and without warning to the others.

To carry the analogy further, we may conceive of a vast arena in which the game goes on continuously. On the playing field, the players have formed subordinate groupings of different sizes, and these subgroupings share common goals which they pursue against all of the other players. The very large players have gathered around them a number of followers; some follow willingly and others are coerced into supporting the larger player. Periodically, fights break out among the players, and they can develop into real riots (for there is no referee) and involve all of the players at once. Sometimes a few of the smaller players engage in fisticuffs while the larger players sit around and watch the progress of the battle. All of the players belong to a single sporting club called the United Nations and all attend meetings where they quarrel about the game that is in progress on the playing field. The United Nations tries to get the players to accept a referee in their game and bring an end to the riots, but each player feels that the referee would interfere with his style of play and perhaps cost him the game, so they all refuse. The game has been going on for centuries, always in the same fashion, and always without any conclusive results. Despite the length of the game, no one has yet been able to define clearly the goals the players are aiming for, yet all players are deadly serious and play to win at all costs. It is a very perplexing way for men to behave.

Obviously, we cannot hope to write the rule book for a game of this sort. We must sit on the sidelines, trying to remain objective and produce an accurate description of the progress of the game, pointing out the goals being pursued, the alliances and coalitions made among the players, and the rules that particular players follow. We can describe the players themselves, giving statistics about their size, strength, and other characteristics. We can try to look at the game through the eyes of one of the participants—study his "foreign policy" in relation to the other players on the field. We may even try to predict future developments in the game, though it is obvious that we cannot project such predictions very far, for there are so many contingencies that our predictions are little better than educated guesses. Unfortunately, each player keeps his real intentions secret, and we can only guess at what he is thinking at any given point in the game; this leaves a serious gap in our knowledge and makes it very difficult to produce an accurate description of the game.

This, in sum, is what is involved in the study of international affairs. We can attempt to systematize our approach to the subject, and we can be as objective as possible in our analysis, but in the final judgment, it is an imprecise and woolly subject which cannot be pinned to one definite framework. We can identify and describe the individual states, study the factors which make them weak or powerful, observe their behavior, make note of the machinery they use, examine the goals they seek. We can take a different perspective and look at the foreign policy of a particular state, study the machinery which it uses to "play the game," the goals it seeks, the means it uses to achieve them. That is the general framework of the present chapter.

Explanations of international relations. In the years since international relations entered its modern period, there have been dozens of attempts to produce an overall explanation of the nature of the international "game." Some have approached the subject from the geographer's standpoint, and argued that geography explained the behavior of states better than any other; others have looked to history and tradition, to military power or psychology, or to trends toward a unified world system for their connecting thread. It is unlikely that any explanation which depends primarily upon a single aspect of the game or a single player can be conclusive or complete; some approaches to the subject throw light upon aspects of the game not illuminated by others.

Power. Perhaps the most common perspective used in the study of international relations makes use of power as the central theme of the international system. This approach argues that the best way to study international relations is to think in terms of the accumulation of power and the exercise of power by states and groups of states. One of the oldest and most famous of all books on international relations, Niccolo Machiavelli's *The Prince,* uses this theme. Machiavelli argued that the accumulation of power and maintenance or expansion of the independent state is the final goal in all international relations; hence any action needed to produce this effect should be taken, whatever its moral status. Thus Machiavelli argued that the ruler should be cunning, as a fox, when necessary, and that he should lie, cheat, and swindle when it suited his purposes; at other times he should be the lion, willing to use force ruthlessly for his own ends. The approach is completely amoral, for morality has no place in a system founded on power alone. International relations becomes a jungle in which success is its own justification and no law exists beyond the law of the jungle. Machiavelli was not arguing that this was a good thing; instead, he was describing the manner in which international relations were actually conducted in Italy in his time, and the description is not inaccurate.

Modern theories of power may be more sophisticated, and students have made a more methodical exploration of the meaning of power which takes into consideration its psychological, moral, and ideological aspects as well as sheer brute force. Nevertheless, the central thesis remains the same, that is, that power and power alone determines the direction of international affairs. Of course, power may be used for ends which we consider either moral or immoral, and if the viewpoint we approve accumulates the most power in the system, then we approve of the outcome. In any case, it is the relative power of the conflicting viewpoints that must be considered.

The national interest. A variant on the work of the power school appears in the writings of those who believe that international affairs are best explained in terms of the "national interest" of each state, or that action is determined by the congeries of beliefs about what constitutes the vital interests of society at a given point in time. Supporters of this view, like Prof. Hans J. Morgenthau, argue that each state acts to maintain the national interest as that state conceives it at the time. What must be done, then, is to define the national interest of each society and the manner in which it is pursued.

This approach to international affairs is sometimes denounced as amoral, but that is not really the case when we examine it closely. For it is quite possible for a state to conceive of its national interest in moral terms and to believe that the pursuit of moral ends by moral means is also in the national interest. Britain, for example, may be said to have regarded the maintenance of international law as a basic part of her own national interests in the nineteenth century, and it is a historical fact that British policy during this period did lead to a unique era in the history of international law. The United States, to take a current example, may believe that it is in the national interest for the United States to pursue its goals abroad by means which world opinion approves—by moral means—because of the value of world opinion to her policies. It is true that the supporters of the national interest theory postulate selfishness as the ultimate rationale of foreign relations, and this is annoying to those who believe that some small element of humanitarianism is at work in the affairs of men. The parallel can be found in the position of the businessman who contributes heavily to charity; is he then acting only in his own business interests, or is he also acting in a humanitarian way? Which is primary when he is making the contribution? It is exceedingly difficult to say, of course.

The principal difficulty with the national interest approach to international affairs is simply that the central concept, the national interest, cannot be defined very easily. There is always the danger that it will be defined as every action of government, and this is not very helpful. But as a central thread to which information can be related systematically, it is extremely useful.

Geography. A third body of opinion related to the power theory finds the central explanatory fact in international relations in the influence of geography; many geographers belong to this group. The belief that geography and climate influence human affairs is at least as old as Aristotle. In modern times, however, geography has been linked to military power and military domination, particularly by the students of "geopolitics," to use the name originated by Rudolph Kjellen (1864–1922), one of the earliest proponents of the thesis.

The central idea in geopolitics was laid down by Sir Halford Mackinder, who argued that the world order would eventually depend upon control of particular geographic regions and the military supremacy which this control implied. The central part of Asia, north of the vast mountain ranges that cross the northern border of India, Mackinder designated as the "heartland" or critical region. The border region surrounding the Asian core he called the "rimland." Those who controlled the heartland, he thought, would eventually control the world, for this was geographically the only potential site of a gigantic bastion that could dominate all of the surrounding territory. Mackinder's ideas were very important in modern Germany, for his disciple, Karl Haushofer, became one of Hitler's advisors. With Hitler's aid, Haushofer established an Institute of Geopolitics in Munich which was very influential in German military circles until Haushofer fell from grace, and from circulation, for opposing the attack on Russia in 1941.

In the United States, geopolitics has also been popular in military schools and in some schools of international relations. The leading figure was Nicholas J. Spykman, who disputed Mackinder's theory of the importance of the heartland and preferred to emphasize the significance of the rimland. Another noted figure in geopolitics is Robert Strausz-Hupé, who is a more orthodox follower of Mackinder's theories. The ideas of these men have had a considerable influence on military strategy, both in the United States and abroad. Whether they are truly crucial in international relations is difficult to say; much depends upon the manner in which they are used. No one would deny that geography does influence international relations, though modern technology has diminished this influence somewhat; but long-range, deterministic conceptions of a dichotomy between "heartland" and "rimland" are more speculative and fanciful and less likely as a substantial explanation of international processes.

Other views. We cannot catalog the entire list of approaches to international relations that have been used by various students of the subject. Most of the major theories are included in one of the three groups outlined above. Other writers have wandered into psychological and psychiatric explanations of the behavior of states, particularly the aggressive nations like Germany, and explained at length that the "state of mind" of the German population in some way predisposes them to militarism or external aggression. Some have produced "devil" theories in which the forces of good (our side) are pitted against the forces of evil (them). Some explain international politics as a sequence of attempts by one nation or another to achieve world domination and the effort made by others to prevent this—the "balance of power" theory. There have also been more serious philosophical attempts to explain historical events in international affairs. Hegel, for example, argued that the driving force of civilization, the undefined "spirit" of the universe, moved from one nation to another, and its influence accounts for the behavior of states. The Marxists explained international relations in terms of the internal contradictions in capitalism, pointing to periodic expansion into colonial areas—the stages of imperialism—as evidence in support of the thesis.

Most recently, a number of attempts have been made to produce a systematic and "scientific" theory of international relations, to provide a framework in which international policy can be studied, measured, and interpreted, and which will permit accurate predictions of the future behavior of states. One theory postulates the international arena as a "system of action" in which the behavior of a given state is the outcome of a number of influences which can be reduced to "parameters" that can be arranged systematically. Another postulates the international scene as a "field" of three dimensions in which the individual states worm and twist their way according to the various influences which operate on them internally and externally. Such designs may be quite useful for systematic explanation, though they do not take us very far in the direction of establishing the precise nature of the influences which cause given behavior or of explaining why such behavior is caused.

Almost every approach to international affairs produces some information which is useful and in some respects different from other approaches. We cannot say that one point of view is "better" than another in any absolute sense, though some may be more useful in a given situation. The student needs to realize the range of possibilities, the approaches that can be used, but his choice of technique will very likely depend upon the type of problem that concerns him. Pure power theory may be very useful in explaining the behavior of the Soviet Union, and yet not very helpful when we are examining the international policy of Holland or India or Afghanistan, for example.

The formative factors in international relations. In general terms, the international political system has a character of its own, and this character—the nature of the system—exists apart from the characteristics of the individual states. The point is a trifle obscure, perhaps, but if we think of the relation between the character of big-league baseball in a given year and the characteristics of the member teams in the league, this may help to establish the parallel. The quality of a system is not the same as the quality of its members, any more than the quality of a baseball team is the same as the quality of the individual players, for it is possible to have a poor team made up of excellent players, and a less-talented group of indiviual players may be molded into a superb team.

The character of the international system is not static; it changes constantly. Thus we find a considerable difference between the climate of international relations in the century from 1815, when Napoleon was finally defeated, to 1914, and the climate between 1914 and 1939. The former period was surprisingly stable, though the amalgamation of Germany and Italy and the dismemberment of the Ottoman Empire changed its quality somewhat; the latter period was marked by the rise of militaristic dictatorships and the expansion of the international system to include the Far East, making Europe relinquish some of its preeminence in international affairs. To take another illustration, a liberal democracy in a world made up of other liberal democracies would find itself faced with quite a different situation from that met by a liberal democracy in a world in which all other states were military dictatorships. Similarly, technological changes can offset the influences of geography, climate, and other physical factors that condition national power.

Thus in every age, there are different prerequisites for national power. In one era, it is control of the sea; in another, powerful land forces; in a third, control of the air. In the contemporary world, power is a combination of population, resources, scientific and technological competence, and the industrial capacity to translate potential into the instruments of power, and, perhaps, a program of behavior which can command the support of other nations. All of these factors are needed to make a great power; some will suffice for the influential. India, oddly enough, has a considerable measure of influence in international affairs, yet her "power" is quite limited, at least in the traditional sense. The fact of India's influence is explicable in terms of her relation to the general climate of the system at the present time, for in other days, India might count for little or nothing in world affairs.

Other factors that are important in determining the character of the system are the state of technology, the amount of tension and antagonism between major powers, or their level of real cooperation, the state of military preparations, the character of the major governments, the status of international law, and the tradition or historical context in which states carry on their relations with one another. The world since 1945 has been characterized by growing tension, increased armaments, alliances and coalitions, and the gradual polarization of international affairs into two major groups, each hostile to the other. The external conditions influence not only the foreign policies of the countries concerned, but their internal policies as well, for the requirements of foreign policy have a great influence on the type of governmental control and regulation that is needed within the state.

Probably the simplest way to demonstrate the influence of the character of the international system on the individual powers is to think of the difference between the contemporary world as it is, and the world that might have been had the United States, Britain, and the Soviet Union remained friendly and cooperative. The whole character of the system would then be different, and the internal and external policy of every nation on earth would be changed. Consider the task facing the emerging nations in a world dominated by a British-American-Soviet alliance and in a world in which they are divided in two armed camps. The machinery provided by the United Nations could function perfectly, in security matters as well as in economic and cultural affairs, if the Great Powers were agreed. The economic structure of the world could be revolutionized, for technology is rapidly approaching the point at which it will be possible to improve the lot of all of mankind to a degree never before possible in human history, and the principal obstacle in the path of this renovation is Great Power antagonisms. Internally, the life of the American people would be similarly affected, for resources now used for military preparations might then be used for social improvements, development of a still higher standard of living, scientific investigations, and other peaceful projects. This is not wishful thinking, for it is obvious that we cannot return to the *status quo ante bellum* merely by wishing that things were different from what they are. But it does illustrate how different affairs might be if the climate of international relations were different.

We might also point to one hopeful, or interesting, new development in world affairs that dates only as far back as World War II, and that is the development of a fairly definite and meaningful phenomenon that we call world opinion. The immediacy of world conflict, and the fact that its effects would be felt by the whole of mankind should it occur, has stimulated interest in foreign affairs to an unusual degree; the world has become foreign-policy conscious, and technology has provided the means for making known what is going on in the world. Out of this interest has grown an intangible but meaningful body of world opinion which is beginning to exert some influence on world affairs, and this may well be a hopeful augur for the future.

INTERNATIONAL INSTITUTIONS

As society grows and develops, it produces the institutions and customs that are needed to keep its daily affairs in motion, the basic structure on which social relations can grow. Some of these social institutions are formalized; others remain informal and *ad hoc*. Some endure for long periods of time; others are used temporarily and then abandoned in favor of something new or different. Institutions are the tools of social relationships, the instruments by which we arrange our affairs with other persons.

The same phenomenon has appeared in the relations among states, for international relations has its own institutions, its own machinery, rules and procedures, and customs, which control and formalize international relationships. The customary rules of international behavior have been gathered together to form a body of international law which, if not binding in the same sense as municipal law, is nevertheless usually followed in international intercourse by most states. The institution of diplomacy has been very firmly grounded, and is now highly formalized and complex. International organizations have appeared as formal structures within which the states may deal with one another. Where these instruments proved inadequate, the states have turned to other devices, to the use of special emissaries, special conferences, including those between heads of state, regional organizations, and systems of alliances. Such institutions as intelligence and espionage provide the states with information about one another's affairs which are not widely published. And finally the institution of war appears rather too frequently as final arbiter in disputes among states.

These techniques are quite old, well established, and supplied with their own rules of operation. Their status varies with time and place, and governments may choose whichever of the instruments of international relations they believe best suited to the moment. The instruments themselves are morally neutral; it is the manner in which they are used that matters. Even espionage and intelligence have rules which are tacitly accepted by all states; so long as the game is played according to the rules, relations proceed "normally," though the general public may find such a definition of normality a trifle strange. We cannot hope to examine the details of every major institution in international relations, for they form a subject in themselves, but we can indicate some of the more significant aspects of the major institutions.

Diplomacy. Diplomatic relations are the formal base from which all international relations proceed. Diplomacy is the institution which keeps each of the nations of the world in touch with all other nations, and the breaking off of diplomatic relations, a very serious matter, means in fact severing one member of the family from his place at the international table. When a new state joins the family of nations, its first act is usually to exchange diplomatic missions with the other nations.

The *diplomatic mission* consists of a mission head, who is the representative of the head of state, and the persons needed to assist him; it is now usually resident in the country to which it is assigned. The mission is accredited to the head of the receiving state, and the head of mission must be acceptable to the receiving state; the latter may declare him *persona non grata* (unacceptable) at will, and he must then be recalled. In normal times, each state has a diplomatic mission attached to every other state, nowadays most often headed by a full ambassador, the highest diplomatic rank. Obviously, the diplomatic groups in the various national capitals throughout the world make up a complex network which must have rules to guide behavior if chaos is not to ensue. Today, diplomacy is highly formalized, and few major problems arise for which protocol has not already been settled. Some four hundred years ago, however, matters of rank, precedence, etc., were not formalized, and some incredible and lengthy arguments grew out of conflicts between diplomats assigned to the same country. Two ambassadors once argued for hours, for example, over whose carriage had the right to pass on the "honored" side and who was to take second place.

The diplomatic mission is not a permanent fixture; either the sending or the receiving country may terminate it. A declaration of war puts a formal end to the mission, as does the severing of diplomatic relations (often a prelude to war), or the death, resignation, or recall of the head of mission. While it exists, the mission is the formal channel through which a steady stream of messages moves in both directions; this is the channel by which heads of state ordinarily communicate with one another. By international law, the mission is protected against arrest, molestation, and infringement of the right to secrecy. Diplomatic correspondence may move freely from one country to another without passing through customs, as may the diplomats themselves. Indeed, the receiving state has the responsibility for protecting the diplomatic mission, and failure to provide adequate protection can be very embarrassing.

The *consular mission* is a different matter, for the consuls are not official representatives of the state but public agents of the commercial interests of the sending country. The consul's job is to smooth economic and commercial relations between the two countries. He provides information for both countries, or their nationals, and aids those seeking to do business with his own countrymen. In practice, the consular officers cooperate with the regular diplomatic mission, but they are formally and functionally separate.

Diplomatic functions. The diplomatic mission has a number of formal functions which it must perform. First, it has the task of presenting the views of its own nation to the government to which it is accredited, both by transmitting official messages from its home government and more informally by making known the attitude of its own government in informal conversations. Such informal opinions may be very useful, particularly where the ambassador is well liked in the receiving country. The diplomatic mission also conducts formal negotiations with the host government, though this is less significant today than fifty years ago when most matters were handled through regular diplomatic channels. Today, many important matters are handled by special conferences or meetings which are outside the jurisdiction of the regular mission. The third major function of the diplomatic mission is to gather information for the home government. Much of this information is obtained from official sources or directly from the foreign office in the host government, but the mission can also obtain less formal but equally useful information from the local press or from local contacts. All in all, a very substantial body of data is forwarded to the State Department each month by American diplomats; this is today one of the major functions of the mission and occupies the time of much of the staff. Finally, the diplomatic mission has the task of protecting its own nationals during their stay in the country, and if there is difficulty with passports, inoculations, or violations of local laws, the diplomatic mission will intervene and attempt to protect the rights of the visiting national. This is often a real nuisance and time consumer, particularly during the tourist season; missions in such countries as France and England maintain a considerable staff to handle the problems arising out of tourism. Commercial questions are generally handled by consular officers, but even here there is often need for political cooperation. In addition, the embassy maintains contact with any special missions stationed in the country, such as NATO forces, special naval units, or visiting teams from one of the departments in the executive branch.

In general, the importance of the diplomatic mission has changed greatly in the past century. Communication techniques make it possible for the mission head to communicate rapidly and easily with his own government and obtain precise instructions covering his actions in any particular situation. Hence the freedom to make policy that once belonged to an ambassador is no longer common; ambassadors tend to transmit policy rather than form their own judgments. Further, the development of extraordinary conferences, the use of special emissaries, and even the meetings of heads of states, which have become common since 1945, have all eaten into the authority of the regular diplomatic mission, leaving a mass of routine work to be performed. This is not a reflection on the competence of the members of the mission, though the American practice of appointing ambassadors as payment for political debts has often led to rank amateurism. Most of the permanent diplomatic officials are well trained and quite capable; the fact is simply that the role of the diplomatic mission today is quite different from what it was in the nineteenth century.

Special emissaries. One of the newer techniques that has diminished the authority of the regular diplomatic mission is the use of a special emissary or personal ambassador. Examples of this type of diplomatic practice are President Wilson's use of Colonel House, Franklin D. Roosevelt's use of Harry Hopkins as a personal ambassador, or Winston Churchill's use of Lord Beaverbrook for special missions. The special emissary has various advantages over the regular diplomatic service. He can usually do his work more quickly and efficiently, for one thing, for he may operate less formally, often with a high-ranking representative of the host government or even with the head of state himself. Thus Harry Hopkins went to Russia in the spring of 1945 for President Truman and talked directly with Stalin, an advantage that the regular ambassador seldom enjoyed. Further, the special emissary is usually a personal representative of the head of state, and has the full confidence of the sending government; as such, he commands greater respect in the host country and speaks with greater authority. The principal drawback to the use of special representatives is probably the demoralizing effect of the practice on the regular diplomatic mission. A second possible danger is that the special representative, lacking an adequate acquaintance with current affairs between the two nations, may make commitments which have implications that are not fully realized. Nothing pleases the regular diplomatic mission so little as the special ambassador who arrives, visits the head of state, and manages in a few hours to disrupt the results of weeks of patient negotiations. It can, certainly, happen.

Meetings of heads of state. Before the twentieth century, the American President seldom traveled abroad, though the crowned heads of Europe did meet occasionally in the nineteenth century and earlier. The precedent was first broken by President Wilson when he attended the Versailles meetings after World War I. Since that time, Presidents have occasionally embarked on "good will" tours and state visits. President Franklin D. Roosevelt shattered all precedents by his meetings with Churchill and Stalin and his various tours. Opinion is somewhat divided on the value of meetings between heads of state. For one thing, no one is quite certain that such meetings are a good thing. If the heads of state take a personal liking or dislike for one another, for example, this might well color their judgment of policy in a manner that is not desirable. Some believe that it is undignified for heads of state to gather in this manner, that such meetings are best left to underlings. When heads of state meet, there is immense publicity for the meeting and great pressure for decisions, for "something to give to the press," and this can lead to hasty decisions. Further, when heads of state announce the results of their meetings, they are likely to be overoptimistic about their achievements, and this can be highly misleading. On the other hand, such meetings are very efficient, for each of the parties to the meeting has the necessary powers to conclude agreements. Further, their meetings are usually confined to a few outstanding subjects; hence accurate discussion is usually possible. Finally, the personal relationship can be useful, if it is not overdone or used unwisely.

Special conferences. It is probably only another sign of the growing complexity of our age, but special conferences for dealing with specific questions are coming more and more into use in the field of international relations. Where such conferences concern technical matters like trade and finance, control of atomic energy, or the dozens of technological and industrial matters that arise in international relations, the justification for special meetings is obvious. Expert opinion can be concentrated at the conference, the range of items under consideration can be limited, and detailed discussion of technical points can be carried on quickly and efficiently. We have had any number of such special meetings since World War II, dealing with problems ranging from armaments to tariffs and social policy. Considering the growing technicality of international relations, it seems likely that the use of such special meetings will expand rather than decline in the future.

The one serious danger in the use of special conferences, of course, is that delegates dealing with a single problem area may lose sight of the overall perspective that must be maintained. It is easy to attach too much significance to the immediate task, forgetting the importance of long-range interests. In addition, it cannot be denied that the regular diplomatic services suffer from the use of such conferences, for they remove yet another area from the purview of the regular mission.

Intelligence and espionage. Cloak and dagger work is always interesting—in theory and in detective stories. In fact, of course, most intelligence work, and one suspects, most espionage work as well, is dreary and monotonous, though the latter is spiced with danger. Intelligence work consists largely of the careful sifting of great masses of information, the bulk of which is useless or unimportant, seeking the bit here and the bit there that may provide a useful pattern. A large share of our data about foreign countries is obtained from information which the foreign country itself publishes, or which appears in newspapers, magazines, journals, etc., and all of this material must be reviewed. Of course, there is also a network of spies and secret agents, unknown in size, but doubtless quite large where possible, which operates in foreign countries, both those which are friendly and those which are not. There are also subsidiary techniques for obtaining information by monitoring the internal information system through listening posts on the border, or by high-altitude flights over foreign territory, though the legal status of the latter technique is as yet uncertain. There was, for a time, a tunnel under East Berlin which was used to tap telephone circuits in the Communist zone, though it was discovered and closed. Similar devices are doubtless used when feasible, and embassies often serve as espionage centers; witness the notorious spy trials in Canada shortly after World War II, when members of the Soviet Embassy were found to be the center of a national spy ring. The aim is to provide a steady stream of information which can be evaluated and collated by experts. Most of this activity is recognized in international custom, and even espionage, which is severely punished when detected, has a sort of status, for all countries engage in it.

Space diplomacy. One of the more interesting recent innovations in the field of international relations stems from the great importance now attached to scientific and technological achievement, particularly in military hardware and in space technology. Much of the responsibility for what is really an unfortunate situation rests with the press, which has managed to create a "race for space" where none existed and where none is either needed or wanted. The use of space achievement for advertising national achievement is peculiar and dangerous, for failure to produce results that are easily observed may have repercussions at home as well as abroad, and lead to the growth of unjustified fear. To some extent the United States is the unwitting victim of this development, and the question which country first plants a rocket on the moon, on Mars, or Venus has been made into a matter of real moment. This is grossly unfair to the countries concerned and it may produce a serious distortion in national expenditure.

The point is that the general public is usually not qualified to interpret the significance of particular technological accomplishments or to appreciate technical comparison of achievements in science. As an illustration, American space technology is largely oriented to military purposes, and each development project has a specific purpose, to produce an instrument or tool that will accomplish certain clearly specified purposes. The pattern of development is intended to produce a weapon with particular characteristics at a particular date. This may or may not be the type of instrument which can be used for spectacular demonstration for the general public. In other words, there may be a serious discrepancy between the types of equipment needed for modern Fourth-of-July-style demonstrations and the real military needs of the moment. Taking time, resources, skilled men, and facilities from the military task and using them to produce "fireworks" may seriously impede the development of equipment that is genuinely needed.

Person to person. Another rather naïve attitude that is often met in conversations about foreign affairs is the belief that "if only the people of countries A and B could get together, they would soon learn that all people are much the same and there would soon be no international problems." The assumption is that international tensions arise out of disagreements among people. The intention may be laudable, but it mistakes the nature of the problem completely. It may well be, for example, that there are Americans who believe that all Russians have horns and spiked tails, and visiting Russia would certainly remove this delusion. But visiting Russia may also confirm the original views of the visitor, for visits are usually brief, the language barrier is always a problem, and people do tend to see what they expect to see in a foreign country. That is, even if the difficulties in the international field arose out of misunderstandings between people, it is doubtful that the brief visit, the interchange of a handful of unimportant individuals, would make very much of an impression on the problem.

However, even that is beside the point, for the real issue in international relations is between *governments,* not between people, and no amount of personal interchange is going to be effective. Even when political government is responsive to public opinion, it would take an inordinate amount of visiting to produce any substantial segment of opinion favoring a particular policy toward a particular country. In those nations where public opinion is largely ignored, the goal is futile.

The influence or effect of tourism, government-sponsored broadcasts, and cultural invasion is also much debated. Critics of the system argue that tourism is, if anything, an international disaster, for the best tourist remains unidentified and the worst is all too easily identified. Similarly, broadcasts to "iron curtain" countries are held to be about as effective as Soviet broadcasts to the United States, and for much the same reasons. On the other hand, few observers have denied the value of cultural interchange when it is conducted properly and really high-quality products are exported. Europeans, for example, are surprised and pleased to learn that the United States actually has an indigenous culture, and American artists, dancers, musicians, and symphonies, to mention only a few, have had an excellent reception abroad. Perhaps best of all, in the author's personal experience, is the American library abroad. Foreign nationals find these libraries to be impressive monuments to the extent to which freedom of expression and free criticism exist in the United States. Many of the libraries in Europe have fine record libraries containing much of the best work that has been produced by native American composers; these are extremely well received. Occasional art exhibitions, concerts, lectures, etc., contribute substantially to the creation of a more reasonably accurate image of American society in the eyes of foreign peoples.

INTERNATIONAL ORGANIZATIONS

Although there were international organizations like the Phocian League and the Achean League in ancient Greek times, the idea of a continuing international organization, in more or less permanent session, is relatively new. The Swiss Federation, formed in the fourteenth century for defensive purposes, is not really a good example to the contrary, and the Hanseatic League of some fifty cities that flourished in Europe from the thirteenth to the sixteenth century was concerned principally though not entirely with trade. Temporary conferences or "congresses" began to appear in the eighteenth century; they consisted of a number of states, some of which were not interested in the particular issue at hand and served as mediators. Thus the Conference at Cambrai in 1722 was attended by Austria, Spain, Britain, France, Netherlands, and several of the German states, not all of whom had a vital interest in the discussion. In the nineteenth century, the Congress of Vienna, following the Napoleonic Wars, was attended by some two hundred delegations and several of the crowned heads of Europe. They did not assemble to make peace, as happened at Versailles in 1919, for peace was made earlier at Paris. Instead, they dealt with boundary disputes, trade disputes, the status of Jews, diplomatic ranking, the slave trade, river navigation, and a variety of allied subjects. In the years following the Congress of Vienna, a number of supplementary consultations between the large powers dealt with political questions such as the relations between Russia and the Ottoman Empire—the so-called Eastern Question.

The League of Nations. The era of congresses and consultations came to an end with World War I. Discussion of the need for a continuing international organization to preserve peace began quite soon after war was declared. Lord Cecil prepared a memorandum on world organization for the British government, and the French government appointed a committee to inquire into the question. In the United States, Colonel House prepared a tentative sketch of a world organization for President Wilson. When the peacemakers finally met at Paris in 1919, they agreed on the need for a world organization and appointed a committee—including Wilson, General Smuts of South Africa, Lord Cecil, and Orlando of Italy—to produce a draft. The plan for the League of Nations that was finally accepted was simple and clear. An executive Council, consisting of Britain, France, Italy, Japan, and four smaller powers, and an Assembly of forty-two states were the two basic parts of the structure. A permanent Secretariat was included to provide administrative support for the League. Various other agencies charged with world health, trade, colonies, etc., were part of the structure, as was the Permanent Court of International Justice.

In operation, the League assumed the equality of all states (which seems naïve, in retrospect), and unanimous approval was required for all decisions. This handcuffed the League later when it sought to carry out its primary purpose of preventing war and settling disputes peacefully.

In nonsecurity matters, the League of Nations was a fairly successful endeavor. It assumed control over the colonial areas taken from Germany and Turkey and supervised their administration under the "Mandate" system. It was made responsible for the protection of minorities, and for the coordination of national legislation in the fields of transportation and communication, care of refugees, etc. Its work in the field of labor legislation, to mention only one example, was outstanding.

The principal failure of the League was in the field of security. Many had hoped (perhaps without too much justification) that the League would put an end to war and substitute arbitration and court decisions for military decisions. Members were asked to accept arbitration in all disputes and to make use of the International Court; they could not be forced to do so, of course. And even in the case of armed conflict, the League Covenant provided machinery which might have halted military aggression if it were firmly applied. Thus Article 16 of the League Covenant provided for quite formidable collective measures against aggressor nations in the event of war. Because the provisions are much misunderstood and misquoted, they are worth quoting:

Should any member of the League resort to war in disregard of its covenants under Articles 12, 13, or 15, it shall *ipso facto* be deemed to have committed an act of war against all other members of the League, which hereby undertake immediately to subject it to the severance of all trade or financial relations, the prohibition of all intercourse between their nationals and the nationals of the covenant-breaking State. . . .

It shall be the duty of the Council in such cases to recommend to the several Governments concerned what effective military, naval, or air force the Members of the League shall severally contribute to the armed forces to be used to protect the covenants of the League.

The article did not *force* the members of the League to produce military forces for preventing aggression, but made it possible and legal to do so if the powers were willing. Further, economic sanctions, in which the drafters of the League had great faith, were automatic. The League had ample authority—if the members chose to act. That the League could have forced action, even by majority vote, is unlikely in any case.

The sorry tale of the collapse of the League of Nations under the pressure of advancing dictatorship in Europe and Asia is too well known to repeat in detail. At first, the League placed great faith in disarmament, in the belief (mistaken or not) that if there were no armaments, war was unlikely. Repeated efforts were made to achieve disarmament in the 1920s; they were only partially successful. The 1930s saw the beginning of aggressive warfare, first in China, where the Japanese attack began in 1931, and then in Africa, where fighting between Italy and Abyssinia (Ethiopia) began in 1934. In 1935, Hitler denounced the League of Nations and marched into the Rhineland, a move expressly forbidden in the Versailles Treaty; nothing was done beyond ineffectual protest. When Russia attacked Finland in 1939, the League roused itself for one last valiant effort and expelled the Soviet Union; but the League was already dead. It failed, very simply, because its members did not provide the support necessary to make it work, and perhaps because of the provision for *liberum veto,* for one nation could annul an action by voting against it.

The United Nations. If the League of Nations was discredited, the principle of international organization, the desirability of having a permanent international agency, including all of the nations on earth, was still accepted. Discussion of a new international organization began early in World War II among the allied powers, and though the Soviet Union was lukewarm (perhaps because of her experience with the League and the Finnish War), Britain was friendly and the United States was enthusiastic. To avoid a repetition of the experience with the League of Nations, which the United States did not join, an extensive program of public education was undertaken to convince the American general public of the desirability of a new international organization to keep the peace. If anything, the program was too successful, for the general public was led to expect results from the United Nations which it was unlikely from the outset that the organization could achieve. Both the Senate and the House of Representatives passed resolutions favoring American participation in a new international organization while the preliminary terms of the association were being hammered out. By 1944, a draft had been prepared at the Dumbarton Oaks Conference; it was released to the general public in October, 1944, with much hullabaloo. The draft left various problems unsolved, however, including the matter of voting in the Security Council, and these arrangements were made at the Yalta Conference early in 1945.

The United Nations, like the League of Nations, was a compromise. None of the countries involved was really willing to hand over control of internal or external affairs to an international agency, and since all nations were sovereign, they could not be forced to agree to provisions which they found unacceptable. The Great Powers in particular were not willing to agree to a system in which they would have no control over the use of armed force against themselves or their followers. When these questions were finally thrashed out, the five Great Powers in the Security Council—Russia, the United States, Britain, France, and China—each had a veto on substantive questions, though not on procedural matters. That is, questions like "Shall we discuss . . ." could not be vetoed, but questions like "Shall we *do* . . ." were subject to the veto; if one of the five permanent members of the Council voted against the measure it did not pass. In effect, the United Nations provided machinery which the great powers could use for controlling the use of force in international relations, but only if they chose to cooperate. Unfortunately, it was already clear by the summer of 1945 that cooperation was not very likely. Later, when the Security Council proved unable to act because of the indiscriminate use of the veto power, the United States sponsored a resolution—called the "Uniting for Peace Resolution"—which made it possible to transfer disputes from the Security Council to the General Assembly where there is no veto. But in principle, this may have been a poor move, for the United Nations cannot coerce a major power without war, whatever the method of voting in the Security Council. Furthermore, the resolution may be a two-edged weapon, which can be used against the United States in the future if the balance of power in the General Assembly should shift.

The United Nations, as it is now constituted, is a large and very complex organization. The Security Council serves as a kind of executive committee, meeting regularly, and dealing particularly with matters that might affect the maintenance of peace. The General Assembly, which is sometimes called a sounding board for world opinion, contains representatives from nearly every country on earth, and has wide powers of discussion, but only a limited ability to act. In addition there is a large permanent Secretariat, the United Nations Economic and Social Council, a Trusteeship Council, and the International Court of Justice. Within the Economic and Social Council in particular there are any number of specialized agencies and commissions for dealing with particular problems. Many of these agencies do useful and important work, surveying natural resources, offering technical assistance, eliminating traffic in dangerous drugs, finding homes for refugees, aiding children, etc.

So far as maintaining the peace goes, the United Nations has been reasonably successful when the Great Powers were agreed, usually where their own interests were not involved; but where the Great Powers' interests were at stake, and this area widened considerably as the cold war deepened, not too much has been accomplished. True, the United Nations was able to act in Korea in 1950, but the Soviet representative had left the Security Council and was unable to cast a veto. Furthermore, the decision to act was fundamentally American-made and American-supported, and this might have been possible with or without United Nations approval. In areas related to security—control of atomic energy and general disarmament, for example—the special agencies arranged under United Nations auspices accomplished nothing.

Regional arrangements. During World War II, it was thought that the United Nations would provide a single central association for dealing with threats to the peace or security matters; once it was clear that the UN was unable to perform that function too well, the Great Powers returned once again to their more traditional method of guaranteeing security—alliances and mutual defense pacts. Article 51 of the UN Charter allows the formation of such regional defense arrangements; hence there is no conflict between UN obligations and regional alliances. Most of the regional arrangements are military pacts, though some have a window dressing of cultural and economic aims added to the military base. Both the United States and the Soviet Union have been quite active in this sphere, and there are now a number of such associations, varying in size and significance. Some are operative and meaningful; others are mostly "paper" organizations, without troops or materiel, and hence of little significance.

The Organization of American States. One of the oldest existing regional arrangements in the world is the association among the nations of the Western Hemisphere. It originated in 1889–1890 as the Pan-American Union, and if it was not particularly effective before the 1930s, it did provide a meeting place at which common policies could be worked out, usually under the leadership of the United States. In 1947, the Pan-American Union arranged the negotiation of a mutual defense pact for the Western Hemisphere (the Inter-American Treaty of Reciprocal Assistance), and when the new organization (Organization of American States or OAS) was formed, the Pan-American Union was incorporated as a bureau. The member nations already had an extensive set of mutual arrangements for settling disputes among themselves, and had agreed earlier to consider an attack against one of them as an attack against all. What was needed was machinery, and this the OAS was intended to provide. In effect, each state is required to provide assistance to a member of OAS that has been attacked, though they must consent to the use of their armed forces. Consultation is required immediately, at which time the members decide, by a two-thirds vote, what further action shall be taken.

The North Atlantic Treaty Organization. The most important and active regional group in the West is certainly the North Atlantic Treaty Organization (NATO), which originated in 1949. It includes the nations of Western Europe, the United States, Canada, and some countries like Greece and Turkey that are rather far removed from the Atlantic Ocean. Like OAS, NATO is a collective defense system; each member is pledged to consider an attack on one member as an attack on itself, and to assist in repelling invaders. NATO is well organized and fairly well armed, for the member nations "earmark" troops for NATO use, and the United States supplies substantial forces for the group.

When the North Atlantic Treaty was signed in 1949, no measures were taken to make NATO into an effective military force. It remained a "paper organization" until the Korean conflict begin. Probably one of the basic purposes of the treaty was to bind the United States firmly and irrevocably to the defense of Western Europe—an offer made in 1946 but not formalized. Europeans were doubtless glad of the added assurance which the treaty provided. Its precise military function is not really clear, despite the plethora of high-level commands which have been organized. American Strategic Air Command Forces are not really a part of the structure, and the American policy of "massive retaliation" seems not compatible with the firm commitment to the land defense of Europe implied in the treaty. Soviet land forces in Europe are extremely powerful—much stronger than the NATO forces—and military experts have been skeptical of NATO's ability to contain a Soviet ground attack. However, it is doubtless useful as a coordinating organization, at the very least, and it may have greater military significance than appears on the surface.

Southeast Asia Treaty Organization. Finally, Pakistan, Thailand, the Philippines, France, Australia, New Zealand, Britain, and the United States negotiated the Southeast Asia Treaty in 1954, creating the Southeast Asia Treaty Organization (SEATO). India, Burma, Ceylon and Indonesia refused to take part. There is no really effective military organization to support the treaty, and the commitment involved is not automatic in the sense that "an attack on one is to be considered an attack on all." There is no real obligation to do more than consult together following an attack and decide at that time what action, if any, should be taken.

Military alliances. Military alliances were also restored to popularity as the UN declined in importance. The United States in particular entered upon an unprecedented period of "pactomania" while John Foster Dulles was Secretary of State. From February, 1778, until April 4, 1949 (NATO), the United States did not sign a single military alliance with a foreign country. The flood broke after the Korean conflict began. A hasty treaty was arranged with Japan (by Dulles), following a peace settlement which was highly disliked by the Asian nations. As a sop to outraged opinion in the Pacific area, the United States also signed a mutual defense pact with the Philippine Republic and a mutual defense pact with Australia and New Zealand (ANZUS). In 1952, treaties of peace and alliance were signed with West Germany. In 1954, an alliance was concluded with Nationalist China (Formosa). Bilateral defense treaties have been signed with Korea, Lebanon, Spain, Morocco, Libya, Saudi Arabia, Ethiopia, Panama, and Israel, to mention a few, and others still have been refused by the other country (India, for example). If we include the nations whose security has been guaranteed by OAS, NATO, and SEATO, we begin to get some notion of how extensive this alliance system has become. Since most of these engagements also involve military or economic assistance, chiefly the former, United States commitments are both extensive and expensive.

INTERNATIONAL LAW

Every organized society has rules and regulations which order the behavior of the members of the society and provide the means of solving peacefully the problems which arise out of the society's operations. In the relations between states, we find a peculiar situation, for since the individual states are sovereign, they cannot by definition be subject to regulation by any external agency. Yet they must have relations with one another, and this produces a need for rules, because relations that are not governed by regular rules are chaotic. Hence we find that over the years a body of customs and practices, of reasonable rules of behavior, has evolved, and though the states cannot be forced to accept this body of rules or "laws" they nevertheless do so most of the time. Because international law has sources and sanctions that are different from those of the municipal law to which we are accustomed, it is sometimes said that there is no such thing as international law. But the body of law among nations is not insignificant; in most cases it is followed regularly.

Sources of international law.

International law resembles medieval law much more closely than modern municipal law, for we have come to accept the notion that laws are made by legislatures through formal procedures. In the Middle Ages, the customs of the community, and "sensible" generalizations of these customs, were accepted as law, binding upon everyone in the community, including the ruler. International law originates in much the same way. In their relations with one another, the states have adopted certain customary practices, and in time these practices have become a part of international law. In some cases, the major states have gathered together and deliberately produced agreements relating to diplomatic practice or to rules of warfare, and such agreements are also part of international law. Finally, we find that some international agencies have been given authority to make rules that are binding upon the members of the state system, and these rules too are part of international law.

Since the law is really what the state is willing to accept, the best source of international law lies in the written agreements that states have concluded with one another, for it is a basic principle in law that obligations must be fulfilled once they have been made (*pacta sunt servanda*—the treaty must be carried out) though there is also a corollary principle—*rebus sic stantibus*—the treaty must be carried out only so long as conditions remain the same. Of course, the state may deny the validity of its treaty obligations, as Nazi Germany did so often while Hitler was ruler, in which case there is no legal sanction against the offender. But states which fail to keep their obligations soon find that other nations will not conclude treaties with them, and this is too serious a handicap in international affairs to risk lightly. Also, there are always cases in which the accepted rule is changed unilaterally by one state, and others follow suit. In this case, the status of the law is not really clear. For example, the limit of a state's jurisdiction extends for 3 miles into the oceans surrounding her shores, but the Soviet Union and some other nations have now claimed a 12-mile limit around their shores, and if they are willing and able to enforce that limit, they may well inaugurate a new rule in the law of jurisdiction.

Sanctions. If individual states may violate the law of nations with impunity, for there is no government to punish them, and no coercion can be applied, at least to the Great Powers, to enforce legal maxims, why do they usually obey the rules? Obviously, one of the more significant sanctions behind international law is the fear of retaliation. If state A mistreats the diplomatic mission of state B, state B will repay the mistreatment, often with interest, in its dealings with the diplomatic mission from state A. The Soviet government, for example, has placed travel restrictions on American diplomats in the U.S.S.R. at various times, and when this occurs, the United States government usually places the same or more severe restrictions on the movement of Soviet diplomats in the United States. When there are no real sanctions governing group behavior, the golden rule is a good general policy. Another factor in the process is doubtless habit; when international behavior runs in well-worn channels there is a tendency to think of them as the only technique for conducting mutual affairs, and the practice continues. Further, we must realize that states stand to gain by maintaining relations with one another, and violation of the rules of international law interrupts and confuses these relations; hence a violation of the law may well operate against the self-interest of the state concerned. Of course, when it is clearly in the interest of the state to violate the law, this limitation does not hold, and we generally find that international law breaks down most frequently in such circumstances. Finally, it must be said that international law is often followed simply because the government concerned believes that justice demands that it accede, even though its self-interest may not be served by doing so.

Subject matter. The subject matter of international law is varied and diverse. We must realize that it deals only with states, and in effect attempts to define the rights and privileges of states in their relations with one another. Private persons have no status in international law and cannot be recognized by the International Court. An individual with a grievance against a national state—and this often happens, as for example when a state fails to make payments of debts accumulated by the sale of bonds to private firms—must have his own government take up the matter on his behalf. International law as such deals with the definition of state, the rules of recognition, diplomatic procedures, boundary regulations, rules of the sea, and similar matters. A very substantial part of international law deals with the rules of warfare, and de Groot's early work is aptly titled *Concerning the Law of War and Peace*, for he wished to mitigate some of the horrors of contemporary warfare. Thus there were regular rules for protecting the innocent civilian population, for dealing with war prisoners, for protecting the rights of neutrals, and for regulating other questions connected with the conduct of war.

Trends in international law. Among the outstanding trends of contemporary international law is the breakdown of the laws of war. The whole conception of total war, whether or not it includes deliberate "frightfulness" or terrorization of the civilian population, makes nonsense of the distinction between civilian and military targets. The mass bombing of cities was carried out by both sides in World War II, and the devastation wrought by the Germans on the territories conquered in Russia was the most terrible ravaging seen in Eastern Europe since the days of the Mongol hordes. Further, though the Germans were very careful in their treatment of prisoners of war, the Japanese were not, and little of the established rules of conduct survived in the Far Eastern theater of operations. Finally, of course, the initiation of atomic warfare broke all precedents for annihilation of civilian populations, and if both Nagasaki and Hiroshima contained war production plants, few cities cannot be defined as military targets in this sense. In any event, the distinction is only academic, for no one doubts that should full-scale nuclear war begin, the prime targets would be the large population concentrations found in urban areas, and a weapon which literally dissolves everything can hardly be said to have a purely military target.

Even more important in some ways is the rapid decline in good faith among the Great Powers after 1945, for this has made international law almost an impossibility. All legal arrangements proceed in some measure from good faith, and in domestic politics, the absence of good faith very frequently if not always leads to the breakdown of the system. Much the same condition is true of international relations, and an age in which suspicion and tension override faith in the willingness of others to abide by their obligations is likely to see little advancement of the principles of international law. Legal controls are bypassed in favor of more positive measures for ensuring against treachery, and protection of self-interest overrides any consideration for justice that might ordinarily count heavily in policy making. Thus international law has had very heavy going in the past two decades. Some argue that the solution to this problem is some form of international government, or world government, which can make and enforce laws against the states themselves. But surely this eludes the point, for conditions which make possible this type of political structure would also remove the cause of the present discontent with the international system.

War. There was a time when the distinction between war and peace was clear and distinct, when wars were fought with mercenary troops and had little effect on the general population. Today, with "cold" wars, psychological wars, economic wars, "races for space," and various other stratagems for obtaining an imbalance of power in favor of one's own side, the line between war and peace has been blurred and we must invent new terms to distinguish one shade of conflict from another. Even open military conflict is now differentiated into wars of aggression (which are usually waged by losers), police actions (which are apparently military actions sanctified by the United Nations), self-defense (which is "our" reason for going to war), limited wars (wars which do not affect the vital interests of the Great Powers), and total wars (wars which do affect the vital interests of the Great Powers). We are also told of our potential to wage wars in outer space, which seems a good place for them, biological wars, push-button wars, and so forth. The formal and precise terms in which international law distinguishes between neutrality and belligerency have lost their meaning in contemporary international affairs.

War is a phenomenon that is peculiar to man, for no other beast produces organized attacks on its neighbors aiming at the annihilation of the enemy for purposes that are not nutritional. It is not a universal human trait, and comparative anthropology tells us that it cannot really be an "instinct," for there are some few benighted tribes, such as the Eskimo, who know nothing of war and think it ludicrous or unbelievable. For thousands of years, moralists have decried the use of force, yet war continues and indeed becomes increasingly destructive. In economic terms, war is a crude and savage waste of resources, both human and physical, which serves no economic purpose except, perhaps, to maintain the population within bounds. Morally, all wars, except those in which one's own country is involved, are insane, though there have been a few Hitlers and Mussolinis to praise the glories of war in absolute terms, and patriotism usually accomplishes the same end in time of war. No one can look at war in moral terms and comprehend why it is that men engage in these orgies of self-destruction.

Unfortunately, war makes sense in political terms, though that may imply that politics is a senseless occupation. For the old cant that "wars never settle anything" is untenable; wars have settled a great many things. In fact, the reason why war is useful is that it can and does settle things, and often with finality. It may be true that new "things" arise immediately that also need settlement and that wars never achieve a final settlement, but neither does politics; that is the nature of the process. This does not mean that wars are fought for reasonable purposes, for war can settle unreasonable as well as reasonable questions. But it does mean that in the last analysis war is a means of settling disputes that is open to men both individually and collectively, and if men have given up the use of war in their individual relations that is only because a final solution can be obtained by political means within the framework of the state. In international relations, however, there is presently no substitute for war as a final arbiter, and so long as the sovereign national state continues to exist unhindered, it is hard to see how a substitute can be produced.

The reasons men give for fighting wars are often very strange. They fight to attain their "destiny" or to save humanity from the current Mephistopheles of the international opera season. They fight to gain lebensraum or to acquire colonies, or to leave colonial status and become independent, or to promote peace. Indeed, it sometimes appears that the sole purpose of peace is to prepare adequately for the next war and that making war is man's primary occupation. Certainly man spends more of his worldly goods on this form of amusement than on any other. It used to be thought, rather naïvely, that wars were due to armaments, that private armament manufacturers were a sinister influence behind the international scene who fomented wars, and hence that the elimination of war was possible if private armament manufacturers were eliminated. "Take the profit out of war," they said, "and there will be no more war." The same charge has been made against the *Comité des Forges,* the I. G. Farben interests, and "Wall Street," and the *agent provocateur* of the mystery novels of the interwar period is testimony to the degree to which the myth was accepted. Wars have also been blamed on the professional soldiers, on the seemingly reasonable grounds that their *raison d'être* is war, but it is not really true that military leaders make war. War is a political decision, fought for political and not military ends (a point that American generals have at times been unable to grasp), and much too important to be left to decisions by professional soldiers.

Is there hope for the future? If wars truly are fought because they are the only means available of attaining a final settlement in international affairs when attempts to reach agreement fail, then the only possible alternative appears to be the creation of some authority which can settle such questions peacefully. Some men argue, of course, that war has become so utterly destructive that it defeats its own purpose, that no one can really win a war in the future, hence that war will be abandoned. There is perhaps some truth in the matter, but that is still no protection against fanatics, and as the twentieth century has shown all too clearly, such men occasionally become the rulers of large and powerful political associations. Further, men have an amazing capacity to hope, and already we have heard discussion of what ought to be done in the period after an attack, based upon the presumption that the initial phases of nuclear war will exterminate millions of persons. People dig holes a few feet in the earth as protection against weapons which blast pits in the ocean floor nearly half a mile deep. War may indeed be unthinkable, but it is not for that reason impossible. Yet it would be quite unrealistic to suppose that men are yet at the stage where they would be willing to abandon their traditions to the point needed to create the kind of political organization which could truly guarantee against an outbreak of war. Some observers, like Lord Bertrand Russell, are pessimistic and presume that war will occur in a few decades at most; others are more hopeful. No decisive answer can be given.

THE UNITED STATES IN WORLD AFFAIRS

Let us now look at international affairs from the point of view of the single nation, examine the problems it raises, the machinery that is needed, the procedures used to handle international problems. We shall use the United States as an example, but every country must deal with the same fundamental problems and has need for the same machinery. Of course, the precise manner in which political decisions are made differs from one country to the next, and since foreign policy questions are political matters par excellence, there will be considerable differences in the machinery for decision making, but the formal structure is remarkably similar in most countries. We will note some of these similarities and differences as we proceed.

Control of foreign relations. Control of foreign relations is generally placed in the hands of the executive, whatever the political system of the nation concerned, and the United States is no exception to the general rule. In the American federal system, authority to deal with foreign affairs is clearly and decisively placed in the hands of the Federal government, and the states are explicitly excluded from the area. Further, authority is placed mainly in the hands of the executive branch, with certain limitations, such as the right of the Senate to approve formal treaties. Actually, the Constitution implies that the Senate should also take part in the negotiation of treaties, but President Washington found this impractical, and custom has established the point so firmly that the Supreme Court has ruled that the Senate may not intrude in treaty negotiation—its task is limited to ratification. The states too may, in practice, interfere in foreign affairs indirectly, as when they pass laws that encourage or permit racial discrimination in public places; such laws are not really subject to Federal control and may prove extremely embarrassing in the Federal government's relations with other countries. Racial discrimination in and around Washington, D.C., for example, has created some very serious complications for the government when foreign dignitaries feel insulted by their treatment in restaurants, etc.

President and Congress in foreign affairs. Foreign relations, then, are controlled by the President and by Congress, with the scales heavily weighted in favor of the former. The President has the appointing power, the right to conduct negotiations, control over military forces, the right of representation abroad and the right to receive diplomatic missions from other countries, the power to recognize, the right to make agreements without senatorial approval so long as treaties are not signed, full access to all information coming from abroad, and control of all of the agencies primarily concerned with the conduct of foreign relations. The President, for all practical purposes, represents the United States in its foreign relations. All diplomats are accredited to him; all messages are sent to him; all eyes, here and abroad, tend to turn to him for policy statements.

This is an agglomeration of authority that Congress cannot hope to match. True, the Senate has the right to confirm appointments and to ratify treaties, which is sometimes significant. Congress has the sole power to declare war, but in this area the President has a considerable measure of influence on the decision. Congress has control over appropriations, and this is probably its most potent weapon. Finally, Congress may use its investigating powers to involve itself to some extent in foreign relations. Of course, the opinions of Congress are influential, because the President is, after all, a political leader and must mend his fences with the rest. But even here, we must recall that the President is the formal head of his own party, and has it in his power to coerce the congressmen to some extent through his control of patronage and through the immense power of publicity that is at his command. It is not a well-matched battle, even in the best of conditions, and the likelihood that Congress can really control presidential policy is actually quite small.

Even though primary control over foreign affairs is vested in the executive branch, the Congress retains enough influence to create some fairly serious problems in foreign relations. The classic illustration of the point is the League of Nations, which President Wilson sponsored and helped draft, but which the Senate refused to accept. Foreign nations will obviously be reluctant to engage in lengthy and complex negotiations with the executive when there is a danger that the Senate will refuse to ratify the ensuing treaty. Where a formal treaty is needed, the President will usually attempt to gain support for the treaty well in advance, as was the case with the treaty that established the United Nations, and the houses of Congress may pass formal resolutions indicating their support for a particular measure to smooth the President's path. However, the President is free to make any of the less formal kinds of agreements, and these are just as binding as treaties.

Only a few major changes have been proposed in the basic machinery of American foreign policy: one suggestion was that the requirement for a two-thirds vote in the Senate be lowered when treaties were brought before it. This would have increased the authority of the President, and made it much easier to obtain ratification. On the other hand, the "Bricker amendment" to the Constitution, proposed by Senator Bricker of Ohio in 1952, would have made very substantial changes in favor of Congress, including the need to have legislative agreement to all international pacts, whether treaties or not, but the amendment was not successful. The balance of authority, then, remains heavily weighted in favor of the executive branch, and seems likely to remain that way in the future, for it would be extremely awkward for Congress to attempt to intervene in the day-to-day conduct of foreign relations.

The basic machinery. A surprising number of governmental agencies, including the Treasury Department, the Defense Department, the Department of Agriculture, the Department of Commerce, etc., not only have an interest in foreign affairs but may even have their own missions abroad on different ventures. But the formal machinery for carrying out American policy is more limited. The President is, of course, personally preeminent in the field, and all foreign affairs are carried on in his name. The Department of State is the principal agency for maintaining relations with other countries, subject, of course, to presidential direction. The National Security Council, which was established by law in 1947, is the principal advisory body on foreign affairs. The Central Intelligence Agency, which is part of the National Security Council, is the center for acquisition and collation of information about other nations. Finally, the military services are active abroad, and the Department of Defense plays an important advisory role in policy formulation, as we might expect.

The State Department. The Department of State is the center for all diplomatic activity abroad and an important element in planning and implementing foreign policy, though its policy-making functions have been reduced somewhat in recent years as new agencies have appeared. There are something like 6,000 persons in the State Department, which is administered by an appointed Secretary of State who is a prominent member of the President's Cabinet. The State Department is fundamentally a vast information service; it is in constant touch with all of our diplomatic missions abroad, sending and receiving information which is collated and organized inside the Department. A steady flow of information moves from the Department to the Secretary of State, advising him of changes, of situations which require attention, etc., and usually outlining conditions in a given area and attempting to delineate the alternate lines of policy open to the government and the consequences likely to follow from each alternate policy. The Department does not make policy as such, but it has a significant role in planning and framing the alternatives.

Secretary of State. The role of the Secretary of State in foreign affairs differs greatly with the incumbent; some men play a minor role in that status while others become extremely influential. A Secretary of State like John Foster

Dulles, with the full confidence and support of the President, may be able to "make" a great deal of American policy on his own; Cordell Hull, on the other hand, worked with Franklin D. Roosevelt at a time when Roosevelt was literally his own Secretary of State; consequently, Hull had little say in policy decisions. An important part of the Secretary's job is to maintain good relations with Congress, particularly with the committees that deal either directly or indirectly with foreign relations. He may supply information, appear at hearings, and in general maintain close contact with those in Congress whose support is essential for the administration.

The overseas mission. The overseas mission is almost literally a listening post and a transmitting station; it has only an indirect role in policy making. The United States maintains some eighty overseas missions; most are now headed by a full ambassador, sometimes because of the importance of the mission (Britain, U.S.S.R., France) and sometimes as a matter of courtesy (Latin America). Missions vary greatly in size, some including two hundred or more Americans plus a substantial number of local clerical staff, others containing a mere handful of people. The overseas staff was once supplied by the Foreign Service, which had a completely separate personnel department with its own rules and requirements. Since 1954, the Foreign Service has been integrated with the regular State Department staff. The heads of missions are usually political appointees, but there is now some pressure to appoint professional foreign service officers to ambassadorial posts. The chief difficulty is perhaps fiscal, for it is very expensive indeed to act as ambassador to a large country, and professional foreign service officers living on their departmental salary cannot possibly accept such a post.

The personnel problem. It would be almost impolite to pass along without at least mentioning the basic problem facing the State Department—finding and keeping suitably qualified men—for personnel has been a headache for the Department for many years. Much of the work of the young foreign service officer, or State Department junior official, is deadly routine—reading and writing endless reports and summaries. There is a need for men with emotional stability and dependability, for obvious reasons. The selection system used is revised from time to time, yet in the nature of things it encounters serious problems. Brilliance is much less important than steady performance, and the pressure to conform and avoid conflict once appointed is great. Yet the "timeserver" is not really the best man for a sensitive post of this sort, surely. Further, frequent rotation of personnel makes it virtually impossible for the foreign service officer to become really expert and familiar with the country to which he is assigned. Whereas the British may retain a man in one country for most of his official life in the department, American foreign service officers seldom remain in the same country for more than three or four years. This creates quite a different relationship between the members of a diplomatic mission and the government to which they are accredited, for there is little time to develop the personal relationships and the expertise that are needed for accurate reporting.

The National Security Council. The National Security Council, which was established by Congress in 1947 as a primary policy-making body in foreign affairs, is not really well known, so far as operation and function are concerned. It consists of the President, the Vice President, the Secretary of State, the Secretary of Defense, and the Director of the Office of Civil and Defense Mobilization, plus any other persons that the President chooses to invite. President Eisenhower, for example, commonly included the Secretary of the Treasury in the weekly meetings. The Council has its own secretariat, and it is attached directly to the President. The Central Intelligence Agency is attached to the Council as an information arm. Major policy decisions are not made by the Council, for the President has the final word in such matters, but the Council will meet to discuss major changes in policy, or crises that arise suddenly, as well as long-term policy problems. And since each person attending the meetings has an opportunity to be heard, the President's final choice is doubtless much influenced by the opinions expressed in these meetings.

Policy making. Although the most important single factor in the making of foreign policy is certainly the views of the President, he cannot and does not act in a vacuum. The fact is that foreign policy is the outcome of a very complex process, in most cases, which may involve various members of the government, congressional leaders, major interest groups, the general public, and even world opinion. As a political leader, the President can hardly ignore the various political pressures arising out of the structure in which he functions. He offends Congress at his peril. He must also obtain the assent of the general public; relations with Israel, for example, will be much influenced by the views of the prominent Jewish organizations in the country, just as relations with Poland will be influenced by the views of the very large Polish groups in the United States. Economic policy is influenced by the views of the business community, farming interests, and others whose economic position may be affected by policy. Thus there is a constant balancing of interests, an attempt to obtain prior agreement so that major conflicts may be settled at home. There are exceptions, of course. President Truman was forced to make a very rapid decision in 1947 to support Greece and Turkey with military aid after the economic crisis in Britain forced her to drop her commitments to these two countries. Similarly, the decision to intervene in the Korean outbreak was made quickly, and with no time to refer to public opinion. If time permits, however, opinion is carefully sounded beforehand.

Perhaps an illustration will make the point clear. In 1946, the government began planning a very large-scale program of economic assistance to the devastated countries of Europe. The need for the program was obvious, for there was no alternate source of aid, and the economic collapse of the Western European region would have worked havoc with the world economic structure and had a massive effect on the American economy as well. Further, relations with Russia were growing more and more strained, though this factor was not emphasized during the early planning stages of the aid program. Toward the end of 1946, the principles involved in the aid program were "tried out" on different audiences—business groups, congressional leaders, and so forth—to obtain a reaction. In the spring of 1947, further "trial balloons" were floated on the subject, this time in more detail. Again the results were apparently satisfactory, for in June, 1947, Secretary of State George C. Marshall proposed the aid program in a speech at Harvard University, and thus inaugurated formally one of the major steps in foreign relations in the early postwar years. Behind the announcement made by Marshall there lay months of planning, coordination, consultation, etc., designed to ensure the support of the major interest groups in the country at large and in Congress. This is more or less typical of the approach that is used to policy making when there is ample time.

Some contemporary problems. In most respects, the United States takes part in international affairs on the same basis as any other country, but with one great difference: the United States is today one of the two superpowers in the world and as such her policies have influence on many other nations in the world. The impact of American political, economic, and military policy reaches to the borders of the Soviet sphere of influence, and American and Soviet influence intermingle and compete in a vast and undefined region between the two nations. American primary interests now reach from the Scandinavian peninsula to the shores of Japan, and from the Arctic Circle to the vast wastes of Antarctica. In a few short decades, the United States moved from isolation and neutrality to a position of world leadership. The speed of the transition, and its scope, placed an enormous strain upon the machinery used to make and carry out policy and upon the principles to which policy formerly adhered, for it is not possible for an active Great Power to retain the same machinery and policy principles as an isolationist nation. For better or worse, the United States is now fully committed to the international community, to share its problems, its dangers, and its frustrations. Much of the world looks to the United States for leadership, and at times, looks with trepidation. New machinery, new attitudes, new concepts, and new principles have had to be developed in a relatively short period of time; not surprisingly, the transition has not been made without contest and dispute, and the road ahead is far from settled.

The American tradition, for example, includes a number of principles which the government has found it extremely difficult to apply as a world power. America has traditionally opposed colonialism and sided with colonial aspirations, yet at times our government has found it necessary to support France and Britain in their attempts to retain control of their colonial possessions, and has thus been unable to support the colonies as much as it might wish to do. Again, the United States has traditionally supported the liberal democracies and opposed dictatorial rule both at home and abroad, yet it has found itself in alliance with dictatorial rule in Spain, in the Middle East and the Far East, in Yugoslavia, and even in South America, as it sought to maintain stability and order. Traditionally, the United States has taken a highly moralistic attitude toward international affairs, condemning the immorality of power politics and doctrines of national interest, yet since 1947, the United States too has had to limit the extent to which it could apply moral principle in its foreign relations, and has had to undertake the same struggle for power that it formerly condemned in others.

Finally, America has traditionally favored the peaceful solution of international problems and opposed militarism, the maintenance of large armies, and the use of force in political affairs, yet it finds itself maintaining a very large military establishment and an enormous nuclear potential, spending a substantial part of its natural resources on military equipment, and even resorting to physical force itself, as in the case of Korea or South East Asia. Many of these changes have been difficult to stomach, or rationalize, and they have not been made without opposition. But no great power, however strong, can act without reference to the behavior patterns of the other states, and the United States has been forced to accept and use the same tactics that other states employ as they seek their international goals. This is only one of the many changes that occur when a nation moves from neutrality to active Great Power status, and the end is not yet in sight.

Summary

International relations can be studied in a variety of contexts: as a struggle for power, as pursuit of the national interest, as a reflection of geographic influences, and in various other systematic ways. Each approach has its own uses and throws some light on particular aspects of the total process.

In their relations with one another, national states have developed a number of useful institutions, all more or less formalized. Of particular importance are the rules of diplomacy, consular practice, special conferences and meetings, intelligence and espionage activity, and personal meetings. Each has its own uses and limits.

A major development in the twentieth century has been the attempt to produce an international organization which can maintain peace. The League of Nations foundered because the nations concerned were unwilling to make use of the machinery it provided. The United Nations has proved able to limit conflict when the interests of the Great Powers have not been involved, but is less useful when the Great Powers come face to face. Its nonsecurity activities in health, education, etc., are invaluable. The nations themselves have turned to regional arrangements, special treaty arrangements, etc., in their search for security and peace. NATO, the OAS, and SEATO are typical examples of this type of arrangement.

International law, though different from municipal law, nevertheless serves an important function in international relations and is generally observed, though it lacks formal sanctions. The laws of war, however, have tended to break down in this century, and there has been an alarming decline in the good faith on which international law depends.

War remains as the final arbiter in disputes among nations, and though there are various legal categories of wars, their character really depends upon the nations involved.

In the United States, foreign relations rest in the hands of the executive and the legislature, with the balance of power leaning heavily toward the executive. The principal organs of foreign policy are the Department of State, the National Security Council, the overseas mission, and the presidency. In policy making, the President has the final word but the nature of the subject matter forces him to depend substantially upon advice, or choice of alternatives, which take into consideration all of the military, economic, political, and other factors involved. Thus careful consultation with affected interests is an important part of the policy making process.

With this brief survey of an enormous topic, we conclude our discussion of the basic principles of politics. We return to the subject in Chapter 19 where we consider some of the major political problems facing the United States at the present time. In the chapters that follow, we turn to the examination of the third major facet of human society— economic activity.

Review questions

1. Comment on the importance of sovereignty in the study of international relations.

2. List four of the different approaches to the study of international affairs, together with their strengths and weaknesses.

3. What are some of the factors that help determine the "character" of the international system at any given point in time?

4. What function does diplomacy perform in international affairs?

5. Differentiate between a diplomatic mission and a consular mission.

6. List some of the techniques used in the conduct of international affairs (outside regular diplomatic channels) and give the advantages and disadvantages of each technique.

7. Compare the League of Nations and the United Nations in organization, function, and usefulness.

8. List three of the major regional arrangements in the Western world, giving their purpose, scope, and status.

9. Give some of the major reasons why sovereign states follow international law. What sanctions are applied to support it?

10. What are some of the major current trends in international law?

11. What is the political function of war?

12. Contrast the authority of the President and Congress in the control of foreign affairs.

13. What is the National Security Council?

14. What are some of the principal problems in American foreign relations at the present time?

15. What is the nature and function of the Department of State? What role does it play in foreign affairs?

For further study

1. What problems can you foresee in any attempt to produce an international organization with authority to coerce member nations?

2. Do you think it likely that the international laws of war will be revived in the near future? Why?

3. Make a list of the factors that the President must take into consideration when he is making a major policy decision in relation to foreign policy. Separate foreign from domestic factors.

4. Do you believe that it is a good thing for heads of state to meet and negotiate? What reasons can you give for your answer?

5. Do you believe that an international telephone system that would allow direct communication between heads of state would be desirable? Why?

6. What do you believe is the future role of the United Nations in world affairs?

7. Do you feel that war has become "impossible"? What consequences would you expect to flow from a massive nuclear war?

8. Does war have a function in a nuclear age, when every country is bound to "lose" in some sense?

9. Do you believe that the machinery of government may be inadequate to the needs of modern foreign relations?

10. How much information about foreign relations should governments make public? All? Only some small part?

SELECTED READINGS

On the Study of Politics

Butler, D. E.: *The Study of Political Behavior,* Hutchinson & Co. (Publishers), Ltd., London, 1958.

Charlesworth, James C. (ed.): *The Limits of Behavioralism in Political Science,* American Academy of Political and Social Science, Philadelphia, 1962.

Easton, David: *The Political System,* Alfred A. Knopf, Inc., New York, 1959.

Hyneman, Charles S.: *The Study of Politics: The Present State of American Political Science,* The University of Illinois Press, Urbana, Ill., 1959.

Storing, Herbert J. (ed.): *Essays on the Scientific Study of Politics,* Holt, Rinehart and Winston, Inc., New York, 1962.

Ulmer, S. Sidney (ed.): *Introductory Readings in Political Behavior,* Rand McNally & Company, Chicago, 1961.

Van Dyke, Vernon: *Political Science: A Philosophical Analysis,* Stanford University Press, Stanford, Calif., 1960.

Young, Roland (ed.): *Approaches to the Study of Politics,* Northwestern University Press, Evanston, Ill., 1958.

Chapter 6: The Changing Pattern of Politics

Adcock, Frank E.: *Roman Political Ideas and Practices,* The University of Michigan Press, Ann Arbor, Mich., 1959.

Aristotle: *The Politics.*

Bloch, Marie L. B.: *Feudal Society,* L. A. Manyon (trans.), Routledge & Kegan Paul, Ltd., London, 1961.

Gierke, Otto: *Political Theories of the Middle Age,* William Maitland (trans.), Beacon Press, Boston, 1958. First printed, 1900.

Girvetz, Harry K.: *The Evolution of Liberalism,* Collier Books, a division of Crowell-Collier Publishing Co., New York, 1963.

Hayes, Carlton J. H.: *Nationalism: A Religion,* The Macmillan Company, New York, 1960.

Hertz, F.: *Nationality in History and Politics,* Routledge & Kegan Paul, Ltd., London, 1944.

Huizinga, J.: *The Waning of the Middle Ages,* Whitefriars Press, London, 1955.

Kohn, Hans: *Nationalism: Its Meaning and History,* D. Van Nostrand Company, Inc., Princeton, N. J., 1955.

Lane, Robert E.: *Political Life,* The Free Press of Glencoe, New York, 1959.

Laski, Harold J.: *The Rise of European Liberalism,* George Allen & Unwin, Ltd., London, 1936.

Lipset, Seymour M.: *Political Man: The Social Bases of Politics,* Doubleday & Company, Inc., Garden City, N. Y., 1960.

Machiavelli, N.: *The Prince.*

MacIver, R.: *The Web of Government,* The Macmillan Company, New York, 1947.

Chapter 7: *Political Authority in the Modern State*

Adler, Mortimer J.: *The Idea of Freedom,* Doubleday & Company, Inc., Garden City, N. Y., 1958.

Barker, Ernest: *Social Contract,* Oxford University Press, Fair Lawn, N. J., 1961.

Benson, George C. S., et al.: *Essays in Federalism,* Institute for Studies in Federalism, Claremont, 1961.

Dewey, John: *The Public and Its Problems,* Holt, Rinehart and Winston, Inc., New York, 1927.

The Federalist Papers.

Handlin, Oscar, and Mary Handlin: *The Dimensions of Liberty,* Harvard University Press, Cambridge, Mass., 1961.

Hobbes, Thomas: *Leviathan.*

de Jouvenal, Bertrand: *Sovereignty,* J. F. Huntington (trans.), The University of Chicago Press, Chicago, 1957.

Locke, John: *Second Treatise on Civil Government.*

Macmahon, Arthur W. (ed.): *Federalism: Mature and Emergent,* Doubleday & Company, Inc., Garden City, N. Y., 1955.

Mayo, H. B.: *Introduction to Marxist Theory,* Oxford University Press, Fair Lawn, N. J., 1960.

McIlwain, Charles H.: *Constitutionalism: Ancient and Modern,* Cornell University Press, Ithaca, N. Y., 1940.

Mill, J. S.: *On Liberty.*

Mills, C. Wright: *The Power Elite,* Oxford University Press, Fair Lawn, N. J., 1956.

Rousseau, Jean Jacques: *The Social Contract.*

Schattschneider, E. E.: *Party Government,* Holt, Rinehart and Winston, Inc., New York, 1960.

Wheare, Kenneth C.: *Federal Government,* 3d ed., Oxford University Press, Fair Lawn, N. J., 1953.

Chapter 8: *The Political Process*

Bailey, Stephen K.: *The Condition of Our National Political Parties,* Fund for the Republic, New York, 1959.

Banfield, Edward C.: *Political Influence,* The Free Press of Glencoe, New York, 1961.

Barron, Richard W.: *Parties and Politics in Modern France,* Public Affairs Press, Washington, D.C., 1959.

Beard, Charles A.: *The Economic Basis of Politics,* Alfred A. Knopf, Inc., New York, 1945.

Beloff, Max: *American Federal Government,* Oxford University Press, Fair Lawn, N. J., 1959.

Blaisdell, Donald C.: *American Democracy under Pressure,* The Ronald Press Company, New York, 1957.

Blau, Peter M.: *Bureaucracy in Modern Society,* Random House, Inc., New York, 1956.

Cannon, James M.: *Politics, U.S.A.: A Practical Guide to Winning Public Office,* Doubleday & Company, Inc., Garden City, N. Y., 1960.

Carter, Gwendolyn M., and John H. Hertz: *Government and Politics in the Twentieth Century,* Frederick A. Praeger, Inc., New York, 1961.

Carter, John F.: *Power and Persuasion,* Duell, Sloan & Pearce, Inc., New York, 1960.

Dahl, Robert A.: *A Preface to Democratic Theory,* The University of Chicago Press, Chicago, 1956.

Duverger, Maurice: *Political Parties: Their Organization and Activity in the Modern State,* John Wiley & Sons, Inc., New York, 1954.

Froman, Lewis A.: *People and Politics: An Analysis of the American Political System,* Prentice-Hall, Inc., Englewood Cliffs, N. J., 1962.

de Grazia, Sebastian: *The Political Community: A Study of Anomie,* The University of Chicago Press, Chicago, 1948.

Harris, Seymour E.: *The Economics of the Political Parties,* The Macmillan Company, New York, 1962.

Hook, Sidney: *Political Power and Personal Freedom: Critical Studies in Democracy, Communism, and Civil Rights,* Criterion Books, New York, 1959.

Jennings, Sir William I.: *Party Politics,* Cambridge University Press, London, 1960.

Key, V. O., Jr.: *Politics, Parties, and Pressure Groups,* 4th ed., Crowell-Collier Publishing Co., New York, 1958.

Leiserson, Avery: *Parties and Politics: An Institutional and Behavioral Approach,* Alfred A. Knopf, Inc., New York, 1958.

Lindsay, A. D.: *The Modern Democratic State,* Oxford University Press, Fair Lawn, N. J., 1947.

Lippmann, Walter: *The Public Philosophy,* Little, Brown and Company, Boston, 1955.

McDonald, Neil A.: *The Study of Political Parties,* Random House, Inc., New York, 1956.

McKenzie, R. T.: *British Political Parties,* St Martin's Press, Inc., New York, 1955.

Nash, Howard P.: *Third Parties in American Politics,* Public Affairs Press, Washington, D.C., 1959.

Neumann, Sigmund (ed.): *Modern Political Parties,* The University of Chicago Press, Chicago, 1956.

Powell, Theodore (ed.): *Democracy in Action: The Voices of Men in American Government and Politics,* The Macmillan Company, New York, 1962.

Rossiter, Clinton: *Parties and Politics in America,* Cornell University Press, Ithaca, N. Y., 1960.

Schattschneider, E. E.: *Party Government,* Holt, Rinehart and Winston, Inc., New York, 1942.

————: *The Semi-Sovereign People,* Holt, Rinehart and Winston, Inc., New York, 1961.

Schettler, Clarence: *Public Opinion in America,* Harper & Brothers, New York, 1960.

Thorsen, Thomas L.: *The Logic of Democracy,* Holt, Rinehart and Winston, Inc., New York, 1962.

Truman, David B.: *The Governmental Process,* Alfred A. Knopf, Inc., New York, 1951.

Williamson, Chilton: *American Suffrage from Property to Democracy,* Princeton University Press, Princeton, N. J., 1961.

Chapter 9: Politics and Economics

Boulding, Kenneth E.: *Principles of Economic Policy,* Prentice-Hall, Inc., Englewood Cliffs, N. J., 1958.

Burnham, James: *The Managerial Revolution,* The John Day Company, Inc., New York, 1941.

Drucker, P.: *The End of Economic Man,* The John Day Company, Inc., New York, 1939.

Ebenstein, William: *Today's Isms: Communism, Fascism, Capitalism, Socialism,* 3d ed., Prentice-Hall, Inc., Englewood Cliffs, N. J., 1961.

The Fabian Essays.

Fainsod, Merle, Lincoln Gordon, and Joseph C. Palamountain: *Government and the American Economy,* W. W. Norton & Company, Inc., New York, 1959.

Finer, Herman: *The Road to Reaction,* Little, Brown and Company, Boston, 1945.

Gabriel, R. H.: *The Course of American Democratic Thought,* 2d ed., The Ronald Press Company, New York, 1956.

Galbraith, John K.: *The Affluent Society,* Houghton Mifflin Company, Boston, 1958.

————: *American Capitalism,* Houghton Mifflin Company, Boston, 1956.

Hamilton, W.: *The Politics of Industry,* Alfred A. Knopf, Inc., New York, 1957.

Hayek, Friedrich A. von: *The Constitution of Liberty,* The University of Chicago Press, Chicago, 1960.

————: *The Road to Serfdom,* The University of Chicago Press, Chicago, 1944.

Hofstadter, Richard: *Social Darwinism in American Thought*, rev. ed., Beacon Press, Boston, 1955.

Hoover, Calvin B.: *The Economy, Liberty, and the State*, The Twentieth Century Fund, New York, 1959.

Lenin, V. I.: *State and Revolution*.

Marx, Karl: *Capital*.

————: *The Communist Manifesto*.

————: *Critique of the Gotha Program*.

Mayo, Henry B.: *Democracy and Marxism*, Oxford University Press, Fair Lawn, N. J., 1955.

————: *Introduction to Marxist Theory*, Oxford University Press, Fair Lawn, N. J., 1960.

Mendel, A. P. (ed.): *Essential Works of Marxism*, Bantam Books, Inc., New York, 1961.

Meyer, A. G.: *Leninism*, Frederick A. Praeger, Inc., New York, 1957.

Oakeshott, Michael: *The Social and Political Doctrines of Contemporary Europe*, The Macmillan Company, New York, 1947.

Schumpeter, Joseph: *Capitalism, Socialism, and Democracy*, 3d ed., Harper & Brothers, New York, 1950.

Taft, Philip: *Movements for Economic Reform*, Holt, Rinehart and Winston, Inc., New York, 1950.

Tawney, R. H.: *The Acquisitive Society*, Harcourt, Brace & World, Inc., New York, 1920.

————: *Religion and the Rise of Capitalism*, Harcourt, Brace & World, Inc., New York, 1926.

Weber, Max: *The Protestant Ethic and the Spirit of Capitalism*, Talcott Parsons (trans.), Charles Scribner's Sons, New York, 1958.

Wootton, Barbara: *Freedom under Planning*, The University of North Carolina Press, Chapel Hill, N.C., 1945.

Chapter 10: Relations among States

Almond, Gabriel A.: *The American People and Foreign Policy*, Harcourt, Brace & World, Inc., New York, 1950.

Birrenbach, Kurt: *The Future of the Atlantic Community*, Frederick A. Praeger, Inc., New York, 1963.

Bloomfield, Lincoln E.: *The United Nations and U.S. Foreign Policy*, Little, Brown and Company, Boston, 1960.

Brierly, J. L.: *The Law of Nations*, Oxford University Press, Fair Lawn, N. J., 1955.

Carleton, William G.: *The Revolution in American Foreign Policy*, rev. ed., Random House, Inc., New York, 1963.

Claude, Inis L., Jr.: *Power and International Relations*, Random House, Inc., New York, 1962.

————: *Swords into Plowshares: The Problems and Progress of International Organization,* Random House, Inc., New York, 1956.

Cohen, Bernard C.: *The Political Process and Foreign Policy,* Princeton University Press, Princeton, N. J., 1957.

Dahl, Robert A.: *Congress and Foreign Policy,* Harcourt, Brace & World, Inc., New York, 1950.

Furniss, Edgar S., Jr.: *American Military Policy,* Holt, Rinehart and Winston, Inc., New York, 1957.

Goldsen, Joseph M. (ed.): *Outer Space in World Politics,* Frederick A. Praeger, Inc., New York, 1963.

Goldwin, Robert A. (ed.): *America Armed,* Rand McNally & Company, Chicago, 1963.

———— (ed.), with Ralph Lerner and Gerald Stourzh: *Readings in American Foreign Policy,* Oxford University Press, Fair Lawn, N. J., 1959.

Goodspeed, Stephen S.: *The Nature and Function of International Organization,* Oxford University Press, Fair Lawn, N. J., 1954.

Kennan, George F.: *American Diplomacy 1900–1950,* The University of Chicago Press, Chicago, 1951.

Lawson, Ruth C. (ed.): *International Regional Organizations,* Frederick A. Praeger, Inc., New York, 1962.

Lerche, Charles O., Jr.: *America in World Affairs,* McGraw-Hill Book Company, Inc., New York, 1963.

Macridis, Roy C. (ed.): *Foreign Policy in World Politics,* 2d ed., Prentice-Hall, Inc., Englewood Cliffs, N. J., 1962.

Morgenthau, Hans J.: *Politics among Nations,* 3d ed., Alfred A. Knopf, Inc., New York, 1960.

————: *Politics in the 20th Century,* The University of Chicago Press, Chicago, 1962, vols. I, II, III, especially vol. II, *The Impasse in American Foreign Policy.*

Northrup, F. S. C.: *European Union and United States Foreign Policy,* The Macmillan Company, New York, 1954.

Rosenau, James N.: *Public Opinion and Foreign Policy,* Random House, Inc., New York, 1961.

Schuman, Frederick L.: *International Politics,* 6th ed., McGraw-Hill Book Company, Inc., New York, 1960.

Seabury, Paul: *Power, Freedom, and Diplomacy,* Random House, Inc., New York, 1963.

Snyder, Richard C., and Edgar S. Furniss, Jr., *American Foreign Policy,* rev. ed., Holt, Rinehart and Winston, Inc., New York, 1959.

Spanier, John: *American Foreign Policy since World War II,* Frederick A. Praeger, Inc., New York, 1962.

Strauss, E.: *Common Sense about the Common Market,* Holt, Rinehart and Winston, Inc., New York, 1958.

Whitaker, Urban G., Jr. (ed.): *Propaganda and International Relations,* Chandler Publishing Co., San Francisco, 1961.

PART 3

The

Economic

Order

Economic affairs are so firmly interwoven in the fabric of modern society that it is hardly necessary to argue the importance of economics in the education of modern man. Without some knowledge of basic economic principles, intelligent discussion of some of the most fundamental problems in human life is literally impossible. The person who has never made a systematic study of economics is handicapped in even attempting to think about such questions. He is like a deaf man trying to appreciate a great symphony. This does not mean that a course in economics, or even a dozen courses in economics, will give answers to these problems once and for all. Economics deals with particular aspects of human life and human life does not lend itself to easy and precise answers. Economics can, however, provide men with a reasonable basis for discussing their problems within a well-defined and integrated framework, and that is no small accomplishment.

"For Whom the Bell Tolls." What are some of the questions that economics seeks to explain or answer? There are, first of all, those which deal with our personal economic situation. What kinds of jobs are there to do? How much do they pay? How much will our wages buy? Will there be enough jobs in the future? And so on through an almost endless list.

Economics, as we have already learned, also has a great deal to do with the political decisions each individual citizen must make. Should I urge the government to add to my taxes in order to help unemployed miners? Or are there other things that government can do to mitigate the problem of unemployment? Should I vote to build a new school or road now, or should this job be put aside until business slackens and prices drop and more jobs are needed? Should married women be made ineligible for public employment in order to keep men from being thrown out of work? Will automation in factories lead to surplus workers and starvation, and is some measure of government control needed in this area? Should I press my representative in government to urge stronger and tighter antitrust legislation and closer supervision of monopolistic pricing?

Economics can also help us come to grips with the crucial issues facing the whole nation. In what sense does a growing population pose a problem for the present and for the future? Will our rate of growth depend upon the extent to which we sacrifice consumer's goods today, in order to produce machines and industrial equipment, or is the inventiveness of scientists, engineers, and workmen the key to growth and development? And perhaps most important of all, is the Soviet Union likely to overtake the United States as the most affluent society in the world in the near future? Or as the most powerful military power? Which approach to economic organization, the Soviet or the Western, offers the common man in India or the Congo the best opportunity for the future?

Finally, economics deals with business affairs, with the rise and fall of stock prices and the prices of goods on the open market, with the cost of living, with inflation and deflation, with money and banking and saving, with agriculture, and with all of the multitude of problems that arise out of business activity.

Every one of these questions requires the study of economics before any progress can be made toward providing an answer, and indeed in many cases before the exact meaning of the question itself can be made clear.

Light and fruit. It would be unfair to characterize economic study as a purely "useful" subject; it has its own fascinations as well. For some two centuries, educated men have found in the study of economics both an intrinsic interest generated by its importance and an element of aesthetic satisfaction. Economic principles display some of the logical beauty of Euclid's geometry, and anyone with a feeling for logic and structure can find some aesthetic pleasure in them. That such mental constructs really do have a life-and-death significance for billions of souls all over the world is a source of continuing wonder and amazement, a source of great satisfaction. Of course, mere beauty of structure is not enough, in economics or in a mate; if at the end of a long life the economist felt that he had done nothing but muse about beautiful forms, his sense of accomplishment would be extremely limited. There is an even greater sense of achievement when the fruits of one's labor have made a difference in the affairs of men. One studies economics for the light it sheds, and any pleasure along the way is an incidental bonus, though not to be despised on that account.

What economics is. Years ago, beginners wanted a one-sentence definition of the subjects they studied, and dozens of such definitions were duly produced. Economics has been defined variously as:

1. The study of those activities involving money and exchange transactions among people
2. The study of how men choose to use scarce or limited production resources (land, labor, capital goods, and knowledge) to produce various commodities and distribute them to the members of society
3. The study of men in their ordinary business life, earning and enjoying a living
4. The study of wealth

The list is a good one, but far from complete. It is always hard to compress a large subject into a few words or lines. Economics certainly involves all of the elements included in the general definitions listed above and many more.

Today, experts would probably incline toward the second definition if they were forced to choose. They know that money is important, but that economic affairs can continue without its use; they realize that limiting economics to business matters calls attention to the fact that it cannot describe subjective human experiences, pleasures and pains derived from psychic relations with others—the best things of life are not free, nor are they for sale in the market place. No single definition is precise, and a precise definition is not really needed. An informative introductory description would be something like the following:

Economics is the study of how men and society choose, with or without the use of money, to employ scarce productive resources to produce various commodities over time and distribute them for consumption, now and in the future, among various people and groups in society.

What economics is not. Economics is sometimes confused with activities that lie beyond its range. For example, economics is not:

1. Home economics—how to bake cakes, or keep household accounts

2. Business management—how to make a million dollars, devise advertising strategy, or anticipate the stock market

3. Engineering—how to build dams, make penicillin, or pollinate corn

Economics touches on these areas, of course. It takes for granted the work of the engineer, and it recognizes the limitations imposed by nature and by man's knowledge. It may even influence the activity of technicians. We do not call an economist when a motor breaks down, but when the production system as a whole breaks down, leading to a depression, then the economist may have a great deal to offer both the engineer and the general public.

Similarly, the economist is interested in the way families choose to spend their money, but not in the same way as a home economist or a marriage counselor. The economist describes the behavior of consumers, but his description is not a substitute for business experience. A knowledge of economics, and the appreciation of the great social forces in a modern economy that it implies, may be quite useful to the person who wishes to make money in the stock market, but a more practical way of entering and getting ahead in the business world is to apprentice yourself to a going concern.

Economic description and analysis. It is the first task of modern economic science to describe, to analyze, to explain, and to correlate the behavior of production, unemployment, prices, and similar phenomena. If descriptions are to be significant, they must be more than a series of disconnected narratives. They must be fitted into a systematic pattern, and that is what is meant by true analysis. Because of the complexity of human behavior, we cannot hope to attain the precision in economics achieved by the physical sciences. We cannot perform controlled experiments; we must, like the astronomer, be content with precise observation. Fortunately, we do not need answers correct to five decimal places; so long as the right general direction can be established, we have made a tremendous step forward in the explanation of economic cause and effect.

Economic policy. Although knowledge and understanding are worthwhile for their own sake, most of us also hope that the knowledge we acquire will be useful, that it will help us to solve human problems as well as understand the universe in which we live. This brings us to the important problem of economic policy, for our understanding of economics should, ultimately, lead to greater control over and improvement of our economic system. How can the vagaries of the business cycle be diminished? How can economic progress best be furthered? How can we make adequate standards of living available on a wider basis? What, in other words, should our economic policy be?

At every point of our analysis we shall try to shed light on these policy problems. To succeed, we must seek to cultivate an objective and detached ability to see things as they are, regardless of our personal likes and dislikes, avoiding, if we can, Bacon's Idols of the Tribe and the Cave. Economic matters arouse emotional responses in almost everyone, and blood pressure rises and voices grow shrill when deep-seated prejudices are involved in discussion. Economic theory speaks the truth as best it can, and for all men. There are not separate theories for employers and employees, for Republicans and Democrats. This does not mean that economists always agree in the policy field. One may argue for full employment at any cost; another for growth; still another for price stabilization. But when they argue in this manner, they argue as citizens, and not as economic theorists; such questions lie in the realm of ethics or value theory and cannot be settled by scientific observation.

Common sense and nonsense. Economic policy is often controversial. The world of prices, wages, interest rates, stocks and bonds, banks and credit, taxes, and expenditure is a complicated one. Yet from childhood days, everyone knows something of economics and this acquaintance is both helpful and deceptive. It helps because much knowledge can be taken for granted; it is deceptive because we acquire a great deal of economic nonsense along with our economic facts when we deal with the subject unsystematically or within the limits of our own personal experience. The union leader who has negotiated several labor contracts may feel that he is an expert on the economics of wages, just as the businessman who has "met a payroll" or the banker who can balance his books may conclude that his views on price control or fiscal operations are valid or even final. Both may be mistaken.

Further, we must fight against the perfectly natural tendency to consider the consequences of particular economic phenomena on ourselves and those around us. A worker who has lost his job recently cannot be expected to reflect on the value to the whole society of the new jobs created by the technological change which cost him his employment, yet in the study of economics we must attempt to do this. The economist is interested in the operation of the *whole* economy; he does not examine it from the viewpoint of any one group. His goals are social and national policies rather than individual policies. That is why economics cannot tell you how to run a bank or a business or how to acquire wealth in the stock market. We can only hope that general economics will provide a useful and even an essential background to such activities.

The economist at work. In the complex world of economic phenomena, the economist must work under conditions that are far from ideal. He cannot, like the physicist or physiologist, determine particular effects of particular causes by carefully designed experiments. If, for example, he wishes to determine the effect of a gasoline tax on fuel consumption, he may be vexed by the fact that in the same year that the tax was imposed, pipelines were also introduced—how can their effects be separated? Nevertheless, he must try, if only mentally, to isolate the effects of the tax on an "other things being equal" basis. This limit on our ability to ascribe causal relations accurately means that our quantitative knowledge of economics is far from complete. We have, of course, a great deal of statistical information available, but before this information is useful it must be treated—simplified, abstracted, and fitted into a framework. The economist will *idealize,* omitting details and attempting to relate the mass of available facts by simple patterns. Every theory distorts reality to some extent because of this oversimplification and abstraction process. But if it is a good theory, what is omitted is greatly outweighed by the illumination and understanding gained through its application. Properly understood, theory and observation, deduction and induction, go hand in hand. The test of a theory's usefulness is its ability to illuminate and explain observed facts. Consequently, when a student says, "That's all right in theory but not in practice," he is really saying, "That's not all right in the relevant theory," or else he is talking nonsense.

Some economic fallacies. The first principle in economics is that things are often not what they seem. For example, all of the following statements are true, yet all appear somewhat paradoxical.

1. If all farmers work hard and produce a bumper crop, farm income may *fall,* and probably will.

2. One man may solve his unemployment problem by personal ingenuity; but all unemployed persons cannot necessarily solve their problems in this way.

3. It may pay the United States to reduce her tariffs even if other countries refuse to do likewise.

4. Attempts by individuals to save more in a depression may actually reduce the community's total savings.

We will resolve each of these seeming paradoxes, and more, in the course of the material that follows. Here we may mention that each of them in fact depends upon what logicians call the "fallacy of composition," the belief that what is true of a part is necessarily true of the whole. In economics, one of the first things we learn is that what may be true for individuals is not always true for society, and conversely that what is true for all may be false for any one individual. If one person carries a soapbox to get a better view of a parade, he may succeed; but what if everyone in the crowd brings a box?

We have come to the end of our brief introduction. Perhaps a preview of the economic material to be covered in the text will be useful as a conclusion. We begin in Chapter 11 with the fundamental tools needed to analyze economic facts and institutions in modern society, working our way steadily toward the basic concept of national income, presented in Chapter 13. We then move to the causes of prosperity and depression, to the manner in which saving and investment interact to determine the overall level of economic activity—purchasing power, income, and employment—and to the way that public monetary and fiscal policies can stabilize business activity at a healthy level of progressive growth.

We then turn to the forces of competition and monopoly and the manner in which they act through supply and demand to help determine the composition of the national income, in terms of both goods and services. From that point, we move to a discussion of the various kinds of income—wages, rent, interest, and profits. We conclude with a discussion of international trade.

Finally, we attack some of our most vital current economic problems and attempt to make use of the economic tools we have learned. Here we try to deal with the pressing and urgent problem of underdeveloped areas, with such challenging problems as the promotion of economic growth and the control of inflation, and with the questions that arise when we compare the American economic system with the structure found in the U.S.S.R.

CHAPTER 11

Basic
Economic
Concepts

Any society, whether it consists of a totally collectivized communistic state, a capitalistic industrial nation, or even a colony of bees, must somehow produce a solution to each of three fundamental and interdependent economic problems:

1. *What* commodities shall be produced and in what quantities? That is, how much of and which of alternative goods and services shall be produced?

2. *How* shall goods be produced? That 'is, by whom, and using what resources and technology?

3. *For Whom* shall goods be produced? That is, who is to enjoy and benefit from the goods which the economic system provides? Or to put the same point in another way: How is the total national product to be *distributed* among the members of the society?

These three fundamental questions are common to all economies but they are answered differently by different societies. In a primitive society, custom may decide the answers in each case. In a bee colony, such problems are solved by "biological instincts." We can also imagine an omnipotent, benevolent or malevolent dictator who decides What, How, and For Whom by decree. The same decisions can be made by a democratic representative body or by some planning authority established by that body. Finally, in a so-called "capitalist free enterprise economy" a system of prices and markets, or profits and losses, primarily (though not completely) determines What, How, and For Whom.

Scarcity. What to produce, How, and For Whom would not be problems if our resources were unlimited and an infinite amount of every good could be produced, for human wants could then be completely satisfied. It would not matter if too much of any particular good were produced, or if labor and materials were combined unwisely. And since everyone could have as much as he pleased it would not matter how goods were distributed. For under these conditions, all goods would be *free goods* like air; there would be no *economic goods*, i.e., goods that are relatively scarce, or goods that not everyone may have. In this case, the study of economics or "economizing" would not be particularly useful.

But in the world as it is, even little children are supposed to learn that "both" is not an admissible answer to the question "which one?" Compared with the backward or underdeveloped nations, or with previous centuries, the modern industrial society is very wealthy indeed. But higher levels of production have brought in their train higher standards of consumption. In *The Affluent Society,* Harvard's Galbraith has eloquently pointed out that Americans today have for the most part moved beyond the level of physiological necessity in their purchases, and he argues that the time has come to spend more on public needs and less on private needs.[1] Without challenging his thesis, one may properly point out that our total product would have to be many times larger than at present if everyone were to have the opportunity to live at the economic level of the moderately well-off doctor or lawyer, to say nothing of the level of the really well-to-do. Even if the total national income in the United States were divided equally among the members of the society— and it clearly cannot be—there would be only about $50 per week for each person. Economics must contend with scarcity as a basic condition, even in "affluent" America.

THE TECHNOLOGICAL CHOICES OPEN TO SOCIETY

Since our resources are scarce, and total resources are limited and not infinite, we must always choose among relatively scarce commodities; we may have some, but not all, of the things which the economy can produce, and by

[1] John Kenneth Galbraith, *The Affluent Society,* Houghton Mifflin Company, Boston, 1958.

choosing some we forego others. An economy contains only so many people, so much technological knowledge, so many tools and factories, and so much land and resources. The economy must somehow decide just how these resources are to be allocated among thousands of different possibilities. How much land should be used for wheat cultivation? For pasturage? How much skilled labor should go into machine shops? Toy making? Such problems are complicated to discuss, let alone solve, but there are certain general principles that apply to the discussion and we can demonstrate these principles most clearly by simplifying our economic system.

Let us assume, then, that there are only two alternative classes of economic goods, and for dramatic purposes, concentrate on the famous economic pair—guns and butter. Society can and must choose between them, and the principles involved in the choice are basic to the study of economics. Obviously, there are two possible extremes. On the one hand, all of our resources may be used to produce butter, which will maximize butter production, the exact output depending upon the quantitative and qualitative resources of the economy and the efficiency of its technology. No guns will be produced. At the other extreme, 100 per cent of the economy's resources may be devoted to gun production, maximizing the output of guns and eliminating butter production. Let us say that if we devote all our resources to butter production we can produce 5 million pounds of it, whereas we can produce 15,000 guns if all of our resources are directed toward this goal. Of course, there are other possibilities. We may give up *some* butter and produce a few guns, and should we find a need for more, produce more guns by giving up more butter. These possibilities are summarized in Table 1. As we give up butter to obtain more guns, we "transform" butter into guns. The transformation is not physical, naturally, but by diverting resources from one use to the other we in fact obtain guns by using resources that could also be used to produce butter.

With full employment of scarce resources, society must choose between guns or butter:

Possibilities	Guns, thousands	Butter, millions of pounds
A	15	0
B	14	1
C	12	2
D	9	3
E	5	4
F	0	5

Table 1. Alternative possibilities in the production of butter and guns. Economic resources can be shifted from butter production to gun production, in effect enabling us to transform butter into guns.

The production-possibility curve. The economist finds it very useful to reduce the information in Table 1 to a graph or curve of the type shown in Figure 1. Each of the alternate possibilities shown in Table 1 is plotted as a point on the grid (A, B, C, D, E, F) and the points are connected by a smooth curve. The result is called the *production-possibility* or *transformation* curve and we shall speak of it often in the pages that follow. The curve shows us the range of choice that lies before us. Further, it has some extremely important properties, depending upon its shape and position on the graph.

In a full-employment economy, society must always give up one good to produce another; it must choose among alternate possibilities. This assumes, of course, that at least some resources can be transferred from the production of one good to production of another, e.g., that steel can be used to produce either guns or butter (as farm machinery, for example).

The production-possibility curve shown in Figure 1 has been drawn at the full-employment level. But what if there had been widespread unemployment of resources, idle men and land and factories? In that case, our economic law might be quite different. For with unemployment, the economy is not operating at full blast; instead, it is working somewhere *inside* the production-possibility curve (toward the zero or lower left-hand corner of the grid), perhaps at the point marked U. By putting idle resources to work, we may then obtain more butter *and* more guns. We can move the production-possibility curve outward from U to a *higher* level. Thus the position of the curve is directly affected by the level of employment within the economy.

However, the location of the production-possibility curve on the grid

We can picture production possibilities by drawing a smooth curve:

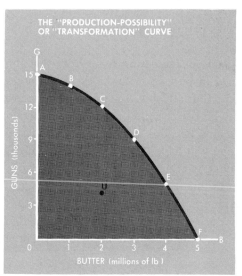

Fig. 1. This shows how society can choose to substitute guns for butter, assuming a given state of technology and a given total of resources. At any point inside the curve, such as *U*, resources are not being fully employed in the best known way.

will also depend upon two other factors: (1) the fixed total of the economy's resources, and (2) the technological level of society. We can see why this is true if we ask ourselves two questions. First, what will happen to the production-possibility curve if the labor force (population) increases? Second, what follows if scientists and engineers discover better (more efficient) ways of producing goods? Clearly, the result in both cases is to shift the curve outward to a higher level, to make it possible to have more guns *and* more butter.

Increasing costs. We have learned from our production-possibility curve, then, that the choice of economic goods requires substitution, the sacrifice of one good for another. That is the reason why the curve slopes downward from left to right, for we obtain more of the goods measured along the horizontal axis at the price of fewer goods measured on the vertical axis.

We can learn still another basic economic principle by examining the production-possibility curve. Notice that the curve is "bowed out" from the zero point—it looks convex from above. This shows that the rate at which we transform goods is not equal; we must trade more of one good to obtain another as we increase our production of the second good. The principle is:

As we demand more of one good (butter) we must usually pay a higher cost for it in terms of the good sacrificed (guns); i.e., we must give up extra amounts of other goods for each extra unit of the goods we want.

The figures in Table 1 show the principle quite clearly. If we are producing guns alone and wish to produce butter, we can obtain *one* unit of butter by sacrificing *one* unit of guns. But if we want to produce *two* units of butter, we must sacrifice *three* units of guns. The second unit of butter costs us twice as much as the first. Each extra unit of butter will demand an extra sacrifice of guns. The same condition holds if we reverse the process, for the production-possibility curve is symmetrical; it follows precisely the same pattern in both directions.

What is the common sense of this law of increasing cost? Note that the first few guns we make can be produced in part with the kinds of resources that are not very useful in butter production anyhow. But if more guns are wanted, we must use resources that may be better suited to butter production than to gun production; hence our economy becomes less efficient. And if we insist on producing nothing but guns, we will have to make use of resources which are quite unsuited to gun production, thus decreasing our efficiency much more. This will certainly lead to an increase in real cost. Only if guns and butter used land, labor, and other factors in exactly the same proportions would the sacrifice of one unit of butter release exactly the resources needed to produce one unit of guns. In this case, the production-possibility curve would be a straight line (try it and see).

The law of diminishing returns. The fact that we obtain more of one good only at an increasing cost in terms of another is somewhat related to a much more famous technological economic relationship—the "law of diminishing returns." This law deals with the relationship between inputs of economic factors (such as labor) and the resulting output of goods (such as corn) when the other production factors are held constant. More specifically, it refers to the *extra output* we get when we add *extra inputs* of some production factors to a *fixed amount of some other input.*

As an example, suppose that we combine two inputs, land and labor, to produce corn. Let us maintain the land input at a constant level of 100 acres, and vary the labor input by adding extra units of labor to the land. To determine the result, we must conduct an experiment and learn the actual output of corn obtained from extra inputs of labor. The results of a hypothetical experiment are shown in Table 2. Obviously, there is no return in corn when no labor units are added to the land. When we add one unit of labor to the land, we obtain a return of 2,000 bushels of corn. But when we add an *extra* unit of labor, it produces only 1,000 extra bushels of corn, and another extra unit of labor produces still less extra corn. In practice, the law of diminishing returns may not appear quite so quickly, and we may have to add several units of labor to our fixed amount of land before extra production per unit of labor diminishes.

It is very important to note that the law of diminishing returns applies only when some inputs are *fixed,* while others are varied. For if all inputs are varied (more land *and* more labor) we have an entirely different situation—we "increase the scale of operations." In many industrial processes, when *all* of the inputs are doubled, output is *more than doubled,* because of the so-called "economies of mass production." If production is large enough to make it worthwhile to set up a fairly elaborate productive organization, then the use

Diminishing returns is a fundamental law of economics and technology:

Man-years of labor	Total product, bushels	Extra output added by additional unit of labor	
0	0		Table 2. Returns of corn when units of labor are added to fixed land. Law of diminishing returns refers to successively lower *extra* outputs gained from adding equal doses of a variable input to a constant amount of fixed input.
1	2,000	2,000	
2	3,000	1,000	
3	3,500	500	
4	3,800	300	
5	3,900	100	

of automatic machinery, standardization of parts, and elaborate specialization of function (as in the automobile production line, for example) may lead to great increases in output.

When some of the inputs are *fixed*, however, this does not occur. For with some inputs fixed, an increase in other inputs means that we change the ratio of one input to the other (5 workers on a 100-acre plot have 20 acres apiece to work; when 100 workers are employed on the plot the ratio is reduced to a single acre of land per man and production *per man* will probably decrease). When the ratio becomes too small, inefficiency will probably follow. To summarize, then, the law of diminishing returns states that:

An increase in some inputs relative to other fixed inputs will cause total output to increase, but after a point is reached the extra output resulting from the addition of the same amounts of extra inputs is likely to become less and less.

Population and economics. We have already met some of the principles of demography and current population trends in our study of sociology. Here, we are interested in a slightly different perspective. You will recall that Malthus argued that there was a tendency for the population to grow geometrically (1, 2, 4, 8, 16, 32, 64, 128) while the food supply increased arithmetically (1, 2, 3, 4, 5, 6). It is true that Malthus did not anticipate the miracles of the Industrial Revolution, for in the next century technical innovation shifted the production-possibility curve outward very rapidly and made possible a higher living standard for everyone even though medical advances were actually reducing natural checks on population growth. More important still, Malthus failed to anticipate that after 1870, in most Western nations at least, family *fertility* (actual number of children born) would begin to fall short of family *fecundity* (biological capacity to reproduce). Nevertheless, the germs of truth in his doctrine are still important for understanding population behavior in areas such as China and India and in other areas where the balance between food supply and numbers is vital.

Do America and Europe face depopulation? In the 1920s men still feared the overpopulation of the Western world that Malthus had predicted, and they wrote books with such alarming titles as *The World Faces Overpopulation* and *Standing Room Only!* But as these books were coming off the press, population trends in Western Europe and the United States began to change. A generation later, a new problem had arisen, and the books produced then were entitled *The Twilight of Parenthood* and *England without People.* How can we account for the sudden change of tune? The records show that the birth rate did not fall below the death rate in the Western nations. Yet a closer investigation revealed that a "real" drop in birth rate had occurred but that it had been masked by the unusually large percentage of the female population in the childbearing age range. The number of children per female parent had declined precipitously.

The net reproduction rate. The facts were revealed by an ingenious technique for investigating population trends which moved away from the study of total births and total deaths, and asked instead: What is the total number of daughters born to 1,000 newborn girl babies by the time they have completed their life span? If 1,000 women give birth to 1,000 female children during their life span, then the net reproduction rate (NRR) is 1.0 and the population will remain steady in the long run. But if only 900 girl babies are born to 1,000 women, the NRR is 0.9 and the population will ultimately decrease at the rate of 10 per cent per generation (about 25 years). If 1,000 women leave behind 2,000 daughters, on the other hand, the NRR is 2.0 and the population will double every generation.

Some recent trends. Before World War II, there was good reason for the population expert to despair for the future of the population of the Western nations. The rich produced fewer children than the poor, and students of Harvard and Vassar, Oberlin and Michigan State University, among others, were not reproducing themselves. Yet the trend changed suddenly, for reasons which the experts cannot yet explain. During and after World War II, the fertility rate began to climb, and now each year brings a crop of about 4 million babies.

Some of the reasons for the change are obvious. War brought prosperity and an increase in the marriage rate. More important still, there was a sharp increase in the rate at which married couples had children. Wartime savings reduced the shock of parentage, and new medical developments lessened fear of childbirth. Government encouragement, including "family allowances," also contributed to the trend. Further, man is an imitative animal, and it became fashionable for the middle class to have numerous children. The end result, as can be seen from Table 3, is that the United States has come to have a net reproductive rate that is one of the highest in the world or in recent history. Will the trend continue? This nobody knows. It depends upon whether the number of *unmarried* adults remains at its present low level and whether the typical married couple thinks that a boy and girl are enough or aspires toward a large family. So far, the odds favor larger families in the future.

The economic impact of population growth is already very noticeable. Our suburbs teem with children, and our schools are overcrowded. The bulge of war births has also hit our colleges; by 1975, we expect college enrollment to be double that of 1960! Ice cream and piano sales similarly reflect the increasing number of young persons in our society. There has been an enormous

Net reproduction rates make correction for changing age distribution:

Table 3. Net reproduction rates for various countries. An NRR (net reproduction rate) permanently greater than 1 means ultimate population growth. An NRR less than 1 means ultimate population decline. The NRR for the United States is now substantially above 1. (Source: *Population Index*, April, 1963, Office of Population Research, Princeton, N.J.)

United States	*Total*	0.98	(1930–40)	Belgium	0.86	(1939)
		1.72	(1960)		1.13	(1960)
	White	0.96	(1935–40)	Netherlands	1.15	(1935–40)
		1.66	(1960)		1.46	(1960)
	Nonwhite	1.14	(1935–40)	Australia	0.96	(1932–34)
		2.09	(1960)		1.61	(1960)
United Kingdom		0.77	(1931–35)	Palestine *Moslems*	2.17	(1940)
		1.25	(1960)	*Jews*	1.61	(1945)
France		0.90	(1931–35)	Israel *Jews*	1.62	(1960)
		1.28	(1960)	Japan	1.57	(1930)
Sweden		0.73	(1933–35)		0.92	(1960)
		1.02	(1960)	India	1.25	(1931)
Germany	*Total*	0.70	(1933)		1.31	(1941)
	West	1.11	(1960)	Soviet Union	1.72	(1926)
					1.54	(1938)

increase in the number of persons under twenty years of age and over sixty-five years of age. Those of working age, caught between increased numbers of dependent old and dependent young, will have to support more nonworkers. Is our population upsurge a good thing? Economics alone cannot answer such a general question. The joys and aches of family life are not to be measured in mere dollars and cents. Because the growing population makes for high money spending, it may act against unemployment, though it could also aggravate inflationary trends. On the other hand, a much higher *level* of population threatens us with the law of diminishing returns. It fills our countryside with people and fills our roads with cars; it spoils the countryside and invades our privacy. Economic analysis must weigh so complex a matter as population change carefully before it can provide the citizen and statesman with the knowledge needed for understanding the problems such a change brings.

FUNCTIONING OF A MIXED CAPITALISTIC ENTERPRISE SYSTEM

Our attention will be devoted primarily to the special features of economic life in the twentieth-century industrial nations (with the exception of the Soviet Union). In most of these countries, what is loosely called "free private enterprise" or "competitive capitalism" has developed steadily in the past few centuries. However, long before this trend reached full *laissez faire,* the tide began to run the other way. Since the late nineteenth century the economic functions of government have increased steadily in almost every capitalistic country. The resulting economic system, which we refer to as a "mixed" free enterprise system, contains both public and private institutions for conducting and regulating economic activity.

Solving the basic economic problems. In a system of free private enterprise, no individual or organization is consciously concerned with our triad of economic problems—What, How, and For Whom. This is really remark-able. Without a constant flow of goods in and out of our large cities, they would be on the verge of starvation in a matter of days, yet the millions of people who live in the cities show no fear of a breakdown of the elaborate economic process upon which city life depends. No central organization ensures the city's needs or directs economic operations. This alone is convincing proof that a competitive system of markets and prices, whatever else it may be, is not chaotic. There is a certain order and orderliness. It works. A competitive system is an elaborate social mechanism which uses a system of markets and prices for coordinating the activities of millions of diverse individuals. Without a central intelligence, it solves one of the most complex problems imaginable. Nobody designed it; it evolved. Its character changes continually. The functioning of the market produces one of the real "miracles" of social organization every day of our lives, and does it so smoothly that we are hardly aware of the job being done.

If students of economics must avoid the error of supposing that the price mechanism will lead to chaos if it is not controlled, they must also avoid the error of becoming so enamored with the beauty of the pricing mechanism that they regard it as perfect, an illustration of providential harmony and beyond the touch of human hands. Adam Smith, for example, was thrilled beyond measure by the recognition of order in the economic system and was led to proclaim the principle of the "Invisible Hand" directing its operation, and the corollary that any interference with the system was almost certain to be injurious. While Smith realized some of the practical limitations on this doc-trine, some of his followers were less prescient. Economists now realize that the virtues claimed for free enterprise are fully realized only when the com-plete checks and balances of "perfect competition" are present.

Perfect competition is a technical term denoting the case where no farmer, businessman, or laborer has any personal influence on market price, when no economic agent is large enough to depress or elevate market prices. Perfect competition, defined in this way, certainly does not exist today, and historians quarrel over the question whether or not it ever existed. We do not even know whether competition is becoming more or less intense, though the statistics available suggest a slight weakening of monopolistic concentration of power. In any case, the challenge is to work out our laws and customs so as to improve the operation of our less-than-perfect competitive system. The polar cases of *laissez faire* and totalitarian dictatorship may dramatize economic principles, but the relevant choice today is not a decision between these extremes. Rather it is a choice of the degree to which public policy should do more or less to modify the operation of particular private economic activities.

The price system. In a competitive profit-and-loss system, *everything has a price.* Human labor, consumer goods, land, capital, and services are bought and sold on the open market. The general principle on which the system operates is easily described. An increase in demand for a particular good or service (a flood of new orders) will cause a rise in price, and the higher price will tempt the producer into increasing his output. Conversely, a decrease in demand for goods (fewer orders) will lower prices, causing producers to reduce their output. However, as prices rise, there is a tendency for consumption to drop off, and as prices fall, consumption tends to rise. The result of this interplay of forces is an equilibrium system of prices and production, a vast system of trial and error which tends to balance out the supply of goods and the demand for goods. The operation of this price system helps solve our three basic economic problems simultaneously.

1. *What* is produced is determined by the votes of the consumer, by his decision to purchase or not to purchase particular goods. The price paid by the consumer ultimately provides the payrolls, rents, and dividends of the producers, and these in turn make up the consumer's income. The system is closed and complete.

2. *How* things are produced is determined by competition for sales among the various producers. The method that is cheapest at any one time will displace more costly methods.

3. *For Whom* is determined by supply and demand in the market—by wage rates, land rents, interest, and profits—for this determines everyone's income. Of course, the character of the resulting distribution of income is highly dependent upon the initial distribution of property ownership and on acquired or inherited abilities.

In Figure 2, we have a bird's-eye view of the way market pricing reconciles public demand and supply with business demand and supply. Note that the connecting device between business and the public is the market. Twenty minutes of poring over this diagram may be worth hours of disconnected musing about economic pricing.

This picture of a competitive market system is highly oversimplified, and it does not work perfectly. Even if it did, many would not consider it ideal.

The competitive price system uses supply-demand markets to solve the basic economic problems—What, How, and For Whom:

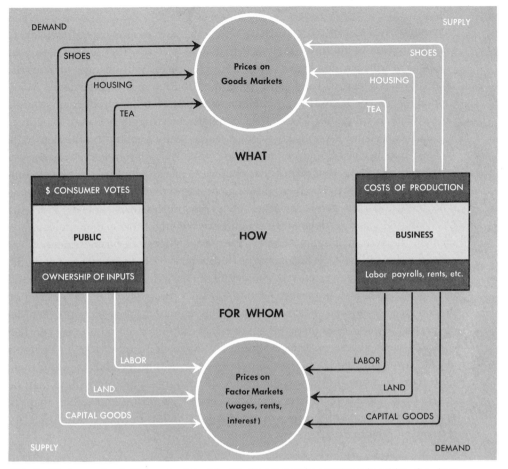

Fig. 2. All demand relations are shown in black; all supply relations in white. See how consumer dollar votes of demand interact in the upper goods markets with business-cost supply decisions, thus helping determine What is produced. And how business demand for inputs or productive factors meets the public's supply of labor and other inputs in factor markets to help determine wage, rent, and interest income—or For Whom goods are produced. Business competition to buy factor inputs and sell goods most cheaply determines How goods are to be produced. (**Warning:** All parts of the diagram interact together. **What** depends on the lower part, just as **For Whom** depends on the upper part—carpenter wages depend on housing demand, and demand for yachts depends on oil-land royalties.)

In the first place, goods go where there are the most dollars—the greatest demand. A rich man's dog may receive milk that a poor child needs to avoid rickets. New machinery may reduce the income of the poor and raise the income of the wealthy. Inherited property may lead to vast inequalities in income. Such problems go beyond the mechanics of economic study into the field of ethics and politics, and they cannot be solved in economic terms.

Imperfections of competition. As we said earlier, one drawback to our description of the price system is that in fact competition is nowhere near "perfect." Firms do not know when consumer tastes will change, and by the time they have learned from experience, the situation may change again. Many producers do not know the production methods of other producers, so costs do not fall to minimum levels. In a competitive struggle one can sometimes succeed as well by keeping knowledge scarce as by keeping production high.

A more serious imperfection in the competitive system is the existence of *monopoly elements*. Remember that the economist's definition of perfect competition is very strict. The mere presence of a few rivals is not enough. Anyone who buys and sells goods in large enough quantities to be able to affect the price of that good is defined as an imperfect competitor, a monopolistic element in the system. To some degree, this means almost all businessmen, except possibly the millions of farmers who individually produce only a negligible fraction of the total crop. All economic life is a blend of competitive and monopoly elements; imperfect (monopolistic) competition is the prevailing mode. This is simply a fact, not a moral condemnation. A good approximation of perfect competition may be all we can hope for. Furthermore, perfect competition is not necessarily desirable for everyone. Trademarks and patents are often responsible for market imperfections, yet most persons consider them quite fair. In some industries, the economies of large-scale production may be lost if there are large numbers of producers. It would be impossible, then, to create perfect competition by legislation, and it might be very costly to society if we attempted to do so.

The economic role of government. Ours is a mixed capitalistic system, in which elements of government control are intermingled with private production and consumption and a market system. As we have seen, democratic countries are not satisfied today with the consequences of an unrestrained market system. Therefore government steps in with its own expenditure to supplement the incomes of some individuals (by providing hospital beds or monthly allowances for the needy or in other ways ensuring minimum standards of life for all of its citizens).

More than this, government provides certain indispensable public services without which community life would be unthinkable and which by their nature cannot appropriately be left to private enterprises. Obvious examples are the maintenance of national defense, internal law and order, and the administration of justice. By and large, government influences the market system in the same way as any other purchaser; by bidding for certain goods it causes resources to flow into their production. The price system continues to work as if these were individual rather than collective needs.

If governments financed their expenditures by printing money or by endless borrowing, that would be almost the whole story. Actually, most government expenditure is paid for by taxes, and this introduces an important element of *coercion* into the system. For taxes must be paid, and the relative burden of taxes on the individual taxpayer is determined by the government. This has a number of significant economic consequences.

Finally, government provides the framework in which private enterprise functions, and modifies the direction of that functioning. Universal political laws regulate many aspects of economic behavior, and there are far more than the Ten Commandments found in the Bible: thou shalt not sell false weights; thou shalt not sell opium; thou may not employ children in thy factories; thou shalt not charge more than the ceiling price for food; thou shalt not pay wages below the minimum set by law; and so on almost ad infinitum. All of these factors need to be taken into account when we come to a more detailed examination of the operation of the market system.

Capital, division of labor, and money. There are three further important features of modern economic society: (1) the use of vast amounts of capital, in the form of elaborate machinery, large factories, and immense stores of unfinished and partly finished materials; (2) an incredibly elaborate degree of specialization and an intricate division of labor; and (3) the extensive use of money, which is the lifeblood of the system and the measuring rod of economic values. All of these features are interrelated with each other and with the price mechanism.

Capital and time. It is obvious that economic production can result from the combination of land and labor, or labor and natural resources generally. Since neither land nor labor result from economic process, but exist by virtue of physical and biological factors, they are often called the primary factors of production. Capital, which is also a production factor, is different in that it is an output of the economy; it has been produced by the economic system. Capital can, of course, also be regarded as an input to be used for further production.

When we combine land and labor to produce goods, we are employing a simple and direct method of production, taking production factors as they appear in nature. A striking feature of capitalistic production is the extent to which it is roundabout and not direct. Capital is itself a product of the economic system, and it be produced only if we are willing to *forego present consumption of goods.* The caveman who combines his labor with the natural resources of the forest can produce food directly. If, however, he is willing to forego food production (and he has the technology or know-how) he can use his labor to produce an ax or club (a bit of capital). The capital can then be employed to produce food. Obviously, this is only worthwhile if the caveman can produce more food with the use of capital than with his bare hands. Further, he must be able to survive during the period of time it takes to produce the club; he must have a backlog of food to meet his immediate needs. This offers us a useful clue to the difficulty encountered in capital formation in the underdeveloped countries, where a large portion of present production must be used to maintain the life of the population and there is little left for the production of capital goods. Time, in other words, is needed to get the process going in the first place. Modern economic activity is "future-oriented," and an outside observer is struck by the fact that no one seems to be producing finished goods. Production is based largely on indirect methods which consume more time but effect great efficiencies in total production. Each person in the system performs his own job, without concern for the total production process, once the circular paths are all established.

To the extent that people are willing to save—to abstain from consumption in the present and await the future—society can devote its resources to capital formation. To the extent that people "dissave"—snatch present pleasures at the expense of the future—resources are taken away from the endless task of maintaining and replacing capital and used to produce extra goods in the present. In progressive societies, some fraction of current production is devoted to new or *net capital formation*, thereby sacrificing some current consumption to increase production in the future.

Specialization, exchange, and division of labor. The economies of mass production simply would not be possible if production still took place in self-sufficient farm households or provinces. *Specialization* makes it possible for each person or region to use its peculiar skills or resources to best advantage. Even in a primitive economy men learn that it is better to allocate particular kinds of work to particular persons—to institute a *division of labor*—and exchange individual production for other needed goods. Specialization may depend upon existing resources, or it may create new resources (like special skills) which are advantageous. Even where there are no natural or acquired differences in ability, specialization will sometimes pay. Identical Indian twins might find it better for one to make all of the bows while the other made arrows, because in this way each could make enough of one item to warrant the use of new tools and techniques. As Adam Smith pointed out, a single man can make only a few imperfect pins in the course of a day, while a small group of men each performing simple repetitive operations can produce hundreds of thousands of perfect pins in the same time. Specialization increases production, for it lends itself to mechanization and the use of labor-saving capital, while it avoids duplication of tools and time loss in production.

Clearly, specialization and division of labor demand interdependence; they make it impossible for the individual workman to consume his own product and thereby survive; each man must depend upon many others for his total needs. In modern economic society, this process is carried to the nth degree, and no man makes the smallest fraction of the commodities he consumes. This makes possible enormous gains in total production, but it also involves hidden "social costs" like worker boredom and loss of pride in the final product or loss of the feeling of individuality.

Barter versus money. Without the use of money, our present division of labor and exchange would be quite impossible. To be sure, we can imagine the use of *barter*—direct exchange of one good for another—and when we peel away the obscuring layer of money, we find that trade between individuals or nations boils down largely to barter. But if barter is a great improvement over conditions in which each man must produce everything he needs for survival, money is even a further improvement, for it is money that permits the degree of specialization and division of labor we have currently reached.

In only the most primitive cultures do men directly exchange one good for another. Instead, they sell one good for money and use the money to buy other goods. This may seem to complicate matters, replacing a single transaction with two transactions, but in practice, the two transactions are usually simpler than a straight barter arrangement. It would be a very unusual coincidence to find a person who desires exactly what another wishes to trade, and has available precisely what the second person is willing to accept. Hence money does simplify economic life. But do not forget that a mere increase in the total money supply does not permit people to consume more than the real products which the economy has made available.

Commodity money, paper money, and bank money. Money has two basic functions: (1) as a *medium of exchange* and (2) as a *standard unit of value* or account. It is also a means of storing wealth. The distinction between these uses is illustrated in a perfect clearing system, where a careful record of all transactions is kept and where what each person has coming to him is ultimately canceled by what he owes. In such a system, no medium of exchange is needed. But a common denominator of value, which allows us to compare and evaluate diverse items, such as chewing gum and automobiles, is needed.

Historically, a wide variety of materials have been used as money, including cattle, leather and furs, olive oil, wampum beads, and wives. Each has its own advantages and disadvantages. Cattle are not readily divisible into small change, but while such "money" is being hoarded it is likely to increase by reproduction, giving the lie to Aristotle's assertion that "money is barren." Beer does not improve with keeping, though wine may; iron rusts, and is of so little value that one would need a cart for a pocketbook. All of these illustrations are *commodity money,* and they are interesting inasmuch as they may be valued for themselves (food or decoration, for example) as well as for their exchange use.

The essence of money, its intrinsic nature, is typified by *paper money,* for it is wanted for what it will buy and not for its own sake. Money is an artificial or social convention, and if a substance is used as money, all people tend to value it whether or not it has intrinsic usefulness for them. As long as things can be bought or sold for a given substance, people will be content to buy and sell with it. This creates something of a paradox; money is accepted because it is accepted.

The use of paper currency has become widespread because of its great convenience. Currency is easily carried or stored. It can be made as divisible as we wish. Careful engraving can protect against counterfeiting or adulteration. And the fact that private individuals cannot create it at will keeps it scarce; i.e., it is an economic rather than a free good. Given this limitation in supply, modern currencies have value. The public neither knows nor cares whether its currency is in the form of "silver certificates," Federal Reserve notes, or coin. So long as each form of money can be converted into any other at fixed terms, the best is as good as the worst.

Finally, our own age has witnessed an enormous expansion in the amount of *bank money* employed in the economy. Today, at least nine-tenths of all transactions, by value if not by number, take place by check. Salaries may be paid directly into a bank account, rent and other bills paid by check, and many expenses "charged" and paid later, also by check. Except for petty cash for lunches or carfare, modern man may handle very little cash in the course of a year.

The basic functions of money—as a medium of exchange and as a standard unit of account—both involve the passage of time. There is always an interval between receiving and spending money, though this interval is usually small, for it is economically unwise to hold substantial amounts of money idle. Money serves, then, as a *store of value,* a way of holding personal wealth on tap. When prices are unstable or extreme inflation is in progress, money may serve very badly as a store of value, for its real purchasing power may decline drastically and abruptly.

THE FORMS OF BUSINESS ORGANIZATION

To understand our business civilization, we must first understand the organization and functioning of business enterprise. This may take various forms, but the most important form of business organization is certainly the modern corporation, particularly the giants who deal in large-scale production.

In 1964, there were over five million business units in America. All but a tiny fraction of these enterprises were small-scale units owned by a single person. Most small businesses are here today and gone tomorrow; the average life expectancy of a business is only six years. Some end in bankruptcy, others die quietly, and some end when the proprietor takes a regular job and leaves business. Though businesses die rapidly, others spring up to take their place, and the total number has grown steadily in the past.

By number, the tiny and transient "individual proprietorship" is the dominant form of American business. But in terms of value, political and economic power, payrolls, employment, and production, a few hundred giant corporations occupy a strategic position in the economy. Small businesses are small in capital, workers, and in profits, usually. Their owners work long hours, trying to stretch a small capital investment into a decent income. Owning a small business is a perilous occupation, generally, but there are always people who want to start out on their own, and if they succeed only to the extent of providing their own living, there is something attractive about being able to make their own plans and carry on the variety of tasks associated with small enterprise.

The three principal forms of business organization are the single proprietorship, the partnership, and the corporation. Each has its own uses and limitations, and these are best demonstrated by following the history of a small business as it grows from a single proprietorship into a corporation. The special problems of the very large corporation will be considered later.

The single proprietorship. Let us suppose that you decide to start a business to produce toothpaste. You obtain a formula for the preparation and begin making the toothpaste. As simply as that, you become a single proprietor. You may hire or fire, buy and sell, and dispose of the profits (if any) as you see fit. The losses of the business are yours, too, and if your business cannot cover your obligations, your personal assets are liable to be placed on the block to satisfy your creditors. This is one of the principal disadvantages of the single proprietorship; the liability of the owner is unlimited and his personal property may be attached by the courts to pay his debts if the business fails. It is also difficult for the single proprietor to borrow enough funds to expand his business very rapidly, and this serves as a check on growth. If your toothpaste business is growing, and you desperately need capital to increase your production, chances are that you will have to look around for a partner to invest in your firm.

The partnership. Suppose again that your brother-in-law is willing to invest $25,000 in the business in return for a share in the profits and a regular job with the firm. All that is needed to form a partnership is an oral agreement, though it is wiser to have a written agreement because it avoids misunderstandings later. Each partner is personally liable for the debts of the business, and each is entitled to a share in the profits of the firm. Profits are taxed by the government as personal income, just as the profits of a single proprietorship are counted as personal income. Usually, each partner has an equal voice in the management of the firm.

Let us say that your business continues to grow, and you find yourself once again in need of additional funds. One possibility is to admit new partners into the enterprise, for there is no limit to the number of partners you can have. However, every time a new partner enters the business, or another dies or resigns, a whole new partnership must be formed. Further, the law of partnerships makes it impossible for any partner to sell his share to another party without the consent of the partners, and if agreement cannot be secured, a costly liquidation of assets may be inevitable. In addition, each new partner has a voice in management, and the result of adding partners is a dilution of control over the business.

These disadvantages of the partnership form are serious enough, but there is another even greater problem: each partner is liable without limit to the full extent of his personal fortune for all debts contracted by the partnership. The partner who owns only 1 per cent of the firm is presumably liable to 1 per cent of the bills if the business fails. But if the other partners cannot pay their share, he may be called upon to pay *all* of the firm's liabilities even though it means selling his home and other assets. This unlimited liability feature shows us why partnerships are usually confined to small, personal enterprises. Each partner has broad powers to act as an agent for the whole partnership, and placing one's personal fortune in the hands of another partner over whom you do not have control is not an attractive business risk.

The modern corporation. At some point, then, you will probably decide to form a corporation rather than a partnership. Usually, you will incorporate in the state in which you live or do business, though if your firm is large enough, it may be worthwhile to establish token headquarters in one of the states, such as New Jersey or Delaware, which have rules that are meant to attract corporations. In any case, a lawyer will prepare the necessary papers for a small fee, including in the charter almost any powers you wish, and the state will automatically grant the charter. You have then formed a corporation. Since this is far and away the most important form of business enterprise today, we shall examine the procedure a little more closely.

Incoporation. Suppose you decide to issue 20,000 shares of common stock in your toothpaste company: 6,600 shares go to you, 3,300 to your partner, 100 to your wife, and the remaining 10,000 are to be sold to outside interests.

Although each share is to have an initial stated value of $10, your lawyer advises to make them "no-par" shares, since "par value" has no particular significance anyway.

The 10,000 shares are to be marketed through one of the local *investment banking* firms. These firms are simply security merchandisers, and they earn profits by selling securities at higher prices than the price they pay for them. Since you own a small business, the investment banking firm may drive a hard bargain and offer you only $10 per share, though it plans to sell the shares at $12.50. Had you been a large company, you might have held out for as much as $12.25 or even $12.40 per share because of eager competitive bidding by the different investment banking syndicates. Further, the investment banker might *underwrite,* or purchase outright, all of the shares issued, and if they could not be sold, he would absorb the loss. But since you are small and a risky undertaking, he takes your issue on a "best effort" basis. If he cannot sell all the shares, you end up with less capital than you planned.

Fortunately, all goes well and the investment banker pays you $100,000 in cash for your securities. Unlike in the partnership, you need not concern yourself with the people to whom the shares have been sold, or with the fact that they may be resold. The names of the owners are registered with the company just for the record and so that you will know where to send dividend checks or announcements of stockholders' meetings. Ordinarily, the owner of each share of stock has one vote in corporation affairs and is entitled to share in corporate earnings in direct proportion to the number of shares he owns. Has the buyer any guarantees of performance? Actually, the answer is no! *Caveat emptor*—let the buyer beware—is still the rule. The Securities and Exchange Commission (SEC) examines all sizable new issues to make certain there are no misleading claims before it permits the issue to be "floated," but the SEC does not pass judgment on or certify the value of the stock.

Advantages and disadvantages of the corporate form. The corporation solves most of the problems that plague the partnership. It is a nearly perfect device for raising large sums of capital. First, every stockholder's liability is *limited;* he can lose as much as he has invested in stock and no more; no personal liability is involved in stock purchases. Further, the stock owner can buy or sell shares without permission. Even if he dies, the corporation is not affected. That is, the corporation is a legal "person"; it can sue and be sued, and it is perpetual, in the sense that the corporation continues despite changes in stock ownership. Since a corporation operates on the principle of majority rule, business decisions are easily made. Finally, no group of shareholders can force any other group to sell or retain their stock holdings. The corporation is really a very useful and flexible organizational tool.

The most serious disadvantage of the corporate form is that the Federal government taxes corporate income separately. Thus most corporations pay a tax of 48 cents on each extra dollar of income, and this is in addition to the personal income tax that stockholders must pay on distributed corporate earnings. Of course, the corporate tax rate is lower than the rate for personal income, and corporate profits which are not distributed, which are "plowed back" into the corporation, are not subject to personal income tax. In a sense, this only puts off the day of reckoning, for the dividends received later will be subject to personal income tax; in some cases, however, the delay in tax payment may be a genuine advantage. Further, corporation executives may avoid the perils of double taxation by voting themselves high salaries, padding expense accounts, and employing their relatives in various capacities. The Treasury Department tries to check on such techniques for avoiding taxation, but it is always hard to know whether a given second cousin is or is not worth $15,000 per year, or whether a trip to a Bermuda convention is truly a business rather than a personal expense.

Raising corporate capital. Let us suppose that your corporation continues to grow as a result of new products, economies of mass production, advertising, horizontal combination (buying out competitors, for example), or vertical combination (buying out suppliers or wholesalers). Besides borrowing on promissory notes or mortgages or buying on credit, what new forms of financing are now available to you as a corporation?

Bonds. First, you may issue bonds. These are nothing but special kinds of promissory notes, nicely printed on gilt paper, issued in denominations of $1,000 or some even amount. A bond is a security, a promise to pay a certain number of dollars every six months for a stated number of years until the bond matures. At that time (maturity) the borrowing company promises to pay off the principal of the bond at its face value. The dollar installments paid each six months are the interest earnings, usually called "coupon" payments because the owner clips off a small part of the bond each six months and mails it in to receive his interest payment. Ordinarily, payments of interest and principal must be made on time, whether or not the company has been earning; otherwise the company is in default and can be taken to court like any other debtor. Since the company must be well enough known to interest the lender, this means of raising capital is usually limited to large corporations, though there is no particular reason why partnerships and sole proprietorships may not issue bonds.

Common stocks. Common stock entitles the owner to a share in the profits and in the control of business decisions, but he must also share losses; hence common stocks are more risky to own than bonds. Stockholders do not receive dividends until all fixed charges have been paid by the corporation. The bondholder gets a nominally lower but steadier income.

Preferred stocks. Intermediate between bonds and common stocks are the so-called "preferred stocks." They pay *at most* a stated dividend no matter how profitable the business may be. However, the holder of preferred stock is more likely to get a dividend than the holder of common stock, for he stands next in line after the bondholder. The common stockholder gets no dividends until the full dividend on preferred stock has been paid. Sometimes preferred stock is "cumulative." This means that if the company pays no dividends for, say, five years, when good times return the "cumulated" interest on preferred stock (interest for the past five years) must be paid before dividends are available for the common stockholder.

Advantages of different securities. From the standpoint of the investor, bonds, preferred stocks, and common stocks form a sequence of increasing risk balanced by an increased chance of high earnings or capital gains. Thus a "gilt-edged" bond may yield about 4½ per cent, a "good" preferred stock about 5 per cent. Common stocks, because they may rise in value and give capital gains, now usually have dividends that are lower even than the yield from bonds. The reader should make sure that he understands why common stocks tend to be a better investment than bonds or preferred stocks during an inflationary period, for this will test his understanding of the three forms of securities.

Bonds are not, of course, perfectly safe investments. The basic risk in all corporate investment is a possible loss of earning power by the corporation, which will reduce greatly the value of its assets. Sometimes a company will undergo reorganization in which the stockholders are squeezed out entirely.

From the corporation's point of view, bond debt creates a low but inflexible charge on earnings. In bad times, such a debt may be embarrassing. Preferred stock is slightly more flexible but still represents a fixed charge of sorts. Equity capital, obtained from the sale of common stock, is best of all because it creates a less serious obligation in hard times.

The giant corporation. Let us now examine the "high-society" list in the family of corporations, the giant enterprises like United States Steel, General Motors, Standard Oil of New Jersey, or the Chase Manhattan Bank. The tremendous concentration of economic power in giant corporations can be gauged by the following facts: alone they own 40 per cent of the total assets of all nonfinancial corporations, more than 33 per cent of all banking assets, and 85 per cent of all life-insurance assets. The largest 200 corporations hold between a fifth and a fourth of all income-producing national wealth. They employ 1 of every 8 workers. There are 5 corporations that individually handle more money than any of our 50 states.

These giants did not emerge overnight; they have been growing steadily since the turn of the century. Recent economic research suggests that they are not, contrary to popular opinion, gulping up more and more of modern industry. Statistics suggest, rather, that the giants have probably lost a little ground in the past fifty years. We find a few newcomers among the giants and a few dropouts, but taken altogether they are a remarkably stable group.

Ownership and control in the large corporation. Perhaps the most striking feature of the internal workings of the giant corporation is the *diversification of ownership* among thousands and thousands of small stockholders. In 1964, more than 2.2 million different people owned shares of AT&T stock. To be sure, half these people had fewer than ten shares, and no single owner has as much as 1 per cent of the total. Yet it seems that the New York Stock Exchange goal of "people's capitalism" is being achieved, for some 18 million persons own some common stocks, though fewer than 1 in 10 gets any appreciable return from them at present.

In a path-breaking study, Berle and Means pointed out that this wide diversification of stockholding had resulted in a *separation of ownership and control* of giant corporations.[2] Recent studies show that in the typical giant corporation, all of management together holds only about 3 per cent of the outstanding common stock. The largest single minority ownership groups typically hold about 20 per cent of all voting stock. Such a small percentage has been deemed more than enough to maintain "working control."[3]

Amplification of control by the pyramiding of holding companies. The ratio between stock held and stock controlled depends on various factors, such as the amount of nonvoting stock that has been sold. But a ratio of 5 to 1 is common and in many cases the ratio is nearer to 10 to 1. That is, with $100,000, one can hope to control a million-dollar corporation. But what if that corporation is a holding company whose sole function is to control a 10-million-dollar company by owning 10 per cent of that company's stock? And the latter is in turn another holding company controlling a 100-million-dollar corporation? A small amount of money at the apex of an inverted pyramid can be given enormous leverage simply by adding layers to the structure, resulting in an amplification factor of 1,000 to 1 or even more. The Securities and Exchange Commission, under the terms of the Public Utility Holding Company Act of 1935, now limits such systems, and they are gradually dissolving.

A managerial revolution? Who makes corporate decisions? Primarily, major decisions are falling into the hands of a group of *professional managers*. The

[2] A. A. Berle, Jr., and Gardner C. Means, *The Modern Corporation and Private Property*, Commerce Clearing House, Inc., New York, 1932.

[3] See R. A. Gordon, *Business Leadership in the Large Corporation*, The Brookings Institution, Washington, D.C., 1945, chap. II.

oldtime captain of industry, for all his creativeness and ability to calculate risks, had something of the buccaneer in his makeup and an irresponsible "public be damned" attitude. In company after company, the original founders have been replaced by a new type of executive, adept at public relations and personnel work. He is necessarily more the "bureaucrat," often as much interested in preserving the *status quo* as taking risks. Typically the dominant man is president of the corporation, and as he begins to feel his years he may be made chairman of the board of directors where he can act as an elder statesman. The role of the board of directors varies, but on the whole it is not too much to say that it acts as a rubber stamp for decisions already taken by company officers.

The evil of monopoly. In most important American industries, a few large corporations produce the lion's share of the output. In Figure 3, there is a list of large industries showing the degree of concentration in terms of the relative proportion of total industry employment controlled by the four largest corporations, compared with the percentage of total employment of the next four companies.

In the past seventy-five years, there has been great concern over the breakdown of competitive markets under the impact of large-scale enterprise. From an economic viewpoint, it is irrelevant whether high prices are due to mergers of competitors, cooperative pools or "cartel agreements," interlocking directorates, tacit collusion, or "fair-price" legislation. Excessive prices, waste of

Some industries are dominated by a very few sellers:

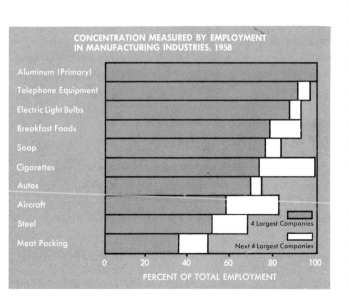

CONCENTRATION MEASURED BY EMPLOYMENT IN MANUFACTURING INDUSTRIES, 1958

Aluminum (Primary)
Telephone Equipment
Electric Light Bulbs
Breakfast Foods
Soap
Cigarettes
Autos
Aircraft
Steel
Meat Packing

4 Largest Companies
Next 4 Largest Companies

0   20   40   60   80   100
PERCENT OF TOTAL EMPLOYMENT

Fig. 3. In aluminum, autos, steel, and many other industries, a few firms get most of the business. This is in contrast to the notion of perfect competition among innumerable small sellers (e.g., farmers), each too small to affect the market price. But MIT's expert, M. A. Adelman, thinks concentration was probably even greater back in 1900. (Source: Federal Trade Commission.)

resources, and monopoly profits are economic evils, however they are brought about. We shall discuss the point at greater length below.

But is bigness itself a bad thing? Undoubtedly there is much popular hostility toward large corporations. Even if they could do so, very large corporations like U.S. Steel would be most reluctant to swallow up competitors because of the effect on public opinion. Yet the problem remains, is public antagonism directed toward bigness, or toward its consequences? What should public policy be toward a "well-behaved" giant corporation, for example?

The so-called "A & P" case provides an illustration of this point. The A & P chain of food stores has long been noted for its low prices, but it was prosecuted by the Department of Justice under the antitrust laws. The Federal courts seemed to say, in the decision, that just growing large as a result of efficiency and low prices was a crime.

Yet when the government wished to produce an atomic weapon, it turned to the du Pont Company and gave it a cost-plus-one-dollar contract; the scientific know-how of the giant corporation is an invaluable national asset. It may well be, moreover, that the giant corporation has been the primary factor responsible for the rise in the standard of living, and not a means of keeping that standard down. This suggests that the problem in the future may be to devise ways of improving the social and economic performance of large corporate aggregates in order to keep the tremendous creative ability of the corporation working toward the public good, rather than try to curtail size in itself.

Summary

In this chapter, we have examined the fundamentals of economic study. We learned that because goods are relatively scarce, society must somehow decide What will be produced, How it will be produced, and For Whom it will be produced, and that there are many ways to do this. Our own mixed capitalistic system depends mainly upon a market and price system to solve these problems.

We learned that society always has a range of choices among various types of goods; this can be summarized in a production-possibility curve, showing the rate at which goods of one type are transformed into another. Such a curve is usually "bowed-out," showing that increased production is usually attended by increasing costs, that we must sacrifice *more* of one good as we demand extra production of another. We also saw that after a point, if we add extra inputs to a fixed input, such as land, the amount of extra product decreases (the law of diminishing returns). However, a third law, the economies of mass production, points out that if all of the inputs are increased, output is sometimes very much increased, thus overpowering the law of diminishing returns, at least for a time.

After a brief look at population problems, we turned to the operation of a mixed capitalistic economy, noting how the working of supply and demand and the price mechanism solved our basic economic problems in a competitive system. Here we found that "dollar votes" by the consumer guided the producer to the right selection of What to produce, but that competition drove him to the cheapest possible production methods, solving the How question. The question For Whom is determined by competitive bidding for production factors, raising or lowering wage rates, land rents, and returns to capital.

A closer look at the system showed that capital goods have the capacity to increase production enormously; hence it may be worthwhile to refrain from current consumption to obtain higher production in the future. These roundabout production systems are slow to start, but produce at a very high level once established. Other features of the system were the private ownership of capital, conditioned, of course, by government laws, and the growth of specialization and division of labor, made possible by the use of money as a medium of exchange. We found that money performs other economic services, acting as a standard unit for measuring value, as a medium of exchange, and as a means of storing value, though the latter use is conditioned by price changes.

Finally, we examined the forms of business organization, showing how enterprises grow, how they acquire capital, and how in most cases the larger organizations turn to the corporation form as an ideal because it facilitates borrowing and reduces the risk element for the investor. The corporation borrows by selling common stocks, preferred stocks, or bonds on the open market; each type of security has its own advantages and disadvantages. We concluded with a brief discussion of the major problems created by the separation of ownership and control in the modern giant corporation and the special social problem created by the concentration of economic power in the hands of a small number of these giants. This problem will be discussed further in Chapter 15 when we examine imperfect competition and antitrust policies.

Review Questions

1. Be able to define and give examples of each of the following concepts:
   a. transformation schedule and transformation curve
   b. production-possibility curve
   c. law of diminishing returns
   d. perfect competition
   e. net capital formation

2. In what ways are bonds, common stocks, and preferred stocks different? Give the advantages and disadvantages of each.

3. Define the three major forms of business organization, giving the advantages and disadvantages of each.

4. Differentiate between free goods and economic goods.

5. Give the three major uses of money.

6. What are the characteristic features of the modern economy?

7. How does the price system solve the three basic economic problems?

8. List some of the major factors that alter the operation of the price system.

9. What is a holding company? What effect does it have on business?

10. What conditions are necessary for capital formation?

For Further Study

1. What would happen to society's production-possibility curve if all of the production factors increased together? What if all of the improvements were valid only in particular kinds of production?

2. What determines the amount of sugar consumed when rationing is in effect?

3. What is the advantage of using bank deposits rather than paper money? Are there disadvantages?

4. How would people's spending habits change if the value of every dollar bill decreased 10 per cent each month?

5. If China cannot borrow from abroad in the years ahead, what must she do to become an efficient industrialized nation?

6. What is the difference between a monopoly element modifying the price system and government intervention in the price mechanism?

7. What is meant by the "managerial revolution" and what are some of its implications?

8. Work out an argument in favor of "bigness" in industry.

9. Imagine that you are starting a new business. List the devices you could actually use to raise money and the type of organizational structure that would best suit your purposes.

CHAPTER *12*

Income

and

Government

One does not have to know anything of the laws of economics to appreciate the importance of income or the growing significance of governmental economic activity. Given a knowledge of a man's income, we can make a rough guess of his political views, his tastes, education, age, and even his life expectancy. Nor is income related only to materialistic activities, for it influences education, travel, cultural activities, reading, and even religious activity like donations to charity. In this chapter, we examine some of the basic characteristics of American income, the range and variations that occur in personal income and level of income. We then continue to an examination of the economic role of government. In the next chapter, these materials are brought together in the vital concept of national income.

INDIVIDUAL AND FAMILY INCOME

In 1964, at the pinnacle of American prosperity, per capita income in the United States was around $2,600 per year, or about $50 per week. An average figure like this has little meaning, for it assumes that all of American income is equally distributed among the population. In real life, income is distributed far from equally, and there is no guarantee that an attempt to divide income equally would not change the total. Recent statistics on the subject are summarized in Table 4.

We can see from the table that it would be a great mistake to think that the poor and the rich are equally distributed around the middle of the income groups. There may always be "room at the top," but only because it is so hard to get there. If we made an income pyramid out of child's blocks, with each layer representing $1,000 of income, the peak would be far higher than the Eiffel Tower, but almost all of us would be within a yard of the ground.

Is family income adequate? A few years ago, social service workers made careful estimates of certain minimum family budgets, classified as follows:

1. Basic subsistence—no movies, practically no meat, no dental care, no newspapers, little new clothing, and so forth

2. Minimum health and decency—occasional movie or recreational expenditure, cheap cuts of meat at intervals, some medical and dental care, and so forth

3. Minimum comfort—adequate diet, occasional vacation and amusement, some tobacco and books, and so forth

The cost of the first budget in 1962 was about $3,000, of the second about $4,100, and of the third about $5,200. If we examine the actual 1962 statistics in Table 4, it appears that about 1 in every 7 of the population did not reach the level of income required for minimum comfort, and 30 per cent of the population earned less than the $5,200 needed for minimum health and decency. Even allowing for the fact that it costs less to live in the country than in town, there is good cause for public concern for the "lower third" of the population.

Trends in inequality among income classes. Roughly half of all Americans fall in the income range $3,500–$8,800; one-fourth lie below $3,500 and an equal number have incomes above $8,800. Of course, this does not mean that each group receives the same percentage of the total income. Actually, the lowest fourth of the population receives one-fourth as much income as the highest fourth; if incomes were absolutely uniformly divided, the lowest fourth would receive exactly one-fourth of the total income.

Scholars have found that there is somewhat less inequality of income

Few families in America reach income level of $15,000:

Table 4. Distribution of incomes of American families and individuals, 1962. Half of these families and individuals are below the median income of $5,800. The average (or arithmetic mean) income that each would get if total income were distributed exactly equally is about $7,100. More families and individuals have incomes around the $4,700 level than around any other income. (Source: U.S. Department of Commerce.)

Income class (1)	Percentage of all families and individuals in this class (2)	Percentage of total income received by families and individuals in this class (3)	Percentage of families and individuals in this class and lower ones (4)	Percentage of income received by this class and lower ones (5)
Under $2,000	12	2	12	2
$ 2,000–$ 3,999	19	8	31	10
4,000– 5,999	21	14	52	24
6,000– 7,999	18	18	70	42
8,000– 9,999	11	14	81	56
10,000– 15,000	12	20	93	76
Over $15,000	7	24	100	100
Total	100	100		

in America today than there was in 1929. Other countries, like Ceylon or Italy, show a much greater degree of inequality than we find in the United States or Britain. On the other hand, we cannot tell which country today has the most equal income distribution, mainly because we cannot compare the results in Communist systems, such as the U.S.S.R. or China, with the mixed systems in the Western countries.

Some factors associated with income differences. In recent years, doctors have without question had the highest earnings of all professional groups. They have mean earnings of about $26,000 per year, as compared with $17,000 for lawyers and $14,500 for dentists. The lowest paid of all professional workers are the ministers, for their median salary is scarcely above $4,000! Thus the choice of a profession may entail a considerable difference in anticipated salary. The highest-paid minister in the country would be unlikely to command a salary equal to the earnings of the best-paid member of the legal profession.

For the lowest-paid manual worker, there can be little expectation that income will increase with age. For manual work, a man is at his best in his early twenties, and after that he goes downhill. In the professions and in executive positions, earnings do increase with age. A doctor reaches his earning prime around fifty, as does a lawyer, and both can hope to work beyond the normal retirement age.

How do education and training affect lifetime income? Financially, there is no doubt of their value. Even if you have to borrow at 6 per cent interest, put off years of gainful employment, live away from home, and pay for food, lodging, and books, your earnings in the professions open only to college graduates will probably turn out to be more than compensatory. Furthermore, good grades help, and the "grind" ends up with slightly more pay than the campus politician or the anonymous student. More important, perhaps, is the fact that college graduates report less mental illness and greater happiness. True, they tend to be more introspective, but coupled with this is a greater sense of well-being and satisfaction. Their perspectives are broader and they aspire to higher levels of accomplishment; when they do worry, their troubles tend to be genuine and not imagined.

Another factor that helps explain differences in income, certainly, is differences in people—physical, mental, temperamental, or even moral. Individual differences may be acquired or inherited, permanent or temporary, slight or considerable. We cannot, of course, answer the question whether it is better to be born intelligent or born to wealthy parents, but a little thought about differences in *capacity* will indicate the direction in which human differences affect and influence earning power.

Membership in particular minority groups can have a serious effect on income. In general, men still outearn women, and whites earn more than Negroes. Oddly enough, there is a great deal of contradictory evidence on this point. Some competent observers have asserted that discrimination against women or Negroes by paying different rates for the same jobs is not common; others assert that such differentials are still very important. In any case, it is certain that women and Negroes are often barred from some types of higher-paid jobs completely, whether or not they are paid the same wages as males or whites for others. Furthermore, it is quite clear that there are many jobs which could be performed by members of any sex, or any race, which are in fact filled on a limited basis. And we must not forget that the older worker is often subject to discrimination, particularly when he seeks reemployment. Paradoxically, such humanitarian measures as pension schemes, which were meant to improve the position of the older worker, are partly to blame for the difficulty, for older workers are relatively more expensive to hire than younger ones.

The land of opportunity. Traditionally, America has been conceived as a land in which anyone with ability can "get ahead" on his own merits. Though the Horatio Alger success legends are doubtless overdrawn, there have always

Anyone can climb the ladder of success, but it helps to start high:

Table 5. Social origin of successful leaders in America. Though laborers far outnumber businessmen in the population at large, most successful businessmen had a businessman father. What trends do you see in this table? How would you explain them? (Source: F. W. Taussig and C. S. Joslyn, *American Business Leaders*, Macmillan, New York, 1932; *Fortune.*)

Occupation of father	Persons listed in *Who's Who*, 1912, per cent	American millionaires, living in 1925, per cent	American business leaders, 1928, per cent	American business leaders, 1952, per cent	American business leaders under 50, 1952, per cent
Businessman	35.3	75.0	60.0	61.8	67.8
Professional man	34.3	10.5	13.4	13.5	14.8
Farmer	23.4	7.3	12.4	12.7	11.1
Laborer	6.7	1.6	12.5	7.8	2.5
Other	0.3	5.6	1.7	4.2	3.8
Total	100.0	100.0	100.0	100.0	100.0

been elements of truth to the claim, certainly when compared with opportunities in the older European countries. Nevertheless, a careful questionnaire investigation of successful businessmen produced some surprising facts, which are summarized in Table 5.

It seems that the typical American business executive does not come off the farm or out of the working districts; more likely, his father was also a businessman or possibly a member of one of the professions.

Does this mean that American economic society is hardening along caste lines? As Taussig and Joslyn point out, there are two possible explanations of the available facts: (1) that in the past, there was a high measure of social mobility in America and all of the cream rose to the top, leaving those less gifted behind; (2) that there are now strong and perhaps increasing barriers to circulation between economic classes. Taussig and Joslyn incline to the first view; many sociologists would disagree.[1] The facts are not sufficient for a final judgment, certainly, nor is there any reason to suppose that present trends are irreversible, whatever their direction. In any event, human resources are the nation's most important form of social capital, talent is always worth seeking out and developing, and it seems that public policy has grasped this vital point quite firmly in recent years.

[1] F. W. Taussig and C. S. Joslyn, *American Business Leaders*, The Macmillan Company, New York, 1932.

THE ECONOMIC ROLE OF GOVERNMENT

Let us look at the role of government in the economic system here in the United States. For the economist, the activities of the state are becoming increasingly important with each passing decade. This is reflected in the quantitative growth of government expenditure and in the great expansion of direct government regulation of economic life. From the economist's point of view, government activity falls into one of three categories: first, the government spends large amounts of money; second, it regulates and controls; third, the government taxes, and the effect of taxation on economic activity can be very considerable.

The growth of government expenditure. Before World War I, Federal, state, and local government expenditure amounted to little more than one-twelfth of our national income. During World War II, this proportion increased so that government consumed about half of the nation's greatly expanded national output. Within the space of a third of a century, the cost of all government in the United States rose from a mere $3 billion per year (1913) to more than $150 billion per year (1960s).

If this remarkable increase were a temporary wartime condition, it could be shrugged off. Actually, the exact reverse is the case. For more than a century, national income and production have been rising, and at the same time, in all countries and cultures, government expenditure has been rising even faster. Each period of emergency—each war, each depression—expands the activity of government. After each emergency has passed, expenditures never seem to return to their previous levels. Nor is the end in sight. Government expenditure receded from its wartime peak after 1945, but it did not drop to the prewar level of less than $10 billion per year, though this figure was once considered alarmingly high. In the years ahead, the trend of government expenditure at all levels appears to be rising, and it is unlikely that this will be affected by the political character of the administration. The facts about public expenditure are clear, as Figure 4 indicates. Further, rich countries tend to spend relatively more on government than do poor countries. We may deplore these facts, or we may like them. However we feel about them, they make clear the increasingly important economic role of government.

Federal, state, and local functions. The overall figures of expenditure become more meaningful if we break them down to see just what activity they represent and which branch of government they pertain to. Every American is faced with three basic levels of government: Federal, state, and local. Surprising as it may appear, the states have always been less important than the other two, and this remains true today. Prior to World War I, local gov-

Government expenditures show rising trend relative to growth in national income:

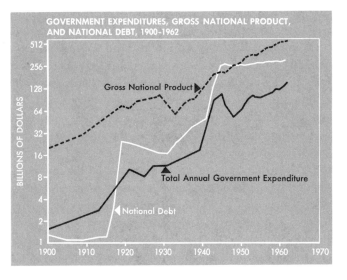

Fig. 4. Government expenditures include Federal, state, and local annual expenditures. Note the relative trends. Also note that this is a "ratio," or "semilog," chart, with vertical distances arranged to reflect percentage changes. (Source: National Industrial Conference Board and Tax Foundation, U.S. Department of Commerce.)

Government share of national product is biggest in wealthy developed countries:

Developed countries	Postwar average tax, per cent	Less developed countries	Postwar average tax, per cent
United Kingdom	35	Ceylon	19
France	31	Brazil	18
Canada	27	Puerto Rico	17
West Germany	27	Indonesia	15
United States	26	Colombia	10
Australia	25	Mexico	10
Japan	22	Pakistan	10
Italy	20	India	8

Table 6. Government receipts as percentages of gross national product. Poor, underdeveloped countries show a persistent tendency to tax and spend less, relative to national product, than do more advanced countries. With higher income comes greater interdependence and less need to spend on private necessities. (Source: H. T. Oshima, *American Economic Review,* 1957, pp. 382–383. Data include all tax and nontax receipts.)

ernment did most of the spending in government circles. The Federal government did little more than finance a few public works and pay for national defense, pensions, and interest on past wars, in addition, of course, to paying public salaries. Most of its taxes came from liquor and tobacco excises and from tariff duties levied on imports. Life was simple in those days; local government performed most governmental functions and collected most of the tax revenue, primarily from taxes on property. The changes that have occurred since World War I are shown in Figure 5. Though nondefense spending has grown relatively less than the total of local and state spending, the combined spending of the Federal government is still far ahead of the others.

Federal expenditure. The United States government is the biggest business on earth. It buys more typewriters and more cement, meets a bigger payroll, and handles more money than any other organization anywhere. The numbers involved in Federal finance are astronomical: not millions, or hundreds of millions, but literally billions (thousands of millions) are needed to keep track of spending. Obviously, such magnitudes convey no meaning to the human mind. We all know what it means to be a mile from home, but assertions that the sun is 93 million miles from the earth leave us unimpressed and somewhat cold. Perhaps public expenditure will have more meaning if we remember that each billion dollars amounts to about $5 for each American man, woman, and child. A current annual Federal budget of 100 billion dollars is equivalent to about $500 per capita, or about 2 months of a year's income.

What does government buy? Chiefly insurance against disaster in the form of national security measures. Table 7 shows the estimated share of

Local and state spending has been rising faster than Federal nondefense spending:

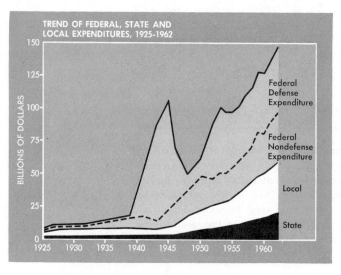

TREND OF FEDERAL, STATE AND LOCAL EXPENDITURES, 1925-1962

Fig. 5. Federal expenditure rose sharply in the Great Depression, and even more during the war. Defense expenditure has remained high; but it is local and state expenditure on schools, sewers, and roads that shows the steepest upward trend. (Source: National Industrial Conference Board and Tax Foundation.)

different categories of Federal expenditure in the fiscal year 1964 (July 1, 1963, to June 30, 1964). The first five items represent the cost of past and future wars, and together they account for four-fifths of all Federal expenditure as well as for most of the increase in Federal expenditure over prewar levels. The figures are only estimates, but they are reasonably representative.

Much of the sixth item (natural resources) goes to support conservation programs, such as TVA and the St. Lawrence Seaway project. The other items are for the most part self-explanatory. We might note, though, that the final category includes the cost of running Congress, the courts, and the executive branch of government. It is to be emphasized that the bulk of Federal expenditure and debt is a consequence of hot and cold war, not of depression and welfare programs.

The changing function of government. The last quarter of a century has witnessed great political changes in the United States as elsewhere. How great have the economic changes actually been? How many departures have been made from the traditional capitalistic system? We can best answer these questions by considering the scope of governmental activity in four main categories: direct controls, social consumption, governmental production, and welfare expenditures.

Direct controls. There has been a great increase in the amount of control that government exercises over economic activity. But little of this body of regu-

Most Federal expenditure goes to pay for defense and past wars:

	Estimate, billions of dollars	Percentage of total
1. National security	$55.4	56
2. Veterans services and benefits	5.5	5½
3. Interest on public debt	10.1	10
4. International affairs and finance	2.7	3
5. Space research and technology	4.2	4
6. Natural resources	2.5	2½
7. Agriculture and agricultural resources	5.7	6
8. Health, education, labor, and welfare	7.1	7
9. Commerce and housing	3.7	4
10. Other, including general government	1.9	2
Total expenditure	$98.8	100

Table 7. Estimated Federal expenditure in fiscal year 1964. The first five items are 79 per cent of total expenditure. Hence, purely civilian expenditure for domestic peace-time purposes is about one-fifth of the total. In the prewar era the proportions would have been reversed. (Source: Bureau of the Budget.)

lation can be dignified by the title of "planning." Market prices still direct most economic activities.

Social consumption. The increase in government expenditure means that as a nation we are consuming more of our national product socially rather than individually. Rather than pay directly to ride on the public roads, we pay indirectly through our taxes. We also contribute substantially, though indirectly, to the immense cost of defending our society. But we ought to notice that most of the goods and services which are consumed socially are produced by free private enterprise. And so it is with most government expenditure on productive goods. The government may pay for a hospital or a machine, but each of these items is still produced by free enterprise.

Governmental production. We find that there has been little expansion of direct governmental production in recent decades. Historically, our government has performed certain direct productive functions and not others. Airports, but not railway terminals, are usually owned by the government; similarly, the government operates the postal service, but not the telegraph service. The reasons for drawing the line at any one place are partly historical and are to some degree changing. Economically, the distinction is not completely arbitrary, for the courts have held that in the special case of "public utilities affected with public interest" there is only limited opportunity for competition among independent producers, so they must be publicly owned or regulated. But one would not expect the production of soap to be a candidate for governmental operation.

Whatever the merits of government ownership, there has in fact been only one direction in which an expansion of government ownership has occurred in the last forty years—namely the hydroelectric power field (Tennessee Valley Authority, Bonneville Dam, Hoover Dam, and so forth). If words are used in their traditional meanings, it is not incorrect to call TVA "creeping socialism." The fact to note, however, is how little of that sort of thing has taken place in recent years.

The atomic-energy program was a post-New Deal development: it shows how poorly traditional words and concepts are adapted to describe the complexities of modern social life. When the government pays General Electric a negligible fixed fee to start and run a vast nuclear industry, is this private or public enterprise? Private, in that the workers are GE employees and not civil servants. But the government puts up all the money, and certainly audits all major decisions. So the whole development of the atomic and hydrogen bombs could by some be called "galloping socialism."

We should also recognize, in this connection, that there has been a substantial rise in the Federal payroll and in the number of government employees. Many of the latter are in Washington, D.C., executive offices, in regional laboratories, in the armed services, and so forth. Even if they are not directly producing private goods and services in competition with private industry, such resources are being directly used by the government; as we shall see, it behooves us all as citizens to see that they be used wisely and in amounts relative to the importance of our different national needs.

Welfare expenditure. Finally, we turn to an activity of government that did expand tremendously in the 1930s and that will continue to loom large in the decades ahead, namely, government welfare expenditures, which *transfer* purchasing power to the needy or the worthy without the recipients performing any service in return. Payments are made to veterans, old people, the handicapped, pensioned workers and their families, and unemployed people. Expenditures of this type have given our modern governmental system the name "welfare state."

A government check received by a veteran's widow differs economically from a check received by a postal clerk or a man who sells typewriters to the government. It is important to understand why, because our later discussion of national income will involve this same distinction between "transfer items" and payments we can count as a true part of the national product or income. The latter type of payment is included in national income because it is made for services rendered. These purchases do use up resources and production facilities, and they do provide for collective consumption, direct or indirect, by the citizens of the United States. Whether they are financed by taxes, or the sale of postage stamps, the government uses its dollars to provide services for public use. Such dollars are part of the national income.

The widow's pension is something else again. Socially, it may be one of our most desirable expenditures, but it is nevertheless not part of the national income. Why? Because payment is not made for services rendered in exchange for the pension. The widow provides no labor, no land, and no capital for society. The pension increases her purchasing power and permits her to live more adequately and buy goods and services from others. The goods she buys are part of the national income and output. But they are attributable to the people who produced them, and not to her.

Transfer expenditures have grown rapidly in recent years, partly as a result of the Great Depression, which made relief expenditures necessary, but mostly because new minimum standards of health, nutrition, and security have been set up by the collective conscience of the American people. Society now rules that children shall not have rickets because of the bad luck or weakness of their parents, that poor people shall not die young because of insufficient money for operations and needed care, that the old shall be able to live out their years with some minimum of income. Are such expenditures anticapitalistic, or noncapitalistic? Not necessarily, for the production induced by expenditure of these funds is both privately produced and privately consumed. Unless transfer expenditures are financed by printing money, larger taxes will be needed to make the payments. Often the more fortunate citizens are paying for the consumption of the less fortunate; and perhaps, within reasonable limits, most people will feel that this is not improper.

Financing government expenditure. Where does the money come from to meet government expenditures? It comes from three sources: (1) taxes and the sale of miscellaneous assets such as surplus equipment; (2) borrowing in the form of interest-paying government bonds; or (3) some kind of issue of printed currency and coin, with no interest being paid to the holders. Normally, taxes are the most important source of government income, but during the Revolutionary War paper money was of greatest importance, and during World War II borrowing was just as important as taxes. We shall examine this question further in a moment.

Analysis of government activity. Every society, at any point in time, may choose between *private* goods and services and *governmental* expenditure; that is, purchase of goods may be made individually, or the government may purchase on behalf of the whole society. At one extreme, which is only theoretical, all purchases are made publicly; at the other, private purchase accounts for 100 per cent of all buying. All societies lie somewhere within this range, and we can chart the range of choice in Figure 6.

The United States presently lies at about point E on the curve, which shows that about one-fifth of resources are devoted to government, and the remainder to private activity. How do we decide upon point E? The answer is simple—legislative action. The government decides how much of expenditure will be public and how much will be private. But within the area left to private decision, the choice of goods and services is determined by market activity, by voluntary individual choice. If international tension eased, so that taxes were reduced, more money would be left for the individual to spend and point E would move further to the right. But if the electorate accepted J. K. Galbraith's thesis and decided that it would prefer more public spending and less private spending, the point E would move back to the left.

Figure 6 also shows how the transformation curve can be used to disentangle a common confusion. Government expenditure can be reduced in two quite different ways: first, public activities can be made more efficient; second, the scope of government can be reduced, by having government drop many of the functions it now performs. The result of increasing the *efficiency* of government is shown on the curve C*G**; we now obtain more goods for the same sacrifice of resources from the private economy. The old curve, C*G*

To reduce costs by cutting waste is not the same as to reduce them by cutting the scope of government activities:

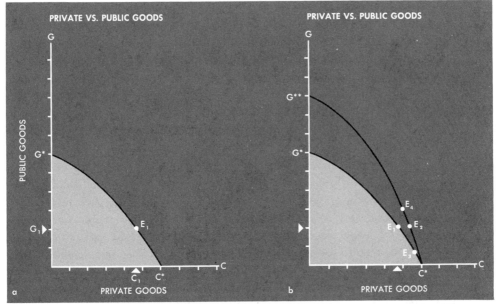

Fig. 6. On society's production-possibility curve (choices between private and public expenditure on goods and services) America has been at a point such as E, with by far the largest fraction of goods going to satisfy private wants.

shifts upward. Where is the new E point to be if the scope of government remains unchanged? It will move to the right from the old point (E_1) to the position at E_2. Private consumption has now increased because of the savings produced by greater efficiency. But if the scope of government is cut down, there is no change in efficiency, and no new curve. The point E simply moves to the right and down on the old C^*G^* curve. Of course, the electorate might want both greater efficiency and an increase in the scope of government, and this would move the E point to E_4.

What does this economic analysis suggest for practical policy? Students of administration seem generally to believe that the government is not so inefficient relative to private industry these days as it was in decades past. Auditing procedures, mechanization, and improved quality of civil servants indicate to these observers that the vast increase in public expenditure must be traced to new functions and an expanded scope rather than to inefficiency. Of course, informed men of good will are agreed on the desirability of increasing efficiency in both the public and private sectors of the economy. What is necessarily a more controversial and philosophical problem has to do with the scope of governmental activity. It is here that representative government must respond to the desires of the majority of citizens.

What light can economic analysis throw on the reasons why governmental use of goods and services is ever required at all? In the first place, suppose all goods could be produced efficiently by perfectly competitive enterprise at any scale of operations. Then suppose that all such goods were like loaves of bread, the total of which can be definitely divided into separate consumptions by different individuals, so that the more I consume the less you consume out of the toal. Now suppose that there were no altruism toward other people and no envy of them; and suppose that each person could be thought of as having equal initial access to human and natural resources, as having equal opportunities in every sense, and as being able to carry on his activities independently of others, much as in frontier days.

If *all* these idealized conditions were met, would there be any need whatsoever for a mixed economy? Why would there be any government functions at all? Indeed, why speak of a society, since the world could then be regarded as an array of independent atoms with absolutely no organic connections among them? Clearly such a case of zero government is at one extreme pole. Yet even so, if there were to be a division of labor between people and regions, and if a pricing system were to work, there would soon have to appear courts and policemen to ensure honesty, fulfillment of contract, nonfraudulent and nonviolent behavior, freedom from theft and from external aggression, and guarantee of the legislated rights of property. This would be *laissez faire* with minimal government, and a very good system it might be if the ideal conditions presupposed for it were truly present.

But each and every one of the idealized conditions enumerated above is lacking to some degree in real life as mankind has always known it. Abilities, opportunities, and ownership of property exhibit disparities in each economy, depending on biological and social history. It is a fact that many kinds of production can take place most efficiently only in units too large for "perfect competition" as defined by the economist; and many other imperfections mar the simplicity of the scenario. All this forms the subject of economic analysis in the chapters that follow—analysis designed to provide a perspective for the important compromises that a free society will want to make. But here we shall concentrate on the factors that call for governmental activity.

Let us consider national defense. Nothing is more vital to a threatened society than its security. How different national defense is, regarded as a commodity, from a commodity such as bread or typewriters. Loaves of bread can be divided in many ways among members of a group; national defense has to be provided for all. Most individuals appreciate national defense, much as they appreciate the quantities of bread; but even among them some would be more willing, if necessary, to give up more bread for a given level of defense than others would. Could *laissez faire*, with no political voting and coercion, give the group the national defense desired by the majority? Evidently not.

If I knew that I was going to benefit anyway from the defense you had paid for, why should I come into the market place and exercise a dollar demand for it? The point is that benefits from a social good, unlike those from a purely private good, are seen to involve external consumption effects on more than one individual. But if the good can be subdivided so that each part can be sold competitively to a different individual with no external effects on others in the group, it is not a likely candidate for governmental control.

Federal taxation and local finance. Our discussion of public finance now continues with a survey of the Federal tax system, followed by a brief examination of expenditure and taxation at the state and local levels. But first some discussion of economic fundamentals will be useful.

Economic nature of taxation. The state needs money to pay its bills. It gets the dollars to pay for its expenditures primarily from taxes. However, what the state really needs to build a battleship or run a lighthouse is not so much money as real economic resources: steel and watchmen—in short, the use of society's scarce supplies of labor, land, and capital goods. In deciding how to tax themselves, therefore, the people are really deciding how resources needed for social wants shall be taken away from the various families and the enterprises they own and made available for governmental goods and services.

We have noted that the state also spends money on welfare transfers which go to particular individuals in the community to spend on their private needs and wants. Again, money is the important veil that cloaks the *redistribution* of command over real goods and services which results from the action by the state to tax some and give to others. Recall also that even if there were no welfare transfers, the state is altering the distribution of incomes that results from *laissez faire* in the following way. In deciding who shall be made to pay for the resources spent on social goods and services, the electorate can vote taxes that will fall heavily on the rich rather than on the poor, on the energetic rather than on the lethargic, on the owners of tangible assets such as land and property as against the owners of labor power, and so forth. In this way, too, taxation affects the distribution of private incomes.

In the distant past, taxes were levied by those in power in a most arbitrary manner. A wealthy nobleman at the court of the king might get off scot-free while a merchant or busy peasant was sorely burdened by the weight of taxation. When scholars finally tried to produce a more rational guide to taxation, certain general principles emerged which are still important and basic.

On the one hand, there is the general notion that different people shall be taxed in proportion to the "benefits" which they can be expected to receive from public activity. On the other hand, there is the general principle that people should be taxed in such a way as to lead to a desirable pattern of "sacrifice," or what is really the same thing, that taxation should be so arranged as to accomplish whatever the good society regards as a proper redistribution of market-determined incomes. Such principles are useful, but they do not obviate difficult decisions with respect to just what is a desirable structure of taxes.

For instance, consider benefit taxation. If you and I were exactly alike, then the benefit we receive from the armed services, the public roads, and other governmental services would be the same and we ought then to pay equal taxes. If the redistribution principle is used, the amount of sacrifice we should be expected to make would be identical if we are equal. No one will quarrel with the dictum "Those who are essentially equals should be taxed equally." If A and B are alike in every respect except that A has red hair while B has brown, this is presumably not a legitimate reason for taxing them differently, any more than, under the rule of law, the fact that A is a friend of the President should relieve him of taxation. As we shall see, the fact that tax laws have loopholes makes it necessary that we do not forget this dictum.

However, there is a corollary to the principle which raises the same problems all over again, for if equals are to be taxed equally, it is presumed that unequals are to be taxed unequally. On this basis, neither the general benefit nor the sacrifice criterion will resolve tax policy problems in society.

Suppose that A and B are alike in every respect except that B has ten times the property and income of A. Is B then to pay the same absolute tax for police protection as A? Or since the police will spend more time protecting B's property than A's, should B pay more than A for police protection? This important question is still unanswered: How differently should unequals be taxed?

Pragmatic compromises in taxation. How have modern mixed societies of the past century resolved these difficult questions? Democracies have generally favored pragmatic solutions which please neither the zealots who favor the benefit principle nor their counterparts who support a thoroughgoing redistributional-sacrifice principle. Where various public services at the local and national level are peculiarly suited to recognizable groups, and where those groups have no special claim for favorable or unfavorable treatment by virtue of their average incomes or other characteristics, modern governments generally rely upon taxes of the benefit type. Thus, local roads are usually paid for by local residents; taxes collected on gasoline may on the whole be devoted more specifically to road construction than to schools or libraries. However, large areas of taxation do not function in such clearly defined circumstances, and other rules of thumb are needed.

Extensive reliance has been placed on the graduated income tax, which taxes a man with an income of $20,000 more than a man with an income of $10,000 even if the former claims to benefit very little from public services. Not only does the man with the higher income pay a higher absolute tax, he also pays a higher fraction of his total income as tax. This is in contrast to a proportional tax structure in which each person pays the same proportion of his income, regardless of its size. Often people speak of such a graduated tax as a *progressive* tax, meaning that it bears down progressively harder upon those in the higher income brackets. A progressive tax increases more in relation to income than a proportional tax; it takes a larger fraction of higher incomes and a smaller fraction of lower incomes. Its opposite, a *regressive* tax, grows less in proportion to a rise in income; a higher proportion of lower incomes is taken in taxes. This often happens in taxes placed upon essential commodities, such as milk or bread. Persons in low-income brackets spend a higher proportion of their income on milk or bread than those in the high-income brackets. Hence they pay a much larger portion of their income in bread tax than does the high-income group. (What if the government levied a heavy tax on fine old wine? Is the tax then regressive, proportional, or progressive? Why?)

Taxes may also be classified as *direct* or *indirect*. A tax on income or inheritance is a direct tax, where the person benefiting or using the item taxed pays the tax himself. Taxes on bread, or gasoline, are indirect taxes levied as excises on particular goods. The lines between them may be hard to draw. A poll tax of $2 on every voter is a direct tax and a very regressive one, because its burden on the wealthy in relation to their income is much smaller than its burden on the poor. An excise tax of $1 per cigar or $5 per quart of rare brandy would be an indirect tax, and probably a progressive tax.

Modern tax systems are, to repeat, a compromise. They give some weight to the benefit which the individual receives from society, some weight to equality of sacrifice, and, one may add, some weight to political obligations and expediency. Nor can we forget the psychological impact of taxation, the effect that taxes may have on human incentives and on the efficiency of society's use of resources.

Federal taxation. The great variety of taxes presently collected by the Federal government is shown in Table 8. The first two, personal income taxes and death (or inheritance) and gift taxes bear most heavily on those with higher incomes and larger accumulations of property; they are progressive taxes. Payroll and sales taxes are regressive in that they take a larger fraction of the poor man's income than of the rich man's. Corporation taxes are in one sense progressive, for corporate dividends usually go to persons with higher incomes, but to the extent that corporations pass on the tax to the consumer in the form

Personal and corporate income taxes are main Federal revenue sources:

	Kind of Tax		Receipts in billions
Progressive	Personal income taxes		$ 45.8
	Death and gift taxes		2.1
Intermediate	Corporation income taxes		23.8
Regressive	Employment or payroll taxes		19.4
	Excise taxes		18.5
	Tobacco and liquor	$5.9	
	Manufacturing and retail excises	6.2	
	Customs duties	1.4	
	Highway trust fund	3.3	
	Miscellaneous	1.7	
	Other taxes and receipts		2.6
	Total tax collections		$112.2

Table 8. Estimated tax receipts of Federal government, fiscal year of 1964. Five-eighths of Federal tax revenues now come from personal and corporate income taxes. These respond quickly to changes in national income. Note that inheritance or death taxes do little these days to redistribute wealth and income. (Total rounded; Source: Bureau of the Budget.)

of higher prices, they may be regressive. In general, the Federal tax structure is more progressive today than twenty-five years ago, or than the tax systems used by state and local government. A brief glance at various Federal taxes may be helpful.

Sales and excise taxes. These are perhaps the most regressive of all taxes, and they have long been the subject of controversy. The Federal government has compromised on the question, avoiding a general sales tax but adding excise taxes to cigarettes, liquor, cosmetics, travel, and certain other goods. But many states and local communities make use of both sales and excise taxes.

Social security, payroll, and employment taxes. Most industries now come under the Social Security Act, and employer and employee each contribute a percentage of all wage income below $4,800 per year to provide the funds for old-age retirement benefits and so forth. Taken alone, such a payroll tax is regressive, but when combined with social security benefit payments it is much less regressive in effect.

Corporation income taxes. After a corporation has paid all of its expenses and reckoned its annual income, it must pay part of that income to the Federal government before it distributes dividends. In 1965 a small corporation has to pay 22 cents of each dollar of net income as taxes; when corporate earnings rise above $25,000 per year, the corporation must pay 48 cents of each dollar as tax. Many people think that the corporate tax rate is too high, that corporations are discouraged from venturing into worthwhile but risky job-making investments. They argue that a small corporation would be able to grow more rapidly if it could plow some of its earnings back into the business and not pay them out in taxes. Further, they argue that the "double taxation" involved is unfair, for the stockholder must also pay personal income tax on dividends received from a corporation. They advise a cut in corporate taxes or more generous tax credits for those who receive dividends from corporations.

On the other side, there are some who argue that corporations should be taxed more heavily than they now are, with the larger corporations taxed proportionately higher than the small corporations. These people believe that if the government must collect large sums of money, and increases in personal income taxes are not feasible, then a tax on corporations is better than any other tax available. They point out that corporations do not distribute all of their earnings to the stockholders, but reinvest some portion of earnings in the corporation. The stockholder may avoid personal income tax on these savings by capital-gains loopholes, as we shall see. According to these critics, a corporation tax will at least partially remedy the situation. The problem is, of course, too complex for a complete evaluation here.

The progressive personal income tax. Spring used to be an unhappy season as people prepared to make a lump-sum payment of taxes on their previous year's income—often money already spent. Now things are better, for the employer withholds automatically enough money to pay the government our tax bill. This puts everyone on a pay-as-you-go basis, or almost everyone. For some 20 million families, with incomes below $5,000, that is all there is to it. They simply turn in their withholding statement at the end of the year and the Treasury computes their tax and refunds any excess they may have paid. For still other millions with moderate incomes and no extraordinary expenses for medicine or charity, there is a short tax form which can be computed quite rapidly. Those with sizable incomes, however, must complete a long and fairly complex form, or even several forms, to fulfill their tax obligations and compute their liability.

How much does a typical person have to pay at each income level? Table 9 gives the approximate tax schedule for 1965, and though the rates change, it is fairly representative. Note that the tax starts at a very low figure for those with low incomes and rises very rapidly in relation to income. Indeed, when annual income climbs to $1 million, 67 per cent of the total will go to the government. Column 3 shows how progressive the tax really is. A $10,000-a-year man pays 15.6 per cent rather than the 8.7 per cent taken from a $3,000-per-year man, and as the income rises to $50,000 the portion due the government rises to 32.9 per cent. Column 4 shows an interesting fact, namely, the

The income-tax schedule climbs progressively as income grows:

Table 9. Amount of Federal income tax to be paid at different income levels by a childless couple, 1965. A bachelor would pay more; the large family less.

Net income before exemptions (but after all deductions) (1)	Personal income tax (2)	Average tax rate, per cent [= (2) ÷ (1)] (3)	Marginal tax rate (= tax on extra dollar) (4)	Disposable income after taxes [= (1) − (2)] (5)
Below $ 1,200	$ 0	0	0	$ 1,200
2,000	112	5.6	14	1,888
3,000	260	8.7	15	2,740
4,000	418	10.5	16	3,582
5,000	586	11.7	17	4,414
10,000	1,556	15.6	22	8,444
20,000	4,044	20.2	28	15,956
50,000	16,460	32.9	50	33,540
100,000	44,460	44.5	60	55,540
200,000	109,972	55	69	90,028
400,000	250,140	62.5	70	149,860
1,000,000	670,140	67.0	70	329,860
10,000,000	6,970,140	69.7	70	3,029,860

fraction of an *extra* dollar that taxes will take. Note that this begins at the "normal" level of 14 per cent and rises little until we reach the $10,000 income level. This margin or "extra" tax rate finally reaches 70 per cent. As new tax laws are passed, these rates may be changed somewhat.

Of course, it still pays to get more income, as column 5 indicates, for the amount of disposable income left after taxes continues to increase, even when an heiress moves into a higher income-tax bracket. The government never takes the full 100 cents out of each extra dollar. The income tax tends to reduce the inequality of disposable income, though it is not a penalty tax which confiscates *all* income above a certain level.

Progressive taxes, investment, and spending. Do high income taxes, and progressive taxes in particular, discourage effort and risk taking? So far as effort is concerned, this is not an easy question to answer, since we shall see that taxation causes some people to work harder in order to make their million. Many doctors, scientists, artists, and businessmen who enjoy their jobs and the sense of power or accomplishment that they obtain from them act the same whether their income is $30,000 or $100,000; others may prefer to work less and take more leisure time because of the effect of progressive taxation. The net result is hard to evaluate.

The effects of progressive taxation on risky investments are less doubtful. They can be quite adverse because in part the government says to the tax-payer, "Heads I win, tails you lose." Progressive taxation can also have an opposite effect. To the extent that dollars are taken from the frugal wealthy persons who spend only a small fraction of their extra dollars, rather than from the poor ready-spenders, progressive taxes may tend to keep spending at a high level—at too high a level if inflation is threatened. Statistics on how people spend extra dollars suggest that this effect on total spending may not be terribly great.

State and local expenditures. Although the Federal government's multi-billion-dollar expenditures are quantitatively greater than those of the states and the small individual localities, the latter are not unimportant. Where do the states and localities obtain their funds, and what do they spend them for? Figures 7 and 8 give a concise answer to these questions.

Schools are the number-one state and local expense:

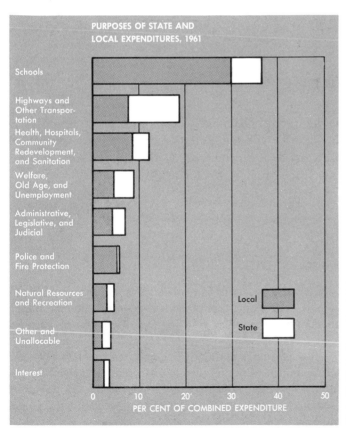

PURPOSES OF STATE AND
LOCAL EXPENDITURES, 1961

Schools

Highways and
Other Transpor-
tation

Health, Hospitals,
Community
Redevelopment,
and Sanitation

Welfare,
Old Age, and
Unemployment

Administrative,
Legislative, and
Judicial

Police and
Fire Protection

Natural Resources
and Recreation

Other and
Unallocable

Interest

Local

State

0   10   20'   30   40   50
PER CENT OF COMBINED EXPENDITURE

Fig. 7. The population outburst and move to the suburbs has put a strain on local and state finance, necessitating increased state and local debt issue. (Source: Bureau of the Census.)

The real-estate property tax still dominates local and state finance:

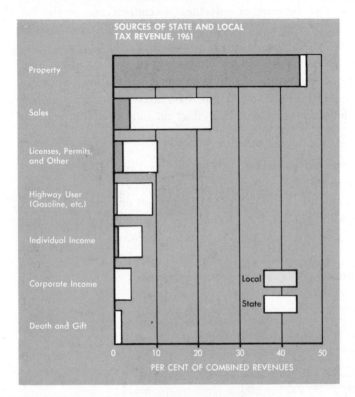

SOURCES OF STATE AND LOCAL
TAX REVENUE, 1961

Property

Sales

Licenses, Permits,
and Other

Highway User
(Gasoline, etc.)

Individual Income

Corporate Income

Local

State

Death and Gift

0   10   20   30   40   50
PER CENT OF COMBINED REVENUES

Fig. 8. Most local and state taxes are still of the regressive type, not easy to expand as needs grow. (Source: Bureau of the Census.)

Notice the overwhelming predominance of school costs in state and local budgets; together with highways and transportation costs, they constitute more than 55 per cent of state and local expenditures. Notice also how heavily local government depends upon the property tax for its revenue.

Summary

This chapter has treated some current aspects of individual and family income in the United States, and then analyzed governmental economic activity in a general way, as preparation for the discussion of national income that follows.

In relation to individual and family income, we need to note the adequacy of income of the different groups in society, as well as the general distribution of income and the relative equality or inequality of income. We have seen how choice of occupation, education, and genetic inheritance can affect our incomes and the way in which we spend them.

The economic role of government has increased steadily in this century and the trend seems likely to continue. The Federal government is now a predominant partner in our economic activity, and the importance of state and local government has diminished relative to the importance of the Federal government. Increased economic activity by the government has not, however, led to government production of goods; most of the increases have come through controls exercised over the system and from social consumption of goods and services.

Finally, we examined the consequences of taxation and the nature of the different taxes which governments employ to obtain their funds. Here we are concerned with both the type of tax (direct or indirect) and its effects (regressive, progressive). We found that the Federal government depends heavily upon income taxes, both personal and corporate, while state and local governments most often make use of property taxes. The effects of these taxes are quite different, and economic analysis can provide us with very useful information about those effects.

Review Questions

1. List the basic causes of income differences. List the consequences of income differences.

2. What three functions does government perform in the economic system?

3. What are some of the more recent trends in the area of government interference in the economic system?

4. What are the major sources of funds of the Federal, state, and local governments?

5. What are the major expenditures at the Federal, state, and local level?

6. What are the two common bases of tax policy?

7. Differentiate between a progressive and a regressive tax. Give examples of each.

8. Differentiate between direct and indirect taxes, and give examples of each.

9. List some of the consequences of taxation on spending and investment.

10. In what way does a government salary check differ from a pension check?

11. What is the significance of the size of the public debt?

For Further Study

1. Why don't people change their smoking habits as a result of taxation?

2. Is regressive taxation likely to lead to higher levels of saving?

3. What factors limit the total amount of indebtedness that the nation can carry safely and easily?

4. As local government increases its expenditures, what consequences can you foresee for the local resident?

5. Make up a model budget for a family earning $4,800 per year. Then consider the changes that would occur in the budget if the family income was reduced by 25 per cent. Increased by 100 per cent.

6. Do you believe that all incomes should be equal? Justify your answer, and if you believe incomes should be unequal, state the basis on which you would make the division.

7. Should the citizens of New York be taxed to provide better schools for the people of Arkansas or Mississippi? Why?

8. Do you favor the use of a sales tax in your community? Give reasons for your answer.

9. Suppose government could be made perfectly efficient. Would the cost of government then decline rapidly?

10. Do you believe that the community should consume more or less of its product socially? Why?

CHAPTER 13

National

Income

We turn now to the subject that is central in any approach to economics: the study of national income and the manner in which it is determined. Oddly enough, we did not even collect national income statistics thirty years ago, but in recent years, we have come to realize their significance, and the Department of Commerce now produces national income measurements on a yearly, quarterly, and monthly basis. No well-informed observer can neglect this vital information about the national economy, and the United Nations tries to get all countries to collect national income data. As a result of this intense interest in matters relating to national income we now have available a vast accumulation of information relating to the national incomes of various countries and the manner in which they change from one year to the next. The study of national income, of the factors that cause changes in income levels, and of the means that may be employed to maintain the national income at a stable level, is today one of the key areas in the whole field of economics.

NATIONAL INCOME: YARDSTICK OF ECONOMIC PERFORMANCE

What does national income mean? It is the loose name we give for the money measure of the overall annual flow of goods and services in the economy. Often we use the almost equivalent terms "national product" or "net national product" as synonyms for national income. Later, we shall distinguish between net national product (NNP) and gross national product (GNP). If we measure all of the things which society produces annually with its land, labor, and capital resources, using money as a standard measuring rod, we arrive at a total that we call the national income or national product.

Two measures of national product: Goods flow or earnings flow. How is the national product, or NNP, actually measured? The general idea is simple enough, and it can be diagramed as a circular or closed system like that shown in Figure 9.

We may measure national income in either the upper half of the loop or the lower half of the loop; both approaches produce the same result, though the measurement is made rather differently.

In the flow-of-product approach to national income, we try to measure what the public consumes each year (the goods, like apples or bread, and the services, like haircuts). The public spends dollars for these goods and services,

Net national product is measured as flow of output or as equal flow of costs:

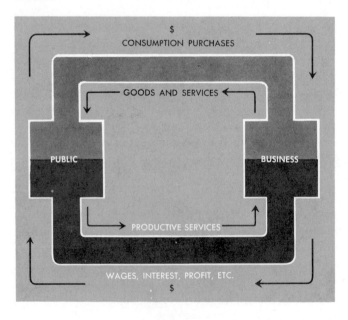

Fig. 9. In the upper loop, people spend their money on final goods; the total flow of these goods each year is one measure of NNP. The lower loop measures the annual flow of costs of output: the earnings that business pays out in wages, rent, interest, dividends, and accrued profits. With profit properly reckoned as a residual, the two measures of NNP must always be identical.

and the flow of goods in one direction and dollars in return is shown in the upper loop of Figure 9. If we add together all of the dollars spent for such goods and services, we arrive at a total figure for the NNP. We use the market prices of goods as a measure of their value, for the market price reflects the relative desirability of the different goods and services that are available. In this approach, the net national product, NNP, or "national income evaluated at market prices" is therefore definable as *the total money value of the flow of final products in the community.*

The earnings or income approach to national income gives the same result, but the calculations are made in the lower loop in Figure 9. Here we learn what business is paying out to the public in wages, interest, rents, and profit. These figures represent the *costs* of producing the flow of goods. Note that the economist, unlike the accountant, includes profit as a cost item in his calculations. The statistician can measure the total of such costs, again producing a figure for NNP. In this case, NNP is defined as *the total factor earnings that are the costs of production of society's final goods.*

Both totals will be exactly the same. The reason is simple. If profit is added to the costs that appear in the lower loop of Figure 9, and profit is what remains after the product has been sold and all costs deducted from income, then the selling price of goods and services is the same as the cost of the goods plus the profit made on the sale of goods.

In our calculations, current market prices serve as a measuring rod; therefore, we must take into consideration the changes in the purchasing power of money that occur from day to day. Usually, this is done by "deflating" the value of money, using some particular year like 1929 as a base. An example is shown in Table 10.

Notice that column 1 shows national income in 1933 equal to exactly one-half of national income in 1929, but that column 3 shows a ratio of 3:2 between

We deflate by a price index to correct for our rubber money yardstick:

Date	Money NNP, billions of current dollars (1)	Index number of prices (2)	Real NNP, in billions of 1929 dollars (3) $\left[= \dfrac{(1)}{(2)} \times 100 \right]$
1929	96	100	$\dfrac{96}{100} \times 100 = 96$
1933	48	75	$\dfrac{48}{75} \times 100 = 64$

Table 10. Sample calculation of real NNP. Using price index of column 2, we deflate column 1 to get real NNP, column 3. (Riddle: Can you show that 1929's real NNP was $72 billion in terms of 1933 prices? Hint: With 1933 as a base, 1929's price index is 133⅓.)

the two years. This gives us an idea of the extent to which changes in money value can alter our calculations.

Avoiding "double counting." When we calculate the national income by adding together all of the goods and services which are produced by the economy each year, we must be careful to avoid "double counting." Bread, for example, is sold directly to the consumer, and the price paid by the consumer is counted as part of the national income. But we must not count the cost of the flour that was used to make the bread, for that is already included in the final cost of the loaf of bread. Such "intermediate products" are hidden, and our accounting system must dig them out and eliminate them.

Usually, this is done by computing the "value added" at each stage in production. This approach does not include *all* of the expenses of every firm in the country; instead, all purchases of materials and services from other business firms are excluded. Thus we would not count the cost of flour and other materials in a baker's expenses, but we would count his overhead, labor costs, and other operating costs. When purchases from other firms are deducted, we have a measurement of the actual value added to the product by the bakery. This is exactly equal to the sum of wages, interest costs, rent, and profits.

Net investment or capital formation. Thus far, our discussion of national income has not mentioned capital growth. We have talked only of present consumption of goods and services such as bread or haircuts. But we may also save part of our national product, using it to build new machines or buildings or to enlarge our stock of goods. The goods and services used to produce new capital, our "net investment" in capital equipment of all sorts, must certainly be considered part of our national product. When we measure the flow of goods in the upper loop of our diagram (Figure 9), we must include net investment (capital goods) as well as consumer goods. We must therefore modify our definition of NNP to read as follows: Net national product is the *sum* of *all* final products, including consumption goods, services, *and net investment.*

Net investment itself comprises three kinds of additions to our stock of goods: (1) buildings, (2) equipment, and (3) inventories. We therefore add to our NNP the cost of all new buildings, equipment, and additions to existing inventories.

How is this done? First, the statistician adds together the value of all the new buildings constructed, all of the new machinery produced, and the net change in inventory for the year. Of course, this figure is too large, for it includes capital that has been used to replace worn-out capital. The statistician must take into account the amount of *depreciation*, the amount of capital that has been used up, during the year. So he calls his first figure *gross investment,* and when he subtracts depreciation from gross investment, he arrives at the amount of *net investment* that has taken place during that year. Depreciation is hard to calculate, but it changes fairly slowly. Therefore most economists are willing to use *gross investment* for their work, bearing in mind, of course, that it includes depreciation.

Gross national product and net national product. We have said that national product is equal to the sum of all final products, including investment. If we use *gross investment* figures, we obtain a total for the national income that is called *gross national product* (GNP). If we use *net investment* (gross investment minus depreciation), we obtain a total for *net national product* (NNP). The only difference between them is the figure for depreciation. We shall make use of NNP in most of our discussions.

National income and government expenditures. We have been

discussing the national income or GNP in terms of consumer goods and services and gross investment. Now we must add one final consumer, and it is a large one—the Federal, state, and local governments. Our GNP concept must somehow take into account the billions of dollars' worth of goods and services which the nation consumes collectively. That is, we have added consumption (C) and investment (I) together to form GNP. Now we must add the effect of government (G) to our calculations.

How is this done? After some debate, American statisticians (and United Nations statisticians) decided to make use of the simplest method available. They simply add *all government expenditures on goods and services* to the total of private consumption and investment. Our formula for GNP now reads C (consumption) $+ I$ (investment) $+ G$ (government expenditures) $=$ GNP (including depreciation). You will see this formula very frequently in economic writings.

The point is that government expenditures represent real consumption of national production, and a jet bomber is just as much a part of our national product as a loaf of bread or a baker's wages. In short, all government payroll expenditures for employees plus all expenditures for goods purchased from private industry form part of G—government expenditure on goods and services. Their relative importance in the national income can be seen in Figure 10. Note that the chart uses *net* investment; depreciation is excluded.

Exclusion of transfer payments. Now, this does not mean that every dollar which government spends is included in GNP, for some government dollars are spent for things other than goods and services. Such expenditures are called *transfer payments,* and we met them before in our discussion of welfare.

NNP is sum of consumption, investment, and government expenditures:

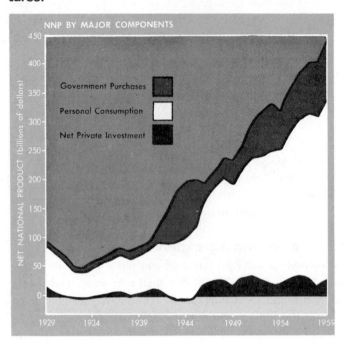

Fig. 10. Though consumption dominates NNP, note the war and postwar growth in government expenditure and in investment. (Source: U.S. Department of Commerce.)

The widow's pension is not included in GNP, for the government has not purchased goods or services with the pension check. Or to put it another way, the pension payment adds nothing to the national product, and it is the total national product that we are trying to measure. The major item now excluded from GNP as a transfer item is interest on the public debt.

Taxes. If we calculate NNP by using the flow-of-product approach ($C + I + G$) we need not worry about taxes or government finance methods. Whether the government acquires money by taxation, by issuing interest-bearing bonds, or by printing noninterest IOUs (money), the statistician computes G as the value of government expenditure on goods and services based on actual cost to the government and disregarding the source of income.

If we take the lower-loop approach, we must take taxes into consideration. Part of the salary paid to workers in society is taken by the government in the form of personal income taxes, and these direct taxes are included in the wage component of the lower loop. This is also true of direct taxes on interest, rent, and profit. Indirect taxes added to the selling price of gasoline or diamonds or other products will also have a direct bearing on the cost of the item to the final consumer (as all automobile owners know); hence this too must be included in the lower-loop approach to NNP.

A FINAL DEFINITION. Now that we have brought government into the picture, our structure is complete and we can give a comprehensive definition of GNP and NNP:

GNP and NNP are definable as the sum of three major components: (1) personal consumption expenditure on goods and services, (2) government expenditure on goods and services, (3) investment expenditure. It is understood that in GNP gross investment expenditure on all new machines and construction is included, whereas in NNP only the net investment expenditure is included, there having been subtracted from the gross births of capital goods an appropriate allowance for depreciation. GNP and NNP can also be defined as a lower-loop total of costs: to factor-costs such as wages, interest, rents, and profit (excluding double counting) there must be added all the indirect business taxes that appear as an expense incurred producing the flow of products; and in the case of GNP there will also be included depreciation expense, whereas NNP will be less than GNP by the amount of depreciation.

America's GNP and NNP.

Armed with an understanding of the concepts involved in GNP and NNP, we can now turn to the actual data and examine both the flow-of-product approach and the flow-of-cost approach.

Flow of product. The left-hand side of Table 11 shows the upper-loop, flow-of-product approach to GNP. Note the distinction between domestic and foreign investment, which adds a new classification to our concept of GNP. Foreign investment represents the excess of exports of goods and services over imports of goods and services, and may be either positive or negative. The GNP of $554.9 billion represents the performance of the American economy in 1962 stated in money terms.

Flow of cost. The right-hand side of the table shows the flow-of-cost approach to NNP, using the value-added method of calculation. A few explanations are in order here. Wages and other employee supplements include all take-home pay and fringe benefits, plus taxes withheld by the employer. Net interest includes all interest except that paid on government bonds (this item, you will remember, is treated as a transfer item). Rent includes "self-payment" by homeowners as well as ordinary rent paid to a landlord. This is an "imputed" item which is estimated, but it must be included if we are to get a realistic picture of housing services and their cost.

Lastly, we turn to profit, which is the residual or leftover after all other items have been accounted for. There are two kinds of profit: corporation profits and profits from unincorporated businesses (proprietorships and partnerships). Profit includes both farmer and professional income, and a good deal of it is really a return to people for labor, capital, and land provided for

The two ways of looking at NNP and GNP in actual numbers:

Table 11. Net national product, 1962 (in billions of current dollars). The left side measures flow of product (at market prices). The right side measures flow of costs (factor earnings plus indirect taxes). GNP, which includes depreciation, is also shown. Be sure you understand the main items. (Source: U.S. Department of Commerce. The starred item includes the "statistical discrepancy" and arises from imperfect measurement of upper- and lower-loop data.)

FLOW-OF-PRODUCT APPROACH			EARNINGS AND COST APPROACH		
1. Personal consumption expenditure		$355.3	Wages and other employee supplements		$322.9
Durable goods	$ 48.2		Net interest		22.0
Nondurable goods	161.4		Rent income of persons		12.0
Services	145.7		Indirect business taxes and adjustments*		51.8
2. Government purchases of goods and services		117.0	Income of unincorporated enterprises (adjusted)		49.8
3. Net private domestic investment (78.8 − 49.4)		29.4	Corporate profits before taxes (adjusted)		47.0
4. Net export of goods and services (28.9 exports			Dividends	$16.5	
− 25.1 imports)		3.8	Undistributed profits	8.1	
			Corporate profits taxes	22.2	
			Reported profits (unadj.)	$46.8	
			Inventory valuation adjustment	+0.2	
Net National Product		$505.5	**Net National Product**		$505.5
Depreciation (or capital consumption allowance)		49.4	Depreciation (or capital consumption allowance)		49.4
Gross National Product		$554.9	**Gross National Product**		$554.9

their own businesses. Finally, "corporate profit before taxes (adjusted)" includes corporate profit taxes of $22.2 billion. The remainder of the $46.8 billion goes to dividends or is "plowed back" into the business—what is called "net corporate savings."

Of course, the GNP or NNP figures are identical whichever loop we use to make our calculations.

Disposable income. How many dollars per year do private individuals and families have available to them to spend? Broadly, this is the same as "take-home" pay, or pay remaining after taxes. Hence to obtain disposable income, we subtract all direct or indirect taxes from NNP, all corporate earnings not paid out as dividends, and add transfer payments for welfare or interest on Federal debts. The result is what gets into public hands for disposal. This is the actual sum that people divide between spending and saving. In recent years, about 93 per cent of disposable income (*DI*) has gone into consumption and about 7 per cent into net personal saving. Obviously, such information is very important indeed to retail stores and others concerned with public spending.

DETERMINATION OF NATIONAL INCOME

We are now ready to move beyond the anatomy of national income and consider its physiology, to ask ourselves what causes national income to rise or fall or remain at some particular level. The analysis that we use, which is called "modern theory of income analysis," stresses the significance of the *level of total spending as determined by the interplay of the monetary forces of saving and investment.* Much of the analysis stems from the work of John Maynard Keynes (Lord Keynes), the English economist. But the broad fundamentals of the approach are today accepted by most economists, though many do not share Keynes's opinions about what governmental policy ought to be in particular economic situations. Thus we are not here concerned with "Keynesian" versus "anti-Keynesian" economics, but with a synthesis of what is valuable in economic theory, whether "classical" or "Keynesian." The result might be called "neo-classical economics" if we insist upon labeling our approach.

Saving, consumption, and investment. Our analysis begins with a fact: in practice, saving and investment are done by different people and for different reasons. This was not always so; for the primitive farmer, they were the same thing, and were undertaken for the same reason. The farmer who drained his field (invested time and work in drainage) was also saving (he did not use the time for current production). If there were no investment opportunities (fields to be drained) he wouldn't dream of saving, nor would there be any way for him to save if he were foolish enough to make the attempt.

In our modern economy, investment (net capital formation) is carried on by business enterprises, especially corporations. Of course, when a corporation has opportunities to invest, its owners are tempted to plow earnings back into the business; hence business saving does depend directly upon investment opportunities to some degree. But saving is also done by an entirely different group—by individuals, families, or households, who do not have an opportunity for investment or capital formation. Instead, they save to provide for future expenses or security, for the future of the family, or merely because they believe saving and thrift are "good." Such savings have little or nothing to do with investment opportunities. Bear in mind that we mean by investment the formation of capital (equipment, buildings, or inventory) and not the purchase of a piece of land in Florida; for the economist, the latter is only a transfer item, not a true investment.

The variability of investment. We are left, then, with the proposition: *saving and investing are often done by different individuals and for different reasons.* To this we must now add a second fact: *the amount of investment is extremely variable.* This is reasonable once we realize that opportunities for investment depend upon the dynamic and relatively unpredictable factors which determine economic growth. Investment opportunities occur where there are *new* products to be made, *new* markets to be filled, *higher* income levels to purchase the additional goods, and so on. Economic growth springs from a variety of factors, technological change, politics, public optimism, governmental policy, taxes, etc.

Now, as we shall see below, the relationship between the amount of savings and the opportunities that exist for investing these savings is a vital factor in the health of the economy. Yet an industrial system like our own has no way that it can guarantee enough investment opportunities to maintain full employment and maximum production. If there is too little investment, deflation and unemployment will follow; if there is too much investment, inflation will occur. The optimum condition is a dynamic equilibrium in which there is just enough investment to maintain full employment. We have said that the system cannot achieve this goal unaided. Fortunately, things need not be left to Dame Fortune to decide. As we shall see, a sensible combination of public and private economic policy can greatly enhance economic stability. It cannot, of course, eliminate all fluctuations from the economy; but the fluctuations in employment and prices can be very considerably reduced.

Some basic concepts. Before we proceed with our analysis, we must clarify some of the relationships that economists have discovered between consumption, saving, and income. In particular, we find that the income level is an important factor in determining saving and consumption levels. We have all observed that the very poor seldom save anything from their income, while the wealthy commonly save a good deal. The actual differences unearthed by studies made in the 1960s are shown in Table 12.

Three aspects of the table are particularly interesting to the economist: (1) the total amount of consumption at each income level (propensity to consume); (2) the total amount of saving at each income level (propensity to save); and (3) the percentage of each *extra* dollar of income that is consumed (marginal propensity to consume). We shall now examine each of these concepts in more detail.

Propensity to consume. Examine column 3 in Table 12. This is called the consumption schedule, and it shows our propensity to consume. Note that the

Most saving is done by families with incomes above the average:

Disposable income after taxes (1)	Net saving (+) or dissaving (−) (2)	Consumption (3)
$ 3,000	$ −170	$3,170
4,000	−110	4,110
5,000	0	5,000
6,000	+150	5,850
7,000	+400	6,600
8,000	+760	7,240
9,000	+1,170	7,830
10,000	+1,640	8,360
11,000	+2,150	8,850

Table 12. Postwar propensity of families to save and consume. The break-even point at which people cease to dissave and begin to do positive saving is here shown at $5,000. How much of each extra dollar do people around this income devote to extra consumption? How much to extra saving?

level of consumption increases absolutely with a rise in income level, though it declines in proportion to total income. We can transfer this schedule to a graph, producing a curve similar to that shown in Figure 11.

The 45° line drawn on the graph is extremely useful, for at any point on that line consumption is exactly equal to disposable income. Note that the consumption curve touches the 45° line at an income level of $5,000 per year—

A graph of the propensity-to-consume schedule:

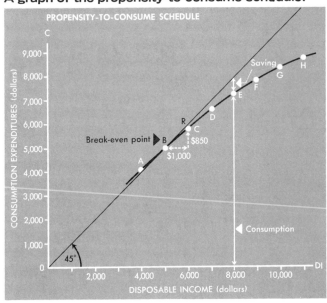

Fig. 11. The curve through A, B, . . ., H is the consumption schedule, or the propensity to consume. Its slope at any point — measured by forming a little triangle and relating altitude to base — is the MPC, the marginal propensity to consume. The 45° line helps locate the break-even point and helps our eye measure net saving. Can you see how?

The saving schedule is the exact twin of the consumption schedule:

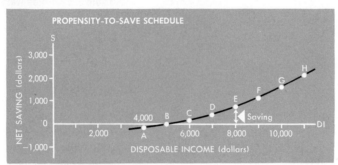

Fig. 12. This saving schedule comes from subtracting consumption from income. (Graphically, we vertically subtracted the consumption schedule from the 45° helping line.) Note the break-even point *B* is at the same $5,000 level as in Fig. 11. Why? Measure MPS by the curve's slope at any point. Does MPS + MPC = 1 everywhere? (It had better!)

our "break-even" point in the schedule. Any family whose level of consumption lies above the 45° line (as at point *A*) is dissaving; a family whose propensity to consume lies *below* the 45° line is performing net positive saving.

Propensity to save. Obviously, the difference between income and spending (column 2 of Table 12) is our net saving or dissaving. This schedule too can be illustrated by a graph or curve (Figure 12). In this graph, the amount of saving is shown by the distance between the horizontal white line and the income curve. When the saving schedule lies *to the left of* the "break-even" point, the family is dissaving. When it lies *on* the point, the family is breaking even. When it is *to the right of* the point, the family is saving.

Marginal propensity to consume. The economist has also found it very useful to examine the effect of an *increase* of income on the propensity to save or consume. That is, he wants to know what happens when the family receives *added income*. Will it all be spent? If not, what part of the new income will be spent? Let us rearrange our consumption schedule to show how the family disposes of *extra* income (Table 13). Between A and B, the family receives $1,000 in added income. Of this $1,000, the family consumes $890 and saves $110. The decimal fraction of the added income which is devoted to consumption (column 4) is given the special name *marginal propensity to consume* (MPC).

We can make the same type of calculation for the portion of each extra dollar that is saved, and this gives us the *marginal propensity to save* (MPS).

MPC and MPS are Siamese twins, for if MPC is .85, the MPS must be .15; added together they account for 100 per cent of the extra disposable income. In other words, *saving + consumption = disposable income.*

The community's overall consumption schedule. So far we have been talking about family consumption at different income levels. To study the national income, we are interested in a propensity-to-consume schedule that is slightly different from a family budget schedule. We must relate total consumption and disposable income at the national level. We find that aggregate income, though not the only factor involved, definitely influences our level of consumption. Note how closely consumption follows yearly disposable income in Figure 13.

However, certain warnings are in order. The national consumption schedule must in some sense be an aggregation of family schedules. But even if family schedules were known, we would still have to know something about the distribution of increased incomes before we could plot total consumption on a national schedule. A second point arises out of gross changes in income. If my income suddenly jumps from $5,000 to $40,000 per year, would I save and spend in the same way that other people in that income bracket spend and save? Not necessarily, especially at the beginning. A third factor that must be considered is that each man's consumption depends upon the incomes and

How we depict important consumption-income and saving-income patterns:

Table 13. Propensity to consume and propensity to save. Each dollar of income not consumed is saved. And each extra dollar of income goes into extra consumption or extra saving—giving us two important concepts we are to study: the MPC and MPS.

	Disposable income, $ (after taxes) (1)	Added income, $ (2)	Amount of added income consumed, $ (3)	Marginal propensity to consume: (3) ÷ (2) (4)
A.	3,000			
B.	4,000	1,000	890	$\frac{890}{1000} = .89$
C.	5,000	1,000	850	$\frac{850}{1000} = .85$
D.	6,000	1,000	750	$\frac{750}{1000} = .75$
E.	7,000	1,000	640	$\frac{640}{1000} = .64$
F.	8,000	1,000	590	$\frac{590}{1000} = .59$

National consumption did move with national income:

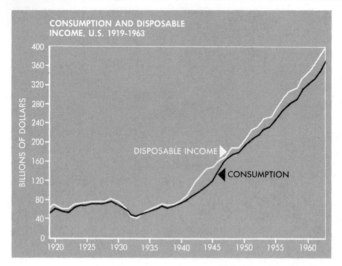

CONSUMPTION AND DISPOSABLE
INCOME, U.S. 1919-1963

DISPOSABLE INCOME

◀ CONSUMPTION

Fig. 13. Can you see how great saving became during wartime goods shortage and rationing? (Source: U.S. Department of Commerce.)

consumptions of others. What is regarded as adequate today may not be so considered a few years from now, and this can produce significant changes in our national consumption schedule. Other factors like price changes, population growth, and that most unpredictable of all things—human desire—increase the economist's margin for error and remind us once again that we are not dealing with an exact science.

THE THEORY OF INCOME DETERMINATION

Economists are agreed that investment is the factor which has the greatest influence on employment and income fluctuation. That is, the level of investment tends to determine whether we live in an inflationary economic situation in which prices rise rapidly, or in a frigid state of mass unemployment. The importance of income itself needs little emphasis; it affects our lives in a thousand different ways.

How saving and investment affect national income. The general principle that we now wish to demonstrate is that *income will tend toward a point where there is an equilibrium between saving and investment*. It is clear that there will be different amounts of saving and investment at different levels of national income. The point here is that income will move toward the level of national income at which saving and investment are equal.

For simplicity, let us first suppose that available investment opportunities are such that net investment will be exactly $40 billion each year regardless of the level of NNP. There are three cases that we must then consider. First, the amount that people actually save may be just *equal* to $40 billion; in this case everyone will be content to go on as before. Business firms will not find inventories increasing on their shelves, nor will business be so good that firms will want to produce more goods. Production, employment, and income spending will then remain about the same. The system is in equilibrium.

In the second case, people actually save *more* than the $40 billion which business firms want to invest. Now we find pressure at work to induce changes in the saving pattern. For this increased saving is possible only if consumption is decreased, and business firms will find themselves piling up inventories. Since this is poor business policy, production will be reduced and workers laid off, thus gradually reducing the NNP. The reduction will continue until savings and investment are once again in balance. That is, a slowing down of production will cause a reduction in income, and consequently a reduction in savings until savings reaches the 40-billion-dollar level.

In the third case, people are saving *less* than the $40 billion per year which business wants to invest. This results in the consumption of more goods than are currently being produced. Business inventories begin to disappear, and businessmen are then motivated to expand production. They employ more men and create more income. This increases savings (remember the propensity-to-save curve) until it reaches the 40-billion-dollar level.

In all three cases, the conclusion is that the national income will stabilize only at a level at which investment and savings are equal. At any other national income level, the desired savings of the population will not match the desired investment of business. This imbalance will cause production and employment changes which alter the operation of the economic system in such a way that the income level moves toward a point at which savings and investment balance. The equilibrium level may, of course, occur at a very low level of production, and equilibrium is not a "good thing" in itself. Governments today are much concerned with the level at which equilibrium occurs, seeking to raise or lower the level to obtain optimum production and full employment.

Arithmetic demonstration of income determination.

A thoughtful reader may still want more on *why* the equilibrium point will be located at the intersection of the saving and investment schedules. A numerical illustration may help clarify this basic point. In Table 14 a very simple pattern of the propensity to save at different income levels has been recorded. The break-even level is assumed at $380 billion. Each income change of $60 billion is assumed to lead to a 20-billion-dollar change in saving and a 40-billion-dollar change in consumption. In other words MPC is assumed as a constant 2/3, and MPS as a constant 1/3. For simplicity, the investment level is taken at exactly $40 billion.

Now, the crucial data are in columns 5 and 6. Column 5 shows how much

The tendency toward equilibrium is shown by an arithmetic table:

Table 14. Income determination by saving and investment (in billions of dollars). The unshaded row depicts the equilibrium NNP, where the $40 billion that businessmen will be willing to continue to invest is just matched by families' intended saving. (In higher rows, firms will be forced into unintended inventory investment and will respond by cutting production and NNP back to equilibrium. Interpret similarly the expansion arrows of the lower rows.)

Levels of NNP and *DI* (1)	Scheduled con- sumption (2)	Scheduled or planned or main- tainable saving (3)[=(1)−(2)]	Scheduled or planned or main- tainable invest- ment (4)	Expense incurrable by business to produce NNP (5)[=(1)]	Scheduled spending that would permanently come back to businesses (6)[=(2)+(4)]	Resulting tendency of income (7)
$620	$540	$80	$40	$620 >	$580	Contraction
560	500	60	40	560 >	540	Contraction
500	460	40	40	500 =	500	Equilibrium
440	420	20	40	440 <	460	Expansion
380	380	0	40	380 <	420	Expansion
320	340	−20	40	320 <	380	Expansion

total expense business firms undergo at each level of national production (expenses for wages, interest, rent, and profit). Column 6, on the other hand, shows what business firms would actually *get back* in the long run (spending for consumption plus investment).

When business firms as a whole are temporarily producing more than what consumers will buy plus what business will invest, businessmen will find themselves piling up unsold and uninvested goods. Meanwhile, their revenue from sales will be pressed downward and profits will decrease. They will therefore seek to contract their operations, and NNP will tend to fall. In the opposite case, when they are producing less than the sum of public consumption and business investment, businessmen will find sales increasing and profits up; this situation will lead them to expand production, inducing a rise in NNP.

In other words, when business firms as a whole are temporarily producing at an expense greater than what they can recover, they will want to contract their operations, and NNP will tend to fall. When they are getting back more than their current expense for production, they will increase production and NNP will rise. Only when the level of scheduled savings in column 3 is exactly equal to the scheduled investment in column 4 will business firms tend to maintain their present rate of production, and NNP will be in equilibrium.

A RESTATEMENT. Figure 14 pulls together the main elements of income determination in a simplified way. Without saving and investment there would

Dynamic investment pumps national income up and down:

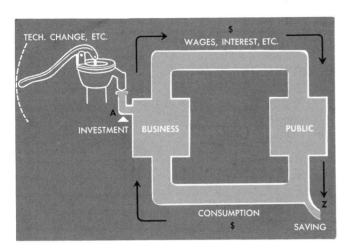

Fig. 14. Technological change, population growth, and other dynamic factors keep the investment pump handle going. Income rises and falls with changes in investment, its maintainable equilibrium level being realized only when intended saving at *Z* continues to match intended investment at *A*.

be a circular flow of income between business and the public. Business payments in wages, interest, rents, and profits would be exactly balanced by public payments for goods and services consumed. But in practice, the public will save a part of its income, so business cannot get back all of its payments by selling its production. Some monetary cranks think that this saving necessarily means unemployment and depression, but that is simply not correct. If there are opportunities for investment, business firms will pay out part of their costs for new investment goods rather than for consumption goods. Hence they need only receive a part of the total costs paid to the public as consumption income—the part which covers the cost of goods produced for current consumption. Public saving cannot be harmful so long as it is not greater than the amount that business can profitably invest.

Investment and income. We have sketched briefly the outlines of modern theory of income determination. Naturally, there are many important qualifications (like the effect of government finance on income analysis) still to be explored. Before we go into these questions, however, we need to look a little further into the relation between income and investment.

The multiplier. Our first point is that an increase in private investment will cause national income to expand, and a decrease in private investment will cause national income to contract. This is not very surprising, for investment is one part of NNP, and when one of the parts increases in value, we would expect the value of the whole to rise. But that is only part of the story. The theory of income determination states that the amount of the increase in income is *greater than* the amount of investment. This is called the "multiplier" doctrine. The *multiplier* is a numerical coefficient which shows how great an increase in income results from each increase in investment spending. Thus if a 5-billion-dollar increase in investment causes a 15-billion-dollar increase in income, the multiplier is 3.

We have not yet attempted to "prove" the multiplier effect, but common sense can show us that it exists. If I spend $1,000 to build a garage, I provide $1,000 in income for the contractor who builds the garage. But that is not the end of the story. If the contractor has a marginal propensity to consume of 2/3, he will spend $666.67 of his money on consumption goods. The producers of these goods now have an extra income of $666.67, and if their MPC is also 2/3, they will spend $444.44 of that sum, thus creating additional income for those who supply them with goods, and so on.

In this way, an endless chain of secondary consumption is started by each new primary investment. It is a dwindling chain, and it adds up to a finite amount which can be calculated arithmetically, or by using the geometric progression $1 + MPC + MPC^2 + MPC^3 \ldots = 1/(1 - MPC)$. With an MPC of 2/3, the multiplier is 3 (1 unit of primary spending and 2 extra units of secondary spending). If the MPC were 3/4, the multiplier would then be 4. The general formula we arrive at is

$$\text{Change in income} = \frac{1}{1 - MPC} \times \text{change in investment}$$

In other words, the greater the extra consumption spending, the larger the multiplier; the greater the saving, the smaller the multiplier.

Thriftiness and income. If changes in investment affect income, so do changes in the savings pattern. If the investment schedule remains the same, an increase in savings will tend to *lower the equilibrium level* of income. Common sense again tells us why. If people consume less, and business does not invest more, sales will fall, and production will soon be reduced. How far? Until national income has dropped enough to make people feel so poor that they quit trying to save more. How fast? We find that the multiplier effect works in reverse as well, and a $1 upward shift of savings will kill off more than $1 of income, just as a $1 downward shift in savings creates more than $1 in income.

This brings us to what is called the "paradox of thrift." In practice, businessmen are much more likely to add new plant and equipment (invest) when sales are high relative to plant capacity. Thus an increase in employment and production may induce a higher level of new investment. Anything that increases national income is likely to be beneficial to capital goods industries; anything that decreases national income is likely to be harmful. Under certain conditions, thrift, oddly enough, can be definitely harmful. If everyone attempts to increase savings, there may be a real decline in the savings of the community. Much depends upon prevailing economic conditions. At the full-employment level, where production is maximized, thrift is good for both the individual and the whole community. But during a severe depression, when there is much unemployment, the attempt to save may actually reduce saving—the individual who saves reduces his consumption, and therefore passes on less purchasing power to others.

The deflationary gap. Socially, the most desirable level of national income is that which provides full employment, and this level cannot be maintained, if our analysis is correct, unless business investment can make use of all of the savings at full-employment income level. If, for example, the amount of savings at the full-employment level is *greater* than what business will invest, there is said to be a "deflationary gap" which must be closed, else production will decline until a new equilibrium is reached. We must bear in mind the effect of the multiplier, which works both positively and negatively, increasing income or decreasing income as investment increases or decreases.

The inflationary gap. We may also have an inflationary gap when scheduled investment is greater than full-employment saving, for in this case more goods will be demanded than business can produce, and prices will begin to rise. Since everyone is already employed, an increase in production cannot produce the goods required for investment. This leads to spiraling prices, and rising prices can lead to attempts by labor to secure pay increases (increase production costs), which in turn cause still higher prices, and so on into the dizzy heights of inflation. The movement will continue until the gap is removed, either by investment or consumption demand falling off, or through corrective governmental policies.

Government fiscal policy and income determination. Fiscal policy is the general name given to government tax and spending policies; fiscal policy can play an important role in setting or altering the equilibrium level of national income. To simplify our task, we shall first consider the effect of government spending with taxes held constant.

We have already learned that net national product consists of three basic parts: NNP = consumption expenditure + private net investment + government expenditure on goods and services ($NNP = C + I + G$). Governmental expenditure must be added to private expenditure when we are considering overall consumption in the society. Furthermore, government spending produces the same multiplier effect as private investment so long as we disregard taxes. The reason, of course, is that a chain of respending is set into motion by those whom the government pays to build roads, etc.

Taxation, on the other hand, acts to depress the NNP level. Common sense tells us that if the government takes more from us in taxes and holds its own spending at a constant level, the extra taxes mean lower disposable incomes and lower consumption. Obviously, if both private investment and government spending remain the same, a reduction in consumption spending will reduce net national product and lead to unemployment. Or, if we already have an inflationary gap, the new taxes will help close the gap and wipe out excessive inflationary price increases.

We can easily reverse our analysis to show why tax reductions help fight a bad depression. Each dollar of tax reduction increases disposable income and leads to more consumption spending. Hence dollars of tax reduction are almost as powerful a weapon against mass unemployment as are increases in dollar expenditure. Such a program may involve a larger budget deficit than an expenditure program, but it also means an expansion of the private rather than the government sector of the economic system.

Summary

The national income concept, which is basic to economic study and analysis, has certain characteristics:

1. Net national product (NNP) is most simply interpreted as a flow of product: the sum of consumption plus net investment (domestic and foreign) and government expenditure for goods and services. That is, $NNP = C + I + G$.

2. A price index can be used to "deflate" NNP in current dollars and arrive at a more accurate measure of "real NNP expressed in dollars based on one particular year's purchasing power." This eliminates the distorting effects of price-level changes.

3. We can also measure NNP by following the flow of cost in the lower loop, bearing in mind the definition of residual profit. This approach to NNP uses factor earnings, determined by carefully computing the value added at each stage of production and eliminating all double counting. After adding before-tax wages, interest, rent, and profit incomes, we add all indirect business taxes to obtain NNP. NNP does not include transfer items like interest on government bonds or welfare payments.

4. Net investment is positive when people devote part of society's resources to creating more buildings, equipment, or inventory than are currently being used up by depreciation. Net investment is equal to gross investment minus depreciation. Since depreciation is hard to estimate, statisticians have more confidence in the gross figure.

5. For the same reasons, official statistics usually make use of gross national product (GNP) rather than NNP, where GNP = NNP + depreciation. Depreciation is sluggish and rarely varies much from one-twelfth to one-eleventh of NNP; hence the two concepts can be used interchangeably for practical purposes.

Income determination depends largely on the interaction of saving and investment. Yet each is carried out by different persons for different reasons. Income level seems the principal determinant of saving, and the relationship is stated as the propensity-to-save or propensity-to-consume schedules. Investment, however, depends on autonomous factors, such as population changes, inventions, or technology.

National income tends to an equilibrium determined by savings and investment. The level may be high or low. In the simplest case, investment calls the tune; it causes income to rise or fall until saving adjusts itself to the level of maintainable investment.

Investment has a multiplier effect on income. When investment changes, there is an equal primary change in national income, and this sets in motion a whole chain of additional secondary consumption spending. This multiplier works in both directions, increasing or reducing national income accordingly.

To avoid inflationary and deflationary gaps, we must match full-employment saving to investment. An increase in government expenditure, with taxes and investment unchanged, tends to expand production much like net investment. The $C + I + G$ schedule shifts upward. An increase in taxes, with I and G unchanged, depresses production because it shifts the consumption schedule downward, reducing consumption spending. Governmental fiscal policies properly managed are therefore a powerful source of stability in the economy.

Review Questions

1. What is meant by the concept "national income"?

2. Describe in detail, including a diagram, the two ways in which the national income can be measured.

3. What are some of the problems and dangers that face the statistician when he attempts to compute the national income? How are they avoided?

4. Give a careful differentiation between GNP and NNP.

5. What is meant by disposable income?

6. What are some of the basic factors involved in income determination?

7. Define as accurately as you can the basic principle which the economist uses to explain changes in national income.

8. What is meant by the paradox of thrift?

9. Differentiate between an inflationary gap and a deflationary gap.

10. Differentiate between the effect of government spending and government taxation on national income.

11. Discuss the differences between savings and investment. Who carries them out? What determines their total size?

12. Explain the principle on which the multiplier works, using an illustration from your personal experience.

For Further Study

1. Why must dollar measures of income be "deflated"?

2. What factors determine opportunities for investment? What would happen if savings were very high but investment opportunities were low?

3. Try to prove that the level of national income will tend toward the point at which savings and investment are equal. Use either the arithmetic or geometric demonstration.

4. Discuss the factors that influence propensity to save or consume among the population.

5. Is the size of the national income unaffected by the manner in which the government obtains its funds? Why?

6. Does inflation affect the size of the national income? In what way?

7. Why is it always true that MPC + MPS = 1?

8. Give arguments for and against thriftiness. Relate this to the fallacy of composition.

CHAPTER 14

Money,
Prices,
Banking

We have seen that the modern economist finds it convenient to analyze the forces that expand or contract money income in terms of savings or investment schedules, or what is the same thing, in terms of consumption, investment, and government spending. For the most part, it was assumed tacitly that all schedules were expressed in terms of dollars that had been corrected for changes in the price-level "measuring rod." Until now, a shift upward in the $C + I + G$ schedule could be thought of as stimulating an expansion in employment and production.

PRICES AND MONEY

Now we need to focus on changes in price levels. Why do prices rise swiftly in wartime? Why do prices creep up even before an expansion of $C + I + G$ raises the economic system to full or high employment? Why may prices and wages rise even when there is idle plant capacity and slack labor markets? Our program for examining these issues is as follows: first, we trace the facts about price changes and their effects; then we discuss the concept of money supply and its movement in relation to long-term prices. This provides the background we need for the subsequent examination of banking and Federal Reserve monetary policies.

Prices. Figure 15 shows the history of wholesale prices since 1770. Each war is clearly marked by a peak, and though a first glance may seem to indicate no clear trend, there has in fact been a general movement upward—as we can see by the chart of consumer prices. Since today's college student was born, the value of the dollar, as measured by its purchasing power, has been halved. And as an omen for the future, we can note that since World War II there has been no price decline comparable to what followed previous wars. Wages and prices seem to have become sticky. Further, government now acts quickly to stem any depression that is beginning to get under way. If prices rise in good times and do not fall much in bad times, what is the long-term direction of prices? The question answers itself.

Inflation and deflation. By inflation we mean a time of generally rising prices for commodities and factors of production; deflation is a time when most prices are falling. In neither case do all prices move in the same direction or in the same proportion. As a result of relative changes in prices and in total spending, inflation and deflation cause definite and characteristic changes in (1) the

Wars bring sharpest price rises:

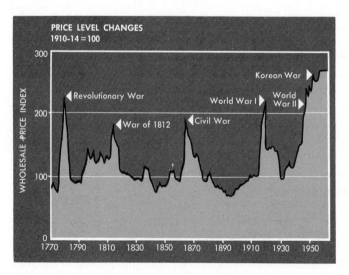

Fig. 15. In each successive postwar period there has been slightly less of a price drop. Indeed, after the last war, there was no significant drop. For 65 years the price trend has seemed definitely upward.

distribution of income among economic classes and in (2) total output. In general, unforeseen inflation tends to favor debtors and profit receivers at the expense of creditors and fixed-income receivers. Deflation has the opposite effect.

If you lent $1,000 today to be repaid in one year, inflation would reduce the purchasing power of the money repaid, while deflation would increase the value of the money repaid. If prices increased a trillionfold, as happened in Germany between 1920 and 1923, the $1,000 would be worthless. Creditors' wealth is virtually wiped out by extreme inflation. Since World War II, the interest paid on savings bonds has not always been enough to maintain the value of the purchase price. A bond bought for $75 in 1949 was worth $100 in 1959, but the one hundred 1959 dollars had less purchasing power than the seventy-five 1949 dollars.

In general, persons living on fixed pensions and regular salaries are most seriously affected by inflation. Some workers in highly organized occupations can keep ahead of the rising cost of living by militant bargaining, but many find their real wages lagging. On the other hand, anyone who invests in real estate, in common stocks, or in real goods may achieve a large money profit during inflationary periods. The effect of deflation is just the converse.

Further, modern research suggests that inflation generally redistributes money from older people to younger people. The dollars put aside for retirement often shrink in purchasing power. If prices rise at an average rate of 3 per cent per year, for example, the real purchasing power of a dollar held for 45 years will halve and halve again in that period.

Prices, output, and employment. An increase in prices is usually associated with high employment. In mild inflation, the wheels of industry are well lubricated, and output is near capacity. Private investment is brisk and jobs are plentiful. Thus many businessmen and union spokesmen tend to think of mild inflation as a lesser evil than mild deflation. The losses to fixed-income groups are usually less than the gains to the rest of the community. Even workers with relatively fixed wages are better off because of improved employment opportunities and greater take-home pay.

In deflation, on the other hand, growing unemployment of labor and capital reduces the community's total well-being. In fact, in a deep depression everyone suffers, including the creditor—who is left with uncollectible debts. This shows why an increase in consumption or investment spending is considered a good thing during unemployment periods, even though it causes some pressure on prices, for most of the increased spending goes to increase production and create jobs. But the same reasoning shows that once full employment of labor and capital is reached, further increases in spending are likely to be wasted completely in price-tag increases.

Galloping inflation. A price increase of 2 per cent per year is one thing; but if each price rise is the signal for a general increase in wages and costs, we may soon be in the midst of a malignant, galloping hyperinflation. Nothing good can be said for excessive price rises, such as those which took place in Germany between 1920 and 1923 or more recently in China and Hungary. Production— and even the whole social order—may be disrupted. The wealth of large groups in the population is wiped out as money loses its value. Debtors ruthlessly pursue creditors to pay off their obligation in valueless money. Speculators profiteer. Housewives rush to spend the husband's paycheck before prices rise further, and in doing so, they bid prices up even higher.

Fortunately, hyperinflation is rare except during war or revolution. The primary fear today is of a steady upward creep of prices. Will the creep necessarily become a full gallop? No definitive answer can be given. Most economists do not regard galloping inflation as inevitable, but they are still concerned with too fast and steady a price rise. In fact, the early postwar years led some to the view that a price-fixing board was essential to maintain full employment and price stability. But it is not yet clear that those who value freedom of enterprise and dislike authoritarian government controls need to despair over the question and resign themselves to regulatory boards of this sort.

Goals of long-term price behavior. Ideally, we all want a progressive full-employment economy in which the excess fluctuations of the business cycle are moderated or "damped." We want prices to be reasonably stable. But there are three possible programs offered as a compromise solution to long-term pricing questions, and each has its defenders:

1. *Prices, on the average, are to be stable.* Increased output over time, owing to population increase, capital formation, and technological progress, will increase total spending. Money wages and real wages also rise as a result of increases in productivity.

2. *Prices are to be gently rising.* As high-employment output increases, total dollar spending rises even faster than prices. Money wages also rise steadily; but the increase in real wages is not quite so great because of the upward trend in the cost of living.

3. *Prices are to be falling steadily.* The total of money wages and property income remains almost constant. Increased output resulting from technological gains is passed to the consumer in the form of lower prices. Real wages rise even though money wages remain constant.

All three solutions are tolerable if unemployment is kept at a low figure. And in some ideal system, it would not matter which pattern was chosen so long as trends in prices could be foreseen and suitable adjustments made. However, our experience suggests that the third possibility is least likely to maintain high employment. Most of the vigorous periods in the history of capitalistic development have come when prices were stable or gently rising. It is probably best not to prejudge the issue, but to withhold judgment until we have mastered the tools used for macroeconomic analysis.

The money supply. In modern times, money is the standard unit used for exchange and for expressing prices and debts. Money and credit affect the balance of saving and investment expenditure, and control over these factors is exercised by the Federal Reserve System as it seeks to curb inflation and fight depressions. Let us now look more systematically at these important components of economic activity.

Kinds of money: Small coins, paper, and bank deposits. The three main kinds of money in use today are small coins, paper currency, and checking-account bank-deposit money. Each has its own characteristics.

The coins we use for small change (pennies, nickels, dimes, etc.) are called "fractional currency." Because the metal in the coins is worth less than their face value, they are also called "token money." Although children think them important, they do not add up to more than a thirteenth of all the community's cash. They are valuable chiefly because they can be converted into other kinds of money.

Paper money is far more important than small coins. If you examine a ten-dollar bill, you will find that it is a "Federal Reserve note." Federal Reserve notes are "legal tender" and must be accepted as payment of obligations. Essntially, paper money is money because the government decrees that it is money and because we all accept it. Both gold and silver certificates have been used as paper money (they could be exchanged for either gold or silver at the Treasury), but gold was withdrawn from circulation in 1933, and silver certificates are no longer issued.

It is probably just as well that the gold has been withdrawn from circulation, for it certainly makes it easier to understand the nature of money. Earlier generations believed commonly that "gold backing" gave money its value. But the sensible reason why a staunch conservative wants to return to gold-coin money is not that the gold gives money its value. Rather, he knows that government can strongly influence the value of money, and he is convinced that governments cannot be trusted not to abuse this power. So he favors taking from Congress, the Executive, and the Federal Reserve System the power to control these matters and trusting the vicissitudes of mine discoveries rather than fallible or "corrupt" governments. Gold still influences the total amount of money available, and this is its true role in twentieth-century economics.

The third category of money is what is called "bank money"—the bank deposits subject to checking on demand. If I have a sum of money in a checking account in a bank, that deposit is considered money because I can pay for purchases by writing checks against it. Note that it is the balance, and not the check itself, that is considered money. The deposit serves as a standard of value and unit of account just as paper currency or small coins do, so there is no reason why it should not be counted in the money supply. Actually, bank money is quantitatively more important than currency today, for most transactions are now made by check.

Liquid assets: "Near-money." The concept of "near-money" is defined differently by different economists. It includes those holdings which can be converted into cash very quickly, like savings deposits or government bonds. These items have many of the properties of money. You cannot pay monthly expenses with government bonds, so we hesitate to call them money, but such bonds are so easily converted into cash that current spending habits are probably affected by bond ownership in much the same way as they are affected by a larger bank deposit.

Because it is difficult to draw a clear line between money and "near-money," the exact definition of the money supply is partly a matter of taste and not scientific necessity. A century ago, demand deposits would not have been included in the total supply; today, they usually are. For simplicity, this book will follow common practice and define the total money supply as the sum of coin and currency in circulation outside the banks, plus checkable demand deposits.

THE BANKING SYSTEM

Today there are over thirteen thousand banks in the United States that accept checking deposits. About a third of these banks are national banks; the remainder are under state supervision. All national banks are automatically members of the Federal Reserve System, as are most of the larger state institutions. About half of all banks do not belong to the Federal Reserve System, but they are so small that their deposits are only about one-seventh of the total. In any case, almost all commercial banks have had their deposits insured by the Federal Deposit Insurance Corporation (FDIC) since 1933 (up to $10,000 per deposit). This has made bank failure, which was once quite common, a rarity.

The primary economic function of commercial banks is to hold demand deposits and honor checks drawn upon them. A second major function is to lend money to local merchants, farmers, and industrialists. Banks also perform a variety of functions in competition with other financial institutions. Thus they compete with "mutual savings banks" for savings deposits or time deposits on which they pay interest. They also compete with cooperative building and loan societies and federal savings societies. They sell money orders or travelers checks, handle estates and "trusts," and even sell insurance in a few states, such as New York and Massachusetts.

Though commercial banks are not our only financial institutions, they are by definition the only organizations able to provide "bank money," i.e., checkable demand deposits that can be used as a medium of exchange. Therein lies their primary economic importance and chief economic interest. Their credit function is also interesting to the economist, and doubtless to the prospective borrower as well.

The Federal Reserve System. The Federal Reserve Act was passed by Congress in 1913, largely as a result of the outcry over the panic of 1907 and the epidemic of bank failures that followed. The country was divided into twelve Federal Reserve districts, each with its own Federal Reserve Bank. The capital for each Reserve Bank was subscribed by the commercial banks who joined the system, so that *nominally* the Federal Reserve Banks are owned by their members. Their actions are coordinated by a seven-man Board of Governors in Washington, D.C. There is also a twelve-man Federal Open Market Committee, consisting of the Board of Governors and five representatives from the districts.

The Federal Reserve Board, plus the twelve regional banks, constitutes our American "central bank." Every modern country has such a bank (Bank of England, Deutsche Bundesbank of Germany, etc.). This is the bank that handles government transactions, controls and coordinates the commercial banks, and most important of all, helps with the task of regulating the nation's money supply and credit conditions.

In actuality, the Federal Reserve (or "Fed" as it is usually called by the financial press) is directly responsible to Congress, and when there is a conflict between making a profit and acting in the public interest it chooses the latter without hesitation. It pays fixed and nominal dividends to its members, and is so profitable that it contributes substantially to the government. The members of the system do not dictate the action of the Board, but regard the Fed as a public or quasi-public agency. While the members of the Board are appointed by the President, the Board owes allegiance primarily to Congress. This is unlike the usual situation abroad, where the central bank is directed by the executive. We shall hear a great deal more about the activities of the Federal Reserve Board and the Open Market Committee in our further discussions of finance.

Legal reserve requirements. Bankers, as is well known, invest part of the money deposited with them in bonds, mortgages, or other earning investments.

How much of their deposits may they use in this way? The modern bank is required to keep a substantial part of its assets—about one-sixth or one-seventh of the total—uninvested. Usually, they are deposited with the regional Federal Reserve Bank, though the Fed now allows members to count vault cash as part of their reserve holdings. These nonearning holdings are known as bank *reserves*. Bankers tend to chafe at the reserve requirements set by the Federal Reserve Banks, and some banks which are not members of the Federal Reserve System do not maintain them. But from the standpoint of the Federal Reserve System, bank reserves are part of the mechanism used to control bank activity; the purpose of the reserves is not simply to ensure the viability of the bank.

Making banks safe. Banks are today much safer (for the depositor) than they used to be before the Great Depression, but this has little to do with legal reserve requirements. Banks are safe because we realize that governments must support them if there should be another avalanche of panicky "runs" on the banking system. No bank can turn all its deposits into cash on the spot; all banks keep "fractional deposits," and fractional systems are "fair-weather" systems if the government does not stand behind them.

Although the peril of a nationwide banking run has been conquered, that does not mean that bankers can stop worrying about their own banks. Various reforms have been introduced in recent decades to increase the safety of the deposits in individual banks and to reduce the instability of laissez-faire banking:

1. Bank formation and activity have been regulated. Capital required to start a bank is set by the government, and bank examiners periodically scrutinize bank assets and pass on the bank's solvency.

2. The Federal Reserve System was another great step toward banking stability, giving us a "Rock of Gibraltar" in time of panic and a central bank to control the money supply and credit conditions.

3. The Federal Deposit Insurance Corporation, which insures bank deposits up to $10,000 for members of the Federal Reserve System, was formed in 1933. All members of the System and most state banks belong to FDIC. Even if the bank should go bankrupt, depositors are insured against loss of deposits. In 1961, there were more than 100 million depositors whose accounts were insured by FDIC, and the $10,000 limit *fully insured* 98 per cent of that group.

Creation of bank deposits. We now turn to one of the most interesting aspects of money and credit, the process called "multiple expansion of bank deposits." Most people have heard that banks can, in some mysterious manner, create money, but few really understand how the process works. Actually it is simple enough if we remember that bank deposits count as money, and any increase in these deposits is in effect an increase in the money supply.

Let us begin with a brand new deposit of $1,000. When the money is deposited, it creates $1,000 of bank money, and withdraws $1,000 in cash from circulation. If the bank kept 100 per cent reserves, nothing further would happen. Now if the bank has to maintain 20 per cent reserves, it can invest $800 of the new deposit by lending it out. So far as the *first* bank is concerned, this is the end of the transaction; it has received $1,000 in deposits, of which it now holds $200 in cash—$800 has been loaned out. But notice that it retains the $1,000 in *bank money* (the original deposit) even though it has only $200 left in the vault. It has in fact created a net increase of $800 in the supply of money.

Now let us turn to the "chain repercussions" in other banks. The $800 which bank No. 1 loaned out will find its way back to *other banks,* less any amounts that "leak" out of the system. The $800 in new deposits will be treated just like any other original deposit; 20 per cent ($160) will be retained, and $640 will be loaned or invested, creating an additional $640 in circulating money. And so on through a chain of deposits and loans until it is used up. When each bank holds 20 per cent reserves, the *banking system* can create five times as much money as the amount of its deposits.

Obviously, the process will work in reverse when $1,000 is permanently withdrawn from a bank. You can test your knowledge of the system by calculating the steps by which this occurs.

Through this chain process the banking system eventually creates total deposits equal to five times the original new reserves:

Position of bank	New deposits	New loans and investments	Reserves
Original banks	$1,000.00	$ 800.00	$ 200.00
2d-generation banks	800.00	640.00	160.00
3d-generation banks	640.00	512.00	128.00
4th-generation banks	512.00	409.60	102.40
5th-generation banks	409.60	327.68	81.92
6th-generation banks	327.68	262.14	65.54
7th-generation banks	262.14	209.72	52.42
8th-generation banks	209.72	167.77	41.95
9th-generation banks	167.77	134.22	33.55
10th-generation banks	134.22	107.37	26.85
Sum of first 10 generation banks	$4,463.13	$3,570.50	$ 892.63
Sum of remaining generation banks	536.87	429.50	107.37
Total for banking system as a whole	$5,000.00	$4,000.00	$1,000.00

Table 15. Multiple expansion of bank deposits through the banking system. (From the 7th generation on all data have been rounded off to two decimal places.) Note that in every generation each small bank has "created" new money in the following sense: It ends up with final bank deposit five times the reserves it finally retains from the rest of the economy.

FEDERAL RESERVE AND CENTRAL BANK MONETARY POLICY

The Federal Reserve is a central bank, a bank for bankers and for the government. It has one prime function: *to control the economy's supply of money and credit.* If business is worsening and jobs are getting scarce, the Federal Reserve Board will try to expand money and credit; if spending threatens to become excessive, then the Fed will do everything possible to step on the brakes and contract money and credit. The Fed has the task of "leaning against the prevailing economic winds."

How monetary policy works to control spending. What is the exact process that Reserve authorities use to influence general spending? Basically, it is a five-step process:

1. The first step, when the Fed wants to put on the monetary brakes, is to cut down on the amount of money available to the bank for lending or investing. It "reduces the reserves" of member banks (not the legal minimum reserve limit). So important are these *reserves* that we shall capitalize the word in the rest of this section.

2. Each dollar of contraction in bank Reserves forces about a 5:1 contraction in total bank money.

3. The contraction of the money supply M makes credit "tight," which means more expensive (to borrow) and less available. Less M raises interest rates for those who wish to borrow, and makes borrowing more difficult.

4. The contraction of M will tend to reduce private and public investment. Why? Because decisions to build new houses or new plant usually depend upon financing conditions, upon the amount that can be borrowed and the interest rate that must be paid. If the rate is high, and money is hard to borrow, investment will be deferred. This applies to both private investors and state and local governments.

5. Finally, the downward shift in the $C + I + G$ schedule will have a depressing effect on income, on spending, on prices, and on jobs.

If the Fed has been right in its diagnosis of inflationary conditions, the drop in money income will be just what the doctor ordered to help the situation. The Fed's action will reduce the size of the inflationary gap, and congratulations will be in order.

In the opposite situation, where signs of a depression are growing, the Fed reverses its actions to expand income and loosen credit. You can test your grasp of the principle involved by outlining the steps involved in such an expansion.

The Federal Reserve System in action. We have surveyed monetary policy briefly with a telescope; now we can look at the mechanism in more detail. We cannot pretend to a complete treatment of the subject—that is the task of an intermediate course in money and banking—but we can get a general view of exactly what weapons the Fed can use to affect bank Reserves.

Like any other bank, the Fed has both assets and liabilities. Table 16 shows the combined balance sheet of the twelve Federal Reserve Banks in June, 1963.

Taking assets first, the gold certificates are simply warehouse receipts from the Treasury showing the amount of gold deposited there. Most of the remaining assets are United States government securities, and their significance will be explained later. The smaller items consist primarily of loans or advances to member banks. The interest on such loans, which is called the "discount rate," can be varied by the Fed to supplement its monetary policies.

The liabilities include the capital subscribed by the member banks plus surplus (which would be very large if it were not turned back into the Treasury). Federal Reserve notes (the five- and ten-dollar bills we carry) are the principal liability. They cost the Fed no interest, and the power to issue such notes is granted by Congress. The most important item is the member bank's *reserve balances,* the amount kept on deposit with the Federal Reserve Banks. These are the *Reserves* which the Fed attempts to control in order to expand and contract the money and credit supply.

Discretionary monetary policies by the Federal Reserve. The Federal Reserve has three main weapons for its stabilization policy. In the order of their importance, they are: (1) open-market operations; (2) discount-rate policy; (3) changing the legal reserve requirements of member banks. Four supplementary weapons, used from time to time, are: (4) the use of "moral suasion"; (5) selective controls over margin requirements for loans made to buy stocks; (6)

Federal Reserve notes and deposits underlie our money supply:

Table 16. Combined balance sheet of 12 Federal Reserve Banks, June 30, 1963 (in billions of dollars). By (a) controlling its earning assets (government securities and discounts), the Fed (b) controls its liabilities (deposits and Federal Reserve notes)— thereby (c) controlling the economy's money supply (currency and demand deposits).

ASSETS		LIABILITIES AND NET WORTH	
Gold certificates and other cash	$15.9	Capital accounts	$ 1.5
U.S. government securities	32.0	Federal Reserve notes	30.4
Discounts, loans, and acceptances	0.1	Deposits:	
Miscellaneous other assets	5.7	**Member bank Reserves**	17.0
(primarily "uncollected		U.S. Treasury	0.8
items")		Foreign and other	0.4
		Miscellaneous liabilities	3.6
Total	$53.7	Total	$53.7

selective credit controls over installment contracts and other forms of consumer credit; (7) selective controls over the terms of housing mortgage contracts. Congress allowed the last two powers to lapse in 1952 and 1953.

Open-market operations. The most important stabilizing weapon available to the Fed is "open-market operations"—the buying or selling of government bonds in the open market (mostly New York City). At frequent intervals, the Open Market Committee meets to decide whether to pump more Reserves into the banking system by buying government bills (short-term bonds) or whether to tighten things up by selling bills. The process goes on continuously. How does this affect bank Reserves?

Suppose that the Fed thinks the economic winds are blowing up a little inflation. The Open Market Committee, in secret session, decides to sell $1 billion worth of government bonds from the Federal Reserve portfolio. To whom are they sold? No one knows. Buyers' names are not revealed, but we can guess that they are primarily insurance companies, big business firms, and commercial banks. Not many ribbon clerks deal in bills. The buyer will likely pay for the bills by a check drawn on his bank account, and the Fed will present his check to the member bank for payment. The member bank holding the account loses an equivalent amount of its balances with the Federal Reserve. Thus $1 billion of Reserves, and demand deposits owed to the bond buyer, have been eliminated. But that is not the end of the story, for it is likely that a five-billion-dollar cut in the money supply M will follow. The reasons for this have already been covered. The Fed's open-market sale has put a 5:1 contractionary pressure on bank deposits. You can test your understanding of the process by outlining the steps taken to expand the amount of money in circulation.

Discount-rate policy. Federal Reserve Banks make loans to member banks, called "discounts." When discounts are growing, the banks are borrowing from the Fed, and this helps bank Reserves to grow. The Fed is not free to make discount policy exactly as it pleases, and it cannot simply drum up more discounts when it wants to expand them, but it can name the *discount rate*, i.e., the interest charge on these loans, and thus make them more or less attractive to members. This indirect pressure can produce changes in bank Reserves within certain limits.

Changing reserve requirements. The Federal Reserve Board has limited power to raise or lower the required legal reserve ratio—the Reserves that member banks must maintain with the Federal Reserve Bank. Using this control, the Fed can tighten credit very quickly by raising the required ratio. For example, if the required reserve ratio is 20 per cent, banks can create deposits at a 5:1 rate; if the legal requirement is raised to 25 per cent, the deposit creation ratio drops immediately to 4:1 and a one-fifth drop in all deposits will follow immediately, for every bank is deficient in legal Reserves as soon as the rate is raised. Banks will sell some of their bonds and call in enough loans to make up the difference. Bond buyers will liquidate deposits to pay for bonds they have purchased. The process continues until deposits have been reduced to the new ratio. The change is drastic, and may affect the entire economy; hence it is used very sparingly.[1]

FISCAL POLICY AND FULL EMPLOYMENT WITHOUT INFLATION

The behavior of saving and investment determines national income and employment levels. We have seen that investment and other spending often fluctuate widely from year to year, producing painful and wasteful instability, chronic slump, and snowballing inflation. What prescription follows from the economic diagnosis? No single answer can be given, for there is no panacea for the economic ills of society. Business, labor, and agriculture must pursue price and wage policies aimed at stable, high-employment economic activity. The Federal Reserve System must do its part by controlling interest and monetary policy toward the same ends. And powerful aid is needed from public fiscal policy (government taxation and expenditure). The subject is still in the controversial stage, and economists are far from complete agreement on particular policies. But we can attempt an objective analysis of the issues involved that will help each person to form his own opinion on these matters.

The task of fiscal policy. A positive fiscal policy is the process of shaping public taxation and public expenditure to help dampen the swings of the business cycle and contribute to the maintenance of a growing high-employment economy free from excessive inflation or deflation. Fiscal policy is an extremely powerful weapon, and some believe it really too powerful to be used. But no nation can today stand aside while its economy stagnates, so there is no choice but to try to lead fiscal policy along sound economic lines rather than destructive channels.

The task is clear. When the economy shows signs of weakening, or is threatened by a deflationary gap, the Federal Reserve must use an expansionary monetary policy to stimulate private investment so far as it can. If it is

---

[1] The Fed can use various minor weapons for controlling the economy. It can persuade bank officials to adopt a policy by informal argument (jawbone control), or adopt other informal policies which in fact control banking activity. It can also limit stock buying and installment buying by changing legal requirements of payment.

not successful, Congress and the President can then introduce tax and public-expenditure policies designed to help the economy achieve stable full employment once again. The goal is a high-employment and growing economy free from price inflation.

Our built-in stabilizers. We do not wish to give the impression that the economy will remain stable only so long as government officials are carefully watching trends and anticipating future movements of the economy and taking appropriate measures. In fact, our modern fiscal system has inherent automatic stabilizing properties, factors which operate whether or not the government intervenes. Let us look at the more important of these stabilizers:

1. Our tax system is so constructed that there are *automatic changes in tax receipts* as the national income rises and falls (roughly a 3.5-billion-dollar drop in tax receipts for each 10-billion-dollar drop in NNP). As income drops, so does the amount of tax collected; this reduction in tax collection has the same effect as an increase in disposable income, and thus helps to offset the initial fall in income. As income increases during a boom, more taxes are collected, thus reducing disposable income and helping to dampen the boom.

2. We now have an elaborate system of unemployment compensation and other *welfare transfers,* so that workers who are laid off begin receiving unemployment compensation very shortly thereafter. When they return to work, payments cease. The taxes used to finance these funds increase greatly when employment is high. Thus this program acts as a stabilizing influence in both prosperous and bad times, taking in funds during the former and paying them out in the latter.

3. The various *farm-aid programs* also act as stabilizers, moving government dollars into the farm-income area when prices drop off and spending decreases. When inflation brews and prices soar, government warehouses sell their goods and absorb dollars, again cushioning the effect of the cycle.

4. Finally, *saving* by families and corporations is a stabilizing influence in the economy. To the extent that both families and corporations attempt to stabilize their own spending and saving they contribute greatly to the overall stability of the economy.

Of course, these automatic stabilizers have limits; they are not sufficient to maintain full stability without aid, and their use in preference to discretionary programs (government action) raises social questions of a very broad nature.

Discretionary fiscal policy. The area in which government may act deliberately to alter the operation of the economy is subject to discretionary fiscal policy. This encompasses three principal types of activity: (1) public works and other expenditure programs; (2) transfer expenditures; (3) tax variations. Each has its advantages and drawbacks.

Public works. In the 1930s, the use of public works programs to offset the effects of the Depression was widespread and often ill-organized. The day is now long past when a modern nation will allow its economy to come so near to complete collapse. Emphasis has therefore shifted away from "make-work" projects. Indeed, economists would much prefer to rely on temporary tax reductions to offset recessions than to turn to public works. The principal reason is doubtless the time involved; it takes months or even years to put a large-scale works program into action.

This ought not to be construed as an argument against public works as such. Slum clearance, urban rehabilitation, road building, and other public construction may be among the most urgent of national needs. But they should be pressed for their own sake, and not under the guise of short-run economic stabilization. It might be wise to keep a long-term public-expenditure program fully prepared, so that it could be moved forward in time and made immediately effective, but that is another matter.

Welfare expenditures. In addition to the built-in stabilizers we have already mentioned, it is possible for the government to institute various discretionary welfare programs to further stabilization. Thus veteran's bonuses could be delayed during inflationary periods, and pressed during depressions. Parity payments could be lowered during boom periods, and raised during depressions. Most important of all, the Federal government could moderate the effect of prolonged periods of unemployment by helping the states to extend the period during which the jobless draw unemployment benefits. A major problem, of course, is that short-run welfare programs of this sort may be difficult to terminate once they have served their purpose.

Variations of the tax rate. If there is good reason to suppose that a recession will be brief, a temporary cut in income tax rates is a very good way of keeping disposable income at a high level or of keeping the rate of decline relatively low. It has the advantage of being effective immediately, for employers can simply withhold less from the weekly or monthly paycheck. Again, it is politically a difficult subject, for it may not be easy to restore tax rates to their prerecession level after the recession is past, but the policy is economically sound and has much to commend it.

Surplus and deficit financing. When an inflationary gap calls for contractionary fiscal policies, the principle of a balanced budget will almost certainly conflict with the need for higher tax rates and a reduction of expenditure. Similarly, a successful attempt to offset a deflationary gap may put the budget into a deficit. If the business cycle were regular, we would not worry much about this so long as the budget balanced over the complete cycle. But how can we be sure that the cycle is regular? What if America faces what Harvard's

Alvin Hansen called "secular stagnation"—a long period of slowing population increase, the end of free land, high corporate saving, and vast accumulations of capital goods with a bias toward inventions which will depress investment schedules? Or suppose that population soars, new inventions appear at every turn, and investment is generally excessive? Finally, suppose a nation deliberately attempts to accelerate its own rate of growth, how can it correlate the measures needed to stimulate growth and yet remain free of inflation? Obviously, a thorough discussion of fiscal policy will hinge in some respects on the issues raised by the general question of the public debt.

THE PUBLIC DEBT

The public debt of the United States is now almost one-third of a trillion dollars. What economic problems are created by such a debt? Are there any false or pseudo problems associated with it? What noneconomic factors must be reckoned in any adequate discussion of this vital political issue? These are the questions to which we now turn.

Genesis of the public debt. Let us be clear about the matter to which we are referring. Our interest is the same problem that concerns the man in the street; i.e., as a consequence of the war, the United States now has a public debt of just under one-third of a trillion dollars. During the war, the government pared civilian consumption and investment to the bone by rationing and direct controls. It attempted to maximize output by increasing hours of labor, both daily and weekly. Plant and machinery were not replaced or fully maintained. Inventories were depleted. As a first approximation, one can say that the country ended up with the minimum stock of capital goods consistent with winning the war in a given time. No change in this inheritance could have been made by any alternative financing plan. The shortage of goods in the postwar world was a direct consequence of the need to win the war, and quickly. The war burden will remain for as long as we must do without the capital goods that might otherwise have been produced in the war period. In this simplified form, the burden of war has nothing to do with the public debt. The missing capital would still be missing however the war was financed.

Are there then no effects of the war-created public debt? We find that the type of effect we get depends on the nature of the debt. When it is *internal,* the debt involves internal transfer effects between individuals of the same or different ages. Thus the persons who saved money and purchased bonds during the war now receive a larger share of consumption than those who did not, and the nonsavers are taxed more than would otherwise be the case in order to make these transfer payments.

A large *external* debt, on the other hand, would be a real burden. As a nation, we would be forced to ship valuable goods and services abroad to meet interest charges and amortization. If 10 per cent of the national income were sent abroad the burden would be extremely heavy, if not intolerable. Americans would have to work longer and would still have less to show for their efforts than they have today.

The most important lesson to be grasped, then, is that there is a great difference between the effect of internal and external national debts. Interest on internal debts is paid by Americans to Americans; there is no direct loss of goods and services to the whole economy, nor is there a loss of total income, for one man's loss is another's gain. Fortunately, the United States came out of the most costly war in history with little impairment of capital equipment and little external debt.

Borrowing and shifting economic burdens through time. It is often said— wrongly—"When we borrow rather than tax in order to fight a war, then the true economic burden is really shifted to unborn generations who will have to pay interest and principal on the debt." In relation to an external debt, this is certainly true. But in reference to an internal debt, it is economically naïve and misleading.

Wars are fought with real goods, expended here and now. If we borrow our munitions from another society and pledge our grandchildren to repay them in goods and services, we have truly shifted the economic burden to unborn generations. But if no outside nation lends us munitions, we must produce our own goods; and if the government cannot obtain the necessary money through taxation, we must resort to borrowing, and we acquire a large internal debt. But it is the present generation which gives up the resources needed to produce munitions; that cannot be done in the future, it must be done here and now.

What does happen to this internal debt? Decades after the war, certain of our unborn grandchildren will be taxed to pay interest and perhaps principal to other as yet unborn grandchildren. This transfer is important, of course, but it does not transfer the economic burden to the shoulders of future generations. That simply cannot be done. But it would be wrong to jump to the hasty conclusion that no burden of any kind is involved. There is an indirect distortion burden that may be very important. First, although money goes from one pocket to another, the trousers may be worn by different people. Nearly every person has some share of the national debt, but statistical evidence suggests that the people who receive bond interest are *on the average* not in the lower-income brackets. Thus the debt is criticized as a "regressive" element in the fiscal system—a case of "soaking the poor to pay the rich."

However, this is not the most important single indirect burden involved in the debt. More important, transferring tax money from Peter to pay bond interest to the same Peter will involve a heavy indirect burden on the economy, for taxation always has some distorting effect on people's economic behavior. Taxation at a high level can affect willingness to work or to take risks in capital investment, and can result in less technological progress and fewer jobs.

Attitudes and the debt. Nor can we forget that a tremendous amount of emotion is generated by the debt. People used to predict the end of the economic system when the debt reached one-hundredth of its present level. Such attitudes may affect private investment by frightening off potential investors. Or in an inflationary situation, fears of the debt might actually accentuate inflationary tendencies. Obviously, the only way to counteract such tendencies is with facts, and it is to facts that we must look for our own assessment of the

Growing debt holds little peril for a dynamically growing economy:

Table 17. National debt and interest charges relative to national income. The 40-billion-dollar debt that so worried people in the 1930's looks small against the subsequent rise in our income. (Source: *Economic Almanac*, U.S. Department of Commerce; U.S. Treasury; United Nations; *Colwyn Report; Statistical Abstract of the United Kingdom.* Data rounded off.)

Year (1)	National debt (2)	Interest charges on national debt (3)	National income (4)	Size of debt in years of national income (5) [= (2) ÷ (4)]	Interest charges as a percentage of national income (6) [÷ 100 = (3) ÷ (4)]
United States (billions):					
1962	$298.2	$9.52	$453.7	0.7	2.1
1945	258.7	4.96	181.2	1.4	2.7
1939	40.4	1.04	72.8	0.6	1.4
1929	16.9	0.66	87.8	0.2	0.8
1920	24.3	1.02	79.1	0.3	1.3
1916	1.2	0.02	38.7	0.0+	0.0+
1868	2.6	0.13	6.8	0.4	1.9
Britain (millions):					
1962	£29,000	£700	£22,000	1.3	3.2
1946	24,000	500	8,100	3.0	6.2
1923	7,700	325	3,950	1.9	8.2
1913	625	20	2,400	0.3	0.8
1818	840	31	400	2.1	7.7

problem. Table 17 compares the present debt with the past, and with the British debt.

In 1963, our national debt of about $300 billion was much less than one year of national income, and interest payments amounted to about 2 per cent of national net product. Note that England had a debt *double* her national income in 1818, 1923, and 1946, and her interest payments were a far greater proportion of NNP than we can anticipate. Yet in the century before World War I, Britain was at the peak of her economic power. The steady growth of national income soon swallowed the "enormous" national debt.

The reader must form his own judgment as to whether the debt presently constitutes a problem of the first magnitude. All we can ask is a reasonable attempt to remain within the facts, and an unimpassioned attitude. We must avoid the error of forgetting that the real NNP of the United States is growing steadily and quite rapidly. The population is increasing lustily. Productivity continues to mount. What seemed an enormous debt in 1790 would today be nothing. How are we to say what our grandchildren will regard as a massive amount of indebtedness? There are many major problems ahead for our economy: inflation, slump, conservation, congestion, adequate growth, international balance of payments, and many others. In a sober man's tabulation of grave economic problems, does the public debt rank very high on the list?

CONCLUSION: A SYNTHESIS. The Employment Act of 1946 stated that the government felt a responsibility for maintaining high employment and moderating cyclical instability, and many have suggested that it be amended to include responsibility for maintaining reasonable stability in prices. Even if there were no legislative proclamations, the populace of modern mixed economies require their governments to assume these responsibilities. And we may reasonably conclude here that appropriate monetary and fiscal policies can ensure a fairly stable economic environment. Succinctly, the synthesis goes as follows:

By means of appropriate reinforcing monetary and fiscal policies our mixed-enterprise system can avoid the excesses of boom and slump and can look forward to healthy progressive growth. This fundamental being understood, the paradoxes that robbed the older classical principles dealing with small-scale "microeconomics" of much of their relevance and validity—these paradoxes now lose their sting. In short, mastery of the modern analysis of income determination genuinely validates the basic classical pricing principles; and the economist is now justified in saying that the broad cleavage between microeconomics and macroeconomics has been closed.

With good conscience, we can now turn to the analysis of the means by which the great social aggregates of national income and employment are determined.

Summary

Prices. The expansion of investment and other spending produces changes in price levels as well as changes in employment and output. The study of inflation (general rise in wages and prices) and deflation (general fall in prices) is a basic part of modern economics. War tends to produce the greatest variation in prices, but in this century there has been a long-range trend upward which the end of World War II did not interrupt.

Inflations and deflations are never "balanced" in the sense that all wages and prices move equally. In the past, inflations have typically favored debtors, profit seekers, and risk-taking speculators. They have hurt creditors, fixed-income classes, and conservative investors. Aside from the redistributional effects of inflation, mild inflationary pressures are considered more conducive to high employment levels than deflationary trends, so long as the threat of galloping inflation is not ignored. That is, a pattern of gently rising prices is preferred to a pattern of slowly falling prices or even a pattern of stable prices.

Money. The money supply M includes token coins, paper currency, and demand deposits, plus some important near-money or liquid-asset items like time or saving deposits and government bonds. However defined, the total money supply M has increased enormously in this century, particularly since 1939. The size of the money supply affects prices directly, in the sense that government action which influences the availability of money to investor borrowers and interest costs helps determine the consumption + investment + government spending level, and thus influences both prices and wage rates.

Banking. The American banking system consists primarily of relatively small-scale units, chartered by the national government or by the states. Less than half of the banks are members of the Federal Reserve System, but member banks handle six-sevenths of all demand deposits. Commercial banks have the primary function of handling demand deposits, honoring and collecting checks; such demand deposits are our most important single money supply.

The Federal Reserve System includes all member banks, the twelve Federal Reserve Banks, and the Board of Governors in Washington. Although nominally owned by the member banks, the banks are in fact almost branches of the Federal government, and are concerned with the public interest rather than with profits. It is the primary responsibility of Reserve authorities to use their powers to prevent any collapse of the banking system and to contribute to full employment and stable prices.

Demand deposits serve as a medium of exchange; they are money.

The banking system as a whole has the ability to "create" bank deposits, thus increasing the money supply, because they do not maintain 100 per cent cash reserves against their deposits. Roughly one-sixth of the total amount of money deposited must be held in Reserves; five-sixths may be loaned or invested. As these loans find their way into other banks, they create further deposits, of which five-sixths may again be loaned, thus creating a chain or multiplier effect which will produce $6 in deposits for each dollar of new deposits.

Federal Reserve Policy. The Federal Reserve is a banker's bank, a central bank, which controls the community's money supply. The weapons it uses are: (1) open-market operations, (2) discount policy, (3) changing legal reserve requirements, (4) minor weapons like moral suasion. Its operations follow a five-step procedure: (1) It contracts bank Reserves; (2) this causes a contraction in total deposits; (3) credit becomes expensive and hard to obtain; (4) this depresses investment spending; (5) money income and prices are thereby damped.

Monetary policy of the central bank is an important way of shifting the saving and investment schedules. The chain of causation moves from increased money to a lower interest rate and readily available credit, to increased investment spending (and perhaps some increase in spending by local government). The increased investment has the effect of expanding production, which means more jobs, higher income, and sometimes higher prices. When the process is reversed, the effect is precisely the opposite.

Fiscal policy—government tax and spending policies—also influences the national income by shifting spending schedules. When the government spends, it raises the G component in the $C + I + G$ schedule, and thus raises the equilibrium level of income of the economy. Taxes have the opposite effect of spending. A reduction in taxes increases the amount of disposable income, thereby shifting the consumption schedule upward and hence increasing total spending. Increased tax rates have the opposite effect.

The modern economy has a number of "built-in" stabilizers, such as the change in tax receipts that accompanies a change of income, and unemployment insurance that is collected during prosperous periods and paid out in hard times. It is the function of monetary and fiscal policy to supplement these processes whenever additional stabilization is needed.

Modern governments are able to ensure high-level employment and high-level income and to avoid chronic slumps or inflations by the appropriate combination of monetary and fiscal policies. This mastery of modern income analysis enables us to move on to discuss the classical principles of pricing and complete the synthesis of modern macroeconomics and classical microeconomics.

Review Questions

1. Differentiate between inflation and deflation.

2. What are the three possible kinds of long-term price behavior, and what are the advantages and disadvantages of each?

3. What are the kinds of money and what purposes do they serve? Which is most important?

4. Explain the general organization and operation of the Federal Reserve System. What purposes does it serve?

5. Differentiate between fiscal policy and monetary policy.

6. What is meant by "legal reserves"?

7. Why are banks today safer than those of a century ago?

8. Explain the process by which bank deposits are created, beginning with a deposit of $1,000 and assuming a 20 per cent reserve requirement. Make a diagram to show the flow of money as it creates new deposits.

9. What are the weapons used by the Federal Reserve Board to achieve its economic goals?

10. What are some of the stabilizers built into the economy and how do they operate?

11. What is the difference between an internal and external debt?

12. Explain, as clearly as you can, the policy which the Fed would follow if it appeared that a recession was likely.

For Further Study

1. What would happen if the supply of money were seriously curtailed? How could this be done?

2. Could a single monopoly bank with many branches create deposits?

3. What effect would a severe inflation have on your family? A severe deflation?

4. What would occur if prices tended to fall in the long run?

5. What is the role of government in the money supply? How does government know how much money to issue?

6. What happens if a bank invests unwisely? What consequences can you foresee for the economy if many banks make faulty investments?

7. Do you believe that a government can maintain full employment and a stable economy through wise monetary and fiscal policies? Could you convince your parents of your belief?

8. What are the respective merits of a tax cut and public works projects as weapons against depression?

9. What factors affect the size of the public debt that the nation can tolerate?

CHAPTER 15

Composition and Pricing of National Output

In Chapters 11 through 14, we were concerned with the basic characteristics of the mixed-capitalistic economic system, with the nature of national income, and with the modern theory of income determination. We wanted to know how the system operates, how and why income fluctuates, and how money and banking fit into income analysis. And perhaps most important of all, we tried to show how government monetary and fiscal policies, properly directed, can keep the economic system working tolerably well.

In this chapter and the next we ask a different type of question: What determines the prices of goods? How do we break down the national income into various kinds of goods and services? To answer such questions, we must study the tools of supply and demand in greater detail, and the closely related problem of analyzing the prices of the factors of production.

Microeconomics and macroeconomics. Sometimes this type of detailed analysis of market pricing is called "microeconomics," to distinguish it from "macroeconomics." The latter deals with the big picture, with aggregate income, employment, and price levels in the system. But that does not mean that microeconomics deals with unimportant details, nor that there is some kind of opposition between micro- and macroeconomics. Both are absolutely vital. A few decades ago, macroeconomics was so poorly understood that microeconomics was virtually ignored while economists devoted their time to the overall picture of the system. Today man has considerable mastery over macroeconomic problems, and his attention is once again turned toward the detailed and classic problems of microeconomics.

SUPPLY—DEMAND—PRICE

In a mixed economy, the basic economic problems—What, How, and For Whom—are solved by a system of markets and prices. Although the system is not directed, there is a definite relationship between the amount of goods available, the demand for goods, and the selling price of goods—between supply, demand, and price. A clear understanding of this relationship is basic to economic study.

Demand. Let us begin with demand. Everyone has observed that how much people will buy at any one time depends on price; the higher the price charged for an article, the less the quantity of it bought. And other things being equal, the lower the market price, the more units that people will buy. This definite relationship between market price and quantity demanded can be tabulated in a *demand schedule*, such as Table 18.

A demand schedule relates quantity demanded and price:

	Price ($ per bu.) P (1)	Quantity demanded, million bu. per month Q (2)
A	$5	9
B	4	10
C	3	12
D	2	15
E	1	20

Table 18. Demand schedule for wheat. At each market price, there will at any time be a definite quantity of wheat demanded. At lower prices, the quantity demanded will go up as more people substitute this food for other goods and feel they can afford to gratify their less important wants for wheat.

The schedule shows the relation between the price of wheat per bushel and the number of bushels of wheat that can be sold at that price.

The demand curve. Economists find it very useful to produce a graphic interpretation of the demand schedule, which is called the *demand curve*. The demand curve is constructed in the same way as the production-possibility curve we met earlier (see pages 417–418). The demand schedule shown in Table 18 is reproduced in graphic form as Figure 16. Each item in the schedule is plotted as a point on the graph (*A, B, C, D, E*) and the points are connected as a smooth curve (*dd*), which shows the relationship between demand and price.

We can learn a great deal from a careful examination of the demand curve. Note, for example, that price and quantity are *inversely* related, that an increase in price leads to a reduction in demand. This important principle is sometimes stated as the *law of downward-sloping demand* (for the curve slopes downward from left to right), and it applies to practically all com-

A downward-sloping curve portrays demand:

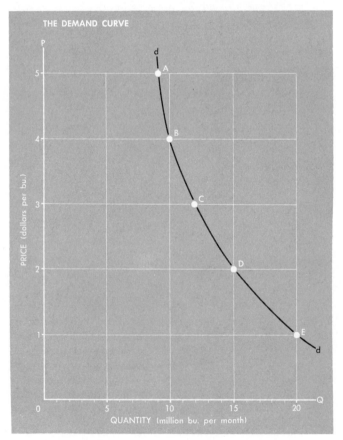

Fig. 16. Prices are measured on the vertical axis, and quantities demanded on the horizontal axis. Each pair of *Q, P* numbers from Table 18 is plotted here as a point, and a smooth curve passed through the points gives us the demand curve. The fact that *dd* goes downward and to the right portrays the very important "law of downward-sloping demand."

modities. Formally, the law states that: When the price of a good is raised (all other things being equal) less of it will be demanded. Or, if a greater quantity of a good is placed on the market, then (other things being equal) it can be sold only at a lower price.

Reasons for downward-sloping demand. The law of downward-sloping demand accords with common sense, and has been known, in a vague way, since the beginning of recorded history. People differ in wealth, or the ability to spend; hence when the price of wheat is sky-high, only rich men can afford it, even though everyone might like to purchase wheat rather than rye or some other grain. If the price is lowered, men of more moderate means can afford wheat, and will buy some. If wheat becomes very cheap, within the means of everyone, then demand for wheat reaches its maximum. The point is that each drop in price *brings in new buyers.*

Further, lowering prices has an effect on the amount that each purchaser buys. The man of moderate means may purchase meat once each week when meat prices are high, but eat meat daily when meat is very cheap. That is, each price reduction may coax out some *extra purchases* by each of the good's consumers. And, of course, a rise in price may cause them to buy less. As prices rise, the buyer seeks *substitutes* (tea for coffee, for example). Furthermore, a rise in prices has the effect of reducing real income; it reduces the purchasing power of each person's income, causing him to buy less, even though he may spend the same amount.

Supply. The price of goods can be related to the supply of goods in a similar manner. From the seller's point of view, the amount of goods that producers are willing to produce and sell will also depend upon price. In general, the higher the price of a good, the more of that good producers are willing to supply. This information can also be represented by a *supply schedule* (Table 19) and plotted as a *supply curve.* The supply curve inversely relates to the demand curve, for it *rises* from left to right.

The supply schedule relates price and quantity supplied:

	Possible prices per bu.	Quantity sellers will supply, million bu. per month
A	$5	18
B	4	16
C	3	12
D	2	7
E	1	0

Table 19. Supply schedule for wheat. At each *P*, there is listed the *Q* that producers will want to supply.

The supply curve relates price and quantity supplied:

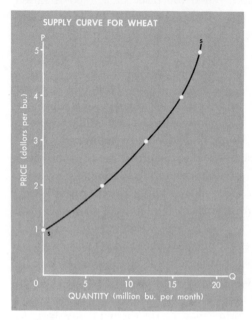

Fig. 17. Each Q, P pair of Table 19 is here plotted as a point. A smooth curve passed through them gives the upward-sloping supply curve *ss*.

The reason for the position and shape of the curve is fairly obvious. At a higher wheat price, farmers will take acreage formerly used for other crops and devote it to wheat cultivation, thus increasing the total wheat supply. Further, farmers can now afford more fertilizer, more labor, and more machinery, and can even afford to grow extra wheat on poorer land. All this tends to increase output when prices are high.

Equilibrium of supply and demand. We can now combine our analysis of demand and supply and see how market price is determined. That is, we can concern ourselves with the question "What will prices actually be?" rather than with "What prices are possible?" Neither the supply schedule nor the demand schedule alone can tell us the answer; we must combine them, as in Table 20. To understand how the table is constructed, consider what would happen if an auctioneer was selling wheat at each of the listed prices. If he set the price at $5 per bushel, producers would bring 18 million bushels of wheat to market each month. But the demand for wheat at $5 per bushel is only 9 million bushels per month. Therefore, this price could not prevail for any length of time. As the wheat piled up, competitive sellers would cut the price, bringing in new buyers, and increasing the amount of wheat sold. The price would fall. But it would not fall to zero. Instead, it would fall to the point at which the supply of wheat equaled demand. Further, if the price of wheat was very low, say, $1 per bushel, the demand would be quite large

Equilibrium market price is at the point where supply and demand match:

	Possible prices per bu. (1)	Quantity demanded, million bu. per month (2)	Quantity supplied, million bu. per month (3)	Pressure on price (4)
A	$5	9	18	Falling
B	4	10	16	Falling
C	3	12	12	Neutral
D	2	15	7	Rising
E	1	20	0	Rising

Table 20. Supply and demand schedules for wheat. Only at $3 will quantity demanded by consumers equal quantity supplied by producers. At any lower price, demand would exceed supply; at any higher price, supply would exceed demand.

(20 million bushels), and storehouses would empty rapidly. Disappointed demanders would then tend to bid up the price, and the higher price would tempt new producers into the market. Thus prices would rise to the equilibrium point. Only at a price of $3 per bushel do we find the sale of wheat stabilizing.

The equilibrium market price is where demand and supply curves intersect:

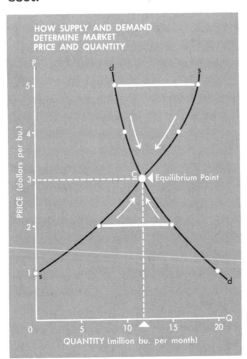

HOW SUPPLY AND DEMAND DETERMINE MARKET PRICE AND QUANTITY

Fig. 18. At the C intersection, the amount supplied just matches the amount demanded. At any lower P, the excess of demand will force P back up; and at any P higher than the equilibrium, the amount supplied will be excessive and P will be forced back down to the equilibrium level.

At this point the amount of wheat demanded just equals the amount of wheat produced. Of course, this stationary price may not be reached immediately, and prices may vacillate around the equilibrium point before they finally settle down.

Figure 18 shows the same relationship obtained by combining the supply and demand curves. The point at which they intersect (*C*) is the equilibrium price and quantity. The white bars show the excess of supply over demand at a higher price (above equilibrium) and the excess of demand over supply at a price below the equilibrium level. Competition among *sellers* will tend to move the price downward; competition among *buyers* will tend to move prices upward. Only at point *C* do we reach a balance between supply and demand.

Effect of a shift in supply and demand. Gregory King, an English writer of the seventeenth century, noticed that when the harvest was bad, food rose in price, and when it was plentiful, the farmers got a lower price for their products. We can explain this phenomenon very easily by using our supply and demand graph.

A spell of bad weather has the effect of reducing the wheat supply, and

Diagrams show effects on price of demand and supply shifts:

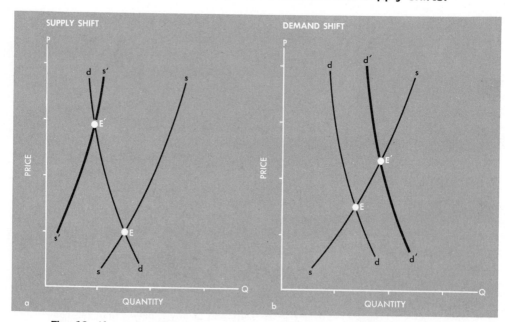

Fig. 19. If supply shifts leftward for any reason, the equilibrium price intersection will travel up the demand curve, giving higher *P* and lower *Q*. If demand shifts rightward, the equilibrium will travel up the supply curve.

this moves the supply curve to the left (Figure 19a). The demand curve does not change. The effect is to move the equilibrium point from E to E', or from a lower to a higher price. The effect of a good harvest, on the other hand, is to move the supply curve to the right. Try drawing in a new supply curve and note the position of the new equilibrium point.

The same apparatus can be used to analyze the effect of changes in demand. If rising family incomes make everyone want more wheat, the demand curve shifts to the right (Figure 19b), and more wheat will be demanded at each price in the range covered by the graph.

It is worth noting briefly that these graphs show the conditions that obtain only if *other things are equal*. This may be very difficult to establish in practice, for a rise in wheat supply may be accompanied by a decrease in the supply of some other commodity that has the effect of increasing the price of wheat. However, difficult as it may be, it is very important that our thinking about economics be clear and logical so that we may recognize and evaluate the various factors that actually influence the movement of prices in the market place.

What supply and demand accomplish. Having seen how supply and demand work, let us take stock of what has been accomplished. The scarce goods of society have been rationed out among the users by the auctioneering mechanism of competitive price. For Whom was *partially* determined by who was willing to pay for them. If you had the money and desired the goods, you got the goods; lacking either the money or the desire for the goods, you did without them. At the same time, the What question was also being partially answered. A rise in market price was the signal to coax out a higher supply of goods, for high wheat prices meant that farmers could afford more equipment and other materials to speed production. We say *partially* in all these cases because we have been considering only *one* market. As we shall see later, pricing involves interdependent markets and not just the "partial equilibrium" of a single market.

Of course, the supply and demand curves apply strictly only in a perfectly competitive market where some kind of standardized commodity such as wheat is being auctioned by an organized exchange that registers transactions of numerous sellers. The economist's curves are useful ways of idealizing the behavior of such markets, but they do not pretend to give an accurate microscopic description of what is going on at each moment. Rather they are used to summarize important average relationships that result over a long period of time from such organized trading exchanges.

The diagrams in Figure 20 illustrate how the tools of supply and demand may be used to give a good approximate description of various economic situations.

Supply and demand tools have many applications:

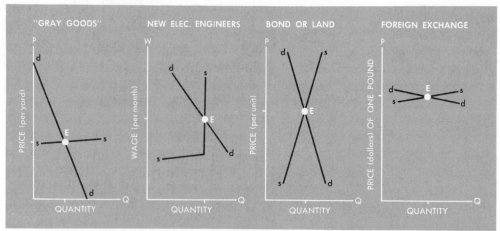

Fig. 20. Here are a few examples of the many uses of supply and demand. Note that these diagrams have used straight lines rather than the curved lines of previous figures: In connection with supply and demand and many other diagrams, the economist often uses such simplified drawings merely because the eye takes them in rapidly; usually this is a tolerably good approximation to the true empirical curves, but when this is not so, it is easy to modify the straight lines. (Example: The supply of graduating electrical engineers is a relatively fixed number, and this fact is depicted in the vertical supply line in the second diagram; however, this is an exaggeration in view of the fact that, as the wage gets low enough, some graduates will take jobs in other fields and some will go to graduate school—which is the reason why the *ss* curve bends to the southwest at low wages.)

DETERMINATION OF PRICE BY SUPPLY AND DEMAND

Our principal task now is to put the tools of supply and demand to work. We must attempt to show how supply and demand help explain changes in price, both in the short run and in the long run, how they help us to predict the effect of taxation on competitive prices, and how they aid us in our evaluation of policies that affect the operation of supply and demand.

Elasticity of demand and supply. In our discussion of supply and demand and price, we found that for any given condition of supply and demand, an equilibrium point was reached at which a given quantity of goods could be sold for a stated price. An increase in supply above the equilibrium level will generally lower the price; a decrease in supply will cause the price to rise. This much is obvious. What may not be obvious is a point also noted by Gregory King—that farmers as a whole received *less total revenue* when the harvest was good than when it was bad. In other words, if quantity sold (Q) is low, and prices (P) are high, then $P \times Q$ is *greater* than when quantity sold (Q) is high, and prices (P) are low.

This fact, that high agricultural production (and lower prices) tends to be associated with *low total farm income* is one that every American President has had to face in dealing with the farm problem.

Elasticity of demand. To discuss this problem adequately, we need a new and important concept: *elasticity of demand.* This is a measure of the degree to which the quantity Q of goods bought responds to changes in the price P and is independent of the units used to measure P and Q. A cut of 1 per cent in wheat price may increase wheat sales much less than 1 per cent, while a 1 per cent cut in the price of automobiles may increase sales much more than 1 per cent. The former case is called *inelastic demand;* the latter, *elastic demand.* In between is the borderline case where the relationship is direct and equal (a 1 per cent decrease in price causes a 1 per cent increase in sales), called *unitary elasticity of demand.*

Elasticity of demand helps us to distinguish between three special cases of the relation between demand and price. The crucial point to concentrate on is the total dollar revenue paid to sellers, or the product of $P \times Q$. Elasticity of demand is a good indicator of the way total revenue changes when a fall in price induces a rise in the demand for particular goods. For goods with elastic demand, a cut in price raises the quantity sold high enough to *increase* total revenue. For goods with unitary elasticity of demand, a cut in price will raise sales high enough to leave total revenue *unchanged.* For goods with inelastic demand, a cut in price will raise the quantity sold so little that total revenue will *fall.*

An example may help make the case clear. Table salt is a commodity which we need and use without too much regard for price. That is, if the price of salt dropped a penny or two per box, people would not rush out and buy large quantities of salt. Similarly, a small increase in price would hardly influence the amount of salt sold. The demand for salt is thus *inelastic* and a reduction in its price would mean a reduction of the total revenue for salt makers. But if television sets were reduced 50 per cent in price many more people might buy a second or third set, thus raising sales (Q) much more than 50 per cent, and thus increasing total revenue. In this case, demand is elastic. How elastic do you think the demand for cigarettes might be? Gasoline? Coffee? What reason can you give for your answer?

Elasticity of supply. What we did for demand we can also do for supply. Economists use the conception "elasticity of supply" to indicate the increase in supply that results from a change in competitive price. If the amount of goods supplied to the market is fixed (as with the supply of perishable fish brought to market each day), supply is perfectly *inelastic*. At the other extreme, if the supply is such that the slightest cut in price will cause the amount supplied to become zero, and the slightest increase in price will coax out an indefinitely large supply, then it is said to be *perfectly elastic*. Between the two extremes, obviously, there are varying degrees of elasticity, depending upon the percentage increase in supply that follows from a given increase in price.

Applications and qualifications of supply and demand.
Other things being equal, there is a clear and definite relation between supply and demand in any period of time. But other things will not remain equal. The demand for cotton has declined over the years because of reductions in the price of synthetic fibers. The supply of gasoline is increasing because technological progress enables us to produce more at the same cost. As costs and tastes change, as incomes vary, as the prices of rival products (coffee in relation to tea) or cooperating products (sugar in relation to tea) change, our demand and supply schedules shift. What effect does this have on consumption, production, and price? That we must now study.

The beginning student of economics is here warned against a common error. Do not confuse an increase in *demand at the same price* with an increase in *quantity demanded that results from a lowering of prices*. By "demand" we mean the whole demand curve. Quantity bought or demanded at a particular price is only *one point* on the demand curve. When we change price, we move to a different point on the demand curve; the curve itself does not change.

Incidence of tax. We can illustrate the point by referring to the supply and demand schedules for wheat. Suppose they intersect at an equilibrium price of $3 per bushel; at this figure, supply and demand are equal. Let us then introduce a new factor into the system which upsets the equilibrium—say, a $1 per bushel tax on the producer. On every sale, the producer pays a $1 per bushel tax. What is the final effect of this tax? What is its "incidence," as economists say? Who actually pays it? We can find the answer by considering the effect of the tax on our supply and demand curves.

There is no reason for the demand curve to change at all. Suppose that 12 million bushels can be sold at a price of $3 per bushel. So far as the consumer is concerned, he neither knows nor cares whether the producers are paying a tax on wheat.

But the supply curve will alter radically, for the producers will actually supply less wheat at any given price level because of the tax. Before they will bring 12 million units to the market, the price must be raised to, say, $4 per bushel. *The supply curve will shift* everywhere by the $1 tax.

A tax on wheat falls on both consumer and producer:

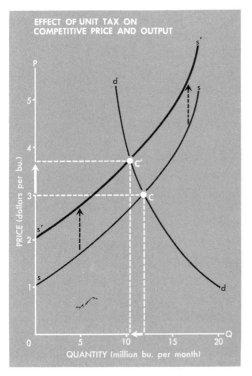

EFFECT OF UNIT TAX ON
COMPETITIVE PRICE AND OUTPUT

Fig. 21. A $1 tax shifts *ss* up $1 everywhere to give *s's'*. This intersects *dd* in new equilibrium at *C'*, where price to consumer has risen $2/3 above old *C* equilibrium and where price to producer has fallen by $1/3. The thick white arrows show change in *P* and *Q*. (Had *dd* been very elastic and flat relative to *ss*, most of the $1 tax would have fallen on the producer. Had *ss* been completely horizontal, the whole $1 tax would have been shifted forward onto the consumer.)

Where will the new equilibrium price be? We find the answer in Figure 21 where the demand curve intersects with the *new* supply curve. Because the supply has decreased, the price is higher, and the amount bought and sold is less. The graph tells us that the new equilibrium level is about $3.67, and the new equilibrium output is 10.6 million bushels, rather than 12 million bushels. Who pays the tax? Well, the wheat farmers do in part, for they now receive $2.67 rather than $3 for each bushel of wheat sold. But the consumer shares the burden, for his price has *risen* to $3.67, an increase of 67 cents per bushel. The consumer pays two-thirds of the tax, the producer, one-third. Finally, there may be an indirect cost to society as a whole in that the reduction of wheat consumed may have significant effects on the health and well-being of the members of society.

The student should check his understanding of this process by considering, step by step, the effect of a $1 a bushel *subsidy* to wheat producers. What is the new price? Quantity? Who benefits? How much?

A common fallacy. A tax, then, has the effect of raising the price to the consumer. Or does it? What about the following argument, so often seen in the press, or heard from the platform:

The effect of a tax on a commodity might seem at first sight to be an advance in price to the consumer. But an advance in price will diminish the demand; and a reduced demand will send the price down again. Therefore it is not certain, after all, that a tax will really raise the price.

Well, what about it? Here our warning against confusing a movement *along* the curve (price change) with an actual shift in the curve. One of the four sentences in the quotation is false because the word "demand" is used in the wrong sense. The correct reply would be more or less as follows:

A tax will raise the price to the consumer and will lower the price received by the producer, the difference going to the government. At the higher price a smaller quantity will be bought by consumers. And supplies are bringing a smaller quantity to market. Thus the amounts bought and sold are in balance where the new supply and demand schedules intersect and there will be no further price change.

Is the law of supply and demand immutable? Competitive price and quantity are determined by supply and demand. But do not prices depend on other factors as well? Actually they do, but such factors are not *in addition* to supply and demand—they work *through* supply and demand. If new gold production raises incomes it will shift the demand curves and raise prices, but the competitive price is still determined by supply and demand.

At this point, the thoughtful reader will protest: "What about the cost of production and its effect on price?" But again our answer must be that competitive price is affected by the cost of production only to the extent that production costs influence supply. If God sends manna from heaven at no cost but in limited supply, its price will not be zero, but will be given by the intersection of the supply and demand curves. And if it cost $50,000 to engrave the national anthem on a pinhead, but there was no demand for the item, its price would not be $50,000 plus profit; in fact, it would not be produced at all, and we leave to the reader the task of naming the market price of nonexistent things.

Cost of production is important, certainly, particularly in competitive conditions, but its importance shows itself *through its effects on supply*. Businessmen produce for profit. If they cannot get a price high enough to cover their past costs, then they will not like it. Nevertheless, once the crop is in, so to speak, there is not much they can do about it under competition. But they will not continue to produce these goods in the future at prices that fail to cover the extra costs incurred in their production. Thus supply depends intimately on costs, especially "extra" costs, and so too must price.

Moreover, to say that price equals cost does not in itself tell us which causes which. In many cases where an industry uses a productive factor that is highly specialized (baseball players, opera singers, grapevines, etc.), *price determines cost* rather than the converse. Grain land is dear because the price of grain is high. So we see that supply and demand are not ultimate explanations of price. They are simply useful catch-all categories for analyzing and describing a multitude of forces, causes, and factors that impinge on price. Rather than being final answers, supply and demand are initial questions, and our work is far from completed.

This should help debunk the tendency for neophytes to become confused by the use of the terms "supply" and "demand" and insist that the law of supply and demand cannot be repealed and that governmental activity cannot interfere in its operation. It would be better never to have learned any economics than to be left with this opinion. Of course government can affect price, through either supply or demand. The Brazilian government has burned coffee to raise its price; Britain has artificially controlled the price of rubber; sugar prices are still under international control. These governmental activities do not violate the law of supply and demand. They work through it.

Prices fixed by law. One important kind of interference with supply and demand which we must analyze is legal controls over wages or prices. During the war, ceiling prices were placed on some items in the normal household budget, and a floor has now been placed under hourly wages for most factory workers. These interferences work quite differently from other governmental activities, for they do not influence price through supply or demand.

Let us suppose that the government places a ceiling on the price of sugar of 7 cents a pound (retail). Now, because of prosperity or poor crops, let the demand be so high and the supply so small that the equilibrium price would contribute to profiteering in the sugar industry, and would represent a heavy "tax" on the poor who could least afford it.

However, we have a legal price ceiling of 7 cents per pound. Now what will happen? Supply and demand, of course, do not match. Consumers want thousands of pounds of sugar in excess of what producers are willing to supply. The gap is so large that some people will have to go without sugar, and if it were not for the price ceiling, someone would gladly bid up the price to much more than 7 cents a pound. But it is illegal to sell sugar for more than 7 cents per pound, and illegal to pay more than that price. There follows a period of frustration and shortage. The normal price system does not act to ration the supply of sugar, and a policy of "first come, first served" only leaves out those at the end of the line.

Once rationing is adopted most people heave a sigh of relief, for sellers need not turn people away and buyers can count on getting their fair quota of the limited sugar supply. Of course, there are always a few critics, longer on intuition than brains, who blame their troubles on the rationing mechanism rather than on the actual sugar shortage. They dream of the day when the government will "print more coupons" as if this would increase the supply.

Clearly, the rationing agency must try to issue just enough coupons to lower demand to the actual supply level. If too many coupons are issued, demand is still too high, and some people will still go without. If too few coupons are issued, stocks of sugar will pile up. With careful management, and a little luck, a reasonable balance can be maintained.

DEMAND AND UTILITY

So much for the general question of demand and supply. Now let us go just a little more deeply into the economic principles that lie behind the demand and supply schedules. First we calculate the demand curve of each individual customer—say, for a commodity such as beef—and then add together all of the individual demand curves to obtain the market demand curve for the whole society. The demand curve will generally slope downward from left to right across the graph—a very important characteristic, as we learned before.

Causes of shifts in demand. We know that a change in the price of a commodity such as beef will change the quantity demanded, though this may not change the curve itself. In addition, budget studies, historical experience, and careful thought tell us that other factors can also change the demand curve. Perhaps the most important of these factors is a change in income. Normally, an increase in income tends to increase the amount we are willing to buy of any kind of goods, though necessities are usually less responsive to income changes than are luxuries. A few "inferior" goods, like potatoes or rye bread, may actually be demanded *less* as income rises, but they are rare and we can safely neglect them.

What does all this mean in terms of our old friend, the demand curve? The curve shows the response in terms of quantity of a good purchased that comes from a change in the price of the good. But the quantity purchased may also change because of a change in the price of *other goods* or because of a change in consumer income. The demand curve is drawn on the assumption that they will not change. But what if they do? Figure 22 shows the effect of such changes. The original curve, *dd*, is drawn on the basis of fixed income and steady prices for other goods. Suppose the consumer's income rises? He will probably buy more tea than before, and his demand curve will shift to the right to *d'd'*. If his income falls, his demand for tea will shift to the left to *d''d''*.

Income is only one of many factors that position the demand curve. If tea became fashionable, the demand curve would also shift to the right. If the

Change in income or other-good's price shifts demand curve:

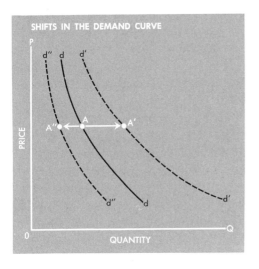

SHIFTS IN THE DEMAND CURVE

Fig. 22. Higher income will shift *dd* to *d'd'*. (Explain why; and why lowering income will shift *dd* to *d"d".*) Similarly, a rise in coffee price might shift tea's *dd* out to *d'd'*. (What would a cut in coffee price do? Or a great rise in lemon price?) A change in tastes, population, or expectations about future price movements would also shift the *dd* schedule.

price of coffee rose very sharply, this too could increase the demand for tea as a cheaper substitute.[1]

The law of diminishing marginal utility. The law of downward-sloping demand is so important that we need to touch on some of the economic principles that justify and explain it, though we can only sketch the basic notions here. The first principle to be grasped is that customers purchase goods because the goods give satisfaction or "utility." The first unit of a good bought (the first ice-cream cone) gives a certain amount of psychological utility. Now imagine consuming a second unit (ice-cream cone). The total utility rises, for the second cone gives some satisfaction, perhaps as much as or more than the first. But what of the third, fourth, or fifth? Obviously, there will come a point where each *additional* ice-cream cone gives less satisfaction than its predecessors. This decrease of utility, which resembles the law of diminishing returns, leads us to the *law of diminishing marginal utility:* as the amount consumed of a good increases, the marginal utility of the good (the "extra utility added by the last unit consumed") tends to decrease. The total utility may increase, but the rate of increase diminishes. In advanced economics, this law is used to help explain the downward slope of the demand curve.

[1] A rise in the price of tea will decrease the amount of tea demanded on the market; it will also affect the amounts of other commodities, such as coffee, that are demanded. Tea and coffee are called rival or competing products *(substitutes)*, while tea and lemon are *complementary* products. Pairs like tea and salt are said to represent *independent* commodities; demand for one does not affect demand for the other.

The process of rational choice. We can also use the concept of marginal utility to determine whether or not a consumer is spending his income so as to maximize his utility or well-being. If he has arranged his consumption so that the marginal utility he obtains from each good consumed is exactly proportional to its cost, then he has reached an equilibrium point at which he is best off. If we divide the marginal utility of several goods by their dollar price, we get the *marginal utility per dollar* of each good; the marginal utility of different goods can then be compared, giving us an index of utility "value" of each expenditure. If any good gives more marginal utility per dollar than other goods, one would gain by taking money away from other goods and spending more on that one good—to the point where your purchases brought its marginal utility per dollar down to equality with other goods.

We need not apply this principle just to spending money. Suppose you have only a certain number of hours to spend studying for examinations? If you are so uncreative as to seek merely to maximize your grade score, how should you allocate your time? By spending equal hours on each course? Not necessarily. You must shift from one subject to another until you are getting the same marginal grade advantage from the last minute spent on each alternative use. If an extra hour on chemistry is worth more than that same hour spent on economics, you are well advised to spend the time that way (if you need the higher score in chemistry, for example).

Substitution-effect. Diminishing consumption due to price rises can obviously be ascribed to the use of substitute goods which are cheaper. When butter prices soar, consumption of margarine increases; an increase in the price of coffee may lead to increased consumption of tea or cocoa. The consumer simply substitutes cheap production units for those which are expensive. By substitution, he produces the same result at least total cost.

Income-effect. Even when money income is fixed, high prices have the same relative effect as a decrease in income, particularly when all prices are high. This "lower" real income means the consumer can afford to buy less of every good, and unless the good whose price has risen is of the "inferior" variety, like potatoes, the consumer ordinarily buys less of it once real income has fallen.

Of course, the quantitative importance of the substitution-effect and income-effect varies with the good in question and with the consumer. Under some conditions, the resulting demand curve is very *elastic*—as in the case of a commodity which has been bought in large quantities and where there are ready substitutes (beef, for example). But demand for a commodity such as salt, which involves only a small part of the budget, is not easily replaced, and then demand will tend to be *inelastic*.

The paradox of value. We can now explain a famous problem that much troubled Adam Smith, whose book, *The Wealth of Nations* (1776), marks the beginning of modern economics. He asked, "How is it that water, which is so very useful that life is impossible without it, has such a low price—while diamonds, which are quite unnecessary, have such a high price?" Today, even the beginning student can give a correct answer to this problem. The supply and demand curves for water are such that they intersect at a very low price; the curves for diamonds intersect at a high price.

While this answer is not incorrect, we are still entitled to ask, "Why do supply and demand for water intersect at such a low price?" The answer must be phrased in two parts. First, diamonds are very scarce and the cost of adding to our stock is high; water is relatively abundant and its cost low in most areas of the world. Second, the *total* utility of water does not determine demand or price. Only the relative marginal utility and cost of water, the utility and cost of the *last little bit of water we use*, determines its price. And since every unit of water is exactly like another, and there is only one competitive price, every unit must sell for what the last useful unit sells for. The more there is of a commodity, the less becomes the relative desirability of the last unit, even though total usefulness always grows as the supply increases. The later units pull down the market value of all units. This is why air is actually a free good.

Consumer's surplus. This discussion underlines the fact that the accounting system which records the "total economic value" of a good differs from the measurement needed to record "total welfare." The total economic value of air is zero; its contribution to welfare incalculable. Similarly, if we increase the quantity produced of a commodity, such as wheat, we obviously increase the community's welfare, but if its demand is inelastic, we destroy some of the economic value of the commodity.

Thus there is always a sort of gap between total utility and total market value. This gap is in the nature of a surplus, which the consumer gets because he "receives more than he pays for." Not that he benefits at the expense of the seller, for in a swap neither party loses what the other gains. The well-being of all parties may be increased by trade. Each unit of a good that the consumer buys costs him only as much as the last unit is worth. By our fundamental law of diminishing marginal utility, the earlier units are worth more (have greater utility) than the later. Therefore he enjoys a surplus on each of the earlier units. When he stops receiving the surplus, he stops buying.

Many ingenious ways to measure consumer's surplus have been devised, but the important point for us to note is how lucky the citizens of modern industrial communities really are. The privilege of being able to buy a vast array of goods at low prices cannot be overestimated. All of us reap the benefits of the complex economic world in which we live, but which we did not make. We need only to think of what we would be able to provide for ourselves alone and unaided to realize what this means. For if we take away the social factor from economic activity, we are not left with a Robinson Crusoe with his salvage from the wreck and his acquired knowledge. No indeed. We have left a naked savage, living on roots, berries, and vermin, and nothing more.

COST AND SUPPLY

Turning to the fundamentals of cost that provide the background to the supply curve, we find that the concept of marginal cost, which is analogous to the concept of marginal utility, is basic. Again, we can deal only with fundamentals, reserving technical problems for advanced discussion. Suffice it to say that the supply curve is obtained in the same manner as the demand curve—by adding together the supply curves of each individual producer. The total supply of goods brought to market is simply the sum of what each producer will market at any given price.

Diversity of production conditions among firms. Firms engaged in production of the same goods may be quite different from one another in size, efficiency, amount of capital goods, etc. Though one firm may supply one hundred times as much goods to the market as another, so long as no one firm can supply a significant portion of total output, there is no monopolistic threat to perfect competition. But in some cases, the larger firm or the more efficient firm may continue to supply goods to the market even after the price has fallen so low that the smaller or less efficient firm ceases to produce. The owner of a modern, efficient fishing boat, for example, may continue to fish after the owner of an older or obsolete boat finds it will cut losses simply to stop fishing. And when market prices rise to the point that the inefficient producer can earn a reasonable return, the owner of the more efficient producing unit can often show a handsome profit.

This diversity of costs is peculiarly evident in mining and farming. A high-grade copper mine may continue to operate at prices that are much too low for a low-grade mine to continue. Farms with good soil may stay in production when farms with poorer soils cannot survive. Even when natural resources are not involved, the same disparities appear. A fast typist may be able to eke out a living at a low rate per page, while another person less skilled may find it impossible to continue the attempt to earn a living by typing. This sometimes causes peculiar problems. For example, the price of copper soared during World War I, and as prices rose, abandoned mines were brought back into production because they could operate at a profit with the high price levels. Obviously, efficient producers made handsome profits at these same prices. Price controllers found this rather puzzling. If they placed low ceiling prices on copper, they were faced with a shortage. If they let the price rise high enough to coax out the extra production from inefficient mines, they created what looked like "profiteering" on the part of advantageous producers.

Entry and exit of firms. Economists use a technical term to refer to the fact that a higher price will bring new firms into production and keep old firms in the industry. They call the last firms willing to stay in industry at the stipulated price M "marginal firms" at that price. In a loose sense, such firms are just "breaking even" so far as the decision to remain in the industry is concerned. The freedom to come in or go out of an industry is an important element making for efficiency. No competitor, even one who has been efficient, can rest on his oars. Technological changes, new ideas and techniques for producing goods, changing prices, etc., bring about changing conditions within the industry, and the firm that used to be a low-cost producer may find that new competition has brought the market price down so low that it is now one of the marginal producers in the industry.

Marginal costs. Even more important, for the economist, is the fact that the amount of goods supplied in the short and long run by a single firm is also subject to variation in price. That is, a rise in the price of goods may be needed to coax out additional output from existing firms. When the price of fish is high, a larger crew will pay, even though the extra output per extra crew member declines, and it will become worthwhile to fish in distant waters that previously would have been too expensive to reach.

It is at this point that the economist brings in the concept of *marginal cost* to explain what it is that determines the shape of a firm's supply curve—or what is the same thing, the degree to which its output varies internally in response to high and low prices. The prime determinant is the "marginal cost" concept. Most simply put, marginal cost is the *extra* cost incurred to produce one extra unit of output.[2] The marginal cost of fish is the difference between the total cost of producting 1,000 barrels of fish, say, and the total cost of producing 999 barrels.

Notice in Table 21 that the cost of producing the first unit is $8,000. The marginal cost of the second is $4,200; the third costs $5,800, and so on.

The marginal cost schedule is identical to the firm's supply curve. This is very useful. For example, if a firm can sell all of the goods it wishes at $5 per unit, it will in fact choose to produce at a level where its marginal cost is

---

[2] In economics, anything with the adjective "marginal" refers to "extra."

Marginal cost can be shown by numbers or curves:

Output q (1)	Total cost TC (2)	Marginal cost MC (3)
1	$ 8,000	
		$4,200
2	12,200	
		5,800
3	18,000	
		8,000
4	26,000	

Table 21. Going from 1 to 2 units involves $4,200 of marginal cost. In every case we get marginal cost in column 3 by reckoning extra costs as the difference between successive totals of column 2.

exactly $5; to produce more would involve a loss on each item. Each unit sold would bring in $5, but the cost of producing the unit would be greater than $5.

An interesting sidelight of marginal cost calculations is that if we think through the process we find that only when the price of goods is equal to marginal cost is the economy squeezing from its scarce resources and limited technological knowledge the maximum number of outputs. This is true of every society, whether capitalist, communist, or mixed. Further, if different firms have different marginal costs, it would pay us to cut back a little on the high-marginal-cost source and produce that extra little bit from the low-marginal-cost source. If we repeat the process, we eventually arrive at a balance with minimum total costs to society, for there will then be no divergencies in marginal cost. Thus this analysis can be used, if we are careful, to detect inefficiency in any institutional setup.

Short-run shutdown conditions. The "short run" is defined as a period of time in which certain equipment, resources, and commitments of the firm are fixed, though some variation in labor, raw materials, and so on is possible. This gives the firm a certain "fixed cost," defined as the total costs that will go on anyway because of fixed commitments—such costs as bond interest, rent, overhead, salaries, franchise taxes. The rest of the firm's "total cost" is made up of those costs which vary with output, the so-called "variable cost" of production. This would include materials, wages, and so forth. At what price level is it to the advantage of the firm to discontinue production, considering the short-run time period as a standard?

Every firm has the option of producing nothing at all, but that does not put an end to its costs. For with revenue at zero, the fixed costs against the business remain; when the plant is shut down, its losses are exactly equal to fixed costs. It follows that when the selling price of goods falls so low that the firm obtains less revenue than the amount of its variable costs, the firm will prefer to shut down completely, since continuing production means incurring a greater loss than the loss coming from a shutdown.

Long-run break-even conditions. Once a producer is stuck with a body of fixed costs, he will continue to produce in the short run even though he does not cover *all* of his costs. But if he is to stay in business, he must earn enough in the long run to cover all costs: (1) all labor, materials, equipment, taxes, and similar expenses; (2) all wage payments; (3) the interest yield on investment that could be obtained by capital invested in another industry. These "full competitive costs" include more than what accountants usually include in cost, in that they cover a normal return to both capital and management, the amount determined by returns in competitive firms and industries with similar risks. In the long run, then, earnings must cover all of these costs. If prices are so low that firms cannot do this, some will leave the field, thus reducing the supply and raising the price. We must also note that if prices remain above this level, others firms will enter the field, thus increasing the supply and tending to depress the price to the "break-even" point.

Long-run costs, then, include a return to the factors of production; for the economist, this return is extremely important, regardless of how the factor happens to be owned, and it is given a new name—"implicit costs." Thus the return to labor provided by the owner of labor is called "implicit wages" (self-employed) while the return to labor hired from outside is simply called "wages." Through miscalculation or ignorance, small businesses sometimes fail to receive this part of real costs in the short run.

An even broader conception of long-run costs takes into consideration the fact that some costs mean *foregone opportunities;* something has been sacrificed to meet the cost factor, and the sacrifice means that other opportunities have been passed by. This sacrifice of doing something else is called "opportunity cost," and it exists even when the personal choice of the individual concerned has been satisfied with the choice. Robinson Crusoe may prefer picking strawberries to picking blackberries, but he realizes that choosing one task means that the other must be laid aside.

How does this apply to industry supply and break-even costs? If the labor I use raising wheat could be used to grow rye, or even be employed by another farmer, then its value in those uses must be met or I will not continue to supply it to my own wheat patch. If I calculate, for example, that I earn $2 per hour working for myself, and I can earn $3 per hour working for someone else, there are good economic reasons for doing the latter.

SUPPLY AND DEMAND IN AGRICULTURE

The economist's model of perfect competition, in which a homogeneous product is produced by many different people and auctioned off in a well-organized market, does not fit most of American economic life at all closely. We must therefore supplement it with the new tools of imperfect and monopolistic competition. There is, however, one great area that provides us with a valuable application of the basic tools of supply and demand—agriculture. This is a vital national problem area, for it makes news, shifts votes, and affects our economic well-being, directly or indirectly.

General conditions of American agriculture. Farming is still America's largest single industry. But the percentage of people engaged in farming has declined steadily for the past 200 years. We are no longer a nation of farmers; though farmers swing much political weight, only one out of any thirteen American workers is employed in agriculture. Various factors have contributed to this shift away from farming. People seek the higher incomes, shorter hours, and better social life of the city. Perhaps this is a good thing, for the birth rate is higher in the country than in the city, and if the migration to the city ended, the population on the land might increase enough to evoke the law of diminishing returns and substantially reduce our total income, since more people would be used in food production than necessary, leaving fewer for other kinds of production. Technological change, which makes possible increased farm production with fewer workers through labor-saving devices of various sorts, and the change in our pattern of tastes, which leads us to consume more manufactured goods and not increase food consumption as we grow wealthier, have both contributed to the decline in farm workers.

Agriculture's long-run decline. Over the decades, farm prices have tended to fall relative to other prices (see Figure 24). Were it not for the temporary shortages of food and fiber created by World War II, this trend would be even more marked. We know that population growth and higher real incomes make people want to consume more food at the same price. But we also know that basic foods are the kinds of necessities which do not increase in the share of the family budget proportionately to increases in real income, and of course the American population simply is not growing so rapidly as it once was. The amount which the demand curve shifts to the right as a result of population growth and increased income, then, is relatively modest. Productivity, on the other hand, has increased even more rapidly in agriculture than in industry, moving the supply curve toward the right at a relatively rapid rate.

Now, without government interference, a shift in supply that moves more rapidly than a shift in demand will certainly lead to lower market prices. This

One diagram goes far to explain the farm problem:

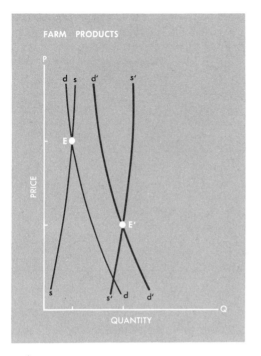

FARM PRODUCTS

Fig. 23. As the years go by, the increase in demand for farm products generated by population and income growth tends to be less than the vast increase in supply generated by technological productivity improvements. Thus free prices fall. With both schedules highly inelastic, prices fall hard. And small shifts in inelastic curves generate large price fluctuations.

trend toward declining prices (excluding inflationary effects) means financial pressure and hardship on all farmers whose efficiency has not increased greatly; this increases the pressure on rural workers to seek employment in industry. It also means that the community pays lower food prices, and the economy is reallocating its resources toward the things that are now most demanded by our growing society. And, as we know, it means strong political pressure for government aid to agriculture.

Poverty in agriculture. The "family farm" is an enduring American vision. Consisting of parents and children, with perhaps some outside help, it is reasonably efficient and produces a minimum income for everyone in the family. The facts hardly support the vision. Professor Theodore Schultz of the University of Chicago has pointed out that this definition automatically excludes numerous sharecroppers, and that country residences, nonfamily farms, and subsistence farmers with low cash incomes ought also to be eliminated. This leaves a good deal less than 3 million farms that *might* be classed as family farms. But those with gross incomes of less than $2,500 could not represent a reasonably efficient use of resources, so in the end we find that only a fraction of all American farms are today like the American dream (Table 22).

The farm problem centers mostly around small farmers:

Table 22. Distribution of farms by sales. The 4 per cent largest commercial farms produce 32 per cent of total product. Three out of five full-time farmers collect less than $5,000 of gross annual sales, from which all their business and living expenses must be met. (Source: *Census of Agriculture,* 1954; all part-time, institutional, and residential farmers have been excluded.)

Sales per farm	Number of farms, thousands	Percentage of all farms	Percentage of value of product sold
$25,000 and over	134	4.0	32.0
$10,000 to $24,999	449	13.5	27.5
$ 5,000 to $ 9,999	707	21.3	20.9
$ 2,500 to $ 4,999	812	24.4	12.4
$ 1,200 to $ 2,499	763	22.9	5.8
$ 250 to $ 1,199	462	13.9	1.4
Total	3,327	100.0	100.0

Most family farms are not sharing fully in the nation's economic progress, for the sad fact is that 134,000 farmers with the largest farms produce more than do the 2 million poorest farm families. Most farmland, then, is very low-producing, and a hidden population surplus exists in the form of low-productivity, marginal farm residents. Further, the paid laborer on the farm was, before the war, one of the lowest paid of all workers; two-fifths of the 2.5 million farm laborers earned less than $250 per year above their keep. And only one-fifth received more than $500. Even in 1960, farm wages, though much increased as far as percentages are concerned, still averaged little more than $45 per week, plus housing but without board.

The Southern white or Negro sharecropper, who owns neither land nor tools, and lives on credit during the year, is a more complex case. In an ordinary year, he is lucky if his crop brings enough to pay off the IOUs that he has incurred. Often he is chained to risking everything in a single crop such as cotton because it cannot be eaten or stolen easily. A week after the harvest, he is again in debt. Only in exceptional years does he earn enough to pay off past debts and leave a margin or surplus.

The tenant farmer is intermediate between farm owner and laborer. Ordinarily, he rents land for a fixed price or on a sharing basis. He may live on the farm, provide all of the labor, and perhaps own some of the equipment and livestock. Under the most favorable circumstances, tenant farming is the stepladder by which a young farmer climbs to farm ownership. But when farming is depressed, mortgage foreclosures tend to eliminate more independent farmers, and the traffic on the ladder may be predominantly downward.

Instability in agriculture. Farming is an up-and-down industry. Corn, wheat, beef, pork, and other farm products sell in highly competitive markets, and prices change yearly, weekly, daily, hourly, and even by the minute. The farmer swings at the very end of the economic chain. Good times bring him great percentage increases in income; depressions lower his cash income to almost nothing. Wartime demands are usually beneficial to farmers, and unlike most of the community, farmers can ride out periods of inflation. Yet since 1947, farm income has been sliding downward relative to other incomes, both in total and in per capita terms.

Though farm incomes fluctuate greatly between boom and bust, farm *production* is remarkably stable. Even the weather does not cause sizable fluctuations in total farm crops over the whole nation. In the last quarter century, agricultural production has had less than a 4 per cent average variation per year, while industrial production has varied about 12 per cent.

The farmer's supply curves are relatively inelastic despite his efforts to increase output when prices are low as he tries desperately to maintain his income, and many of his costs are fixed, whether he produces much or little. He cannot save by cutting quantity of output. Further, the demand for farm products is relatively inelastic in its response to price changes. Hence we have a combination of inelastic supply and inelastic demand; a very small shift in supply or demand can cause a disastrous reduction in income.

Government aid to agriculture.

Agriculture may be the unlucky stepchild of nature, but it is often the favored foster child of government. The public seems always to have hated a landlord and loved a farmer. So there is fairly widespread support among the electorate at large for aid to the farmer, even though the farmer's voting strength has shrunk considerably. Prior to 1929, government aid to farmers came principally through public-land policy, which aimed to place acreage into the hands of settlers, and through elaborate assistance programs to improve farming methods. The work in agricultural experimental stations and the "land-grant colleges" is well known, and the work of government-paid county agents is an important source of skilled assistance for the farmer. In 1929, under the Hoover administration, the Federal Farm Board was organized, and a new era of direct aid to farmers began. Subsequently, the government has established elaborate organizations for aiding farmers by increasing the stability and level of farm incomes.

The parity concept. The years from 1910 to 1914 are often looked back upon as the golden age of agriculture, and over the years there has been considerable political pressure to have the government somehow guarantee prices as relatively favorable to the farmers as those prevailing then. This is the root notion of "parity"—the simple feeling that if a bushel of wheat sold for enough in that

Parity is the ratio of prices the farmer gets to prices that he pays:

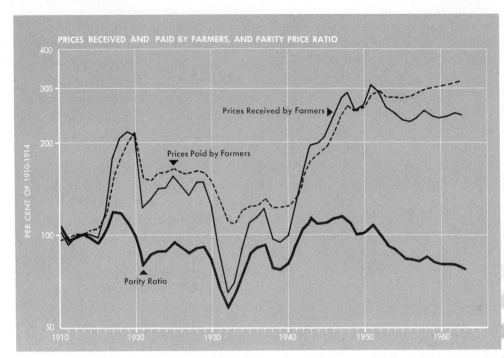

PRICES RECEIVED AND PAID BY FARMERS, AND PARITY PRICE RATIO

Prices Received by Farmers ▶

Prices Paid by Farmers ▼

Parity Ratio ▲

PER CENT OF 1910-1914

Fig. 24. If the change since 1910–1914 in prices farmers receive for their products just matched the change in the prices they pay for goods, the parity-price ratio curve would be at 100. Its being recently around 80 shows that prices received by farmers have not risen as much as have prices they must pay.

period to buy a certain amount of goods then a bushel of wheat should buy an equivalent amount of goods in 1960.

In practice, parity formulas contain some complications. As Figure 24 shows, the prices of the goods farmers buy have risen, and it would not be enough to simply restore wheat prices to the 1910–1914 level. To arrive at the parity figure, we must compare the purchasing power of the farmer's income in 1910–1914 with its purchasing power today. Thus if the goods which one bushel of wheat would purchase in 1910–1914 now cost the income from *two* bushels of wheat, the farmer's income is effectively cut in half, and the price he is receiving for his wheat is only 50 per cent of the parity price. Formally, we take the relation between today's prices of farm products and the price levels of 1910–1914. If the price of wheat has doubled, while the price of goods purchased by farmers has quadrupled, then farmers prices have fallen behind other prices by 50 per cent.

Parity sounds simple enough, and perhaps even fair. Why then do fights erupt when the government drops its fixed support prices (prices at which it will buy all farm products on the market) in favor of "flexible price supports" at lower percentages of parity, or even abandons all price supports?

Deeper analysis of the problem shows that as demand and supply change over the long run, the attempt to peg prices at an arbitrary high level brings an avalanche of surplus farm goods on the market. The dollar cost of price supports grows astronomically high, and distortion of production becomes cumulatively greater. Government storage bins are bursting, the mothball fleet of abandoned warships is used for storage, and in some places, grain is simply stored on the ground, yet the end is not in sight. The reason for this is simple. Rapid technological progress has greatly increased food production per hour of labor; the real costs of farm production have gone down. Pegging prices at the old levels calls forth a supply of farm products much larger than what parity figures brought to the market in 1910–1914. It means very large incomes for efficient farmers, and it also keeps inefficient farmers from going into other occupations. Though farmers boast of their independence and claim they wish to "earn" their subsidies, there is no escaping the fact that more than half of what the farmers have collected in the market place for certain crops since World War II has come from government aid programs.

Forms of government aid. There are five principal economic mechanisms which government uses to help, or seem to help, the farmer:

1. Outright gift or relief payments, given principally to farmers who have established their need and misery

2. Programs that aim to increase the demand for farm crops, or cut their real cost of production

3. Crop-limitation programs that aim to cut supply or raise price

4. Purchase-loan storage programs to guarantee or support prices

5. Purchase-and-resale differential subsidy plans (the "Benson" plan and the "Brannan" plan, named for Eisenhower's and Truman's respective secretaries of agriculture)

Issues in farm aid. In the early years of the New Deal, the emphasis in farm aid was placed on crop reduction, and there was much editorial weeping for the little pigs killed and the crops aborted. After the Supreme Court declared the Agricultural Adjustment Act unconstitutional, emphasis shifted to price supports through government purchase and loans. Huge gluts of surplus naturally resulted, but World War II made these warehouse surpluses worthwhile. After the war, the old problem of surplus production returned. To continue price supports at parity or even 90 per cent of parity would have been colossally expensive in view of the great improvements in farm productivity, and it would have produced more surpluses than government warehouses could hold. The farm prosperity of palmy days (1945–1947) ebbed steadily, and the 90 per cent parity program was abandoned.

Even the flexible price support program at 70 per cent of parity has resulted in such tremendous production of farm crops as to bring the emphasis back to crop restriction in the guise of the soil bank. But each cut in acreage has produced ingenious devices for growing more per acre, and this too can only be a stopgap. Another stopgap, dumping our surpluses abroad for less than at home, has infuriated our friends like Canada, who produce the same type of goods for export. And it infuriates our domestic textile producers to have foreign rivals produce textiles at a competitive advantage out of American cotton that has been sold abroad for less than we charge at home. Such dumping has, on the other hand, been a blessing to India and other poorer countries of the world.

What economic analysis can suggest. We have seen that there is often a strong case for sticking to a competitive market system unless there is some good reason for preferring those who are assisted to those who are hurt by interference with the market system. How does this apply to the farm problem? Many tough-minded economists argue that much government aid now goes to very prosperous commercial farmers, and that the public would not approve such aid if it knew how much of it went to farmers earning incomes far above the median income level and how little filters down to the really poor and needy farmer.

What is suggested? One remedy involves giving whatever aid you decide to give to farmers in a more efficient way—so as to leave the rest of us with more than the present inefficient arrangements provide, and so as to pinpoint the aid given and mark it for those who actually need help. Such a turnabout would involve more reliance on market forces to determine food and fiber prices. Lower prices would enable consumers to purchase more, especially of the more expensive protein foods such as milk and meat. Commercial farmers would then be pressed to greater efficiency and many would find their incomes so low that they would leave agriculture for industry. The really poor farmers would be given welfare aid on the same basis as any other families.

Does all this sound cruel, heartless, and hardboiled? Speaking as but one citizen, I must confess I do find it a bit extreme in that it may give too little weight to the argument that a civilization is happier which seeks to protect any group in it from sudden and drastic changes in status. An ideal program might perhaps involve the following points: (1) transitional aids to ease readjustment for those who are losing income; (2) continued retraining and transportation subsidies to help rural migrants prepare for and locate jobs; (3) effective full-employment policies to ensure availability of new jobs; (4) permanent welfare expenditures for those in need, whether from town or country. However, there is little danger of a ruthless program of action in the near future; the politics of agricultural aid is too intense for that.

Nevertheless, the only ultimate solution, as Vanderbilt's W. H. Nicholls has pointed out, is to reduce our surplus of farmers. Doubtless, this must be done gradually, and it is actually happening now as each year finds fewer persons remaining in farming.

IMPERFECT COMPETITION

Thus far, our study of the workings of competitive supply and demand have dealt mostly with what economists call the case of "perfect competition." In economic terms, perfect competition is rather strictly defined, and though it is an important special case, it remains a special case. Certainly it cannot faithfully represent many of the facts of modern industry. The real world as we know it—in America, Europe, or Asia—contains significant mixtures of monopoly imperfections along with elements of competition. For the most part, then, the real economic world falls in the realm of "imperfect competition," for it is neither perfectly competitive nor perfectly monopolistic, and our analysis must be modified accordingly.

Perfect competition. The economist defines perfect competition very stringently indeed. He says that competition is not really perfect unless numerous producers sell an exactly identical product, and unless no single producer has the means to raise the market price above prevailing levels. A perfectly competitive industry is made up exclusively of perfect competitors, and usually it has an organized auction mechanism or exchange market for the sale of goods. Notice how strict this definition of perfect competition is. In many industries, such as steel, a few firms produce a large fraction of the total output. Although each firm produces an identical product, it can significantly affect the price of steel by its selling practices.

Actually, when we go down the list, we find that only potatoes, tobacco, wheat, and cotton fall within the terms of the definition: there is perfect competition in the production and sale of these goods. There are thousands of different producers, each producing an identical product. No single producer can affect the price of the goods significantly, for the total production is so large that no single producer markets a significant fraction of the total output. Finally, there is a regular "auction place" for buying and selling these products. Of course, we mar the perfection of the industry to the extent that the government is drawn into its activities, and farm programs which affect either the production or sale of wheat, cotton, potatoes, etc., bring monopolistic imperfections into the picture.

Acid test for imperfect competition is slope of firm's demand:

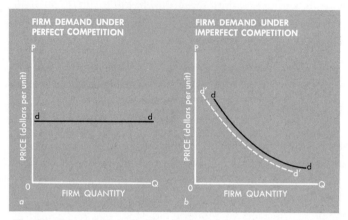

Fig. 25. The perfect-competitor firm can sell all it wants to along its horizontal *dd* curve, never depressing market price. But the imperfect-competitor firm will find its demand curve slopes downward, as its increased *Q* forces down the *P* it can get. And unless it is a sheltered monopolist, a cut in its rivals' *P*'s will appreciably shift its own *dd* leftward to *d'd'*.

Figure 25 shows the acid test to determine whether a given producer is a "perfect competitor" or "imperfect competitor." If the demand curve is horizontal, he has no control over price at all and can sell all he wants at the going price; if the demand curve is not horizontal, then competition is imperfect.

Imperfect competition. If an "imperfect competitor" is any firm whose demand curve slopes downward, as in Figure 25, this means that should the firm throw more goods on the market, the price will be depressed. Note that this does not mean that the owner is of poor character, that he beats his wife, or fails to pay his bills. Nor does the fact that a firm is an imperfect competitor mean that it does not try to outsell its rivals. Intense commercial rivalry is not the same thing as perfect competition. Indeed, wheat producers do not bother to advertise at all, though they are perfect competitors. Why should they? They can sell all of their wheat without depressing market price. Meanwhile a tobacco company, which is an imperfect competitor, may spend much of its energies trying to outsell its rivals.

The final test, then, is the shape and position of the demand curve. It does not matter whether the firm is profitable or unprofitable, whether it is efficient or inefficient; if the demand curve is horizontal, the economist's definition of perfect competition has been met.

Monopoly. How imperfect can competition get? The extreme case is obviously the *single* seller with almost complete monopoly power. He is the only firm in his industry, and no other industry produces an adequate substitute. Exclusive monopolies, like telephones or public utilities, are generally regulated by the government, and even they must take into account the potential competition of alternative products—oil for gas, cables for telephones. Complete monopolies are relatively unimportant in our economic structure.

Oligopoly. This horrible-sounding word means "few sellers" and it comes in two distinct types. An oligopolist may be one of a few sellers who produce an identical or almost-identical product. In this case, a relatively small difference in price will drive the consumer to another producer, so no one in the small group is a monopolist; yet the number of sellers is limited and each has an appreciable effect on market price. This type of oligopoly is thought to be common in a number of our basic industries, where the product is fairly homogeneous and each enterprise is very large (aluminum or nylon).

The second type of oligopoly arises when there are a few sellers who sell *differentiated* products. The Big Three in the auto industry (Ford, Chevrolet, and Plymouth) are examples, for though they dominate the industry, the cars they make are somewhat differentiated. In the cigarette industry, a few large sellers own numerous brands and types and sell a major fraction of the total consumed.

Many differentiated sellers. The third kind of imperfect competition arises when there are many sellers, who produce "differentiated products," i.e., products which differ somewhat in real qualities or which the buyer thinks differ in real qualities. Toothpaste production, for example, fits into this category.

Table 23 gives a brief picture of the various possible categories of imperfect and perfect competition. Note that the categories tend to overlap, and there are considerable differences in the degree of competition in different industries.

Price quantity and total revenue.

Under perfect competition, the producer has little trouble deciding on his output level. Since by definition he can sell all of his product without affecting the market price, he simply produces as much as he can as cheaply as he can. But the imperfect competitor has a different problem, for his sales affect the price of the goods. Hence he must try to decide on the level of production that will bring maximum profits. The imperfect competitor, or even the monopolist, will not, as we might think, set his prices sky-high and wait for the profits to roll in. As his prices rise, the amount of his product demanded will drop, and he will eventually lose profits by setting prices too high. But he will not set prices so low as a perfect com-

Most industries are imperfectly competitive—a blend of monopoly and competition:

Table 23. Types of competition.

Kind of competition	Number of producers and degree of product differentiation	Part of economy applicable to:	Degree of control over price	Methods of marketing
Perfect competition	many producers; identical products	a few agricultural industries	none	market exchange or auction
Imperfect competition:				
Many differentiated sellers	many producers; many real or fancied differences in product	toothpaste, retail trade	some	advertising and quality rivalry; administered prices
Oligopoly	few producers; little or no difference in product	steel, aluminum		
	few producers; some differentiation of products	autos, machinery		
Complete monopoly	single producer; single product without close substitutes	a few utilities	considerable	promotional and "institutional" public-relations advertising

petitor either, and that is the difficulty with imperfect competition. In practice, many factors will have to be considered, including costs, total revenue, marginal costs, and profit at each different level of production.

When competition is not perfect, the economist needs the concept of marginal revenue to discuss the behavior of the firm. Just as we defined marginal cost as the extra cost of an extra unit of goods, we define marginal revenue as the *extra* revenue obtained by selling an *extra* unit of goods. Under perfect competition, marginal revenue and price are equal, for the firm can sell all it wants at a given market price. But under imperfect competition, when the firm's demand curve slopes downward, the firm can sell more units only by forcing down the price of all previous units sold. Generally speaking, then, marginal revenue is less than price except in the case of perfect competition. We can now bring all of these factors together in a single table (Table 24).

Of course, the firm is most interested in the column that shows total profit, but a comparison of marginal revenue (column 6) and marginal cost (column 7) will also serve as a guide, for so long as extra output gives more marginal revenue than marginal cost, profits are increasing and we continue to increase production. Whenever marginal cost exceeds marginal revenue, we reduce output. Best-Profit position, then, is reached when marginal cost and marginal revenue are equal.

Imperfect competition and resource allocation. How do the imperfections of competition affect the efficiency with which a free-price system solves the important problems of What, How, and For Whom. Suppose that under free pricing firms definitely face a sloping demand curve, so that marginal revenue is below price. Under these conditions, will the competitors who pursue their own self-interest intelligently be guided by Adam Smith's "Invisible Hand" to act in the general interest of the whole society?

The answer is, No, they will not! For there is now a flaw in the general picture. When the businessman takes "marginal revenue" into account he is making sure that he does not "spoil the market." He in fact is trying to keep his commodity scarce and not reduce his own receipts. What are the effects of

The intelligent firm seeks its Best-Profit point:

Table 24. This brings together all demand and cost data. See that the firm will find its Best-profit point at unshaded row where $Q = 6$, $P = \$84$, and Profit = \$104, the maximum. For $Q < 6$, $MR > MC$ and firm expands; for $Q > 6$, $MR < MC$ and firm will contract output. (If you accurately interpolate MR and MC to get them at exactly $Q = 6.0$ and not between 5 and 6 or 6 and 7, you will find $MR = \$24 = MC$ there exactly.) $MR = MC$ is the condition for maximum profit.

Quantity Q (1)	Price P (2)	Total revenue $R = P \times Q$ (3)	Total Cost $TC = FC + VC$ (4)	Total Profit Pro (5) $[=(3) - (4)]$	Marginal revenue MR (6)	Marginal Cost MC (7)
0	$144+	$ 0	$256	−$256		
					$134	$ 64
1	134	134	320	−186		
					114	20
2	124	248	340	−92		
					94	15
3	114	342	355	−13		
					74	13
4	104	416	368	+48		
					54	13
5	94	470	381	+89		
					34	19
6	84	504	400	+104		
					14	31
7	74	518	431	+87		
					−6	49
8	64	512	480	+32		
					−26	73
9	54	486	553	−67		
					−46	103
10	44	440	656	−216		

this policy? The imperfect competitor may be earning more than he would if the government somehow made him compete like a perfect competitor. The man in the street tends to worry about the evil effects of imperfect competition on the distribution of income. But the economist is interested in the fact that imperfect competition may also represent an important economic evil.

The point is that price is the signal that consumers use to show how much they value various goods. Costs, and particularly marginal cost, indicate how much of society's resources are used to produce the goods. Competitive firms in effect give people what they want most, and they produce to the point where price and marginal cost are equal ($P = MC$), where goods are worth what they cost. Though the imperfect competitor does not force people to buy from him, he does have some control over price. And he can use his power to keep things a little scarce, thereby maximizing his profits. So society does not get quite as much of his goods as it really wants in terms of what they really cost to produce, for if the price were lower, they would buy more. This does not make the producer a villain, but the illustration does show that self-interest cannot perform the miracle that Smith expected to occur.

IMPERFECT COMPETITION AND ANTITRUST POLICY

We have now paved the way for a bird's-eye view of the market structure of modern-day industry. What is the role of the theoretical economic tools we have been developing to analyze profit maximization? What are some of the important patterns of imperfect competition? What issues do they raise for antitrust policy? To these important questions, we now turn.

Do firms maximize profits? To what extent do businessmen actually try to maximize profits? Do they succeed? These are not easy questions to give precise answers to. Certainly this much is true: if a firm is absolutely reckless in calculating costs and revenues, it will probably be eliminated from the economic scene. Therefore those which survive cannot be oblivious to profit maximization. But that does not mean that every imperfect competitor is seeking desperately to squeeze the last ounce of profit from every transaction. Once a firm is large enough to enjoy some control over prices it can often afford to relax its profit maximizing somewhat. Further, this may in the long run be good business practice.

Even a firm that is maximizing profits in a fairly sensible manner is not really calculating elaborate geometric curves of cost and revenue. Nevertheless, the firm that is not self-conscious about its use of theoretical economic tools, *to the extent that it makes a pretty fair guess as to where its highest profits can be realized,* succeeds in making marginal revenue and marginal cost approximately equal. It does so, usually without curves and graphs, simply feeling its way by trial and error.

Some of the wastes of imperfect competition.

Before going into the legal, historical, and institutional aspects of antitrust legislation, we ought to remind ourselves of the economic ills associated with monopolies and other imperfections of competition.

Monopoly restrictions. To drive home the point that excessive profit is not the greatest evil of monopoly but a result of its tendency to *set too high a price in relation to social marginal-cost pricing,* consider the following simple case. Suppose a monopoly arbitrarily sets a price higher than the actual cost of producing goods and that government then places a tax on the monopoly equal to its profits. Would this correct the evil? Clearly, the monopoly would end up with no profit; that would go to the state. But the consumer would still be getting too little of the product and paying too high a price for it. The only change would be in the recipient of the monopoly profit—which would now be the state—for the misallocation of resources would simply continue as before. Only if the state forced the monopoly to equate price to costs rather than to revenue would society as a whole benefit. The true economic burden of monopoly is in the divergence that appears between price and marginal costs.

Overentry and "sick" industries. Many industries are characterized by an excessive number of firms. Most such firms do a small business, and remain in the industry only until they have lost their original capital. Grocery stores, taverns, restaurants, nightclubs, and gasoline stations are typical examples in the retail trade area, and the same conditions are found in textiles, dressmaking, and many others that require little initial capital. Don't unprofitable firms leave the industry? Yes, but as fast as they leave, new firms enter, leaving the total unchanged or even increased.

Why do new firms enter industry in the face of the fact that most firms already operating are losing money? Partly, of course, from ignorance, and partly from overoptimism. Each new entrepreneur hopes, and perhaps prays, that *his* attempt will be different. All too often the newcomers are quite wrong. Occasionally, one "hits the jackpot," and this seems enough to spur others to join the sweepstakes. The only thing that can be said for such small businesses is that they make jobs. But the jobs they make are largely an illusion so far as pay is concerned, for they are really eating up capital already accumulated.

Chronically overcrowded industries need not be "perfectly competitive," although in farming and "cotton gray goods" this is approximately the case. In a competitive industry, the consumer gains, through lower prices, what the producer is losing. But too many firms in a competitive industry is economically wasteful. In most cases, the competition is imperfect, and the small concerns, being inefficient producers, do not sell very cheaply. Instead of competing on a price basis, they tend to charge fairly high prices and simply divide the existing market. The amount of economic waste may be even greater than under monopoly conditions. Not only is the price excessive, but valuable resources are wasted because each firm has too much idle plant and manpower. Producers incur losses, resources are wasted, and prices are too high—a triple loss.

Oligopoly. During the railroad price wars of the past century, each of the three or four trunk lines took turns undercutting the existing rates, and since customers always pick the route that offers even a few pennies of saving, a disastrously low rate level was reached. At the same time, the railroads boosted prices on short hauls where shippers had no alternative means of transportation. This created an anomalous, discriminatory rate pattern which was costly for everyone. The Interstate Commerce Commission was established in 1887 to regulate and control precisely this kind of activity.

Even without government intervention, the industries which have heavy overhead costs and identical products have come to realize that competition can be ruinous. Therefore, tacitly or explicitly, firms try to agree on a price that maximizes long-run profits for everyone. Trade associations, with one eye on the Justice Department lawyers who enforce the Sherman Antitrust Act, may impose penalties on any chiseler in the industry who makes secret price concessions. Occasionally, as new conditions or new firms upset the *status quo* in the industry, price wars break out and last until everyone has learned his lesson and the morale—and prices—of the industry are restored.

When we appraise the effects of oligopoly, we must bear in mind that the desire of corporations to earn a fair return on past investment can at times conflict with the well-being of the consumer. Too much plant capacity may have been built in the past, and this cannot be accepted as a justification for continuing high prices. Competition, which the businessman regards as destructive and ruinous, may be the only way to force the firm to either make use of its plant capacity or cease maintaining it. For if society has made the mistake of building excess capacity, there is no point in compounding the error by failing to use it to good advantage. Losses or subnormal profits is the free-enterprise way of discouraging excess capacity.

We can see illustrations of this pattern of imperfect competition in the steel and other metal industries. In 1960, the economy slowed a bit and steel production was reduced to one-half of existing capacity. Some feared that this would initiate a wave of price cuts which would reduce steel companies' earnings to the break-even point or below. Did it work out that way? Not quite.

The industry discovered that it could still make money at levels far below capacity.

In a perfectly competitive industry, a reduction of demand will lower prices, and profits will decline greatly. Yet the amount of goods sold may not decline very much, for goods are sold for whatever they will fetch. The consumer does benefit from what the producer loses, and in time output will adjust to the new state of demand. But under an oligopoly, prices tend to remain firm, with output varying instead of prices. Plants stand idle, but the product is not cheapened in the hope of coaxing out new quantity demanded. This inflexibility of prices, many economists fear, adds to the danger of creeping inflation. Why? Because if prices and costs rarely ever fall, there is only one way for the price index to go—up!

Dynamic research and monopoly. They say, "It is an ill wind that blows no one any good," and this is the case with imperfect competition, for it has some virtues as well as vices. A common argument in favor of imperfect competition is that a firm with considerable control over price by virtue of technological efficiency, patents, etc., makes use of its "monopoly profits" to underwrite further research and advertising so that it can keep ahead of its rivals. General Electric, RCA, and Du Pont are perhaps typical of such companies.

Because research and advertising are expensive, and their results are cumulative, success tends to breed success and profits to breed profits. Small business therefore claims that it cannot always compete effectively with large firms. In other words, industrial research may be subject to economies of large scale that cannot be enjoyed by small businesses. Large firms also "pool their risk," since statistically an aggregate of independent risks tends to cancel out some of the variations. Advertising and research are, of course, quite different things: witness the examples of beer, cigarettes, and soap. Advertising is meant to persuade people of the merits of a product; it does not actually produce those merits. Yet in some cases, it is not easy to decide whether a particular bit of applied industrial research is meant for technical improvement or for market improvement.

What to do about monopoly imperfections. Must we conclude that there is no hope for limiting monopoly and oligopoly? Of course not. For one thing, if we keep barriers to free entry at a minimum, fear of competition—and its actuality—may help keep oligopoly under control. Secondly, the government can enforce its antitrust policies vigorously, cracking down at the slightest sign of collusion to keep prices firm or control production. This will tend to force the oligopolists to keep their prices near the true marginal cost of the goods.

Finally, some economists like Chicago's George J. Stigler argue that large firms should be broken into small pieces. Stigler and others believe this can be done without sacrificing any of the economies gained from large-scale production. With numerous sellers, competition would approach perfect competition more closely than at present, and this would be beneficial to society as a whole. Needless to say, Stigler is opposed to any mergers that would reduce the number of firms still further, and he believes that many of today's giants were born out of earlier mergers which aimed at monopoly control over markets and not at production efficiency. Plainly, this is a controversial area. Even the Supreme Court changes its position on the questions involved. For example, the Standard Oil Company of New Jersey was dissolved by the Court in the days of John D. Rockefeller, Sr., as was the American Tobacco Company, yet the United States Steel Corporation, for all its size, was permitted to remain as a unit. In another case, the Court plainly welcomed the end of Alcoa's monopoly position in aluminum when Reynolds and Kaiser became important producers, and it has forced the large motion-picture producers to get out of the theater business. Yet the position is still far from completely defined.

Publicly regulated monopolies. To show what government can do about monopoly, let us consider in detail monopolies licensed by the state and under government regulation. Such monopolies include gas and light companies, telephone and communication services, railroads and public carriers, and so forth. Since it seems uneconomical to have two sets of local telephone wires, an exclusive franchise is given to a single company. (Why is not the same thing true of milk delivery?) But having given the monopoly to the utility company, the state proceeds to protect the consumer by regulating the cost and quality of the service provided (usually by a commission).

Ordinarily maximum prices for utility services are set so as to allow the company a "fair" return on its investment (rates such as 5, 6, or 7 per cent). In the main, rates are not guaranteed, for this raises the broader question of the effect of guarantees on efficiency and cost-consciousness. But, even without this stumbling block, there are some major questions to be solved. What, for example, is the capital value base which the company uses to compute a "fair return"? Three standards have been suggested: (1) original cost (minus depreciation), or the sum of all prudent past investments; (2) current reproduction or replacement cost (minus depreciation), or the cost of replacing the company's equipment at present prices, corrected for age and condition of property; and (3) capitalized market value of the company's securities and assets.

Of the three methods, the third is usually recognized as nonsensical, for the market value of any income-earning property is given by capitalizing its annual return by an interest rate, and for a regulating authority to use capitalized market value as a base for measuring capital would be tantamount to recognizing any level of earnings, high or low, as fair. Once having been capitalized into a new base, excessively high earnings will appear as only moderate interest returns, and the same is true of excessively low earnings. This method of computing begs the question which it is intended to solve.

The American courts have usually vacillated between original cost and reproduction cost as a fair basis for determining earning level. So long as the price level remains steady, the two are not very different. But over a period of decades, when prices increase greatly, reproduction costs will involve higher earnings and rates than original cost. In periods of declining prices, the reverse is true. Neither method is ideal when considered from the standpoint adopted in advanced discussions of "welfare economics," but reproduction cost leads to a more flexible price structure and gives less weight to the dead hand of past costs.

Antitrust policy. Toward the end of the nineteenth century, the public became greatly concerned with the development of large-scale industrial combinations, called trusts, involving as they did the threat of monopoly. In 1890, the Sherman Antitrust Act was passed, making it illegal to monopolize trade or combine or conspire "in restraint of trade." On paper, this was a major setback to the trusts, but in practice few persons were clear about its purpose or the type of combination against which it should be used. Early in the twentieth century, the Roosevelt and Taft administrations made use of the Sherman Act to prevent some mergers and to dissolve the American Tobacco Company and the Standard Oil Company. The act was also used to attack labor unions, a purpose for which it was probably not really intended. The Clayton Antitrust Act of 1914 was meant to exclude labor from antitrust action and to define illegal behavior more precisely than the "rule of reason" enunciated by the Court— that *unreasonable* combinations would be subject to the law. However, the Clayton Act was not an unqualified success and the position remained cloudy. During the 1920s, actions against "trusts" were infrequent, and with the Depression of the 1930s, few persons were concerned with price increases—they were trying to keep prices up.

The antitrust laws as such have contributed enormously to the maintenance of competition in our system, and agencies like the Federal Trade Commission have performed valuable service in this area. Unfortunately, the Depression tended to weaken the government's attitude toward the trusts, and in the first two Roosevelt administrations, legislation actually fostered the growth of monopolistic practices. Thus the NRA (National Recovery Act of 1933) promoted industry-wide codes and cartels and collusive price maintenance. The Robinson-Patman Act of 1936 tried to keep businessmen from cutting prices by selling the same product under different brand names, and in various other ways limited competition. Still other laws provide for resale price maintenance (Miller-Tydings and McGuire Acts) and make it difficult if not impossible for a merchant to undersell a competitor on given brand-name merchandise. These laws have been heavily attacked in recent years and may perhaps be eliminated.

Sometimes the legislators, lawyers, and judges have simply been opposed to bigness, even though they admitted that it promoted efficiency and produced lower consumer prices. Thus in the A & P case, the grocery chain's biggest crime was that its size permitted it to sell groceries at a much smaller markup than its myriad of individual competitors could afford. Terrified by the quite unrealistic possibility that its price cutting would drive out all competitors and *then* permit it to raise its prices high, critics of the A & P tried to use the antitrust laws against it. These perversions of antitrust philosophy show how far removed the economist's preoccupation with the way in which the price system determines What, How, and For Whom is from the preoccupation of the courts with Who is a nasty man, What has he been doing, and To Whom has he been doing it.

Future of antitrust policy. Fortunately, the government took up its antitrust policies with renewed vigor in the late 1930s. Thurman Arnold, head of the Antitrust Division, even tried to tackle the building industries with their notoriously backward technologies, and such industries as glass, cigarettes, and cement, among others. All this means costly litigation; the Antitrust Division has expanded many many times in size, and the number of prosecutions under way has increased greatly. Since the war, various important cases have been settled—the 1946 cigarette case, the 1948 cement case, and in 1957, the order by the Supreme Court that Du Pont must disgorge its holdings in the General Motors Corporation. Other proposed mergers (Bethlehem and Youngstown Steel, for example) have been vetoed by the Attorney General. Both political parties have been pursuing antitrust policies with greater vigor and enthusiasm, and the effects of this policy are clearly apparent in the standards practiced by American industry today. Judgments are tougher, and the power of the firm to exploit its patents and market advantages is consistently weakened. The use of "consent decrees" which allow the courts to control policies for a number of years serves to tighten legal control.

The economist and the lawyer do not always see eye to eye on these issues. The economist often feels that the courts and the lawyers have concentrated too much on the letter of the law without trying to define its spirit and its economic rationale. A businessman indiscreet enough to keep a record of certain illicit transactions gets "the book," while his confederate, who is more discreet, is immune from punishment. The legal mind is less concerned with price distortions than with the means used to set prices. Yet it seems that today economist and lawyer are drifting toward some measure of agreement. While no one would claim that American antitrust legislation and enforcement have been completely logical or anywhere near completely successful, one has only to look abroad to realize how much worse off we might be. American enterprise is kept on the defensive and would never dream of making use of the flagrant devices that are all too common in other parts of the world. America has been the pioneer in antitrust legislation, and though such legislation is beginning to take hold in Britain, Germany, and Japan, most of the rest of the world is far from even beginning an attack on entrenched monopolistic and oligopolistic interests.

We cannot expect competition to become "perfectly perfect" in the economist's sense. But we can strive for what Columbia's venerable economist J. M. Clark years ago called "workable competition." By public and private policies we can hope to improve the efficiency with which market prices reflect underlying individual needs, desires, and wants against the background of true costs of goods—costs in terms of alternative goods that could be produced and in terms of used-up scarce productive factors which involve sweat and disutility.

Summary

A closer look at supply and demand—microeconomics—shows that demand varies more with a change in price for some goods than for others. This elasticity of demand determines the effect of price changes on total revenue. Beginners must avoid confusing the expression "an increase in demand," which is a movement outward of the whole demand curve, with "an increase in quantity demanded," which follows from a reduction in price.

Price is affected by many factors, but in a free competitive market, they act through supply and demand, though the government may sometimes interfere with the working of competitive markets. In general, interference with supply and demand, like monopoly interference, is harmful, and even if the purpose is approved there may be hidden costs involved.

Market demand is derived by adding the separate demand curves for each consumer. Shifts in the demand curve may be due to many factors, such as an increase in income, population changes, etc. The concept of marginal utility is an important part of the economist's explanation of the movement and shape of the demand curve, particularly the law of downward-sloping demand. Marginal utility also enables us to explain such phenomena as Adam Smith's paradox of value—that a good like air or water has no money value.

The supply curve is calculated in the same manner as the demand curve, by adding together the curves of each individual supplier. The supplier is much concerned with his short-run costs, short run being defined as that period of time in which some of the firm's productive factors and costs are fixed and some variable.

The marginal cost of production, the cost of producing an additional unit of goods, is a very important concept for the perfectly competitive firm. When marginal cost is just equal to the price of the goods, the firm is maximizing its profits, or minimizing its losses. In the long run, the firm must cover all of its long-run costs, including profit and implicit wages, rents, etc., to remain in business.

When there is free entry, and no one firm has special advantages, excess profits will be absorbed by the entry of new firms if profits rise sharply.

The improvement in agricultural technology has greatly increased the supply of food, while decreasing the labor supply needed to produce it, and the demand for food has not kept pace with the supply. Free equilibrium prices tend to fall, and farm income tends to be low and unstable. The government has adopted a variety of programs to support farm prices and maintain farm incomes.

Pegging prices, though it sounds fair, ignores basic changes in demand and real costs of production. This produces high surpluses or wasteful low quotas and distortions of efficiency. Aid programs need no deep economic analysis, though supply and demand are needed to explain crop limitation, price support, and other governmental policies.

In the real world, market situations lie somewhere between perfect competition and complete monopoly. Imperfect competition involves some control by each firm over the price of its product. Oligopoly (few sellers produce a given product) is an important form of imperfect competition in several basic American industries.

Total costs can be divided into fixed cost and variable cost. Marginal cost represents the change in total cost that follows the production of an extra unit of output. It is not the same as average cost per unit. A firm will find its maximum profit position when the last unit it sells brings in extra revenue just equal to its extra cost. *Marginal revenue = marginal cost* is the equilibrium position of maximum profit.

The consequences of imperfect competition may be very severe, and they are not limited to monopolistic profits. Overentry may waste resources; monopolistic and oligopolistic pricing above true marginal costs may cause a distortion of resource allocation even if excess profits are taxed away. Some economists argue that the dynamic efficiency of monopoly and oligopoly must be weighed against the evils we have discussed. Furthermore, it is sometimes argued that many of the wastes of imperfect competition can be eliminated by government regulation.

Review Questions

1. What is the law of downward-sloping demand? Why is it valid?
2. Explain how market price is determined by the interaction of supply and demand.
3. What factors influence the position of the demand curve? The supply curve?
4. What is meant by elasticity of supply or demand? What is the effect of elasticity on price? Cite illustrations of goods that are very elastic. That are inelastic.
5. Differentiate between an increase in demand at the same price and an increase in demand that results from the lowering of price.
6. Explain the effect of a subsidy and a tax on price in terms of supply and demand. Give an example.
7. How does rationing affect demand? Supply?
8. What are some causes of shifts in the demand curve?
9. Explain the law of diminishing marginal utility and its relation to the price of goods.
10. Explain why the price of water is low, though water is absolutely necessary for human life.
11. What is meant by marginal cost, and why is it important?
12. What is the difference between fixed costs and long-run costs?
13. What is meant by parity?
14. What are the principal forms of government aid to agriculture?
15. What does the economist mean by perfect competition?
16. Distinguish between monopoly, oligopoly, and competitive production.
17. What are the principal consequences of imperfect competition?

For Further Study

1. Draw a demand schedule showing your demand for soft drinks.
2. Try to make an analysis of your time and effort and the manner in which they are allocated, using supply and demand as a framework.
3. Can you imagine any good for which utility increases with greater supply? What about opium for addicts?
4. How can both persons in a barter arrangement obtain more than they give from the transaction?
5. Explain how you would decide whether to continue operating your business if sales were very slow.

6. Prepare a reasoned defense of monopoly. Of oligopoly.

7. If you were charged with responsibility for the operation of the Antitrust Division of the Department of Justice, what standard would you use to decide whether prosecution of a particular firm was necessary or desirable?

8. Do you believe that the government should continue aid to farmers? Why?

9. If you owned a monopoly producing a daily necessity, what price would you charge for your product? How would you decide on the price?

10. Can you explain why total farm income is low in years in which production is very large?

CHAPTER *16*

Distribution
of
Income

When the economist speaks of "distribution" he does not refer to the market-ing of goods and services. What he is concerned with is the way in which the factors of production are priced in the market place. How does the economic system determine: (1) *rents* of land and other resources; (2) *wages* of various kinds of labor; (3) *interest* rates on capital assets; and (4) *profit?* The "prob-lem of distribution" deals with rents, wages, interest, and profit, and the price of each in the market place.

The pricing of production factors interests the economist simply because it helps determine For Whom goods are produced, and more important still, it helps solve the problem How goods are produced. If we wish to understand why wages make up three-fourths of the total national product we must study the forces that determine market wage rates, land rentals, and interest rates. This is the type of analysis that is used to investigate the distribution problem.

THEORY OF PRODUCTION

The key to factor pricing is provided by the economic theory of production. Here we must master yet another "marginal" concept—the concept of *marginal-product*. It is closely related to the law of diminishing returns, and like other marginal conceptions, deals with the *extra* unit of production, and with its cost.

The "production function." The theory of production begins with a body of specific engineering information. If you have a certain amount of labor, land, and other inputs, such as machines or raw materials, how much output of a particular good can you get? The answer depends on the state of technology, of course, but at any given time there is always a maximum possible output from given amounts of factor inputs. The rule relating economic inputs and outputs is extremely important; it is called a *production function*, and is defined as the technical relationship which states the output that can be obtained from any set of specified inputs or factors of production.

Here is an example. An agricultural engineer knows the various combinations of land and labor that will produce different amounts of corn. A thick handbook shows all of the combinations of inputs that will produce different outputs—that is the production function. There are thousands of production functions in the economy, of course, and they determine a firm's total cost curve. That is, they provide the basis on which the firm demands the land, labor, capital, and other productive inputs which it buys on the market.

Each producing firm sits poised between two markets. (1) On the *commodity market*, it appears as a supplier, selling its products along the demand curve of its customers; (2) in the market for *factors of production* it appears as a buyer, purchasing those inputs that will minimize cost and produce a maximum-profit position. This second market puts price tags on the various factors of production which the company uses, and thus determines the distribution of income to wages, rent, interest, and profit.

The aggregate American production function. Let us take an overall look at the aggregate of labor, capital, and product in American manufacturing. Such magnitudes must be measured with care, but they are useful as a broad description of economic society. The total production function is not easily measured, but intensive studies of the subject suggest that the single most important factor of production is labor, in a sense at least. Both labor and capital are needed for production, and if all capital is taken away, or all of labor, production is negligible. A 1 per cent increase in labor, however, seems to increase output about three times as much as a 1 per cent increase in capital. This corresponds roughly with the known fact that wages are about three-fourths of the national product while property incomes are about one-fourth. A few other major findings in this area might be noted:

1. The productivity of both labor and capital has increased through the century as a result of improved skill and technology. The average rate of improvement seems to be about 1½ per cent per year.

2. The amount of capital has been growing at a faster rate than the labor supply because of increased thrift by society as a whole. Each laborer therefore has more capital to work with, and his productivity wages have risen even more rapidly than the 1½ per cent due to technological change.

3. The return for each unit of capital might appear subject to the law of diminishing returns because each unit of capital has less labor to cooperate with it, yet capital's return per unit has in fact remained about the same. Why? Technological progress. The total income of capital has therefore risen as the amount of capital has increased, but the rate of growth of the total return has been held down. The law of diminishing returns cancels some of the fruits of technological progress. Yet capital's share of the social pie has remained fairly constant—about one-fourth of the total—and this is remarkable when we consider the growing union movement, changes in the overall economy, and the widespread notion that automation has downgraded the value of human brain-power and skills.

Marginal-products. If we hold all other inputs constant and measure the output produced by one extra unit of a single factor of production, we obtain the *marginal-product* of that factor. Thus if land, capital, and raw materials are held constant, and one extra unit of labor is added to the production process, the amount of extra production obtained is the marginal-product of labor. The term marginal-physical-product is often used in this context because the product is usually expressed in terms of physical output. The marginal-physical-product behaves exactly according to the law of diminishing returns, and we might really call the latter the "law of diminishing marginal-physical-product." As we add successive units of one factor, holding the others constant, the added output—the marginal-physical-product—decreases steadily for all factors of production, a very important characteristic of production.

Substitution of production factors. There are various ways in which the factors of production can be combined to produce a given output. We may use more labor and less land, or less labor and more machinery, and still achieve a given level of production. Obviously, our choice of factors, the combination we use, will depend upon relative cost. When labor is expensive and land is cheap, we use fewer workers and more land; when labor is cheap and land is dear, we reverse our combination. In either case, the realization that the factors of production can be combined in various ways is an important element in the businessman's efforts to minimize the cost of production.

The successful firm achieves least-cost production only when it uses the cheapest possible inputs that will produce the output required. The choice depends on the cost of the input and its marginal product. If 1 acre of land and 1 unit of labor each cost $2, we achieve least-cost production by substituting labor for land or land for labor so long as the marginal-product of one is greater than the other. When the marginal-product of each is exactly even, we are getting the most for each dollar spent on production factors and we have reached the least-cost production point for a given output.

The general least-cost substitution principle. The example we have used, where land and labor costs were identical, is a special case. If land costs ten times as much as labor, it would be silly to stop when marginal-product is equal. We would continue substitution until the marginal-product of land is ten times as large as the marginal-product of labor. The general rule is as follows: Least cost is achieved by substituting production factors until their marginal-physical-products are exactly proportional to their respective factor prices. Then marginal-physical-product per last dollar spent on each will be exactly the same. That is the least-cost position. This rule will hold for any factor, or any combination of factors, and give the least-cost position for a given output.

Final factor demand at Best-Profit output. We can now calculate factor demand at each level of production, but we have still to decide which production level to choose. To do this, we combine cost and revenue to obtain the Best-Profit position.

Table 24 shows the method used to calculate Best-Profit position and thereby determine the demand for the different productive factors. Comparing costs (column 4) and total revenue (column 3) we find that when output is at 6 units we have reached our Best-Profit position. Marginal cost is now equal to marginal revenue. In real life, the calculation tends to be done by trial and error, but we have oversimplified to illustrate the principle at work. The important point to note is that the factor demand appropriate to this least-cost, Best-Profit position that gives us the optimum amount of factors demanded by the firm.

In some production processes, the factor inputs are so closely related that an increase in one input gives zero extra product, and a decrease in one factor eliminates all production. In this case, the factors must be changed in combination, but least-cost, Best-Profit calculations can still be made.

Demand for factors is a derived demand. The businessman demands production factors for different reasons than the consumer demands an overcoat or a magazine. The latter is concerned with his own satisfaction; the businessman hopes to produce goods that will bring him revenue in the future. His demand is derived *indirectly* from consumer demand. Many stages of demand may intervene between producer and final consumer, but in each case, all previous demands depend on the demand of the final consumer.

Another peculiarity of factor input demand is that factors do not usually work alone. A shovel produces nothing without a man to use it. The quantity of goods produced depends on combinations of inputs. In practice, inputs are inseparable, for they interact and usually reinforce one another. This means that demand for one factor will depend in some measure on demand for all other factors. The amount of labor demanded will certainly depend on the wage rate, but it will also depend on the price of machines—a point of some significance.

PRICING THE FACTORS OF PRODUCTION: RENTS

We can now examine the manner in which a market system distributes income to the owners of the different factors of production. We have seen how market factor-prices determine the demand of each firm for the different production factors. When the factor demands of all individual firms are summed, we have the aggregate market demand for the factors of production. This demand curve, together with the supply curve of the factors, determines the market price of the production factors and the distribution of income to the owners of the factors. The interesting special case of rents paid for the use of land serves to illustrate these principles clearly and accurately.

Aggregate market demand for outputs and inputs. The demand for a given factor input (cornland) can be derived from the final consumer's demand for the output it produces (corn), assuming, of course, that the price of other inputs remains constant. The farmer must decide on the Best-Profit production level and the least-cost combination of inputs according to prevailing prices for these factors. If the price of one factor changes, demand for that factor will vary until the value of the marginal-product (marginal-revenue-product) of that factor is equal to its market cost. The relationship between demand for outputs and inputs such as corn and cornland is shown in Figure 26.

Since the industry is competitive, and no single producer can affect price, the farmer need not worry about spoiling the market by overselling. Consequently, marginal revenue and price are the same. And marginal-revenue-product will be the same as marginal-physical-product multiplied by the price of corn.

Factor-price determination by supply and demand. Obviously, all of the firms together determine a factor's market price, since the demand for a factor, in-

Demand for factors is derived from demand for the goods they produce:

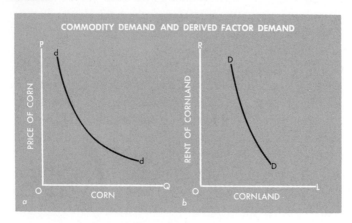

COMMODITY DEMAND AND DERIVED FACTOR DEMAND

Fig. 26. The derived demand for corn-land *DD* comes from the commodity demand for corn *dd*. Move *dd* up, and up goes *DD*. (Make *dd* more inelastic and vertical, and same tends to happen to *DD*.)

teracting with the supply of the factor, will determine factor-price. The demand for land, combined with the supply curve for land, tells us the market price of land—the amount of rent that must be paid for its use.

The total land supply is fixed by nature, and can be neither augmented nor diminished when factor-prices change. The supply curve is therefore a vertical line; supply is completely inelastic. The intersection of the supply and demand curves (point E) is the factor-price toward which land rent will tend.

The reasoning? If rent rose above E the amount of land demanded by

Fixed land must work for what demanders will bid:

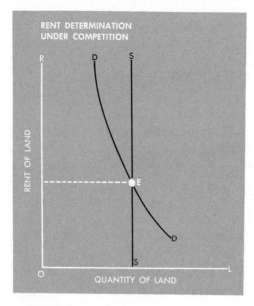

RENT DETERMINATION UNDER COMPETITION

Fig. 27. Perfect inelasticity of supply characterizes the case of so-called "pure economic rent." We run up *SS* curve to demand curve to determine rent. (Aside from land, oil and mining properties may also involve rent considerations.)

producers would be less than the supply and some owners would be unable to rent their land at all. They would therefore offer land at lower rents until they found a buyer. Similarly, if the rent were too low, demand would exceed supply, and prices would tend to rise until equilibrium was reached. In this sense, supply and demand determine the price of any factor of production. It is the productivity of the factor (land in this case) that is being paid for.

Even the productivity of land is not something absolute. If the price of corn fell drastically because people wanted something else, the derived demand for cornland would shift downward and to the left and the rentals which landlords receive would also sink to a new equilibrium intersection. The land has lost no fertility, but the demand for the factor has changed.

A production factor like cornland is said to earn "pure, economic rent" because (1) total supply is regarded as perfectly inelastic, and (2) we assume that land has no other uses. As David Ricardo noted early in the nineteenth century, it is not really true that the price of corn is high because the price of cornland is high. Actually, the reverse is more nearly the truth. For supply is inelastic, and land will always work for whatever it receives in a competitive market. The value of land is derived from the value of the product, and not vice versa. Other production factors may also be said to earn pure economic rent (where supply is entirely fixed) or quasi rent (where supply is fixed, except in the long run)—heavy and elaborate machinery, for example.

Rent and costs. Because land will work at any price, some economists have gone so far as to say that rent does not enter into the cost of production. There is a grain of truth here, but the terms are dangerous and misleading. A farmer who raises corn would soon find that his landlord expects to be paid like anyone else, and rent paid for land is certainly part of production costs. Even where the farmer owns his own land, rent figures into production costs. After all bills are paid, including wages to the farmer, there must remain an amount equal to the market rental value of the land, for if there is not, the farmer would soon find it better to rent the farm and hire himself out as a laborer.

Sometimes, economists call rent paid by the owner to himself "implicit" rather than "explicit" to differentiate the two cases. But implicit rent is clearly as much a part of long-run costs as any other cost. The same can be said for implicit wages or interest, or the return on any factor that could be sold rather than used personally.

Henry George's single-tax movement. Late in the nineteenth century, open land was still abundant in the West, but as the population increased, each acre of land acquired more people to work it. In a sense, land became more productive, and its rental value tended to rise. This created handsome profits for those lucky or farsighted enough to get in on the ground floor. Various people began to ask why such lucky landowners should be permitted to receive these so-called "unearned land increments." Henry George, a printer by trade, crystallized these sentiments into what is called the "single-tax" movement. George's arguments were widely supported about a half century ago, and there are still some adherents of the single-tax, though it is unlikely that anyone will come so close to being elected mayor of New York City on the single-tax platform as Henry George did in 1886. Nor is it likely that anyone will soon come along to write so persuasive a bible for the movement as George did in his *Progress and Poverty*, a book which sold millions of copies here and abroad.

This is not the place to assess the merits of the single-tax movement as a political force, but the central economic principle of the movement—that land rent is in the nature of a surplus which can be taxed heavily *without distorting production incentives*—can be analyzed to illustrate one principle of distribution and taxation.

Suppose that supply and demand create an equilibrium land rent. What now happens if a 50 per cent tax is placed on all land rents? We are not taxing buildings or improvements, for that would certainly affect construction activity. All we are taxing is the yield of the fixed supply of agricultural and urban land sites. There is no change in the total demand for land, and purchasing firms are willing to pay the same amount as before for a given quantity of land. With the supply of land fixed, the market price will remain the same. Why? Because neither supply nor demand has changed. The situation is seen in graphic form in Figure 28.

What has changed? Only the difference between what the farmer pays and what the landlord receives. In the case of the landlord, the effect of the 50 per cent tax is identical to a shift in demand from *DD* to *D'D'*. The landlord's equilibrium return after taxes is now only as high as E', or just half as great as it had been at E. The whole of the tax has shifted to the owners of land. The landowner may not like this, of course, but under competition nothing can be done about it, since the supply of land cannot be altered.

Whether or not it is fair to take away part of the landowner's return is a question we cannot decide on economic grounds. What is relevant is that a similar 50 per cent tax on a factor of production whose supply is not completely inelastic would alter the factor-prices charged in a competitive market. Such a tax would distort the production pattern and shift some of the burden forward onto the users of the factor and the consumer. If an acre of land were taxed differently when it was used for corn rather than wheat, for example, this would certainly distort the price of wheat relative to the price of corn. But on completely inelastic land, the distortion does **not** appear.

Tax on fixed land is shifted back on landlords, skimming off pure rent:

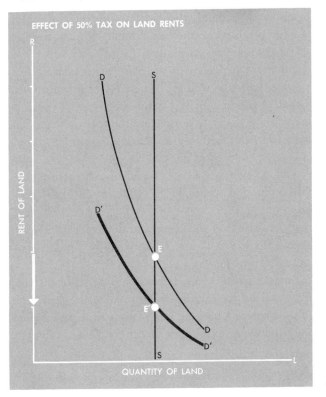

EFFECT OF 50% TAX ON LAND RENTS

RENT OF LAND

QUANTITY OF LAND

Fig. 28. A tax on fixed land leaves rentals paid by users unchanged at E but reduces rent retained by landowners to E'. (What can the landowners do but accept less return?)

Supply and demand for any factor. The determination of land rent through the interaction of supply and demand is only one type of analysis that can be made of any factor of production. How is the weekly rental price of a tractor determined in the competitive market? We first sum the derived demands of all business firms for tractors, and then calculate the supply curve for tractors (which need not be inelastic). The supply curve may be inelastic and vertical, positively elastic or negatively elastic, but in all cases it can be calculated, and the intersection of the supply and demand curves will set the final equilibrium factor-price for tractors. If the demand curve shifts upward, the market price will tend to rise; if the supply offered for sale increases, shifting the supply curve to the right, the factor-price will tend to fall. All factor-prices are determined in this way.

Factor pricing and efficiency. For Whom, as we have seen, is determined by competitive supply and demand, and whether or not we like the solution, we must admit that it contributes to efficiency. How is solved in a similar manner. Each of the production factors, land, labor, etc., has a price which fluctuates with supply and demand. The producer, seeking his least-cost combination (lest he go bankrupt) substitutes one factor for another where there is a difference in marginal cost. Supply and demand, then, determine the particular combination of factors used for production; they determine How as well as For Whom. And the resulting commodity prices tend to make us substitute cheaper goods in our diet for more expensive items. The price system thus signals the best commodity substitutions as well as the best factor substitutions.

Do you now believe that charging rent has a function, even if part of it is later taxed away? Then you are ready to appreciate the fact that some of our economic troubles derive from our inability to charge appropriate rents. Here are some examples:

ITEM. The sea is free to all, so everyone fishes excessively, threatening the supply of fish. If rent could be charged we might all be better off in the long run, including the fisherman.

ITEM. Our roads are very crowded on weekends and during rush periods, yet we cannot usually charge rents for their use. If we could, we might coax drivers into the use of less crowded time periods.

ITEM. Even if collections from parking meters paid only a part of the cost of the meter system, it might still be socially desirable to keep the tolls high enough to create rational use of space. Charging rents can lead to an efficient How, even though they may produce a For Whom that is considered ethically dubious.

COMPETITIVE WAGES AND COLLECTIVE BARGAINING

A man is much more than a commodity. Yet men do rent their services for a price, and this price is the wage rate. Of all the prices in the economy, the wage rate is by far the most important. For most of the population, the wage rate determines family income, and since much of the income of farmers and unincorporated businesses is really a form of labor income, wages must constitute almost 80 per cent of the total national income. It is hard to discuss wages objectively and dispassionately because our welfare is so intimately bound to the wage rate. In fact, the sociological importance of wages has economic implications which the student of the labor market must always bear in mind.

Wage levels and differentials. Wage rates differ enormously, and the average wage is as hard to define as the average man. An auto executive may earn $500,000 in a year, while a clerk earns $4,000 and a farmhand $2,000. Part of any wage theory must explain these differentials as well as the vital question of general wage levels. We begin with the factors that determine wage rates under competitive conditions. Then we shall investigate the effect of deviations from competitive conditions and analyze the economics of collective bargaining between union and employer.

Wage determination under perfect competition. Let us begin with the simple case of a single category of workers all exactly alike in skill, effort, and every other respect. Wage rates under competition would be exactly equal for all members of this category, for no employer would pay more for the work of one than of another, and no worker could demand more for his services than the others obtain.

How is this wage rate determined? By our old friend supply and demand. For the competitive equilibrium point (Figure 29) at point E, where the supply and demand curves intersect, will set the wage rate. If wages rise, a surplus of labor will bid them down; if they fall, bidding by prospective employers will restore them.

We are, of course, interested in *real wages,* and not just in money amounts. Wages used in our illustrations must be corrected to show real purchasing power of goods, for if money wages doubled between 1946 and 1950

Favorable resources and technology explain high American wages:

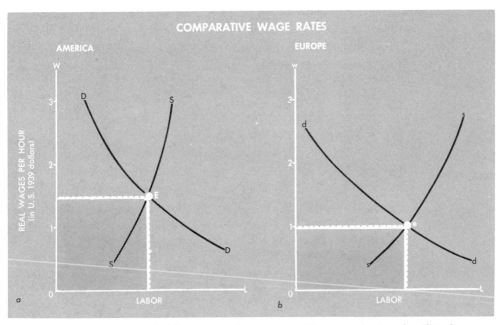

Fig. 29. Supply and demand determine a higher competitive wage in America than in Europe.

while prices increased 50 per cent in the same period, real wages would increase by one-third—200/150 = 1⅓.

National resources and high productivity. Why, then, are wages so much higher in America than in Europe? Superficially, the answer is that supply and demand in America and Europe are different. But we must look behind these schedules to find a meaningful answer.

The derived demand schedule for labor slopes downward, and the law of diminishing returns suggests that adding more labor to existing resources will tend to diminish labor productivity and wage rates. If the American population increased enough to shift the labor supply curve to the right, the wage might fall to the European level or even lower. One important explanation of high American wage levels, then, is that America is generously supplied with resources proportional to the population. The per capita supply of these materials is lower in Europe, and lower still in other parts of the world.

Technology, capital, and high productivity. Economic geography does not, of course, tell the whole story of different wage levels. Two regions may have exactly the same resources, but if one of them uses superior technological methods, its productivity and real wages may be much higher than the other's. Superior technology is partly a matter of know-how, scientific progress, and economic laws and practices, and partly a matter of the relative abundance of capital goods—machinery, etc. We do not understand exactly why the United States achieved its technological superiority, and our lead seems to be narrowing as technical competence spreads, but the facts of the superiority are not subject to much dispute.

Immigration and restrictions on the labor supply. Obviously, we then want to know why Europeans do not move from their low-wage areas to our high-wage area. Again, the answer is quite clear. People *did* migrate to America in large numbers before this century, but laws restricting the entry of immigrants were passed early in the century severely restricting the flow. This is our first example of interference with the free play of competition in the wage market. By keeping the labor supply limited, immigration restrictions tend to keep wages high. As a basic principle, any limit on the supply of a particular grade of labor relative to the supply of all other productive factors will tend to raise the wage rate. An increase in the supply, other things being equal, will tend to depress wages.

The counterlaw of increasing returns. We have already noted that if we add increased quantities of *all* of the factors of production, we begin to obtain greater productivity and economies from the mass-production system that follows. The law of increasing returns, or the law of the economies of mass production, works against the law of diminishing returns, within limits. This law helps explain why America is so prosperous. Modern mass-production systems require large plants and very large markets to consume the goods, and when these are available the benefits of mass production can be reaped. The United States has both, since the whole nation is a single *free trade area* in which goods may move freely.

Theory of optimum population. The law of increasing returns raises the question whether population growth necessarily leads to diminishing returns as the labor supply increases. Might it not make possible further economies of mass production? This suggests an interesting theory of population. Why not take advantage of mass-production economies by aiming at a population which remains stable at the point where increasing returns end and diminishing returns begin? This point, at which the highest level of real wages is attained, is called the "optimum population" point. Certainly it would maximize the returns to society if the point could be reached, but unfortunately, no economist knows what the curve looks like. Should we welcome more immigrants for purely selfish reasons? Or are we now at a point where a high birth rate should be discouraged? Which policy would move us closer to the optimum population level? At the present time, we simply do not know.

The iron law of wages: Malthus and Marx. According to Thomas Malthus, who formulated the "iron law of wages," the wage level will, in the long run, tend to the lowest standard of living at which the population will reproduce itself. The belief that wages tend toward the bare subsistence minimum was widely accepted in the nineteenth century, and economics was in fact called the "dismal science" for that reason. Our survey of living standards in recent years shows how unrealistic this notion is for the modern world, but the argument survives in the works of Karl Marx, where it is stated in somewhat different form.

Marx placed great emphasis on the "reserve army of the unemployed," the men who are surplus and cannot find jobs. This group, always willing to work for whatever is offered, pressed downward on the wage rates. Since subsistence is the lowest level of wages that man can accept, wages move to this level. Below that point men cannot work; above this level, the unemployed will be willing to work for less to obtain a position.

The argument is diagrammed in Figure 30, assuming a wage of $2 per hour at 1939 prices. Employment is at the level indicated at A. The number of unemployed is represented by the distance from A to B. This would certainly put downward pressure on wages, but does this mean that they would tend to drop to the subsistence level? Not at all. Given adequate resources, the com-

Karl Marx exaggerated power of reserve army of the unemployed:

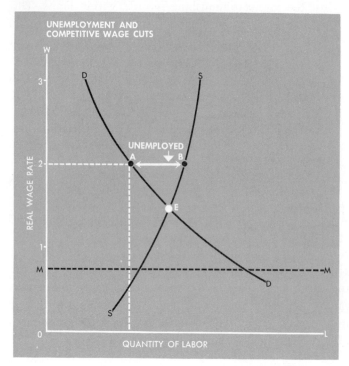

Fig. 30. Contrary to Marx, the "reserve army of the unemployed" — as shown by *AB*—need not depress real wages to the *MM* "minimum-subsistence" level. It can only depress competitive wages from *A* to E. If labor supply became so abundant that *SS* intersected *DD* at *MM*, the wage would be at a minimum level, as in many underdeveloped regions; but institutional or legal changes can do little when marginal productivity remains abysmally low.

petitive equilibrium wage might be very comfortable indeed, though in a less fortunate country it would be lower. If competition is really perfect, the employer cannot set the wage rate arbitrarily, for he must bid competitively for labor. If he obtains none, he makes no profit. So long as employers are numerous, seeking profits, and not acting in collusion, the demand for labor will bid the wage rate to the equilibrium level, and this level depends on many factors other than the employer's desires.

Unions and hours. The law of diminishing returns helps us to understand why labor unions have favored restrictions on immigration. The same analysis will help explain why they have urged: (1) a shorter week and longer vacations, (2) restrictions on child labor and early retirement, (3) restrictions on the rate of activity at work. Today, union policy is not uniform in these matters. The AFL-CIO, for example, has in fact supported a more liberal immigration policy.

Economics alone does not explain why unions fight for shorter hours. Labor fears unemployment, and tends to think that the total amount of work is constant in the short run; hence it does not wish to exhaust the amount of work by increasing the labor supply. This is sometimes called the "lump of labor" fallacy. The notion may be true in relation to particular workers, but it is not true if it implies that there is only so much work to be done in an economic system. There is no need for mass unemployment if proper fiscal, monetary, and pricing policies are pursued. Technological unemployment is a serious matter, of course, but its optimal solution lies in offsetting policies which create new job opportunities, not in restrictions on production.

The thirty-hour week? Should the working week be further reduced? As living standards rise, it is only reasonable that we should seek more leisure, but at this stage of history one wonders if the American worker would really be willing to buy ten hours of leisure each week if it meant foregoing a sizable fraction of his potential real income—say, 20 per cent. A decade of full employment has greatly reduced agitation for a thirty-hour week, which suggests that unemployment really carries the most weight in the argument. Moreover, union leaders like Walter Reuther, who support a shorter workweek, also insist that there be no reduction in take-home pay. No worker would oppose a free present of leisure time, of course, and that is what this proposal means.

Economically speaking, one aspect of the shorter workweek bears closer scrutiny. Past experience shows that when the working day is cut by one hour, output does not fall by the same percentage. This suggests that a 25 per cent reduction in hours might not require a 25 per cent cut in take-home pay. But that is a far cry from the claim that hours can be reduced 20 per cent without *any* reduction in total production. The Bureau of Labor Statistics made a careful study of the evidence which lends little credence to the claim. Doubtless Saturday work will become increasingly rare in American industry, and vacations with pay will increase. Time off is one of the benefits of technological progress. But the amount of time that can be taken away from production is still limited by the total output achieved during the shorter workweek.

The general supply curve for labor. Returning to the case of perfect competition, what does the labor supply curve look like? How does the wage rate affect population? Will higher wages lead to more effective work? These questions show that the labor supply involves various factors, four of which are particularly important: (1) population, (2) proportion of the population actually in the labor force, (3) average number of hours worked each week and year, and (4) the quantity and quality of skill and effort provided by the workers. The third of these factors is most clearly subject to economic forces; sociological factors, law, custom, etc., will influence the others.

Equalizing differences in wages. Let us now turn to the vital problem of *differentials in competitive wages* among different categories of people and jobs. Some observed pay differentials are easily explained. Jobs differ in unpleasantness; hence wages may be raised to coax people into less attractive jobs. Such differentials simply compensate for nonmoney differences among jobs and are called "equalizing differences." Thus steeplejacks are paid more than janitors, and workers often receive extra pay for the "undesirable" 4 P.M. to 12 P.M. work shift.

Equalizing pay is usually found where jobs involve dirt, nerve strain, tedium, low social prestige, seasonal layoffs, or much dull training. To recruit workers for such occupations, you raise pay. Pleasant and attractive jobs may be filled with lower wage rates, which accounts for the low wages of clerical workers. A wage differential is "equalizing" when people qualified for both jobs are hesitant to accept that which pays the higher wage rate, for the higher-paid job is probably not really more attractive when all of the conditions involved are weighed.

Nonequalizing differentials: Labor quality. If all labor were homogeneous, all wage differentials would be equalizing. But in real life, we all know that most higher-paid jobs are also more pleasant; the wage differential is not of the equalizing type. Of course, this may be due simply to imperfections in competition, for workers do not have anything like a perfect knowledge of job opportunities, and hence do not compete for all jobs for which they are qualified. Further, labor unions, minimum-wage laws, or monopolies by the workers in particular occupations may also explain differentials.

But many wage differentials have little to do with imperfections in competition, and they would persist even if all monopoly elements in the system were eliminated. They are due to qualitative differentials among people. Men do not contribute equally to production, even if they occupy identical positions in a firm. There are many different kinds of labor, many skills and aptitudes, that make up the labor market; labor is not a single lump that is the same all the way through.

Older economists called these different categories of labor "noncompeting groups in the labor market," but that terminology is liable to be misunderstood, for the "noncompetitive" groups would remain even in a perfectly competitive system. Further, they do compete, though not perfectly; they are *partial* rather than *perfect* substitutes for each other.

General equilibrium of labor market. In real life, there is some mobility between different jobs, though there are certain permanent barriers to mobility that depend on irreducible biological and social differences. Hence wage differentials arising from these differences will probably persist, even in the long run. We can reduce the differentials by training and better knowledge of job opportunities, but in the long run the supply and demand for labor skills will tend to an equilibrium for each wage group, and the resulting pattern of wage differentials will represent a general equilibrium of the labor market at that point.

IMPERFECTIONS OF THE LABOR MARKET

In the real labor market, human beings cannot be graded neatly into market categories like eggs or wheat. There is no auctioneer who allocates workers to the highest bidder. There are considerable long- and short-run immobilities. Through ignorance, inertia, sentiment, etc., workers often fail to move to higher-paying jobs. All of these factors tend to produce wage differentials.

Two tests can indicate that the labor market is imperfect: (1) if a considerable amount of unemployment (as in 1960) does not produce a drop in wages (wage stickiness); and (2) if every sizable firm *must* have a wage policy. In a perfectly competitive system, a firm would not make pay-schedule decisions; they would be made by the market system. A raise in wages would bring in more workers; a cut in wages would reduce the labor force.

However, this does not mean that the labor market is totally uncompetitive. There is a blend of competition and some degree of monopoly power over the wages to be paid. A firm that sets wages too low soon finds its workers quitting at a somewhat faster rate than would otherwise be the case, and recruitment of new workers becomes increasingly difficult. There would probably be some slackening of performance by those who remained.

Availability of labor does, then, affect the wage rate under imperfect competition. A small firm may even bargain and haggle with prospective workers to keep wages at a minimum. Larger firms tend to set wages for each type of job, altering the rate according to the number and type of applicants. In practice, optimal wage policy is a puzzling problem, even in the absence of unions. Should the employer pay the "going wage," or try to obtain the cream of the local market by paying slightly more than average? Or should he try to pay minimal wages and obtain what work he can from the workers, knowing that they will leave as soon as another job is available?

Labor unions. Labor markets are imperfect, even when labor unions are not involved. One of the reasons given for starting unions was the feeling that unorganized workers lacked "equality of bargaining power" when they faced the financially strong employers. Have the unions accomplished their task? It is very hard to say, for bargaining power is not easily measured. Various features of the labor market that are commonly associated with union activity are in fact present when there are no unions. Standard pay rates and wage stickiness, for example, are found in large companies where there are no unions. Many of our findings are applicable to all labor markets, though we shall concentrate on imperfections related to trade unionism. Further, we shall limit our discussion mainly to the economic function of unions—to wage rates, pensions, hours, etc.—though we ought not to forget their noneconomic functions—political, social, etc.

Three ways unions try to raise wages. Dropping the oversimplified picture of perfect competition, we can use economic theory to analyze the actual operation of trade unions. Unions have three main methods of raising wages in particular industries, all closely interrelated: (1) they seek to reduce the labor supply, (2) they use collective bargaining power to raise standard wages directly, (3) they can cause the derived demand curve for labor to shift upward. The three devices often reinforce one another, but they are not identical.

Restriction of labor supply. The labor supply may be limited in various ways. Immigration barriers, maximum-hour legislation, high initiation fees, long apprenticeships, refusal to admit new members to the union or to let nonunion workers hold jobs—all these work to restrict the labor supply. In addition, there are more subtle restrictions like work-load limits and other "featherbedding" practices or implicit understandings that force a slowdown of the work pace.

Raising standard wage rates. Direct limits on the labor supply are no longer necessary to unions except to reinforce their ability to secure higher wage rates. If the employer will pay a high standard wage, the labor supply takes care of itself. Surplus job candidates are automatically excluded from the market by the limited needs of employers, so long as they cannot underbid for the job.

Figure 31 compares the two techniques for raising wages. In Figure 31a the labor supply has been reduced, raising wages from E to E'. In Figure 31b, the employer has agreed to the E' wage rate, and the workers from E' to F are automatically excluded from the market in any case.

Shifting the derived demand curve upward. Any policy that improves the demand for labor acts to raise wages, and unions have used this principle in various ways. Thus the International Ladies Garment Workers Union studied means of reducing garment prices by improving productivity and by helping the industry to advertise its products. In other cases, a union may agitate for high tariffs, hoping to raise the demand curve for domestic workers, or write

To raise pay, unions restrict supply and enforce standard wage rate:

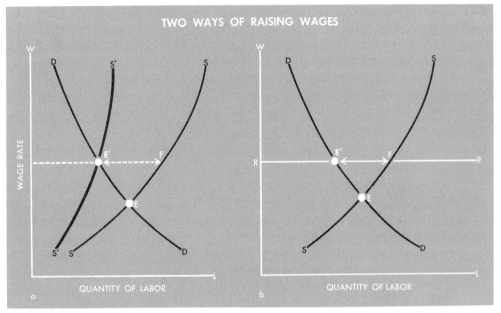

TWO WAYS OF RAISING WAGES

Fig. 31. Raising the standard wage to *RR* in (*b*) has exactly the same effect on wages as reducing the effective supply from *SS* to *S'S'* in (*a*); the workers from E' to F are excluded from employment in either case.

"featherbedding" provisions into building codes, or help maintain a monopoly price so long as some of the extra profits go to higher wages.

Further, if increasing wages raises the productivity of labor, then labor shifts its own demand curve upward. The traditional illustration of this principle was the case where malnourished workers were made more effective by higher wages. Even today, when this is not a pressing problem, too low wages are bad business if only because of their psychological impact on productivity.

Finally, some argue that high wage rates make management more efficient, for industry must then develop tools and methods that can meet the high wage bill. There may be this "shock effect" on the employer, of course, but how much it influences him no one knows, and the concept should be used with caution.

Wage increases and reductions in unemployment. If rising wages means simply moving up the existing demand curve for labor, then employment will decrease, for the demand curve always slopes upward from right to left. The amount of unemployment created depends on the elasticity of the demand curve for particular kinds of labor.

In some cases, unions have recognized this relationship and accepted lower earnings to maintain employment, as in the Massachusetts shoe industry (which was losing firms to other areas). On the other hand, the United Mine Workers has pressed for higher wages even though this meant a reduction of the hours of work per year and a large increase in the sale of oil as a substitute for coal.

Unions are seldom able to practice much wage restraint, for members tend to regard an increase in wages as intrinsically a good thing, and the union tends to pay most attention to the interests of those who will remain in the industry, disregarding the interests of those who lose their employment. Finally, the demand curve for union labor is actually inelastic, or is *thought to be* inelastic anyhow.

Collective bargaining. If unions sometimes realize that higher wages are not in their own best interests, management sometimes believes that a wage increase will improve long-term corporate earnings. But these are exceptional opinions. Usually, a collective-bargaining conference finds workers urging higher wages and management wishing to pay less. A demand for a 30-cent per hour increase may be made in the realization that perhaps half that much will be granted, and a 5-cent per hour increase may be offered in the realization that 15 cents per hour may have to be accepted. What will the final terms of the agreement be? Economic theory can tell us little here. The result depends on politics, psychology, and a thousand other intangibles. The economist views the outcome as indeterminate.

Arguments used in collective bargaining. Seven main arguments will appear in collective bargaining, in most cases. (1) If living costs are rising, the unions concentrate on the workers' *standard of living;* if prices are falling, the employer stresses this point. (2) If the company is prosperous, the union stresses *ability to pay;* if not, the employer stresses the point. (3) If *productivity* has risen or fallen, one or the other of the parties will include it in his argument. (4) *Going wages* in similar firms is another common basis for discussion. (5) Labor tends to support high wages as a means of bolstering *purchasing power;* management stresses the *higher cost of production involved.* (6) If a *national pattern* has been set in the large industries, this will carry great weight at the bargaining table. (7) Finally, both workers and employers have grown accustomed to wage increases, and many firms have built into their labor contracts a provision for a steady upward trend in wage rates.

Strikes. Usually, collective bargaining requires neither a strike nor a lockout, but both sides must realize that a failure to agree can lead to a costly work stoppage. Either side may "cause" the strike by refusing the other side's terms, and both sides, plus the general public, are generally hurt by strikes. Some commentators wonder why workers bother to strike for a small pay increase when it may take years to make up lost earnings at the new rate. The workers look at the strike differently, pointing out that the employer loses more than the cost of paying the extra hourly wage rate. In any case, workers do not strike *only* because of the last few cents of a wage demand. Workers feel that the threat of a strike forces the employer to agree to higher wages, and they realize that threats are hollow if both parties are not prepared to accept a strike at some point rather than give way. If the employer could not refuse a wage demand, or a union could not strike, collective bargaining would be without meaning.

Collective bargaining and the public interest. Within the framework provided by present legislation, the government does not interfere in collective bargaining; it is based on voluntary cooperation of labor and management. The results are not perfect, but experts are uncertain that government intervention would help. However, we all realize that the public interest is strongly affected by collective bargaining in the vital industries of the nation. There are *three* parties to every labor dispute, one being the general public. In emergencies, then, voluntary collective bargaining will always be superseded when it endangers national security. The government can and will keep the railroads running and the steel mills at work. Once government has superseded collective bargaining, what principles does it apply to set wages? Fact-finding boards simply re-phrase the question. Is a "fair wage" to be defined economically, politically, or in the court of public opinion? There are no easy answers here, but we can stress the fact that a stable and progressive economic system requires all parties to exercise self-control when they use their political powers.

INTEREST AND CAPITAL

Capital, the third great production factor, also has its special price— "interest." Capital theory is one of the most difficult parts of economic theory, and an introduction can only summarize some of the basic points made in all standard treatments of the subject, perhaps touching on a few qualifications that must be made. The interested student is urged to seek out some of the specialized literature for more information on the topic.

Land, labor, and capital. Traditionally, productive factors are divided arbitrarily into three categories: (1) *natural resources* provided by nature in fixed supply, the return being what we have called *rent;* (2) *human labor,* not produced in response to economic conditions, the return to which is called *wages;* (3) *capital goods,* which are produced by the economic system itself and used for further production of goods and services. Land and labor are called the "primary factors of production" because they are located largely outside the economic system. Capital goods may have a long or a short life, and they can be rented out in the competitive market like land or labor. The rental paid for capital (not pure economic rent, like payment for land) is determined by the same conditions that apply to land and labor.

However, traditional theory calls the return to capital by another name, *interest per annum*, measured as a pure percentage per unit of time, independent of dollar or other value units. But we usually calculate interest rate in terms of dollar value, for you cannot add hammers and turbines and thread meaningfully in physical terms. In competitive markets, these items have a dollar market value determined by supply and demand. There is no reason why these dollar values cannot be added, giving us the money value of all capital assets. Interest per annum can be calculated on this base.

Net productivity of capital. Why do people bother to transform the primary factors of land and labor into capital or intermediate capital goods? The answer is a technological fact of life. We get *more future consumption product* if we use indirect or roundabout production methods. By investing in capital, we make possible a much higher yield in the future. The primitive caveman who took time from hunting to "make" a stone club had to forego current consumption while he was forging his "capital," but he found it worth while because the club increased his future yield. It is this *net productivity*, this capacity to increase future production, that makes capital worthwhile.

Let us look at a more complex illustration. Imagine two islands exactly alike, supplied with identical quantities of the primary factors—labor and land. On island A, the primary factors are used to produce goods for current consumption; no capital goods are produced and everything is consumed. On island B, some of the goods are capital goods, and some are consumed currently. During a given time period, island A has enjoyed a higher standard of living than B, for the goods per capita were larger, but island A has no capital. Island B has consumed at a lower level, but has a stock of capital goods in hand (machinery, tools, etc.). After a period of "net capital formation," island B is ready to use its capital goods for further production.

Suppose that island B did without 100 consumption units in order to accumulate its stock of capital. That is, island B consumed 100 units less than island A, and placed this "saving" into capital goods. Clearly, island B would not do this unless the 100 units saved have the capacity to produce *more* than 100 units of goods in the future. And that is exactly what happens. Roundabout production methods, which take time and abstinence to get started, in fact produce more than direct processes. That is a basic fact of technology. We can therefore draw the very important conclusion that after allowing for depreciation and upkeep, capital has *net productivity,* which can be expressed as a percentage per annum of its original cost.

Interest determination: A bird's-eye view.

We can now see how the interest rate is determined over time. Capital formation proceeds at a rate which varies with current consumption; the more that is consumed now, the less capital we form. But as the supply of capital increases, the amount of extra production we obtain from new capital decreases because of the law of diminishing returns. Further, some kinds of capital investment produce much greater amounts of productivity than others. In general, investors will place their funds in those projects which offer the greatest return—projects whose net productivity is high. Such investments yield a high interest rate. As high-return projects are completed, investors must turn to capital formation which yields a lower return, and this causes the interest rate to drop. Ultimately, then, the abundance or scarcity of the stock of capital goods—which is determined by the community's past and present willingness to abstain from consumption and to save—determines the net productivity of capital or the interest rate that capital can earn.

SOME MAJOR QUALIFICATIONS. This traditional account of capital theory, much oversimplified, needs some important qualifications. We can only mention the more important of them, leaving the reader to seek a more advanced text in economics for further enlightenment.

1. *Technological disturbance* may affect the interest rate pattern outlined above, for in real life we cannot hold everything constant while our system accumulates capital and moves to the point at which the law of diminishing returns sets in. New discoveries are particularly significant here, for they often raise net productivity, and hence raise the interest rates that capital can earn. In fact, historical studies suggest that the tendency for the interest rate to fall has actually been canceled out by technological progress, for though wages have risen steadily, the interest on capital has not really dropped as we might expect. If technical innovation ceased, the interest rate might move toward zero, or the point at which no savings took place, but this is unlikely in the near future.

2. Our simplified theory ignored *uncertainty*. We assumed perfect foresight regarding the future. Yet in real life we are faced with uncertainty and vagueness; we cannot predict with certainty and we make mistakes. This element of uncertainty plays a vital role in profit theory. Lack of certainty can lead the investor to change his mind very rapidly, and investment relations are shiftable, changing with opinion and rumor, with technological innovation, and with many other factors.

3. The *effect of income changes*—shifts in schedules—was also ignored. That is, we failed to consider the fact that changes in the level of real income

have a profound effect on the saving and investment schedules at each interest rate. That is a serious weakness in traditional capital theory which many classical economists failed to realize.

PROFITS AND INCENTIVES

In addition to wages, interest, and rent, economists talk often of a fourth category of income—*profit*. Wages are the return to labor, interest the return to capital, and rent the return to land. What is profit a return to? The economist's answer is complex but significant. The term "profit" has many uses, but the economist, after careful analysis, relates profit to dynamic innovation and uncertainty, or to the problem of monopoly and incentives. We begin with the main notions of profit, then discuss briefly the role that profit and loss play in the market-pricing solution to our What, How, and For Whom questions.

Meaning of profit. When a U.S. Department of Commerce statistician gives newspaper reporters a figure involving profits, he usually means *corporation earnings*, whether paid out as dividends or held as undistributed profits, and he sometimes includes corporate taxes, though they may be omitted. The statistician may also "adjust" corporate profits for changes in inventory value due to price changes. Clearly we must be careful when we use published statistics like these. The statistician also provides figures for income of unincorporated enterprises (farmers, self-employed persons) which sounds like profits, obtained by subtracting all costs from sales revenue.

Implicit factor returns. To the economist, such statistical reports are a hodgepodge of different elements. Obviously, at least part of reported profits are merely the return to the owners of a firm for the factors of production supplied by them. Part may be a return for personal work by the owner; part may be rent on self-owned resources; part the equivalent of interest on the owner's capital. This shows us the first principle of profit. Much of what is ordinarily considered profit is really nothing but interest, rents, and wages, under a different name. Such returns are called *implicit interest* or *implicit rent* to show that they are earnings on self-owned factors.

Reward to enterprise and innovation. In a world where competition was perfect, the future predictable, and no innovations were permitted or possible, the economist would have no profits to report. The statistician might still report profit figures to the press, but economists would know that under these ideal conditions, profits would in fact be implicit returns to labor and property supplied by owners. Why? Because owners would hire out their factors on the market if they did not get equal rewards by using them in their own businesses, and those who had previously hired out their labor and property would soon enter business for themselves. Perfectly free entry of numerous competitors, in a static world with perfect knowledge, would bring price down to cost and squeeze out all profits above competitive wages, interest, and rent.

In real life, this does not happen. Someone must be boss; someone must make business decisions. This always involves some risk, a hazard on the future which may produce losses. And someone must introduce new ideas or inventions into the economic system. Let us call the man who does these things an *entrepreneur.* We can try to keep him separate from the manager or executive who simply keeps things running, and if this is possible, economists like Joseph Schumpeter believe that wages received by managers and executives should not be considered profits. Instead, profits should be defined as the returns to the entrepreneur or innovator, though the distinction is not always easy to make. The innovator in any case is a man with vision, originality, and daring. He may not invent new processes, but he introduces them. Many try this, and few succeed, but in Schumpeter's definition, it is the returns to this small group that are properly entitled profits.

Risk, uncertainty, and profit. Innovation depends on uncertainty, for if the future were certain there would be no opportunity for it. And innovation involves risk. One famous economist, Frank Knight of Chicago, argued that all true profit is therefore linked with uncertainty. From this view, profit is not simply a fourth factor return, like wages or rent, but a *part* of these factor returns. A worker unlucky enough to pick a trade that becomes obsolete may also suffer losses, and he takes risks; hence some of his wages must be considered profit for risk taking.

Profit as monopoly return. Those with a hazy notion of a capitalist as a fat man with a large cigar and a penchant for arithmetic who exploits the rest of the community may assume that profit is nothing more than the earnings of monopoly. This is obviously a caricature and not an economic concept. However, if we are objective we know that competition is not perfect in the economist's sense, and if there is great inequality in the distribution of property a very rich and perhaps idle minority may emerge. Is their income really monopoly profit? Whenever there is an appreciable deviation from perfect competition, it will pay the producer to take into account the fact that he may spoil the market if he offers too much of his product for sale. Hence it pays to limit the supply of production factors. These are called "contrived scarcities," and some texts, taking this into account, define monopoly profits as a *return from contrived scarcity.* It may take the form of rent, wages, or interest, depending on the factor in question and the relationship used to handle the specific situation.

The ethics of profit. Public-opinion polls invariably show that there is some hostility to profit, and this seems to indicate a lack of understanding of the complexity of the term. A scientist recently asked businessmen, for example, if they tried to "maximize profit," and was told in every case that they did not. Yet when he asked whether they thought a change in prices would make them better off in the long run, every one replied that they were doing as well as they could hope to do. Clearly, this is a consequence of the public attitude toward the term.

Actually, it is misleading to talk of a "profit system," for ours is a *profit-and-loss* system, in which profits are the carrot, the incentive to efficiency, while losses are the "stick" used to penalize the inefficient producer. The pursuit of profit simply means that the businessman is trying to get as much as he can for the resources at his disposal within the framework supplied by law and custom. This is not different from the worker who seeks to "better himself" by changing jobs or joining a union. In perfect competition, there would be no excess profits, and competitors would have to run hard just to stay in place, but that does not mean that there would be no profits under perfect competition. Production factors (land, labor, etc.) would still earn a return as wages, interest, and rent. Much of the hostility to profit is in fact directed toward extreme inequality in the distribution of incomes that results from unequal factor ownership. This should be kept separate from hostility toward profits created by imperfections in the competitive system.

Measuring profit. There is no way of knowing how large the different categories of profit may be, and we are unlikely to be able to measure them in the future. So far as the economist is concerned, it is not clear that we would gain very much by being able to do so, though social reformers might urge that contrived scarcity *should* be eliminated.

Taxation and profit. Even for those who oppose high profits, taxing profits is a risky business. For taxes have a drastic effect on the economy which must be weighed before a tax is imposed. A tax on each of our conceptions of profit, for example, would produce quite different results.

1. If implicit interest is taxed more heavily than explicit interest paid to bondholders, as is actually the case with corporation income tax, what is the effect? If this were the only point to be considered, a company like Standard Oil, which pays the government about 50 cents of each dollar earned on capital supplied by stockholders would rely on bonds for capitalization since it need not pay corporate taxes on them. Similarly, when I quit my job for a week to paint my house, I switch from explicit to implicit wages and the latter is not taxed as personal income. The reader can ponder for himself the tendencies produced by this difference in tax structure.

2. If the innovator's income is taxed, the result is even clearer, for the innovator cannot then look forward to reaping a tidy sum for his new ideas. He may instead decide to take a job with the civil service and never innovate anything. If old innovations are taxed, it will certainly affect the prospects of innovations yet to come.

3. If taxes affect risky enterprises more than routine activities, people will naturally avoid venturesome fields and gravitate toward the routine. Yet all of us have a stake in promoting vigorous exploration of new ways of doing things. Investment in venturesome projects is just what the doctor ordered to avoid depression and mass unemployment, and technological progress has long been the secret of material progress. We tamper with these projects only at our peril.

However, tax experts know that many investors, particularly those with high incomes, deliberately seek out risky investments because they expect windfall gains from such ventures to be taxed as capital gains while their costs can be charged against high-rate taxable income. In fact, some claim that the loopholes in the tax system encourage too much risk taking by capital. No simple answer is possible in such a controversial field, but the problem is evident.

Incentives, surpluses, and equity. Voters usually favor measures that tax the rich relatively more than the poor, or tend to reduce inequality of incomes. The decision is ethical and political, not economic. However, the public ought to weigh in the balance the effect of these measures on venturesomeness, effort, and thriftiness. The hostility is aimed at the surplus the factors earn, and we must grant that when prices are high, extra production is coaxed out from less efficient factors, allowing very efficient factors to earn at a high rate. Thus every factor income has some element of surplus in it and some element of incentive payment. But we cannot divide the two, for they are hopelessly integrated, and an attack on one can hardly avoid affecting the other.

A sermon on profit and economic activity.

We have shown how the price system helps society solve the basic economic problems, What, How, and For Whom. We have examined the tools of supply and demand, and noted how they determine competitive market price. And we have noted the important effects of monopolistic imperfections in competition. Finally, we dealt with the distribution of income by factor pricing. It is fitting, therefore, to end with a summary of the role of profit and loss in the overall pricing process.

1. Each person seeks his own advantage: workers seek high wages; landowners, high rents; owners of capital, high interest returns. Some of these returns are implicit, others explicit. Some may be called profit and others may not.

2. In the most general sense, profit means seeking self-advantage. Does this lead to the *lex talionis*—the law of the jungle? Not if there are competitive checks and balances.

3. Under perfect competition an ordered pattern emerges, a pattern of efficiency. But it has nothing to do with the poor becoming prosperous or the rich being brought down to the mean level.

4. When government does not like the For Whom pattern that results from *laissez faire*, it uses taxation, regulations, subsidies, etc., to change the pattern. This helps some and hurts others; the cost is both direct and indirect. There is also a lessening of the efficiency of the market system.

5. Profits and losses signal the advantages and disadvantages of particular economic activities. When a man is performing properly, producing what others want, his wages or profits rise. If he overdoes, he is penalized. If a better performer enters the picture, he is also penalized. He must then adapt or take losses. Profits and high factor returns are the bait that tempt men to new enterprises; losses are the penalties applied to the inefficient.

6. Under perfect competition, a man could get ahead only by doing things of value to himself or someone else. He could not spread false rumors or make false advertising claims. He could not control market price, and he could gain nothing by withholding production from the market, for his price would be exactly equal to marginal cost. Monopoly profits from contrived scarcity would be impossible. And if the pricing system were really perfect, no one would pour smoke into the atmosphere without paying the cost that smoke imposes on the rest of the community. No one would refuse to do basic research for fear that he could never tap its full advantage to society and thereby recover his costs. All external benefits or costs of every activity would be counted in accurately. As each person maximized his own advantage, the checks and balances of perfect pricing would ensure that the benefit of all with money votes was being efficiently achieved.

7. Obviously, we cannot produce a perfect system of this sort, nor does *laissez faire* mean perfect competition. But to the degree that public action can lessen monopolistic imperfections in competition, increase our imperfect knowledge of things, and bring total social benefits and costs into closer alignment with private benefits and costs—to this degree there is a creative role for government to play. Of course, the role of government also has its costs, and these too must be weighed with each extension of the functions of government.

This ends our sermon on pricing. Taking into account the real world as we know it, students of modern economics realize why the economy must by its very nature be a mixed economy. Competitive pricing must carry most of the burden of solving society's What, How, and For Whom. But constructive public policies are also needed to keep the system competitive and to provide the favorable environment in which private initiative can achieve the common good.

Summary

Distribution is concerned with the determination of different people's incomes or with the basic question For Whom economic goods are to be produced. Distribution theory studies the way the different factors of production—land, labor, capital, entrepreneurship, or risk taking—are priced in the market place, how supply and demand interact to determine all kinds of wages, rents, interest rates, and profits.

The demand for production factors is a derived demand because it comes from final consumer demand; it is also a joint demand, because the factors interact in the final production process. This leads to the process of substitution of factors to achieve least-cost production, equalizing the marginal-physical-product per dollar spent for each factor. The simultaneous determination of the firm's Best-Profit and least-cost position determines the amount of each productive factor demanded by the firm.

Factor-demand curves are derived from commodity-demand curves. The unchangeable quantity of land is an interesting special case where the supply is perfectly inelastic. In a case like this, pure rent is determined by competition, but the cost factor is more price-determined than price-determining. Despite its inelasticity, land would still be available if it had to work for less, and in that sense, the return on land is a "surplus" rather than a reward needed to coax out a supply of the factor. This is the basis for Henry George's "single-tax" proposal, aimed at the unearned increment in land.

Competitive wage determination is a complex problem. If all men and jobs were alike, there would be no wage differentials. But differences in natural capacity, plus differences in resources and technology, make for differences in wage rates and in wage levels.

The law of diminishing returns suggests that a reduction of the labor supply would increase wages; and this belief leads to pressure to restrict immigration. But there is a tendency for returns to increase as population increases, and in theory, the optimum population is the point where these two tendencies balance.

The labor supply has four dimensions: population size, percentage of people gainfully employed, average number of hours worked per week, and quality of worker effort.

In real life, labor markets are not perfectly competitive, with or without unions. Unions try to influence wages by restricting the labor supply, establishing standard wage rates and shifting the demand schedule for labor upward. If the demand schedule does not change, wage increases will usually lead to unemployment.

Collective bargaining usually centers around six basic points: living standards, ability to pay, productivity trends, "going wages," purchasing power, and "national patterns" in key industries. The threat of strike or lockout, even if it is not carried out, is the major incentive to agreement, though the usual result is a compromise.

Capital has net productivity above replacement costs, expressed as an annual percentage or interest rate. The interest rate also acts to screen investment projects that are most fruitful, though government monetary and fiscal policies play an important part in setting the pattern of interest rates and capital formation. Net productivity is strongly influenced by technological changes, income-level changes, or new expectations.

Profit is a difficult conception which economists view in four different ways: (1) as implicit interest, (2) as temporary high earnings from innovation, (3) as payment for risk taking, and (4) as a return to monopoly, sometimes called contrived scarcity.

For the economist, profit seeking, under perfect pricing conditions, leads to an efficient How. If the distribution of wealth and abilities and opportunities were made ethically optimal and if there were no externalities or monopolistic imperfections of markets or technology, then the checks and balances of perfect competition would lead to a best solution of society's What, How, and For Whom. In a mixed economy, public policies try to provide the necessary correctives that align private and social benefits, in short, to promote the environment in which private initiative can function best.

Review Questions

1. What does the economist mean by rent? Wages? Interest? Profit?
2. What is a production function? What are some of the basic characteristics of American production?
3. What is marginal-product? Why is it important?
4. Explain how the producer arrives at his least-cost production position.
5. Explain how factor-price is determined by supply and demand.
6. Why does Henry George's single-tax system fail to distort production incentives?
7. Differentiate between a wage level and a wage differential.
8. Explain why American wages are generally higher than wages in any other country in the world.
9. What is the iron law of wages? Who proposed it? Why is it important?
10. What are some of the major causes of imperfections in the labor market? What are their effects?
11. How do labor unions seek to raise wages?

12. What arguments are generally encountered in collective bargaining?

13. Explain what is meant by "net productivity of capital." Why is it important? How does it relate to interest rate?

14. What are some of the factors that can influence productivity and qualify the theory of interest determination?

15. What does the economist mean by profit?

For Further Study

1. Is American labor threatened by "cheap labor" in Japan or other parts of Asia? Explain.

2. Try to imagine the "production functions" involved in building a house. How would you weigh and balance them to obtain a house of a given size in a fixed price range?

3. Can you explain how wage differentials would disappear in a perfectly competitive market where all people and all jobs were exactly alike?

4. What are the factors that influence the level of real wages? How can they be linked to the theory of optimum population?

5. Explain the dangers involved in treating the general demand for labor just like a particular group's demand. Show that wages are both costs and sources of demand.

6. How do innovations and expectations affect traditional interest theory?

7. If you had capital to invest, would you invest in the United States or in one of the underdeveloped countries? Explain in detail the factors governing your decision.

8. Are you in favor of a reduction of corporate taxes? Why?

CHAPTER 17

International
Trade
and Finance

Earlier in the text, we took international trade more or less for granted. In this chapter we wish to analyze explicitly the interesting economic problems arising as soon as an economy begins dealing with another economy—arising out of foreign trade. We begin with a discussion of the monetary factors involved in international trade, then turn to the basic factors which underlie the system and which are often obscured by the veil of monetary discussion that arises out of international transactions. You will be introduced to the very significant "Theory of Comparative Advantage," which explains why trade is beneficial to both advanced and underdeveloped economies, and to the system by which foreign trade balances are calculated. These basic factors are essential for a rational appraisal of the problems raised by tariffs and other barriers to an international division of labor. Finally, we shall attempt to put these principles to work to gain some understanding of the contemporary international economic scene, and particularly the goals pursued by the United States in its international economic relations.

THE BALANCE OF INTERNATIONAL PAYMENTS

International trade is important for one very basic reason: foreign trade gives us a "consumption-possibility schedule" that includes goods which our domestic economy alone simply cannot produce. Thus Americans consume rubber and coffee, which our economy does not produce, while Brazilians consume manufactured goods which they do not produce. In the end, each country involved in foreign trade can consume more goods, or more different kinds, than it can consume left to its own devices. So simple. Yet so hard for Congressmen and voters to remember.

Our first task is to examine the mechanics of international trade and finance, including foreign exchange rates, the balance of international payments, foreign lending and giving, tariffs, import quotas, and the so-called principle of comparative advantage which tells us what kinds of trade can take place and why. Finally, we shall look at some of the basic problems facing international trade in the sixties, such as the drain on American gold supplies, the European Common Market, and foreign aid. These are anything but abstract economic problems. They are the news that may break on tomorrow's front page.

Foreign exchange. Within a single country, economic transactions are simple, for when I buy goods I expect to pay in dollars, and the seller expects to receive dollars. But if I want to buy an English sports car directly, matters are a little more complicated. The British manufacturer wants to be paid in British money, in pounds sterling, rather than dollars. I must therefore convert my dollars into British money ("buy" British money) before I can make the purchase. This introduces a new factor into the sale—the foreign exchange rate, the amount of foreign money that I receive for my American dollars. In 1961, a British pound sterling would cost me about $2.80, while a French franc could be had for about 20.4 cents. In fact, there is an exchange rate between American money and the currencies of each and every foreign country. Knowing this rate, I know how many dollars I must spend to buy an item in a foreign country.

However the transaction is handled, we must point out that the foreign seller always wants to be paid in his own currency, while the buyer wishes to pay in his currency. This could create an insoluble problem, except that there are people in other countries who wish to exchange their currency for ours—people also want to buy American goods. Hence when I wish to buy pounds, I find someone who wishes to sell pounds for dollars because he wants to purchase American goods. Remember, American dollars can be spent only in America, in the final analysis. The foreign exchange takes care of the transaction for me by acting as a market for foreign money, where currencies of different countries can be bought and sold.

Determining the exchange rate. So much for the exchange rate itself. As a consumer, you need not worry about the mechanical details of the money market. But your economic knowledge would be incomplete unless you understood the basic economic forces working behind the scenes. How are banks, post offices, and brokers here and abroad able to exchange pounds for dollars and dollars for pounds? The answer lies in the fact that international trade is largely a two-way street. When goods flow in one direction only, serious difficulties arise. It is the reciprocal interplay of import demand and export supply that determines the equilibrium level of international trade and exchange rates.

There are two different cases of exchange-rate determination that we need to consider: (1) the case of freely fluctuating foreign exchange rates, and (2) the case of a stable exchange rate, determined by government adherence to the gold standard or some other explicit standard. The free-exchange case is easier to describe, and is still important, as in American-Canadian trade. The gold-standard stable-exchange case was most important during the past century.

Free exchange rates. The American dollar and Canadian dollar are not precisely the same; that is, one American dollar will not buy exactly one dollar in Canadian money. In the 1940s, for example, a Canadian dollar could be bought for about 90 cents; more recently, it became more expensive and even cost a few cents more than one American dollar. Until recently, the rate of exchange was determined solely by supply and demand; it was a free exchange rate. In the summer, when Americans went to Canada in large numbers, and there was a demand for Canadian money, the price increased slightly; in midwinter, when tourism was lower, the rate dropped slightly.

A free exchange rate is determined by the market forces of supply and demand, like any other freely competitive price. Figure 32 gives a simplified supply-and-demand picture of the manner in which this rate is determined. Various forces act to increase our demand for foreign exchange (tourist spending, aid, goods and services imported, raw materials imported, etc.), and similar factors determine the goods and services which foreign nations wish to purchase from us, and hence determine their demand for American currency. The interrelation of these two sets of factors acts to determine the free foreign exchange rate.

Gold-standard stable exchange rate. Under this system, the rate of exchange between two currencies is dependent upon the price that the two governments are willing to pay for a fixed amount of gold. Suppose that the American government is willing to buy and sell gold at a fixed price of about $35 per ounce. If the British government is willing to buy and sell gold at 35 pounds sterling per ounce, then one dollar is the exact equivalent of one pound sterling. In

Demand bids up and supply bids down a free foreign exchange rate:

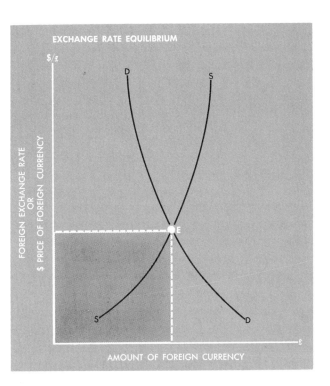

EXCHANGE RATE EQUILIBRIUM

AMOUNT OF FOREIGN CURRENCY

Fig. 32. Behind our *DD* is our desire to import British goods, buy British securities, visit the Bard's grave, and so forth. Behind their *SS* supply of £ to be traded for $ is their desire for our export goods and services. If the rate were above E, there would be an excess of foreign currency that they would want to supply us over what we would want to demand. Such an excess of supply would bid the rate back down to E, where the market of foreign currency for dollars is just cleared.

practice, Britain buys and sells gold at about 12½ pounds sterling per ounce, which gives a parity exchange rate of $2.80 per pound sterling. Except for minor fluctuations around this level caused by delays and the cost of shipping gold across the Atlantic, the exchange rate remains stable, and the value of the two currencies is closely integrated. Obviously, before this system can function, both countries must be willing to buy and sell gold at a fixed price.

Exchange "devaluation" and "depreciation." In 1949, the British pound was "devalued" from $4.02 to $2.80. What precisely does this mean in economic terms? Is this the same as the newspaper term exchange "depreciation"? We now have enough background to define these terms fairly precisely.

We say the pound is *depreciating* relative to the dollar when the dollar price of the pound is falling on the foreign exchange market, that is, when we can buy more pounds with the same amount of dollars. We say the pound is *appreciating* when its rate on the foreign exchange market is rising, e.g., when we must pay $2.90 to buy a pound instead of $2.80. Plainly, in a free exchange market where the rate fluctuates from day to day, or even from hour to hour, currencies are always appreciating or depreciating. And for countries undergoing severe inflation, this is a one-way street, for their currency loses its internal value (the goods it can buy inside the country) and its external value follows suit.

The term *devaluation,* on the other hand, is usually reserved to mean a change in the purchasing price of gold expressed in terms of a given currency. If every country in the world were on the gold standard (would buy and sell gold at a fixed rate) and all countries were to double the buying and selling price at the same time, then we would speak of a worldwide devaluation. If a single country like Britain changes its buying and selling price for gold, we say that Britain has "devalued" the pound. Usually, devaluation is the term used to describe an unusual and rather large change in gold price, rather than day-to-day fluctuations.

When only one country, or a few countries, "devalue" their currency, important economic effects usually follow. When a country leaves the gold standard, and refuses to buy and sell gold at a fixed price, its currency will usually depreciate relative to others. Returning to the gold standard will generally lead to an appreciation of its value. The most significant effect of these changes lies in the field of exports and imports of goods and services. For if Britain devalues the pound, I find that all British goods can now be bought for fewer dollars. If the pound is devalued from $4 to $2, a sweater that costs 5 pounds sterling drops from $20 to $10 in terms of American dollars. Some domestic British goods appear cheaper on the world market. On the other hand, all foreign goods then appear much more expensive to people living in Britain, for their price will in effect have doubled.

What happens in this case? British exports are stimulated, for British goods are now available at a lower price to foreign buyers. And British imports tend to be inhibited because foreign goods are now much more expensive to British buyers. Devaluation then leads to an increase in physical exports and a decrease in imports.

When does a country devalue and why? It will try to devalue, or will have devaluation thrust upon it, when it is having serious "balance-of-payments" difficulties—when the value of the goods and services it exports tends chronically to fall behind the value of the goods and services it imports. For a while, a country in this position may close the gap with foreign loans or gold exports, but it will eventually find itself running short of foreign currencies at the existing exchange rate. It may then devalue, thus reducing physical imports and expanding physical exports, and in this way, usually, improve its balance-of-payments position by obtaining more foreign currencies.

The balance of international payments. The time has come to explain exactly what we mean when we speak of a country's "balance of international payments." The concept in effect summarizes the very important set of relations between the value of all goods, gifts, services, capital loans, and gold coming into a country and the amount of these same items leaving the country. It is the total record of a nation's international transactions. In our country, the U.S. Department of Commerce keeps records and makes official estimates of all international transactions during the year. This includes merchandise exported and imported, money lent abroad or borrowed, gold shipments into and out of the country, tourist spending, interest and dividends received from abroad and paid abroad, shipping and insurance services bought and sold, and so on through a long series of items.

It is convenient to present the data on balance of payments in three sections:

I. CURRENT ACCOUNT
   A. *Private*
      1. Merchandise (trade balance)
      2. Invisibles:
         Transportation (shipping services, etc.)
         Travel expenditure (tourists, etc.)
         Income on investments (interest, dividends)
         Private gifts (immigrant remittances, etc.)
         Miscellaneous
   B. *Governmental*
      1. Government export of military goods
      2. Unilateral grants (aid programs, etc.)

II. CAPITAL MOVEMENTS
   A. *Long term*
      1. Government
      2. Private
   B. *Short term*
      1. Government
      2. Private

III. GOLD MOVEMENTS (out and in)

Let us take a closer look at each of the major elements in the balance sheet.

Current account. All of the items included under section I above are usually referred to as the "balance on current account." This is a summary of the difference between total exports of goods and services and total imports of goods and services. We can leave the discussion of how any surplus or deficit in this account is "financed" by gold and capital movements, and describe some of the major items in the group.

Centuries ago, when merchandise items dominated international trade, economic writers tended to concentrate on this one narrow category. They spoke of a "favorable" balance of trade when exports of these items exceeded imports and an "unfavorable" balance of trade when there was an excess of imports over exports. The choice of terms was not too happy, for an "unfavorable" balance of trade may in fact be a very good thing for the national economy, while a "favorable" balance of trade may not always be desirable.

Today we realize that "visible" or tangible trading items are not the only factors affecting international trade. There is also a vast field of "invisible" imports and exports, consisting of such items as shipping services, insurance, expenditures by tourists, loans and investments, and gifts, which must also be calculated. When an American shipper buys an insurance policy from Lloyds of London, or a tourist buys a drink in a Paris cafe, the effect is precisely the same as importing a British automobile or a bottle of wine. Conversely, when a foreign firm leases an American vessel, this has exactly the same effects on the balance of trade as an export of American automobiles or machinery. A good rule of thumb for classifying expenditures of this sort is to ask whether or not they earn foreign currency, or whether they require payment of foreign currency. In the former case, they are like exports of visible goods; in the latter, they have the same effect as imports. Exports build up our supply of foreign currency, and are classed as "credit" items; imports drain off some of our supply of foreign currency, and are called "debits."

To compute the balance of international payments, each item of trade, whether visible or invisible, is entered into an account book showing the total debits and credits. A sample of the United States balance-of-payments position is shown in Table 25. Note the large debits that accrue from governmental transactions in both the current account and the capital account.

Once the bookkeeping for section I has been completed, we can turn to the movement of capital from one country to the next. This includes all of the long-term and short-term foreign loans made by private citizens and by governmental agencies. We can think of these exchanges most easily as IOUs. When we lend abroad, we are importing IOUs; when we borrow, we are exporting them. Thus lending gives rise to credits, and borrowing to debits. In 1959, the United States was a net long-term foreign lender, but a net importer of short-term credit. This means simply that the United States was making more long-term loans to others than it received from them, but borrowing more on short-term credit than it was lending.

In line 17 of Table 25, the score of all current transactions and long-term capital movements is toted up. The result is a net debit position of over $2 billion—$2,069 million to be exact. Line 20 shows that the deficit was covered partly by $2,187 billion of short-term loans to us. The remainder, shown in Section III, was covered by $907 million worth of gold shipped abroad. The final balance shown in line 23 is of course zero, for all credits and debits

Table 25. United States balance of international payments, 1962 (in millions of dollars).
(Source: Adapted from U.S. Department of Commerce data.)

No.	Items (a)	Credits (b)	Debits (c)	Net credits (+) or debits(−) (d)	
I	**Current:**				
	Private:				
1	Merchandise (adjusted)	$20,479	$16,145	+$4,334	
	Invisibles:				
2	Transportation	1,749	2,055	− 306	
3	Travel expenditures	921	1,905	− 984	
4	Income on investments (interest, dividends, etc.)	3,850	656	+ 3,194	
5	Private remittances		491	− 491	
6	Miscellaneous services	1,475	436	+ 1,039	
7	Current private balance				+$6,786
	United States governmental:				
8	Exports of military goods and services (+)	1,539			
	Military aid payments (−) to allies		1,539	0	
9	Other military transactions	660	3,028	− 2,368	
10	Other grants and payments		2,148	− 2,148	
11	Miscellaneous government transactions	656	739	− 83	
12	Current government transactions				−$4,599
13	Net balance on current account				+$2,187
II	**Capital account, net exports of our IOUs (+) or net imports (−)**				
	Long-term loans (−) or borrowing (+)				
14	Private			− 2,495	
15	Government			− 1,761	
16	Net long-term foreign investment				− 4,256
17	Net balance on current account + long-term loans (the "basic deficit in U.S. balance of payments")				−$2,069
	Short-term loans (−) or borrowing (+)				
18	Private			+ 30	
19	Government			+ 2,157	
20	Net investment in short-term debt				+ 2,187
III	**Net gold exports (+) or imports (−)**				+ 907
21	Errors and omissions				− 1,025
22	Offset to basic U.S. "deficit"				+$2,069
23	Over-all net balance of international payments				0

must cancel out. However, line 17, which shows a deficit in this case, is much more significant, for this amount must be covered either by gold shipments or by borrowing or lending. When newspapers and congressmen speak of a "deficit in the balance of payments" they probably refer to a figure of this sort. Technically, the statement is inaccurate because the balance of payments always comes out at zero when a double-entry bookkeeping system of this sort is used.

International capital movements. Let us now turn to the problem of capital movements. If political problems arising out of nationalism and domestic unemployment did not enter the picture, the fundamentals of international lending would be easy to understand. We could cut through the fog of money and finance and concentrate on the real aspects of international investment in terms of goods and resources.

Within a country, capital grows when we divert labor, land, and other resources away from current consumption goods into capital goods. Instead of consuming current production, we plant trees, build new machinery and buildings, and so on. All these things add to our future income. We postpone present consumption for greater consumption in the future, greater because capital goods have net productivity, which can be expressed as an interest rate on investment.

Now, different parts of the world have varying amounts of resources, and if it were not for ignorance and political boundaries, no one would invest in North America for a 3 per cent return when opportunities for a 6 per cent return existed elsewhere in the world. Some capital would certainly be invested abroad. This would raise the wages of foreign labor and increase foreign production enough to pay for replacement of capital and interest or dividend return on the investment. In effect, capital would then be going into areas where its productivity is highest, and we would be using capital very efficiently.

When would our loan be repaid (our principal)? So long as we earn a good return, there is no reason to wish to see it repaid. But if the country in which the loan is invested becomes prosperous, it may wish to reduce its own consumption and buy out our investments. We, on the other hand, may wish to retain these investments, so we raise our selling price and accept a smaller percentage of return on the investment. Thus there is no reason why a country should ever be paid off for past lending unless it has become older and relatively poorer.

When nationalism rears its head, however, matters change. Inside the United States, interest and dividends may move from one region or state to another without limit, and if people grumble from time to time about absentee ownership, the courts and police see to it that property rights are respected. Not so between nations. When a country is poor, it may be anxious to borrow, but after it grows richer, it dislikes paying interest and dividends to foreigners.

It chooses to forget that its prosperity may depend upon this past borrowing, for there is more than an economic principle involved here. Dislike for "furriners" or absentee owners may grow very strong, and international liabilities may be removed by paying them off at a fair price, at an unfair price, or often by outright seizure or default.

Financial versus real aspects of foreign lending. Money tends to throw a veil over these real aspects of capital movements. Usually, a foreigner borrows *money* from us rather than capital goods. He gives us his IOU in the form of a bond, note, or stock certificate; we give him dollars. If he simply puts these dollars in an American bank, or holds them, or invests them in American security, there has been no net capital movement at all. We have his IOU, he has ours, and they cancel each other in the balance of payments. Only when the foreign borrower uses the loan to import goods and services or gold in excess of his exports has a real and a financial capital movement taken place.

When the time comes for interest payment, the foreign borrower must sell more goods than he buys to get the extra dollars needed for payment. Our balance of international payments will then show an import surplus balanced by a visible credit item, interest and dividends.

If we never had to worry about unemployment, exports would probably be a bad thing, for the goods we export might better serve our own well-being. For it is imports, not exports, that add to national well-being, as John Stuart Mill pointed out a century ago. Before World War II, the problem of maintaining full employment was so badly handled that nations put the cart before the horse and placed excessive emphasis on exports. Fortunately, we have now learned how to use our economic tools better, and to this degree Mill's sensible emphasis on imports will come back into its own.

THE THEORY OF COMPARATIVE ADVANTAGE

Again and again in our study of economics we have seen how specialization increases productivity and raises standards of living. Now we must show how this works out in the field of international trade, going behind the facade and confusion of international finance. Why, for example, did the United States specialize in the production of agricultural goods in the early nineteenth century and exchange these products for the manufacturing output of Europe? Why is she today able to export highly complex mass-produced goods to the far corners of the globe? Why is the agriculture of Australia so different from that of Austria or Belgium? How great would be the costs of complete self-sufficiency (autarky) for a modern country? In what way do all countries benefit from trade?

The key to the correct answers to such questions, and many more, is provided by the theory of comparative advantage or comparative cost. Developed more than a century ago by David Ricardo, John Stuart Mill, and other English followers of Adam Smith, the theory of comparative advantage is a closely reasoned doctrine which, properly stated, is unassailable. With it, we are able to weed out the gross fallacies in political propaganda in favor of protective tariffs which aim to limit imports. At the same time, the theory helps us to identify the germs of truth that sometimes emerge in the heated claims made for tariff protection.

Diversity of conditions between regions or countries. For the sake of simplicity, let us imagine two countries or continents, each endowed with certain quantities of natural resources, capital goods, kinds of labor, and technical knowledge or know-how. The first point to be made in the development of comparative-cost theory is that the conditions of production are quite different from one country to another. Specifically, this means that the production possibilities of the different countries and regions are different. Though people could try to produce some of every commodity in any region, it is obvious that they would not succeed, or if they did succeed, that the cost would be enormous. Using hothouses and forcing techniques, it might be possible to grow wine grapes in Scotland, for example, but the cost in terms of economic resources would be exorbitant, and the resulting product would hardly be fit to drink anyway. Similar diversities appear between almost any two regions in the world.

Even if by chance two countries can both produce the same commodities, they will usually find that it pays for each to concentrate its production especially on some goods and trade them for other goods. If we consider trade between, say, the northern temperate zones and the southern tropics, this proposition seems both true and a little trivial. Of course, resources near the equator are more productive in the growing of bananas, and the northern resources are better designed for wheat growing. In this case, everyone can see that specialization and trade will increase the amount of world production of both goods and also each country's capacity to consume both goods.

It is not so immediately obvious, but it is no less true, that international trade is mutually profitable even when one of two countries can produce *every commodity* more cheaply (in terms of labor hours or all resources) than the other country. One country may, in effect, be absolutely more efficient than the other in the production of every product. But inside that very efficient country, there are differences in the efficiency with which it produces different products, and this difference in relative efficiency *internally* makes the rule of comparative advantage work. Suppose that country A can produce both wheat and sugar more efficiently than country B. But inside country A, wheat is produced much more efficiently than sugar. It may then pay country A to concentrate on wheat production, leaving country B to produce the sugar, because it gains more by concentrating on wheat. That is, so long as there are differences in the relative efficiencies of production, we can always be sure that even a poor country has a *comparative advantage* in producing those commodities in which it is most efficient. The rich efficient country will find that it should specialize in those fields of production where it has a comparative advantage, planning to export its goods and import the commodities in which it has a comparative disadvantage.

A traditional example used to illustrate the seeming paradox of comparative advantage is the case of the man who is both the best lawyer and the best typist in town. Will he not specialize in law and leave typing to a secretary? How could he afford to give up precious time from the legal field, where his comparative advantage is very great, to perform typing work at which he is also very efficient, but in which he lacks comparative advantage? From the secretary's point of view, she is less efficient than the lawyer in both activities, but her relative disadvantage compared with him is least in typing. Relatively speaking, she has a comparative advantage in typing.

Because of the rule of comparative advantage, trade between America and Europe in food and clothing would be mutually advantageous even if America could produce both these items more efficiently than Europe in terms of all economic resources used in production. Moreover, barter between America and Asia is especially advantageous to us even though the Indian laborer receives only a fraction of the real wages going to productive American labor. We shall see in a moment why this is so.

The law of comparative advantage. David Ricardo, stockbroker and self-made millionaire, expert on the theory of land rent and of currency, came up in 1817 with the beautiful proof that international specialization pays for a nation. This is the famous theory of comparative advantage or, as it is sometimes called, the "theory of comparative cost."

For simplicity, Ricardo worked with only two regions (say, America and Europe) and with only two goods (food and clothing in our illustration). Also for simplicity, Ricardo chose to measure all costs in terms of hours of labor; we shall do the same, though we realize that more advanced treatises must make some qualifications on this oversimplified set of assumptions. The germ of truth in the original principle stated by Ricardo still remains.

Common sense tells us that trade between America and Europe is likely to be mutually profitable if America can in one day produce the same amount of food which Europe takes three days to produce, while America takes longer than Europe to produce a unit of clothing. We do not need Ricardo to tell us that in this case America will specialize in food production, exporting food to Europe in exchange for clothing.

But Ricardo showed much more than this. He demonstrated beyond doubt that even if American resources or labor are more productive than European labor in both food and clothing, trade is still likely to be mutually advantageous.

Table 26 illustrates Ricardo's principle. In America, one unit of food costs one day's labor, and a unit of clothing two days' labor. In Europe, food costs three days' labor and clothing four days' labor. By using these ratios, Ricardo was able to prove conclusively that America and Europe would both benefit if America specialized in food, while Europe specialized in clothing.

How does the European man in the street regard this proposition? Good heavens, he says, trade could never be profitable for us with that American colossus. Her efficiency would enable her to undersell us in every line—food and clothing. We must have import tariffs to protect the honest European worker against an inundation of American goods.

Meanwhile, the American man in the street and the congressman who has not yet grasped the law of comparative advantage are producing their own argument against trade with Europe. The European wage level, they say, is most assuredly far below American wage rates, since America is the most prosperous and productive nation on earth. If we force American workers to compete with Europeans whose wages are lower than ours, the real wage of the American worker will assuredly fall. We must have a protective tariff against cheap imports if we are to maintain the American standard of living.

Ricardo shows that both arguments are wrong. International trade can provide higher real wages for *both* the European and the American worker, and prohibitive tariffs on either side or both sides will reduce real wages in both places. And we may add that in our day there are better tools than protective tariffs to make sure that there are plenty of job opportunities and stable price levels in both places, e.g., proper fiscal and central bank monetary policies.

Before trade. If we start with a prohibitive tariff that has killed off all international trade, Table 26 shows that the real wage of the American worker for a day's work will be one unit of food or one-half unit of clothing. The European worker is even less well off, for he gets only one-third unit of food or one-fourth unit of clothing for his day's work.

After trade. Now we repeal the protective tariff and make trade free. The relative prices of clothing and food must now come to a common level, as the water in two connecting pipes must come to a common level when you remove the barrier between them. Competitive merchants buy where things are cheap and sell where they are dear. With clothing relatively more expensive in America, merchants will soon ship clothing from Europe to America and

Comparative advantage depends only on productivity ratios:

Product	In America	In Europe
1 unit of food	1 day's labor	3 days' labor
1 unit of clothing	2 days' labor	4 days' labor

Table 26. American and European labor requirements for production. Even though America's 1 and 2 are respectively less than Europe's 3 and 4, we have comparative advantage in food and Europe has it in clothing. Why? Because our 1 ÷ her 3 is less than our 2 ÷ her 4 (or equivalently because our 1:2 is less than her 3:4).

ship food from America to the European markets where it has been relatively dear. Our clothing industry will feel the keen price competition of imports, and if the values in Table 26 do not change, it will lose *all* its workers to the American food industry. In Europe, the opposite effect occurs, for workers will leave the food industry for the clothing industry in which Europe has a comparative advantage.

Note that America as a whole has benefited. Like any merchant who will buy electric power from another firm if he cannot produce it as cheaply himself, America has taken advantage of the fact that clothing does cost us less by barter than by domestic production. Europe has benefited in a similar manner.

But if Ricardo has shown that both countries have benefited from specialization in accordance with comparative advantage, what about the workers in both places? We find that real wages have improved in both places, for both are now producing the goods they produce most efficiently. The American worker's day of labor will buy the same amount of food as before, but he gets *more* imported clothing for a day's labor than before, and can now afford to consume more of both goods. The European laborer now obtains more food, and the same amount of clothing from one day's labor, and he too is better off in terms of real wages.

To sum up, the principle of comparative advantage states that whether or not one of two regions is absolutely more efficient in the production of every good than is the other, if each specializes in the products in which it has a comparative advantage (greatest relative efficiency) trade will be mutually profitable to both regions. Real wages of productive factors will rise in both places. An ill-designed prohibitive tariff, far from helping the protected factor of production, will instead reduce real wages by making imports expensive and by making the whole world less productive by eliminating the efficiency obtained by using the best pattern of specialization and division of labor possible.

QUALIFICATIONS AND CONCLUSIONS. Of course, comparative advantage holds for any two countries and any goods, not just for Europe and America and for food and clothing. The rule can be generalized to handle any number of regions or products. Transport costs can also be treated, as can movements of productive factors between regions. Instead of using simple labor-cost examples we can easily measure costs in terms of "doses" of labor, land, and capital goods of fixed proportions. It is also possible to allow for changing factor proportions and diminishing returns within the framework of the principle.

A serious defect of comparative advantage is its static assumptions. The theory disregards stickiness of prices and wages, all transitional and deflationary gaps, and all balance-of-payments problems. It pretends that when workers leave one industry they always go to another which is more efficient —never into chronic unemployment. No wonder the abstract theory was lightly regarded during the Depression. Recently, its prestige has been increasing again, and to the extent that we can count on the success of the neoclassical synthesis of economics the old classical theory of comparative advantage will have social relevance. It is an elegant logical structure, even though it is highly simplified. We cannot simply rush out and apply it to real life without qualification, certainly, yet it provides us with an important glimpse of economic truth. Political economy has found few more pregnant principles, and a nation that neglects comparative advantage may have to pay a heavy price in terms of living standards and potential rate of growth.

TARIFF PROTECTION AND FREE TRADE

It would be absurd to try to decide whether God exists or not by counting on the one hand all arguments in the affirmative and on the other hand all arguments in the negative and then awarding the decision to the side with the greatest number of points. It is just as absurd to evaluate the case for tariff protection by a mere count of equally irrelevant pros and cons. Indeed, there is essentially only one argument for free or freer trade, but it is exceedingly powerful: unhampered trade promotes a mutually profitable international division of labor, greatly enhances the potential real national product of all countries, and makes possible higher standards of living all over the globe. We have already elaborated the point in our discussion of comparative advantage.

How is the comparative advantage argument affected by tariffs and import quotas? Putting on a tariff duty (tax) discourages imports and raises prices to the domestic consumer. By killing off the potentially fruitful international division of labor, it offers a protective shield for the inefficient domestic producer and raises the profits of the efficient domestic producer.

How then are protective tariffs justified? Generally, there are three basic classes of arguments for high protection against competition from foreign imports: (1) those that are definitely economically false; some so obviously and palpably false that they hardly merit discussion, though others are more subtle and less easily detected; (2) a few arguments that have no validity in a perfectly competitive "classical" static, full-employment world, but contain some elements of truth in the world as it is, subject to unemployment and undergoing economic development; (3) certain noneconomic arguments that may make it desirable for national policy to sacrifice economic welfare in order to subsidize activities which are not economically efficient.

Noneconomic goals. Let us begin with the last class of arguments, for they are most simply disposed of. If you are ever on a debating team and are given the assignment of defending free trade, you will strengthen your case greatly by conceding at the outset that economic welfare is not the sole purpose of human life. It may therefore be necessary to become partially self-sufficient in certain lines of economic activity for political or social reasons, such as fear of war.

An example is the production of oil. If oil reserves and capacity are considered essential for national defense, and if the amount needed cannot be attained under a system of free trade, the economist cannot assert that national policy should avoid protecting this industry. That is a political decision. But he can make clear the real cost involved, and he may suggest that a subsidy should be used to sustain domestic production at the required level because this would bring the domestic price down to the international price instead of raising the price to the domestic consumer. The subsidy would also show clearly what the total costs of national defense are and enable the public to decide whether benefits are worth the price paid for them.

The question of a national policy to foster the development of the American merchant marine is a similar example. The United States doubtless does *not* have a comparative advantage in building or operating a merchant fleet. As soon as American seamen, through unions or on their own, insist on living conditions and wages resembling those of Seattle factory workers, we cannot compete with English, Greek, Japanese, and Norwegian ships. If we give no weight to the "glorious seafaring tradition" of the past—long past—and consider purely economic factors, the correct policy is obvious. If America has a comparative advantage in factory production, let men go to Seattle factories where their real productivity is high and stay out of merchant ships. American international trade need not suffer by being carried in other countries' ships. But if national defense makes a large merchant marine necessary, that is another matter. Mail subsidies and subsidies for shipbuilders may then be justified.

The problem of deciding how much to spend on national defense is perplexing, especially since armament races are both cause and effect of international disunity. The economist can claim no special competence to advise on this problem. He can point out that selfish economic interests often wrap themselves in the flag and try to justify uneconomic projects in terms of national defense. He can ask suspiciously, Was the recent increase in tariffs on Swiss watches really justified by our defense needs for precision workers? Or was it a case of political pressure? The economist can also point out that mutually profitable international trade may help promote international understanding and unity and that political interference with trade has in the past provided some of the frictions that lead to war.

In conclusion, there may well be noneconomic goals that deserve consideration. Society may feel that there is some special sanctity in farm life, something worth preserving in the way of life of the "happy peasant," though it is doubtful that people who rhapsodize about farm life in this way have ever lived and worked on a farm. A deliberate decentralization of industry may be forced upon us by military considerations, and other noneconomic proposals may have to be adopted for social or military reasons. But in such cases, a direct subsidy is a better alternative than a tariff, for the latter is only a clumsy form of subsidy which draws our attention from the real problem at issue.

Of course, not all political arguments favor high tariffs. Every congressman knows that America has a tremendous interest these days in winning and retaining allies abroad, and nothing is less conducive to international friendship than a high-tariff policy. Actually, our tariff policies have grown increasingly moderate in recent decades, and it remains in the national interest to resist the pressures that make for such restrictions on international trade.

Grossly fallacious arguments for tariffs. In the seventeenth and eighteenth centuries, economic writers who followed "mercantilist" policies argued that a high tariff would "keep money in the country." They believed that a country which could export goods and receive a steady inflow of gold was extremely fortunate. Nowadays, of course, we realize that it is the amount of goods available for consumption that determines our standard of living, and that in times of full employment an increase in the money supply can only lead to an increase in prices, but the fallacy still appears from time to time in naïve economic suggestions.

A second major fallacy is the belief that high tariffs lead to higher real wages. It is generally agreed that extreme protection can raise prices and attract gold into the country—if other countries do not retaliate. The tariff may even increase money wages, but it will tend to raise the cost of living by more than the increase in money wages; hence real wages actually fall.

An important problem in the tariff field is the enormous political pressure exerted by interest groups in favor of protective tariffs for their interests. In the freer days, bribery and corruption figured prominently in setting tariff policy. Today, this type of influence has been subjected to legal control, but powerful lobbies in Washington continue to drum up enthusiasm for the good old crockery, watch, or buttonhook industry. Such groups are fully aware of the benefits *they* will reap from a high tariff, whatever its effect on total production and consumption. Politically, the pressure for protection is often stronger than the pressure for freer trade. Why? Because free trade helps everybody a little, while protection helps a few people a lot. If those who benefit most are politically very active, they are usually more influential in the halls of power than the many who obtain slight benefits from free trade and are only slightly injured by protection. If political votes were in exact proportion to total economic benefit, every country would selfishly legislate most of its tariffs out of existence.

Some less obvious fallacies. A very old argument in American economic thought is that the tariff should be used to raise revenue, as readers of the *Federalist* papers know. The difficulty here is that a tariff is one form of regressive sales tax, and a peculiarly obnoxious specimen, for it draws economic resources away from their best uses. If those who support this view were really sincere, they would advocate a sales tax which would also fall on domestic production, and this would provide no protection at all. And we need only recall that a prohibitively high tariff which protected us perfectly would collect no revenue at all, for there would be no imports!

A second subtly fallacious argument, often advanced by Henry Clay about a century ago, is that tariffs enlarge the home market. Farmers, for example, would sell more of their own crops if they had a protective tariff. But isolation from international trade tends to reduce the total national product, and hence reduce real income. The total domestic demand for farm products, or any others, would certainly be less at a low level of real income than at a high level. So unless it can be buttressed by some quite different argument, the slogan about "creating a home market" is seen once again to be fallacious.

A third argument, already touched upon indirectly, is that tariffs protect American wages from cheap foreign labor competition, that the American standard of living will fall if goods produced by cheap labor are admitted duty free. The discussion of the law of comparative advantage can take care of this particular bit of cant. In fact, it shows that we benefit most by trading with countries in the Far East or other areas very different from ourselves. Furthermore, comparative advantage shows that absolute wage levels have nothing to do with the long-run increase in national income that resulted from trade.

So much from a theoretical point of view. In the real world, the argument is even less useful. Europeans and Asians also beg for high tariffs to protect them from the "high-paid, efficient" American worker. The rest of the world fears direct competition from American mass-production industries. They claim that the high efficiency more than offsets the difference in money wage rate. This is perhaps an overstatement, but it is near to an important truth: American real wages are high because of high efficiency, and they are no handicap in foreign competition.

There is one theoretical case in which the argument might have some validity. Free trade in goods may under some circumstances be considered a substitute for immigration of labor into the United States. This implies that labor scarcity in the United States could be alleviated by our international specialization in labor-economizing products and that real wages might actually fall under free trade. Real national product would go up, but the relative and absolute share of labor would decline.

Although admitting this as a slight theoretical possibility, most economists are inclined to think that its grain of truth is more than outweighed by other realistic considerations. Particular laborers like textile workers certainly might be injured temporarily if tariffs were removed. But since labor is such an important and flexible factor of production with many alternate uses, it seems likely that workers who were displaced as a result of tariff changes would find other work and in the end gain more than they lose by virtue of the resulting expansion of trade and the gain in national product. Objectivity demands that we set forth the proposal as fairly as possible, but it seems unlikely that the special case involved is a genuine possibility.

A fourth argument for tariffs revolves around their use as a weapon against other countries who impose tariffs on our goods—on their value as a retaliatory weapon. But surely it is unwise to harm ourselves further simply because another country has been foolish enough to inflict harm on itself and on us. We merely compound the problem. It is possible that the threat of retaliation may inhibit the imposition of tariffs on American goods by other countries, and our promise to reduce them may persuade others to do likewise. On these grounds, passing an occasional tariff might be tactically useful. But economically, tariffs cannot but be harmful to both the country that imposes them and the country against whom they are imposed.

A more insidious argument appears in the guise of a "scientific" tariff, which sounds modest and rational, but would in effect mean an end to all trade if taken literally. The usual argument is that tariffs should be at a level which would "equalize the cost of production at home and abroad." But we saw before that all the advantage from trade rests on *differences* in cost. If tariffs equalized the cost factor, so that imported goods cost as much as the highest-priced American goods, no goods would come in at all. There is nothing scientific about such a system, and it is a grave reflection on the economic literacy of the country that this gross argument has had tremendous political importance in American history and has even been written into law on occasion.

Finally, there is the belief that tariffs should be kept low unless this results in imports at a level which imperils the existence of a domestic industry. When this "peril point" is reached, duties should be increased and quotas tightened to keep the domestic industry from disappearing altogether or becoming perilously small.

Though this argument sounds moderate, it too runs completely counter to our basic theory of comparative advantage. Our nation gains by specialization, by giving up certain activities and concentrating on others in which our comparative advantage is high. Industries in which we have a great comparative disadvantage should never come into existence. And industries which lose their comparative advantage become a means of wasting resources since they are inefficient producers. Such industries *ought* to be imperiled and driven either to compete or perish. This sounds ruthless indeed, for no industry dies willingly, and no region gladly faces conversion to new factor uses, but it is economically sound.

Perhaps the best policy in such situations is to introduce reductions in the tariff gradually, allowing time for reallocation of production factors. Some economists suggest public aid to retain workers and relocate factors of production, arguing that this speeds the transition and shares the burden among weak and strong. Some current weak sisters are the bicycle, watch, textile, and china industries, oil, wool growing, and the manufacture of large generating equipment. Many of these industries have obtained protective concessions through political pressure.

Fortunately, in a growing economy, the ineffective industries gradually dwindle in importance relative to the dynamic and effective industries. Fortunately, too, the strength of our export industries and the effective use of fiscal and monetary policies can keep overall employment opportunities high, so that with good conscience the nation can strive for the increase in real income to be obtained by specialization according to the principles of comparative advantage.

The "foreigner will pay" argument. After dealing with so many fallacious tariff arguments, it is refreshing to come to one that may be valid—the argument which hopes to shift the "terms of trade" against the foreigner. The argument goes back to John Stuart Mill, more than a century ago—a free trader! Mill argued that a tariff on rubber would raise the price here over its price abroad, but curtail demand. Since our demand is an important part of world demand, the price abroad would come down and part of the tariff would really fall on foreigners. A small country, with little influence on the demand curve, could not use this argument, of course. In these terms, a judicious tariff might actually improve a large nation's terms of trade.

WARNING: A prohibitive tariff, which would suit the absolute protectionist, would kill all trade and could never be justified by this argument. That would in effect eliminate the advantage obtained by shifting the terms of trade in our favor. Mill, and modern economists, insist that the "optimal tariff" is just large enough to improve the terms of trade and just small enough to keep the physical exchange of imports and exports at the level most favorable to your own country. Most argue that this would imply rather low tariff rates for most countries. And they hasten to point out that when all nations pursue this policy the world pattern of production and exchange becomes less efficient. So most, if not all, nations tend to end up worse off than before.

Arguments for protection under dynamic conditions. The "terms of trade" argument is valid only under static conditions. Under dynamic conditions, there are three important arguments that can be used to support tariffs: (1) that tariffs may reduce unemployment; (2) that tariffs may create diversified industries less subject to risk; and (3) that temporary tariff protection for "infant industries" with growth potential may be desirable.

1. Historically, one of the strongest arguments for protection has been the desire to make or protect jobs. Exports and foreign investments tend to have a "multiplier" effect on jobs and domestic spending, while imports tend to the converse. There is no denying that high-tariff policy might increase employment in the short run—until other nations retaliated. But can we accept such measures as a valid part of our national full-employment program? Is not freer trade much like a scientific discovery of new machinery and methods? Both represent increases in our potentially producible level of real national output; but either *might* in the short run tend to lower our actual attained level of output and employment. And yet there is no need, either in the short or long run, to tolerate a gap between actual and potentially producible products, for that represents an unnecessary frittering away of the gains from progress.

How then do we meet the arguments concerning unemployment because of too low tariffs? In the same manner that arguments concerning "technological unemployment" are met—by pointing out that economic slump can be solved by monetary and fiscal policies. If workers displaced by imports can find other employment in a buoyant economy, the protection plea loses its force. Again, we find that the policy weapons which economic analysis gives us can create economic conditions that validate the principles of classical economics.

2. Comparative advantage might tell a country to specialize completely in one good or a few goods, but what would happen if the prices of those goods

dropped or export prices vacillated? National income would be seriously affected, and this would tend to destabilize real income, perhaps leaving permanently unprofitable industry. To avoid the perils of this kind of specialization, Latin American economists advise the use of tariffs to induce diversification.

The argument certainly deserves careful consideration. Note that it assumes (a) that private citizens are neglecting to take into account the riskiness of the industries in which they invest, and (b) that the government is better informed than private investors and able to take into account future price changes. However, if private investors can foresee the risk of price drops, but expect to fire workers when this happens, throwing the unemployed on the state, a genuine problem is created which might justify government intervention. Further, of course, if the diversified industries have no genuine long-run future, there is no real value in creating them within the economy in any case.

3. Alexander Hamilton, in his famous "Report on Manufactures," stated a clear argument for tariffs to protect "infant industries" and give them an opportunity to get started without facing extreme competition. The policy has been endorsed, cautiously, by various other economists. The argument maintains that a nation might enjoy a comparative advantage in many lines of activity if they could once get started. But they are unable to weather the storm of early and fierce competition. They need a breathing space.

There is certainly something to this, at least as a theoretical possibility. The American silk industry has been cited as an example of the process at work, but there are various other industries, like woolen worsteds, where the infant failed to grow to manhood, protection or no. Unfortunately, the industries most likely to receive protection from Congress are not the infants in any case, but the old and hardened vested interests, though we can perhaps except certain war industries like chemicals and optics which began during the First World War.

Quotas and the invisible tariff. Until now, we have spoken of tariffs only, but almost everything we have said would apply equally well to other impediments on international trade. Thus quotas have all the bad effects of tariffs, and are often even more restrictive in their operation. Note too that any increase in transport costs will have the same effects on advantageous trade as artificial restraints imposed by governments.

Finally, we should mention the so-called invisible tariff. In many countries, and the United States is no exception, the effect of the complicated administration of the customs can be as bad as the monetary duty that must be paid, or even worse. If an importer's shipments are unduly delayed, or if foreign exports are refused admittance for complicated reasons, under arbitrary and trivial regulations, then such red tape can be extremely harmful to international trade.

This completes our discussion of the tariff controversy. No fair-minded reader who takes the trouble to think the matter through can fail to see how shallow are most of the arguments for tariff protection. The only serious exception is the infant-industry or young-economy argument. It is not surprising, then, that economists—who supposedly agree on almost nothing—were unanimously opposed to the extreme tariffs of the early thirties and have been overwhelmingly in favor of reciprocal trade agreements and other policies aimed at lowering trade barriers.

CURRENT INTERNATIONAL ECONOMIC PROBLEMS

Let us now turn to the main international economic problems facing the United States and the rest of the world in the immediate future. What is the significance of the basic facts? What policies ought we to avoid? What policies should we follow? These are questions of considerable moment for those who are charged with the responsibility for conducting the affairs of state. In the seventeenth and eighteenth centuries, the mercantilists concerned themselves with the gold question and with the problem of generating job opportunities at home by means of "favorable" trade balances. Adam Smith and the classical economists turned the discussion to the benefits of cheap imports from abroad, which acted to increase the supply of goods available in the home economy.

In the 1960s, as America faces a chronic problem of gold drains and deficits in her balance on current account, the emphasis has once again shifted to the effects of foreign trade on employment conditions at home. Our problem is to see what true causal connections can be found in mercantilism while avoiding the distorted policy recommendations that the mercantilists put forward and distorted because they did not really understand the basic principles of modern macroeconomics and microeconomics.

Exports and jobs. Historically, exports have been a stimulating factor for the American economy, along with domestic private or public investment. In the years 1915–1916, before we entered World War I, France, Russia, and England suddenly became avid customers for our exports, sending us gold and gilt-edged certificates in return, and the result was a shift from depression to great prosperity. After we entered the war, shipments of economically useless shot and shell again produced all of the trappings of prosperity. In the 1920s, when we were making many foolish private loans to the rest of the world and whooping it up for tariffs to "protect the worker's standard of living," one of the contributing factors to our favorable balance of saving and investment seemed to be heavy foreign lending. *Current* jobs and prices were favorably influenced by lending, even though the loans might turn out to be worthless in a few years. As Leon Fraser put it: "It is better to have lent and lost than never to have lent at all."

Foreign investment and inflationary pressures. The expansionary effects of foreign investment are due to a "multiplier" effect, which begins with an increase in domestic private or public investment, or in *net foreign investment,* and multiplies the total amount of income created by a factor determined by the marginal propensity to consume. It is the multiplier which increases national income at home when foreigners buy more from us than we from them, for the balance of saving and investment then shifts upward to intersect at a higher American national income.

Is that a good thing? It depends on previous economic conditions. If the economy has been operating below the full-employment level, new foreign investment will give jobs to the unemployed and expand production. But if the economy is already going at full blast, the added demand from abroad cannot increase production or expand the labor supply. Hence it can only result in increased prices. In short, when domestic demand is already excessive, expansion of exports relative to imports will add to inflationary pressure, and new foreign investment will be a "bad thing."

Though this may sound academic and unrealistic, it is really nothing of the sort. Between 1945 and 1948, domestic demand was very high because of wartime shortages, and at the same time, Europe needed our help to get back on her feet. We gave the assistance, as loans or gifts, and sold goods in return for gold. The result was some increase in inflationary pressures and a further rise in our already zooming prices. The same thing happened in the period 1915–1917. In 1958–1960 we find a different story, because more than 5 per cent of the labor force was unemployed and firms would have welcomed export orders to use excess capacity. There were bitter complaints about competitive imports in steel, autos, and generating equipment. Our current balance was unfavorable and the foreign-trade multiplier was working against us and not for us.

Throw one loaf on the waters to get two in return? While it seems unlikely that the world will soon slip back to the deep slump conditions of the 1930s, we had better not be too smug and too quick to forget some of the costly lessons we learned then. When unemployment is high, every nation attempts to "export" some of it by discouraging imports and encouraging exports. Of course, not every country can succeed, but each can try, and with each trying, all can end up worse off than before.

Why does a rational nation try to export goods rather than import? Why, outside a lunatic asylum, would you want deliberately to give goods away rather than get them? The answer seems to lie, of course, in the fact that under conditions of mass unemployment, different considerations are important. Here we meet again the "paradox of thrift," the fact that when individuals attempt to increase their savings in such periods this may result in less actual saving and investment because of harmful effects of saving on income and employment. Compared with doing nothing at all to cure depression unemployment, a nation may find it better to increase exports and refuse imports. This much is obvious, but what may not be quite so clear is that such giveaway programs may actually produce more domestic consumption. If we remember the multiplier and its effect, we can see that although the amount sent abroad may be lost, the effects of the multiplier are felt at home in the form of extra jobs and extra production. So the paradox, though second-rate as a policy, does have to be recognized as a possibility under certain exceptional circumstances.

Beggar-my-neighbor policies. A little knowledge can be dangerous, and a congressman who has grasped the possibility of creating jobs and domestic consumption by increasing exports and refusing imports might set out to create a "favorable" trade balance for America assuming that these benefits would then follow. We could increase tariffs, sponsor "Buy American" campaigns, or pass laws setting import quotas. We could also impose exchange controls, require a license for imports, subsidize exports, and make special agreements with other countries controlling the quantity of goods flowing in each direction. Finally, the dollar could be depreciated drastically, making our exports very cheap and imports very expensive. We might also offer foreigners international loans at low interest rates or even make large gifts abroad, though the foreign country is not necessarily beggared as a result.

An opportunistic congressman should be able to think up a few more such devices for achieving the same results. Now, any intelligent person who agrees that the United States must play an important role in international relations will oppose the above policies strongly in times of worldwide recession because they attempt to snatch prosperity for ourselves at the expense of the rest of the world. But even if we are cold and hardboiled about it, we must still regard such policies as rather foolish. For one thing, other nations will not simply stand by and accept our activities without retaliation; they too will try to reduce imports and increase exports. The result is logically necessary; both cannot succeed. The effect is even worse than one canceling the other, for the drop in international trade that will follow makes matters worse for both nations. Similarly, devaluation can work only if other countries maintain their exchange rates at a stable level. If they too seek to make their exports attractive by devaluation, the result is again a standoff. Indeed, we may not even be able to give things away, for if free goods enter the country, more domestic workers may be thrown out of work, a condition no red-blooded nationalist could permit.

The moral of the tale is simple: strong nations like the United States cannot sensibly regard international trade as a way of solving future unemployment problems. Our only real hope here is to conquer the problem of unemployment by domestic policies and use our international trade to increase our present or future consumption standards or to serve our political aspirations and responsibilities.

AMERICAN GOALS AND INTERNATIONAL COOPERATION

Economic isolation simply will not work. On this, if nothing else, 99 44/100 per cent of all economists are agreed. Nevertheless, isolationism may again appear in this country because nations who ignore history too often repeat it. Let us turn to the major problems ahead, then, bearing in mind that the goals we seek are full and efficient employment at home, with a rising standard of living and increasing productivity and with peaceful, profitable trade relations with our neighbors.

Foreign lending and the International Bank. The United States is more highly developed industrially than most of the rest of the world. The nations of South America, the Far East, Africa, and so on, could use our capital for their industrial development. Such capital could be expected to increase their production enough to pay a generous interest and repay the capital because of its net productivity. But private citizens have been reluctant to lend abroad. American corporations will build branch plants abroad and invest in oil or mineral resources, but substantial lending disappeared sometime in 1929, seemingly forever. Yet American citizens have put aside savings which they would be glad to lend abroad if such capital transactions could be made secure, and the nation would benefit by a higher future standard of living from sound foreign lending. How can this problem be solved?

In 1944, the leading nations of the world (except Soviet Russia) formed the International Bank for Reconstruction and Development, and a sister institution, the International Monetary Fund. The Bank was intended to provide sound long-term loans for reconstruction and economic development; the Fund is concerned with short-term credit and stabilization of foreign exchange rates.

The operation of the International Bank is fairly simple. The leading nations subscribe capital in proportion to their economic importance ($21 billion to date); the American quota is about one-third or $6.3 billion. The Bank uses its capital to make international loans to people or countries whose projects seem economically sound and reasonable but who cannot obtain private loans at reasonably low interest rates.

So far, each country has been called upon to put up less than 10 per cent of its full quota and the bank does not plan to call for the remainder. Obviously, this is not very much money by international standards. But the International Bank's true importance does not depend on the amount of money it has to lend. More significant is its ability to float bonds and use the proceeds to make loans. It has already floated such bonds in the United States, in Switzerland, and elsewhere. The bonds are safe because they are backed by the credit of all member nations up to the full amount of their quotas. And the bank can insure loans in return for a ½ or 1 per cent premium, making it possible for private parties to subscribe to loans knowing that the Bank's credit is behind the loan.

As a result of these techniques for extending long-term credit, we can expect goods and services to flow out of the United States in the years ahead and into areas in need of industrial development. If the loans are sound, they will be repaid in full; if some go sour, the loss will be spread over all member nations—it will not fall on Uncle Sam alone. Meanwhile, the lending nations (like the United States) will be getting jobs, or even some increase in inflation problems, from current activity; while the loans are being "serviced" or repaid, America should have an import surplus of useful goods. Production in the borrowing nation can be expected to increase more than enough to repay the loans plus interest. Already we can say that the Bank is definitely a financial success. In fact, it has been overly conservative, if anything, in its lending policy.

In addition, the United States has organized its own Export-Import Bank, which makes foreign loans, e.g., to prospective purchasers of American goods. Some of these loans are "tied" in the sense that they must be spent in the United States, even though we often criticize this policy when others follow it. The Eisenhower administration also set up an International Finance Corporation, as a subsidiary to the World Bank, to provide venture capital for economic development. There is also an International Development Association, which is part of the United Nations. An internal Development Loan Fund (which "ties" its loans to purchase of American goods) is still another foreign-lending agency. Later we shall see exactly what the pattern of lending has been in the past two decades.

Stable exchange rates, freer trade, and the Monetary Fund. Daily variations in exchange rates increase the risks of international trading and lending and reduce their volume. World specialization and productivity is in consequence reduced, and when nations begin competing in the manipulation of exchange rates, world trade ends up on its back. The gold standard, while it operated, kept exchange rates stable, but it made each country a slave rather than master of its own economic destiny. To keep the system stable, every country had to inflate and deflate as the rest of the world inflated and deflated. The gold standard was a casualty of World War I, and few finance ministers have wept at the loss.

The International Monetary Fund, along with the International Bank, was born at the conferences held at Bretton Woods, New Hampshire, in 1944. The Fund hopes to secure the stability offered by the gold standard, without accepting all of its disadvantages, through international cooperation. It also aims to reduce direct controls over imports. In 1947, for example, the Fund set exchange rates for most of its members. In 1949, however, most countries of the British Empire and Western Europe depreciated their currencies 30 per cent, stabilizing the exchange rate at a new figure. Even with fixed exchange rates, the economic upheaval that followed World War II made it unlikely that perfect balance would be achieved. Some countries would end up owing money to others, and stable exchange rates would be subjected to great pressure.

This is where the International Monetary Fund comes in. It provides short-term credits for debtor countries and tries to set up rules and procedures which will prevent one country from digging itself deeper into debt with each passing year. After a certain level of indebtedness has been reached, penalties are applied, and more important, the Fund's directors consult with the country and recommend remedial procedures. They cannot tell a country to create a depression which will lower national income to a point where imports are reduced, of course, but they can permit a 10 per cent depreciation of national currency, and this will tend to restore trade equilibrium by expanding exports and contracting imports. If this is not enough, further depreciation may be permitted. The important point is that all these changes take place in an orderly way. International stability remains unshaken while the one country attempts to solve its basic international problems.

Operation of the International Monetary Fund. Briefly, and untechnically, the Fund extends short-term credits in a simple manner. Each member nation has a quota proportional to income and volume of international trade, payable largely in national currency, and partly in gold. The quota paid into the Fund is used for stabilization. The United States contributes about one-third of the total, about $4 billion.

Suppose that England needs short-term credit from the Fund because of an imbalance in current account. The Fund aids her by extending "purchasing rights"—it allows Britain to buy some of the Fund's dollar holdings with British pounds sterling. To keep the Fund balanced, no country can buy more than one-fourth of its original quota, and the Fund will never hold more than twice the original quota of British pounds. However, once Britain's balance-of-payments position has improved, she is expected to buy back the pounds used to purchase dollars or gold. In this way, the Fund maintains its stock of currency in balance.

At first the Fund was rather disappointing, for the postwar strains turned out to be rather more severe than people expected in 1944, and the Fund's resources were not adequate to cope with these disequilibria. Fortunately, some of the burden was taken over by the European Payments Union, which was set up after the Marshall aid program to act as a clearinghouse for Western European nations, and by the Organization for European Economic Cooperation (OEEC), which provided for consultation among member nations in case of payments problems. Later, as the world economy stabilized and the major reconstruction period ended, the Fund began to perform more adequately, and experts now believe that it has a great role to play in the future.

Marshall Plan, military aid, and other programs. Since World War II, American economic assistance to other countries has reached astronomical proportions. Immediate postwar emergency needs were met largely through the United Nations Relief and Rehabilitation Administration (UNRRA) to which America contributed heavily. In 1947, the European Recovery Program (Marshall aid program) was introduced, principally to aid the countries in Western Europe. Concurrently, the "Truman Doctrine" provided economic and military aid for Greece and Turkey. Substantial grants have been made to our various military allies through the North Atlantic Treaty Organization (NATO) and other military alliances. Even Communist Yugoslavia has received aid, together with the Chinese Nationalists, the South Koreans, the French in Indochina, etc. In all history there is no precedent for the aid given for economic development in the years after the war.

Doubtless, fear of communism inspired many of these aid programs. But a close study of events leading to the Marshall Plan and other foreign-aid programs shows that there was also a strong element of altruism involved. We have come to realize that the globe holds fifteen non-Americans for every American, making our future depend upon a stable international order that is not hostile to Western society nor to its basic value structure. Close study of the facts will in any case discredit the view that we embraced aid programs because that was the only way to prevent a great depression at home. On the contrary, we have been most enthusiastic about aid at times when domestic inflationary pressures were already severe, thus aggravating our own problems very seriously.

Point Four: The bold new program. Aside from providing substantial material aid to underdeveloped foreign countries, there is one thing we can do that helps them a great deal and costs very little, namely, help them acquire the technical know-how that will enable them to increase productivity and living standards. The American program designed to do this became known as the "Point Four" program because it was the fourth point in President Truman's Inaugural Address in 1949. The aim is contained in this direct quotation from Truman:

Fourth, we must embark on a bold new program for making the benefits of our scientific advances and industrial progress available for the improvement and growth of underdeveloped areas. . . . I believe that we should make available to peace-loving peoples the benefits of our store of technical knowledge in order to help them realize their aspirations for a better life. . . . We invite other countries to pool their technological resources in this . . . world-wide effort for the achievement of peace, plenty, and freedom.

We have also been exporting "know-how" privately, of course. Many large companies have branch factories abroad, often capitalized abroad but staffed by American technicians. Some shortsighted people raise their hands in horror at the thought of helping foreign nations to become our industrial competitors, but they forget that trade is largest between industrial nations, not between developed and backward areas. Even in selfish terms, our best policy in the long run is to help others to develop as fully and rapidly as possible.

The European Common Market and free-trade area. We have already analyzed the economic gains to be had from freer trade. One way of removing impediments to free trade is to form customs unions, groups of countries in which tariffs and quotas are reduced drastically or banished completely. Externally, the group must be treated like a single country or trading area. The United States can be thought of as a large customs union or free-trade area patterned along these lines. More than a century ago, the independent German states formed a *Zollverein* or customs union, and more recently Belgium, Luxembourg, and the Netherlands have formed the Benelux union. A proposed union of France and Italy did not materialize.

One of the most exciting developments along these lines was the formation of the six-nation European Common Market in 1957. The same group of countries also formed a common nuclear-energy pool. Belgium, France, Italy, Luxembourg, the Netherlands, and Western Germany agreed to eliminate gradually tariffs and import quotas on nonfarm goods produced within the area, and to set up common tariffs against goods from countries outside the Common Market. They also agreed to allow free movement of capital and labor and to organize an investment bank, with contributions from each member, for economic development. Farm goods have not yet been included in the proposal, and the difficult problem of relating the Common Market to the overseas territories of the member nations has not yet been clarified. Nevertheless, the progress made by the Common Market in recent years has been astounding.

The Common Market could become the second-largest free-trade area in the world, and if Britain had been able to join, it would have become the largest market area in the world. British commitments to the Commonwealth nations and to the remains of her imperial holdings have made her hesitate, but there may yet be a reconciliation of interests on the question. The anxiety created by the Common Market among nonmember nations led to the formation of the "Outer Seven," another free-trade area consisting of Austria, Denmark, Norway, Portugal, Sweden, Switzerland, and the United Kingdom. This very loose federation also looks toward eventual free trade, but its development to date cannot compare with the progress made by the Common Market.

Some economists are uncertain that lowering tariffs between the members of a bloc of nations is really moving toward a more efficient pattern of world production. They fear that the lower-than-average tariffs will distort "normal" trade patterns even more than national tariffs. But others believe that any movement in the direction of freer trade is a step in the right direction, and perhaps hope that once a few large free-trade areas are in existence these can be merged into a single worldwide unit. No definitive answer will cover every case, though most economists would perhaps agree that lowering tariffs in Europe could have such salutary effects on the division of labor as to make the experiment very worthwhile.

World trade patterns: Dollar shortage to trade deficit? We can conclude with a brief summary of one of the most striking changes to take place in the pattern of world trade in recent decades. After World War II, American exports soared as the rest of the world tried desperately to obtain goods to replace and rebuild those destroyed or used up, or never owned, during the war. This was particularly true of the countries devastated by war and postwar disruption—Germany, Japan, Greece, Italy, Britain—of enemy and ally alike.

"Dollar shortage." The demand for American goods was coupled with a basic inability to make payment for those goods—with a serious dollar shortage which was almost worldwide. This necessitated aid programs, like Marshall aid, unilateral gifts, and loans. In addition, other nations relied heavily on exchange controls, strict rationing of imports, quotas, licensing, and various other devices to limit the demand for American exports. Finally, a large number of Western countries felt obliged to resort to devaluation of their currency, hoping that the result would improve their balance-of-payments position. Until 1950, a condition best described as "chronic dollar shortage" seriously limited a large part of international trade.

Then in 1950, America became involved in the Korean conflict, and for some years afterward we had a great need for foreign currencies to meet our increasing military obligations. Early in the 1950s, the tide was already beginning to turn. The governmental deficit on current account began to rise while the surplus on private account reached its peak in 1947 and began to decline slowly. Gradually, we began to move into an actual deficit on current account. And our continued lending abroad, largely in the form of direct investment by private corporations, added to the debit items in our balance of payments.

By the last half of the 1950s it would have become obvious that America was beginning to lose gold and undergo net borrowing abroad on short-term account had it not been for the Suez Canal incident. For when Egypt took over the canal, and Near East shipping was blocked temporarily, there was a tremendous but temporary increase in American exports of oil and other materials, which concealed the trend through 1957.

Since 1957, the problem has been clearly recognized. Our deficit on current account, plus long-term net lending abroad, has left us with a total deficit which may be paid in gold or by giving foreigners short-term dollar obligations. They may take their choice, and they have actually done both. By 1961, our gold reserves had dropped from the postwar peak of $24 billion to less than $18 billion. Even more, foreigners have been taking on our short-term obligations at a rate of billions of dollars each year.

There is no more talk of dollar shortage. Quite the reverse, for we now speak of America's seemingly chronic international deficit. As Western Germany accumulates gold by the billion, talk is heard of a "mark shortage" and Germany is urged to expand her imports, to appreciate the mark, to share aid and military burdens, and to have more domestic inflation. Nor is Germany alone in this enviable position. Japanese transistor radios and other goods are eagerly bought here and elsewhere, giving Japan a sizable surplus on international account.

Reasons for a chronic international deficit. Various reasons are given for the turn that has occurred in international trade balances, most with some element of truth in them. But as we shall see, the most influential change is probably to be found in the vast improvement of technical productivity abroad in recent years. Let us look at some of the common causes to which this turn of events is attributed.

Too much inflation at home. If a country has more rapid wage and price increases than its neighbors, and if these increases are not matched by compensating gains in productivity, then a deficit in the balance of international payments is to be expected. Going from theory to fact, we find that there has not been more inflation here than abroad, either in terms of price levels or money wage rates. Nevertheless, there is a grain of truth in the point. If we examine certain important sectors of the economy, we find that American steel prices, for example, have been rising relative to prices abroad. No wonder that Japanese steel invades Pacific Coast markets and that foreign steel products, such as barbed wire, have taken over many traditional American markets.

Lengthy domestic strikes have helped England and Belgium to get a foothold in other markets. Similar occurrences are found in various of our machine industries.

Overgenerosity in aid and military programs. It is natural, in a time of international deficits, to think of cutting foreign aid and military spending. But it is misleading to think that such a cut will be reflected intact by the balance of payments. Many of our credit items are included in the balance of payments only because government programs supply foreigners with the funds they need to pay for them. If these funds are cut out, some of our exports will go with them. How much, we cannot estimate very accurately. In any event, it seems clear that our deficit has not been caused primarily by generosity to foreigners. Such programs have not grown much in relative size, and it is more the case that a lowering of the surplus on private account has left us less able to be generous. Our income abroad has dropped.

Lack of trust in the dollar. It is a fact that many foreigners have had so much faith in the dollar that they have kept their holdings of short-term liquid assets in dollars rather than in gold. Nevertheless, uneasiness has undoubtedly been growing abroad, and a reduction in our domestic short-term interest rate causes many foreigners to transfer their money to other foreign investments which yield higher earnings. Hence they demand gold or payments in other currencies. True, America still has more gold than any other nation. Too much, many say, in terms of total world distribution. But it is not just a question of losing some gold now and then reaching an equilibrium, for there is no equilibrium in sight. Hence the experts are anxious, in some measure, about the future of the dollar, with the consequences we have already noted.

Discrimination against American goods. While the dollar was in short supply, barriers to American exports were common and understandable. But there is now good reason to argue that the time for such limits is past and that remaining discriminations ought to be removed or drastically reduced; much has, in fact, been done lately along these lines.

Growth of productivity abroad. From the long-run point of view, the fundamental cause for the change in America's international position seems to be the remarkable rate at which productivity has increased in Western Europe and Japan. Their production technology is still behind ours, but the gap, particularly in those goods which we customarily export and specialize in, has been narrowing quickly. Even with real wages rising more rapidly abroad than in the United States, foreigners can produce for themselves more cheaply than we can produce for them. Hence they can outsell us in other markets and even in our own market, in some cases.

This means that the patterns of comparative advantage are changing, and such transition periods are generally uncomfortable, perhaps more so for those already at the top. Moreover, it is not simply a question of our shifting factors from one industry to another. So long as our dollar costs are high all around, American currency can be said to be "overvalued currency." A country with overvalued currency tends to incur international deficits, to be undersold in most goods, and to be threatened with high unemployment and excess capacity. What may be needed is for her money prices and wages to fall relative to those abroad, either falling absolutely or rising less rapidly than theirs. Even if no real-wage change were needed, we know that it is very far from easy in a modern mixed democratic society to have a deflation in wage and other costs and in prices.

As a result of these developments, American leaders face some very real international problems in the immediate future, problems which require long, careful, and deadly serious consideration.

Therapy for a chronic deficit. Economists know generally what is needed to reverse a chronic international deficit, but it is rather easier to preach a solution than to put it into practice. Some of the basic remedies are sketched briefly below.

1. American workers and industry can be urged to *increase domestic technical production.* Of course, urging does not always accomplish much, but public pressure on unions and management may help, as will aids to research and innovation.

2. American exporters can be urged to *improve selling practices* abroad. Since foreign salesmen are also being urged in the same way, mere exhortation may not lead to much improvement in the overall situation.

3. We can press for further reductions in discriminations against the dollar abroad. There are still some left.

4. We can ask that the prospering nations of the free world take up a larger share of the aid, development, and defense burdens.

5. We could keep our economy depressed at home, eschewing low interest rates needed for expansion and growth, diminishing our demand for imports, and putting pressure on profit margins in export industries. Such a solution lacks appeal for those concerned with high employment and growth, and they urge greater reliance on fiscal rather than monetary policy.

6. We could revert to protectionism. Tariffs and quotas will not raise real wages, for the reasons we have already seen, but they can compensate a little for sticky money wages by raising our prices generally. Such a solution will be deplored by all who value the advantages that come from specialization according to comparative advantage and for all who think America's political advantage lies in our living down our old reputation as a bad neighbor.

7. There could be a depreciation of the dollar relative to other currencies

by unilateral devaluation relative to gold. Such an event seems remote, despite the fears of continental speculators.

Perhaps the most likely possibility for the near future is a period when all the major nations will find it desirable to increase the price of gold to compensate for the fact that world production and trade have been growing more rapidly than the supply of mined gold, with a resulting tendency toward underliquidity around the world. Of course, this is very speculative, for there is also possible a more elaborate monetary scheme, of the type proposed by Yale's Robert Triffin, that would introduce an international unit of currency rather than continuing the use of gold. No doubt the International Fund will take on new functions.

While the new trade trend creates problems for America, we must note that it implies a great improvement for the rest of the world. No mature nation expects things always to go its way, and to the degree that we are cosmopolitan in our outlook we should welcome improvements in living standards wherever they occur. At the same time, one realizes that there will be difficult decisions to make at home. With the cost-push phenomena at work, and with a balance-of-payments problem, the challenge facing the economy is great, and the opportunity to make use of our neoclassical synthesis equally significant. It would be a tragedy if, after learning so much about stability and growth, modern nations were to fall back into the slough of depressions where the classical precepts are in danger of losing much of their relevance.

Summary

Buying and selling abroad presupposes a foreign exchange rate between home and foreign currencies. Supply and demand set each day's free exchange rate, but countries on a gold standard have a stable exchange rate set by the price at which they buy or sell gold. The balance of payments refers to all transactions which use foreign exchange, the total value of exports and imports, including both visible and invisible items.

As soon as production is diversified within a country, specialization and exchange become profitable; the same conditions hold for nations. The benefit of trade between dissimilar producers is obvious. But the principle of comparative advantage shows us that trade may be beneficial even among countries which produce the same items. So long as there is a difference in relative efficiency, powerful benefits can be derived from specializing in goods where advantage is maximized. Both countries are then better off, and real wages are improved. Prohibitive tariffs hurt real wages and factor returns.

The law of comparative advantage must be qualified to take into account such factors as rigid wage rates and poor fiscal policies, for the latter may lead to unemployment.

The case for freer trade rests on the increased productivity that specialization according to the law of comparative advantage makes possible. Higher world production is then possible, and all countries can have higher living standards. Trade between countries with different standards of living is likely to be especially mutually profitable. Most arguments in favor of protection are simply rationalizations of special benefits to particular interest groups and cannot withstand analysis.

An important exception to the law of comparative advantage arises out of the need to favor uneconomical production in the interests of national safety or self-defense. An outright government subsidy might be preferable in such a case. The only other exception of any practical importance, aside from the use of tariffs to relieve unemployment, is the case for infant industries or young economies which need temporary protection to realize their true long-run comparative advantages. Generally, when public planning for development can discern long-range trends better than the free market can, tariff and other interventions may turn out to be beneficial.

Review Questions

1. What is the basic reason why international trade is important to all people?

2. Explain why it is true that American dollars can be spent only in the United States.

3. What are the two methods of determining the exchange rate? Give an illustration of each of them.

4. Differentiate between devaluation and depreciation. What is the effect of each on imports? Exports?

5. List the major items considered in calculations of the balance of payments. Why is the balance always zero at the end of each year?

6. What is meant by a "deficit on current account"?

7. What noneconomic factors influence the international movement of capital?

8. Explain the theory of comparative advantage in your own words. Give an example from your own knowledge. What are the more important qualifications that must be made to the theory?

9. What are the major arguments in favor of protective tariffs? Evaluate each of them in economic terms. In political terms.

10. What are the three arguments for protection under "dynamic conditions"?

11. Distinguish between a quota and a tariff.

12. Explain why foreign investment has an inflationary effect. Use the concept of the multiplier to do so.

13. What are some of the major institutions for international economic and financial dealing with which the United States is involved? What function do they perform?

14. In what sense does the European Common Market create conditions in Europe somewhat analogous to conditions inside the United States?

15. What is the "dollar shortage"? Can you explain its history since 1945?

16. What are the principal reasons why a nation has a chronic international deficit? Which of these causes are applicable to the United States? How can the deficit be overcome?

For Further Study

1. How would the balance-of-payments positions of a young debtor nation (such as the United States in 1800), an older nation (Britain in 1960), and a new and powerful nation (the United States in 1960) differ?

2. Do we really care if international loans are repaid so long as interest payments are maintained? Why?

3. Is it better to buy cheap machinery from Europe even if our own machinery industry is languishing? Explain your position.

4. What would be the consequences if an extremely high American tariff were imposed suddenly by the Congress?

5. Can you think of an industry in which the "infant industry" argument for protection would be valid?

6. Is it a good thing to export goods and take gold in return? Would it have been a good thing in 1933 at the nadir of the Depression?

7. What effect does military activity have on the balance of payments?

8. What do you consider the major international problems in economics at the present time? How many of them can be solved by a single country working alone?

9. What consequences can you foresee from the European Common Market? What would be the effect of applying this principle in the Western Hemisphere?

SELECTED READINGS

Texts (use latest edition)

Bach, George L.: *Economics: An Introduction to Analysis and Policy,* 3d ed., Prentice-Hall, Inc., Englewood Cliffs, N.J., 1960.

Dodd, J. H., and Thomas J. Hailstones: *Economics: Principles and Applications,* 4th ed., South-Western Publishing Company, Cincinnati, Ohio, 1961.

Harriss, C. Lowell: *The American Economy,* Richard D. Irwin, Inc., Homewood, Ill., 1962.

McConnell, Campbell R.: *Economics: Principles, Problems, and Policies,* McGraw-Hill Book Company, Inc., New York, 1963.

Reynolds, Lloyd G.: *Economics: A General Introduction,* Richard D. Irwin, Inc., Homewood, Ill., 1963.

Samuelson, Paul A.: *Economics: An Introductory Analysis,* 6th ed., McGraw-Hill Book Company, Inc., New York, 1964.

Readings

Grey, Arthur L., and John E. Elliot: *Economic Issues and Policies,* Houghton Mifflin Company, Boston, 1961.

McConnell, C. R., and R. Bingham: *Economic Issues,* McGraw-Hill Book Company, Inc., New York, 1964.

Samuelson, Paul A., R. L. Bishop, and J. R. Coleman: *Readings in Economics,* McGraw-Hill Book Company, Inc., New York, 1958.

Slesinger, Reuben E., and Asher Isaacs: *Contemporary Economics: Selected Readings,* Allyn and Bacon, Inc., Boston, 1963.

Works of General Interest

Ebenstein, William: *Today's Isms: Communism, Fascism, Capitalism, Socialism,* Prentice-Hall, Inc., Englewood Cliffs, N.J., 1961.

Friedman, Milton, *Capitalism and Freedom,* The University of Chicago Press, Chicago, 1962.

Galbraith, John K.: *American Capitalism,* rev. ed., Houghton Mifflin Company, Boston, 1956.

———: *The Affluent Society,* Houghton Mifflin Company, Boston, 1958.

Heilbroner, Robert: *The Worldly Philosophers,* Simon and Schuster, Inc., New York, 1961.

———: *Making of Economic Society,* Prentice-Hall, Inc., Englewood Cliffs, N.J., 1962.

Loucks, William N.: *Comparative Economic Systems,* 6th ed., Harper & Row, Publishers, Incorporated, New York, 1961.

Marx, Karl: *Capital and Other Writings,* Modern Library, Inc., New York.

Myrdal, Gunnar: *Rich Lands and Poor: The Road to World Prosperity,* Harper & Row, Publishers, Incorporated, New York, 1958.

Robertson, D. H.: *Money,* The University of Chicago Press, Chicago, 1959.

Veblen, Thorstein: *Theory of the Leisure Class,* Modern Library, Inc., New York, 1934.

Wilcox, Clair: *Public Policies toward Business,* Richard D. Irwin, Inc., Homewood, Ill., 1955.

PART 4

Contemporary Problems: Social, Political, Economic

We come now to the discussion of contemporary social problems as they appear to the sociologist, the political scientist, and the economist. This is doubtless the most difficult part of textbook preparation. The social processes that we live with from day to day are so complex and so closely intermingled that it is not always easy to assess them properly. We may ignore really fundamental social problems and attach great significance to what is only peripheral and transient simply because the basic problems are, for the moment, overshadowed by more immediate if more trivial concerns. Furthermore, it is not always an easy matter to phrase our problems correctly, even when they can be identified. Think of how hard it would be to explain to a person from another planet the basis for the current tension between the United States and the U.S.S.R. or to make clear why some nations are under-developed while others are not. Are these matters intrinsically significant, or do they flow from some more fundamental condition of human society which is as yet only imperfectly understood? Such questions are not easily answered, even in the areas in which our knowledge of human affairs is greatest.

In general, social problems fall into one of three broad categories: first, there are matters which we are unable to explain—areas in which our knowledge is simply inadequate; second, there are aspects of social action which we are unable to control—goals which we cannot achieve; finally, there are broad areas in which we are unable to choose with finality among the various alternatives which present themselves—areas in which we are unable, for one reason or another, to choose the goal that ought to be pursued. Each of these three types of problem appears in every society in every age, and all three are represented in the chapters that follow.

It may be surprising to learn that there are still basic social problems that cannot be resolved because we lack the knowledge or explanatory capacity to solve them. Yet our ability to explain social phenomena is often much overrated, perhaps because we have advanced so rapidly in technology and certain areas of science. It often appears, when we examine the daily press, that all of our problems will eventually be solved and that all we must have is time to work out solutions. In the social sciences, nothing could be further from the truth. There are basic problems in society that men have been examining for centuries without success, and their nature is such that no amount of scientific information will produce a final solution. In Chapter 18, for example, we examine the problem of social change—the explanation of why and how society changes. We find that men have sought for an explanation in almost every phase of human behavior and environment—in geography, biology, demography, military and political activity, through technology, economics, or ideology—always without producing a theory that contains no flaws. Perhaps a theory of this sort is impossible; that we cannot really know. In any event, all of the theories formulated thus far have been faulty. That does not mean, of course, that they are useless. A theory may be very useful even though it is inadequate. But the problem of social change remains a good illustration of the type of social problem that is presently beyond our capacity to explain or solve.

Man has achieved a considerable measure of control over his natural environment. He crosses mountains, irrigates deserts, cools and heats his homes. Yet there are natural phenomena he cannot control—hurricanes, earthquakes, the seasons, the movement of the tides, etc. Similarly, there are a great many social goals that nearly everyone agrees upon which have proved extremely difficult to achieve. In politics, for example, the basic civil liberties are fairly well defined, but they have not yet become social realities, despite our best efforts. In Chapter 19, we look at the means that have been used to achieve civil liberties here in the United States and at the problems that have arisen in our pursuit of these social goals. In Chapter 20, we examine the problem of underdevelopment—another situation in which the goals to be achieved are agreed and the means of achieving them well known, but the achievement proves impossible in the short run. A multitude of similar social problems could be sorted out for detailed discussion in every branch of social science.

In classic ethics, one of the dilemmas that is often used to illustrate the problem of moral choice is as follows: If you were placed in a burning building with your mother and a priceless invention and could save only one or the other, which would you save? This matter of choosing between values, each desirable in itself, is a serious problem for every society, for there are hundreds of such choices to be made in every generation. Thus in Chapter 20, we find a conflict between price stability and the stimulation of economic growth that economic theory must resolve, and in Chapter 19, the same problem appears as a conflict between national security and personal freedom. Such questions cannot be solved here, but we can gain some insight into the nature of the problem and the manner in which they are attacked in different disciplines.

CHAPTER 18

The Problem of Social Change

Candor and confession are good for the soul, or so it is said, and no less so for the sociologist than for others. Candor compels us to confess at the outset that the discussion of social and cultural change which follows will be unsatisfactory to the undergraduate who studies it, to the instructor who teaches it, and to any sociologist who may happen to read it. It is indeed unsatisfactory to the author himself. Sociology simply does not yet possess a solution to the vast and complex problem of social change, though this problem is in a sense the *ultima ratio,* the ultimate reason, for the discipline. A cogent theory of the process of history is the acid test of sociological inquiry, and this, at the moment, is a test that sociology cannot pass.

We begin hesitantly, then, by inviting the reader to reflect on the wisdom of an ancient Greek philosopher named Heraclitus, who said that it is impossible for a man to step into the same river twice, for on the second occasion the river is not the same, nor is it the same man. The time interval has produced changes, however minute, in both man and river. Belief in the reality of change was the central theme of Heraclitus's philosophy; everything save change itself was in a constant flux. In the same era, another Greek philosopher named Parmenides produced precisely the opposite philosophy by asserting boldly that change is only an illusion, that everything remains the same and that the only reality is "being." The Western tradition has produced supporters for both of these points of view, and many others. The question is important, for it involves a serious and difficult metaphysical problem. But in this form, it is a problem for philosophy and not for sociology.

Sociology cannot be content with the identification of structure, for the social order is, after all, a changing order. The question of social statics, of discovering what society is, may be basic to sociology, but it must be wedded to social dynamics, to the question how society changes. Indeed, there is a sense in which sociologists have concerned themselves with social statics only because they are essential to an adequate study of social dynamics. Accurate prediction is beyond the capacity of the sociologist, of course, but we at least want to know the factors that have brought present societies into being, the factors that explain their structure and account for their culture.

The sociologist, then, is not satisfied with an outline of the structure of society. He must also seek its causes. The generations of humanity pass one after another in response to inexorable biological process, and in passing they alter the character of human society. What are the factors that first form societies and then change them in ceaseless flux and flow? The question itself has a kind of splendor. It is the most sublime of all sociological inquiries. It cannot be approached without due consideration to the dimension of time, which we must now introduce into our inquiry.

Unfortunately, social change is a most complex and difficult problem, for societies, like men and women, appear in endless variety. No two of them are alike. All of them serve the needs of their members in some degree, but these needs are different in different cultures. In all societies there are regularities and recurrences, but there are also differences in detail, in spirit, and in meaning—in idea, norm, and value. The history of society follows no single track, and the metronome of history beats more rapidly for one people than for another, more slowly in one epoch than in its successor. The difficulty, clearly, is to find a point at which to begin.

First of all, we must seek a proper level of discourse for our discussion. Obviously, a problem of such magnitude demands a sustained attack by scholars from many disciplines—not only sociologists, but philosophers, historians, and other social scientists. Indeed, it would be a species of forensic arrogance to claim the question as distinctively or exclusively sociological. Let us, therefore, carve out the elements which are more properly historical or philosophical and concentrate on those areas proper to sociology, bearing in mind that the subtracted concerns have ultimate sociological significance, just as the eye specialist is ultimately concerned with the problem of human health.

A philosophical problem. Among the more vexing questions in this theater of inquiry is the meaning of the "social causation" that we seek. What precisely do we mean when we say that events have "causes," or that ideas influence human society? What is a cause or an influence in this sense? This is a philosophical, or more specifically, a methodological problem, and no satisfactory answer has been supplied by more than two millenniums of speculation.

Although we all "know" what a cause is, the principle of causality eludes explanation, and neither reason nor experience, nor both together, can guarantee the validity of the principle. The Scottish philosopher, David Hume (1711–1776), pointed out that we never experience causation—only succession. We see one billiard ball strike a second, and we see the second ball move. But all that we have actually seen is a succession of events, and we have no proof that the first event caused the second. Nor can such proof be derived by the techniques of logic. Some contemporary philosophers, unable to answer Hume, would abandon the concept of "cause" altogether and substitute a probability principle, but that issue is too complex and technical for a beginning text.

The sociologist cannot answer Hume any better than the philosopher, but he must nevertheless accept the validity of the causation principle and think accordingly. For the assumption of causality is a necessary preface to all intellectual inquiry—without causation we simply could not think. Unless we assume that events have causes, the world of nature dissolves into pure confusion and caprice, knowledge becomes fortuitous, and science impossible. To attribute the behavior of the universe to fortune or luck is only to plead ignorance of the causal factors involved in an explanation, and neither the scientist nor the man in the street can do this. This does not "solve" the causation problem, of course, but so long as the assumption is clearly stated it can do no harm. Hence the reader is invited to join the author in assuming that social change is a matter of cause and effect and not of chance, keeping in mind that this is an assumption and not a "known" fact.

An historiographical problem. Sociology is an abstract and not a concrete science. The task of describing singular and concrete events belongs to history rather than to sociology. The historian seeks to describe changing situations, series of happenings that lead to other events, tied in an endless chain. He may write of the political state, or art or literature, of science or religion; in all cases, the task is to tell the story of events as completely and accurately as the data permit. The historian seeks to go beyond mere description, to weigh and estimate as carefully as he can the factors that led to particular consequences. Such explanations, of course, involve a search for causes; history cannot be a mere catalog of dated events unmotivated by causal concern. In this sense, all history has sociological significance and sociologists would be helpless without the evidence that history supplies.

But historical inquiries are concrete, and not sociological in emphasis and focus. For sociology is not concerned with historical events in themselves, but with the patterns that historical events reveal, patterns that repeat themselves in time and space. Thus sociology is concerned with war in general, and not with particular wars, with capitalism in general, and not with the development of some particular capitalistic enterprise such as the United States Steel Corporation. The causal inquiries of sociology, in short, are directed to patterns rather than to particulars, to classes of events rather than to the events themselves. In our discussions, we often ignore the causes of particular events for this reason. However, the reader is cautioned to remember that historians and sociologists are colleagues in a great inquiry, and that it would be a serious error to contrast too sharply their separate questions and endeavors.

The factors of sociocultural change. There is another methodological difference between the historical and the sociological approach to social and cultural change—a difference in the direction of the inquiry. The historian moves from effect to cause; the sociologist from cause to effect. That is, the historian begins with particulars and seeks multiple causes from single particulars; the sociologist begins with multiple consequences and seeks the causes which create them. These classes of causes, what we may call "factors," are the sources of social change. In the discussion that follows, we single out certain factors that social thinkers have emphasized in their efforts to explain social change. Each factor, singly or in combination with others, is associated with a particular theory of social change.

Theories of social change are themselves subject to classification, for theory sometimes ceases to be sociological and becomes speculative and metaphysical. At what point does this occur? It is not always possible to say. But we can point to philosophers of history, such as Hegel, who made logic into a force, a destiny, or an idea that threads its way through history in response to an inevitable and eternal dialectic of thesis, antithesis, and synthesis, and identify them as metaphysicians. Theories of this kind we shall ignore, except for some of the more recent ones, less metaphysical than Hegel's, that attract our attention because of their intrinsic and contemporary interest.

Our procedure will be first to discuss the factor theories of social change and then several of the theories built upon principles rather than factors. There are a great many factor theories, some of them almost too fantastic to win any credence; we shall include a few of the more fanciful for the sake of completeness. Other factor theories—those emphasizing the geographic, biological, and demographic factors—have already been treated in detail, and our present discussion of them can accordingly be brief.

The geographic factor. Geographic theories of social change, as we suggested earlier, are necessary but not sufficient as explanations. They range from a variety of theories that attribute social commotions to cosmic disturbances of one kind or another to the belief that the stars somehow guide and control our destinies. Various writers have suggested that sunspots, those vast eruptions on the face of the sun, are responsible for fluctuations in human activity, that great masses of energy are somehow transferred to our human population, stirring us to new activity in new directions. Others have insisted that the conjunction of constellations on the date of birth has something to do with the course of life, with progressions and change in human society.

Even if geographic speculations are more reasonable than the theories put forward by the astrologer, there is no reason to assume that they are in any way a *sufficient* explanation of social change. For no period of human history do we have information of a geographic character that will adequately account for the social changes that occurred. The arguments offered earlier will suffice also for our present purposes, and we may even say, this time misquoting Santayana, that although geography does explain one man's habitat, it cannot by itself explain his history.

The biological factor. Sometimes a biological factor like race is elevated to supreme importance in theories of social change. But as we pointed out in great detail earlier, there is no evidence whatever that the slight physical differences between the various racial groups of mankind imply differential intelligence and none that they exert any particular influence on the course of history. We have, of course, been subjected in recent centuries to theories that arrogantly explain social developments in terms of the "master race" or a superior hereditary endowment. And the notion that "blood will tell" is as old as history. Such theories are found in every society in every part of the world and in every epoch. Only in a sociologically sophisticated society, it seems, can men really discover that racial theories are only a primitive form of ethnocentrism.

The theory that biological or racial differences explain the superiority or inferiority of nations and the changes that occur in them is, in short, one that no present evidence will support. But the *belief* that such differences as skin color or slant of eye are important is a factor to be reckoned by sociology. When men believe that racial differences matter, then that belief has real social consequences, and they may not be too different from those which would occur if the situation were actually what it is believed to be. For this reason, racial interpretations of social change attract our attention, but in this sense we are dealing with ideas and attitudes, and not with racial differences as such. It is not the situation, but the "definition of the situation" that is a factor in social change.

The demographic factor. Other theories of social change attribute causal efficacy to demographic developments. Again, this is a subject already discussed at length. The importance of size, and changes in size, for the study of society has been emphasized again and again. Very small societies seldom rise to eminence; very large societies may influence not only their neighbors but the whole subsequent course of history. An expanding population brings different consequences for man than a contracting population, particularly in economics. Population pressures, actual or presumed, have often been cited as a cause of war. Differential fertility rates in various classes of the population have been held to account for changes in the group structure of society.

Many other demographic phenomena influence society and its institutions. Along with gross size and differential fertility rates, we should include general age distribution, regional distribution, ethnic composition, sex ratio, differential mortality and morbidity rates, ratio of population to total land area and to area of arable land, rural-urban ratios, ratio of population to the general technological level of the culture, emigration and immigration rates, and many others. Some of these factors are causes of effects which are not known with certainty, and all of them are the effects of still other unknown causes. Taken all together, it is evident that they cannot be discounted in any attempt to find a solution to the problem of social change.

Political and military factors. Some writers find the secret of social change in the story of military wars and battles, in victory and defeat. Indeed, history itself was until quite recently written almost exclusively in terms of military power. Accordingly, we have a military theory of society and of social change. The function of society, in terms of this theory, is to support the soldiers— the stars of the endless show that we call history. History is understood, in these terms, as a succession of crucial battles, and the story of these battles is the story of social change. The conquest of an army becomes the single factor that explains multifarious changes in the development of a society.

This is an ancient tale, hardly discussable in a brief space. We may pause only to suggest that in so far as it elevates force to a position of preeminence in social change, it suffers from certain sociological inadequacies. Force is always applied in a social context and not in a vacuum, and the character of the context cannot be understood in terms of military power alone. By itself, the military theory of history cannot even explain the sociology of war, a phenomenon with which it is most intimately related.

Furthermore, it is difficult if not impossible to separate the military factor from the political, since wars and revolutions are in most cases political phenomena. Indeed, war has been defined as the continuation of diplomacy by other means, and it has also been said that history is past politics and politics is present history. Certainly political government is a basic social problem for all men, today or many millenniums ago. But the sociological significance of political influences is as yet far from clear.

The role of the "great men." The political or military interpretation of social change leads quickly and easily into the so-called "great man" theory of history. History, it is said, never recovers from the impact of the great man (or perhaps woman); writers like Carlyle or Nietzsche never tired of praising the "hero" or "superman." History, in this sense, is a serialized biography of great men and is to be understood in terms of the achievement of men of genius.

This poses a tantalizing question, Do men make history or does history make men? The greatest of American Presidents, we may note, held office in times of war—Lincoln, Washington, Roosevelt, etc.—and the question of their status in peacetime is not easily settled. Perhaps a case can be made for both sides, but no one can weigh the influence of single individuals in the process of social change with any degree of confidence or any measure of precision. Sociologists in general, in contrast to biographers and most historians, are inclined to be chary of attributing major influence to the activity of a single great man. Human personality is, after all, shaped and formed by the patterns of culture and historical circumstance, and the sociologist tends to interpret social change in terms of deep-lying phenomena of which great men are only surface representations. The question can be debated endlessly; all we can do here is ask it and then go on, not waiting for a reply.

Ultimately, of course, all social change occurs because of the actions of men and women. Culture is not self-innovating, nor are ideas and technology self-creating. Somehow, somewhere in society, they arise in the minds of men. Traditions can be broken, new techniques devised and tried, new ideas or discoveries circulated, and when that happens the stream of culture is disturbed. The ripples may go on indefinitely, or they may die immediately. But in some such way, social change is born.

Other factors. We have mentioned only a few of the factor theories of social and cultural change. The list could be continued indefinitely, for an astonishing variety of factors have some influence on society. Three others, however, merit special attention—the technological, the economic, and the ideological. Accordingly we turn to them in the pages that follow, not, perhaps, because they are more cogent than those we neglect, but because they have received a more comprehensive discussion in the literature of sociology.

The technological factor. Many writers on sociology and allied subjects are proponents of the technological explanation of social change. We cannot consider all of their separate views—they are too numerous—but a detailed discussion of the theory advanced and developed by the prominent sociologist William F. Ogburn will demonstrate the type of approach to social change that concerns us here.

Professor Ogburn begins by dividing culture into two large categories: material culture and nonmaterial culture. He then suggests that changes usually occur first in material culture (though the converse does happen) and that nonmaterial culture then adjusts to these changes. In other words, changes in material culture cause changes in nonmaterial culture, the latter lagging behind and adjusting to the former. In these terms, technological innovation becomes the primary force in cultural change.

Ogburn's theory is not without its appeal, particularly when we consider the changes in living patterns that followed the invention of the steam engine, the printing press, the automobile, and so on. Many other illustrations of the relationship can be culled from history, and Ogburn even suggests that the self-starter on automobiles placed women on an equal footing with men and helped liberate them from masculine dominance. And if the emancipation of women seems like a vast social effect to attribute to a single invention, the answer to that is that other inventions also contributed to the change, particularly those laborsaving devices in the home which electricity made possible. Without such inventions, it is contended, the emancipation of women could not have occurred. Similarly, Ogburn suggests that the invention of the elevator, which made possible the construction of tall apartment buildings had a depressing effect on the urban birth rate because it was difficult to rear children in such surroundings.[1]

To take another example from Ogburn, the Civil War, whose cause has long puzzled historians and sociologists, is attributed to the invention of the cotton gin by Eli Whitney. The explanation which Ogburn gives is as follows:

An invention has a succession of effects, attached more or less as the links of a chain follow one another. The cotton gin seems to have increased the number of slaves, making it possible to increase the planting of cotton, which had the effect of stimulating trade with England, the best policy for which was free trade. The economic system of the South, where cotton was King, then led to conflict with the economic system of the North, based upon a protective tariff favoring infant industries, and ended in the War Between the States.[2]

[1] Cf. William F. Ogburn, *The Social Effects of Aviation*, Houghton Mifflin Company, Boston, 1946, p. 5, and *Machines and Tomorrow's World*, rev. ed., Public Affairs Pamphlets, no. 25, 1946, p. 6.

[2] William F. Ogburn and Meyer F. Nimkoff, *Sociology*, 2d ed., Houghton Mifflin Company, Boston, 1950, plate 20, facing p. 514.

A technological factor, in short, led to a conflict of economic interests and finally to a conflict of arms.

How are we to evaluate this proposition? First of all, we have to relieve Professor Ogburn of any charge of dogmatism, for he does not say that the cotton gin was *the* cause of the Civil War, nor even that the cotton gin was the sole cause of the increase in cotton production. Indeed, he carefully qualifies his thesis, as all competent scholars must, by noting the other factors also operating to produce this effect and other consequences deriving from the same cause. Nevertheless, his emphasis upon the cotton gin is unmistakable, and his preference for a technological explanation of social change is clear.

In the second place, we cannot say what would have happened if the cotton gin had not been invented. The process of history is irreversible, like the passage of time; we cannot repeat history with one of the variables omitted in order to test its influence. We must therefore be prepared to concede that this invention did indeed exert an influence and that it had something causally to do with the events that followed.

But the concession has an interesting and perhaps unfortunate logical consequence, for if the cotton gin is responsible for the War between the States, it is also responsible for everything associated with that war. By a process of free association we can in fact attribute to the cotton gin almost everything that has occurred in American history, and much of what has gone on elsewhere, since its invention. Once the theory is accepted, it proves too much. For if the cotton gin caused the war, it is also responsible for the weakness of the Republican party in the South, for the bolt of the Dixiecrats from the Democratic party in 1948, and for all of the filibusters that have taken place on civil rights bills in the Senate. The theory has the defects of its virtues. If it explains the Civil War, it explains everything remotely connected with that event.

Further, the progression from cause (technological change) to effect (social change) is seldom an easy or automatic process. Some innovations are so reasonable or so efficient that they are adopted almost immediately, and effects follow quickly; others meet strong resistance. Some of the greatest blessings that science and technology have offered man have been resisted for years before they were finally put into use. Inventions alone are not enough; they must also be accepted. Once again we meet the concept of cultural lag, the condition where one part of culture changes more rapidly than other parts, producing a dislocation between them. The ensuing shock often takes a very long time to be absorbed in the tissue of society.

Technological changes in the automobile industry, for example, proceed more rapidly than the highway system can adjust to them. Automobile engineers created automobiles that could travel 80 miles per hour long before the highways could accommodate this speed with safety. In fact, the great turnpikes across the countryside are almost obsolete on the day they are opened to traffic, and the traffic problems of the present seem almost beyond all hope of solution. And this is only one of thousands of possible examples of this type of cultural lag.

Professor Ogburn classifies culture into two great compartments—material culture and nonmaterial culture—and since innovations may appear in either classification, there are four possible causal relationships that may appear: (1) mechanical inventions cause social inventions, (2) mechanical inventions cause other mechanical inventions, (3) social inventions cause other social inventions, and (4) social inventions cause mechanical inventions. The fourth possibility is illustrated by the true-false type of examination, which is a social invention; it gave rise, in time, to mechanical graders that survey thousands of test papers very rapidly.

If innovations may appear in any of these four compartments, the question arises which sequence is more likely. While noting the element of uncertainty involved, Ogburn points out that it is easier to find examples of technological change inducing changes in the social structure than to find examples to the converse, hence that the hypothesis favoring technological change followed by social change seems more likely than its opposite. The point is well taken, and we must concede that the theory is remarkably cogent in these terms, that supporting evidence is common while the theory is almost impossible to disprove. The principal drawback to the theory is doubtless its tendency to prove too much.

A brief glance at history readily demonstrates the strength of the technological theory of social change. For the differences in material culture between the past and present are very striking, and it is frequently remarked that Socrates would have been less surprised by the world of Leonardo da Vinci, a Renaissance man, than by the sight of a modern city such as New York. The Industrial Revolution has changed the physical contours of society and brought a new civilization into being, and the Industrial Revolution was preeminently a technological revolution.

Some questions, however, remain, for even here we meet the very complex problem of uncaused cause. What, we may ask, caused the Industrial Revolution? What encourages man to invent, to search for new techniques? Why are some inventions accepted while others are rejected? What determines when society is "ready" for a particular invention? And how does it happen that the same invention will be made simultaneously and independently by a number of different people? Some of these questions are probably unanswerable. All of them suggest the difficulty of arriving at a definitive evaluation of the technological theory of social and cultural change. However convincing it may appear, must it not at least be supplemented by reference to factors of another kind? The answer would seem to be affirmative.

The economic factor. The economic interpretation of social change is most closely associated with the name of Karl Marx, the "spiritual" father of Communist Russia. This fact makes it unusually difficult to discuss this theory with balance and judgment at the present time. Anything associated with communism is immediately suspect and by some kind of principle of association, any arguments in favor of the economic interpretation of social change are likely to be misconstrued as arguments in favor of the Soviet system of government. This is bad logic. The fact that some 200 million Russians are required to believe the economic interpretation of history does not make the theory true, and for precisely the same reason, it does not make it false either. Nor can logic be distorted to fit another line of reasoning that is sometimes met in these matters: (1) Communists believe that social change has an economic base; (2) some sociologists, economists, and political scientists believe in the same principles; therefore (3) such persons are Communists. This thinking is as sound as the argument that since apples are round and some balloons are round, some balloons are apples.

Actually, the economic interpretation of social change far antedates the life and work of Karl Marx. P. A. Sorokin finds the theory in the works of the ancient Chinese sages, Confucius and Mencius, in the sacred books of the East, and in the Christian Bible.[3] One also finds it expressed, sometimes with great force and clarity, in the writings of Greek historians and philosophers. Thucydides emphasizes the significance of wealth, production, and commerce in determining social change and notes particularly the effect of love of gain on social behavior. And Plato, in the *Republic*, divides the population of his cities into the rich and the poor, noting that they are at war with one another. It is hard to imagine the theory of class conflict ignored completely by any writer on human society, ancient or modern, so important has the economic factor been in human life.

If the number of people who adhere to a doctrine is not a valid criterion of its truth, neither is the age of a doctrine nor the reputation of its proponents. Truth and falsity are both independent of the character of those who promote their various doctrines; that is one of the lessons to be learned from the study of the liberal arts. If the economic interpretation of society is not true because Plato espoused it, neither is it false because it was favored by Stalin. Sociological theory must be evaluated on its own merits.

Actually, there is good reason why men have placed a great deal of emphasis upon the role of economics in human life. It is a biological truism that we must eat to live, and in all but a few cases, we must work in order to eat. Hence the factors involved in the production and distribution of food are in a sense paramount in human life. One of the most important things about

---

[3] Pitirim A. Sorokin, *Contemporary Sociological Theories*, Harper & Brothers, New York, 1928, pp. 514ff. See Sorokin's entire chapter on this subject, pp. 514–599.

us as social creatures is the manner by which we earn our living. And one of the most important facts about any society is the way in which its members produce and distribute goods. All goods, as we have seen, are scarce, and economics is concerned with the allocation of scarce resources among the members of society. All men have economic problems, in this sense, and they develop their own norms and from them the basic character of society. We have here a theory that emphasizes as the prime factor in social change not a change in materiel, as does the technological theory, but a change in the basic norms governing economic relations within society.

Perhaps the most powerful statement of the theory comes from Marx, and since it has been very influential in our own time, perhaps we can use it as a paradigm. In the *Critique of Political Economy,* we find Marx describing the relationship in the following manner:

> In the social production which men carry on, they enter into definite relations that are indispensable and independent of their will; these relations of production correspond to a definite stage of development of their material power of production. The sum total of these relations of production constitutes the economic structure of society—the real foundation, on which rise legal and political superstructures and to which correspond definite forms of social consciousness. The mode of production in material life determines the general character of the social, political, and spiritual processes of life. It is not the consciousness of men that determines their existence, but, on the contrary, their social existence determines their consciousness. At a certain stage of their development, the material forces of production in society come in conflict with the existing relations of production, or what is but a legal expression of the same thing—with the property relations within which they had been at work before. From forms of development of the forces of production these relations turn into their fetters. Then comes the period of social revolution. With the change of the economic foundations, the entire immense superstructure is more or less rapidly transformed.[4]

And in the *Communist Manifesto,* we find these famous lines on the class struggle:

> The history of all hitherto existing society is the history of class struggle. Freeman and slave, patrician and plebeian, lord and serf, guild-master and journeyman, oppressor and oppressed, stood in constant opposition to one another, carried on an uninterrupted, now hidden, now open fight, a fight that each time ended either in a revolutionary reconstitution of society at large, or in the common ruin of the contending classes.

Marx, then, conceives society to be composed of highly differentiated economic interests, pitted against one another for economic advantage, and in this situation, the class struggle is inevitable. At the time when Marx was writing, this

---

[4] Quoted in Sorokin, *op. cit.,* p. 524.

process had crystallized. As he put it, "Society as a whole is more and more splitting into two great, hostile camps, into two great classes directly facing each other; Bourgeoisie and Proletariat." The next century, he thought, would bring open conflict between the two classes, a conflict that would certainly result in victory for the proletariat, who had nothing to lose but their chains, and the classless society would then become a reality. This would be the final revolution in human history; men would henceforth dwell in a communist utopia where no one owned anything and everyone owned everything; and since there would be no property, there would be no social classes.

It is unnecessary to write an extensive refutation of this theory, for in the stark terms in which Marx expressed it, the theory is a vast oversimplification of the process of history. That economic factors are significant in human life no one who works for a living would be inclined to deny. But that all other factors are unimportant is too much to believe. A great many changes occur in society that are only remotely related to changes in the mode of production, and it is surely an exaggeration even to imply that the history of human society is nothing but a record of class conflict.

The sociological theory of Karl Marx is an excessive, dogmatic, and radical variant of an extremely ancient theme. In Marx, the theory acquires a curious inconsistency, for he argues on the one hand that economic factors are all-important and on the other that they will eventually cease to operate. That is, once the classless society is attained, the modes of production apparently cease their changing, or if change continues, they no longer have social consequences. Here, clearly, is political dogmatism and not sociological theory. An otherwise respectable theory of social change is thus subordinated to political expediency and the political freight is more than the sociological locomotive can haul.

Nevertheless, in less extreme and less Marxist terms, there is no doubt that economic factors do play a significant role in social change. It has been possible to correlate changes in economic variables with changes in other variables in society in specific and significant ways. There are, for example, correlations between economic conditions and health, mortality and morbidity rates, marriage and divorce rates, suicide and crime, immigration and emigration, and so on. The business cycle affects these variables and many others in complex and varied ways. Future sociological research will doubtless throw still more light on this fruitful set of relationships. Economic and political phenomena, for example, are very closely related, though even here it is desirable to avoid definitive inferences with respect to the influence of economic factors. Sharp political changes often occur without any noticeable change in the economic variables or the modes of production.

The causal influence, furthermore, is not always a one-sided affair. Political decisions have economic consequences, some of them unanticipated.

Thus the waning of the British Empire in the twentieth century can be attributed in large measure to the effects of two world wars, but the wars themselves cannot be explained completely by examining the economic issues which affected the relations among European nations. The present political alignment in the United States can be illuminated by reference to the Civil War, whether or not the primary causes of that war can be discovered in the operation of economic factors. The notion that the party in power cannot be defeated in periods of prosperity was disproved in 1952. Many other illustrations of the point can be given. It is therefore an error to conclude that when a relationship is established between economic and political phenomena, the former always have causal priority. The situation in society is more complex than that, and simple explanations seem prima facie open to suspicion.

We must, then, hedge our conclusions about the role of economic factors in social change with some caution. The enthusiasm of the Marxist writers stems more from faith in the future than knowledge of the past and present. In certain areas of human behavior, such as politics, the relationship between economics and politics is clear to the careful observer, but in many other parts of human life the relationship may be very obscure. Indeed, an economic explanation of art or music or cathedral building on Marxist lines would be little more than an unsupported bit of speculation. Economic man must eat, certainly, but the whole man must also think and love and create and seek to understand. There is therefore no reason to assume that economic factors are an independent, universal, and sufficient explanation of social and cultural change.

The ideological factor. There remains the theory that deals with the role of ideas in society and concerns itself with what may be called the ideological factor. Earlier, we distinguished between ideas and ideologies, defining the latter as ideas that people in a given society have a moral obligation to believe—an ideology is made of the ideas which the society's norms support. Here we shall consider ideas and ideologies together and attempt to show that they are powerful motivating forces in social change. What people think, in short, determines in very large measure what they do and what they want. It is not surprising, then, that many sociologists should single out ideas as the most important initiating impulses in social change and give to ideological innovations a place of precedence in the solution of this problem.

Once again, we find a rich mass of material to illustrate the thesis, and to keep the discussion within reasonable limits we shall select only one theory, that of the distinguished German sociologist, Max Weber, author of one of the most remarkable pieces of sociological research ever accomplished.[5]

[5] Max Weber, *The Protestant Ethic and the Spirit of Capitalism,* Talcott Parsons (trans.), George Allen & Unwin, Ltd., London, 1930.

Karl Marx had conceived of economic factors as the real fundamentals of human society, as the bottom layer of the cultural pyramid. Social and political organization, art, science, philosophy, etc., were only a superstructure erected on this base. Weber accepted the importance of the economic factor, but he did not accept the Marxian thesis. Instead, he asserted that other factors, including religion or other beliefs, should be taken into consideration.

Weber was too careful a scholar to subscribe to any single-factor theory of social change—a fact that his critics sometimes overlooked—but the net result of his work was to place a heavy emphasis on the ideological interpretation of social change. In effect, when Weber's careful qualifications are ignored, his work stands as a complete repudiation of Marx. Whereas Marx thought that the economic factor determined everything, including religious beliefs, Weber states that economic phenomena themselves rest on an ideological base. He has, in effect, turned Marx upside down.

Let us follow the general pattern of Weber's argument. First of all, he confines himself to one particular economic phenomenon—capitalism—and one particular religious phenomenon—Protestantism—and he refuses to indulge in sweeping and speculative generalizations. The Marxists saw the Protestant Reformation as a consequence of such economic forces as the German revolt against Papal exploitation, or the economic dislocation caused by the influx of gold from the New World. Such assertions are too unsophisticated for Weber. He takes as his thesis the proposition that the development of modern capitalism is at least partly attributable to the Protestant Reformation. He agrees that the profit motive may operate in all civilized societies, but such psychological factors, if they are universal, must also be constant, and they cannot therefore explain a particular social phenomenon appearing at a particular time in history, such as capitalism. It is Weber's thesis that there is something in Protestantism that helped create the system of economic norms that we call capitalism and that it was the Reformation that gave a direct impetus to the development of a capitalistic economy.

Weber develops a new and interesting method by which to study this relationship. What is capitalism? Protestantism? There is no "pure" case of either in history, for they always exist as part of a complex cultural situation, never as isolated phenomena. To avoid this difficulty, Weber introduces the notion of an "ideal type." He will study the ideal type of capitalism, capitalism as it would be if it were historically "pure," and similarly, the ideal type of Protestantism. He knows that these ideal types are not precisely like the capitalism or Protestantism we find in everyday society, but he hopes to learn something of their operation by examining them in this pure form.

Capitalism, in its market phase, is simply a rational bureaucratic organization devoted to the acquisition of pecuniary profit. And Protestantism? Here Weber is less interested in theological doctrine than in what he calls the Protestant *Wirtschaftsethik*, the economic ethic of Protestantism. And this economic ethic he finds ideally exemplified in the aphorisms of Benjamin Franklin as they appear in his *Autobiography*, his *Advice to a Young Trades-man*, and his *Necessary Hints to Those Who Would Be Rich*. Here we find the maxims so familiar to American students, both at home and in school. "Honesty is the best policy." "A penny saved is a penny earned." "Time is money." And so on. Added together, they say in effect that work is a virtue and that it is right and proper and good to earn and save money.

Now this notion that work is a good thing is something relatively new in the history of Western civilization. It is a Protestant idea, for it cannot be found in the Catholic ethic. The latter accords leisure, not work, the higher place. In Genesis, the punishment visited on Adam and Eve for their trans-gressions is plain: Eve and her daughters would henceforth bear their chil-dren in pain, and Adam and his sons would earn their bread by the sweat of their brows. Labor, in this ethic, is no virtue; it is a punishment. One cannot add one cubit to one's spiritual stature by work; work is only a re-minder of original sin. How different the Protestant attitude, where work is something to be done for its own sake, something that is good to do, and even more important, something that contributes to the glory of God.

This attitude toward work has prevailed in Protestant societies since the Reformation, and all of us in the United States, whether Catholic, Protestant, or Jewish, are deeply imbued with the idea. We think that too much leisure is somehow wrong; we must work even when there is nothing to do. Indeed, most of us, when we speak truly, feel a little uncomfortable about sleeping too late in the morning. Our conscience disturbs us. We must work, do some-thing, even if the work is not meant for financial gain.

The first Protestant contribution to capitalism, then, is a changed atti-tude toward work. The Protestant ethic supports gainful enterprise and makes a virtue of what had formerly been a punitive necessity. The new attitude, whether encouraged officially by Protestant preachers or not, became an in-timate part of the ordinary Protestant's beliefs and practices. The stimulus of the new attitude to the development of capitalistic enterprise is obvious.

The second Protestant contribution to incipient capitalism which Weber discovers in his study was the concept of a "calling." It does not appear in Lutheranism; but in Calvinism (Presbyterianism today), the doctrine of pre-destination—the belief that every soul is predestined at birth for heaven or for hell and that nothing the individual does in this life can affect his ultimate fate—is clearly maintained. No one, of course, knows with certainty what his fate will be, but there are signs that may reveal that one is a member of the fortunate group destined for heaven. One of those signs is success in his work or "calling." This may be one of the signals by which God indicates to society those who are predestined for heaven. It is therefore worthwhile to work hard at one's calling, for success can indicate a favorable future, whether the calling is the ministry or the pursuit of pecuniary gain. In any case, hard work contributes to the glory of God, since the calling is part of God's plan for the individual.

To the contemporary reader, this may sound like an uncomfortable doctrine, but so long as it was held by the rising business classes of the sixteenth and seventeenth centuries, it added its share to the general economic climate. Capitalistic enterprise, like any other calling, is part of a master plan, predestined for all eternity, and grace may therefore attach to those who indulge in it. It is easy to see that in terms of this estimation of a calling, one need not enter a monastery, make pilgrimages, or devote himself to poverty, charity, and obedience in order to serve God. One can practice religion in the market place quite as well as in the parish church.

The third contribution of the Protestant ethic to capitalism that appears in Weber's study was also Calvinistic rather than Lutheran. A new attitude toward the collection of interest on loans was produced. Aristotle had said that money could not breed money, and that view was firmly entrenched in Catholic thought in the Middle Ages. Catholic theologians wrote strictures on usury, by which they meant the taking of *any* interest on loans, and not the taking of excessive interest. Before the Reformation, interest and usury were synonyms. Christians could not operate openly as moneylenders because of theological proscription. As a result, the Jews, who suffered no such disability, became the moneylenders of the age, and this was one of the prime sources of medieval anti-Semitism. The prohibition was evaded, of course, but it acted to discourage the accumulation of capital—an essential prerequisite for capitalistic development.

After the advent of Calvinism, the attitude toward interest taking changed completely, and we might say, "officially." In 1545, Calvin wrote a famous letter sanctioning the collection of interest on loans, thus approving a practice that had been forbidden previously. Money could now be openly loaned at interest, capital could accumulate, and money could be "hired" without incurring religious disapproval or jeopardizing the soul. Again, it is easy to appreciate the stimulus which this new idea gave to capitalistic development. The Protestant ethic harmonizes perfectly with the spirit of capitalism. So perfectly, in fact, that it is unlikely that the reader has ever entertained the thought that interest was immoral or improper, yet the belief that it is not is a fairly recent innovation in Western thought.

Weber found various other aspects of the Protestant ethic which favored the development of capitalism. Strictures on the use of alcoholic liquors, for example, are generally somewhat less severe in Catholicism than in Protestantism. Indeed, the prohibition movement in the United States was a Protestant movement almost exclusively. One might say, with only slight exaggeration, that sobriety is more of a Protestant than a Catholic virtue, so long as we avoid the implication that Catholics drink and Protestants do not, for that is not the meaning. The importance of the point for capitalism? As Charles A. Beard wryly commented, "Grass may grow and sheep may graze if the peasant lies drunk under the hedge occasionally, but the wheels of mills cannot turn steadily if the boiler stokers must have frequent debauches."[6]

A growing literacy, encouraged by the Protestant belief that every individual should read his own Bible, together with Luther's translation of the Bible from the Latin to the German, also contributed something to the rational procedures of capitalism. The intoxicated peasant need not be able to read, but the factory foreman must be literate in order to do his job efficiently.

Finally, we may note one further difference between the Protestant and the Catholic ethic which has economic implications. The Catholic calendar is filled with holy days that are not found in its Protestant counterpart. This too is due in part to the contrast beween Catholic belief that leisure is needed to honor God in a suitable manner with meditation or celebration and the Protestant belief that work itself contributes to the glory of God. Work, in short, is more frequently interrupted in one case than in the other. Too many holidays would make the kind of continuous action found in modern factories quite impossible. Capital equipment cannot be employed to full efficiency in the face of frequent interruptions, and the Protestant calendar, coupled with the Protestant attitude toward work, contributed therefore to the efficacy of the capitalistic system.

When we gather these various components of the Protestant ethic together—attitude toward work, exaltation of sobriety, the concept of calling, and the distinction between usury and interest, emphasis on literacy, and reduction of holidays—and note that they are absent from the Catholic ethic, we can begin to appreciate the full significance of the Reformation and more particularly the impact of Calvinism on the development of capitalism. Changing ideas introduced changing norms into the economic structure of society. New ideas brought new practices into being and encouraged the increased production of economic goods (why "goods"?), thus serving as a potent force in the rise of capitalism. In stating this conclusion, we want to remind the reader again that, as important as Protestantism may have been, other factors too were at work in this vast historical process.

We may now ask whether this theory is merely a matter of argument, however reasonable or compelling, or whether there is empirical evidence to support it. The answer is that there is very good empirical evidence indeed on its behalf. All of the countries in which capitalism has attained its highest development are Protestant. In countries where the religious beliefs of the population are divided between Catholicism and Protestantism, it is clear from Weber's evidence that it has been the Protestants, by and large, who

[6] "Individualism and Capitalism," *Encyclopedia of the Social Sciences*, The Macmillan Company, New York, 1930, vol. I, p. 149.

became capitalistic entrepreneurs and who responded to the challenge of the Industrial Revolution. Even the persecuted Protestants, like the Huguenots of France, demonstrated their business acumen in the countries that gave them sanctuary, especially England, Germany, the Netherlands, and the United States. Most striking of all, if one compares the industrial and capitalistic development of Spain and her colonies on the one hand and England and her colonies on the other, the evidence in support of Weber's theory becomes very impressive indeed. After the Reformation, England prospered while Spain declined. Mexico, a Catholic country, is still, like Spain, largely unindustrialized, whereas her neighbor to the north is the exemplification of industrial might.

This, then, is the Protestant ethic, and this is the manner in which an idea, or a series of related ideas, can influence the structure of an economy or a society and become a factor in social change. We have noted that Weber, a careful and studious sociologist, does not weaken his theory by overstatement. Nor does he indulge in sweeping generalizations about the role of ideas in the entire course of historical development. Among the many ideological interpretations of social change, his theory assumes a very high rank. Sociologists who, like Weber, support the ideological interpretation do not deny that economic, political, geographic, and demographic factors disturb the tenor of society as they move through time. But they are convinced that what people think, the ideas they have or acquire, their basic philosophies, have much to do with the character of culture and with the changes that occur within societies.

We have now concluded our examination, in all cases too brief, of the various single-factor theories of social change. This is not the place in which to commit ourselves or our readers to any one of them or even to any combination of them (multiple-factor theories). The problem is too large for introductory treatment and we shall have to be content with the foregoing summary and examples. In the next part of the chapter, we want to look at a different kind of theory, one that appeals to a principle rather than to a factor.

The idea of progress. The notion that each succeeding society, or each succeeding age, is somewhat "better" than or "superior" to its predecessors is so much a part of the American tradition that it may come as a surprise to them to learn that the idea is in fact not very old. It was unknown in Western civilization until the sixteenth century and has never made an appearance in some other societies and civilizations. We have somehow come to accept improvement as a matter of course and to view history as a story of continuous rise or improvement of the quality of society. The future, by inference, will be even brighter than the past.

The notion of progress is wholly foreign to Greek thought. To the Greeks, the golden age lay in the remote and distant past, and each succeeding generation moved further away from perfection. In some of their reflections, this notion is coupled with the idea of eternal recurrence, the belief that everything that has happened will someday occur again, and this is inconsistent. But even in this cyclic conception of history, there is no room for a theory of progress.

Nor does the idea of progress occur in the Middle Ages. The medieval mind was oriented to another world, and the here and now was of little import, scarcely worth expending energy or curiosity upon. Attention was focused on the Day of Judgment, the awesome climax to human life when every man would stand before his Maker and be consigned to torment or to bliss. Here too there is no room for a theory of progress, nor indeed any interest in such a conception as it applied to mundane affairs.

With the Renaissance, social philosophers turned their attention to earthly events and to man, and found there some evidence of progress. We cannot trace the history of the idea here, but the story has been told brilliantly by the late, eminent English historian, J. B. Bury.[7] In the nineteenth century, the idea of progress received additional impetus from an unexpected source —the biological theories of Charles Darwin. It was the sociologist Herbert Spencer who translated the idea into the language of Darwinian evolution, producing a theory which had a great vogue in the United States. Social darwinism dominated late nineteenth and early twentieth century thought, and the history of everything from science to art was written in evolutionary terms. Society itself came to be viewed as a continuous development through regular stages, and all societies were presumed to pass through these stages, necessarily and inevitably, as they evolved.

At the turn of the century, it was rather easy to believe in progress, prosperity, and peace. The century from Waterloo to Sarajevo, as is often remarked, was almost unique in Western history by virtue of its stability and order and enhancement of material possessions. But the First World War, not to mention later events, brought disenchantment, and sociologists began to deny the necessity of progress. The term acquired a normative connotation and lost its "scientific" status. If progress means development in a desirable direction, then it must be said that what some people find desirable others find abhorrent. Several attempts have been made to define progress scientifically and accurately, but sociology has had to abandon the concept. In the process, the concept of evolution, as applied to society and history, was also abandoned. There is some reason to believe that we may have acted too hastily in the case of evolution, for certain changes do occur in society as they grow and mature and these may reasonably be analyzed as evolutionary. But

[7] J. B. Bury, *The Idea of Progress*, The Macmillan Company, New York, 1932.

in the sense in which the term was used in the nineteenth century, it is no longer viable.

Some general theories of social change.

In recent decades, various general theories of social change, new philosophies of history, have appeared, and though we cannot discuss them all in the limited space available here, three of the more prominent theories—those of Oswald Spengler, Arnold J. Toynbee, and Pitirim A. Sorokin—can serve as an introduction to the type of work being done.

Oswald Spengler. Oswald Spengler, once an unknown German schoolmaster, achieved immediate international fame in 1918 with the publication of the first volume of *The Decline of the West.* In this book, Spengler denounces all previous historical writing as based on an erroneous conception of historical time. There is not one linear time, Spengler declares, but as many "times" as there are historical civilizations. Neglecting all primitive societies as "history-less," Spengler discovers eight high civilizations with a similar pattern of development and a similar destiny. Each had an existence like that of a great organism—a birth-adolescence, a maturity, a decline, and a period of decay and disintegration. Spengler refers to the rising phase of a society as a "culture" and to the falling phase as a "civilization." All creativity occurs in the culture period, and when this efflorescence is ended, society turns to the elaboration of techniques and becomes a civilization. Decline is then inevitable. Spengler, in other words, studied the unique history of each civilization, and not the continuous history of man, beginning with an organic framework. He considers Caesar and Cromwell, for example, identical men living in different civilizations; both were inevitable consequences of their civilizations.

In beautiful but pessimistic prose, Spengler announces that our own civilization, one of eight, has passed its peak and that there is nothing left for the future but decay and decline. War and urbanization, he believes, are the portents of this decay.

Spengler's thesis is a curious amalgam of old and new. The view that societies are like organisms is as old as social thought, though few writers have exploited it so extravagantly. The cyclic theory of history, with its ineluctable patterns, is also common in previous historical writing. The combination which Spengler produced, and its application to present civilization, doubtless accounts for the great interest which it generated. The thesis was developed with great learning and literary power, and its importance may be judged by the fact that books and articles about the author and his work still find their way into print. Few modern sociologists, however, will assent to this mystical and speculative doctrine of human history.

Arnold J. Toynbee. Arnold J. Toynbee, the English historian, is the author of a massive project entitled *A Study of History.*[8] It is not in fact, a history of anything at all but a work of pure speculative sociology. Where Spengler discovered eight civilizations, Toynbee finds twenty-one, and with these "cases" before him, he seeks a common pattern of growth, a key to their development, a principle of social change.

Once again, we find it impossible to enter into a detailed discussion of so comprehensive a work, and it would be unfair to the author to outline only the bare essentials. Nevertheless, we must indicate the basic structure of Toynbee's sociological theory, which relies heavily upon two major concepts—the "challenge" and the "response." Every literate society begins life, Toynbee claims, in response to a challenge and works out its destiny in response to further challenges. The initial challenge comes from the environment, the geographic conditions in which society exists. They must not be so favorable that no effort is required to adjust to them, nor so severe that the mere struggle for survival exhausts the energies of the population. When this optimal condition of challenge is met, the society is in a sense started on its way.

Once the initial geographic challenge is met, succeeding challenges tend to be social rather than geographic. They are provided by the internal and external proletariat. Societies survive some of these challenges and succumb to others. And this, in brief, is the story of their development. It is a tale of challenge and response, of withdrawal and return, of rally and rout, transfiguration and integration.

The tone of Toynbee's work is optimistic, in contrast to Spengler. Some societies can utilize the experiences of earlier societies and thus rise to greater heights. The course of history is cyclical, but it is also cumulative, for each cycle may be slightly larger than its predecessors. The interpretation may be called "helical"—like a circular staircase—rather than cyclical. Toynbee's optimism is sustained by his religious faith, by his belief that the Anglican religion represents the highest achievement of mankind. Indeed, his resource to this kind of estimate has induced an adverse critic to remark that Toynbee has buried philosophy of history in an Anglican churchyard.

An evaluation of Toynbee's thesis would be entirely inappropriate here. His scope is spectacular, his learning impressive, and his concepts imaginative. But his conclusions are also unverified, and in a sense unverifiable. Neither the pessimism of Spengler nor the optimism of Toynbee can be justified at present, even by the best historical evidence. We are indebted, nevertheless,

[8] Three volumes appeared in 1933, three in 1939, and four more in 1954, all published by the Royal Institute of International Affairs in London. There is an excellent one-volume abridgement of the first six volumes by D. C. Somervell, Oxford University Press, Fair Lawn, N. J., 1947.

to Toynbee and others like him for their courage, and for an exciting adventure in historical speculation.

Pitirim A. Sorokin. Pitirim A. Sorokin, the distinguished Russian-American sociologist, has also made a major assault on the vast problem of social change in a four-volume work entitled *Social and Cultural Dynamics.*[9] Sorokin sees the course of history as a continuous but irregular fluctuation between two basic kinds of culture, the "sensate" on the one hand and the "ideational" on the other. A "culture" is a system of items and traits that possess some kind of unity, that belong together in some kind of logico-meaningful integration. Not all collections of cultural items have this unity. Some are so heterogeneous that they are mere "congeries," and not systems. A system is built out of consistent items and can be represented, on a small scale, by such things as the multiplication table, an internal-combustion engine, scholastic philosophy, or the musical works of Bach. These systems build into "supersystems," and it is the supersystems which are ultimately either ideational or sensate. A mixed or transitional culture, which Sorokin calls "idealistic," lies between them.

The sensate culture is one in which all human expressions—art, literature, religion, law, ethics, social relations, etc.—appeal to the senses and satisfy sensual needs or desires. An ideational culture, on the other hand, is one in which these expressions appeal to the soul, the mind, or the spirit. Sensate art, for example, is visual, sensational, and photographic; ideational art is symbolic, religious, and often abstract. Sensate sculpture emphasizes the nude human body realistically; ideational sculpture clothes the body in religious vestments. Sensate philosophy invokes the truth of the senses (empiricism), whereas ideational philosophy relies upon the truth of faith (fideism). Sensate psychology is behavioristic while ideational psychology is introspective. Sensate ethics, law, and social relations are "compulsory" and "contractual," rather than "cooperative" and "familistic."

Sorokin devotes several thousand pages to contrasting these two kinds of culture. They are even distinct in mood and temper, for the sensate man says, *"Carpe diem"* (literally, seize the day, or "eat, drink, and be merry, for tomorrow you may die"), while the ideational man preaches the golden rule and turns the other cheek. Science and invention, in these terms, are almost completely sensate accomplishments, and are not to be expected in an ideational culture. Religion, on the other hand, falters in a sensate culture. In sum, the contrast between these two cultures can be expressed briefly by saying that sensate culture is scientific, while ideational culture is religious, and this fundamental distinction pervades every compartment of art and thought and life.

Now Sorokin does not contend that history ever gives us an example of

[9] American Book Company, New York, 1937, 1941.

either type of culture in pure form. He maintains, however, that in various periods of history societies approach these polar positions. The Middle Ages, for example, is a good illustration of an ideational culture; our own century an example of "overripe" sensate culture. Contending that the entire course of Western history can be viewed in terms of these contrasting cultural poles, Sorokin argues that an excess of sensatism produces a reaction which leads to ideationalism, which in turn leads eventually back to sensatism once again.

If this process is inevitable, it is also irregular. History does not move in cycles so much as in fluctuations, and though culture is always moving toward one pole or the other, it does not always reach its limits. It cannot, in any case, move always in one direction; there are limits at which it must turn. This is the "principle of limits," which can be illustrated by a simple but graphic example. If a piano key is struck, a sound emerges from the piano. If the key is struck harder, the sound gets louder. But there is a limit, a point at which you can get a broken piano and not a louder sound. And so with cultures. There comes a time when increasing sensatism produces a reaction, and not further sensatism.

The question arises, of course, as to the basic motivating force in this process. What is the dynamic, the nisus, the urge, or the cause of all this activity? Sorokin answers by appealing to something he calls an immanent self-directing principle of change. Cultures change from ideational to sensate and back because it is in their nature to change thus. An acorn becomes an oak because that is its nature; so also with society. We have once again met the biological analogy. Societies, like organisms, may be destroyed before they complete their natural careers, but in the absence of external destructive factors, the inherent, internal, immanent causes carry the society to its ideational or sensate destiny. Societies change because it is in their nature to change.

What can we say about so imposing a theory? First of all, we must pay deserved tribute to the erudition and industry which produced the theory. But then we must ask some questions. And if we hesitate to accept the theory as it appears, it is because there are three major questions which plague our thoughts when the reading is completed.

We notice, for example, that Sorokin's concepts of "ideational" and "sensate" culture, though perhaps adequately defined, are ultimately subjective rather than objective categories. The author's prejudices "show through" his arguments. The style of the work displays Sorokin's preference for the ideational, and his dislike for the sensate. There is an easily discerned nostalgia for the Middle Ages, a period when truth was established and certain and when all doubts were stilled by authoritarian utterance. There is an animosity to modern science, to technical and industrial civilization, which is plainly evident.

Such sentiments are defensible, and Sorokin, like other men, has every right to express them. There was much of value in medieval life, and much that appears in our own time is tawdry and superficial. It is useful to be reminded that the solution of the world's problems lies in universal acceptance of the golden rule and in the conversion of man to altruism and love. But the sociologist needs to know the cultural and social conditions in which these ethical norms can operate, the conditions that encourage or discourage conformity to them, the reasons why they appear in some societies and not in others, and the factors which make them acceptable to society. These questions Sorokin leaves unanswered.

Nor does it suffice to say, on the sociological level, that cultures change because it is their nature to do so. This criticism Sorokin's work cannot well sustain. One does not explain a phenomenon by asserting that it behaves "naturally," by positing immanent but unknown causes for its operation. An automobile moved by "immanent causation" is satisfactory only to those who know nothing of the mechanics of internal-combustion engines. And similarly for societies. It may be in their nature to change, but this gives us very little knowledge of their dynamics.

Finally, as a third source of skepticism regarding Sorokin's theory, we may suggest that the ideational culture whose virtues he extols is to some extent a creation of his own imagination; it has never been approximated in history. It is a kind of utopia that appears nowhere. Poverty, cruelty, and ignorance are no more admirable in the thirteenth century than in the twentieth, and it is fruitless to deny that these traits characterized the thirteenth century as well as the twentieth. By taking what is best in the Middle Ages, and contrasting it with what is worst in modern times, the earlier age can be made to seem utopian indeed. But such comparisons are just as illicit as the contrary, and they reveal more of the prejudices of the investigator than of the processes of history.

In short, Sorokin has produced a stimulating piece of work and an original theory. It may be said that he avoids some of the pitfalls that trapped his predecessors. But new assaults on the secrets of history are still needed, if indeed there are such secrets.

Summary

We have taken a very long journey in this chapter, and one that has no destination. The problem of social and cultural change remains unsolved. For this, we offer no apologies. A more advanced treatment of the subject would have the same result, though it would involve a more detailed distinction between process and change, single- and multiple-factor theories of change, and a more detailed analysis of social causation.

Here we have only described the problem, suggested its magnitude and magnificence, and indicated some of the solutions that have been proposed. Since the entire chapter is in the nature of a summary, we need not review our conclusions. But we would like to point out that it is here that history, philosophy, and sociology meet, and it may be hoped that the combined efforts of scholars in these disciplines will eventually produce new and more stimulating answers to the ultimate social question.

Review Questions

1. Contrast the study of social statics and social dynamics, and explain why each is necessary for the study of sociology.

2. Differentiate between observation of "cause" and observation of succession. Why is this important?

3. Compare the historian's approach to society with the approach taken by the sociologist.

4. List the major factors that have been used to explain social change, enumerating the advantages and disadvantages or weaknesses of each.

5. Outline briefly the classification of cultures made by William F. Ogburn.

6. What is the significance of economics in social change? What was the value of Marx's contribution to this area?

7. Trace the thesis expounded by Max Weber to show the interaction between religious belief and economic activity.

8. Criticize the idea of "progress."

9. Outline the theory of social change produced by Oswald Spengler.

10. What are the two kinds of culture discerned by Pitirim Sorokin, and what are the characteristics of each?

For Further Study

1. Why is it impossible to think without using the conception of "causality"?

2. Suppose it were definitely proven that the life of man was utterly meaningless. What effect would this have on human behavior?

3. How would you argue for the belief that it is possible to produce a general theory of human social development? Against it?

4. Could you develop a theory of society for an ant colony?

5. Can you defend the idea that mankind is not really progressing at all?

CHAPTER 19

Contemporary
Political
Issues

In this chapter, we move from the discussion of broad and general political questions that arise in every society in every era to the more detailed and specific problems that confront mankind, and our own society in particular, in the present age. Since we are all so directly involved in these matters, it is peculiarly difficult to maintain our objectivity and detachment—to avoid the influence of the Baconian "Idols." A discussion of American-Soviet relations or of the civil rights issue is less likely to pass without controversy than a discussion of eighteenth-century politics. This places a special burden on both the reader and the author. The course of the argument must be followed more closely and self-consciously than usual, and the argument should be evaluated, so far as is possible, on its merits. Despite the hazards, the task is worth undertaking, for political study must serve the present as best it can, and some awareness of contemporary political issues is essential to political competence and sound citizenship.

We shall limit our discussion to two major points: First, to the character of the world system as it has developed in recent decades; second, to the major issues in current American politics, particularly the issue of civil rights. The first type of problem obviously requires the cooperative efforts of several states for solution; the second affects only our own society, though it is often intimately related to the first—domestic problems cannot be completely separated from international problems. We cannot hope to "solve" any of the questions that are raised by these issues, or even to delineate them fully in a brief space, but the exposition can serve to remind us of the immense diversity of politics and of the different impact of politics on the lives of members of our own and other societies.

CONTEMPORARY WORLD PROBLEMS

The present-day state system is a complex and diversified structure in which tension and conflict seem the norm rather than the exception. The political observer who surveys the path of world politics in the mid-twentieth century can hardly avoid being struck by the extent to which political problems occupy mankind and by the degree to which international problems have come to affect the entire population of the world. True, there are still areas of the globe in which people are essentially unconcerned with political matters, but interest in world affairs is certainly growing, and with good reason. A second striking feature of the world system is the rate at which change is taking place, for it is probably true that human institutions are altering more rapidly today than ever before in man's history. Given this kaleidoscope of political activity, it is not easy to separate what is permanent and enduring and significant from what is transient and fleeting and irrelevant. One cannot easily discern fundamentals in the welter of detail that modern research has uncovered. Yet there are certain fundamentals which are clearly significant for us all, and on these matters we shall concentrate in the discussion that follows.

The state system. The national state is still the dominant political institution in the contemporary world, though it has undergone some basic changes in the past three centuries. The states themselves are unique and variegated. Some are rich; others are poor. Some are large; others small. Some are old; some new. Some are democratically governed; others are authoritarian despotisms. Each state remains legally and technically sovereign, bound only when it chooses to be bound. Thus the international system is basically anarchistic, like Hobbes's "state of nature" in which the normal relationship between individuals was assumed to be a war of "all against all." The short-term future of the state systems seems assured. The long-range future, however, is less sanguine, for as we have already remarked, there are good reasons to suppose that the state is growing increasingly less capable of performing its essential political functions—protection of the population against external attack and maintenance of internal order and stability.

No state can today guarantee the safety of its population by its own efforts, and it is even doubtful that the guarantee can be made in concert with others. This is obvious when we consider the position of the smaller states, and modern weapons technology has placed the very large states in the same fix. Hence we find the states, large and small, joining together to maximize their individual security. And the smaller states are often faced with a forced choice which is peculiarly difficult to make. The political activities which may lead to conflict are not of their doing, yet the consequences of war will affect them equally with the active participants—nuclear effects do not differentiate between combatant and noncombatant. Security, in other words, has really become a world problem, demanding the cooperation and concern of the whole family of nations. It is utterly beyond the power of any single state, though it might be solved by agreement among the major powers.

Significantly, recent political events seem to indicate that the smaller national state is growing less able to maintain its own internal order—though this is not true of the major powers. For example, it is commonplace for one political society to seek economic assistance from others or even military assistance for a struggle against domestic opponents. Further, it sometimes happens that the large states interfere in the domestic affairs of small states with or without a request for assistance. In both cases, domestic politics ceases to be a means by which domestic problems are solved and becomes an arena in which the issues of world politics are fought. When the government of a Middle Eastern nation asks for American or Soviet assistance to maintain internal order it is really admitting the bankruptcy of its own political system. And when the United States and the U.S.S.R. support opposing factions in Laos or Vietnam, they have simply transferred international politics to another battleground; the issues at stake may have nothing whatever to do with the political or economic needs of those who occupy the field of battle.

Polarization. Much of this activity can be attributed to a second major characteristic of the contemporary political world—the division of the world into two immense power blocs, one led by the United States and the other by the Soviet Union. This may well be the most significant political fact of our times, for the fate of the world, or even the future of man, seems to depend on the manner in which the blocs carry on their mutual relations, on the goals they seek, and on the means they employ to achieve them. This much is of course commonplace, but a more detailed examination of the structure reveals some interesting conditions that might escape a cursory glance.

For one thing, not all of the nations of the world have gravitated into the bipolar world system, and some observers have claimed that the trend to polarization has in fact diminished in recent years. The nature of the conflict between the two blocs has tended to press the antagonists into competition in these uncommitted areas, thus avoiding head-on collisions. Each side seeks support from world opinion, and each hopes to gain support among the uncommitted nations. Both seek to extend their influence into areas where there is a "power vacuum." Obviously, neither side has need for military assistance from these countries, for each is well supplied with the equipment needed to devastate the other. In fact, the quest for "uncommitted" support has generally proved expensive, and not infrequently has been very embarrassing to both sides. The United States, for example, finds it somewhat difficult to rationalize its support for reactionary regimes in Asia and the Middle East, for the fascist dictatorship in Spain, and even the Communist dictatorship in Yugoslavia, and the U.S.S.R. has been embarrassed on occasion by the behavior of its ally, Communist China, particularly in India and other parts of Southeast Asia. Support, in other words, is often bought at very high prices.

What is the purpose of polarization? What do the power blocs seek? Nominally, each seeks its own safety and protection, and each assumes hostility and antagonism on the other's part; hence it seeks to thwart the intentions of the other as far as possible. They do not, of course, seek a balance of power; rather they are concerned to achieve an imbalance of power in their own favor. Each side, in other words, fears the efforts of the other to achieve world hegemony, and each is in some measure driven to seek world hegemony in order to impede the efforts of the other. Both sides assert that they are prepared, under conditions not clearly defined, to undertake nuclear war. Each has the capacity to destroy the other. Neither side can at present prevent retaliation in kind. Hence the end result is a sort of nuclear stalemate, a "balance of terror," as it has been called, which has continued since the 1950s. Neither side intended this outcome, but the impasse can be broken only by war, by a major technological advance which would give one or the other an overwhelming advantage, or by mutual agreement. Neither alternative seems likely in the immediate future.

How did this situation come about? Basically, the polarized world is the outcome of the breakdown of Great Power cooperation in World War II and the search for individual security that followed. The actual cause of the breakdown, the location of fault, is complex and obscure, though each side convinces itself that its own position is just and that the other is totally at fault. Soviet fear and ambition must certainly weigh heavily in the scales as a source of disunity, though what was due to fear and what to ambition no one can say. For the Western part, if intentions were not always clear and unambiguous, and if some elements of Western opinion were decidedly hostile and even aggressive toward the U.S.S.R. after 1945, it remains true that the Western nations made a prolonged and serious attempt to secure Soviet friendship, even though the delay badly hampered the economic rehabilitation of Europe. It is probably too easy to look back and ascribe to the U.S.S.R. an expansive and aggressive urge based on present performance, an urge to world conquest fostered by an expansive ideology and a desire for world domination. But the historian will probably conclude that the major share of the responsibility lies with the insular, hostile, and myopic rulers of the Soviet state.

There were, of course, excellent grounds for Soviet fear and suspicion of the West in 1945. The history of Soviet-Western relations was hardly conducive to mutual trust, excluding the wartime period. Russia had been invaded in 1919, the "White" forces of anticommunism had been assisted materially by Western powers in their attempt to overthrow the Bolshevik regime. The Soviet Union was unlikely to forget that fascism had been nurtured on anticommunism, and applauded for its attitude, nor that many members of the family of nations had refused all dealings with the Soviet regime for years. Yet when all this is said and done, fear alone will not suffice to explain Soviet conduct after 1945. Ambition too played its part, and hostility to the West or contempt for Western institutions and traditions were ill-concealed at best. We should be aware of the conditions that existed in 1945, but that need not lead to apologetics.

If we examine the development of a polarized world from the Western point of view we get quite a different picture. In general, public opinion was friendly toward Russia after 1945, and official opinion, if suspicious, was certainly not fearful. The United States, after all, allowed its military establishment to be reduced to almost nothing in the two years following the war, and made no serious effort to rearm until after the Korean conflict. As the years passed, suspicion turned to fear and hostility and, at times, to something near mass hysteria—particularly in the United States. The events which led to this change of attitude are too numerous to catalog, but we can mention the activities of the Communist parties in Italy and France and Greece, the rapid consolidation of Soviet influence in Eastern Europe, and Soviet intransigence in Germany as major factors. The real break came in 1947, when the U.S.S.R. refused to take part in the Marshall aid program, and forced her satellites to do likewise, meanwhile consolidating her hold over Eastern Europe by a series of repressive purges of the existing coalition governments.

There followed a period of mounting hostility, between 1947 and 1950, though even then the United States did not really show alarm and begin to rearm. The Berlin blockade caused great concern in the West, though fear died down when the initial crisis passed. The Communist victory in China in 1949 was a great blow, to the United States particularly, though it is hard to see what might have been done to change the outcome short of full-scale warfare—for which the United States was not prepared. Various preliminary moves were made, in 1948 and 1949 (NATO, etc.) which reflected this increased tension and uneasiness and concern with Soviet intentions.

The final straw was the Korean conflict, widely accepted as an illustration of Soviet willingness to risk war for expansion (a dubious proposition, in this case). It began a decade of rapid militarization in the West, largely under strong American pressure. The disaffection of some few American troops in Korea produced, for a time, an almost pathological fear of "communism," poorly defined, augmented by the discovery of minor subversion at home. This paved the way for the rather unpalatable activities of Senator McCarthy and his followers in the early 1950s. For a time, it is unlikely that any American government could have reached a genuine agreement with the U.S.S.R. without running the risk of being denounced for treason—a most unhealthy situation. Since the mid-1950s, some measure of calm has been restored, though serious negotiation is still very difficult to achieve.

Much of Western fear of Russia is a consequence of the authoritarian nature of its political regime and the techniques it has used to control its own population and its satellites. Russia achieved domination in Eastern Europe by a combination of force and coercion and subversion; it maintains its position by using repressive police regimes, backed by Soviet military force. The possibility that these same techniques might be extended to Western Europe, or even to the United States, has strongly influenced Western opinion —rightly or not. The American people in particular have viewed Soviet policy with a curious amalgam of moral indignation, idealism, naïveté, and hard-headed realism that is very hard to describe accurately.

There is, at bottom, a well-founded belief that dictatorship is dangerous, militaristic, and aggressive, that it will eventuate in another world conflict, and that Russia is a dictatorship. It is certainly true that totalitarianism has had a sorry history in this century. Invariably, it has been accompanied by all of the paraphernalia of the police state, and in every case, it has led to war. The line of reasoning is simple and attractive. Russia is totalitarian. Totalitarianism is aggressive and warlike. Ergo, Russia is bent on world domination. If this means only that the U.S.S.R. will seek to expand its influence by every means available, the attitude is tenable. But it cannot mean that the Soviet Union is deliberately seeking a world war as a means to world domination. In fact, the terms of the Marxist ideology would lead to quite a different conclusion: why risk a trial at arms when your side is bound to win in the long run in any event? Further, wars are not won or lost in these days of nuclear power, as everyone, including the rulers of Russia, knows full well. The recent rulers of Russia are hostile and determined, but they seem not to be maniacs. They pursue their own interests vigorously and with every means available to them. But it is hard to see, on rational grounds at least, how these interests could possibly include a world war.

While it would not be exactly true to say that the world has polarized along lines which separate the democracies from the dictatorships, the assertion is generally true and worth consideration. On the Western side, the hard core of the bloc is made of nations of Western Europe and the Western Hemisphere which are part of the liberal-democratic tradition; the hard core of the Soviet bloc is certainly dominated by the totalitarian states. One bloc holds together by agreement, the other by force and repression. Although the Western bloc includes nations or governments that cannot meet the test of democratic standards, like fascist Spain or the military dictatorships in most of South America, there is nevertheless a fundamental distinction between the two sides. There is a difference in outlook, in values, and in techniques of political action, and Western observers quite naturally consider this distinction vital. The point is valid, so long as the difference is not caricatured into the terms of a television Western, with the "good guys" on one side and the "bad guys" on the other. The popular press often takes this line, and this is unfortunate, for partly informed cynicism may lead to the belief that the distinction between the blocs is wholly without meaning. This is not really the case, though some of the neutral nations at times imply that there is little to choose between the two sides. A distinction can be made, not sharp and clear-cut, perhaps, but quite significant for those reared in the liberal-democratic tradition. It has to do with respect for the individual, with belief in the fundamental integrity of man, and with other similar assumptions, and it ought not to be blurred by indiscriminate and oversimplified generalizations.

Militarization. A third characteristic of modern world politics, one of the causes and the effects of world tension, has been the steady militarization of the two great power blocs. Military forces have each year grown larger, more complex, and more costly. And perhaps more important, military considerations have come to exercise an increasing influence over the domestic and international policies of the governments in both blocs. The implications of this development are both extensive and very important.

Each bloc begins with a basic military establishment which includes a substantial nuclear force whose dimensions are unknown, but which may be assumed capable of destroying a large part of the enemy's population and productive capacity. There is usually a large conventional army, with air and naval equipment to match. Further, no self-respecting Great Power can today do without a very large research establishment, aircraft of all sorts, submarines, rockets, and the other implements of the warrior's trade. Substantial armies are stationed far beyond the nation's borders to guard defense perimeters that reach to the enemy's borders. The Soviet Union is virtually surrounded; the United States is heavily threatened from nearly every direction. Compulsory military training has become an accepted part of national life, and society has had a new dimension added to its thinking.

Militarization, as everyone knows, is an expensive business. How expensive, it is probably impossible to say, when both direct and indirect costs are added together. The adjacent table gives us some idea of the basic direct costs of the American military establishment. Notice the sharp rise in costs after 1950 as the United States began to rearm. About two-thirds of the national budget is now earmarked for security items. Since the Soviet national income is much smaller than ours, we can assume that national defense spending forms an even larger part of government disbursement in Russia.

A high rate of military spending tends, of course, to gear the national economy to military production. The nation accumulates a great deal of specialized capital equipment, trained workers, etc., whose continued employment depends upon a continuation of defense spending. Whole industries may develop around defense contracts, and areas like the state of California, thickly populated by defense plants, depend very heavily upon this kind of income. The long-range effects of this type of spending need careful thought, for if the government spends something over $40 billion each year on military supplies, etc., and the multiplier effect is calculated, we can see how much this affects our total national income.

The indirect social costs of militarization cannot be calculated in dollars and cents or in tax rates. Young men must take time from their education or career to serve with the Armed Forces. There are hidden costs like family

Year	Total budget, billions	Major national security, billions	Per cent of total
1945	98	81	82.7
1946	60	43	71.7
1947	39	14	37.0
1948	33	12	35.7
1949	39	13	32.7
1950	40	13	32.9
1951	44	22	51.1
1952	65	44	67.4
1953	74	50	68.1
1954	68	47	69.6
1962	88	51	58.2

SOURCE: U.S. Bureau of the Census, *Statistical Abstract of the United States:* 1963, 84th ed., Washington, D.C., 1963.

displacement or the development of particular attitudes of mind within the population. The whole community may have to rearrange its social ideals and tolerate activities traditionally enjoined in the society. The voices of military leaders acquire considerable weight in the nation's councils, and political decisions may be predicated increasingly upon military needs, endangering personal rights and social institutions and ideals. Even domestic political matters like taxation or government financial aid to educational institutions may be studied for military implications and planned accordingly. Let us look at an illustration of the point.

Militarization has generally led to the mobilization of science and technology in the service of the state on an unprecedented scale. A very substantial part of our American technological and scientific manpower, for example, is engaged directly or indirectly in military research. The fact that government controls the manufacture and use of nuclear materials forces it to seek out a large body of scientists to carry on this essential work, and most nuclear research is directed primarily toward military and not civilian use. The military services themselves employ thousands of scientists and technicians in their rocket programs, in meteorology, and in various related areas. Many scientists are indirectly engaged in military research because the firm which employs them is working on government contracts. Others are engaged on research projects sponsored by the government and paid for with government funds. In sum, government today controls and directs a very large part of the scientific activity carried on in the nation, largely because of its military needs. We must grant immediately that many research findings have both civilian and military applications, and that this skill and talent are not entirely wasted. But the basic fact remains that a very large part of our most highly trained manpower is directed toward goals not of their own choosing, owing to the increased emphasis upon military security in our time. Science has been "nationalized" to a surprising degree.

"War and Peace." Curiously enough, the institution of war today occupies a somewhat anomalous position, despite the great increase in emphasis upon military preparedness. The search for national security is certainly the most important single political problem of the age, yet it is now widely recognized that the ability to wage war and the actual waging of wars are two different matters. War is not really a way out of the dilemma; it is only an admission that efforts to find a way out of the dilemma have failed.

The reason is fairly obvious. Wars have grown progressively more inclusive and more destructive as technology has placed new weapons in the hands of modern armies. The old distinctions between military and civilian, belligerent and neutral, have largely disappeared. The first milestone along the road to modern war, the destruction of Hiroshima and Nagasaki, has long since been passed. Hydrogen weapons, unlimited in size, and rocket systems beyond the capacity of present defense systems to intercept have made the older fission weapons obsolete. The immediate destructive power of the fusion weapon beggars the imagination; a single bomb could quite easily reduce the whole of Manhattan Island to nothingness. And beyond the direct effects of blast and heat lurk the deadly side effects of radiation and fallout. Fusion weapons can contaminate the whole atmosphere in a matter of hours or render the soil incapable of sustaining life for a century or more. They may alter the genetic structure of children yet unborn, producing mutants whose qualities we may only imagine. No one can today calculate the full effects of exploding hundreds or thousands of these devices in a relatively short period of time. But it is usually conceded that man now has the capacity to exterminate the human race, or at least to reduce man to a mere shadow of his present eminence on earth. It is a very frightening possibility, to say the least.

Here, it might appear, is the weapon that has truly made war impossible by making it so horribly destructive that concepts like winning or losing have no meaning. Yet medieval man thought that gunpowder would accomplish this end. Vain hope! Much the same thing seems to be true today, for war remains very much a possibility in modern politics. It may be that only madmen would deliberately court war under these conditions, yet we must realize that perfectly sane and normal persons spend a great deal of time considering the possible effects of atomic warfare and planning the best course of action to follow should it occur. This is their job and they must do it. Does this mean that man is bent on self-immolation? Were the tragedians of ancient Greece right in their belief that man is driven by forces beyond his power to control to conclusions not of his choosing? If the "lunatic fringe" is excluded, no one today seeks war for its own sake, and no one is prepared to argue that there is anything to be gained by making war. Instead war is universally viewed as an awful tragedy which everyone ought to avoid. No one desires war. Yet everyone realizes that war is very much a possibility.

If war is deplorable on humanitarian grounds and in terms of self-interest as well, how is the security problem to be solved? Some men suggest that war be outlawed, usually by some means left unclear. But this is not really a solution. So long as men accept the right of the national state to defend its own vital interests by any means available, nations will in the last analysis resort to war rather than accept certain eventualities. It would be futile to expect sovereign national states to refuse to make war when their own independence was threatened. A similar dilemma arises when disarmament is suggested, for disarmament depends upon faith, and if the mutual trust needed for disarmament were present, then the need for disarmament would disappear. In any case, disarmament assumes that war cannot be fought without weapons, and modern technology has the capacity to channel its activities into either warlike or peaceful purposes very rapidly. Disarmament might expand the time needed to prepare for war, but it could not eliminate the means of securing arms. That is a consequence of industrialization.

The national states have sought security by other means and have concluded, in the last analysis, that the best way to prevent war is to *increase* armaments to the point that no nation dares attack another for fear of the consequences. This principle underlies the policy of "massive retaliation" followed by the United States during the 1950s. A combination of nuclear weapons and strategic aircraft, or rockets, was expected to serve as an effective deterrent against attack. The program was simple, relatively cheap, and attractive. But its principal strength proved its undoing. If retaliation is to be effective it must be truly frightful. But if it is frighful, it cannot be unleashed without good cause. This poses a real practical problem: What *is* a good cause? A blockade of Berlin? An invasion of Formosa? Bombing of an American city? Stationing rockets on Cuba? And if massive retaliation is not to be used except as a drastic measure, what is to be done about small conflagrations?

More recently, the United States has moved toward a more flexible military apparatus, including highly mobile ground forces, varied air forces, large and complex rocket systems, submarines, etc., which may deal with small local troubles as well as massive world problems. The stalemate therefore continues, with the Western powers seeking now to block up the gap left by concentration on strategic bombing. Neither side has yet gained a sufficient advantage to force the other side to yield, fight, or negotiate.

At this point, the only sensible course of action might appear to be some mutual recognition of the impasse and a negotiated agreement to live and let live. Negotiations have, of course, been carried on, but without any great success. Neither side has been prepared to negotiate on an unequal basis, or even on the basis of equality; they wish to "negotiate from strength," as the phrase goes, which means negotiation from a position of superiority. More important is the almost total absence of good faith or trust on both sides; without it, there can be no successful negotiation. Public opinion, moreover, has been educated to hostility for some years, and neither side can undo the past overnight. There are, in other words, various psychological attitudes at work in the modern world, and to these attitudes we now turn.

Psychological attitudes. The attitudes and beliefs of whole populations, the fears and insecurities, the ideological convictions, the accepted truths of society, these are psychic and psychological factors of the first importance on the present world scene. Every society has its own ideology, its political verities, its attitudes toward itself and others, its stereotypes and caricatures.

They are firmly embedded in the language of society, in the norms, and in the techniques of political discussion. There are objects of hate and fear, of respect and reverence. There is the friend and the enemy. No government can avoid or ignore the psychological factor, whether it is a democracy or a totalitarian system.

Today, fear and insecurity are the common lot of all peoples, but the objects feared or hated are usually different. The newly emerging nations are commonly resentful of the colonial powers and very sensitive about their own status. The American fears or even hates the Soviet Union, or more commonly, the vague and nebulous "thing" that he calls communism. Doubtless the Soviet citizen has a vision of Americans dominated by vicious capitalists, lashing the backs of their exploited wage slaves. Both ideas are wrong, but they are social facts, for beliefs need not be true to be important. They condition the actions of the believer equally in either case. If the American believes that the Soviet rulers are monstrous savages with a lust for blood—his blood—then he will act as though this were true and it might just as well be true so far as he is concerned. Ideologies of this sort produce intolerance, bigotry, and a very dangerous tendency to consider all incoming information in terms of the ideology, rather than in terms of truth or falsity or credibility.

However, when this much has been said, it does not mean that the contemporary world is dominated by a conflict which arises out of ideological differences, or that the polarization of world politics follows ideological lines. Of course, every society has its own national ideology, and in this sense the conflict between the United States and the Soviet Union is a conflict of nationalisms. For the principles of American nationalism presume a hostile and aggressive Soviet Union, and Soviet nationalism contains similar provisions directed toward the United States. In these terms, there is an ideological conflict. But it would be foolish to say that American citizens are torn between their own ideological convictions and those of the Soviet Union, and there is as little likelihood of a Soviet citizen accepting American principles as the converse. Neither side in fact weighs the merits of the other's ideology objectively—that would be "unideological." In fact, it might be considered treason to make the attempt in moments of extreme tension. But in this direct sense, it is probably more accurate to speak of conflicting nationalisms than to picture a conflict between Soviet communism and some vaguely defined American ideology which transcends nationalism.

A true ideological conflict does appear when a third party is involved in the conflict between the two great power blocs, when each bloc seeks support and influence in a third nation. In such cases, each bloc proposes a different body of social and political principles, as we have already mentioned, and the difference between them is meaningful, however difficult it may be to define them perfectly. The trouble is that each peddles abroad an ideal somewhat different from its own practice; each projects its ideal culture rather than its real culture. Thus each bloc claims to be "more democratic" than the other, to offer its citizens a better way of life than the other. One of the major problems in American foreign relations, as we have noted before, is to concentrate on reality rather than preachments, and find some means of convincing the uncommitted that the principles of free society, honestly propounded, are with all their faults more likely to lead to a satisfactory social life than the totalitarian-collectivist alternative which the Soviet Union practices at home.

Interdependence. Despite the deep political divisions that appear on the contemporary international scene, there has been a steady increase in the amount of interdependence among nations in recent decades. In fact, polarization has really acted to underline the growth of interdependence to the degree that it demonstrates the limited capacity of the individual state to ensure its own security and economic well-being. Today, there is growing recognition of the fact that some social and economic and political problems must be solved by all men acting in concert. The security problem is an obvious illustration of the point, but human interdependence today goes far beyond security measures and common defense.

For example, most of the wealthier nations of the world, the fully developed regions, accept some measure of responsibility for the improvement of economic and social conditions throughout the world as a matter of self-interest if for no other reason. In practice, the amount of assistance that has been made available is still small, but the principle is clear. American economic assistance to Europe, for example, involved recognition by the United States that its own prosperity was bound together inextricably with the prosperity of the Europeans. The principle was greatly expanded in the Point Four program, the Peace Corps, and similar measures. Other countries have followed the same principles within the limits of their economic strength.

Oddly enough, interdependence is greatest among the more highly developed nations, leaving aside the fundamental security problem. No modern industrial nation could maintain its economic system without resources from beyond its own borders, and the extent to which industrial progress depends upon the free movement of scientific information across national boundaries is not always appreciated. The general public is, however, growing increasingly aware of the extent to which the nations of the world are interdependent, and this realization has been much stimulated by such events as the International Geophysical Year which call attention to the accomplishments that can be made through international cooperation.

SUMMATION. In the realm of international relations, then, the basic problem is to find or maintain peace and security. The United Nations simply cannot perform this function because it depends upon the very cooperation among the Great Powers that would eliminate polarization and the security problem it produces. Each major power has therefore had recourse to armaments and alliances as a means of maintaining its integrity, and there are strong psychological factors at work within the national boundaries to maintain the existing political arrangement. Over the whole scene we see the awful power of atomic weapons as a grim reminder of the consequences of a serious error in political judgment.

Beyond the security problem lie a whole congeries of political and political-economic difficulties which are sometimes overlooked because of our concern with security. Modern technology has forced an unprecedented degree of interdependence upon the peoples of the world, and modern power standards have sharply altered the balance of power in the world community. Behind the screening influence of military affairs, numerous significant political developments are occurring. One of the most important is the economic unification of Western Europe. Another is the gradual decline of colonialism and the emergence of new nations on the international scene, bringing with them new ambitions, new goals, and new problems.

SOME MAJOR AMERICAN POLITICAL PROBLEMS

The major political problems which the United States faces in the contemporary world are of two types: first, there are problems which stem from or are directly related to the international situation and America's position in the world today; second, there are domestic problems, not necessarily less significant, which may or may not influence foreign affairs, or be influenced by them. We can here consider only a few of these—the effect of the quest for national security on internal affairs and the fundamental problem of civil rights as it appears in the mid-twentieth century. Others perhaps just as significant must be laid aside for more advanced work in political science.

The changing social pattern. Politics operates against the broad background that society as a whole supplies, and the student of politics must take into consideration certain general tendencies in society which influence political behavior in a subtle but significant manner. It is a truism that American society is today changing at amazing speed. The population has increased rapidly; the nation grows more urbanized and mechanized every year; technological change, industrial growth, increased population density, increased social organization—all act to depersonalize and institutionalize social relations and political relations. The individual has lost ground steadily in the race with organization. Today, men must organize to be heard, whatever their goals. It is the group, rather than the individual, that counts, whether we are discussing politics or the sciences or labor unions or even social recreation.

Since World War II, American society has come under detailed and searching analysis from psychologist, sociologist, economist, political scientist, and a host of others concerned to determine the major trends in present-day America. The movement toward regimentation, the impulse to conformity, the pressure to fit personality to group requirements—whatever it may be called by individual scholars—has appeared in every study. Here is a social phenomenon that is most important, though presently inexplicable. It marks a certain loss of concern with personal identity and achievement—a major departure from the traditional value structure of the society. It implies a growing concern with the opinions of others, a tendency to "other-directedness" as against concern for personal interests. The hallmark of the era seems fast becoming the organization man, the small cog in the very large machine, the "integrated" personality. Is this, as Erich Fromm claims, a desire on the part of the individual to escape from the responsibilities of personal freedom? No one can say with certainty, of course. But it seems true that the individual in America has moved from the aggressive self-assertion that characterized society a half century ago toward a more passive identification of social with personal interests. There has been, concurrently, some loss of individual responsibility for social policies, a decline of personal identification with personal aspirations, an increase in "anomie," and a loss of the feeling of personal significance.

What consequences for politics are implied in this trend? Here is one of the more interesting, if speculative, areas in contemporary political discussion. Democracy, some critics of the trend have argued, depends upon a close and meaningful personal relationship between the individual and the political system, some sense of personal involvement in politics, particularly at the local government level. Without some sense of responsibility, some degree of commitment, some desire to master events rather than drift with them, democratic government in the traditional sense of the term is impossible. Such critics suggest that group-oriented social attitudes are incompatible with democratic necessity, that current social trends tend to ready acceptance of charismatic leadership, to making men followers and not leaders. It is argued, moreover, that conformity leads to intolerance and that the regimentation of opinion leads to a decline in the vitality of political speculation and criticism, a tendency to substitute authoritative assertions for discussion and rational argument. Such arguments are perhaps too speculative, or too strongly worded, but the social facts from which they derive are well documented, and the point needs further exploration. Individualism, in other words, is declining in the United States, and social pressures move men to greater conformity, regimentation, and group-oriented behavior. Enormous social forces are at work grinding the individual to fit a mold which he neither chooses nor desires.

A few illustrations may help clarify the point. Substantial numbers of social activities once considered the prerogative of the individual are today social functions, organized and directed by society and, in many cases, operated by professional organizers. Social welfare is now primarily a state rather than a family or personal responsibility. Recreational activities are increasingly organized; "Little League" baseball, for example, replaces the "pick-up" games of three or four decades ago. College athletics are highly organized, semiprofessional affairs in some schools. Professional sports, spectator events, and nonparticipation recreations of various sorts have boomed in the postwar years. Even the sciences have not been immune to the trend, for the day of the individual scientific genius working alone in his laboratory is ended. Today's scientist is part of an integrated team, working toward goals he does not choose for himself, using elaborate and expensive apparatus far beyond the financial capacity of the private citizen. We narrate these items without judgment. They are simply the facts of modern social life, easily seen in almost any phase of human behavior.

What makes the trend very important is the evidence that seems to show that the American people have, for the moment at least, lost direction and begun actively and openly to search for "national goals"—a form of activity unheard of just a few decades ago. It seems that traditional materialism and pragmatism are losing some of their magic. The emotion-laden ideals of the nineteenth century have lost their appeal to some, and the population is growing more knowledgeable, or more cynical. Certainly the modern university student is far better informed and more critical than his grandparents were; he no longer accepts the hoary maxims of Franklin at face value, and he seems less convinced of the desirability of ceaseless ambition, of striving to satisfy the self, of risking all to gain all. He is, according to recent surveys, more willing to sacrifice rewards for security and contentment and less risk. College graduates, for example, willingly accept lower salaries to enter a large corporation where employment is secure, progress slow but reasonably certain, and the pension plan well established. Are we, as one popular author recently said, becoming a "nation of sheep"? If so, what are the political consequences likely to be? It is a point that bears close attention and careful thought.

Civil liberties. The whole concept that we know as political democracy rests on the assumption that each individual citizen has certain rights, privileges, and immunities which government may not transgress or eliminate. Free speech, a free press, freedom of association, free access to information, freedom of criticism—these are fundamentals in our political order. So also are conceptions like the basic equality of all citizens, regardless of race, color, or creed. When government action infringes upon these fundamentals, a whole congeries of questions arises, questions which are referred to broadly as problems of *civil rights*. Few political issues in recent years have generated so much discussion and argument.

The "civil rights" of the American citizen—his rights *against* his government—are defined in the Bill of Rights and in the Thirteenth, Fourteenth, Fifteenth, and Nineteenth Amendments to the Federal Constitution; other provisions are contained in the individual state constitutions. We cannot hope to treat all of the problems that fall under the heading of civil rights in a brief space, or even mention all of them; hence we will confine our discussion to the major problems arising out of the provisions of the First, Fifth, and Fourteenth Amendments to the Constitution:

First: Congress shall make no law respecting an establishment of religion, or prohibiting the free exercise thereof; or abridging the freedom of speech, or of the press; or the right of the people peaceably to assemble, and to petition the government for a redress of grievances.

Fifth: No person . . . shall be compelled in any criminal case to be a witness against himself, nor be deprived of life, liberty, or property, without due process of law.

Fourteenth: All persons born or naturalized in the United States, and subject to the jurisdiction thereof, are citizens of the United States and of the state wherein they reside. No State shall make or enforce any law which shall abridge the privileges or immunities of citizens of the United States; nor shall any State deprive any person of life, liberty, or property, without due process of law; nor deny to any person within its jurisdiction the equal protection of the laws.

Notice particularly that the First and Fifth Amendments apply only to the Federal government; the Fourteenth Amendment, on the other hand, applies specifically to *state* governments. The distinction is quite important.

Notice too that civil-rights questions arise out of the actions of *government,* not the actions of private individuals. That is, the provisions of the Constitution are meant to protect the person against the state or Federal governments, not against private persons.

Finally, the nature of the provisions makes it clear that the courts will play a vital role in the maintenance of civil rights, and the Supreme Court is in fact the basic agency for protecting the individual—through the exercise of its power of judicial review. Of course, the Supreme Court cannot bear the burden alone and in isolation. Public opinion, and its influence on the organs of government, also bears heavily on civil-rights questions. Civil rights, after all, involve a conflict of values, and the Court can do no more than weigh one set of values against the other and hope to find a balance that society will accept. Thus freedom of speech is balanced against the danger of disorder, free access to information against the needs of security. The conclusion reached can hardly avoid reference to the evaluation of these matters made by the general public. Few issues in the civil-rights area can be portrayed in simple black and white terms; there are large areas which are gray, and many different shades of gray at that.

BACKGROUND. If we exclude the special questions raised by the Civil War, civil rights did not become an issue in American politics until the First World War. After the Alien and Sedition Acts were invalidated in 1800, the Federal government made no serious effort to interfere with the rights of its citizens, and state action was considered by the courts to lie beyond the authority of the Bill of Rights. The Espionage Act of 1917 and the spate of restrictive state legislation generated by the war seriously infringed upon civil rights. Cases involving these laws flowed into the court system, and once the crisis was past, the Supreme Court began sorting out principles and seeking a legal standard that could be used to judge questions of this sort. The timing here is typical, and very informative. The Supreme Court has seldom been able— or willing—to intervene and limit the power of legislature or Executive *during* periods of crisis, and at such times civil liberties have frequently been curbed and limited. But in the lull that follows the storm, the Court has usually managed to recoup some of the losses, tempering and mitigating the harshness of crisis legislation and practice.

Between 1925 and 1937, the Supreme Court developed a number of important guidelines or principles for dealing with civil-liberties cases, particularly for protecting the individual against action by the states. Most important of all, perhaps, was a sequence of cases which brought all of the freedoms guaranteed by the First Amendment (speech, religion, etc.) under the aegis of the Fourteenth Amendment, thus making them applicable to state action as well as Federal action. Not every item in the Bill of Rights was applied to the states, of course, but the First Amendment freedoms were singled out, given a special status, and, through the Fourteenth Amendment, made applicable to actions by the states.

World War II, despite its magnitude, raised comparatively few civil-liberties problems. Though the Smith Act of 1940 resembled the Espionage Act of 1917 in some respects, public hysteria did not appear, and the law was less harshly applied. A major exception was the involuntary removal of some seventy thousand Japanese-Americans from the West Coast and their internment in desert camps in the far West for the duration of the war—an action later upheld by the Supreme Court as a military necessity. Another was the suspension of habeas corpus in Hawaii, again grounded on military necessity, but in this case invalidated by the Supreme Court at a later date. With a few exceptions, civil liberties were remarkably well preserved during the hostilities.

Since the war, the civil-liberties issue has very rapidly come to the forefront of American political discussion. Some of the specific issues arose from purely domestic sources—church and state relations or the variety of problems arising out of segregation; others were an indirect consequence of international tensions and governmental efforts to inhibit disloyalty and subversion and thus protect the vital interests or security of the nation. The first class of problems has been handled remarkably well; the second is as yet far from a satisfactory solution.

Religious freedom. The First Amendment contains two provisions relating to religion: first, no laws relating to an establishment; second, the free exercise of religion may not be inhibited. Some controversy has arisen in both areas, though more commonly with relation to the "establishment" clause.

In general, we can say that the exercise of religious freedom is unfettered so long as the individual does not violate the law or injure other persons by his actions. There are some limits on the kinds of activities that can be practiced in the name of religious freedom: the courts have refused to permit polygamy as an exercise of religious freedom, and exemption from military service cannot be obtained on religious grounds unless the law makes provision for such exceptions. On the other hand, freedom to abstain from saluting the flag, freedom to attend church-operated schools, freedom to make use of public facilities without discrimination, and freedom to distribute tracts and solicit funds, among others, have all been upheld as a legitimate exercise of religious freedom. Most of the controversy in this area arises out of local ordinances and the activities of some of the smaller and more active sects; the Federal government is seldom involved in the regulation of religious affairs.

The establishment clause, however, raises some difficult and serious problems. The courts recognize that there are many direct and intimate relations between our government and religion, and Christianity has occupied almost a "preferred status" in our society since its inception. Prayers are offered by the various legislatures, special tax privileges are accorded legitimate religious institutions, and government and religion are bound in a number of different ways. Nevertheless, there is still room for sharp disagreement, particularly with regard to state support for education and similar matters.

Two of the more persistent questions to appear in recent years have to do with financial assistance to church schools from state funds and with the constitutionality of legislation which allows public school students "released time" to attend classes in religious instruction during the regular school hours and perhaps in regular school buildings. On these issues, it appears that the Supreme Court has not been entirely consistent. In 1947, a New Jersey statute which provided transportation costs for children attending parochial schools was upheld. In 1948, the Court invalidated an Illinois program which allowed religious instruction in public school facilities. In 1952, reverting once again, the Court approved a New York program for "released time" on the ground that this was entirely consistent with the American tradition. There the matter rests, seemingly with the Court willing to accept a "reasonable" degree of intermingling so long as no effort is made to actually establish or favor one church. But there are numerous questions that have not been resolved. Can the government in fact provide aid of all kinds so long as it is done on a nondiscriminatory basis? In Congress, several "aid to education" bills have foundered on precisely this point, and the Court has not provided a basis on which the dispute can be resolved.

Discrimination. Another major postwar problem in the civil rights field centers upon the status of the Negro and other minority groups in the United States, particularly upon the right to protection against discrimination, whether in politics, in education, in the use of public facilities, or in access to property. The Court has here followed a clear line, though the problem is far from solved—perhaps because the ultimate solution does not really lie within the Court's power.

In political affairs, for example, and especially with regard to the right to full and equal suffrage, the Court has taken an unequivocal position, though enforcement is still incomplete. The Fourteenth and Fifteenth Amendments were specifically designed to extend the suffrage to the Negro and other minorities, and the attempts that have been made to evade the amendments through state action have invariably been eliminated by the Court. Thus the so-called "grandfather clause," limiting suffrage to those whose grandparents were eligible to vote at a date impossible for the offspring of former slaves, was specifically declared unconstitutional in 1915. Various devices used by the Southern states to exclude Negroes from the primary elections (which are decisive in these states) have been voided. Five states still retain the poll tax (Alabama, Arkansas, Mississippi, Texas, and Virginia) but the Justice Department has the authority to eliminate discriminatory application of the laws. Legislation to eliminate the poll tax has been introduced in Congress, but defeated in committee or by filibuster.

The legal position, then, is perfectly straightforward, and the machinery of the Department of Justice has been strengthened to attain adequate enforcement. However, control over the suffrage is still essentially a state concern, and the techniques now used to deter Negro voting—discriminate application of literacy tests and unofficial coercion—are very difficult to police by Federal action.

Nonpolitical discrimination—segregated schools and other public facilities, etc.—is even more difficult to attack, but again we find that the courts have laid down the necessary legal foundation. In the nineteenth century, the Southern states commonly adopted segregation as a technique for dealing with the Negro population, and the Supreme Court accepted the doctrine that so long as facilities were "separate but equal" there was no discrimination involved. In practice, of course, the "equal" part of the formula was almost ignored, and the differential between white schools and Negro schools, to take one example, was notorious.

Since the mid-1930s, the Court has by stages abandoned the "separate but equal" doctrine. The first step was to insist that facilities truly be equal in meaningful terms. This materially increased the fiscal burden on the states concerned, for as the Court's standards increased in precision, segregation costs rose sharply. By the 1950s, even the existence of fully equal facilities, in the physical sense, was considered inadequate because of the psychological and social barriers involved in separation. Finally, in the very significant *Brown vs. Board of Education* case in 1954, the Court abandoned the doctrine completely, for it said, in effect, that *any* separation is a denial of the equal protection of the laws because of the psychological and social disadvantages involved. This swept away the legal foundation for discriminatory practices in transportation, education, and all other major areas of public policy. The shattering effect of this new conception was mitigated somewhat by allowing the states time to alter their present practices, particularly in schools, but the ultimate legal position is clear and well defined.

Furthermore, by extending the concept of "state action" very broadly, the Court has managed to attack some of the consequences of *private* attempts at discrimination. For example, if a restrictive covenant prohibits the sale of property to a minority group, suits brought against persons who break the covenant will not be accepted by the courts. Private persons, in other words, cannot make use of any part of the governmental apparatus to further discriminatory practices.

Freedom of speech. While everyone realizes that free speech is basic to open society, we also realize that freedom of speech cannot be absolute. One can cause willful and malicious damage by speech as well as by action. At what point, then, is the legitimate exercise of free speech to end and license begin? This is a puzzling question which can perhaps never be answered perfectly. The Supreme Court, in its search for criteria, has produced a number of standards, and has vacillated between one and the other, depending upon circumstances. These criteria are not simple procedural rules, of course, for they must take into consideration all of the factors involved in a case; they are broad generalizations which summarize the main lines which the Court's reasoning follows as it moves toward a judgment.

The problem of free speech did not arise in the nineteenth century; not until the Espionage Act did the Court face the task of formulating a standard for judging limits on free speech. The initial solution to the problem was proposed by Justice Holmes in 1919 when he asserted that speech could be limited only when it involved a "clear and present danger" to society. Holmes offered as an example a rule which prohibited shouting "Fire!" in a crowded theater. A few years later, an alternative rule appeared which held that where free speech showed "evil tendencies" rather than a clear and present danger, the right of the state to limit free speech would be upheld. Two years later, the Court returned once again to the "clear and present danger" doctrine in a carefully reasoned argument by Justice Brandeis. By 1937, the Supreme Court was supporting a position which in effect maximized the significance of individual liberty. The First Amendment freedoms were given "preferred status," meaning that any legislation which limited them was considered prima facie unconstitutional until the government could show that a clear and present danger justified the limitation.

Since 1937, the Court has once again departed in some measure from the clear and present danger doctrine, particularly under the impetus of cold war developments and the search for internal security. Generally, the Court has been willing to accept a more tenuous relationship between free speech and evil tendencies where the evil or danger was great, and has moved back toward the clear and present danger doctrine when the danger seemed less real and immediate.

Civil rights and national security. The growing tensions between East and West pose perhaps the most serious threat civil rights have faced in this century. As American fear and suspicion of the U.S.S.R. increased, various efforts have been made to protect the national interest and secure the nation against subversion, disloyalty, and sabotage or treason. Both the state and national governments have produced legislation aimed to reduce the danger of subversion and ensure the loyalty of government employees. Various investigating committees have probed into governmental and private affairs seeking information that would help locate potential areas of disaffection. Public opinion, balancing the value of liberty against the threat to security, seems to have been inclined to curtail liberty, and the courts have moved in the same direction.

Legislation like the Smith Act of 1940 or the McCarran Act of 1950 has aimed mainly at the elimination of Communist influence in the country at large and in the government in particular by making membership in Communist organization or espousal of Communist doctrine illegal. Loyalty oaths have been required of both new and old public employees at all levels of government. Investigations have combed the files for signs of affiliation with subversive organizations. The Attorney General has been authorized to prepare a list of "subversive" organizations, and membership in these societies has been taken as prima facie evidence of questionable loyalty. Communists have been denied the right to hold government jobs, obtain passports, etc., and membership in the Communist party was made illegal. Perhaps most important, because of its implications for freedom of thought, has been the restriction on advocating or preaching the overthrow of the existing political system and the failure of the courts to apply the clear and present danger doctrine to this limitation.

In general, the Court has been extremely reluctant to intrude into the conflict between government and individual in matters relating to security. In matters relating to loyalty and security, it has refused to pronounce against governmental activity, but has tended to insist upon very strict adherence to procedural limits outlined in authorizing legislation. Some limits have been placed on the Attorney General's power to add organizations to the subversive list, and state loyalty oaths which involved guilt by association have been struck down. But the power of investigation has been conceived in almost absolute terms, and though the Court introduced some limitations in 1957, they have since been abandoned. Investigating committees must stay within the scope of the authority which Congress possesses, and questions must be pertinent to the matter under investigation, nor may witnesses be forced to testify against themselves. However, the latter limit can be eliminated by granting immunity from prosecution, at which point the witness must answer or be cited for contempt.

In the long run, it seems that the Court has moved from the clear and present danger doctrine, eliminating the preferential status of First Amendment freedoms out of deference to the wishes of the legislature and the climate of public opinion. In the Dennis case in 1951, the provisions of the Smith Act which forbids the willful advising, teaching, or advocacy of the overthrow of the government by force or violence, and conspiring to effect this goal, were upheld, though opinions offered by different members of the Court were quite disparate. In 1957, the Yates case drew a distinction between urging others to believe and urging others to act, but it is not yet certain that any fundamental change was made, for the Court insisted that the Dennis case was not affected by the Yates decision.

Some of the major difficulties in this area of civil rights are reasonably clear. For one thing, there is an obvious lack of a standard by which the menace to national security can be judged; hence fear and suspicion rather than well-grounded judgment are likely to prevail. Second, there is a tendency for crisis conditions to equate subversion with nonconformity or to lead to guilt by association—both results would violate the fundamental precepts of liberal democracy. Finally, the extent to which the investigatory power may be abused in the absence of judicial restraint or hostile public opinion has been well demonstrated. Loss of employment, grave social pressures, and an unwarranted airing of private affairs by public bodies, among other consequences, have appeared in the wake of legislative investigations. The unnamed accuser, the unspecified charge, the assumption of guilt until innocence is proved beyond doubt—these are features of closed societies, not liberal democracies. The extent to which they appear in moments of crisis is an adequate measure of the immense significance of the civil-rights issue in our time.

National security and domestic affairs. We can see the influence of international tensions on the political process and on the social life of the nation even more clearly if we move beyond the field of civil rights to consider its more general effects. To some extent at least, foreign policy and its needs have first call upon the resources and ingenuity of every nation, democratic or not. National security is a prime consideration for every state, and national security is, in the nature of things, a concept that is not easily defined. Security is a compound of many factors, some beyond the control of any single state. There is not one road to security, but many, and there is often as much disagreement over means as over ends.

It is therefore worth examining the security concept more closely. Insecurity is clearly a variety of fear, and the search for security arises out of fear of some object—one must fear something or someone, some force, some nation, some consequence. The fear may be justified or it may be imaginary (like the child's fear of darkness, which is a condition of the mind, not of external circumstances). American insecurity, however defined, must arise out of some danger, some threat, before it can have any real meaning. The basic fear is directed at the Soviet Union, of course, or more vaguely, at "communism." Yet we are entitled to ask, How does the U.S.S.R. threaten the United States? What exactly do we fear from her? There are four major possibilities that merit examination: first, fear of atomic attack; second, fear of conquest and occupation; third, fear of internal subversion leading to conquest and domination; and finally, conversion to communism as a system of ideas by persuasion. In each case, the search for security has a different goal, and the means employed to attain it must be different.

Security against atomic attack is, in one sense, impossible. If the Soviet Union once decides to attack the United States with atomic weapons, the United States is powerless to prevent it. The only solution, then, is to create conditions in which the Soviet Union will not make this particular choice. That is the basis of massive retaliation. The problem is not completely solved in this way, however, for it must always rest upon some estimate of the Soviet reaction to particular American policies, and here, doubtless, is the area where the greatest possibility for error is found.

Security against occupation seems to follow naturally from the possession of large stocks of atomic weapons. No nation could occupy the United

States in the sense that Europe or Japan was occupied in World War II. The attempt would be suicidal. Hence this alternative can hardly be taken seriously at the moment. For the same reason, fear of subversion seems also to be an extreme attitude. Subversion must have some point, e.g., weakening the nation so that invasion or occupation is then possible. In practical terms, this too is unlikely at the present time, though there is no doubt that espionage can be an irritating and perhaps costly activity.

Finally, we come to the fear of ideas. This poses some interesting problems, particularly for the liberal democracies. So far as the history of Western civilization can tell us anything, it states that all attempts to suppress ideas have failed. The spread of ideas cannot be inhibited by force. Further, the liberal tradition tells us that any attempt to repress particular political ideas would be a loss to society and might weaken the very freedoms we admire and seek to retain. This poses an interesting dilemma for the democracies, and one that we have not yet completely solved.

The principal difficulty in all cases of subversion is to differentiate the individual who holds a particular set of opinions which most of society does not share (say, the convinced Communist) from the individual who is in fact acting as the agent for a foreign power. It is one thing to suppress foreign agents and quite another matter to suppress the political opinions of a citizen, however distasteful they may be. Freedom of discussion has always been assumed a fundamental part of liberal democracy, and the willingness of society to tolerate a wide range of diversity of opinion is a hallmark of the free society. When societies seek to enforce some particular political orthodoxy upon the citizenry, the essentials of free discussion have been lost. This, broadly, is the point at issue here.

Some effects of security seeking. The search for national security has an influence that runs so deeply into the fabric of society that we are often unaware of its full implications. Let us attempt to sketch some of the major and minor effects of this trend in modern-day America. High on the list of consequences would be the tendency for government to make use of "national security" as a justification for all sorts of political policies, ranging from research expenditures to foreign aid or the suppression of personal freedoms guaranteed by the Constitution. Where military affairs are concerned, the justification is appropriate, but in many cases, the "need to fight communism" has become a catchword used to support measures which have little real relation to security matters. The peculiar indefinability of national security makes this practice an extremely potent weapon in the hands of government. Few persons would deny the government the power to do what is needed to maintain national security. Yet at some point, this justification must be criticized, else government is free to act as it pleases, without restraint. Since military leaders themselves often differ on the best means of attaining security, the nonexpert finds himself in a hopeless position when he seeks to evaluate the argument before him.

Secrecy. The difficulty is much aggravated by the tendency for governments to cloak matters affecting the national security in the protective cover of secrecy. Unfortunately, government is in this case its own judge of those areas in which secrecy is necessary, and those who are suspicious of political authority without checks are much concerned with the consequences of this development. To take an illustration of the problem, the government must certainly control information relating to weapons, military capacity, etc., and this sounds innocuous enough in principle. But in practice, information pertaining to military affairs may be so construed that virtually no information regarding the conduct of foreign affairs can be published. The United States has not, of course, reached this extreme. Yet there is some cause for concern, and where there is no information, there can be no reasoned criticism, and broad areas of public policy are left unquestioned. Government operates in these areas without that ultimate responsibility to the public which is an essential feature of self-government anywhere. The wider the area covered by security regulations, the greater the areas in which the government enjoys complete freedom of action.

How, for example, does one draw the line between information relating to atomic energy which is essential to national security and information that should be circulated among the members of the scientific community? If the scientists are starved for information, their output will certainly be curtailed in some measure and we can expect wasteful duplication of effort. Yet too much information may mean giving data to the enemy, which reduces his research and development time and cost. Many critics of the security system insist that government employees, and military personnel in particular, tend to overclassify information, just to be on the safe side. This is a difficult and complex area, and not easily settled, even in principle. Perhaps the basic point at issue, broadly construed, is the need for democracies to allow the people enough information to govern themselves, or at least, to judge the quality of their government. On principle, the right to know seems inherent in the structure of our society; hence it can only be denied when the need for denial is proved. Few persons disagree with this principle, but in the heat of day-to-day administration, it is not infrequently lost in the hustle and bustle of "getting things done."

Effects of militarization. What effect has the corollary to the search for security, the growth of militarization, had upon our society? Here too we are soon lost in a complex of relationships which is very difficult to untangle.

The role of military leaders in government has certainly increased drastically. Civil-military relations have in fact become a serious problem area in American government in modern times. The United States has a long tradition of civil supremacy; the military services are apolitical service groups, with no power to make political decisions. The founding fathers, rightly or not, had a healthy fear of the influence of military leaders, and took various precautions to ensure against military control over the government. They wanted no praetorian guard and no palace revolutions.

Today, we have moved very far indeed from this tradition. Through the National Security Council and other political machinery, the chiefs of staff make their opinions felt at the very heart of the political system, and as testimony before Congress reveals, their advice is very seldom refused. The facts of military influence on political affairs have been thoroughly scouted and are not in dispute.

What, then, do the critics of militarization fear? In truth, their fears are somewhat vague. There is much concern for the influence of the "military mind," the attitude or outlook generated by long years of training and military service. Various studies of this intangible factor suggest that it is at least partly definable, and support the belief that there is a serious difference between civilian and military thinking. The military mind, it is argued, views political problems in oversimplified, black-and-white terms. It seeks "final" solutions. It is Machiavellian or amoral, unconcerned with right or wrong, and interested only in success or victory as defined by power relationships. Further, it is argued that militarization leads to regimentation, to conformity, to a tendency to accept authority without question; hence it is anti-individual, anti-intellectual, and hostile to the kind of free inquiry which democracy encourages. Militarism, in other words, has overtones which associate it with fascism and totalitarianism, and the unspoken assumption seems to be that an increase in the influence of military leaders will probably lead the United States toward a totalitarian political system. Critics of the military point to the conflict between President Truman and General MacArthur as a case in point, noting that they differed over the means to be employed to achieve national goals, and on the national goals themselves, and citing in particular the General's arrogance and unwillingness to see any viewpoint but his own.

This is, of course, an extreme point of view, and it must now be conditioned or tempered. Few persons argue that American military leaders are deliberately seeking political power; they have in fact had it thrust upon them by the course of events. And there is no question of a grand conspiracy; no attempt is being made to substitute military dictatorship for constitutional political processes. What is involved is a fear that external conditions will increase military influence to such a degree that the nation will slide unwittingly into a militaristic society which no one really wanted. This seems a valid and worthy concern. The role of the military forces in modern society has been examined in a few major works in recent years, and there is no doubt that changing military requirements are working substantial changes in the social structure. The President has gained greatly in power at the expense of Congress. Individual and personal rights have in some cases been threatened by militaristic trends. Foreign policy often produces a conflict between military and civilian needs, and the latter yield to the former more often than not. Such developments demand the closest attention in the years ahead.

The political heritage. In the nineteenth century, the United States was widely regarded as a "great political experiment," an effort to determine whether or not men really were capable of governing themselves. For most of human history, most men have been political subjects, almost slaves, and even today that is the unfortunate lot of the majority of men. A small minority may exercise meaningful political authority and enjoy the social advantages of their position, but for the great mass of men politics has been a kind of activity reserved for others besides themselves. The subject classes have, for the most part, been indifferent to politics, caring little for ruler or dynasty or affairs of state. They accepted political authority, usually with little thought or concern, as part of the scheme of things which they inherited with the rest of their culture. Until modern nationalism initiated a further stage in the intellectual idiocy of mankind, men did not associate their own future with the fate of any particular political regime. The notion of "dying for one's country" would have seemed utterly absurd to the European peasant of the sixteenth century or before. This was a problem for the ruler. For the peasant, the political relationship that mattered most was the occasional contact with the ubiquitous tax collector. Political rights and political obligations were the prerogative of the nobility, the religious leaders, the men of blood.

When did this rather dreary conception of the relationship between state and individual come to an end? To that we must say that it has not yet ended, if we except one very small portion of mankind. It is really as simple as that. Outside the few political democracies, men have no part in their own government, or very little. The point is that we need to realize how atypical the political tradition of the Western world actually is when we set it against the whole world as a backdrop. A few societies, a few decades of self-rule at the most—how fragile it all seems when we look at it this way. The liberal-democratic tradition, a tiny drop in the waterfall of history, made man a citizen and not a subject, and gave meaning to the term individual rights and personal freedoms. In no society has the ideal been achieved. But the hard core of beliefs from which the ideal springs, the set of values which it embodies, seems truly one of the more admirable creations of political thought and it deserves respect, particularly from those who live with its benefits.

Review Questions

1. List some of the deficiencies of the modern state system. How are they currently solved?

2. What is meant by a "polarized" world? Why is it significant? What were the major steps in the development of polarization?

3. Point out some of the signs of militarization in current American society.

4. What is meant by the term "balance of terror"?

5. In what sense is an ideological conflict taking place in world affairs at the present time?

6. Do wealthy countries or poor countries rely more heavily on others? Why?

7. List some of the major changes that are taking place in contemporary American society, and consider their effect on politics.

8. Define the term "civil liberties" as it is used in American political science.

9. What is the content of the First, Fifth, and Fourteenth Amendments? How does the Fourteenth differ from the others?

10. What are the major issues in current "civil-liberties" debates?

11. Discuss the status of the following civil rights:

a. Political freedom

b. Freedom of the press

c. Religious freedom

d. Social equality—discrimination

12. What is the significance of *Brown vs. Board of Education?*

13. What is meant by the "clear and present danger" doctrine? How has it been modified?

14. How have international tensions affected civil rights? Cite particular instances.

15. Discuss some of the problems that arise when national security is threatened. Why are they particularly difficult to handle?

For Further Study

1. Do you believe that atomic weapons are now so horrible that war is no longer possible? How would you support your belief?

2. To what extent is forced militarization a threat to the democratic principles on which American society is based?

3. Would you agree to the statement that "security cannot be defined"? Why?

4. It is sometimes said that in the last analysis, only public opinion can guarantee individual freedom. Do you agree? On what grounds?

5. Do you believe that discrimination can be abolished, or even lessened, through legal action? Justify your answer.

CHAPTER 20

Current
Economic
Problems

We are now ready to make use of the economic principles that we have learned, to apply them to some of the current problems in the field of economics. We shall deal with two major areas: first, with the problem of growth and development in the underdeveloped countries; second, with the problem of economic growth and price stability in an advanced economy such as our own. A brief note on the comparable problems that arise in a directed economy such as that found in the U.S.S.R. completes the chapter.

PROBLEMS OF ECONOMIC GROWTH AND DEVELOPMENT

The problem of the underdeveloped economies is perhaps one of the most challenging issues facing mankind at the present time. There are about three billion people in the world, and at this moment about two-thirds of them are hungry. Only someone who has pursued health or beauty on a temporary diet of 1,500 calories per day will know how food can fill one's dreams and every waking thought during periods of sustained hunger, and perhaps appreciate the problem that people living in these countries must face.

DEFINING UNDERDEVELOPMENT. Writers used to speak of "backward" nations, which naturally irritated the people who live in them. To avoid offense, the United Nations sometimes used the expression "less-developed" nations, but today most people have adopted the expression "underdeveloped" nations to describe these countries. What is meant by the term? Most definitions involve something like the following basic points: An underdeveloped nation is simply one with real per capita income that is low relative to the present-day per capita incomes of such advanced nations as the United States, Britain, or Western Europe generally. Usually, an underdeveloped nation is one regarded as capable of sustained improvement in its income level. Of course, no nation is perfectly developed, and the "advanced" nations were by our definition underdeveloped at one time.

Characteristics of underdeveloped economies.

To bring out the contrasts between advanced and underdeveloped economies, imagine that you are a typical twenty-one-year-old living in one of the underdeveloped nations, say, El Salvador in Central America. You are terribly poor. Your annual family income is less than $100 per head, compared with $2,500 per head in the United States. You are probably illiterate; there are four illiterates in your country for every person who can read. Your life expectancy is about half the life expectancy of an American, and some members of your family have probably died already. You work with about one-twentieth of the mechanical horsepower available to your more prosperous fellow man. Yet you and those like you make up about 70 per cent of the world's population and divide among you only 20 per cent of the world's income. You brood over the fact that the United States, with 6 per cent of the world's population, enjoys some 38 per cent of the world's income.

Urgency of the problem. If there have always been differences between the rich and the poor, why worry about the underdeveloped nations now? There are several good reasons.

Widening differentials. Among the advanced nations, income differentials are currently narrowing, but the divergence between advanced and underdeveloped countries is probably widening. Canada, the United States, and Western Europe have increased their productivity by about 70 per cent since 1938. Many authorities believe that living standards in India, Indonesia, and other underdeveloped countries have deteriorated in this same period.

Ideological struggle. The Communists tend to regard the underdeveloped nations as the Achilles' heel of the Western nations, and they seek to exploit their poverty for political advantage. To turn our backs on the problem of underdevelopment would be to leave these countries open to exploitation and to court future disaster.

"Great Expectations." The people in underdeveloped nations are today acutely aware of their own poverty and they do not like it. They insist on doing something to alleviate economic conditions, and the belief that material comfort ought to be increased for everyone has spread widely in the modern world. This increased awareness comes at a time when government is developing rapidly, and when people want things done, they tend increasingly to turn to government for assistance. Demands for better health, land reform, better methods of cultivation, industrialization, and individual political rights are heard everywhere. Men want these things on quite reasonable grounds— for economic welfare and to gain respect, admiration, and even fear from their fellow man. "Freedom from contempt" is a much-sought goal among underdeveloped peoples.

Desired markets. Altruism and politics aside, advanced economies have a selfish interest in the growth of underdeveloped nations—they will provide markets for international trade. These countries will import more from us as their national incomes grow, and trade, as we have seen, is more beneficial for developed than for underdeveloped nations. The issue is more complex, though, than simple trade advantage. Why do we want more trade? Not just to increase dollar sales, for exporting cannot continue without buying or lending. The point is that as foreign economies grow, they should display those differences in comparative advantage that make international trade fruitful for all parties.

More precisely, then, we want other nations to develop so that we can import from them those goods we produce less economically at home. When our resources can be used to produce exportable goods that can be exchanged for more imported goods than can be produced at home, then international trade is truly advantageous. The United States also has need for raw materials from abroad, and the Paley Raw Materials Study found that each passing decade will expand that need, from 10 per cent today to more than 30 per cent by 1975. Of course, the developing nations may not wish to concentrate on industries that provide us with the greatest comparative advantage, and this may produce a real clash of interests in the future.

Economic imperialism to avert a slump? Expanded exports are in the best interests of the capitalistic nations. Does it follow that Lenin's argument about imperialism as a necessary aspect of capitalism seeking to avert slumps is correct? His argument is roughly as follows: Wealthy capitalistic nations always face a worsening oversaving crisis at home. To keep profits from falling and stave off depression, they must dump goods abroad. For this selfish reason alone, they favor development of backward peoples. In fact, they will enslave the natives and make colonies of them, or even begin wars in their search for such colonial dependencies.

What can one make of the argument? Has colonialism been motivated by the need for markets? Actually, the flag has not really "followed trade" very often, as was once believed. Careful historians have discovered that governments often took the initiative, prodding businessmen into overseas economic investments in areas that had political significance.

Fortunately, we need not involve ourselves in the complexities of the issue. For today we know that the monetary and fiscal tools available to modern nations can effectively avoid depressions, and there is no need to create domestic purchasing power by foreign trade. Depressions can be fought by useful internal programs. We need not buy prosperity by selling goods abroad.

Exploiting colonial peoples? Modern Marxists realize that Marx's prediction of falling real wages and increasing misery for the workers was completely wrong. Real wages have risen steadily in capitalistic nations. How can a Marxist explain this? Not by the actions of reformers and trade unions —that would be a bitter pill to swallow after all that was said to the contrary. So Marxists seek to credit the rise in real wages to the exploitation of colonial workers. Men drive new cars in Dayton, Ohio, because the Burmese peasant starves. So goes the argument. Is there anything to it?

Economics is not an exact science, and so we cannot dismiss the point offhand. But when the evidence is weighed critically, it must be said that it cannot support the argument. The high standard of living in the West does not seem to depend in any significant way upon trade with the underdeveloped nations. In fact, if nylon and synthetic rubber are followed by other substitutes for raw materials, the Western nations may actually decrease their dependence on such trade in the future.

Plain altruism. Finally, it is only the simple truth to mention disinterested altruism as an important reason for helping the underdeveloped nations. The evidence for this is plain. Look at public opinion in the advanced nations. Examine the policy statements of the governments of the fully developed countries. Look, finally, at the efforts which have already been made to ameliorate the lot of the poorer members of the human race, and without political strings attached either. The ethical urge to provide minimum standards for everyone inside the advanced nations, which is very strong, spills over into a desire for assistance to the underdeveloped peoples. Altruism is not something we can with grace dwell upon at length, but it is certainly present in some measure in the overall Western attitude.

Diagnosis and therapy. We have described the general problem of underdevelopment and cleared the ground for a discussion of more specific problems. We can now turn to the constructive task of discovering why some countries are poor and what can be done to hasten their growth and development. The most fruitful approach is through analysis of the four economic fundamentals: population, natural resources, capital formation, and technology.

Population problems. Mere growth in numbers does not necessarily mean economic development. Indeed, as writers since Malthus have warned, it may invoke the law of diminishing returns and actually decrease living standards. Admittedly, some of the underdeveloped nations are repeating the pattern of Western economic development in the eighteenth and nineteenth centuries. Improved medical technology reduces the death rate and the birth rate remains high, producing a rapid growth of the total population. There are two lessons here: first, much of the increased output flowing from technological advance may be absorbed in population increase; second, modern science may lessen the threat of death by disease only to threaten death from famine because disease is conquered more rapidly than the food supply is increased. Will birth rates fall in the developing countries as they did in older nations? We cannot even hazard a guess.

Much constructive planning and programming needs to be done in relation to the labor supply in underdeveloped nations. In particular, control of malnutrition and disease will make people both happier and more productive, and increased education is an essential prerequisite to a major production increase. Accordingly, we need to realize that hospitals, sewage systems, schools, etc., are not frills or luxuries; they are primary necessities. And education must go beyond mere literacy, for the best minds need to be sent abroad and trained in new techniques in agriculture and industry, engineering and medicine. This is perhaps the best of all possible investments.

Another important means of promoting economic development is better utilization of manpower. In poor countries, particularly in rural areas, the manpower supply may be virtually unemployed because there is nothing for men to do. Such people may not be included in the unemployment census, but they are scarcely productive workers, for they live with their kinfolk, find jobs when they can, and have little effect on total production. This same type of disguised unemployment is met in advanced countries when men eke out a bare living at such tasks as door-to-door selling. Governments may find it desirable to pursue expansionary fiscal and monetary policies in order to meet this type of unemployment problem, even though these policies raise problems of inflation and deficits in the international balance of payments.

Natural resources. Poor countries are typically poorly endowed by nature, and such land and minerals as they do possess must be divided among dense populations. The possibilities are therefore somewhat limited, for new discoveries of rich resource supplies are today less likely than before. The more productive regions of the earth are generally settled. Of course, some hidden resources may come to light, and there are cases where the jungle is reclaimed for farmland. But we must balance against these gains the undeniable fact that many underdeveloped nations are actually depleting their supply of resources, and some of their resources are becoming obsolete as new technological innovations appear. If synthetic rubber replaces natural rubber completely, for example, Eastern Asia will find itself unable to maintain even its present low standard of living. In brief, further development must come from better use of existing resources. The opportunities that lay before the early American settlers are gone.

Even without creating or finding new land, nations can make better use of the land they do have. The pattern of land ownership still reflects the medieval system of strip farming in many parts of the world, and these small plots are very inefficient. The cost of consolidation may be high, for it took nearly five centuries to break up the common lands in England, and in the process many peasants were dispossessed and forced into the cities, causing hardship and suffering for many families. The ruthless and not altogether successful collectivization movement in Russia in the 1920s and the more recent collectivization program in China provide us with further models and analogies. In many parts of the world, the painful process of consolidating landholdings into efficient agricultural units is not yet begun, let alone completed.

At the other extreme, we find in many of the underdeveloped nations that the estates held by single families are much too large for efficient operation. Here the land is farmed by tenant farmers, men with no incentive to improve the land, knowing they can be dispossessed and that added benefits will in any event go to the landlord. The landlord in turn has no reason to improve the property since irresponsible tenants may dissipate costly resources with no real increase in production. In such cases, agitation for land reform —for breaking up the large estates—is very powerful, and the Communists have exploited this sentiment fully.

Capital formation. The fingers and brains of men are much alike whether they live in advanced countries or underdeveloped countries. But men in advanced countries work with a plentiful supply of capital goods which they have accumulated. To pile up net capital formation requires, as we saw earlier, a sacrifice of current consumption. For the underdeveloped nations, that is where the shoe pinches, for they are already so poor that they cannot in fact save very much of their current national income for future production. They must consume most of their product simply to stay alive. The advanced nation may set aside 10 to 20 per cent of its income for capital formation. The underdeveloped country may only save 5 per cent or less of its national income. Where population is growing and production methods are primitive, as in Indonesia, only a very small amount is left over from current consumption to be invested in capital.

In the advanced nations, until we learned how to deal with mass unemployment, economists tended to worry about *oversaving*—saving more than was needed for investment. But in the underdeveloped countries, the problem is more often the classic problem of *undersaving*, or more precisely, underinvestment in productive capital. Why don't these countries save more? Poverty is doubtless the prime reason, for people who live on the edge of starvation cannot save very much. There is, however, a sharp distinction between rich and poor in these countries, and this complicates matters. Is this separation a good thing? Does it provide extra savings by producing unequal incomes?

In some countries, this may be the case. But we must also remember that our Industrial Revolution was accompanied by a change in social philosophy; there developed an attitude toward business activity that was unique in the world, already described in the discussion of the Protestant ethic. Weber's thesis was overstated, but there is a hard core of truth in his generalizations. In many of the underdeveloped nations, on the other hand, there remains a tradition which is contemptuous of material progress, commerce, thrift, and business. Further, the rich often live abroad and funnel their expenditures into foreign investment channels rather than into their own countries.

A further problem arises out of the fact that saving and investment in the underdeveloped nations is both quantitatively low and of poor *quality*. Too much of the limited savings of India, for example, goes into hoards of gold and jewelry. Many other underdeveloped countries like Brazil and Chile suffer from chronic inflation, and there is a natural tendency for people to invest in real estate or inventories of goods. When you can earn 20 per cent by hoarding goods, why seek a slightly higher percentage in manufacturing where the risk is greater? Thus over 55 per cent of Brazil's investments in 1947 was in construction. Observers are also struck by the fact that in many of the very poor parts of the world there are luxury apartments and hotels everywhere while industry languishes from lack of new equipment.

Another reason why saving comes hard in poor countries is that the people have a tendency to emulate prosperous foreigners. "Poor" is a relative term, and the underdeveloped peoples are constantly tempted by the comforts of life common in advanced countries; they see movies and magazines, meet tourists, listen to students, and often find themselves spending a sizable part of their income trying to enjoy a few of the things we enjoy in abundance. As the consumption curve rises, the amount left for saving and investment grows progressively smaller.

Nor is this true only of private individuals, for the governments of underdeveloped nations see and emulate social security programs, minimum-wage legislation, factory safety programs, and other social laws common in the advanced nations. Of course, this makes for high levels of government spending, and if the basic economy does not supply enough income, welfare and security programs may also reduce the amount left for investment. Further, governmental regulations may act as an obstacle to venture capital by reducing potential gains through high labor costs, etc.

Capital from abroad. If there are so many obstacles to capital formation at home, why not rely more heavily on foreign sources of capital? After all, the American economy began on capital borrowed from England, and all of the advanced nations have invested heavily in other parts of the world in the past. Is it not true that a rich country which has used up all of its high-interest investment projects can benefit both itself and its poorer neighbors if it shifts investment to high-interest projects abroad?

Actually, economic development did proceed this way prior to 1914. In her heyday, Britain saved about 15 per cent of her national income and invested fully half this amount abroad. If the United States were to match this figure today, it would have to lend or invest about $60 billion abroad every year, many times more than the combined lending of all the foreign-aid programs carried out since World War II. For many reasons, we cannot expect such great things of foreign investment today.

For one thing, pre-1914 loans often followed European migrations to foreign lands, and this is no longer occurring. Remember too that the world was unbelievably cosmopolitan in the latter part of the nineteenth century. You could travel anywhere without a passport, or migrate freely from one country to another. Tariffs were low and there were no trade quotas. The international gold standard allowed free transfer of capital from place to place. Property was safe from government confiscation, both at home and abroad. Finally, it was then possible literally to purchase dictatorial governments and bribe them into making very favorable concessions in mining and other industries.

Though this may sound like an investor's paradise, the facts were not quite so rosy as they appear. Foreign investors often went bankrupt for lack of commercial demand. And people living in the underdeveloped nations were not too happy with the system. But it did work, and it seems to have conferred benefits on both the advanced nations and the backward nations concerned. However, this world is gone for good. Nationalism is today very powerful everywhere, often taking the form of antiforeign sentiment. Underdeveloped nations are no longer willing to sell long-term development rights to foreigners, and investors are no longer willing to risk their savings in bonds and stocks from backward countries. This does not mean that substantial capital investment programs from abroad are impossible, but we need to be realistic and look for new machinery to carry them out. Often we will need governmental agreements which insure the private investor against confiscation under pressure from domestic political interests, for example.

Technological change and innovation. The fourth vital element in our discussion of underdeveloped nations is technology. Here we may be cautiously optimistic, for the underdeveloped nations have one possible advantage: they may take advantage of what has already been done elsewhere, copying whatever is suited to their own economic situation, and thus benefiting from more advanced technology developed elsewhere.

Imitating technology. The new lands do not need to develop their own Isaac Newtons or follow the slow climb through the Industrial Revolution which occurred in the West. They can borrow and imitate, saving endless amounts of development time.

Japan and Russia clearly illustrate the benefits of borrowing in their historical development. Japan joined the industrial race late, but toward the end of the nineteenth century she began importing technology and sending her own people abroad for training at a furious rate. Her government took an active and creative role in stimulating economic development, building railroads and utilities and taxing the newly created increments on land value very heavily. A few energetic, wealthy families were permitted to develop vast industrial empires, and the general population was made to work hard in order to earn a living. Without relying on net foreign capital imports, Japan moved in a few decades to the forefront of industrialized and militarily powerful nations.

Russia also illustrates the possibility of fast development through technological imitation. The very fact that the Russians claim to have invented everything is taken by the rest of the world as a sign of her basic insecurity and late development. Tsarist Russia was developing rapidly around the turn of the century, encouraged by French capital investment. But it came too late to stay the revolutions of 1917, and under Bolshevik rule foreign capital could not be obtained. To force the pace of industrial development, Russia ruthlessly limited current consumption and imported as much technical skill as possible from the West.

Interplay of technology and capital. But if the underdeveloped nations are short of capital goods, how can they be expected to copy superior technology? Is not technology itself embodied in complex capital goods? There is much truth in this suggestion, for technology and capital investment do go hand in hand. All the same, they are analytically distinct, though related, processes. Farming, to take an example, is inefficient in many backward countries. Perhaps an ingenious light plow—simple and cheap—can be found which would pay for itself in a month and lessen the total amount of capital needed while still increasing output. In this case, technological innovation can actually *save* capital rather than use it.

Moreover, even in the poorest countries, there is always some gross capital formation as things wear out and are replaced. Why replace with the same item? Surely it would be much better to put what investment funds there are into the most efficient technological implements available? In this way, the interrelated factors of capital formation and technology can be mutually reinforcing.

Entrepreneurship and innovation. Does all this sound like an easy task? All that the underdeveloped nation must do is telescope into a few years the accomplishments of decades—go abroad, copy efficient methods, put them into effect at home, and sit back and wait for production to roll in. Of course, it does not really work this way, as we know. But too often we seem to think that teams of technical experts can produce an improvement program in a short time and that once the recommendations are "implemented" the problem is solved.

Experts can, in some cases, work wonders, particularly with technological processes. Technologists soon discover, however, that this sort of quick miracle simply cannot be accomplished with the *whole economy.* Indeed, the typical expert soon becomes completely disillusioned, and may indeed be so impressed with the cultural and economic barriers to progress that he resigns himself to defeat.

Experience, in other words, shows that development is a hard and slow process, but not impossible. To hasten the pace, there must develop spontaneous entrepreneurship and innovation on the part of the people themselves. Remember that many of these people begin with contempt for dirty, hard work; often they have contempt for business or moneygrubbing. They must gradually develop for themselves, within their own cultural pattern, a creative group of producers who will try new ways of doing things.

Why emphasize innovation? Because it is by no means a cut and dried task to adapt advanced foreign technology to an underdeveloped country's own use. Remember that advanced technology was developed to fit the special conditions found in advanced countries. What are these conditions? High money wage rates, scarce labor, skilled labor, plentiful supplies of capital, mass-production techniques, etc. These conditions simply do not exist in an underdeveloped country. It has often been easy to obtain a foreign loan to build a model factory in Turkey or Burma only to find that the results are not satisfactory. Rarely is production high; seldom are sales well above costs. Too often such grandiose projects turn out to be unprofitable. The factory that is an optimal investment in New York may be a fiasco in Rangoon or Ankara.

The task of creative innovation is not, however, one for the rugged individualist. Government can do much to provide extension services, agricultural aids for farmers, new methods of cultivation, and training in the use of implements. It can also create vocational schools and training courses where they are needed. In short, the government can also act as a creative innovator in society.

A case study of development: Alertia on the march. To end our discussion, let us consider a concrete but hypothetical case of an underdeveloped country—Alertia. How does it actually go about stimulating its economic growth?

Impatient planners, anxious to accelerate development, must always remember that people are not inanimate objects. Ignore the customs and prejudices and traditions of the country and you will almost certainly fail. Pure economics must be spiced with generous doses of sociology, anthropology, and so on; and the planner must proceed in an evolutionary rather than a discontinuous manner. Each nation is in some respects unique; no master plan will fit every underdeveloped nation.

Alertia is poor and populous. It was long dominated by a European power but won its freedom and independence after World War II. Political freedom did not, however, raise the standard of living, and the government has set up a planning committee in the cabinet to prepare a Plan for Development. With the help of United Nations experts, numerical estimates of national product have been prepared. The Technical Assistance Program of the U.S. Department of State has sent missions to help improve technology. The Food and Agriculture Organization (FAO) has helped develop better methods of cultivation. What more can be done? Several things of considerable importance.

Tax policies. The government has revamped the tax system, thereby increasing revenues substantially. Yet it knows that it cannot really use a modern tax system like that of Canada or the United States. There is too much illiteracy, accounting methods are primitive, and there is a strong tradition of cheating the government out of its tax money. Further, corruption and inefficiency are common in the public service and many of the economic transactions in society are carried on without money.

Expenditure policies. The government does, however, collect a great deal of revenue, much of it coming from the exporters of a few staples. Part of this money is used for important "social overhead capital" projects: roads, schools, hospitals, power dams, railroads, soil improvement, conservation, etc. While many of these projects are invaluable, their benefits are intangible and will not yield profit to private investors. Some projects are too large for the limited private capital markets; others yield a return too far in the future to tempt the investor. Finally, the government must undertake projects to train workers, advise farmers, and help businessmen on a here and now basis.

Foreign experts have told Alertia how vital these "social overhead capital" projects are. Paul Rosenstein-Rodan, who originated the term, uses it to refer not only to roads, dams, railroads, and so on, but to sewers and "invisible" public utilities—those environmental conditions needed to foster private industry. Successful economic development is like airplane flight; a "breakthrough" is needed to get the vehicle off the ground and begin operation.

Public loans. Some of the public revenue is given to the Finance Development Corporation which makes loans to private applicants, choosing those projects which are most likely to have social value. Finally, some of the tax money is used to retire public debt, thereby permitting the central bank and commercial banks to expand their loans to new private ventures.

Inflation and development. In the early stages of independence, the government was plagued by inflation. Part of this was due to international price rises, but some resulted from the government's attempt to force economic development faster than it could increase tax revenues. The Cabinet reminded itself that older capitalistic nations had floated their industrial revolutions on a rising price level and had thereby tended to subsidize the active entrepreneurial classes at the expense of the creditor *rentier* class and wage earners. The Cabinet was therefore willing to accept a little inflation, hoping to speed development and lessen "disguised unemployment."

However, there are limits to the utility of inflation. For as inflation increases investment, it distorts the qualitative composition of investment by shunting it into real estate and inventory speculation. Once people grew accustomed to inflation, they also saved less, for they feared that future price rises would melt the real value of their savings. The government is therefore trying to reduce its dependence on inflation and encourage more personal saving.

Diversification and protection. Bitter experience has warned Alertia to beware of putting all of her export hopes in a few staple crops. New substitutes abroad and cyclical changes in foreign demand and supply could produce great ups and downs for Alertia. So she has come to regard "monoculture" as a condition to be avoided. Instead she seeks to diversify her industries and agricultural output and lessen her dependence on imported foods. To this end, she has introduced tariffs and protective quotas, claiming in justification the usual "infant industry" and "young economy" arguments. Many doubt that some of the protected industries will ever outgrow the need for protection, particularly the imported steel mill and airline, which seem always to need help. But friendly critics are reserving judgment until the future reveals the new comparative advantage situation.

Breaking vicious circles. Sometimes the Minister for Economic Development gets discouraged; he feels caught in a vicious circle. Poverty creates want, and want disourages thrift and capital formation; absence of capital prevents improvement, and limits on mass demand make mass production impossible; absence of mass production makes for poverty; so the vicious circle goes. However, the very interconnectedness of these factors does mean that a breakthrough can have favorable repercussions for the whole economy, leading to ascending spirals of development.

Beyond economics. It is too soon to tell how the desperate race between Alertia's rising population and her development program will turn out. Great issues are still debated politically: How much shall government do? How much private industry? How much reliance shall be placed on domestic rather than foreign resources? And so the endless questioning continues. The greatest problems go beyond pure economics. They involve sociological tensions between the old culture and the new, for the old leaders take a dim view of the trend to materialism and the new have lost their roots. Insecurity, crime, and disorganization are serious problems. The people watch America and Russia carefully, trying to see which way of life offers the greatest promise. All this is a fascinating spectacle for the visiting economist or anthropologist, and no one knows exactly where Alertia is going. This much is clear—she is on her way.

PROBLEMS OF GROWTH AND STABILITY IN AN ADVANCED ECONOMY

There is great popular interest in the economic development of backward countries, but the problems associated with future growth in a mixed economy such as ours, without creeping inflation, are even more exciting. They are truly vital public issues, and anyone can talk about them. Yet in some ways they are more difficult to analyze than the problems facing a poor nation. We can bring order into the question, but alas, not all of the advanced treatises on economics ever written are enough to give confident and conclusive answers in this truly complex area.

The questions to be asked are reasonably clear. How is economic growth to be measured? What have been the past growth patterns in advanced nations? Is creeping inflation of the "cost-push" type a serious hazard? How do we achieve rapid growth without losing price-level stability? Can we have both? Let us examine some of these questions in detail before we turn to a comparison of the American and Soviet economies and the future relationships.

Measuring economic growth. Growth is obviously a many-sided process. Although no single number can portray the varied dimensions of total growth, the real national product, net or gross, is perhaps our best growth indicator. Because NNP and GNP tell largely the same story, and GNP data are more common, we shall concentrate on GNP, but certain cautions need to be observed.

1. For some purposes, such as war, the absolute magnitude of real GNP is vital, but generally we want to deflate GNP for population changes when we are thinking about economic welfare.

2. Leisure is one of life's finest goods, but it does not register in GNP. Some allowance for shortening the labor week and year ought always to be kept in mind.

3. A mere increase in aggregate GNP, if distribution deteriorated seriously, would not mean an improvement. Hence many observers feel that the What problem can never be divorced from the For Whom.

4. Qualitative improvements in goods and services may not register very well in GNP and price-level data, and may thereby tend to give an overly pessimistic view of the economy. Some rough allowance should be made for this.

5. Money cannot measure many of the important spiritual and non-economic aspects of human welfare.

Subject to these qualifications, we shall use real GNP (GNP deflated for price-level changes) as the principal quantitative indicator of economic growth.

Brief history of growth. Economic growth is characteristic of the modern world. Nations have grown in population, in total production, in employment, in real national product, in living standards, in leisure time, in relief from tedium and sweat. Any and all of these changes are aspects of economic growth.

Figure 33 shows the steady advance of GNP per capita for some of the leading advanced nations. All such absolute comparisons are difficult, but we can note that Britain dropped from the top of the heap just after the turn of the century, while American growth permitted us to surpass her.

Growthsmanship. At the beginning of the 1960s, preoccupation with underdevelopment and with the challenge posed by Soviet growth rate has led to great concern over the American growth rate. Is it satisfactory? Can it be improved? Various answers are given to these questions. Some of the more important points of view are:

Laissez faire. Some firm believers in classical economics hold that the economy should grow as fast as the citizenry wants it to grow, as determined by their daily decisions to spend or save. If the population chooses to live

Advanced nations expect rising per-capita welfare:

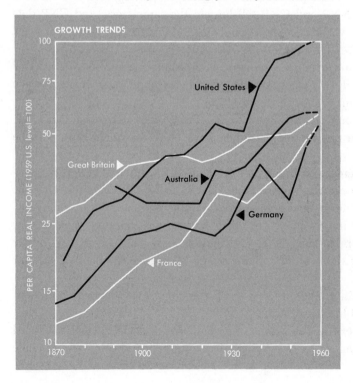

Fig. 33. Relatively small differences in annual growth rates, when accumulated over a long time, can change the relative position of nations. (Source: Adapted by the author from Colin Clark, *Conditions of Economic Progress,* 3d ed., St Martin's, New York, 1957.)

well now and grow less rapidly, that is their choice. This is not a popular view today, but it is entitled to a hearing.

No need for further growth. A similarly complacent view about growth holds that we are already so affluent that there is no great need for further growth. "Why have a third or fourth monstrous car in every garage?" would be a caricature of this position. Observers abroad, already convinced that America is too materialistic, are especially attracted to this view.

Full speed ahead. At the opposite extreme are those who feel that the Soviet threat and our need to keep neutrals out of the Communist bloc make economic growth our nation's first problem. Some are prepared to give the government the authority to force the pace of economic growth; others merely insist that government keep the problem in mind and act accordingly.

Stepping up growth by public and private measures. Many others think that we should not be satisfied with the postwar growth rate and ought to take positive measures to increase it. The reasoning behind the position varies. Some are impressed by the Soviet challenge; others wish to impress the neutral nations with the advantages of mixed economies; still others believe that governmental goods and services are most needed by the population in the years ahead and that it will be politically easier to get these items out of extra growth than to tax current GNP more heavily. Some believe, further, that even if more material goods are not important, society is still happier when it is moving forward. Finally, others glorify group effort and participation and support controlled growth for that reason. These are only a few of the major arguments in favor of controlled increased growth.

How to grow. If we are convinced that faster growth is needed in the decades ahead, how is it obtained in a mixed economy? The answers are by no means obvious. A totalitarian society can grow by ruthlessly channeling goods away from current consumption into capital formation. We cannot simply set a target of 5 per cent growth per year, and then rely on exhortation to supply the needed savings. And we are not prepared to accept the level of coercion that would be needed to enforce savings at the requisite level.

In practice, certain factors must be changed to improve the rate of growth: the quality and quantity of population and natural resources, the stock of capital goods, and the technological efficiency of society are particularly important. These basic factors are the key to a sensible program of growth stimulation within the framework of a free society.

Expanded private and public research. The least controversial measure for enhancing growth is an expanded research program. Everyone agrees that more research in pure science, engineering, development, and management could pay high social dividends in terms of productivity. It can be extended both by government and by private persons. Business firms do much research and can be urged to do more. But actually management can see for itself that research is profitable, and hence can be presumed to extend its maximum effort in any case. Here government can help by direct or indirect support for scientific research, as it has in fact done since 1940.

Expanded education and training. Since the "quality" of the working population is as important as the quality of the machinery used for production, investing in people, in terms of education, can produce greater output. Society can, then, promote growth by spending more for education. Private investment in this area already occurs among the income groups that can afford it; a lawyer with a large income will make sure that his son gets the best possible education, knowing that it is an even better investment than buying General Motors stocks. When the family cannot afford this investment, public assistance in the form of scholarships and tuition aid is clearly called for. And if people still feel that the nation can benefit from an even greater outlay for education, it is the manifest duty of government to increase public support for schools, colleges, and universities.

Maintaining high employment. People are generally as much opposed to unemployment as to Satan, and since putting idle people to work expands output, this type of growth injures no one and benefits everyone. Consequently, a program designed to attain rapid growth by eliminating unemployment is a third noncontroversial path that we can follow. Some qualifications are, however, in order. A reduction of unemployment from 6 per cent to 3 per cent sounds substantial, and in human terms, that is certainly the case. But in terms of product, it means only a rise in employment level from 94 per cent to 97 per cent. This is not to be ignored, but the increase in product will be proportionately smaller than the decrease in unemployment, and we ought not to expect too much.

Moreover, sophisticated economists realize that decreasing unemployment from 6 per cent to 3 per cent might add some 3 per cent to the annual rate of growth, but that such high rates are by nature temporary. A return to full employment is a one-time proposition. The next year, growth will again return to a lower rate since there will be no further labor supply to bring into use. This does not belittle the importance of high employment levels, but it enjoins caution against overoptimism or the extrapolation into the future of growth rates which are characteristic of periods of recovery from past recessions.

Combination of micro- and macroeconomics. Finally, a mixed economy can hope to increase its rate of growth by making use of the fiscal and monetary mechanism explained earlier. By properly blending economic and fiscal policy, a mixed economy can hope to shift the composition of its high-employment NNP toward capital formation and away from current consumption. If this device should turn out to be ineffective, then simple honesty requires us to admit that a mixed economy is very limited in its ability to alter the growth rate.

The control mechanism involved is fairly simple. Federal Reserve monetary policy can help choke off investment spending or capital formation by making credit tight or dear, and alternatively it can hope to stimulate capital formation by making credit easy and interest rates lower. As the interest rate drops, investments not otherwise worthwhile become profitable, and business firms tend to take advantage of opportunities that might be passed by when credit is tight. The whole process by which capital formation is increased as interest rates drop has been given the name "deepening of capital" by the British expert, Sir Ralph Hawtrey. The process is very significant, for if it were not possible, then there would be little point in giving up current consumption to form more capital. In our mixed economy, the process of deepening capital is not always smooth, but the operation of the process can be explained fairly easily.

Monetary and fiscal policy at work. Let us assume that our mixed economy wishes to maintain a high rate of employment, say, 97 per cent, and shift some consumption to capital formation. What steps are to be taken in this case?

1. An expansionary monetary policy will make for deepening of capital and stimulate much capital formation.

2. The tendency of this policy to induce inflation can be offset by an austere fiscal policy—high income tax rates that will reduce disposable income and cause a reduction in consumption, thus releasing resources for investment without causing inflation.

3. Combining steps 1 and 2, a free society can hope to alter its own effective rate of capital formation and growth without adding unnecessarily to its economic controls.

As Professor James Tobin of Yale put the matter: If the United States wants faster growth, it must manage to move from a full-employment economy that devotes 65 per cent of its GNP to private consumption to a full-employment economy that devotes only 60 per cent of its GNP to consumption. This would release 5 per cent of the GNP for capital formation.

Will this policy work? Let us examine some of the qualifications that must be made.

America's international deficit. The United States faces a chronic gold drain, and a policy of low domestic interest rates may cause foreigners to withdraw their dollar claims and convert them into gold. Since our gold supply is not unlimited, easy-credit conditions pursued as a means to growth will be hampered in some degree by international payments problems.

Hitches in the deepening of capital. Another objection arises out of the possibility that expansionary credit may (1) fail to build up capital in the short run, or (2) succeed in the short run but leave behind so much excess capital that the high growth rate cannot be maintained. In short, orthodox banking policies may not be able to produce the desired deepening of capital on a long-run basis. This is a possibility, certainly, for an increase in the supply of capital goods beyond some critical point might cause the extra capital to be worthless. If new investment brought the interest yield on capital to zero or below the minimal-risk figure, then deepening of capital would be impossible and the whole optimistic policy would collapse.

The optimist suggests that there are always ways of using capital and roundabout production processes, pointing to planned economies such as the U.S.S.R. for support. Even when there is already enough capital in industry, there are cost-reducing investments that will pay if resources are available at low enough interest rates. A study of engineering technology also suggests that there are many alternative ways of using more capital.

The optimist must admit, however, that ours is not a planned economy and because of the way risks appear to the individual entrepreneur there might come a time when the easing of credit and cheapening of interest might not induce further capital investment. The reply is that central bank policy would have to be supplemented with courageous new programs of tax subsidy and finance involving public guarantees to offset business risks, thus persuading the businessman to invest further. We cannot reach a definite conclusion here, but most estimates suggest that society is nowhere near being satiated with capital at the present time. If that point is ever reached, there will be no need for an austere fiscal policy.

Cost-push inflation problems. Finally, one of the factors that make growth planning most difficult is the possibility of a cost-push seller's inflation. If it were just a case of avoiding inflationary or deflationary gaps of the demand type, authorities would know where sound fiscal policy lay. But the cost-push phenomenon can complicate policy making greatly since prices rise while the economy contains much slack, creating doubts whether more or less expansion is the best course to follow.

A new inflation? From 1955 to 1958, American prices were generally rising; wholesale prices, farm prices, cost-of-living prices, in fact all but staple prices, rose steadily. Everyone was disturbed by the rise but no one was certain of the cause. Excessive demand? An examination of various industries showed no signs of excessive demand. Autos were not selling well, farm equipment was slow, and the steel industry operated far below 80 per cent of capacity much of the time.

Experts began to wonder if this was a case of "wage-push" rather than "demand-pull" inflation. Money wages rose each year, often by more than the growth of productivity, and not many strikes were needed to accomplish the rise. Both the unionized and nonunionized sectors of the economy were involved. Employers, it was said, did not oppose wage increases, depending on the Fed and the Treasury to keep aggregate demand high enough to buy the higher-cost output. So wages rose, production costs rose, and prices rose. The result was a new kind of inflation, and the weapons used against demand inflation only created unemployment and recession.

Gradually, emphasis shifted from wage-push to a more general cost-push theory. In 1959, the Joint Economic Committee of Congress published research reports suggesting that the increase in the price of steel was by itself responsible for a significant fraction of the increase in the wholesale price index. But the Committee also found that profit margins rose in this administered-price industry, along with wage increases, and concluded that the pressure was not due to wage demands alone.

Are growth and price stability opposing goals?

If the American economy behaved like a frictionless classical economy, wage rates would never rise while significant unemployment persisted. Authorities could blissfully pursue expansionary policies whenever there was unemployment, knowing that growth would be more rapid when more resources were put to work. Similarly, price rises could be attributed to inflationary gaps of the demand-pull type and counteracted by contractionary policies just strong enough to wipe out the price rise and not produce unemployment. But if consumer wholesale and general GNP prices all tend to creep upward at a time when unemployment is at the 4, 5, and even 6 per cent level, what should monetary and fiscal authorities do? Reduce demand, even though that means further unemployment and lower production? Or increase total spending, though that means further price increases?

There is no easy answer, but we can note three major viewpoints on the question:

Price stability at all costs. Some feel that a stable price level is so important that it transcends even high employment and growth. The extreme view supports price stability at all costs. But most adherents to the view are not extremists; they argue that in the long run there is no real clash between price stability, growth, and high employment. Inflation today means depression tomorrow, and only in a stable price environment can efficient business decisions be made. They believe that a little inflation will inevitably be followed by more; hence the best policy is to prevent any inflation at all. They ask, in other words, a sacrifice of some output and employment now as an investment in a higher future growth and employment rate.

Growth at all costs. Leon Keyserling, adviser to President Truman, argues that full employment and growth are the primary goals. He feels that by insisting on growth, society will in fact end up with more stable prices as a bonus. Growth, it is said, brings price stability as well. The argument runs as follows:

1. Higher output means downward pressure on prices, other things being equal.

2. Since workers tend to get money wages that increase rather steadily, a faster growth rate ensures smaller price increases.

3. At high levels of capacity, unit costs drop and lower prices can be charged without affecting profits.

4. High employment and production make people efficient and venturesome.

Exponents of this view would therefore sacrifice price stability in the short run as an investment in future growth and price stability.

Compromising between price stability and growth. A large number of experts reject both extremes. They feel that absolute price stability may detract from high employment and growth, that some slack would be induced into the economy to halt the gentle price rise completely. What follows then? Two points: first, that pressing for full employment and maximum growth without limit will place such a strain on prices that compromise is absolutely essential; second, that if some measure of price creeping is not permitted, economic progress and high employment will probably be sacrificed.

If acquiescence in price rises is at times necessary, this raises one of the most difficult and vital problems in modern economics. Will toleration of price rises and pressure for reasonably high employment inevitably snowball into runaway inflation? The Commission on Money and Credit has produced evidence which suggests that this is not the case, but it would be idle to deny that economic analysis and historical experience are too limited to make a definitive judgment on the question. We need to know more of the means that can be used to minimize price creep, and the level of price creep that can be tolerated. We need more vigorous antitrust activity in the administered-price area, new legislation, a new labor attitude toward money wages, and pressures in collective bargaining to uphold the consumer's interest and the national interest. Doubtless other policies as yet unexplored may also contribute to the solution of the problem.

THE SOVIET ECONOMY

The reader will be interested to know something of the operation of the economic structure in the Soviet Union. How, for example, does the U.S.S.R. solve the three basic economic problems—What, How, and For Whom? We can provide only a brief sketch of the process, but the broad picture is something like this.

Almost all of the factors of production are owned by the state, and workers are paid wages by the state. There is some range of choice of occupation, but by our standards, the range is severely limited.

What to produce? The decision What to produce is made politically. The government decides how much of production will go to defense, to capital formation, and to consumer goods. While a Russian can indicate his preference among the different goods by the way he spends his income, any shortages or gluts that result do not generally produce price changes. So long as goods were very scarce, central planners could count on their output being bought, even if it were not precisely what the public would have preferred, given a free choice.

Now that some of the comforts and even luxuries of life are coming into production, the planners can no longer think only in terms of bare necessities, and the task of planning has become more difficult. When certain goods are not sold, production must be reduced. Since marketing surveys are still in their infancy, it is very difficult to learn what people do or do not want. Actually, Soviet planners find it useful to watch what Americans and others abroad consume and then introduce such products into their own system. The rare comrade who obtains a car, and he is a rare bird indeed, will find that it resembles our cars of the past, and the experts tell us that this imitative pattern works reasonably well.

With respect to capital goods and military expenditure, decisions are made directly by the state. The emphasis to be placed on industrialization, electrification, transportation, mining, research, etc., is determined in broad outline by conscious political decision.

How. Private enterprise is negligible in economic importance, for the typical factory is state-owned and operated by professional management. The manager owns no capital, though he does receive higher wages and other special benefits. He may even get bonuses and quicker promotion if his enterprise meets or surpasses its quotas. In practice, he gives orders like any other boss and expects to have them obeyed. He may even hoard raw materials and labor to make certain that he meets his quotas, and in many cases management has deliberately planned to obtain a small quota, easily filled, by concealing the true efficiency of the plant.

The decision how to combine the various productive factors appears to depend on a mixture of purely economic and technical considerations and the need to adapt to resource availability. A continuous trial-and-error process goes on, and the operation of the system is curiously uneven. A military ballistics plant may achieve a level of precision rivaling anything in the world, while its neighboring plants may use production processes that are unbelievably primitive.

Experts say that there is no elaborate formal structure of planning, but all of Soviet economic life is built around a pyramid with a broad base and a narrow peak. Individual enterprises are grouped together into industries and regions, headed by regional councils. The regional councils are subordinate to the appropriate minister in Moscow. All ministers in turn are subordinated to the planners on the Gosplan. However, organization changes very rapidly, and it would be misleading to emphasize it unduly.

For Whom. To a considerable degree, the Russian economy works for the security of the state and for the future. How much present-generation workers consume is not determined primarily by day-to-day spending; it depends on political decisions which ration and allocate resources. Workers are paid wages, and wage rates are highly differentiated, even more than in the United States in many cases. But the state uses various economic devices to ensure that it gets the distribution it wishes—heavy emphasis on industrialization and military security. For one thing, goods are taxed heavily at every stage of production (the so-called turnover tax), and the resulting elevation of prices ensures that the public can afford only a part of the total output. Another device is to set consumer prices much higher than the price of military or capital goods—in terms of true economic costs. Finally, consumer goods of certain types simply may not be sold to those who do not have special status.

By using such techniques, Soviet authorities fight price inflation, which would occur if the workers tried to spend their entire income on the limited supply of consumer goods. For Whom, then, is in the last analysis decided by the political authorities. But we cannot for that reason assume that everyone in the U.S.S.R. is miserable. Doubtless, few Western citizens would trade their present standard of living for life in the Soviet Union, but the Soviet citizen also thinks of himself as living in paradise compared with life in China. Nor was life a bed of roses under the Tsars, though few now living remember that period. The degree of Russian affluence today must look much more impressive in their eyes than in ours.

Comparative economic growth. Today, we have a great many facts about the Russian economic system, and teams of our economic experts pore over their statistics very carefully. While they find the data incomplete, or even deliberately misleading, it is now assumed to be possible to make an objective appraisal of the rough dimensions of the system. We find, as we might expect, that they are neither too ignorant and stupid to keep a Model T running, nor so efficient that they outstrip everyone else. There are strong spots and weak spots.

The basic facts seem to be as follows. In 1964, Soviet GNP was between two-thirds and one-third of ours, depending upon the price units used. Splitting the difference, we arrive at a reasonable estimate that real GNP in the U.S.S.R. was about one-half of U.S. real GNP in 1964. Since the Soviet population is larger than ours, and since a smaller part of Soviet GNP is devoted to consumption, it follows that real consumption per capita is much smaller than ours. This conclusion is fairly well confirmed by casual observations made by visitors to Russia.

Which economy is growing faster, ours or the Soviet Union's? This issue has dominated discussion since the late 1950s, and though much nonsense has been written and spoken on the subject, there is a nucleus of objective fact that deserves analysis. Depending on the years used for comparison, one can say that America's GNP has been growing at a long-term rate of between 3 and 4 per cent per year. Although the 1960 Democratic platform and various writings associated with Republican Governor Nelson Rockefeller speak of a 5 per cent rate of growth as a goal for the United States, expert economic opinion does not think this likely in the decades ahead.

Estimates of Soviet growth are more difficult. Everyone seems to agree that her recent growth rate has been much greater than ours as a percentage per annum, though she has not surpassed the growth rate of the mixed economies in Western Germany, Japan, or Italy. Further, many experts feel that an economy which begins at a lower gross level of productivity can show a higher initial growth rate than a more advanced economy. They believe that once the U.S.S.R. reaches a stage of development comparable to that of the United States, she will grow at a slower pace and will be likely to lose the advantages of imitation of more advanced technologies. So they caution against blind extrapolation into the future.

There is much that is persuasive in such arguments, yet they also make possible temptingly optimistic rationalizations for those who are wishful about the future. Moreover, Germany and other mixed-economy nations whose growth rate exceeds that of the U.S.S.R. in recent years warn us that such arguments can work in reverse. It is possible to be both optimistic and pessimistic with regard to the same body of facts. Figure 34 shows a spread for the Soviet Union that demonstrates both outlooks.

It is evident from the graph that the Soviet Union is not likely to overtake our real GNP for a long time to come and our per capita welfare level for an even longer time period. This is reassuring, but the economist must warn against two possible sources of error:

First, war strength today is not measured by GNP alone. Military analysts estimate that the U.S.S.R. now mounts about the same military effort as the United States, though her real GNP may be only half as large as ours.

America leads Russia, but will the gap narrow?

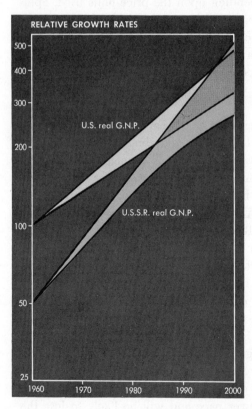

Fig. 34. The range of estimates shown here can make no pretense to accuracy, but they do portray the nature of the Soviet challenge. (Note: All indexes are based upon U.S. real GNP for 1960 = 100 and U.S.S.R. real GNP for 1960 = 50.)

She simply devotes twice as large a fraction of GNP to military expenditures. Further, once both parties are completely armed with nuclear weapons and rockets, it does not follow that extra spending by the United States will produce a military advantage. For those concerned with the power struggle, superiority in GNP is not an adequate basis for complacency.

Secondly, the two systems are in a sense "on trial" in the eyes of many of the uncommitted nations. Even if the United States retains its absolute advantage, if the Soviet Union were to show a rapid improvement proportionately, it might tempt neutrals to imitate the totalitarian pattern in years to come, suppressing democratic and personal freedom by collectivist decisions in order to achieve a high rate of capital formation.

An Optimistic Last Word

We have seen how our modern economy operates, and have subjected the economy to a searching examination with no holds barred. We have looked ever so briefly at the operation of our principal competitor, the Soviet Union. We must grant that our own system is imperfect, though we may argue that its imperfections can be ameliorated within the existing framework of ideas and institutions. It would be easy to compare the imperfections of our own system with some nonexistent ideal that worked perfectly at all times. And it is easy to gloss over the tremendous vitality of our mixed economy, which, with all its faults, has given the world a century of progress unequaled in human history.

We therefore conclude on an optimistic note. The American economy now has more potential than ever before. We number only 6 per cent of the world's population, yet we account for 38 per cent of the world's income. With all its defects, our system has a long record of rapid advance in productivity and rising living standards, and the system can, if the people wish, accommodate to an increased rate of growth quite easily.

Thirty years ago, all of this could not have been said in a textbook. International trade was shrinking, the banking structure was in a state of collapse, unemployment was drastically high, and the grim specter of poverty appeared everywhere in the land. It was a time when one might reasonably despair over the future of free society, and many persons did so. Careful and dispassionate examination of the economic statistics of the past thirty years enables us to take quite a different and more optimistic outlook today. Even more important for the textbook writer, modern economic analysis provides us with a "neoclassical synthesis" that combines the essentials of the theory of aggregate income determination with the older classical theories of relative prices and microeconomics. In a smooth-running system, with monetary and fiscal policies operating to validate the high-employment assumption postulated by classical theory, that classical theory finds new life, and the economist can state with renewed conviction the classic truths and principles of social economy.

Review Questions

1. What is meant by "underdevelopment"? List some of the major characteristics of an underdeveloped nation.

2. Why is the problem of underdevelopment growing increasingly severe? What reasons can you give why the United States or any other country should aid underdeveloped nations?

3. Clarify the population problem as it appears in underdeveloped nations.

4. How can the resource problems of underdeveloped nations be met?

5. Explain why capital formation is peculiarly difficult for underdeveloped nations. Are there any solutions?

6. Explain why technological change and innovation are absolutely essential in the underdeveloped nations. Do they have any advantages in this area? Explain.

7. List some of the major policy decisions that can be made by the government of an underdeveloped nation determined to expand its economy.

8. What are some of the techniques or standards that may be used to measure economic growth? How are they used?

9. What are the alternative policies that may be adopted to stimulate economic growth in advanced countries? What are the advantages and disadvantages of each?

10. What are the factors that influence growth, and how can they be used?

11. Explain how monetary and fiscal policy can influence growth and maintain price stability.

12. How can inflation be avoided while the economy is growing, particularly when it is being stimulated to increase growth?

13. How are the basic economic decisions in the U.S.S.R. made? Contrast with the United States. What are the advantages and disadvantages of the Soviet system?

For Further Study

1. Do you believe that the United States should assist the under-developed nations to the best of its ability? How should this be done? Why? By what measures?

2. What would happen if the Soviet GNP should exceed American GNP in the near future?

3. If the Soviet economic system could be combined with the American political system, would it then be the best possible social structure for the modern world? Justify your answer.

4. If population increases should end, would there still be an urgent need to concern ourselves with economic growth? Explain.

5. Do you think that price stability is more important than growth, or should it be sacrificed to achieve a high growth rate? Explain your answer.

SELECTED READINGS

Chapter 18: The Problem of Social Change

Barnes, Harry Elmer: *Historical Sociology: Its Origins and Development,* Philosophical Library, Inc., New York, 1948.

Barnett, H. G.: *Innovation: The Basis of Cultural Change,* McGraw-Hill Book Company, Inc., New York, 1953.

Berlin, Isaiah: *The Hedgehog and the Fox,* Simon and Schuster, Inc., New York, 1953.

Bury, J. B.: *The Idea of Progress,* The Macmillan Company, New York, 1932.

Ginsberg, Morris: *The Idea of Progress: A Revaluation,* Beacon Press, Boston, 1953.

MacIver, Robert M.: *Social Causation,* Ginn and Company, Boston, 1942.

Sims, N. L. R.: *The Problem of Social Change,* Crowell-Collier Publishing Co., New York, 1939.

Sorokin, Pitirim A.: *Social and Cultural Dynamics,* American Book Company, New York, 4 vols., 1937–1941.

Spengler, Oswald: *The Decline of the West,* Charles Francis Atkinson (trans.), Alfred A. Knopf, Inc., 2 vols., New York, 1939.

Tawney, R. H.: *Religion and the Rise of Capitalism,* Harcourt, Brace & World, Inc., New York, 1926.

Toynbee, Arnold J.: *A Study of History,* Royal Institute of International Affairs, London, 10 vols., 1934–1954. Abridged by D. C. Somervell for Oxford University Press, Fair Lawn, N. J.

Weber, Max: *The Protestant Ethic and the Spirit of Capitalism,* Talcott Parsons (trans.), George Allen & Unwin, Ltd., London, 1930.

Westermarck, Edward: *Christianity and Morals,* The Macmillan Company, New York, 1939.

Znaniecki, Florian: *Cultural Sciences: Their Origin and Development,* The University of Illinois Press, Urbana, Ill., 1952.

Chapter 19: Contemporary Political Problems

Bell, Daniel: *The End of Ideology,* Crowell-Collier Publishing Co., New York, 1961.

Chenery, William L.: *Freedom of the Press,* Harcourt, Brace & World, Inc., New York, 1955.

Cushman, Robert E.: *Civil Liberties in the United States,* Cornell University Press, Ithaca, N. Y., 1956.

Fraenkel, Osmond K.: *The Supreme Court and Civil Liberties,* Oceana, New York, 1960.

Freedman, Leonard, and Cornelius P. Cotter (eds.): *Issues of the Sixties*
   Wadsworth, San Francisco, Calif., 1961.
Fromm, Erich: *Escape from Freedom,* Holt, Rinehart and Winston, Inc., New
   York, 1941.
————: *May Man Prevail?* Doubleday & Company, Inc., Garden City, N. Y.,
   1961.
Hoffer, Eric: *The True Believer,* Mentor Books, New American Library of
   World Literature, Inc., New York, 1951.
Krutch, Joseph W.: *The Measure of Man,* Grosset & Dunlap, Inc., New York,
   1953.
Lasswell, Harold: *National Security and Individual Freedom,* McGraw-Hill
   Book Company, Inc., New York, 1950.
McCloskey, Robert G.: *The American Supreme Court,* Phoenix Books, The
   University of Chicago Press, Chicago, 1962.
Mills, C. Wright: *The Sociological Imagination,* Oxford University Press, Fair
   Lawn, N. J., 1959.
Pound, Roscoe: *The Development of Constitutional Guarantees of Liberty,*
   Yale University Press, New Haven, Conn., 1957.
Riemer, Neal: *The Revival of Democratic Theory,* Appleton-Century-Crofts,
   Inc., New York, 1962.
Riesman, David, Nathan Glaser, and Reuel Denney: *The Lonely Crowd,* Yale
   University Press, New Haven, Conn., 1950.
Roche, John P.: *Courts and Rights,* Random House, Inc., New York, 1961.
Rossiter, Clinton: *Conservatism in America,* Alfred A. Knopf, Inc., New York,
   1955.
Spicer, George W.: *The Supreme Court and Fundamental Freedoms,* Appleton-
   Century-Crofts, Inc., New York, 1959.
Turner, Gordon B., and Richard D. Challener: *National Security in the Nuclear
   Age,* Frederick A. Praeger, Inc., New York, 1961.
Whyte, William: *The Organization Man,* Simon and Schuster, Inc., New York,
   1956.

Chapter 20: Current Economic Problems

Baran, Paul A.: *The Political Economy of Growth,* Monthly Review Press,
   New York, 1957.
Bauer, P. T., and Basil S. Yamel: *The Economics of Underdeveloped Coun-
   tries,* The University of Chicago Press, Chicago, 1957.
Brand, Willem: *The Struggle for a Higher Standard of Living,* The Free Press
   of Glencoe, New York, 1958.
Coale, Ansley J., and Edgar M. Hoover: *Population Growth and Economic De-
   velopment in Low Income Countries,* Princeton University Press, Prince-
   ton, N. J., 1958.
Hoselitz, Berthold F.: *Sociological Aspects of Economic Growth,* The Free
   Press of Glencoe, New York, 1960.

Millikan, Max F., and Donald L. M. Blackmer (eds.): *The Emerging Nations,* Little, Brown and Company, Boston, 1961.

Pentony, DeVere E.: *The Underdeveloped Lands,* Chandler, San Francisco, Calif., 1960.

Samuelson, P. A., R. L. Bishop, and J. R. Coleman (eds.): *Readings in Economics,* 3d ed., McGraw-Hill Book Company, Inc., New York, 1958.

Sievers, Allen M.: *Revolution, Evolution, and the Economic Order,* Prentice-Hall, Inc., Englewood Cliffs, N. J., 1962.

Villard, Henry H.: *Economic Development,* Holt, Rinehart and Winston, Inc., New York, 1959.

Name Index

Subject Index